Contents

KU-338-334

Question index

The headings in this checklist/index indicate the main topics of questions, but questions often cover several different topics. Where necessary, questions have been amended to reflect the new format of the exam from June 2013.

Past exam questions are designated with 'APM' after the question name, along with the date of the exam in which they featured.

ACCA

PAPER P5

ADVANCED PERFORMANCE
MANAGEMENT

P
R
A
C
T
I
C
E

&

R
E
V
I
S
I
O
N

K
I
T

FOR EXAMS IN SEPTEMBER 2016, DECEMBER 2016, MARCH 2017 AND JUNE 2017

First edition 2007
Tenth edition February 2016

ISBN 9781 4727 4446 3
(previous ISBN 9781 4727 2696 4)
e-ISBN 9781 4727 4661 0

British Library Cataloguing-in-Publication Data
A catalogue record for this book
is available from the British Library

Published by

BPP Learning Media Ltd
BPP House, Aldine Place
London W12 8AA

www.bpp.com/learningmedia

Printed in the United Kingdom by Polestar Wheatons

Hennock Road
Marsh Barton
Exeter
EX2 8RP
486769

Your learning materials, published by BPP Learning Media Ltd, are printed on paper obtained from traceable, sustainable sources.

We are grateful to the Association of Chartered Certified Accountants for permission to reproduce past examination questions. The suggested solutions in the practice answer bank have been prepared by BPP Learning Media Ltd, unless otherwise stated.

Part E: Performance evaluation and corporate failure

50 mark (Section A) Questions

Mock exam 1

Mock exam 2

Mock exam 3 (ACCA September/December 2015 Exam)

Important note: Questions 1 and 2 in **Mock exam 2** are past exam questions from June 2012 and December 2011 respectively. Even if you do not attempt the full Mock exam, you are strongly encouraged to complete these two questions as part of your revision.

Topic index

Listed below are the key Paper P5 syllabus topics and the numbers of the questions in this Kit covering those topics.

If you need to concentrate your practice and revision on certain topics or if you want to attempt all available questions that refer to a particular subject, you will find this index useful.

Syllabus topic	Question numbers
Accountability and responsibility accounting	23, 44
Activity-based costing	39, 55
Activity-based management	56
Appraisals and performance management	12(c)
Balanced scorecard	49, 50, 73, 74, 76(d), Mock 3 Qn 4
Benchmarking	3, 76(b), Mock 1 Qn 1
BCG matrix	5(d), 47
Big Data	29
Branding	37(a), 38(c)
Budgeting and types of budget	10, 11, Mock 3 Qn 2
Building blocks model (Fitzgerald and Moon)	54, 74
Business process re-engineering (BPR)	12, 13
Business structure (and performance measurement)	60
Controls and security over information	27
Corporate failure	61 – 65
Costs of quality	39, 40, Mock 2 Qn 2
Critical success factors (CSFs)	7, 8, 55(b), 66, 67, Mock 3 Qn 1
Divisional performance measures	70, Mock 1 Qn 1
Economic value added (EVA™)	32, 33, 48, 57, 72, 75(iii), Mock 3 Qn 1
Environmental management accounting	16
Enterprise resource planning systems (ERPS)	25, Mock 3 Qn 1(iv)
External environment (and impact on organisations)	8, 17, 18, 19, 66
Financial performance	18, 32, 43, 69-72, Mock 1 Qn 1, Mock 2 Qn 1
Five forces (Porter)	8, 20, 62
Goal congruence	2, 9, 30
Information for decision making	1, 4 , 21, 66
Information overload	27, 70
Information systems and IT systems	14, 68, Mock 1 Qn 2, Mock 3 Qn 1
Integrated Reporting	28
JIT	76 (c), Mock 2 Qn 2, Mock 3 Qn 1 (iii; iv)
Joint ventures	59, Mock 2 Qn 3
Kaizen costing	4(d), 40(c), 56(c), Mock 2 Qn 2, Mock 3 Qn 1(iii; iv)
Key performance indicators (KPIs)	7, 9, 53, 55(b), 66, 67, Mock 3 Qn 1
League tables	3, 35, 69, Mock 2 Qn 4
Lean information systems	22, 26

Helping you with your revision

BPP Learning Media – Approved Content Provider

As ACCA's **Approved Content Provider**, BPP Learning Media gives you the **opportunity** to use revision materials reviewed by the ACCA examination team. By incorporating the ACCA examination team's comments and suggestions regarding the depth and breadth of syllabus coverage, the BPP Learning Media Practice & Revision Kit provides excellent, **ACCA-approved** support for your revision.

Tackling revision and the exam

You can significantly improve your chances of passing by tackling revision and the exam in the right ways. Using feedback obtained from the ACCA examination team:

- We look at the dos and don'ts of revising for, and taking, ACCA exams
- We focus on Paper P5; we discuss revising the syllabus, what to do (and what not to do) in the exam, how to approach different types of question and ways of obtaining easy marks

Selecting questions

We provide signposts to help you plan your revision.

- A full **question index**
- A **topic index** listing all the questions that cover key topics, so that you can locate the questions that provide practice on these topics, and see the different ways in which they might be examined

Making the most of question practice

At BPP Learning Media we realise that you need more than just questions and model answers to get the most from your question practice.

- Our **Top tips** included for certain questions provide essential advice on tackling questions, presenting answers and the key points that answers need to include
- We show you how you can pick up **Easy marks** on some questions, as we know that picking up all readily available marks often can make the difference between passing and failing
- We include **marking guides** to show you what the examination team rewards
- We include **comments from the examining team** to show you where students struggled or performed well in the actual exam
- We refer to the **BPP Study Text** for exams in September 2016, December 2016, March 2017 and June 2017 for detailed coverage of the topics covered in questions

Attempting mock exams

There are three mock exams that provide practice at coping with the pressures of the exam day. We strongly recommend that you attempt them under exam conditions. **Mock exams 1 and 2** reflect the question styles and syllabus coverage of the exam; **Mock exam 3** is the ACCA September/December 2015 exam paper.

This exam is compiled from questions selected by ACCA's examination team from the September 2015 and December 2015 exams. It does not reflect the entire September or December exams but contains questions most appropriate for students to practice.

Revising P5

Any part of the syllabus could be tested in the compulsory Section A question. Therefore it is essential to learn the **entire syllabus** to maximise your changes of passing. There are no short cuts – trying to spot topics is dangerous and will significantly reduce the likelihood of success. As this is an advanced paper it also assumes knowledge of topics covered in Paper F5 – *Performance Management*.

That said, the **main capabilities** in the syllabus (which is shown on ACCA's website) take you through what the examination team expects from you when you have completed your studies. There are five key areas for you to concentrate on. These five areas are the syllabus areas covered in the BPP P5 Study Text.

However, whilst it is important that you work through your way through the Study Text and cover all the different syllabus areas, it is also important to try and think how the areas might relate to each other, and how they could be used to help managers in an organisation control and improve the performance of that organisation. Remember, this paper is about performance **management**, as well as performance **measurement**; and you should treat both of these aspects (measurement and management) with equal importance as you are studying for your P5 exam.

Remember to come out of the detail once you have finished a chapter and practised some questions. Take some time to reflect on how the chapter has covered the syllabus and how it feeds back into the capabilities which you will need to display in order to pass this paper.

Question practice

You should use the Passcards and any brief notes you have to revise the syllabus, but you mustn't spend all your revision time simply reading or making notes. **Question practice is vital.** Doing as many questions as you can, in full, will help develop your ability to analyse scenarios and produce relevant discussion and recommendations.

Make sure you leave enough time in your revision schedule to practise 50 mark Section A questions, as the Section A question is compulsory in the exam. The scenarios and requirements of Section A questions are more extensive than Section B questions, and are likely to integrate several parts of the syllabus. Therefore, practice is essential. Also ensure that you attempt all three mock exams, under exam conditions.

Passing the P5 exam

Displaying the right qualities

The P5 technical articles section of ACCA's website include the 'Examiner's approach to Paper P5' which outlined the way the syllabus will be tested and the qualities students should demonstrate when answering P5 questions. The article addresses the five main syllabus areas (A to E) in turn, and identifies and what qualities students should demonstrate under each. We reproduce the main points here.

1. **The application of strategic planning and control models in performance management.** The models stress the need to take an all-encompassing view of the factors that affect a business and to consider them when giving strategic advice on performance. Good candidates at Paper P5 often distinguish themselves by being able to synthesise disparate detailed points into an overall, strategic approach for an organisation.

2. **Factors external to the business.** Candidates need to move beyond the internal factors associated with traditional management accounting to consider the information needs of the strategic level of management as well as the operational and tactical levels.

3. **The information that management require and the systems that are needed for its delivery.** Candidates are expected to be aware of the effect of information technologies on performance management decision making rather than the detail of these technologies. They should be conversant with the broad hardware and software trends and issues and how these interact with the provision of performance information throughout the organization.

4 and 5. **The fourth capability** is the **application** of the techniques and assumed knowledge to specific scenarios. You shouldn't simply discuss theories and models in general terms; you need to apply them specifically to the scenario identified in the question. **The fifth capability** is being able to take this information and turn it into **advice which is commercially valuable for strategic decision makers.** This capability also requires the candidate to be able to recognise and advise on situations where the organisation is in danger of failing.

There will be a small number of **professional marks** available in the compulsory 50 mark Section A question, and it should be possible for a well-prepared student to score most of these. For example, the effective use of appropriate introductions and conclusions, and helpfully breaking the document into properly headed sub-sections, will help to demonstrate a professional approach to writing a report. However, it should be stressed that the approach taken will vary from question to question and the exam tests the candidates' ability to apply their knowledge of professional presentation. In order to score full professional marks, the answer will have to be tailored to the specifics of the scenario in the question recognising the needs of the readers of the document.

Presentation points. First: on rounding. At this final level, candidates should use their own judgment about the level of detail to which they round figures – the basic rule is that there should be enough detail to make a useful conclusion without obscuring it with insignificant figures. However, it is also very important that you round correctly (ie up or down) according to the underlying figures.

Second, short paragraphs are usually clear but single sentence paragraphs are often insufficient and unable to get to the depth required at Paper P5. Bullet points are useful for lists but not if commentary is required. Finally, reading model solutions is not a substitute for actually writing out your own answers.

Summarising the advice ACCA's examining team gives for P5:

Candidates should:

- Understand the objectives of the exam as explained in the *Syllabus* and prepare the detailed topics in the *Study Guide*

- Be very comfortable with the areas tested in Paper F5 *Performance Management* which constitute brought forward knowledge for Paper P5

- Ensure that their preparation for the exam has been based on a programme of study set for the required syllabus and exam structure

- Use an ACCA-approved textbook for Paper P5. They are structured around the syllabus and ACCA's examining team reviews them so that they give an effective coverage of what is examinable

- Practise questions under exam conditions in order to improve speed and presentation skills, ensuring these test discursive, computational and analytic abilities

- Study all the relevant technical articles that are published on ACCA's website

- Be able to clearly communicate understanding and application of knowledge in the context of a Professional level exam

The questions tend to be wide-ranging, as the examination team wants to link topics and mix ideas up. So you are better knowing something about every part of the syllabus than a lot of detail about a few areas only.

Avoiding weaknesses

Our experience of, and examination team feedback from, other higher level exams enables us to predict a number of weaknesses that are likely to occur in many students' answers. You will enhance your chances significantly if you ensure you avoid these mistakes:

- **Failing to provide what the question verbs require** (discussion, evaluation, recommendation) or to write about the topics specified in the question requirements

- **Repeating the same material** in different parts of answers

- **Stating theories and concepts** rather than applying them

- **Quoting chunks of detail** from the question that don't add any value. Whilst it is important that you relate your answer to this scenario, this means using issues highlighted in the scenario to help answer the question – not simply re-writing the question.

- **Forcing irrelevancies into answers**, for example irrelevant definitions or theories, or examples that don't relate to the scenario

- **Failing to make the most of the information** given in the question. Remember, you need to apply your knowledge specifically to the scenario given in the question.

- **Giving long lists or writing down all that you know about a subject area**, without considering whether it is relevant to the question or not

- **Failing to set out workings clearly and separately**

- **Not planning and preparing the answer properly,** taking into account mark allocation. Students often leave part-questions out – either because of poor time management, or because they have failed to read the requirement properly.

- **Unrealistic, vague or impractical recommendations**

- **Not refreshing brought-forward knowledge** (for example, from Paper F5).

- **Failing to answer sufficient questions**, or all parts of a question, because of poor time management

Choosing which questions to answer first

We recommend that you spend time at the beginning of your exam carefully reading through all of the questions in the paper, and each of their requirements. Once you fell familiar with your exam paper, we then recommend that you attempt the compulsory Section A question first, ensuring that you spend adequate time reading and planning before you begin to write up your answer. Comments from examination teams across syllabuses that have similar exam formats suggest that students appear less time-pressured if they do the big compulsory questions first.

During the second half of the exam, you can put Section A aside and concentrate on the two Section B questions you've chosen.

However, our recommendations are not inflexible. If you really think the Section A question looks a lot harder than the Section B questions you've chosen, then do one of those first, but **DON'T run over time on it.** You must leave half of the exam time (one hour and 38 minutes) to tackle the Section A question (which accounts for 50% of the total marks in the paper). If you do one of the Section B questions first, and then come back to the Section A question, you should be able to generate more ideas and find the question is not as bad as it looks.

Remember also that small overruns of time during the first half of the exam can add up to you being very short of time towards the end.

Tackling questions

You'll improve your chances by following a step-by-step approach along the following lines.

Step 1   Read the background

Usually the first couple of paragraphs will give some background on the company and what it is aiming to achieve. By reading this carefully you will be better equipped to relate your answers to the company as much as possible.

Step 2   Read the requirements

There is no point reading the detailed information in the question until you know what it is going to be used for. Don't panic if some of the requirements look challenging – identify the elements you are able to do and look for links between requirements, as well as possible indications of the syllabus areas the question is covering.

Step 3   Identify the action verbs that are used in each requirement

These convey the level of skill you need to exhibit and also the structure your answer should have. A lower level verb such as define will require a more descriptive answer; a higher level verb such as evaluate will require a more applied, critical answer.

ACCA's examination team has indicated that **higher level requirements and verbs** will be most significant in this paper, for example critically evaluating a statement and arguing for or against a given idea or position.

Action verbs that are likely to be frequently used in this exam are listed below, together with their intellectual levels and guidance on their meaning.

Level		
1	Define	Give the meaning of
1	Explain	Make clear
1	Identify	Recognise or select
1	Describe	Give the key features
2	Analyse	Give reasons for the current situation or what has happened
2	Compare and contrast	Explain the similarities and differences between two terms, viewpoints or concepts
3	Assess	Determine the strengths/weaknesses/importance/significance/ability to contribute
3	Discuss	Examine in detail by using arguments for and against
3	Advise	Inform the recipient of an appropriate course of action; or inform the recipient about a fact or situation
3	Recommend	Advise the appropriate actions to pursue in terms the recipient will understand
3	Evaluate	Determine the value of, in the light of the arguments for and against
3	Examine	Critically review in detail

Step 4   Identify what each part of the question requires

Think about what frameworks of theories you could choose to support your answer (if the question doesn't indicate a specific one you need to use).

When planning, look at how the different parts of a question fit together, and make sure you don't end up repeating the same points in more than one part of the question.

Also, you're likely to come across part questions with two requirements; for example a requirement may ask you to evaluate some different approaches to budgeting and then recommend one which is appropriate for an organization. You must ensure that you **fulfil both requirements**, and at the appropriate level indicated by the question verbs.

Step 5   Check the mark allocation to each part

This shows you the depth anticipated and helps allocate time. The P5 exam is 3 hours 15 minutes (195 minutes); which means you should allocate time on the basis of 1.95 minutes per mark.

Step 6   Read the whole scenario carefully, highlighting key data

Put points under headings related to requirements (eg by noting in the margin to what part of the question the scenario detail relates).

It is also important to identify any instructions in the scenario which reinforce the question requirements. For example, a scenario could identify that you (as a management accountant) have been asked for information by the CEO. The requirement could then instruct you to act '… as requested by the CEO.' In this context, it is very important that you pay attention to the original request when preparing your answer, and make sure that your answer addresses any issues which had been highlighted in that original request.

Step 7 — Consider the consequences of the points you've identified

You will often have to provide recommendations based on the information you've been given. Be prepared to criticise the framework or model that you've been told to use, if required. You may have also to bring in wider issues or viewpoints, for example the views of different stakeholders.

Step 8 — Write a brief plan

Your plans should be produced within your answer book.

Make sure you identify all the requirements of the question in your plan – each requirement may have sub-requirements that must also be addressed. If there are professional marks available, highlight in your plan where these may be gained; for example, preparing a report.

Step 9 — Write your answer

Make every effort to present your answer clearly. The pilot paper and exam papers so far indicate that the examination team will be looking for you to make a number of clear points. The best way to demonstrate what you're doing is to put points into separate paragraphs with clear headers.

Discussion questions

Remember that **depth of discussion** will be important. Always bear in mind how many marks are available for the discussion as this will give you an indication of the depth that is required. Ask yourself the following questions as you are tackling a discussion question:

- **Have I made a point in a coherent sentence?**

- **Have I explained the point?** (to answer the 'so what' or 'why' queries; and to demonstrate which the point is important)

- **Have I related the point to the company in the scenario?** (with material or analysis from the scenario, or perhaps even an example from real life)

In the P5 exam a number of requirement verbs will expect you to express a viewpoint or opinion, for example construct an argument, criticise, evaluate. When expressing an opinion, you need to provide:

- **What the question wants.** For instance, if you are asked to criticise something, don't spend time discussing its advantages. In addition if a scenario provides a lot of information about a situation, and you are (say) asked to assess that situation in the light of good practice, your assessment is unlikely to be favourable.

- **Evidence** from theory or the scenario – again we stress that the majority of marks in most questions will be given for applying your knowledge to the scenario.

Gaining the easy marks

Technical knowledge (including knowledge brought forward from F5) should enable you to score a small number of relatively easy marks. There are likely to be some marks available in certain requirements for **definitions** or **explanations** that don't have to be related to the scenario. However don't assume that you can ignore all the scenarios and still pass! The level of marks available in P5 for knowledge (without application) is nowhere near enough to pass the exam.

As this is a Professional level paper, four **professional marks** will be awarded in the compulsory Section A 1question, and some of these should be easy to obtain. For example, there are likely to be marks available for presenting your answer in the format, and style, requested (eg a report).

Reports should always have an appropriate title. They should be **formally written**, with an **introductory paragraph** setting out the aims of the report. You should use **short paragraphs** and **appropriate headings**, with a brief summary of findings as a conclusion.

Exam formulae

Present Value Table

Present value of 1 i.e. $(1 + r)^{-n}$

Where   r = discount rate

          n = number of periods until payment

Discount rate (r)

Periods (n)	1%	2%	3%	4%	5%	6%	7%	8%	9%	10%	
1	0·990	0·980	0·971	0·962	0·952	0·943	0·935	0·926	0·917	0·909	1
2	0·980	0·961	0·943	0·925	0·907	0·890	0·873	0·857	0·842	0·826	2
3	0·971	0·942	0·915	0·889	0·864	0·840	0·816	0·794	0·772	0·751	3
4	0·961	0·924	0·888	0·855	0·823	0·792	0·763	0·735	0·708	0·683	4
5	0·951	0·906	0·863	0·822	0·784	0·747	0·713	0·681	0·650	0·621	5
6	0·942	0·888	0·837	0·790	0·746	0·705	0·666	0·630	0·596	0·564	6
7	0·933	0·871	0·813	0·760	0·711	0·665	0·623	0·583	0·547	0·513	7
8	0·923	0·853	0·789	0·731	0·677	0·627	0·582	0·540	0·502	0·467	8
9	0·914	0·837	0·766	0·703	0·645	0·592	0·544	0·500	0·460	0·424	9
10	0·905	0·820	0·744	0·676	0·614	0·558	0·508	0·463	0·422	0·386	10
11	0·896	0·804	0·722	0·650	0·585	0·527	0·475	0·429	0·388	0·350	11
12	0·887	0·788	0·701	0·625	0·557	0·497	0·444	0·397	0·356	0·319	12
13	0·879	0·773	0·681	0·601	0·530	0·469	0·415	0·368	0·326	0·290	13
14	0·870	0·758	0·661	0·577	0·505	0·442	0·388	0·340	0·299	0·263	14
15	0·861	0·743	0·642	0·555	0·481	0·417	0·362	0·315	0·275	0·239	15

(n)	11%	12%	13%	14%	15%	16%	17%	18%	19%	20%	
1	0·901	0·893	0·885	0·877	0·870	0·862	0·855	0·847	0·840	0·833	1
2	0·812	0·797	0·783	0·769	0·756	0·743	0·731	0·718	0·706	0·694	2
3	0·731	0·712	0·693	0·675	0·658	0·641	0·624	0·609	0·593	0·579	3
4	0·659	0·636	0·613	0·592	0·572	0·552	0·534	0·516	0·499	0·482	4
5	0·593	0·567	0·543	0·519	0·497	0·476	0·456	0·437	0·419	0·402	5
6	0·535	0·507	0·480	0·456	0·432	0·410	0·390	0·370	0·352	0·335	6
7	0·482	0·452	0·425	0·400	0·376	0·354	0·333	0·314	0·296	0·279	7
8	0·434	0·404	0·376	0·351	0·327	0·305	0·285	0·266	0·249	0·233	8
9	0·391	0·361	0·333	0·308	0·284	0·263	0·243	0·225	0·209	0·194	9
10	0·352	0·322	0·295	0·270	0·247	0·227	0·208	0·191	0·176	0·162	10
11	0·317	0·287	0·261	0·237	0·215	0·195	0·178	0·162	0·148	0·135	11
12	0·286	0·257	0·231	0·208	0·187	0·168	0·152	0·137	0·124	0·112	12
13	0·258	0·229	0·204	0·182	0·163	0·145	0·130	0·116	0·104	0·093	13
14	0·232	0·205	0·181	0·160	0·141	0·125	0·111	0·099	0·088	0·078	14
15	0·209	0·183	0·160	0·140	0·123	0·108	0·095	0·084	0·074	0·065	15

Annuity Table

Present value of an annuity of 1 i.e. $\dfrac{1-(1+r)^{-n}}{r}$

Where   r = discount rate
          n = number of periods

Discount rate (r)

Periods (n)	1%	2%	3%	4%	5%	6%	7%	8%	9%	10%	
1	0·990	0·980	0·971	0·962	0·952	0·943	0·935	0·926	0·917	0·909	1
2	1·970	1·942	1·913	1·886	1·859	1·833	1·808	1·783	1·759	1·736	2
3	2·941	2·884	2·829	2·775	2·723	2·673	2·624	2·577	2·531	2·487	3
4	3·902	3·808	3·717	3·630	3·546	3·465	3·387	3·312	3·240	3·170	4
5	4·853	4·713	4·580	4·452	4·329	4·212	4·100	3·993	3·890	3·791	5
6	5·795	5·601	5·417	5·242	5·076	4·917	4·767	4·623	4·486	4·355	6
7	6·728	6·472	6·230	6·002	5·786	5·582	5·389	5·206	5·033	4·868	7
8	7·652	7·325	7·020	6·733	6·463	6·210	5·971	5·747	5·535	5·335	8
9	8·566	8·162	7·786	7·435	7·108	6·802	6·515	6·247	5·995	5·759	9
10	9·471	8·983	8·530	8·111	7·722	7·360	7·024	6·710	6·418	6·145	10
11	10·37	9·787	9·253	8·760	8·306	7·887	7·499	7·139	6·805	6·495	11
12	11·26	10·58	9·954	9·385	8·863	8·384	7·943	7·536	7·161	6·814	12
13	12·13	11·35	10·63	9·986	9·394	8·853	8·358	7·904	7·487	7·103	13
14	13·00	12·11	11·30	10·56	9·899	9·295	8·745	8·244	7·786	7·367	14
15	13·87	12·85	11·94	11·12	10·38	9·712	9·108	8·559	8·061	7·606	15

(n)	11%	12%	13%	14%	15%	16%	17%	18%	19%	20%	
1	0·901	0·893	0·885	0·877	0·870	0·862	0·855	0·847	0·840	0·833	1
2	1·713	1·690	1·668	1·647	1·626	1·605	1·585	1·566	1·547	1·528	2
3	2·444	2·402	2·361	2·322	2·283	2·246	2·210	2·174	2·140	2·106	3
4	3·102	3·037	2·974	2·914	2·855	2·798	2·743	2·690	2·639	2·589	4
5	3·696	3·605	3·517	3·433	3·352	3·274	3·199	3·127	3·058	2·991	5
6	4·231	4·111	3·998	3·889	3·784	3·685	3·589	3·498	3·410	3·326	6
7	4·712	4·564	4·423	4·288	4·160	4·039	3·922	3·812	3·706	3·605	7
8	5·146	4·968	4·799	4·639	4·487	4·344	4·207	4·078	3·954	3·837	8
9	5·537	5·328	5·132	4·946	4·772	4·607	4·451	4·303	4·163	4·031	9
10	5·889	5·650	5·426	5·216	5·019	4·833	4·659	4·494	4·339	4·192	10
11	6·207	5·938	5·687	5·453	5·234	5·029	4·836	4·656	4·486	4·327	11
12	6·492	6·194	5·918	5·660	5·421	5·197	4·988	4·793	4·611	4·439	12
13	6·750	6·424	6·122	5·842	5·583	5·342	5·118	4·910	4·715	4·533	13
14	6·982	6·628	6·302	6·002	5·724	5·468	5·229	5·008	4·802	4·611	14
15	7·191	6·811	6·462	6·142	5·847	5·575	5·324	5·092	4·876	4·675	15

Exam information

The exam paper

Format of the paper

The current format of the P5 exam was introduced in June 2013. It is:

		Number of marks
Section A:	1 compulsory case study	50
Section B:	Choice of 2 from 3 questions (25 marks each)	50
		100

Time: 3 hours and 15 minutes

Note. Although the format of the exams changed from June 2013, the underlying syllabus content and the way in which subjects are examined has not changed, so earlier questions can still provide useful practice. The changes only relate to the **number of questions** in the exam, and the **mark allocations** for each question.

Section A will be a compulsory case study question, typically with four or five sub-requirements relating to the same scenario information. The question will usually assess and link a range of subject areas from across the syllabus. It will require students to demonstrate high-level capabilities to understand the complexities of the case, and evaluate, relate and apply the information in the case study to the requirements.

Professional marks will be available in Section A for presentation, logical flow of argument and quality of argument.

Section B questions are more likely to assess a range of discrete subject areas from the main syllabus section headings; they may require evaluation and synthesis of information contained within short scenarios and application of this information to the question requirements.

Although one subject area is likely to be emphasised in each Section B question, students should not assume that questions will be solely about content from that area. Each question will be based on a short case scenario to contextualise the question.

The **pass mark** for Paper P5 is 50%.

Additional information

The Study Guide provides more detailed guidance on the syllabus.

Exams prior to 2013

Questions and answers for exams prior to 2013 are available on ACCA's website:

www.accaglobal.com/gb/en/student/acca-qual-student-journey/qual-resource/acca-qualification/p5/past-exam-papers.html

Please note, these questions reflect of the format of the exam prior to 2013. In the main body of this Kit, where we have used past exam questions, we have adapted them to fit the format of the exam from June 2013.

Analysis of past papers

The table below provides details of when each element of the syllabus has been examined and whether it was examined as part of a compulsory question ('C') or an optional one ('O'). Please note that up to, and including, December 2012 the exam contained two compulsory questions, whereas exams from 2013 only contain one compulsory question.

With the introduction of the four exam sessions, ACCA will continue to publish the same number of exams, two per year, and at the same times, after the December and June exam sessions. These exams will be compiled from questions selected from the two preceding sessions. The first of these compilations was published in December 2015, incorporating questions from the September 2015 and December 2015 exams.

Covered in Text chapter		Sept/Dec 2015	June 2015	Dec 2014	June 2014	Dec 2013	June 2013	Dec 2012	June 2012	Dec 2011	June 2011
	STRATEGIC PLANNING AND CONTROL										
1	Introduction to strategic management accounting		C	C				O	O		
2	Performance hierarchy	C	C			C				C	
3	Performance management and control of the organisation	O			O			C			
4,5	Business structure, IT developments and other environmental and ethical issues		C	C, O	O		C				C, C
	EXTERNAL INFLUENCES ON ORGANISATIONAL PERFORMANCE										
6	Changing business environment and external factors		C		O	C	O			C	
7, 8	**PERFORMANCE MEASUREMENT SYSTEMS AND DESIGN**	C, O	O		C	O			C	O, O	C
	STRATEGIC PERFORMANCE MEASUREMENT										
9	Scope of strategic performance measures in the private sector	C	O		C			C, O	C		C
10	Divisional performance and transfer pricing issues						O				C
11	Scope of strategic performance measures in not-for-profit organisations			O		O					
12	Non-financial performance indicators		O	O				O	C		
13	The role of quality in management information and performance measurement systems	C, O					O		O	O	
14	Performance measurement: strategy, reward and behaviour		O, O		O	O		C		O	O,O
	PERFORMANCE EVALUATION AND CORPORATE FAILURE										
15	Alternative views of performance measurement and management	O	O	C	C	O	C, O		C	C	C, O
16	Strategic performance issues in complex business structures				O				O		O
17	Predicting and preventing corporate failure			O				O			

IMPORTANT!

The table on the previous page gives a broad idea of how frequently major topics in the syllabus are examined. It should **not be used to question spot** and predict for example that a certain topic will not be examined because it has been examined in the last two sittings. The examination team are well aware that some students try to question spot, and so they try to avoid predictable patterns. Consequently, a topic could well be examined in a number of consecutive sittings. Equally, just because a topic has not been examined for a long time, does not necessarily mean it will be examined in the next exam!

Useful websites

The websites below provide additional sources of information of relevance to your studies for *Advanced Performance Management*.

- www.accaglobal.com

  ACCA's website. The students' section of the website is invaluable for detailed information about the qualification, past exams, technical articles, and a free downloadable Student Planner App.

- www.bpp.com

  Our website provides information about BPP products and services, with a link to the ACCA website.

- www.ft.com

  This website provides information about current international business. You can search for information and articles on specific industry groups as well as individual companies.

- www.economist.com

  Here you can search for business information on a week-by-week basis, search articles by business subject and use the resources of the Economist Intelligence Unit to research sectors, companies or countries.

- www.cfo.com

  This site provides useful news and insights for financial executives.

- www.investmentweek.co.uk

  This site carries business news and articles on markets from Investment Week and International Investment.

Questions

STRATEGIC PLANNING AND CONTROL

Questions 1 to 16 cover strategic planning and control, the subject of Part A of the BPP Study Text for Paper P5.

1 AB Electronics

49 mins

AB Co manufactures, markets and distributes a large range of electronic components, and it is has established a significant market share across Europe and the United States of America.

AB has three different divisions: the Domestic Electronic Components division (DEC), the Industrial Electronic Components division (IEC), and the Specialist Components (SC) division. The DEC division and the IEC division supply standard electronic components for domestic and industrial use, while the SC division supplies specialist components which are often unique and made to specific customer requirements. Each division has its own factory, with DEC and IEC's factories based in the same Eastern European country and SC's factory based in a Western European country.

All three divisions have been profitable over the past five years, although the Board has traditionally taken a relatively cautious approach to providing strategic direction for the company. However, AB's institutional shareholders are now looking for increased growth and profitability. In the past, the institutional shareholders have been critical of AB's board for being overly cautious in their attitude to risk.

In AB's most recent annual report, published in March 20Y0, the Board stated that AB's overall strategic aim is to: 'Achieve growth and increase shareholder returns by continuing to produce and distribute high quality electronic components, and develop our international presence through expansion into new overseas markets.'

Two years earlier, in 20X8, AB established a separate trading company with a local partner in Asia to sell the IEC division's products. The ownership of the company is shared: 50% by AB and 50% with a local entrepreneur. AB chose this structure because of local legal requirements. A further legal requirement is that, in the case of the company ceasing to trade, AB will be required to reimburse the local entrepreneur the full amount of his original investment (which was $500,000).

This expansion was initially very successful, with good levels of demand being experienced for IEC's products. Recently, however, a number of environmental factors have rapidly changed. These include a forecast of declining demand for IEC's products in Asia due to adverse world economic factors (which have slowed the growth in demand for electronic components in total) and a move towards protectionism in some Asian countries. The trading company had originally been forecast to make a profit of $2 million in 20Y1, but this figure has now been re-forecast to $1.6 million.

IEC has also been unfortunate in that its direct labour costs in Asia have increased by more than the planned level. Economic intelligence suggests that this inflation will continue increasing for the next two years.

However, analysis by AB's management accountant shows that the trading company's costs (and in particular its wage costs) are proportionally much higher than its competitors.

Required

(a)   Advise the Board of AB how strategic management accounting could help it manage the performance of the trading company in Asia.   **(8 marks)**

(b)   Discuss the factors which AB should consider before withdrawing from the trading company it has established with its partner in Asia.   **(12 marks)**

(c)   Briefly discuss how the Board's attitude to risk means it may respond to potential new opportunities in a different way than the institutional shareholders would like.   **(5 marks)**

(Total = 25 marks)

2 Megasnack

Megasnack Co operates an extensive chain of fast-food outlets in a number of countries. Most outlets are owned and managed by the company but some are operated under a franchising agreement. The company's strategy is based on conformity – providing a range of standard products at a standard price, in similarly designed stores, using the same service procedures. This means that customers visiting a Megasnack outlet in any country will know what service, what eating environment and what products to expect, and (depending on currency rates) how much they will pay for their food.

The financial strategy of the company has been to achieve targets for gross contribution and net operating profit at all outlets, and to achieve sales growth by meeting customer needs and expectations better than rival fast-food companies, with support from extensive advertising. Two key performance indicators which Megasnack uses to measure the performance of its outlets are: revenue per outlet; and staff costs as a percentage of revenue.

The senior operations management team at head office have become concerned recently by a number of reported incidents in which some local outlets have been deviating from company strategy in order to meet targets for sales growth or profit margins. Several incidents are itemised below:

(1)   Some outlets have been offering special discount prices or special deals ('two-for-the-price-of-one') in order to increase sales, and, for the same reason, some outlets have offered a home delivery service, which is against company policy.

(2)   Some outlets have cut training costs for staff in order to save costs, and head office managers are concerned that this could affect the quality and speed of service given to customers. Other outlets have taken on temporary staff without training them, in order to meet the demand from customers.

(3)   There have been reports that in one country, outlets have been offering extra products on their menu, in addition to the standard Megasnack product range.

(4)   There has been adverse publicity in the media about one outlet that was disposing of food waste in a way that was contrary to health and safety laws, and in breach of the company's health and environmental policies.

(5)   Another adverse media story has been the decision by the manager of one outlet to dismiss all the staff after they took unofficial strike action. The manager took this action without consulting head office or referring to the company's industrial relations policy.

Another source of concern has been a problem with the quality of the pre-preparation of food products. Megasnack's products are pre-prepared at a number of large processing centres, and they are then transported to the outlets each day from these processing centres. Each outlet then finishes the preparation of the products for serving to customers in their own kitchen. Recently, during a period of high demand for products from the Megasnack outlets, the managers of some processing centres had resisted demands to produce more pre-prepared output, on the grounds that this would stretch their resources and damage the quality of the food items produced.

Senior management have recognised that a problem exists with the processing centres and are considering what action to take.

Required

(a)   Briefly evaluate the choice of revenue per outlet, and staff costs as a percentage of revenue as key performance indicators for Megasnack's outlets.

(5 marks)

(b)   With reference to the experiences at Megasnack, discuss the reasons for conflict between the strategic business plans of a large organisation and short-term decision making at local level.   **(10 marks)**

(c)   Recommend the measures that senior management at Megasnack should take to reduce the scope for such conflict and the risk that this conflict might occur.   **(10 marks)**

(Total = 25 marks)

3 Ganymede (APM 6/12, amended)

Ganymede University (GU) is one of the three largest universities in Teeland, which has eight universities in total. All of the universities are in the public sector. GU obtains the vast majority of its revenue through government contracts for academic research and payments per head for teaching students. The economy of Teeland has been in recession in the last year and this has caused the government to cut funding for all the universities in the country.

In order to try to improve efficiency, the chancellor of the university, who leads its executive board, has asked the head administrator to undertake an exercise to benchmark GU's administration departments against the other two large universities in the country, AU and BU. The government education ministry has supported this initiative and has required all three universities to cooperate by supplying information.

The following information has been collected regarding administrative costs for the most recent academic year:

	GU	AU	BU
	$'000	$'000	$'000
Research			
Contract management	14,430	14,574	14,719
Laboratory management	41,810	42,897	42,646
Teaching facilities management	26,993	27,263	26,723
Student support services	2,002	2,022	2,132
Teachers' support services	4,005	4,100	4,441
Accounting	1,614	1,571	1,611
Human resources	1,236	1,203	1,559
IT management	6,471	6,187	6,013
General services	17,049	16,095	18,644
Total	115,610	115,912	118,488

Drivers:			
Student numbers	28,394	22,783	29,061
Staff numbers	7,920	7,709	8,157
Research contract value ($m)	185	167	152

The key drivers of costs and revenues have been assumed to be research contract values supported, student numbers and total staff numbers. The head administrator wants you to complete the benchmarking and make some preliminary comment on your results.

The education ministry in Teeland is also keen that potential students should have as much information as possible to help them choose which University to apply to.

To this end, the ministry has proposed that summary league tables are published showing:

- The value of research funding secured by each university
- The proportion of students gaining first class and upper second (2:1) class degrees
- The proportion of students completing their courses
- The proportion of graduates who have secured full time employment within one year of graduating

However, the chancellors of a number of universities in Teeland have written to the minister for education expressing their concern at the proposal to introduce the league tables.

Required

(a) Assess the progress of the benchmarking exercise to date, explaining the actions that have been undertaken, and those that are still required. **(7 marks)**

(b) Evaluate, as far as possible, Ganymede University's benchmarked position. **(10 marks)**

(c) Evaluate the usefulness of the proposed league tables for students choosing where to study in Teeland. **(8 marks)**

(Total = 25 marks)

BPP
LEARNING MEDIA

4 Wheeler

You have recently been appointed to lead the management accounting department of Wheeler, which is a small engineering company engaged in the manufacture of precision parts. The market in which the company sells its products is small and Wheeler faces severe competition. Due to the production facilities available, the company is able to undertake only small-scale engineering work. Large-scale engineering jobs are turned away as the company does not possess the manufacturing facilities to undertake them. At best, it can act only as agent for another contractor to do the work.

The board of Wheeler is aware that the volume of work which is being turned away is increasing. This is particularly frustrating as the company is unable to utilise its capacity to the fullest extent all the time. Wheeler has achieved a steady increase in profit over the last few years. Nevertheless, the board of the company believes that it could increase profitability still further by expanding and thus being able to carry out the larger scale work which is currently being turned away.

Budgetary control and standard costing information has, for many years, been the sole output of the management accounting department. The previous management accountant prided himself on the punctuality and comprehensiveness of the reports produced. Each job is priced by adding a percentage to its total cost calculated in accordance with the company's standard costing procedures. The annual cost budget is split into monthly parts and flexed to take account of a particular period's actual production. Monthly cost variances, comprising those for direct materials, direct labour, variable and fixed production overheads, are produced and provided to the relevant manager. In addition, sales price and volume variances are produced by the management accounting department each period.

The company does not have a marketing department although new customers are obtained from advertising within professional engineering journals and by attendance at trade shows. At one such recent trade show, the managing director was introduced to the concept of benchmarking. He believes that there may be advantages in Wheeler undertaking benchmarking.

Required

(a)   In consideration of the need for the board of Wheeler to be provided with information which assists its strategic decision making, comment critically on the management accounting reports currently provided.

(5 marks)

(b)   State and justify what changes you, as management accountant, would make in providing information which facilitates strategic planning in the company.

Within your answer, describe what financial and non-financial information you would supply which is different from that already provided.

(10 marks)

(c)   Explain the concept of benchmarking and suggest how it might be applied to information for strategic planning in Wheeler.

(5 marks)

The Finance Director has also suggested that Wheeler may be able to improve its profitability if it moved away from its current standard costing approach and used a Kaizen costing approach instead. However, the other directors have asked the Finance Director for further details about this, because they are not familiar with the Kaizen costing approach.

(d)   Discuss and evaluate the impact of the Kaizen costing approach on the costing systems at Wheeler.

(5 marks)

(Total = 25 marks)

5 BPL Leisure

BPL is a medium-sized hotel and leisure company based in a European country. The hotel and leisure market in BPL's country is very competitive, and in recent years the company has noticed a significant drop in revenue and profits as a result of falling customer numbers.

However, the performance of the hotels division has been worse than that of the other divisions in the company, and the Divisional Managing Director has scheduled a meeting of his senior management team to discuss the division's performance and future strategy. The Managing Director has asked the divisional Management Accountant to prepare a summary of the division's performance for the meeting.

The Accountant's figures included the following information:

	Prior year $m	Current year $m	Forecast (next year) $m
BPL Hotels – Revenue	145	135	120
Operating profit	7.5	6.5	5.3
Market sector – Revenue	14,000	14,300	14,550
IC Hotels (market leader) – Revenue	1,580	1,620	n/a

Despite preparing the performance information, the Accountant has not been invited to the meeting .

The Marketing Director, who has recently joined BPL from the IC Hotels Group has expressed his concern that the Accountant would not be attending the meeting, and suggested to the Managing Director that he felt it was very important that the Accountant should be involved in any discussions about the division's future performance and strategy.

However, the Operations Director argued strongly against this. He told the Marketing Director, "The Management Accountant's role is to provide us with the information we need about the division's financial performance to date, which can then help us make informed decisions about its future strategy. But the Accountant has no part to play in the managerial decision-making process itself."

In an angry exchange, the Marketing Director countered that if such an out-dated approach is indicative of the quality of management across the division, this may help to explain why it has performed so poorly in recent years.

This prompted a wider discussion about what the role of a Management Accountant should be. Among the observations made were the following:

- The HR Director reported the results of a recent international study which ranked the five most important aspects of management accountants' work within their organisations as:

  (1)   Preparation and interpretation of management accounting information
  (2)   Developing and implementing accounting systems and financial controls
  (3)   Cost analysis and control
  (4)   Identifying profit improvements
  (5)   Strategic financial planning

- BPL's IT Director noted that the company had recently introduced a new IT software system, and one of the benefits given to support the business was that it would enable operational staff to produce and monitor some performance information themselves. Another benefit given was that the software would reduce the amount of time the accounting team would need to spend processing information.

Required

(a)   Compare and contrast the Marketing Director and the Operations Director's views on the role of management accountants and management accounting in an organisation.   **(7 marks)**

(b)   Evaluate the extent to which the results of the study cited by the HR director support the idea that the traditional role of the management accountant has been replaced by a role as a business partner.   **(7 marks)**

(c)   Assess how technology and the competitive environment could change the Management Accountant's role in the hotel division at BPL.   **(6 marks)**

BPL's main Board of Directors are also concerned about the hotel division's performance, and are considering a proposal to sell the division.

(d)   With reference to the BCG matrix, briefly evaluate the proposal to sell BPL's hotel division.   **(5 marks)**

(Total = 25 marks)

6 Mentons

Mentons Co is a large private company that produces confectionery and chocolate products at four sites in the UK. The company has been in existence for nearly one hundred years. In the past few years, competition from other European producers has intensified, but Mentons has responded successfully and now exports a large proportion of its products to markets across Europe. Until ten years ago, the company produced a limited range of confectionery and chocolate products, but in response to the increasing competition, it now produces a much wider product range, and is continually trying to innovate. Its recent designs of chocolates for special occasions, such as birthdays and weddings, have been a notable success.

The company now has an integrated IT system that links the four production centres with head office. Authority over operational decisions has largely been delegated to local management, subject to guidance from head office on matters of strategy and risk. Each production centre prepares its own operational and cost data, which is then consolidated at head office for the purpose of reporting to senior management.

At a senior management meeting, the CEO has raised the subject of economising on costs. One suggestion he proposed was to eliminate the role of management accountants within the company. At the moment there is a management accountant at each production centre and two at head office. The CEO doubts how much useful information the management accountants produce which operations management could not extract themselves from the company's computer system, and he is aware that many traditional management accounting techniques, such as standard costing, are no longer required or appropriate. "We have a modern lean manufacturing system based on just-in-time production methods. We need operations managers, not management accountants" the CEO said.

Required

(a)   Explain the reasons why many of the traditional management accounting methods and techniques have lost their relevance in a modern manufacturing environment.
(7 marks)

(b)   With reference to the developments at Mentons, discuss the reasons suggested by Burns and Scapens as to why the role of the management accountant has changed over time.
(9 marks)

(c)   Assess the contribution that the management accountant, or a similarly professionally qualified accountant, can make in a commercial organisation such as Mentons.
(9 marks)

(Total = 25 marks)

7 CFD (APM 12/09, amended)

The 'Care For Dogs Company' (CFD) is a very profitable organisation which was established in 1998. CFD offers accommodation, care and supervision for pet dogs owned by inhabitants of Barkland.

CFD provides temporary accommodation for dogs whose owners are unable to care for them due to holidays, work commitments, illness etc. As part of the service offered to dog owners, CFD collects and returns dogs at the beginning and end of all dog stays.

When CFD was formed, the directors created a mission statement which was 'to provide very high value for money to all of our clients'.

The directors have always attempted to manage CFD in a socially responsible manner. Indeed, they are now considering the creation of a 'Dog Sanctuary' for homeless dogs which would involve an allocation of 20% of the total accommodation available for dogs to the Dog Sanctuary. The Dog Sanctuary would accommodate homeless dogs until such time as a new owner was found for them. CFD would not receive any revenue whatsoever in respect of any homeless dog.

LEARNING MEDIA

Required

(a) (i) Discuss the purpose, potential benefits and potential problems of mission statements. **(8 marks)**
    (ii) Advise the directors of CFD regarding the appropriateness of its mission statement. **(4 marks)**

(b) (i) Explain what 'critical success factors' are, and explain the relationship between critical success factors and key performance indicators. **(4 marks)**
    (ii) Discuss **three** critical success factors for CFD, and highlight a key performance indicators for each critical success factor. **(6 marks)**

(c) Excluding the number of complaints by clients, identify and briefly explain **three** quantitative non-financial performance measures that could be used to assess the 'quality of service' provided by CFD. **(3 marks)**

(Total = 25 marks)

8 ZTC Communications
49 mins

ZTC, a telecommunications company, has recently been privatised by the government of Zeeland after legislation was passed which removed the state monopoly and deregulated the communications market, opening it up to competition from both national and overseas companies.

Prior to the deregulation, ZTC was the sole supplier of telecommunications in Zeeland and was required to provide 'the best telecommunications service the nation can afford'. At that time the government dictated the performance levels required for ZTC, and the level of resources it would be able to bring to bear to meet its objectives.

Following the privatisation, ZTC's shares were floated on the Zeeland Stock Exchange, with 80% being made available to the population of Zeeland and up to 20% being made available to foreign nationals. The government of Zeeland retained a 'golden share' to prevent the acquisition of ZTC by any foreign company.

However, the privatisation meant that many of the traditional ways in which the industry had operated would need to change under the new regulations. Apart from the money received from the flotation, the government privatised ZTC in recognition of both the changing global environment for telecommunications companies, and the overseas expansion opportunities that might exist for the privatised company. The government recognises that foreign companies will enter the home market but feels that this increased competition is likely to make ZTC more effective in the global market.

You have recently been appointed as the management accountant for ZTC and have a background in the commercial sector. The Board of Directors remains unchanged from the time ZTC's was a state monopoly.

Required

(a) With specific reference to ZTC, discuss how the external environment can affect an organisation's performance. **(5 marks)**

(b) Explain to the Board of Directors why the objectives of ZTC will need to change as a result of the privatisation of ZTC and the deregulation of the market. **(10 marks)**

(c) Recommend **two** examples of suitable strategic objectives for ZTC, following its privatisation and the deregulation of the market, and explain why each would be an appropriate long term objective. **(4 marks)**

(d) Explain the link between objectives and critical success factors, and recommend, with reasons, **two** Critical Success Factors (CSFs) which would be appropriate for ZTC as a company. **(6 marks)**

(Total = 25 marks)

9 Stayzee Hotels
49 mins

Stayzee Hotels company ('Stayzee') owns a number of hotels across a European country. Each hotel is wholly owned by the company, but the manager of each hotel has a large amount of autonomy for the day-to-day running of the hotel, and for ensuring the hotels are well maintained.

The hotel managers also have the authority to adjust room prices in their hotels. One of Stayzee's key performance measures is room occupancy rates, and the managers can increase or decrease room prices in response to the number of unoccupied rooms available and expected demand at different times of the year.

Stayzee's managers are entitled to an annual bonus payment. The level of their bonus is determined by the average room occupancy rates in their hotel over the year, as well the net profit margin (%) achieved by their hotel for the year.

Five years ago, Stayzee was bought by a group of investors, and a key part of their strategic plan for the company is increasing its market share within its current country, with a view to subsequently expanding into neighbouring countries.

Stayzee's business model has been to offer high quality accommodation and service for its customers, who include business travellers as well as leisure travellers. There are no plans to change this strategy.

Recently, Stayzee's management have become increasingly concerned about the performance of one its hotels (in Shepham).

A new manager was appointed two years ago, and the Shepham hotel's occupancy rates soon began to increase after his appointment. The hotel's net margin also increased slightly.

However, there have been an increasing number of negative comments about the Shepham hotel posted on online hotel review sites, such as TripAdvisor. Three key themes have emerged from these comments:

- Although rooms have become cheaper at the Shepham, the standard of service has fallen significantly.

- The rooms need cleaning and re-decorating; and the fixtures and fittings need replacing (for example, the beds need new mattresses).

- Business travellers who have stayed at a number of different Stayzee hotels, say the ambience of the Shepham hotel is completely different to the others in the group. It feels more like a budget hotel than a high quality hotel.

Stayzee's Operations Director has arranged an urgent meeting with the manager of the Shepham hotel to discuss the hotel's performance.

In preparation for the meeting, Stayzee's group management accountant has prepared a summary of the key performance indicators for the Shepham hotel, comparing the performance for 20X4 (last year) to 20X1 (under the previous manager). The Shepham hotel has 150 guest bedrooms, and is open for 365 days per year.

KPI	Comment	20X4	20X1
Average room occupancy rates	Number of rooms let/Total number of rooms in hotel	94%	78%
Average daily room rates	Daily revenue from rooms let/Number of rooms let	$65	$90
Service cost per room	Total daily room servicing costs/Number of rooms let	6	8.5
Promotion & marketing costs	Promotion & marketing costs as a % of total revenue	5%	7.5%
Net profit margin	EBIT/Revenue	9.8%	9.7%
Return on investment	EBIT/Total assets	11.2%	11.0%

Note. You should assume that all the hotel's revenue comes from the sale of guest rooms.

Required

(a) With reference to the Shepham hotel's performance, discuss the potential for conflict between Stayzee's long-term objectives and the short-term performance of individual hotels. **(17 marks)**

Note. There are up to 7 marks available for calculations in part (a).

(b) Evaluate the extent to which Stayzee's key performance indicators are consistent with its corporate strategy. **(8 marks)**

(Total = 25 marks)

10 Drinks Group (APM 12/12, amended)   49 mins

The Drinks Group (DG) has been created over the last three years by merging three medium-sized family businesses. These businesses are all involved in making fruit drinks. Fizzy (F) makes and bottles healthy, fruit-based sparkling drinks. Still (S) makes and bottles fruit-flavoured non-sparkling drinks and Healthy (H) buys fruit and squeezes it to make basic fruit juices. The three companies have been divisionalised within the group structure. A fourth division called Marketing (M) exists to market the products of the other divisions to various large retail chains. Marketing has only recently been set up in order to help the business expand. All of the operations and sales of DG occur in Nordland, which is an economically well-developed country with a strong market for healthy non-alcoholic drinks.

The group has recruited a new finance director (FD), who was asked by the board to perform a review of the efficiency and effectiveness of the finance department as her first task on taking office. The finance director has just presented her report to the board regarding some problems at DG.

Extract from finance director's Report to the Board:

'The main area for improvement, which was discussed at the last board meeting, is the need to improve profit margins throughout the business. There is no strong evidence that new products or markets are required but that the most promising area for improvement lies in better internal control practices.

Control

As DG was formed from an integration of the original businesses (F, S, H), there was little immediate effort put into optimising the control systems of these businesses. They have each evolved over time in their own way. Currently, the main method of central control that can be used to drive profit margin improvement is the budget system in each business. The budgeting method used is to take the previous year's figures and simply increment them by estimates of growth in the market that will occur over the next year. These growth estimates are obtained through a discussion between the financial managers at group level and the relevant divisional managers. The management at each division are then given these budgets by head office and their personal targets are set around achieving the relevant budget numbers.

Divisions

H and S divisions are in stable markets where the levels of demand and competition mean that sales growth is unlikely, unless by acquisition of another brand. The main engine for prospective profit growth in these divisions is through margin improvements. The managers at these divisions have been successful in previous years and generally keep to the agreed budgets. As a result, they are usually not comfortable with changing existing practices.

F is faster growing and seen as the star of the Group. However, the Group has been receiving complaints from customers about late deliveries and poor quality control of the F products. The F managers have explained that they are working hard within the budget and capital constraints imposed by the board and have expressed a desire to be less controlled.

The marketing division has only recently been set up and the intention is to run each marketing campaign as an individual project which would be charged to the division whose products are benefiting from the campaign. The managers of the manufacturing divisions are very doubtful of the value of M, as each believes that they have an existing strong reputation with their customers that does not require much additional spending on marketing. However, the board decided at the last meeting that there was scope to create and use a marketing budget effectively at DG, if its costs were carefully controlled. Similar to the other divisions, the marketing division budgets are set by taking the previous year's actual spend and adding a percentage increase. For M, the increase corresponds to the previous year's growth in group turnover.'

End of extract

At present, the finance director is harassed by the introduction of a new information system within the finance department which is straining the resources of the department. However, she needs to respond to the issues raised above at the board meeting and so is considering using different budgeting methods at DG. She has asked you, the management accountant at the Group, to do some preliminary work to help her decide whether and how to change the budget methods. The first task that she believes would be useful is to consider the use of rolling budgets. She thinks that fast-growing F may prove the easiest division in which to introduce new ideas.

F's incremental budget for the current year is given below. You can assume that cost of sales and distribution costs are variable and administrative costs are fixed.

	Q1	Q2	Q3	Q4	Total
	$'000	$'000	$'000	$'000	$'000
Revenue	17,520	17,958	18,407	18,867	72,752
Cost of sales	9,636	9,877	10,124	10,377	40,014
Gross profit	7,884	8,081	8,283	8,490	32,738
Distribution costs	1,577	1,616	1,657	1,698	6,548
Administration costs	4,214	4,214	4,214	4,214	16,856
Operating profit	2,093	2,251	2,412	2,578	9,334

The actual figures for quarter 1 (which has just completed) are:

	$'000
Revenue	17,932
Cost of sales	9,863
Gross profit	8,069
Distribution costs	1,614
Administration costs	4,214
Operating profit	2,241

On the basis of the Q1 results, sales volume growth of 3% per quarter is now expected.

The finance director has also heard you talking about bottom-up budgeting and wants you to evaluate its use at DG.

Required

(a) Evaluate the suitability of incremental budgeting at each division. **(8 marks)**

(b) Recalculate the budget for Fizzy division (F) using rolling budgeting and assess the use of rolling budgeting at F. **(8 marks)**

(c) Recommend, with reasons, a suitable budgeting method which could be used at the marketing division (M). **(3 marks)**

(d) Analyse and recommend the appropriate level of participation in budgeting at Drinks Group (DG). **(6 marks)**

(Total = 25 marks)

11 Godel (APM 6/14, amended)   49 mins

Godel Goodies (Godel) manufactures a variety of own-label sweets for the two largest supermarket chains in Seeland. The business makes several different flavours of the same basic product. The strategy of the business has been to be a cost leader in order to win the supermarkets' business. The sales of Godel vary up and down from quarter to quarter depending on the state of the general economy and competitive forces. Most of the sweet manufacturers have been in business for decades and so the business is mature with little scope to be innovative in new product development. The supermarkets prefer to sign suppliers to long-term contracts and so it is difficult for new entrants to gain a foothold in this market. The management style at Godel is very much command-and-control which fits with the strategy and type of business. Indeed, most employees have been at Godel for many years and have expressed their liking for the straightforward nature of their work.

The chief executive officer (CEO) of Godel has asked your firm of accountants to advise him as his finance director (FD) will be absent for several months due to a recently diagnosed illness. As the CEO is preparing for the next board meeting, he has obtained the operating statement and detailed variance analysis from one of the junior accountants (Appendix 1).

The CEO is happy with the operating statement but wants to understand the detailed operational and planning variances, given in Appendix 1, for the board meeting. He needs to know what action should be taken as a result of these specific variances.

The FD had been looking at the budgeting process before she fell ill. The CEO has decided that you should help him by answering some questions on budgeting at Godel.

Currently, the budget at Godel is set at the start of the year and performance is measured against this. The company uses standard costs for each product and attributes overheads using absorption costing based on machine hours.

No variations are allowed to the standard costs during the year. The standard costs and all budget assumptions are discussed with the relevant operational manager before being set. However, these managers grumble that the budget process is very time-consuming and that the results are ultimately of limited value from their perspective. Some of them also complain that they must frequently explain that the variances are not their fault. The CEO wants to know your views on whether this way of budgeting is appropriate and whether the managers' complaints are justified. He is satisfied that there is no dysfunctional behaviour at Godel which may lead to budget slack or excessive spending and that all managers are working in the best interests of the company.

Shortly before she fell ill, the FD had suggested that in order to stop managers complaining about having to explain variances that were not their fault, the managers should produce their own draft budgets, which would then be reviewed and consolidated centrally. The CEO is not sure what impact this change could have, and wants you to evaluate it before he makes any changes to Godel's current budgeting system.

Required

(a) Advise the CEO on the implications for performance management at Godel of analysing variances into the planning and operational elements as shown in Appendix 1. **(6 marks)**

(b) Evaluate the budgeting system at Godel. **(12 marks)**

(c) Evaluate the FD's proposal to introduce a bottom-up approach to budgeting. **(7 marks)**

(Total = 25 marks)

Appendix 1

(**Note**. You may assume that all figures in this Appendix are correct.)

Operating statement for Godel

Period: May 20X4 (last month)

			$	$	
Budgeted profit				214,200	
Budget fixed production costs				264,180	
Budgeted contribution				478,380	
Sales variances	volume		20,100		Adverse
	price		8,960		Adverse
				29,060	Adverse
Actual sales minus standard cost of sales				449,320	

		Favourable	Adverse		
		$	$		
Variable cost variance					
Material	price		4,200		
	usage	3,500			
Labour	rate	1,100			
	efficiency	24,480			
	idle time		5,600		
Variable overhead	expenditure		1,080		
	efficiency	3,060			
		32,140	10,880		
				21,260	Favourable
Actual contribution				470,580	
Budgeted fixed production overhead			271,728		
Expenditure variance			18,696		Adverse
Actual fixed production overhead				290,424	
Actual profit				180,156	

Detailed variances

Total variable cost variances		$	
	Planning	20,680	Favourable
	Operational	580	Favourable
Sales price variances			
	Planning	15,600	Adverse
	Operational	6,640	Favourable

12 Booxe (APM 6/14)

Booxe is a furniture manufacturing company based in the large, developed country of Teeland. Booxe is the largest furniture manufacturer in Teeland supplying many of the major retail chains with their own-brand furniture and also, making furniture under its own brand (Meson). In a highly competitive market such as Teeland, Booxe has chosen a strategy of cost leadership.

Booxe has been in business for more than 70 years and there is a strong sense of tradition and appreciation of craft skills in the workforce. The average time which an employee has worked for the firm is 18 years. This has led to a bureaucratic culture; for example, the company's information systems are heavily paper based. In addition and in line with this traditional culture, the organisation is divided into a set of functional departments, such as production, warehousing, human resources and finance.

In order to drive down costs, the chief executive officer (CEO) decided to re-engineer the processes at Booxe. She decided that there should be a small pilot project to demonstrate the potential of business process re-engineering (BPR) to benefit Booxe and she selected the goods receiving activity in the company's warehousing operations for this.

The CEO has asked you as a performance management expert to complete the post-implementation review of the pilot project by assessing what it has delivered in financial terms. The project identified that 10 of the warehouse staff spend about half of their time matching goods delivered documents to purchase orders and dealing with subsequent problems. It was noted that 25% of all such matches failed and the staff then had to identify the issue and liaise with the purchasing department in order to get the goods returned to the supplier and a suitable credit note issued. The project introduced a new information system to replace the existing paper-based system. The new system allowed purchase orders to be entered by the purchasing department and then checked online to the goods delivered as they arrived at the warehouse. This allowed warehouse staff to reject incorrect deliveries immediately.

The following are further details provided in relation to the project:

Notes relating to old system:

1   Average staff wage in warehouse $25,000 p.a.
2   Purchasing staff time in handling delivery queries 8·5 days per week
3   Average staff wage in purchasing is $32,000 p.a. for working a 5-day week

Notes relating to new system:

New IT system costs:

		$
4	Hardware for warehouse and purchasing depts	220,000
5	Software total cost	275,000
6	On-going servicing cost (p.a.)	22,500
7	It is expected that the new system will last for eight years.	

The CEO now plans to apply BPR across Booxe and as well as completing the post-implementation review, she also needs to know how BPR will change the accounting information systems and the culture at Booxe. Booxe's current accounting system is a traditional one of overhead absorption based on labour hours with variances to budget used as control indicators. She has heard that an activity-based approach using enterprise resource planning (ERP) systems is fairly common and wants to know how these ideas might link to BPR at Booxe.

The CEO is concerned that middle management unrest may be a problem at Booxe. For example, the warehouse manager was uncomfortable with the cultural change required in the BPR project and decided to take early retirement before the project began. As a result, a temporary manager was put in place to run the warehouse during the project.

The CEO has also begun to reconsider the human resources system at Booxe and she wants your advice on how the staff appraisal process can improve performance in the company. The existing system of manager appraisal is for the staff member to have an annual meeting with their line superior to review the previous year's work and discuss generally how to improve their efforts. Over the years, it has become common for these meetings to be informal and held over lunch at the company's expense. The CEO wants to understand the purpose of a staff appraisal system and how the process can improve the performance of the company. She also wants comments on the appropriate balance between control and staff development as this impacts on staff appraisal at Booxe.

Required

(a) Assess the financial impact of the pilot business process re-engineering (BPR) project in the warehousing operations. **(6 marks)**

(b) Assess the impact of BPR on the culture and management information systems at Booxe. **(11 marks)**

(c) Advise on the appraisal process at Booxe as instructed by the CEO. **(8 marks)**

(Total = 25 marks)

13 Business process re-engineering
49 mins

FCI is one of several insurance companies which offer insurance policies covering general risks relating to individuals and families. Cost efficiency is a major factor in the success of the companies in this industry, because competition within the industry is fierce.

Over the past three years FCI has seen the volume of business increase, but profits have remained static due to declining margins.

Although some of the processes within FCI are computerised, most of the processes which involve communication with customers are still paper-based. Responses to telephone enquiries from customers involve paper-based communications, both with the enquirers and internally within FCI. Additionally, sales staff visit potential customers in their homes to try to sell them insurance policies for their homes and their possessions. These transactions are again paper-based. This process is often slow and has led to complaints from both customers and the company's sales staff.

FCI has also been receiving a regular, and increasing, number of complaints from current and potential customers about errors in the paperwork that they receive.

The Board of Directors of FCI has announced that there is a need for a business process re-engineering programme to be conducted, with the intention of modernising the business, and has asked the management accountant to help with the planning and implementation of the programme.

The intention is to streamline the business model as much as possible, and to increase the profitability of the company. FCI intends to computerise almost all of the work done within the company. However, while some of the staff are enthusiastic about the BPR programme, a number have expressed concern about business process re-engineering and its implications for them.

Required

(a) Briefly explain the principles of business process re-engineering (BPR). **(7 marks)**

(b) (i) Discuss the improvements that the Board of Directors might expect from introducing BPR to FCI's business model. **(10 marks)**

(ii) Recommend, with reasons, TWO performance targets which FCI could introduce to help ensure that the re-engineered processes enable it to achieve its business objectives. **(5 marks)**

(c) Explain why FCI's staff might be concerned about BPR and its implications for them. **(3 marks)**

(Total = 25 marks)

14 BV Entertainments
49 mins

Charles Lee has recently joined BV Entertainments (BVE) as senior management accountant. Previously he worked for DAS, a manufacturer of popular kitchen equipment. BVE arranges entertainment events for corporate clients, such as visits to major sporting events, the theatre and opera, as well as dinners, lunches and formal receptions.

Charles is aware of significant differences between BVE and the company where he worked before. BVE's customers are very demanding, and the entertainment services they require vary considerably. Arrangements are often altered at a late stage, due to changing requirements of the client or even, in the case of sporting events, unexpected weather conditions.

Clients expect a very high quality of service. Some clients approach BVE to arrange an event specifically for them. However, for major sporting events, BVE sells tickets and then either hires a hospitality suite or erects a marquee to provide customers with high-quality meals before, during and after the event. For these events, advertising costs can be high.

Cash flows are often a critical problem for BVE, because it usually has to pay for tickets and venues well in advance of receiving payment from clients.

It is also important for BVE that each individual event should be profitable. Despite wanting high quality, clients are often reluctant to pay high prices and negotiate with BVE's representatives to obtain the best deal they can get. Representatives may therefore be asked to reduce the quoted price, or provide more in the entertainment package: prices are commonly negotiated and agreed on the spot at meetings between BVE representatives and clients.

For major sporting events, BVE buys a block of tickets which it then tries to sell within an entertainment package. Sometimes it is unable to sell all the tickets. On other occasions demand is strong, and BVE then tries to obtain additional tickets to sell.

Required

(a) With reference to BVE, explain how the characteristics of intangibility, heterogeneity, simultaneity and perishability can be used to distinguish services from manufactured products. **(6 marks)**

(b) Discuss how the accounting information requirements of BVE will differ significantly from those in a manufacturing company such as DAS. **(10 marks)**

(c) Discuss how an IT system that provides instant access for management and representatives to a central database can help to improve the quality of information available and the performance of the company. **(9 marks)**

(Total = 25 marks)

15 EEE Chemical company
49 mins

EEE is an established chemical company extracting flavours and oils from plant materials and supplying them to the flavours and fragrances industries. The shareholders include institutional investors (20%), employees and pensioners of the company (20%) and the descendants of the family (30%) who founded the business approximately 100 years ago. The remainder of the shares are in public ownership. The company is reasonably successful but, recently, there has been pressure on margins and its future is not guaranteed.

The majority of the Board of Directors are members of the founding family who have always taken an active part in the management of the business.

When the company was originally started, the surrounding area was mainly used as agricultural land but, over time, a residential area has developed around the factory. Although many of the workers in the factory live locally, some of the housing is quite expensive and has attracted affluent residents from the local city.

The chemical engineers at EEE have recently developed, and patented, a new process which would allow EEE to extract onion oil and garlic oil at far better yields than those obtained by existing processes. The market for these oils is very profitable and presents a significant opportunity for EEE to gain a real competitive advantage in its industry.

The Directors are considering a business case to develop the new extraction process commercially, with a view to it eventually replacing EEE's existing process.

Unfortunately, as with all extraction processes, there will be some leakage from the new process and, although perfectly safe and compliant with all safety legislation, the smell of the oils will offend some of the more affluent residents living near to EEE's factory. They have duly complained to local government officers.

There is very little other industry in the area and EEE is a large contributor to the local economy. One of the trade union representatives working in EEE is also an elected council member serving in the local government.

Required

As management accountant you have been asked to:

(a) Advise the Board of Directors of the advantages to EEE of analysing stakeholders' likely reactions to the proposed investment decision. **(5 marks)**

(b) Analyse the principal stakeholders in EEE in the context of the proposed investment in the new process. **(15 marks)**

(c) Recommend an acceptable course of action to the Board of Directors in the light of the stakeholder analysis conducted in (b). **(5 marks)**

(Total = 25 marks)

16 PLX Refinery (APM Pilot Paper, amended)   49 mins

PLX Refinery Co is a large oil refinery business in Kayland. Kayland is a developing country with a large and growing oil exploration and production business which supplies PLX with crude oil. Currently, the refinery has the capacity to process 200,000 barrels of crude oil per day and makes profits of $146m per year. It employs about 2,000 staff and contractors. The staff are paid $60,000 each per year on average (about twice the national average pay in Kayland).

The government of Kayland has been focused on delivering rapid economic growth over the last 15 years. However, there are increasing signs that the environment is paying a large price for this growth with public health suffering. There is now a growing environmental pressure group, Green Kayland (GK), which is organising protests against the companies that they see as being the major polluters.

Kayland's government wishes to react to the concerns of the public and the pressure groups. It has requested that companies involved in heavy industry contribute to a general improvement in the treatment of the environment in Kayland. The government has identified a national goal to reduce carbon dioxide (CO_2) emissions by 20% in the next five years, and is currently debating a proposal to raise a tax on CO_2 emissions in order to encourage reductions.

As a major participant in the oil industry with ties to the nationalised oil exploration company (Kayex), PLX believes it will be strategically important to be at the forefront of environmental developments. It is working with other companies in the oil industry to improve environmental reporting since there is a belief that this will lead to improved public perception and economic efficiency of the industry. PLX has had a fairly good compliance record in Kayland, with only two major fines (of $1m each) being levied in the last eight years for safety breaches and river pollution. However, main focus of PLX's performance measures remains on financial performance.

The existing information systems within PLX also focus on financial performance. They support financial reporting obligations and allow monitoring of key performance metrics such as earnings per share and operating margins. Recent publications on environmental accounting have suggested that activity-based costing (ABC) and a lifecycle view may be relevant in implementing improvements to these systems.

PLX is considering a major capital expenditure programme to enhance capacity, safety and efficiency at the refinery. This will involve demolishing certain older sections of the refinery and building on newly acquired land adjacent to the site. Overall, the refinery will increase its land area by 20%.

Part of the refinery extension will also manufacture a new plastic, Kayplas. Kayplas is expected to have a limited market life of five years after which it will be replaced by Kayplas2. The refinery accounting team have forecast the following data associated with this product and calculated PLX's traditional performance measure of product profit for the new product:

All figures are $m's

	20X2	20X3	20X4	20X5	20X6
Revenue	25.0	27.5	30.1	33.2	33.6
Costs					
Production costs	13.8	15.1	16.6	18.3	18.5
Marketing costs	5.0	4.0	3.0	3.0	2.0
Development costs	5.6	3.0	0.0	0.0	0.0
Product profit	0.6	5.4	10.5	11.9	13.1

Subsequently, the following environmental costs have been identified from PLX's general overheads as associated with the production of Kayplas.

	20X2	20X3	20X4	20X5	20X6
Waste filtration	1.2	1.4	1.5	1.9	2.1
Carbon dioxide exhaust extraction	0.8	0.9	0.9	1.2	1.5

Additionally, other costs associated with closing down and recycling the equipment in Kayplas production are estimated at $18m in 20X6.

The board wishes to consider how it can contribute to the oil industry's performance in environmental accounting, how it can implement the changes that this might require, and how these changes will benefit the company.

Required

(a)   Discuss and illustrate four different cost categories that would aid transparency in environmental reporting both internally and externally at PLX.   **(6 marks)**

(b)   Explain, and evaluate, how the two environmental accounting techniques mentioned – ABC and lifecycle costing – can assist in managing the environmental and strategic performance of PLX.   **(6 marks)**

(c)   Assess how the increasing focus on environmental accounting will affect PLX's performance metrics and its information systems.   **(6 marks)**

(d)   Evaluate the costing approach used for Kayplas's performance compared to a lifecycle costing approach, performing appropriate calculations.   **(7 marks)**

(Total = 25 marks)

EXTERNAL INFLUENCES ON ORGANISATIONAL PERFORMANCE

Questions 17 to 20 cover economic, fiscal and environmental factors, the subject of Part B of the BPP Study Text for Paper P5.

17 GHG (APM 6/08, amended)   49 mins

The Global Hotel Group (GHG) operates hotels in most of the developed countries throughout the world. The directors of GHG are committed to a policy of achieving 'growth' in terms of geographical coverage and are now considering building and operating another hotel in Tomorrowland. Tomorrowland is a developing country which is situated 3,000 kilometres from the country in which GHG's nearest hotel is located.

The managing director of GHG recently attended a seminar on 'the use of strategic and economic information in planning organisational performance'.

He has called a board meeting to discuss the strategic and economic factors which should be considered before a decision is made to build the hotel in Tomorrowland.

Required

(a)   Discuss the strategic and economic factors which should be considered before a decision is made to build the hotel.   **(14 marks)**

GHG has always used local labour to build and subsequently operate hotels. The directors of GHG are again considering employing a local workforce not only to build the hotel but also to operate it on a daily basis.

Required

(b)   Explain **two** ways in which the possibility of cultural differences might impact on the performance of a local workforce in building and operating a hotel in Tomorrowland.   **(6 marks)**

(c)   Advise the Board of GHG how strategic management accounting could help it manage the performance of the hotel in Tomorrowland.   **(5 marks)**

(Total = 25 marks)

18 CAP (APM 12/09, amended)   49 mins

Cundy Aquatic Pursuits (CAP) was founded 30 years ago by its managing director, Jody Cundy. CAP owns and operates a chain of Aqua Parks in the country of Lizland. Each Aqua Park has a number of large indoor and outdoor swimming pools together with a range of attractions such as water-slides, toboggan runs and surfing rides.

Jody Cundy firmly believes that growth in the number of Aqua Parks is the key to success for CAP, and therefore CAP pursued organic growth which has been financed from retained profits and public share issues. At present, Jody Cundy owns 55% of the ordinary share capital of CAP. Jody has stated on many occasions that 'I always want to control this business'.

It is now December 20X9, and the following information is available:

Year ended 30 November	20X6	20X7	20X8	20X9
Revenue ($m)	330	320	308	280
Operating costs	270	264	256	240
Profit before tax ($m)	60	56	52	40
Number of Aqua Parks	56	58	60	62

Summary Income Statement for year ended 30 November 20X9

	$m
Revenue	280
Operating costs	240
Profit before tax	40
Taxation	(10)
Profit after tax	30

Summary Statement of Financial Position at 30 November 20X9

	$m
Non-current assets	220
Net current assets	30
	250
9% Redeemable preference shares (20Y0)	(100)
	150
Financed by:	
Ordinary shares $1	28
Retained profits	122
	150

Other information:

(1) Jody Cundy considers that it is becoming more and more difficult to earn profits in Lizland and is considering a proposal to expand operations into the country of Robland. CAP would begin construction of forty new Aqua Parks within Robland, on 1 December 20X9. Each Aqua Park will require a capital outlay of $3 million.

(2) Robland is a country which is 3,200 kilometres from Lizland. A market research study commissioned by Jody Cundy indicated 'reasonable' future prospects for Robland. During recent years Robland has experienced some significant variations in its currency, the 'Rob'.

(3) CAP's price earnings ratio at the end of 20X9 was 10 compared to an industry average of 12.

(4) Dividends were paid during the year ended 30 November 20X9 as follows:

	$m
Preference	9
Ordinary	14

(5) Net current assets at 30 November 20X9 were as follows:

	$m
Inventories	30
Trade and other receivables	5
Bank	10
Trade and other payables	(15)
	30

(6) No provision has been made for redemption of the preference shares which are redeemable at a premium of 10% in just under one year's time, on 30 November 20Y0.

(7) Revenue during the year ended 30 November 20X5 amounted to $325 million.

Required

(a) Evaluate the financial performance of CAP. **(6 marks)**

(b) Discuss the principal financial, economic and social considerations that should be considered by Jody Cundy prior to a decision to proceed with the proposed expansion into Robland. **(14 marks)**

(c) Discuss the difficulties which CAP may experience in managing the performance of its operations in Robland, if the proposed expansion goes ahead. **(5 marks)**

(Total = 25 marks)

19 FGH Telecom (APM 12/10, amended)

49 mins

FGH Telecom (FGH) is one of the largest providers of mobile and fixed line telecommunications in Ostland. The company has recently been reviewing its corporate objectives in the light of its changed business environment. The major new addition to the strategic objectives is under the heading: 'Building a more environmentally friendly business for the future'. It has been recognised that the company needs to make a contribution to ensuring sustainable development in Ostland and reducing its environmental footprint. Consequently, it adopted a goal that, by 20Y7, it would have reduced its environmental impact by 60% (compared to year 20X1).

The reasons for the board's concern are that the telecommunications sector is competitive and the economic environment is increasingly harsh with the markets for debt and equities being particularly poor. On environmental issues, the government and public are calling for change from the business community. It appears that increased regulation and legislation will appear to encourage business towards better performance. The board have recognised that there are threats and opportunities from these trends. It wants to ensure that it is monitoring these factors and has asked for an analysis of the business environment with suggestions for performance measurement.

Additionally, the company has a large number of employees working across its network. Therefore, there are large demands for business travel. FGH runs a large fleet of commercial vehicles in order to service its network along with a company car scheme for its managers. The manager in charge of the company's travel budget is reviewing data on carbon dioxide emissions to assess FGH's recent performance.

Recent initiatives within the company to reduce emissions have included:

(a)   The introduction in 20Y0 of a home-working scheme for employees in order to reduce the amount of commuting to and from their offices

(b)   A drive to increase the use of teleconferencing facilities by employees

Data on FGH Telecom:

Carbon Dioxide emissions

Measured in millions of kg	20X1	20X9	20Y0
	Base year		
Commercial Fleet Diesel	105.4	77.7	70.1
Commercial Fleet Petrol	11.6	0.4	0.0
Company Car Diesel	15.1	14.5	12.0
Company Car Petrol	10.3	3.8	2.2
Other road travel (Diesel)	0.5	1.6	1.1
Other road travel (Petrol)	3.1	0.5	0.3
Rail travel	9.2	9.6	3.4
Air travel (short haul)	5.0	4.4	3.1
Air travel (long haul)	5.1	7.1	5.4
Hire Cars (Diesel)	0.6	1.8	2.9
Hire Cars (Petrol)	6.7	6.1	6.1
Total	172.6	127.5	106.6

Required

(a)   Briefly evaluate how well FGH's environmental strategy is aligned to the interests of **three** different stakeholder groups.   **(5 marks)**

(b)   Perform an analysis of FGH's business environment to identify factors which will affect its environmental strategy. For each of these factors, suggest performance indicators which will allow FGH to monitor its progress.   **(8 marks)**

(c)   Evaluate the data given on carbon dioxide emissions using suitable indicators. Identify trends from within the data and comment on whether the company's behaviour is consistent with meeting its targets.   **(9 marks)**

(d)   Suggest further data that the company could collect in order to improve its analysis and explain how this data could be used to measure the effectiveness of the reduction initiatives mentioned.   **(3 marks)**

(Total = 25 marks)

20 Stokeness (APM, 6/13)

Stokeness Engineering (Stokeness) is developing hydrogen fuel cells for use in powering large motor vehicles such as buses and trucks. They will replace standard petrol/diesel engines. The fuel cells have a clear advantage over these older technologies in having lower carbon dioxide (a greenhouse gas) emissions. The governments of many developed countries are keen to see cuts in such emissions and are supportive of a variety of possible technological solutions to this issue (such as fuel cells, electrical batteries and compressed natural gas).

These alternate power technologies would be fitted by the major international vehicle manufacturers into their vehicles for sale to their customers. The vehicle manufacturers will need to form a close partnership with any engine producer in order to make their technologies compatible, and this has already begun to happen, with two of the major manufacturers signing deals with other engine makers recently.

Stokeness's mission is to provide world-leading, reduced-emission, fuel-efficient power products for the motor industry in order to optimise shareholder returns. Stokeness has existed for only five years and is owned by its management and venture capitalists (VCs). The management were all engineers who had been working on the basic research associated with new fuel technologies and saw the opportunity to commercialise their expertise. Stokeness is highly regarded in the industry for its advanced, efficient fuel cell designs. As a result, the VCs were eager to invest in Stokeness and have assisted by placing experienced managers into the business to aid the original engineering team.

It takes five to ten years to develop a viable product for sale in this motor market. Thus, the VCs have stressed the need to analyse competition and competitive advantage in order to understand how to make the business profitable in the long term. A major problem that needs to be overcome with any of these new technologies is that there must be an infrastructure accessible to the end users for refuelling their vehicles (as the petrol station chains do for petrol engine vehicles at present). Governments have indicated their desire to support the development of such technologies to address environmental issues and to try to establish new, high-value industries in their jurisdiction. They may do this through tax breaks and investment to support the development of the refuelling infrastructure.

Production of Stokeness's fuel cells uses a special membrane that requires rare and expensive elements. Also, it has partnered with two other engineering firms to subcontract the production of certain components in the fuel cell. Stokeness has had to share much of its fuel cell design with these firms in order to overcome certain engineering difficulties.

There are a number of companies developing fuel cells but Stokeness is believed to have a two-year lead over them and to be only three years away from commercial launch. Also, there are a number of start-up companies developing the other technologies mentioned above, as well as large, existing diesel and petrol engine manufacturers who are constantly reducing the emissions from their existing engines.

The Chief Executive Officer (CEO) of Stokeness wants to understand the external business environment and its effect on performance management. She has used Porter's five forces model herself in the past for strategic decision-making but here she wants it focused on performance management. In particular, she wants your analysis of the current competitive environment to result in advice about performance management and a properly justified recommendation of one performance measure for each of the five force areas. Stokeness already uses market share to measure its competitive position but the CEO is worried about the way this is calculated, in particular the definition of the market. She has asked for your comments on this as you are a performance management expert.

Required

(a) Using Porter's five forces model, assess the impact of the external business environment on the performance management of Stokeness and give a justified recommendation of one new performance measure for each of the five force areas at Stokeness.
(16 marks)

(b) Discuss how the problems of defining the market in measuring a market share apply for Stokeness.
(4 marks)

(c) Assess the risk appetite of the venture capitalists and discuss how this might impact on performance measurement at Stokeness.
(5 marks)

(Total = 25 marks)

PERFORMANCE MEASUREMENT SYSTEMS AND DESIGN

Questions 21 to 29 cover performance measurement systems and design, the subject of Part C of the BPP Study Text for Paper P5.

21 Handra

49 mins

Handra manufactures equipment for metal testing. It also manufactures the electronic chips that go into the manufacture of the testing equipment.

The company has a well-established cost and management accounting system. The cost accounting system records the actual manufacturing costs for the electronic chips and the testing equipment, and also produces standard unit costs for the purposes of budgeting and variance analysis. The management accountant of Handra is pleased with the management information system that is in place within the company, and is particularly proud of the budgetary control reporting system that provides monthly control reports to the board within one week of the end of each month.

The market for metal testing equipment is growing at a reasonable rate, but there are three other competitors in the market. Competition between them is strong and consequently profit margins are fairly low at the moment, although Handra is operating at a profit. Handra's senior management are not sure what any competitor might do next, although they suspect that at least one of them may be in financial difficulty. Handra's sales director is certain that although low prices are one factor in the buying decisions of customers, customers are much more concerned about the quality, reliability and functional features of the equipment that Handra produces.

At a recent board meeting, the board made two important decisions. The first was a decision not to invest in new equipment for manufacturing electronic chips that would significantly reduce the water and energy consumption in the production process. This decision was taken because the discounted cash flow return on investment was considered insufficient.

The second decision was an agreement that costs needed to be reduced to improve profitability. In relation to this, the board decided that employees in the manufacturing units should be empowered more, and should be given some authority to take decisions affecting production operations.

The board also discussed the current lack of sufficient strategic information within Handra. They were aware that the decision not to invest in the new equipment had not taken into consideration the probability of rising water and energy costs in the future, and they felt they needed more information to help them predict the long term prospects for their industry.

Required

(a)   Explain the difference between strategic, tactical and operational information, and give examples of each that should be used by a company such as Handra.   **(9 marks)**

(b)   Discuss why it will be important for Handra to monitor non-financial aspects of performance as well as financial performance.   **(5 marks)**

(c)   Evaluate the compatibility of the current management accounting system in Handra and the information it provides with the objectives of management accounting.   **(7 marks)**

(d)   Discuss the ways in which the information requirements for a performance management system in Handra would be changed by the delegation of authority to employees working at factory floor level.   **(4 marks)**

(Total = 25 marks)

22 TREN engine components

TREN manufactures standard engine components. It operates a costing system based on absorption costing and standard costs, and the management control system is based on monthly variance analysis reports.

TREN has recently appointed a new CEO, who has begun to introduce changes to the manufacturing systems. He believes in lean manufacturing principles, and has begun to establish a just-in-time manufacturing system, with a focus on reducing inventories and production cycle times, and eliminating waste. Discussions are in progress with major suppliers to introduce just-in-time purchasing arrangements.

The CEO has informed the management accountant that changes will be needed to the company's internal accounting systems, and has indicated that TREN will need a lean management accounting system to support its lean manufacturing system. The CEO is dissatisfied with many of the features of the current management accounting system. There are many errors in data capture for the cost accounting system, and monthly variance reports are not produced until two weeks after the end of each month. He also considers that the wrong information is being reported.

Required

(a)   Explain the main principles of a lean information system and discuss why an organisation may not experience the improvements in productivity and profitability they expect if they implement a lean information system.

(11 marks)

(b)   Discuss the reasons why TREN's current cost and management accounting systems do not fulfil the requirements of lean information systems.

(6 marks)

(c)   Identify the changes that should be made to TREN's management accounting system in order to turn it into a lean information system.

(8 marks)

(Total = 25 marks)

23 KLP divisions

KLP has been growing its business successfully for a number of years, and the business has now grown to a size where the board considers it necessary to establish four divisions as investment centres and delegate more decision-making authority to the management of these divisions.

The authority delegated authority to the divisional managers will include decision-making responsibility for new capital investment projects for their divisions, within overall budget guidelines. The board has also decided that a reward system should be introduced and that divisional managers should receive annual bonuses based on the profitability and return on investment of their division. The board considers that an incentive system of this kind will be necessary to provide the motivation for divisional managers to work for the long-term growth and development of the company.

At the moment, the board receives performance reports for the company as a whole. The most recent annual report is summarised below.

	$m	$m
Revenue		620.2
Manufacturing costs		
Direct manufacturing costs	142.6	
Manufacturing overhead costs	186.3	
		328.9
Gross profit		291.3
Administration costs	69.8	
Selling and distribution costs	105.3	
Finance costs	11.5	
		186.6
Net profit before taxation		104.7

The four divisions are largely independent operating units, although there are transfers of components and services between some divisions. As there is no external market price for most of the services and components transferred, the board has decided that transfers will be priced at cost plus a suitable margin for profit, although the divisional managers should have the freedom to negotiate the transfer prices between themselves.

The group management accountant has been asked to design a performance reporting system that will be appropriate for the new divisional structure and the requirements for responsibility accounting. Several issues have not yet been fully considered.

(1) One of the divisions produces high-technology components. The rate of innovation for new components is rapid, and it has been estimated that an 80% learning curve applies to the manufacturing work in this division.

(2) The group management accountant is concerned about giving too much emphasis to profit and return on investment within the performance reporting system.

(3) The problems of controllability within a responsibility accounting system have not yet been properly addressed.

(4) It is already clear that the managers of the new investment centres will respond to the bonus incentives on offer and that the performance reporting system that is introduced will need to encourage them to take decisions that are in the long-term interests of KLP.

Required

(a) Assess how the requirements for responsibility accounting should affect the design of the new performance reporting system. **(12 marks)**

(b) Assess how the expected behaviour of the divisional managers should affect the design of the new performance reporting system. **(8 marks)**

(c) Management control systems have an important role to play in developing accountability.

Briefly discuss the categories of control mechanism which KLP could use to cope with the problem of organisational control. **(5 marks)**

(Total = 25 marks)

24 Racer deliveries   49 mins

RACER operates a parcel and cargo delivery service for business, government and domestic customers. It has grown successfully over the past twenty years, and now has a sophisticated management accounting system that measures and reports the costs of delivering different types and weights of package between any two locations, and the profitability of its services.

However, the board of directors is concerned about the lack of other information about the company's operations and performance. The directors believe that the success of the company has been built on a reputation for reliable service and strong brand recognition, although they have no firm evidence to support this opinion.

The directors are also aware that RACER's main competitors have introduced cost-saving automated calling systems, whereby the entire process consists of recoded messages and voice recognition, so that customers can request parcel or cargo deliveries without having to speak to anyone. RACER's directors are convinced that automated calls may provide short-term benefits through cost reduction, but that the quality of the service to customers is reduced.

The directors believe that RACER's success is built on its high-quality personal service for callers. RACER does not have an automated calling system; instead it operates a call centre which is staffed by full-time employees. Whenever customers have specific questions to ask or specific problems to handle, the call centre staff are able to use their knowledge to assist them and provide a better service.

The directors' views, however, are a matter of opinion, and there is some concern within the business that unless RACER introduces automated calling systems, it may lose business to its competitors.

The management accountant of RACER has suggested that the board would benefit from the provision of more qualitative information about its services and performance. The directors have opinions about reputation, service quality, reliability, experience and customer satisfaction, but they do not have any evidence on which to base their views or to make decisions about the company's operational systems. The management accountant has suggested that they should use customer surveys to get feedback about how well RACER is performing in key areas of the business, by asking customers to score RACER's performance in each area between 1 (very poor) – 5 (excellent).

Required

(a)   Discuss the qualitative information that may be of benefit to the directors of RACER.   **(10 marks)**

(b)   Discuss the difficulties that would have to be addressed when introducing a reporting system for the board and the company's management to provide information of a qualitative nature.   **(10 marks)**

(c)   Briefly evaluate the usefulness of introducing the customer surveys which the management accountant has suggested.   **(5 marks)**

(Total = 25 marks)

25 Forion Electronics (APM, 6/15)   49 mins

Forion Electronics (Forion) manufactures a range of electronic goods. Its business has grown rapidly over the last ten years and is now complex and international. Forion manufactures over 100 different products, selling into 25 different countries. There is a supplier base of over 200 companies from which Forion sources. As the business has become more complex, the board has found it difficult to pull together all the information that they require in order to make decisions.

The current information systems are developed in-house and are based in the functional departments (such as purchasing, manufacturing, warehousing and delivery, selling and marketing). The organisation uses the financial system as a means of bringing together information for an overview of corporate performance.

There have been a number of examples of problems encountered with information in Forion:

*   there are inefficiencies arising from ordering the wrong amount of subcomponents;

*   there are often stock-outs or obsolescence of unsold goods in the warehouses, although the marketing department prepares good sales forecasts; and

*   sometimes, there are insufficient delivery vehicles available to meet customer deadlines.

The board of Forion believes the problems arise from poor information sharing within the company. They are considering the purchase of an enterprise resource planning system (ERPS) to be the single information system for the whole organisation.

Also, Forion is planning to launch a smartphone. However, in order to make it competitive they need to have high-visibility, durable screens. As the cost of screen development is considerable, it has been decided to form a strategic alliance with a well-known screen manufacturer to provide this key component for the new smartphone. Bon Accord Screens (BAS) has been chosen as the strategic ally, as they have a strong reputation for their quality of manufacturing and new product development. BAS has been trying to break into the smartphone market for several years.

The alliance agreement has stipulated three critical areas of performance for BAS' supply to Forion:

1.   quality of manufacturing, measured by fault rates of screens supplied being within agreed tolerances (so that they fit Forion's phone-bodies);

2.   time of delivery, measured by the number of times a shipment is more than one day overdue; and

3.   the ability to provide technical upgrades to the screens as the market demands.

The service level agreement (SLA) will be based on these three points and there will be financial penalties built into the agreement if BAS fails to meet these.

Required

(a)   Discuss the integration of information systems in an ERPS and how the ERPS may impact on p███
      management issues at Forion.

(b)   Evaluate, from Forion's viewpoint, the usefulness of the three critical areas in the alliance agreement for███
      measuring the performance of BAS.
      (8 marks)

(c)   Evaluate the relative reliability of financial and non-financial data from internal and external sources in the
      context of the alliance between Forion and BAS.
      (7 marks)

      (Total = 25 marks)

26 Quark Healthcare (APM, 12/13)   49 mins

Quark Healthcare (Quark) runs a number of large hospitals which provide general medical care for the people of Veeland. Veeland is an advanced economy and healthcare is considered to be a high skill, high technology and high status industry. It is compulsory for the people of Veeland to purchase health insurance and then the insurance companies reimburse the healthcare providers for services delivered. The insurance companies audit the healthcare providers and grade them for value for money. As there are a number of hospital chains (such as Quark), the insurers will encourage their insured customers to use those which are most efficient. The ultimate sanction for a healthcare provider is for an insurance company to remove them from the list of acceptable providers.

Quark has large amounts of capital tied up in expensive medical equipment and a drug inventory. The existing systems for accounting for these items are traditional ones aimed at avoiding theft and obsolescence. Quark has an inventory system which requires regular (weekly) physical checks of the drugs in inventory in order to update it. It is important that the right drugs must be in easily accessible stores (located throughout the hospital) in order to act quickly in case of a medical emergency. Also, the accounting staff at Quark maintain a non-current asset register (NCAR) which logs the location of all major assets including medical equipment. The problem with the non-current asset register is that it is often out-of-date as doctors will take equipment in time of emergency and not properly log its new location. This often leads to equipment lying unused in one area of the hospital while being searched for in another area, to the detriment of patient care.

Quark has recently instituted a tagging project where radio-frequency identification devices (RFID) will be attached to the most valuable pieces of equipment used in treatment and also to batches of high-value drugs. The hospitals are fitted with WiFi networks which can pick up the RFID signal so that the RFID tags will be detectable throughout a hospital. The tags will identify the object which they are attached to by a unique identification number and will give its location. The identifier number will link to the inventory system which will identify the product, the quantity initially delivered in that batch and the date of delivery. The RFID information will be accessible through the computer terminals throughout the hospitals.

The chief financial officer (CFO) of Quark has asked you to advise him on the impact of this new system on performance management at Quark. He has suggested that you look at the costs and benefits which will be associated with producing the information from the RFID system, the impact of the nature of the information supplied, the changes to performance management reporting and how the new information could be used for improved control at the hospital. He is keen to be seen to be at the forefront of accounting and management developments and has been reading about cost control techniques. Recently, he has heard about 'lean' systems, so wants to know how the RFID system and its impact on the hospital fit with this concept. Given the importance of the medical staff in running the hospital, he also wants to know how their behaviour will be affected by the control information from the RFID system. There is a very strict social order among these staff (in increasing order of skills: nurses, general doctors and specialist doctors) which regularly causes friction when one group feels it is not given its due status. For example, recently, the general doctors agreed to a new method for nurses to record drugs administered to patients but this new system has not been fully implemented due to complaints by the nurses and specialist doctors who were not consulted on the change.

...e radio-frequency identification devices (RFID) system on the performance
...as suggested by the CFO.   **(12 marks)**

...overall management of the hospital can be considered to be 'leaner' as a result of the
...em.   **(7 marks)**

...ical staff's attitudes will influence the design and implementation of the RFID system
...used to promote responsibility and accountability at the hospital.   **(6 marks)**

(Total = 25 marks)

27 Bluefin School (APM 12/11, amended)   49 mins

Bluefin School (Bluefin) is a school for 12 to 17-year-old pupils. It currently has 1,000 pupils attending drawn from its local area. The school is run by an executive group comprising the head of school and two deputy head teachers. This group reports to a board of governors who are part-time and selected from the local community and parents. The school is wholly funded by the government.

The school's ethos is 'to promote learning, citizenship and self-confidence among the pupils. This is developed from a consensus, led by the board of governors and the head of school and informed by the views of the pupils' parents'.

The school information systems are highly decentralised. Each department keeps its own records on a stand-alone PC using basic word processing and spreadsheet packages. The school's administrative department has a small network in its own offices with compatible applications and also a database and financial recording and reporting package for use in schools (provided by the government).

The school is broken down into 11 academic departments such as mathematics, science and history. Each department head must prepare information for reporting to the board by inputting and processing the data. They obtain some help from an administrator who visits each department to spend a few hours per week helping in the recording and preparation of the departmental information. The department heads have different approaches to reporting their performance, with some using average marks in the annual exams for each class and some using pass rates of the annual exams. Some department heads present graphs of their data while most use tables of figures.

The information is passed from each department to the school administration office on a memory stick (USB flash drive). The school administration office prints out the information for each department and adds it to a financial report creating a governors' pack of usually about 13 pages for the annual review board meeting. The financial report is a detailed income and expenditure statement for the period under review (usually a two page print-out from the reporting package). An example of one of the 11 departments' report is given in the Appendix on the next page.

The board of governors meets every quarter and reviews the governors' pack once a year. The board are concerned that the information that they are receiving is not meeting their needs and that there are a number of problems with the control and security of some of the data.

It has been suggested that the school should consider improving its information systems by installing a network across the school to link the departmental computers and the administration department. A single database would be created to store all the performance information. The computers would then be linked to the internet in order to facilitate data transfer to other schools in the region and to the government.

[*Question continues on the next page*]

Appendix

Bluefin School

Mathematics department

Year 20X0/20X1

	Class	Average marks	
		Current yr	Previous yr
		%	%
Year 1	A	63	59
	B	60	61
	C	51	55
	D	47	44
Year 2	A	61	70
	B	58	62
	C	49	47
	D	45	43
Year 3	A	67	67
	B	61	57
	C	50	50
	D	42	41
Year 4	A	62	58
	B	59	59
	C	50	54
	D	46	47
Year 5	A	57	58
	B	51	49
	C	47	48
Year 6		54	53

Notes

Each year contains pupils of the same age.

Annual national exams are set in years 4, 5 and 6.

Each year group is divided into different classes in order to ensure that classes do not exceed 35 pupils.
(Not all pupils take every subject each year.)

Average marks are for the annual examinations.

Required

(a) With reference to the current situation at Bluefin School, discuss the controls and security procedures that are necessary for management information. **(9 marks)**

(b) Using the limited information available, evaluate the usefulness of the pack that is provided to the board of governors. **(6 marks)**

(c) Discuss the usefulness of the different ways the heads of department could use to present their performance information to the board. **(5 marks)**

(d) Evaluate the improvements suggested to the information systems at Bluefin. **(5 marks)**

(Total = 25 marks)

28 Great National Trains

In contrast to many other countries, the railway system in Pecoland remains nationalised, and services are operated by Great National Trains (GNT). The Chairman of the GNT Railways Board reports to senior civil servants in the Ministry of Transport. However, Pecoland also has a rail regulator who has the power to make recommendations directly to the Minister of Transport in relation to all issues relating to the operation and performance of GNT.

The Rail Regulator's role is to ensure that the rail service in Pecoland is delivered in a safe and efficient manner, and in a way which provides high levels of satisfaction to all rail users. GNT's overall strategic objective is to deliver reliable, punctual and safe rail services to customers efficiently and cost effectively, while continuing to reduce its level of carbon emissions.

The Government views cost effectiveness as the key aspect of all public sector services in Pecoland, and it has also imposed the over-riding financial objective that GNT should at least cover its operating costs from the revenue it earns.

Over the last 10 years, GNT has made a significant investment in its rail network and its trains. Diesel trains are being replaced by electric trains following the electrification of the network.

There are three subsidiary companies within GNT:

- Passenger Co runs passenger rail services, which include express services between the major towns and cities, as well as slower services to more remote locations. (The number of services on some rural routes has been reduced significantly in recent years, due to the relatively low number of passengers using them. However, these cut-backs provoked strong opposition from groups of local residents who relied on the railways for their transport.)

- Freight Co runs freight services, transporting bulk goods such as coal, oil, industrial products such as steel; cars; as well as a range of retail products for supermarkets and other retailers. Across the majority of the rail network, freight trains run on the same tracks as passenger trains, although there are a few lines (for example, to power stations) which are used exclusively by freight trains.

- Track Co is responsible for managing, and upgrading, the track, signalling and property for example station buildings.

The majority of Passenger Co's locomotives are now electric as the lines between all the major cities in Pecoland have already been electrified. Most of Freight Co's trains are hauled by diesel locomotives, but it has recently invested in a number of electric engines which are less harmful to the environment. Passenger Co contributes about 50% of GNT's total revenue.

Freight Co contributes about 40% of GNT's total revenue. Its share of the freight haulage market in Pecoland is approximately 10%, and the majority of freight its transported by road. However, the amount of freight carried by rail has begun to increase in recent years due to worsening congestion on Pecoland's roads.

A number of retailers in Pecoland are currently considering the impact of their supply chains on the environment and looking for ways to reduce the impacts of their supply chain. They are currently evaluating the environmental benefits of switching more of their deliveries from road to rail freight. However, the retailers, like many companies in Pecoland also value the convenience of road freight, which allows goods to be delivered directly to their premises.

Key performance indicators

Each of the three subsidiary companies measures their performance against a range of KPIs, based upon meeting GNT's overall strategic objectives. Examples of the KPIs include:

Passenger Co

- The number of customer complaints received
- The percentage of trains arriving at their destination on time
- The number of signals passed at danger

Freight Co

- Train capacity utilisation (the actual load capacity as a proportion of the total available load capacity for a journey)

- The percentage of trains arriving at their destination on time

- Carbon emissions generated (per tonne transported per kilometre travelled)

- The number of signals passed at danger

Track Co

- The number of delays to services per month due to signalling failure
- The number of complaints per month relating to station cleanliness

In recent years, there have been suggestions that GNT is not providing a value for money service for rail users, and that the rail services in Pecoland should be privatised. The Minister of Transport and the Rail Regulator both oppose privatisation, however, and believe that retaining GNT under national control provides the best way of creating value from Pecoland's rail system over the medium and long term.

GNT produces an annual report, which summarises its financial and operating performance for the year, including statistics showing actual performance against target for the KPIs. The group management accountant collates all these figures for the annual report. The annual report also describes the governance structures within the organisation.

However, the Rail Regulator has recently recommended that GNT should produce an integrated report, because this would help to focus attention on the organisation's ability to create value in the medium and long term, as well as on its short term performance. GNT's Board are sceptical of the idea, feeling that the costs involved in producing the amount of non-financial information required for an integrated report will outweigh the benefits of doing so.

Required

(a) Discuss the difficulties faced by GNT, as a public sector organisation, in setting and measuring strategic objectives. **(10 marks)**

(b) Discuss the additional information which GNT would provide to its stakeholders in an integrated report, compared to its current annual report. **(6 marks)**

(c) Evaluate the potential impact on the amount and type of information prepared by the Group management accountant if GNT starts to produce integrated reports, and the issues the management accountant could face in preparing that information. **(9 marks)**

(Total = 25 marks)

29 Amal (APM 6/12, amended)   49 mins

Amal Airline (Amal) is the national airline of Jayland. The airline's objective is to be the best premium global airline.

Amal provides long- and short-haul services all over the world and is based at its hub at Jaycity airport. Amal has been hit by a worldwide reduction in air travel due to poor economic conditions. The most recent financial results show a loss and this has caused the board to reconsider its position and take action to address the changed environment.

Amal has cut its dividend in order to conserve cash and it is trying to rebuild profitability by reducing costs by 14%. The airline is capital intensive as it requires to maintain a large fleet of modern aircraft. The two major costs for the airline are staff and fuel. In trying to renegotiate working conditions and pay, the management have angered the unionised workforce. There has already been some strike action by the unions representing the aircraft crew and ground staff and more is threatened.

Additionally, the board are pushing forward a large project to improve the design of the company website in order to increase the number of passengers who check-in on-line and so would not require as much assistance at the airport. The new design is also aiming to increase the number of passengers who book their tickets through the company's website rather than other resellers' websites or at booking agents.

The board has also been considering taking advantage of new technology in aircraft engines by making a large investment ($450m) in new low-noise, fuel-efficient aircraft in an effort to reduce the environmental complaints surrounding air travel and also cut costs.

The CEO has provided the data below on Amal and two of its main competitors. Kayland Air is a government owned and run airline in the neighbouring country of Kayland. It has a similar mix of business to Amal and targets a similar market. Cheapo Air is currently one of the most successful of the new privately-owned airlines that have gained significant market share over the last 15 years by offering a cheap but basic short-haul service to customers in and around Jayland. Cheapo Air subcontracts many of their activities in order to remain flexible. The CEO wants you to calculate some suitable performance measures and explain the results.

Data provided by the CEO:

Data for the most recent calendar year

		Amal	Kayland Air	Cheapo Air
Passengers ('000s)		23,649	38,272	35,624
Passenger kilometres (millions)		79,618	82,554	40,973
Revenue	$m	5,430	7,350	2,170
Costs				
Fuel	$m	1,480	1,823	535
Staff	$m	1,560	2,998	238
Staff numbers		32,501	56,065	5,372
Operating profit	$m	630	54	127
Number of aircraft		182	361	143
Average aircraft size (seats)		195	163	125
Seat kilometres (millions)		100,654	105,974	46,934

Note. A seat kilometre is generated for every one kilometre flown by an **available** seat on the company's aircraft.

The CEO believes that Amal could be making more use of Big Data. He has recently returned from a conference about 'Big Data in the Airline industry' where one of the speakers talked about the benefits of Big Data in relation to four key areas:

- Identifying trends in passenger demand and using this to set prices

- Understanding and influencing the customer's selection process (in particular reducing the number of potential customers who start booking a flight online but do not go on to complete the transaction)

- Boosting revenue from in-flight sales by optimising the on-board store for individual flights

- Understanding customer sentiment and improving customer satisfaction

Amal currently offers the same selection of in-flight products on all its flights.

The CEO has asked you to explain how using Big Data in these four areas could help Amal improve its performance. However, he also wants to understand the potential implications that using Big Data could have for Amal's management information systems, given that a number of Amal's IT staff are already working on the website upgrade project.

Required

(a) Using the data provided, analyse the three airlines using appropriate performance indicators and comment on your results.

(12 marks)

(b) Explain how Big Data could be used to help Amal's performance, in relation to the four key areas identified at the conference.

(8 marks)

(c) Discuss the potential implications of Big Data for Amal's management information systems. **(5 marks)**

(Total = 25 marks)

STRATEGIC PERFORMANCE MEASUREMENT

Questions 30 to 48 cover strategic performance measurement, the subject of Part D of the BPP Study Text for Paper P5.

30 NCL

49 mins

NCL, which has a divisionalised structure, undertakes civil engineering and mining activities. All applications by divisional management teams for funds with which to undertake capital projects require the authorisation of the board of directors of NCL. Once authorisation has been granted to a capital application, divisional management teams are allowed to choose the project for investment.

Under the terms of the management incentive plan, which is currently in operation, the managers of each division are eligible to receive annual bonus payments which are calculated by reference to the return on investment (ROI) earned during each of the first two years by new investments. ROI is calculated using the average capital employed during the year. NCL depreciates its investments on a straight-line basis.

One of the most profitable divisions during recent years has been the IOA Division, which is engaged in the mining of precious metals. The management of the IOA Division is currently evaluating three projects relating to the extraction of substance 'xxx' from different areas in its country of operation. The management of the IOA Division has been given approval by the board of directors of NCL to spend $24 million on one of the three proposals it is considering (ie North, East and South projects).

The following net present value (NPV) calculations have been prepared by the management accountant of the IOA Division.

	North Project		East Project		South Project	
	Net cash inflow/ (outflow) $'000	Present value at 12% $'000	Net cash inflow/ (outflow) $'000	Present value at 12% $'000	Net cash inflow/ (outflow) $'000	Present value at 12% $'000
Year 0	(24,000.0)	(24,000.0)	(24,000.0)	(24,000.0)	(24,000.0)	(24,000.0)
Year 1	6,000.0	5,358.0	11,500.0	10,269.5	12,000.0	10,716.0
Year 2	8,000.0	6,376.0	11,500.0	9,165.5	10,000.0	7,970.0
Year 3	13,500.0	9,612.0	11,500.0	8,188.0	9,000.0	6,408.0
Year 4	10,500.0	6,678.0	–	–	3,000.0	1,908.0
NPV		4,024.0		3,623.0		3,002.0

The following additional information concerning the three projects is available:

(1)   Each of the above projects has a nil residual value.

(2)   The life of the East project is three years. The North and South projects are expected to have a life of four years.

(3)   The three projects have a similar level of risk.

(4)   Ignore taxation.

Required

(a)   Briefly discuss the benefits and potential drawbacks for an organisation of introducing reward schemes for its employees. **(5 marks)**

(b)   Explain (with relevant calculations) why the interests of the management of the IOA Division might conflict with those of the board of directors of NCL. **(10 marks)**

(c)   Discuss whether the adoption of residual income (RI) might prove to be a superior basis for the management incentive plan operated by NCL.

(**Note**. No illustrative calculations should be incorporated into your explanation.) **(4 marks)**

The IOA Division is also considering whether to undertake an investment in the West of the country (the West Project). An initial cash outlay investment of $12 million will be required and a net cash inflow amounting to $5 million is expected to arise in each of the four years of the life of the project.

The activities involved in the West project will cause the local river to become polluted and discoloured due to the discharge of waste substances from mining operations.

It is estimated that at the end of year four a cash outlay of $2 million would be required to restore the river to its original colour. This would also clear 90% of the pollution caused as a result of the mining activities of the IOA Division.

The remaining 10% of the pollution caused as a result of the mining activities of the IOA Division could be cleared up by a further cash outlay of $2 million.

(d)   Evaluate the West project and, stating your reasons, comment on whether the board of directors of NCL should spend the further $2 million in order to eliminate the remaining 10% of pollution.   **(6 marks)**

(**Note**. You should ignore taxation.)

(Total = 25 marks)

31 Landual Lamps (APM, 6/13)   49 mins

Landual Lamps (Landual) manufactures and delivers floor and table lamps for homes and offices in Beeland. The company sells through its website and uses commercial logistics firms to deliver their products. The markets for its products are highly competitive. The company has traditionally relied on the high quality of its designs to drive demand for its products.

The company is divided into two divisions (components and assembly), plus a head office that provides design, administrative and marketing support. The manufacturing process involves:

(1)   The components division making the housing components and electrical components for the lamp. This is an intricate process as it depends on the specific design of the lamp and so serves as a significant source of competitive advantage for Landual.

(2)   The assembly division assembling the various components into a finished lamp ready for shipment. This is a simple process.

The finance director (FD) of Landual is currently overloaded with work due to changes in financial accounting policies that are being considered at board level. As a result, she has been unable to look at certain management accounting aspects of the business and has asked you to do a review of the transfer pricing policy between the components and assembly divisions.

The current transfer pricing policy at Landual is as follows:

(a)   Market prices for electrical components are used as these are generic components for which there is a competitive external market.

(b)   Prices for housing components based on total actual production costs to the components division are used as there is no external market for these components since they are specially designed for Landual's products.

Currently, the components division produces only for the assembly division in order to meet overall demand without the use of external suppliers for housing and electrical components. If the components division were to sell its electrical components externally, then additional costs of $269,000 would arise for transport, marketing and bad debts.

The FD is considering two separate changes within Landual: one to the transfer pricing policy, and a second one to the divisional structure.

First, the transfer pricing policy for housing components would change to use variable cost to the components division. The FD wants to know the impact of the change in transfer pricing policy on the existing results of the two divisions and the company. (No change is proposed to the transfer price of the electrical components.)

Second, as can be seen from the divisional performance report below, the two divisions are currently treated as profit centres. The FD is considering splitting the components division into two further separate divisions: an electrical components division and a housing components division. If the board agrees to this proposal, then the housing components division will be treated as a cost centre only, charging its total production cost to the assembly division. The electrical components and assembly divisions will remain as profit centres.

The FD needs to understand the impact of this proposed new divisional structure on divisional performance assessment and on the company as a whole. She has asked that, in order to keep the discussion on the new divisional structure simple, you use the existing transfer pricing policy to do illustrative calculations. She stated that she would reallocate head office costs to the two new components divisions in proportion to their cost of sales. You are provided with the following financial and other information for Landual Lamps.

Actual data for Landual Lamps for the year ended 31 March 20X3

	Components Division $'000	Assembly Division $'000	Landual Lamps $'000
Sales Electrical	1,557		
Housing	8,204		
sub-total	9,761	15,794	15,794
Cost of sales			
Electrical	804	1,557	
Housing	6,902	8,204	
sub-total	7,706	9,761	7,706
Fixed production costs			
Electrical	370		
Housing	1,302		
sub-total	1,672	1,268	2,940
Allocated head office costs	461	2,046	2,507
Profit	(78)	2,719	2,641

Note. The components division has had problems meeting budgets recently, with an adverse variance of $575,000 in the last year. This variance arises in relation to the cost of sales for housing component production.

Required

(a) Evaluate the current system of transfer pricing at Landual, using illustrative calculations as appropriate.

(10 marks)

(b) Advise the finance director (FD) on the impact of changing the transfer pricing policy for housing components as suggested by the FD and comment on your results, using illustrative calculations as appropriate.

(6 marks)

(c) Evaluate the impact of the change in proposed divisional structure on the profit in the divisions and the company as directed by the FD.

(9 marks)

(Total = 25 marks)

32 Alpha Division (APM 12/07)   49 mins

Alpha Division, which is part of the Delta Group, is considering an investment opportunity to which the following estimated information relates:

(1) An initial investment of $45m in equipment at the beginning of year 1 will be depreciated on a straight-line basis over a three-year period with a nil residual value at the end of year 3.

(2) Net operating cash inflows in each of years 1 to 3 will be $12.5m, $18.5m and $27m respectively.

(3) The management accountant of Alpha Division has estimated that the NPV of the investment would be $1.937m using a cost of capital of 10%.

(4) A bonus scheme which is based on short-term performance evaluation is in operation in all divisions within the Delta Group.

Required

(a) (i) Calculate the residual income of the proposed investment and comment briefly (using **only** the above information) on the values obtained in reconciling the short-term and long-term decision views likely to be adopted by divisional management regarding the viability of the proposed investment.

(6 marks)

(ii) A possible analysis of divisional profit measurement at Alpha Division might be as follows:

	$m
Sales revenue	XXX
Less: variable costs	XXX
1. Variable short run contribution margin	XXX
Less: controllable fixed costs	XXX
2. Controllable profit	XXX
Less: non-controllable avoidable costs	XXX
3. Divisional profit	XXX

Required

Discuss the relevance of each of the divisional profit measures 1, 2 and 3 in the above analysis as an acceptable measure of divisional management performance and/or divisional economic performance at Alpha Division.

You should use appropriate items from the following list relating to Alpha Division in order to illustrate your discussion:

(i) Sales to customers external to the Delta Group
(ii) Inter-divisional transfers to other divisions within the Delta Group at adjusted market price
(iii) Labour costs or equipment rental costs that are fixed in the short term
(iv) Depreciation of non-current assets at Alpha Division
(v) Head office finance and legal staff costs for services provided to Alpha Division

(8 marks)

(b) Summary financial information for the Gamma Group (which is not connected with the Delta Group) is as follows:

Income statements/financial information:

	20X6	20X7
	$m	$m
Revenue	400	450
Profit before tax	96	117
Income tax expense	(29)	(35)
Profit for the period	67	82
Dividends	(23)	(27)
Retained earnings	44	55

Statements of financial position

	20X6	20X7
	$m	$m
Non-current assets	160	180
Current assets	180	215
	340	395
Financed by:		
Total equity	270	325
Long-term debt	70	70
	340	395

Other information is as follows:

(1)   Capital employed at the end of 20X5 amounted to $279m.

(2)   The Gamma Group had non-capitalised leases valued at $16m in each of the years 20X5 to 20X7 which were not subject to amortisation.

(3)   Amortisation of goodwill amounted to $5m per year in both 20X6 and 20X7. The amount of goodwill written off against reserves on acquisitions in years prior to 20X6 amounted to $45m.

(4)   The Group's pre-tax cost of debt was estimated to be 10%.

(5)   The Group's cost of equity was estimated to be 16% in 20X6 and 18% in 20X7.

(6)   The target capital structure is 50% equity, 50% debt.

(7)   The rate of taxation is 30% in both 20X6 and 20X7.

(8)   Economic depreciation amounted to $40m in 20X6 and $45m in 20X7. These amounts were equal to the depreciation used for tax purposes and depreciation charged in the income statements.

(9)   Interest payable amounted to $6m per year in both 20X6 and 20X7.

(10) Other non-cash expenses amounted to $12m per year in both 20X6 and 20X7.

Required

(i)   Stating clearly any assumptions that you make, estimate the Economic Value Added (EVA™) of the Gamma Group for both 20X6 and 20X7 and comment briefly on the performance of the Group.   **(8 marks)**

(ii) Briefly discuss **three** disadvantages of using EVA™ in the measurement of financial performance.

(3 marks)

(Total = 25 marks)

33 Stillwater Services (APM 12/12, amended)   49 mins

Stillwater Services (SS) is a listed water utility company providing water and sewage services to the public and businesses of a region of Teeland. The company was formed when the government-owned Public Water Company of Teeland was broken up into regional utility companies (one of which was SS) and sold into private ownership over four years ago.

As a vital utility for the economy of Teeland, water services are a government-regulated industry. The regulator is principally concerned that SS does not abuse its monopoly position in the regional market to unjustifiably increase prices. The majority of services (80%) are controlled by the regulator who sets an acceptable return on capital employed (ROCE) level and ensures that the pricing of SS within these areas does not breach this level. The remaining services, such as a bottled water operation and a contract repairs service, are unregulated and SS can charge a market rate for these. The regulator calculates its ROCE figure based on its own valuation of the capital assets being used in regulated services and the operating profit from those regulated services.

The target pre-tax ROCE set by the regulator is 6%. If SS were to breach this figure, then the regulator could fine the company. In the past, other such companies have seen fines amounting to millions of dollars.

The board of SS are trying to drive the performance for the benefit of the shareholders. This is a new experience for many at SS, having been in the public sector until four years ago. In order to try to better communicate the objective of maximising shareholder wealth, the board have decided to introduce economic value added (EVA™) as the key performance indicator.

The finance director has asked you to calculate EVA™ for the company, based on the following financial information for the year ending 30 September 20X2:

Stillwater Services

	Regulated $m	Non-regulated $m	20X2 Total $m
Revenue	276.0	69.0	345.0
Operating costs	230.0	47.0	277.0
Operating profit	46.0	22.0	68.0
Finance charges			23.0
Profit before tax			45.0
Tax at 25%			9.5
Profit after tax			35.5

Capital employed:	20X2 $m	20X1 $m
Measured from published accounts	657.0	637.0
Measured by regulator (for regulated services only)	779.0	761.0

Notes

1 Total operating costs include:

	20X2 $m	20X1 $m
Depreciation	59	57
Provision for doubtful debts	2	0.5
Research and development	12	–
Other non-cash items	7	6

2 Economic depreciation is assessed to be $83million in 20X2.

Economic depreciation includes any appropriate amortisation adjustments.

In previous years, it can be assumed that economic and accounting depreciation were the same.

3 Tax is the cash paid in the current year ($9m) and an adjustment of $0·5m for deferred tax provisions. There was no deferred tax balance prior to 20X2.

4 The provision for doubtful debts was $4·5m on the 20X2 statement of financial position.

5 Research and development is not capitalised in the accounts.

It relates to a new project that will be developed over five years and is expected to be of long-term benefit to the company. 20X2 is the first year of this project.

6 Cost of capital of SS

Equity	16%
Debt (pre-tax)	5%

7 Gearing of SS

40% Equity
60% Debt

Required

(a) Evaluate the performance of SS using EVA™. **(13 marks)**

(b) With reference to the issues involved in managing different stakeholder groups, analyse the potential influence of the regulator, the directors, and the shareholders on performance management at SS. **(5 marks)**

(c) Assess whether SS meets its regulatory ROCE target and comment on the impact of such a constraint on performance management at SS. **(7 marks)**

(Total = 25 marks)

34 Seatown

49 mins

Seatown is located on the coast. The town's main industry is tourism with an emphasis on family holidays and consequently the cleanliness of the town's beaches is a major factor in the town's success.

The town council, which is the local government authority, has a cleaning department that is responsible for keeping the beaches clean and tidy. Early every morning, after the tide has gone out, the beaches are swept, using equipment that is towed behind tractors. This equipment skims the top layer of sand and runs it through a filter to remove any litter, before returning the cleaned sand to the beach. Most of the litter is paper and plastic packaging which tourists have discarded, but the litter can include glass bottles and aluminium cans.

To try to prevent litter being left on the beach the town council also places bins on the beaches above the high water mark. Litter bins need to be emptied regularly, otherwise holidaymakers pile their rubbish beside the bins and that leads to litter being spread by the wind or by seabirds scavenging for food scraps.

The cost of cleaning the beaches is a major expense for the town council. The management team of the town council has asked the internal audit department to investigate whether the town is getting good "value for money" from this expenditure. The head of internal audit has sought clarification from the town managers on whether the audit should focus on the economy and efficiency of the cleaning operations or their effectiveness. Economy and efficiency audits generally focus on whether cost can be reduced for the same level of service and effectiveness audits ask whether better service can be achieved for the same cost.

Required

(a) Recommend, giving reasons, the matters that the town council's internal audit department should study in order to evaluate the economy and efficiency of the beach cleaning activities.

Your answer should include advice on how to obtain the necessary data and information. **(10 marks)**

(b) Recommend, giving reasons, the matters that the town council's internal audit department should study in order to evaluate the effectiveness of the beach cleaning activities.

Your answer should include advice on how to obtain the necessary data and information. **(10 marks)**

Following their investigation, the internal audit department advised the council to consider whether it would be beneficial to outsource the beach cleaning services rather than having an in-house cleaning department. However, the internal audit report also pointed out that if the council does outsource the cleaning services, the council will need to draw up a service level agreement with the outsource partner which it employs to provide the cleaning services.

Required

(c) Briefly discuss the importance of the council having a service level agreement with the outsource partner if the council decides to outsource the beach cleaning services. **(5 marks)**

(Total = 25 marks)

35 Essland Police Forces (APM 12/13)

49 mins

You are a performance management expert brought in by the Chief Executive Officer (CEO) of the Department of the Interior for the country of Essland. The department is a branch of the Essland government which handles security, policing, immigration and border control. The CEO is a civil servant and he reports to the Minister for the Interior. The Minister for the Interior is an elected politician selected by the Prime Minister of Essland, who leads its government.

The newly-elected Minister for the Interior has instructed the CEO to implement his policy for improving the regional police forces' performance by copying the method used for schools. In a recent initiative by the School's Ministry, a league table for the hundreds of schools in Essland was created, showing the best and worst in terms of examination performance only, in order to motivate senior school managers to improve. The league table was used to create targets for assessing the schools' and their managers' performance. Additionally, parents in Essland have the right to choose which school their children attend and so often base their selection on league table performance. Therefore, the Minister has had a policy review body draw up a method of creating a league table for the police forces.

The CEO has requested your help to clarify his own thinking on this new policy for the four regional police forces in Essland (Cashire (C), Dashire (D), Eshire (E) and Fashire (F)). The CEO needs you to assess the use of the league table using the policy review body's suggested method and has collected the data and calculation of the league table given in Appendix 1 to assist you. He also wants to assess whether the table will help in meeting the Department's aim and goals for the police. The overall aim of the Department (and its police forces) is 'to provide a value-for-money service to ensure that the community can live in safety with confidence in their physical and legal security'. The detailed goals of the Department are to:

- Tackle the underlying causes of crime and achieve long-term sustainable solutions
- Bring perpetrators to justice
- Provide protection and support for individuals and communities at risk of harm
- Respond to community needs by being accessible and engaging with their concerns

The CEO warned you, 'I'm not interested in the performance of the forces. I'm interested in the method of assessment, so don't waste time with your ideas on how to improve actual policing.'

The CEO also wishes to understand the strengths and weaknesses of the use of a league table, its link to targets and the likely reaction of employees to this system of performance management, especially as there is a strong union representing the police. He is worried about the employees' attitude to the introduction of the system and its effects on their behaviour and their sense of accountability. He is also concerned about importing the use of a league table from the schools sector, as it might not be appropriate here.

Required

(a) Evaluate the method of calculating and measuring the Force Scores for use in the league table in achieving the Department of the Interior's aims and goals. **(14 marks)**

(b) Discuss the merits of league tables in performance management and address the CEO's concerns over their use in managing the performance of Essland's police forces. **(11 marks)**

(Total = 25 marks)

Appendix 1

The appendix defines the policy review body's method for scoring each force, provides the basic data for each force and then calculates the current force score placing the forces into a league table:

Force score = Rank 1 × 0.25 + Rank 2 × 0.25 + Rank 3 × 0.25 + Rank 4 × 0.25

Where each Rank is the ranking from 4 to 1 which each force gets for each of the following variables (4 is best, 1 is worst):

- Rank 1 is based on the number of crimes per 10,000 of population.
- Rank 2 is based on the solution rate for crimes reported in the year.
- Rank 3 is based on the user satisfaction score (based on a survey of the population).
- Rank 4 is based on the percentage of calls to police answered within 10 seconds.

For example, a force which was top ranked in each of the Ranks would get a Force Score of 4 (= 4 × 0.25 + 4 × 0.25 + 4 × 0.25 + 4 × 0.25).

Data by region:
For the calendar year 20X2

	C	D	E	F
Population	1,250,000	900,000	1,700,000	1,500,000
Number of crimes reported in year	62,500	47,250	83,300	63,000
Number of crimes solved in year	31,250	22,680	45,815	33,390
User satisfaction score	71%	80%	73%	68%
Percentage of calls to police answered within 10 seconds	92%	93%	91%	94%
Number of police force employees	6,200	4,400	8,500	7,900
Cost of police force for year ($m)	404	298	572	510

Calculation of Force Score:

	C	D	E	F
Number of reported crimes per 10,000 of population	500	525	490	420
Rank 1	2	1	3	4
Solution rate for crimes reported in year	50%	48%	55%	53%
Rank 2	2	1	4	3
Rank 3 (user satisfaction)	2	4	3	1
Rank 4 (call handling)	2	3	1	4
Force score	2	2.25	2.75	3

The league table for 20X2 is:

	Force	Score
1.	F	3.00
2.	E	2.75
3.	D	2.25
4.	C	2.00

Note. You should assume that the calculations in Appendix 1 are accurate.

36 Beeshire Local Authority (APM 12/14)   49 mins

Beeshire Local Authority (BLA) is a local government body which provides a range of services for the area of Beeshire within the country of Seeland. Beeshire is a wealthy area within the country with many tourist attractions. One of BLA's tasks is to ensure that waste is collected from the homes and businesses in Beeshire. The goal for BLA's waste management department is 'to maintain Beeshire as a safe, clean and environmentally friendly place where people and businesses want to both stay in and return to.' The need for waste collection is linked to public health concerns, the desire to keep the streets clean and attractive and the desire to increase the amount of rubbish which is recycled. BLA is funded through a single local tax and does not charge its residents or businesses separately for most of its services, including waste collection. There is no public or political appetite for outsourcing services such as waste management.

Waste collection is performed by the workforce using a fleet of vehicles. The waste is either taken to recycling plants or else to landfill sites for burying. BLA obtains revenues from all the recycled waste but this only just covers the cost of running the recycling facilities.

Against a background estimate that waste will increase by 1% p.a. in the future, the national government has ordered local authorities, such as BLA, to promote the recycling of waste and has set a target of 40% of all waste to be recycled by 2015. In order to discourage the creation of non-recyclable waste, the government has imposed a levy per tonne of waste buried in landfill sites and has stated that this levy will rise over the next five years in order to encourage continuing improvement in the amount of recycled waste.

Currently, Seeland is in a long recession and so local authority revenues have fallen as tax revenues reflect the poor state of the economy. Along with other local authorities, BLA has tried to cut costs and so has focused on financial measures of performance. In a recent, private meeting, the chief executive of BLA was heard to say 'keep costs under control and we will worry about quality of service only when complaint levels build to an unacceptable level.' As one of the area's largest employers, cutting staff numbers has been very difficult for BLA due to the impact on the local economy and the reaction of the residents.

The current performance indicators used at BLA are drawn from the existing information systems with national figures given for comparison. Those relating to waste collection for the year ending 31 March 20X4 are:

			BLA	National total
Total cost	($m)		250	2,850
Volume of waste				
	landfilled	(tonnes)	1,250,000	13,750,000
	recycled	(tonnes)	950,000	9,500,000
	total	(tonnes)	2,200,000	23,250,000
No. of staff			3,500	39,900
Staff cost	($m)		110	1,190
No. of households			2,380,952	26,190,476
No. of complaints about waste uncollected			18,250	200,750

	BLA	National average
Frequency of waste collections (days)	14	12

Notes on BLA data:

1   Cost data and no. of households comes from BLA's financial systems.
2   Waste data comes from weighing lorries at the landfill sites and recycling facilities.
3   Staff data is collected from BLA's HR system.
4   Complaints data is based on numbers of letters and phone calls to the waste management department.
5   Frequency of collection data is obtained from the department's vehicle schedules.

Required

(a)   Explain why non-financial indicators are particularly useful for public sector organisations, illustrating your answer with brief examples relevant to BLA.   **(6 marks)**

(b)   Explain how the value for money provision of waste services by BLA should be assessed by suggesting and calculating justified performance indicators using the information in the scenario.   **(12 marks)**

(c)   Discuss the difficulties of measuring qualitative factors of performance, suggesting appropriate solutions for BLA.   **(7 marks)**

(Total = 25 marks)

37 CFE coffee shops   49 mins

CFE was established 15 years ago, and operates a chain of 40 coffee shops across Teeland. It is a privately owned company.

The number of coffee shops in Teeland has increased rapidly over the last decade, and there are now thousands of branded coffee shops operating across the country. Their total turnover now exceeds $1 billion. Although the majority of the branded shops are run by internationally recognised multinational companies, CFE only operates in Teeland.

The range of products offered by the shops has increased over the last few years, in response to customer demand for a larger range of foods and better quality products. The branded coffee shops have been able to command higher than average prices for their products by using quality and service as differentiators. Price appears not to be a particularly sensitive factor, although CFE's prices are largely the same as those charged by the branded shops run by the multi-national companies.

In 20X1, when CFE first opened, most other coffee shops only served a selection of hot and cold drinks and a small range of snacks and cakes. However, right from the outset, CFE also sold a range of freshly made sandwiches and other food items, all made from high quality ingredients.

All CFE's shops operate from rented premises, but before opening they are fitted out to ensure they have the same high standard of shop design and fittings. Having a high quality of shop design creates a good atmosphere, and makes the coffee shops a popular place for people to meet.

CFE's shops generate a high turnover. However, profitability has been lower than some of its competitors. Reasons for this include: high rental costs for some of its city centre shops; high staff costs (as high quality customer service remains a priority for CFE so it pays above the industry average); and lower than average gross margins on some products (due to the high procurement cost of the quality ingredients chosen).

CFE also earns lower margins than some of its rivals on its coffee products because over 80% of its coffee beans are procured from suppliers who deal only with 'Fair Trade' coffee producers. Some of the regional managers have argued that their shops would be more profitable if they stopped using 'Fair Trade' coffee, but CFE's directors remain adamant that the company will continue to buy coffee from Fair Trade suppliers wherever possible, because it is a socially responsible company.

At a recent Board meeting, the Marketing Director said he thought CFE should introduce a loyalty card scheme, and for every six hot drinks loyalty card holders buy, they get their next one free. He argued the card scheme will help CFE's profitability by improving customer loyalty and strengthening the brand.

The Finance Director said that CFE should also consider whether it could increase the prices of its coffee products in order to increase the margins its earns on them.

A summary of CFE's trading results for the last year is shown below:

($'000)	Coffee	Other drinks	Food & snacks	Total
Revenue	19,517	5,541	32,322	57,380
Cost of sales	(3,767)	(2,638)	(13,975)	(20,380)
Gross margin	15,750	2,903	18,347	37,000
Operating profit				5,606

The largest branded coffee chain in Teeland (which has 130 shops) generated revenues of $180m in the last year, with a gross margin of $124m and operating profit of $22.5m.

Required

(a) With reference to the Marketing Director's proposal to introduce a loyalty card scheme, evaluate the importance of brand awareness on CFE's business performance. **(12 marks)**

(b) Discuss the importance of external information in relation to the Finance Director's suggestion for CFE to increase the prices of its coffee products. **(5 marks)**

(c) With reference to the use of 'Fair Trade' suppliers, discuss the potential implications of social obligations on CFE's business performance. **(8 marks)**

(Total = 25 marks)

38 Herman Swan & Co (APM 12/12, amended)   49 mins

Herman Swan & Co (HS) is a family-owned company that has made fashionable clothes and leather goods for men for over 100 years. The company has been successful in building a strong reputation for quality by sourcing from local textile and leather producers. It sells its goods across the world through a chain of owned shops and also from franchised stalls inside large, well-known stores. The company is still owned and run by the family with no other shareholders. The main goal of the company is to organically grow the business for the next generation of the Swan family.

Customers are attracted to HS products due to the history and the family story that goes behind the products. Customers are willing to pay the high prices demanded as they identify with the values of the firm, especially the high quality of manufacturing.

The competition for HS has been increasing for more than ten years. It is made up of other global luxury brands and also the rising national champions in some of the rapidly expanding developing countries. The competitors often try to leverage their brands into many different product types. However, the Swan family have stated their desire to focus on the menswear market after an unsuccessful purchase of a handbag manufacturer five years ago.

The company is divided into a number of strategic business units (SBU). Each production site is an SBU, while the whole retail operation is one SBU. The head office previously functioned as a centre for procurement, finance and

other support activities. The company has recently invested in a new management information system (MIS) that has increased the data available to all managers in the business. This has led to much of the procurement shifting to the production SBUs and the SBU managers taking more responsibility for budgeting. The SBU managers are delighted with their increased responsibilities and with the results from the new information system but feel there is still room for improvement in its use. The system has assisted in a project of flattening the organisation hierarchy by cutting out several layers of head office management.

You are the management accountant at HS and have been trying to persuade your boss, the finance director, that your role should change. You have read about Burns and Scapens' report 'Accounting Change Project' and think that it suggests an interesting change from your current roles of preparing and reviewing budgets and overseeing the production of management and financial accounts. Your boss is sceptical but is willing to listen to your arguments.

He has asked you to submit an explanation of the change that you propose and why it is necessary at HS.

Also, your boss has asked you for an example of how your role as an 'internal consultant' would be valuable at HS by looking at the ideas of brand loyalty and awareness. You should consider their impact on performance management at HS, both from the customer and the internal business process perspectives and how to measure them.

Required

(a)   With reference to HS, briefly explain the increasing importance of non-financial performance measures for organisations.   **(5 marks)**

(b)   Describe the changes in the role of the management accountant based on Burns and Scapens work. Explain what is driving these changes and justify why they are appropriate to HS.   **(12 marks)**

(c)   Using HS as an example, discuss the impact of brand loyalty and awareness on the business both from the customer and the internal business process perspectives and evaluate suitable measures for brand loyalty and awareness.   **(8 marks)**

(Total = 25 marks)

39 Navier Aerials (APM 6/13)   **49 mins**

Navier Aerials Co (Navier) manufactures satellite dishes for receiving satellite television signals. Navier supplies the major satellite TV companies who install standard satellite dishes for their customers. The company also manufactures and installs a small number of specialised satellite dishes to individuals or businesses with specific needs resulting from poor reception in their locations.

The Chief Executive Officer (CEO) wants to initiate a programme of cost reduction at Navier. His plan is to use activity-based management (ABM) to allocate costs more accurately and to identify non-value adding activities. The first department to be analysed is the customer care department, as it has been believed for some time that the current method of cost allocation is giving unrealistic results for the two product types.

At present, the Finance Director (FD) absorbs the cost of customer care into the product cost on a per unit basis using the data in Table 1. He then tries to correct the problem of unrealistic costing, by making rough estimates of the costs to be allocated to each product based on the operations director's impression of the amount of work of the department. In fact, he simply adds $100 above the standard absorbed cost to the cost of a specialised dish to cover the assumed extra work involved at customer care.

The cost accountant has gathered information for the customer care department in Table 2 from interviews with the finance and customer care staff. She has used this information to correctly calculate the total costs of each activity using activity-based costing in Table 3. The CEO wants you, as a senior management accountant, to complete the work required for a comparison of the results of the current standard absorption costing to activity-based costing for the standard and specialised dishes.

Once this is done, the CEO wants you to consider the implications for management of the customer care process of the costs of each activity in that department. The CEO is especially interested in how this information may impact on the identification of non-valued added activities and quality management at Navier.

Navier Dishes (information for the year ending 31 March 20X3)

Customer care (CC) department

Table 1: Existing costing data

	$'000
Salaries	400
Computer time	165
Telephone	79
Stationery and sundries	27
Depreciation of equipment	36
	707

Note. CC cost is currently allocated to each dish based on 16,000 orders a year, where each order contains an average of 5·5 dishes.

Table 2: Activity-costing data

Activities of CC dept	Staff time	Comments
Handling enquiries and preparing quotes for potential orders	40%	relates to 35,000 enquiries/quotes per year
Receiving actual orders	10%	relates to 16,000 orders in the year
Customer credit checks	10%	done once an order is received
Supervision of orders through manufacture to delivery	15%	
Complaints handling	25%	relates to 3,200 complaints per year

Notes

1 Total department cost is allocated using staff time as this drives all of the other costs in the department.

2 90% of both enquiries and orders are for standard dishes. The remainder are for specialised dishes.

3 Handling enquiries and preparing quotes for specialised dishes takes 20% of staff time allocated to this activity.

4 The process for receiving an order, checking customer credit and supervision of the order is the same for both a specialised dish order and a standard dish order.

5 50% of the complaints received are for specialised dish orders.

6 Each standard dish order contains an average of six dishes.

7 Each specialised dish order contains an average of one dish.

Table 3: Activity-based costs

	Total $	Standard $	Specialised $
Handling enquiries and preparing quotes	282,800	226,240	56,560
Receiving actual orders	70,700	63,630	7,070
Customer credit checks	70,700	63,630	7,070
Supervision of order through manufacture to delivery	106,050	95,445	10,605
Complaints handling	176,750	88,375	88,375
Total	707,000	537,320	169,680

Required

(a) Evaluate the impact of using activity-based costing, compared to the existing costing system for customer care, on the cost of both types of product. **(13 marks)**

(b) Assess how the information on each activity can be used and improved upon at Navier in assisting cost reduction and quality management in the customer care department.

Note. There is no need to make comments on the different product types here. **(12 marks)**

(Total = 25 marks)

40 TAW (APM 6/08, amended)

49 mins

Telecoms At Work (TAW) manufactures and markets office communications systems. During the year ended 31 May 20X8 TAW made an operating profit of $30 million on sales of $360 million. However, the directors are concerned that products do not conform to the required level of quality and TAW is therefore not fulfilling its full potential in terms of turnover and profits achieved.

The following information is available in respect of the year ended 31 May 20X8:

(1)   Production data:

Units manufactured and sold	18,000
Units requiring rework	2,100
Units requiring warranty repair service	2,700
Design engineering hours	48,000
Process engineering hours	54,000
Inspection hours (manufacturing)	288,000

(2)   Cost data:

	$
Design engineering per hour	96
Process engineering per hour	70
Inspection per hour (manufacturing)	50
Rework per communication system reworked (manufacturing)	4,800
Customer support per repaired unit (marketing)	240
Transportation costs per repaired unit (distribution)	280
Warranty repairs per repaired unit (customer service)	4,600

(3)   Staff training costs amounted to $180,000 and additional product testing costs of $72,000.

(4)   The marketing director has estimated that sales of 1,800 units were lost as a result of public knowledge of poor quality at TAW. The average contribution per communication system is estimated at $7,200.

Required

(a)   Prepare a cost analysis which shows actual prevention costs, appraisal costs, internal failure costs, and external failure costs for the year ended 31 May 20X8. Your statement should show each cost heading as a % of turnover and clearly show the total cost of quality. Comment briefly on the inclusion of opportunity costs in such an analysis.
(12 marks)

A detailed analysis has revealed that the casings in which the communications systems are housed are often subject to mishandling in transit to TAW's manufacturing premises. The directors are considering two alternative solutions proposed by the design engineering team which are aimed at reducing the quality problems that are currently being experienced. These are as follows:

Option 1 – Increase the number of immediate physical inspections of the casings when they are received from the supplier. This will require an additional 10,000 inspection hours.

Option 2 – Redesign and strengthen the casings and the containers used to transport them to better withstand mishandling during transportation. Redesign will require an additional 2,000 hours of design engineering and an additional 5,000 hours of process engineering.

Internal failure costs of rework for each reworked communication system are as follows:

		$
Variable costs	(including direct materials, direct labour rework and supplies)	1,920
Allocated fixed costs	(equipment, space and allocated overhead)	2,880
Total costs (as per note 2 on cost data)		4,800

The directors of TAW believe that, even if it is able to achieve improvements in quality, it will be unable to save any of the fixed costs of internal and external failure.

If TAW chooses to inspect the casings more carefully, it expects to eliminate re-work on 720 communication systems whereas if it redesigns the casings it expects to eliminate rework on 960 communication systems.

If incoming casings are inspected more carefully, TAW estimates that 600 fewer communication systems will require warranty repair and that it will be able to sell an additional 300 communication systems. If the casing is redesigned, the directors estimate that 840 fewer communication systems will require warranty repair and that an additional 360 communication systems will be sold.

External failure costs of repair for each repaired communication system are as follows:

	Variable costs	Fixed costs	Total costs
	$	$	$
Customer support costs	96	144	240
Transportation costs	210	70	280
Warranty repair costs	1,700	2,900	4,600

Required

(b) Prepare an estimate of the financial consequences of each options and advise the directors at TAW which option should be chosen. **(10 marks)**

(c) Explain how Kaizen principles could be used by TAW to reduce its costs. **(3 marks)**

(Total = 25 marks)

41 Thebe (APM 6/12, amended)   49 mins

Thebe Telecom is a large national telephone business in Fayland. Thebe provides telephone service to more than 11 million customers through its fixed line and mobile services. Thebe has three strategic business units: mobile; fixed line telephone (incorporating broadband); and corporate services (serving other businesses' telephone needs). It has become the largest mobile operator in Fayland through a series of acquisitions of competitors and operating licences.

Thebe's CEO has won many awards for being an innovative businessman who recognises the rapid changes in technology, regulation and competitor action that occur in the sector. Thebe's major competitor in Fayland is the original nationalised telephone company, FayTel, which was privatised 20 years ago but which retains many of the features of a monopoly supplier including a massive infrastructure. As a result, Thebe's CEO realised long ago that competition on the basis of price and volume would not work against such a large competitor and so he has focused on customer service as the key to growing the business.

In order to improve the company's competitive position, the CEO decided that the company should consider a Six Sigma initiative to give an immediate step change improvement to the service quality at Thebe. The initiative involved a number of projects including one to improve the quality of customers' bills. FayTel was publicly criticised by the government's consumer advocate who pointed to occasional misallocations of call minutes to the wrong numbers and also, more frequently, the application of incorrect tariffs in calculating the costs of calls. Thebe's CEO is aware that all telephone businesses (including Thebe) have these problems but this is an area in which Thebe can gain a competitive advantage and has taken a special interest in this project by championing it himself.

The project is focused on improving the accuracy of customers' bills and the handling of complaints. Within the billing department, the company divided activities into normal money collection, credit control on overdue payments and managing complaints. Process diagrams were created for each of these areas and then data was sourced from customer feedback at the various points of interaction with Thebe employees (such as complaint handling) and internal measurables created. The project team was formed from line managers from all three strategic business units and the billing department.

The CEO's involvement in the projects to improve service quality at Thebe made him realise that the performance summary prepared for the monthly board papers does not include any non-financial aspects of performance, and Thebe's key performance indicators also focus solely on financial performance.

Required

(a) Evaluate the benefits of Thebe's board monitoring non-financial aspects of performance as well as financial ones. **(8 marks)**

(b) Explain how the general way in which Six Sigma is implemented helps improve the quality of performance, illustrating your answer with reference to Thebe. **(8 marks)**

(c) Explain and illustrate how the DMAIC method for the implementation of Six Sigma could be applied at Thebe. **(9 marks)**

(Total = 25 marks)

42 There 4 U (APM 6/09, amended) 49 mins

The There 4 U Company (T4UC) commenced trading on 1 January 20X6. It was founded by Ken Matthews, who is the managing director of T4UC.

The initial aim of T4UC was to provide 'good quality' repairs and servicing to customers with domestic central heating systems and domestic 'white goods' (white goods are items such as washing machines, tumble dryers, dishwashers, refrigerators and freezers).

T4UC provides contract services on an annual basis to individual customers who require insurance covering the repair and servicing of their central heating systems and domestic white goods. T4UC charge an annual contract fee and undertake all client repair and servicing requirements without further charge.

Ken, who has a very strong background in sales and marketing, recruited engineers who came from a variety of engineering backgrounds.

Initial growth was prolific with Ken being very successful in establishing a good sized customer base within the first two years of the business. Ken believes that staff utilisation is the key driver of profitability within T4UC.

T4UC set up a website where clients could access product manuals and other diagnostic data as well as being able to book an appointment with a service engineer.

The following data is available:

Year	20X6	20X7	20X8
Number of contracted clients	13,000	15,000	14,800
Number of visits to contracted clients	23,400	30,000	32,000
Number of clients gained via recommendation	200	100	5
Number of telephone calls for product support received	52,500	62,000	59,500
Number of telephone calls for product support answered	52,000	60,000	58,000
Number of product support issues resolved by telephone	46,800	51,000	46,400

At the end of 20X8 Ken became anxious regarding the fact that the growth in the customer base had stopped and that a number of clients had chosen not to renew their contracts with T4UC. In view of these facts, Ken undertook an extensive survey of the customers who had entered into contracts with T4UC since it commenced trading.

Ken received the following comments which were representative of all other comments that he received.

'T4UC ought to adopt a 'right first time' mentality.'

'I booked an engineer for last Monday who never arrived but two engineers turned up on Tuesday!'

'You send me a different engineer each time to inspect my central heating system. Some are here for an hour and yet others are here for the whole day and some of those even have to come back the next day.'

'Your people never seem to have the required parts with them and have to come back the next day!'

'An engineer arrived at my home to repair my washing machine but the required parts which were shipped to my home direct from the manufacturer arrived three days later! I've heard that 'Appliances R Us' is the best organisation in your service sector and that they provide a much more efficient service than T4UC and unlike T4UC is always contactable on a 24 hours basis during every day of the year! When I have tried to contact you on Saturdays and Sundays I have often given up out of sheer frustration!'

Ken also obtained the following data from the 'Centre for Inter-Firm Comparison'.

	T4UC	Appliances R Us	Industry average
Customer satisfaction rating (%)	65	92	75
Remedial visits (%) of client visits	8	1	4
Cost per client per visit ($)	150	75	100
Client to staff ratio	250:1	200:1	225: 1

Ken undertook further investigations which revealed remedial visits were frequently due to staff servicing appliances with which they were not completely familiar.

Required

(a) Describe the Six Sigma methodology for the improvement of an existing process and the varying grades of qualification in Six Sigma that staff involved in the leadership of projects may possess. **(11 marks)**

(b) Explain how the problems at T4UC could be analysed and addressed using the Six Sigma methodology. Your answer should include suggestions regarding additional activities that should be undertaken in order to improve the performance of T4UC. **(14 marks)**

(Total = 25 marks)

43 SSH (APM 12/08)   49 mins

The Superior Software House (SSH) commenced trading on 1 December 20X2 in the country of Bonlandia. SSH develops bespoke software packages on behalf of clients. When requested to do so, SSH also provides training to clients' staff in the use of these software packages. On 1 December 20X6, the directors of SSH established a similar semi-autonomous operation in Karendia. All software packages are produced in Bonlandia and transferred to Karendia at cost plus attributable overheads ie there is no mark-up on the software packages transferred from Bonlandia to Karendia.

Karendia is a country in which the structure of industry has changed during recent years. There has been a major shift from traditional manufacturing businesses to service orientated businesses which place a far greater emphasis upon the use of business software.

The operational managers in both Bonlandia and Karendia have no control over company policies in respect of acquisitions and financing.

The operational manager of Bonlandia receives a bonus of 40% of his basic salary for meeting all client delivery deadlines in respect of Karendia. At a recent meeting he instructed his staff to 'install client software by the due date and we'll worry about fixing any software problems after it's been installed. After all, we always fix software problems eventually'. He also stated that 'it is of vital importance that we grow our revenues in Karendia as quickly as possible. Our clients in Karendia might complain but they have spent a lot of money on our software products and will not be able to go to any of our competitors once we have installed our software as all their businesses would suffer huge disruption'.

Financial data (all stated on an actual basis) in respect of the two divisions for the two years ended 30 November 20X7 and 20X8 are shown on the next page:

Summary Income statements

	Bonlandia 20X8 $'000	Karendia 20X8 $'000	Combined 20X8 $'000	Bonlandia 20X7 $'000	Karendia 20X7 $'000	Combined 20X7 $'000
Revenue	14,600	2,800	17,400	14,000	2,000	16,000
Salaries	4,340	1,248	5,588	4,000	1,200	5,200
Software & consumables	2,040	486	2,526	2,000	450	2,450
Other operating costs	2,880	654	3,534	2,800	600	3,400
	9,260	2,388	11,648	8,800	2,250	11,050
Marketing	2,392	600	2,992	2,100	400	2,500
Interest (Group)			850			900
Depreciation and amortisation	400	160	560	400	100	500
	2,792	760	4,402	2,500	500	3,900
Total costs	12,052	3,148	16,050	11,300	2,750	14,950
Profit/(loss) for the period	2,548	(348)	1,350	2,700	(750)	1,050

Statements of financial position:

	Bonlandia 20X8 $'000	Karendia 20X8 $'000	Combined 20X8 $'000	Bonlandia 20X7 $'000	Karendia 20X7 $'000	Combined 20X7 $'000
Assets						
Non-current assets	9,000	1,600	10,600	8,000	1,000	9,000
Current assets	4,550	1,000	5,550	5,000	800	5,800
Total assets	13,550	2,600	16,150	13,000	1,800	14,800
Equity and liabilities						
Share capital and reserves			9,150			7,800
Non-current liabilities						
Long-term borrowings (Group)			4,000			4,500
Current liabilities	2,400	600	3,000	2,000	500	2,500
Total equity and liabilities			16,150			14,800

Required

(a) Assess the financial performance of SSH and its operations in Bonlandia and Karendia during the years ended 30 November 20X7 and 20X8.

Note. You should highlight additional information that would be required in order to provide a more comprehensive assessment of the financial performance of each operation. **(14 marks)**

(b) Discuss the statements of the operational manager of Bonlandia and assess their implications for SSH.

(4 marks)

(c) Assess the likely criteria which would need to be satisfied for software to be regarded as 'quality software'.

(4 marks)

(d) Suggest a set of **six** performance measures which the directors of SSH could use in order to assess the quality of service provided to its clients. **(3 marks)**

(Total = 25 marks)

44 Albacore (APM Pilot Paper)   49 mins

Albacore Chess Stores (Albacore) is a chain of 12 shops specialising in selling items associated with the game of chess: boards, pieces, clocks, software and books. Three years ago, the company was the subject of a venture capital buyout from a larger group. A new senior management team was put in place after the buyout. They have the aim of running the business in order to maximise profits.

The Chief Financial Officer (CFO), along with the other members of senior management, sets the annual budget and uses a standard costing approach with variance analysis in order to control individual shop performance. The head office handles all capital purchases and brand marketing. All inventory purchasing is done centrally and the shop opening times are set as standard across the company. As an illustration of senior management attitude, the CFO had set the budget for staff costs for 20X1 at $7 per hour for part-time staff, and this was rigorously observed in the period.

Each shop is run by a manager who reports their financial results to head office. The shop managers recruit and manage the staffing of their shop. They have some autonomy in setting prices locally and have been given authority to vary prices by up to 10% from a master list produced by the CFO. They also have a local marketing budget agreed each year by the shop's manager and the marketing director as part of the annual appraisal process.

The shop managers have approached the Chairman of Albacore to complain about the way that they are managed and their remuneration. They feel that their efforts are unrecognised by senior management. One manager commented, 'I have had a successful year in hard economic circumstances. I have run a number of promotions in the shop that have been well received by the customers. However, the budgets that are set are impossible to achieve and as a result I have not been paid any bonus although I feel that I have done everything in my power to bring in good profits.'

The shop managers at Albacore are paid a basic salary of $27,000 with bonuses of up to 30% of basic salary dependent on two factors: performance above budget and the operational director's performance assessment. The budget for the next year is prepared by the CFO and presented at the shop manager's annual appraisal.

The Chairman has come to you to ask if you can consider the system of performance assessment for the shop managers and give an independent perspective on the reward systems at Albacore. She has heard of variance analysis but is unsure about what would be relevant in this situation. She has provided the following illustrative information from the previous year for one shop:

Albacore Chess Stores

Tunny Branch Year to Sept 20X1

		Budget $	Actual $	Variance $
Sales		266,000	237,100	−28,900
Cost of sales		106,400	94,840	11,560
Gross profit		159,600	142,260	−17,340
Marketing		12,000	11,500	500
Staff costs	Manager	27,000	27,000	0
	Part-time staff	38,000	34,000	4,000
Property costs		26,600	26,600	0
Shop profit		56,000	43,160	−12,840

Notes

Property costs includes heating, lighting and rental.
Positive variances are favourable.

The manager of this shop commented at the appraisal meeting that she felt that the assessment was unfair since her failure to make budget was due to general economic conditions. The industry as a whole saw a 12% fall in revenues during the period and the budget for the period was set to be the same as the previous period. She was not paid a bonus for the period.

Required

(a) Evaluate the suitability of the existing branch information given as a means of assessing the shop manager's performance and draft an improved branch report with justifications for changes. **(13 marks)**

(b) Analyse the performance management style and evaluate the performance appraisal system at Albacore. Suggest suitable improvements to its reward system for the shop managers. **(12 marks)**

(Total = 25 marks)

45 Elegant Hotels

49 mins

Elegant Hotels is a chain of twenty hotels across the country. Each hotel is wholly owned by the company. Four years ago the chain was bought by a group of investors who installed a new management team.

The new management team introduced a new reward scheme for the hotel managers in an attempt to motivate managers to improve the revenue and profitability of the chain. The salary package devised for each manager comprised:

- A relatively low fixed salary

- A bonus payment based on high room occupancy rate. The occupancy rate is the percentage of usable hotel beds filled every night. Managers who achieved more than 90% occupancy rate receive a significant bonus. This target is aimed at keeping the hotel full.

- A smaller bonus payment based on the net profit margin achieved by the hotel. This is aimed at improving the profitability of the hotel.

However, despite these incentives the overall performance of the company is still declining. Managers are generally achieving a high occupancy rate but are largely failing to deliver higher net margins. It is also clear that some managers have achieved a high occupancy rate by declaring that some bedrooms were unfit for use or were being used as seminar rooms.

Also, the pursuit of high occupancy and high net profit appears to be affecting the perceived image of the hotel chain. Once regarded as a mid-market hotel chain, the chain now seems to be perceived as a budget buy. A large percentage of bookings are received through the Internet broker lastsecondhotels.com and their view of the chain is given below, together with some visitor quotes from their web site.

Comments

'Great last minute bargain ... very easy to get rooms at half the advertised rate'

'Full of school children on a trip ... will not be using this chain again'

'No Internet connections in the rooms or public areas, very disappointing'

'The bath was cracked and the windows were dirty. Cheap, but badly in need of a clean'

'Receptionists were very off-hand and unable to help. Did not seem to know much about the area surrounding the hotel'

'The staff were surly and uncommunicative. Much worse than last time we visited it. It used to be such a lovely hotel'

'Cheap, but don't eat there. The price for breakfast was extortionate'

'Cheap and cheerful but don't pay the full rate! Always lots of cheap beds available'

'Food was expensive and dull. The serving staff were uncommunicative, the cutlery was dirty and damaged. Staff were more interested in talking to each other than to the customers'

'Restaurant food was very expensive and of poor quality. The two nights I stayed there I was the only customer in the restaurant'

Lastsecondhotels.com says: 'Value for money hotels with rooms always available. Perfect for those last minute breaks'

Required

(a)   Analyse the unanticipated consequences of the management reward scheme at Elegant Hotels.   **(15 marks)**

(b)   The DMAIC methodology of Six Sigma includes five steps: Define, Measure, Analyse, Improve and Control. Evaluate the potential benefits of using the DMAIC methodology at Elegant Hotels.   **(10 marks)**

(Total = 25 marks)

46 Equiguard

Equiguard offers warranties for electrical and electronic equipment to both business and household customers. For a fixed annual fee the company will provide a free fault diagnosis and repair service for equipment covered by the warranty. A warranty lasts for one year and customers are invited to renew their warranty one month before it expires. Equiguard employs 340 full-time engineers around the country to undertake these repairs. It costs about $6,000 to train a newly recruited engineer.

When equipment breaks down the customer telephones a support help line number where their problem is dealt with by a customer support clerk. This clerk has access to the work schedules of the engineers and an appointment is made for a visit from an engineer at the earliest possible time convenient to the customer. When the engineer makes the visit, faults with equipment are diagnosed and are fixed free of charge under the terms of the warranty.

Equiguard is extremely concerned about the relatively high labour turnover of its engineers and has commissioned a report to investigate the situation. Some of the findings of the report are summarised in Table 1, which compares Equiguard with two of its main competitors.

Table 1

Company	Labour turnover*	Average salary ($)	Profit sharing scheme	Average days holiday/year	Performance related pay	Average training spent per year per engineer ($)
Equiguard	12%	24,000	No	20	No	1,000
Safequipe	8%	23,000	Yes	23	Yes	1,500
Guarantor	7%	22,500	Yes	25	Yes	1,250

* Labour turnover is the number of engineers leaving in the last year as a percentage of the number of engineers employed at the beginning of the year

An exit survey of engineers leaving the company recorded the following comments:

(a) 'There is no point in doing a good job, because you get paid no more than doing an ordinary one. Average work is tolerated here.'

(b) 'This is the first place I have worked where learning new skills is not encouraged. There is no incentive to improve yourself. The company seems to believe that employees who gain new skills will inevitably leave, so they discourage learning.'

(c) 'The real problem is that the pay structure does not differentiate between good, average and poor performers. This is really de-motivating.'

The HR director of Equiguard is anxious to address the high turnover issue and believes that quantitative measurement of employee performance is essential in a re-structured reward management scheme. He has suggested that the company should introduce two new performance related pay measures. The first is a team based bonus based on the average time it takes for the company to respond to a repair request. He proposes that this should be based on the time taken between the customer request for a repair being logged and the date of the engineer attending to fix the problem. He argues that customers value quick response times and so the shorter this time the greater the bonus should be for the whole team.

In addition, he proposes an individual bonus. This will be based on the average time taken for an engineer to fix a reported fault once they have arrived. This is the average time taken for the engineer to repair the fault from the start time of the job to its completion. He argues that the company values quick repair time as this increases business efficiency and so the quicker the fix the greater the bonus should be for the individual.

Required

(a) Assess the deficiencies of Equiguard's current rewards management scheme. **(15 marks)**

(b) Analyse the limitations of the proposed performance measures suggested by the HR director. **(10 marks)**

(Total = 25 marks)

47 ENT Entertainments (APM 6/11, amended)

49 mins

ENT Entertainment Co (ENT) is a large, diversified entertainment business based in Teeland. The company's objective is the maximisation of shareholder wealth for its family owners. It has four divisions:

(1)   Restaurants
(2)   Cafes
(3)   Bars
(4)   Dance clubs

Recently, ENT's board have identified that there are problems in managing such a diversified company. They have employed consultants who have recommended that they should perform a Boston Consulting Group (BCG) analysis to understand whether they have the right mix of businesses. The chief executive officer (CEO) has questioned whether using this analysis is helpful in managing the group's performance. A business analyst has prepared information on each division in the table below.

Revenue ($m)	Actual 20X0	Actual 20X1	Forecast 20X2	Forecast 20X3
Restaurants				
ENT	54	56	59	62
Market sector	10,752	10,860	10,968	10,968
Cafes				
ENT	31	34	41	47
Market sector	3,072	3,348	3,717	4,051
Bars				
ENT	349	342	336	336
Market sector	9,984	9,784	9,491	9,206
Dance clubs				
ENT	197	209	219	241
Market sector	1,792	1,900	2,013	2,195

In Teeland, the economy is generally growing at about 2% per annum. The restaurant, cafe and bar sectors are all highly fragmented with many small operators. Consequently, a market share of more than 3·0% is considered large as that is comparable to the share of the largest operators in each sector. There are fewer small late night dance club operators and the market leader currently holds a 15·0% market share. There have not been many new developments within the divisions except for a new wine bar format launched by the bars division which has surprised the board by its success.

Each of the division's performance is measured by economic value-added (EVA™). The divisional managers have a remuneration package that is made up in two equal parts by a salary set according to industry norms and a bonus element which is based on achieving the cost budget numbers set by the company board. The chairman of the board has been examining the consistency of the overall objective of the business, the divisional performance measure and the remuneration packages at divisional level. He has expressed the worry that these are not properly aligned and that this might lead to dysfunctional behaviour by the divisional management.

Required

(a)   Perform a BCG analysis of ENT's business and use this to evaluate the company's performance.   **(7 marks)**

(b)   Critically evaluate this BCG analysis as a performance management system at ENT.   **(7 marks)**

(c)   (i)   Evaluate the divisional managers' remuneration packages in the light of the divisional performance systems and your BCG analysis.   **(6 marks)**

(ii)   Explain the implications of the BCG analysis and divisional performance systems on the management styles which might be appropriate at ENT.   **(5 marks)**

(Total = 25 marks)

48 Beach Foods (APM 6/15)   49 mins

Beach Foods (Beach) is a family-owned business which has grown strongly over its 100 year history. The objective of the business is to maximise the family's wealth through their shareholdings. Beach has three divisions. It manufactures a variety of foods in two of the divisions: Beach Baby Foods (Baby) and Beach Chocolate Foods (Chocolate). Each of these divisions knows its own market and sets prices accordingly. The third division (R&D) researches new products on the instructions of the other divisions and is considered to be vital to the survival and growth of Beach. The board of Beach has been considering the impact of using a divisional structure and has come to you as a performance management consultant to ask for your advice.

There is disagreement at board level about the correct choice of divisional performance measure to be used in the two manufacturing divisions. Currently, the business uses EVA™ but two directors have been questioning its value, complaining that it is complicated to understand. These directors have been promoting the use of either residual income (RI) or return on investment (ROI) as alternatives. The board wants to use the same measure for each division. As well as qualitatively evaluating these different measures, the board needs an assessment of the impact of a change in performance measure on their perception of these divisions' performance. Therefore, as an example, they require you to calculate and discuss the use of ROI and RI at Baby division, given the data in Appendix 1.

The chief executive officer (CEO) of Beach has engaged a business analyst to perform a study of the portfolio of manufacturing businesses which make up Beach. This has been completed in Appendix 2. The CEO wants your comments (based on the categorisation given in Appendix 2) on how this work will impact on the performance management of the divisions. Specifically, the CEO has asked for your recommendations on how to control each division; that is, whether each division should be treated as a cost/profit/investment centre and also, the appropriate management style to use for handling staff in each division. The CEO commented to you:

'I have heard of different approaches to the use of budget information in assessing performance: budget-constrained, profit-conscious and also a non-accounting style. I need to know how these approaches might apply to each division given your other comments.'

All of this work has been partly prompted by complaints from the divisional managers. The Chocolate divisional managers complain that they had to wait for a year to get approval to upgrade their main production line. This production line upgrade has reduced wastage and boosted Chocolate's profit margin by 10 percentage points. The Baby division has been very successful in using the ideas of the R&D division, although Baby's managers do complain about the recharging of R&D costs to their division. Head office managers are worried about Chocolate as it has seemed to be drifting recently with a lack of strategic direction. Chocolate's managers are considered to be good but possibly not sufficiently focused on what benefits Beach as a whole.

Required

(a)   Assess the use of EVA™ as a divisional performance measure for the manufacturing divisions at Beach.
                                                                                        (8 marks)

(b)   Using Appendix 1, calculate the ROI and RI for Baby and assess the impact of the assumptions made when calculating these metrics on the evaluation of the performance of this division and its management.
                                                                                        (7 marks)

(c)   Provide justified recommendations for each division's control and management style as requested by the CEO.
                                                                                       (10 marks)

                                                                               (Total = 25 marks)

Appendix 1

Figures from Beach management accounts for year ended 31 March:

Baby division	20X5
	$m
Revenue	220
Costs	
Divisional operating costs	121
R&D costs recharged	11
Allocated head office management fees	28
Profit before tax	60
Capital employed 4	24

Notes

1   Baby launched a new product with a large publicity campaign during the year.

2   The notional cost of capital for Baby is estimated by the chief financial officer at 11%. WACC for Beach is 7.5%.

3   ROI for similar entities is 20%.

4   EVA™ for Baby is calculated as $35m.

Appendix 2

Star	Problem child
Baby:	
Market growth 18%	
Relative market share 105%	
Cash cow	**Dog**
Chocolate:	
Market growth 3%	
Relative market share 120%	

Relative market share is the market share of the division compared to that of the market leader. If an organisation is a market leader, then its market share is compared to the next largest competitor.

Note. You may assume that the calculations and this categorisation are accurate.

PERFORMANCE EVALUATION AND CORPORATE FAILURE

Questions 49 to 65 cover performance evaluation and corporate failure, the subject of Part E of the BPP Study Text for Paper P5.

49 Pharmaceutical Technologies (APM Pilot Paper)   49 mins

Pharmaceutical Technologies Co (PT) is a developer and manufacturer of medical drugs in Beeland. It is one of the 100 largest listed companies on the national stock exchange. The company focuses on buying prospective drugs (which have shown initial promise in testing) from small bio-engineering companies. PT then leads these drugs through three regulatory stages to launch in the general medical market.

The three stages are:

(1)   to confirm the safety of the drug (does it harm humans?), in small scale trials;
(2)   to test the efficacy of the product (does it help cure?), again in small scale trials; and
(3)   finally, large scale trials to definitively decide on the safety and efficacy of the product.

The drugs are then marketed through the company's large sales force to health care providers and end users (patients). The health care providers are paid by either health insurance companies or the national government dependent on the financial status of the patient.

The Beeland Drug Regulator (BDR) oversees this testing process and makes the final judgement about whether a product can be sold in the country.

Its objectives are to protect, promote and improve public health by ensuring that:

• medicines have an acceptable balance of benefit and risk;
• the users of these medicines understand this risk-benefit profile; and
• new beneficial product development is encouraged.

The regulator is governed by a board of trustees appointed by the government. It is funded directly by the government and also through fees charged to drug companies when granting licences to sell their products in Beeland.

PT has used share price and earnings per share as its principal measures of performance to date. However, the share price has underperformed the market and the health sector in the last two years. The chief executive officer (CEO) has identified that these measures are too narrow and is considering implementing a balanced scorecard approach to address this problem.

A working group has drawn up a suggested balanced scorecard. It began by identifying the objectives from the board's medium-term strategy:

• Create shareholder value by bringing commercially viable drugs to market
• Improve the efficiency of drug development
• Increase shareholder value by innovation in the drug approval process

The working group then considered the stakeholder perspectives:

• Shareholders want a competitive return on their investment
• Payers / Purchasers (governments, insurers and patients) want to pay a reasonable price for the drugs
• Regulators want an efficient process for the validation of drugs
• Doctors want safe and effective drug products
• Patients want to be cured

Finally, this leads to the proposed scorecard of performance measures:

• Financial – share price and earnings per share
• Customer – number of patients using PT products
• Internal business process – exceed industry-standard on design and testing; time to regulatory approval of a product
• Learning and growth – training days undertaken by staff; time to market of new product; percentage of drugs bought by PT that gain final approval

The balanced scorecard now needs to be reviewed to ensure that it will address the company's objectives and the issues that it faces in its business environment.

Required

(a) Evaluate the performance measures proposed for PT's balanced scorecard.   **(10 marks)**

(b) Briefly describe a method of analysing stakeholder influence and analyse the influence of four different external stakeholders on the regulator (BDR).   **(8 marks)**

(c) Using your answer from part (b), describe how the application of the balanced scorecard approach at BDR would differ from the approach within PT.   **(7 marks)**

(Total = 25 marks)

50 Victoria-Yeeland logistics (APM 6/15)   49 mins

Victoria-Yeeland Logistics (Victoria) is a logistics support business, which operates a fleet of lorries to deliver packages of goods on behalf of its customers within the country of Yeeland. Victoria collects packages from its customers' manufacturing sites or from the customers' port of importation and delivers to the final user of the goods. The lorries are run and maintained from a set of depots spread throughout Yeeland.

The overall objective of Victoria is to maximise shareholder wealth. The delivery business in Yeeland is dominated by two international companies and one other domestic business and profit margins are extremely tight. The market is saturated by these large operators and a number of smaller operators. The cost base of Victoria is dominated by staff and fuel, with fuel prices being highly volatile in the last few years.

In order to improve performance measurement and management at Victoria, the chief financial officer (CFO) plans to use the balanced scorecard (BSC). However, she has been pulled away from this project in order to deal with an issue with refinancing the business' principal lending facility. The CFO has already identified some suitable metrics but needs you, as her assistant, to complete her work and address any potential questions which might arise when she makes her presentation on the BSC to the board. The CFO has completed the identification of metrics for three of the perspectives (Appendix 1) but has yet to complete the work on the metrics for the customer perspective. This should be done using the data given in Appendix 2.

Additionally, two issues have arisen in the reward management system at Victoria, one in relation to senior management and the other for operational managers. Currently, senior management gets a fixed salary supplemented by an annual bonus awarded by the board. Shareholders have been complaining that these bonuses are not suitable. The operational managers also get bonuses based on their performance as assessed by their management superiors. The operational managers are unhappy with the system. In order to address this, it has been suggested that they should be involved in bonus target setting as otherwise there is a sense of demotivation from such a system. The CFO wants an evaluation of this system of rewards in light of the introduction of the BSC and best practice.

Required

(a) Discuss how Victoria's success in the customer perspective may impact on the metrics given in the financial perspective.   **(5 marks)**

(b) Recommend, with justification, and calculate a suitable performance metric for each customer perspective success factor. Comment on the problems of using customer complaints to measure whether packages are delivered safely and on time.   **(11 marks)**

(c) Advise Victoria on the reward management issues outlined by the CFO.   **(9 marks)**

(Total = 25 marks)

Appendix 1

Financial perspective

(How do we appear to our shareholders?)
Return on capital employed
Profit margin
Revenue growth

Customer perspective

(How do we appear to our customers?)
Success factors:
Ability to meet customers' transport needs
Ability to deliver packages quickly
Ability to deliver packages on time
Ability to deliver packages safely

Internal process perspective

(What business processes must excel?)
Time taken to load and unload
Lorry capacity utilisation

Learning and growth perspective

(How do we sustain and improve our ability to grow?)
Leadership competence (qualitative judgement)
Training days per employee

Appendix 2

The process: A customer makes a transport request for a package to be collected and delivered to a given destination. The customer is supplied with a time window in which the delivery will occur. Packages are then loaded onto lorries and delivered according to a route specified by the depot's routing manager.

Total number of customer transport requests	610,000
Total number of packages transported	548,000
Total number of lorry journeys	73,000
Total package kilometres	65,760,000
Total package minutes	131,520,000
Number of delivery complaints from customers:	
from damaged packages	8,220
from late delivery (outside agreed time window)	21,920

Notes

1   All figures are for the last financial year.
2   A package kilometre is defined as a kilometre travelled by one package.
3   A package minute is defined as a minute spent in transit by one package.

51 Graviton (APM 12/13)

49 mins

Graviton Clothing (Graviton) is a listed manufacturer of clothing with a strong reputation for producing desirable, fashionable products which can attract high selling prices. The company's objective is to maximise shareholder wealth. Graviton's products are sold through its own chain of stores. Graviton's markets demand designs which are in tune with current fashion trends which can alter every few weeks. Therefore, the business's stated aim is to focus production on these changing market trends by maintaining flexibility to adapt to that market demand through close control of all stages of the supply chain (design, manufacture and distribution).

The chief executive officer (CEO) is unhappy with the current performance measurement system at Graviton. The system was created about five years ago by the finance director who has subsequently retired. The aim of the system was to provide the company with a list of measures which would cover performance at the strategic, tactical and operational levels of management. An example of the most recent performance report is given in Table 1.

Table 1

Graviton Performance Dashboard
Report for the year to Sept 20X3

	20X3	20X2	20X1	Change 20X3/20X2
Financial				
Revenue ($m)	1,723	1,570	1,413	9.7%
Operating Profit ($m)	320	314	308	1.9%
ROCE	15.8%	15.9%	15.9%	
Design				
Design awards won	3	2	3	50.0%
Manufacture				
Average time to market (days)	22.2	22.3	22.1	−0.4%
Distribution				
Deliveries on time	87.0%	86.8%	87.3%	0.2%

Commentary:

- The revenue growth of the business remains strong in a difficult market.

- Return on capital employed matches the industry average of about 16%.

- Time to market for new designs has been maintained at 22 days by paying overtime to designers in order to meet production schedules.

Recent press reports about Graviton have been mixed, with positive comments about the innovative new designs and much admiration over the growth of sales which the business has achieved. However, there has been some criticism from customers of the durability of Graviton's clothes and from institutional investors that the dividend growth is not strong.

The CEO believes that there are major gaps in the current list of key metrics used by Graviton. She wants an evaluation of the current system and suggestions for improvements. However, she has warned you that the board wants a reasoned argument for each measure to be included in the list in order to avoid overloading each level of management with too much data.

Although rapidly growing, Graviton has had some problems in the last few years which have appeared on recent internal audit reports. It was found that a senior manager at factory site 1 has been delaying invoicing for completed orders in order to ensure that profit targets are met in both the current and the next accounting period. At factory site 2, there has been excellent return on a low capital employed figure although there is a significant adverse variance in the equipment repairs account.

The board is dominated by long-serving executives who are sceptical of change, given Graviton's growth over the past three years. At a recent board meeting, they have shared the CEO's concern about data overload and also have pointed out a variety of problems with the use of performance measures. They presented the CEO with a list of three common problems (myopia, gaming, ossification) and argued that the current good performance of the business did not justify changing the performance measurement system. The CEO needs to know if these problems apply to Graviton and if they do, then what can be done to manage them.

Required

(a) Evaluate the current performance measurement system using the Performance Pyramid of Lynch and Cross.
(15 marks)

(b) Assess whether the three problems listed by the board apply to Graviton and suggest appropriate performance management solutions to them.
(10 marks)

(Total = 25 marks)

52 Bettaserve
49 mins

Bettaserve has identified and defined a market in which it wishes to operate. This will provide a 'gold standard' focus for an existing range of services. Bettaserve has identified a number of key competitors and intends to focus on close co-operation with its customers in providing services to meet their specific design and quality requirements. Efforts will be made to improve the effectiveness of all aspects of the cycle from service design to after-sales service to customers. This will require inputs from a number of departments in the achievement of the specific goals of the 'gold standard' range of services. Efforts will be made to improve productivity in conjunction with increased flexibility of methods.

An analysis of financial and non-financial data relating to the 'gold standard' proposal for each of the years 20X7, 20X8 and 20X9 is shown in Schedule 1 below.

Required

(a) Prepare an analysis (both quantitative and discursive) of the 'gold standard' proposal for the period 20X7 to 20X9. You should use the information provided in the question, together with the data in Schedule 1 below. Your analysis should include the following:

(i) A definition of corporate 'vision or mission' and consideration of how the proposal may be seen as identifying and illustrating a specific sub-set of this 'vision or mission'. **(5 marks)**

(ii) Discussion and, where possible, quantification of the proposal in both marketing and financial terms. **(5 marks)**

(iii) Discussion of the external effectiveness of the proposal in the context of ways in which each of Quality and Delivery are expected to affect customer satisfaction and hence the marketing of the product. **(5 marks)**

(iv) Discussion of the internal efficiency of the proposal in the context of ways in which the management of each of Cycle Time and Waste are expected to affect productivity and hence the financial aspects of the proposal. **(4 marks)**

(b) Discuss the links, both vertical and horizontal, of the performance measures investigated in (a). The discussion should include comment on the hierarchy and inter-relationships between the measures, including internal and external aspects of the expected trends in performance.

(**Note**. A diagram may be used to illustrate the links, together with relevant discussion.) **(6 marks)**

(Total = 25 marks)

Schedule 1

'Gold Standard' proposal – estimated statistics

	20X7	20X8	20X9
Total market size ($m)	240	250	260
Bettaserve – sales ($m)	30	36	40
Bettaserve – total costs ($m)	28.2	25.448	25.1

Bettaserve – sundry statistics:

	20X7	20X8	20X9
Services achieving design quality standards (%) and accepted without further rectification	95	97	98
Rectification claims from customers ($m)	0.9	0.54	0.2
Cost of after sales rectification service ($m)	3	2.5	2
Sales meeting planned completion dates (%)	90	95	99
Average cycle time: (customer enquiry to service finalisation) (weeks)	6	5.5	5
Service enquiries not taken up by customers (% of enquiries)	7.50	5.00	2.50
Idle capacity of service personnel (%)	10	6	2

Analysis of total cost:

	$'000	$'000	$'000
Target cost – variable	12,000	14,400	16,000
Target cost – fixed	4,000	4,000	5,000
Internal failure costs	3,200	1,840	1,050
External failure costs	4,000	2,208	1,050
Appraisal costs	1,000	1,000	1,000
Prevention costs	4,000	2,000	1,000
Total cost	28,200	25,448	25,100

53 Cod (APM 12/11, amended)

49 mins

Cod Electrical Motors (Cod) manufactures electrical motors for some of the 24 different European domestic appliance manufacturers. Their motors are used in appliances such as washing machines and refrigerators. Cod has been in business for over 50 years and has obtained a reputation for producing reliable, low cost motors.

Cod has recently rewritten its mission statement, which now reads:

'Cod Electrical Motors is committed to providing competitively priced, high quality products, with service exceeding customer expectations. We will add value to our business relationships by investing in product development and highly trained personnel.'

The board have recognised that their existing key performance indicators (KPIs) do not capture the features of the corporate mission. They are worried that the staff see the mission statement as a public relations exercise rather than the communication of Cod's vision.

The monthly board papers contain a simple performance summary which is used as the key performance measurement system at that level.

Example of board papers for November 20X1:

Cod Electrical Motors

Key performance indicators for November 20X1

	This month	YTD	Comparative
Profit ($m)	2·1	25·6	1·9
Free cashflow ($m)	3·4	17·6	1·6
Return on capital employed (%)	12·4	11·7	11·8

Notes

1   The year end is 31 December.
2   The comparative figure is for the same month in the previous year.
3   ROCE is an annualised figure.
4   YTD means year to date.

There are additional performance indicators not available to the board that line management use for a more detailed picture.

Additional performance information:

	Note 1	20X1	20X0
Activity			
No of orders		2,560	2,449
No of deliveries		1,588	1,660
Staff			
No of staff (FTE basis)	2	1,229	1,226
No of staff training days		2,286	1,762
No of vacant posts	3	11	17
Customers			
No of orders with a complaint	4		
Late delivery		26	25
Product quality		39	31
Customer service		21	24
Other		52	43
Preferential supplier status	5	14	12
Production			
New products			
begun in year to date		2	1
in development at month end		4	3
launched in year to date		1	1
Quality			
internal failure costs ($'000)		3,480	2,766
external failure costs ($'000)		872	693

Notes

1   Figures are year to date with comparatives from the previous year quoted on the same basis.
2   FTE = Full-time equivalent staff numbers.
3   Post is considered vacant if unfilled for more than four months.
4   Complaints are logged and classified into the four categories given when received.
5   Number of customers where Cod holds preferred supplier status.

Required

(a)   With reference to Cod's mission statement and its existing KPIs, discuss why it is important for KPIs to reinforce the features of an organisation's mission. **(6 marks)**

(b)   Explain how the performance pyramid (Lynch and Cross) can help Cod's board to reach its goal of a coherent set of performance measures. **(6 marks)**

(c)   Evaluate the current system using the performance pyramid and apply the performance pyramid to Cod in order to suggest additional KPIs and a set of operational performance measures for Cod. **(13 marks)**

(Total = 25 marks)

54 APX Accountancy (APM 6/11, amended)   49 mins

APX Accountancy (APX) is an accountancy partnership with 12 branches covering each of the main cities of Emland. The business is well established, having organically grown over the last 40 years to become the second largest non-international practice in Emland. The accountancy market is mature and expands and contracts along with the general economic performance of Emland.

APX offers accountancy, audit, tax and business advisory services. The current business environment in Emland is dominated by a recession and the associated insolvency work is covered within the business advisory area of APX.

At present, the practice collects the following information for strategic performance evaluation:

	Audit	Tax	Business Advisory	Total
Revenue ($m)				
APX	69.1	89.2	64.7	223.0
Accounting industry	557.0	573.0	462.0	1,592.0
Change in revenue on previous year				
APX	3.0%	8.0%	22.0%	10.0%
Accounting industry	2.5%	4.5%	16.0%	6.8%
Profit margin at APX	6.4%	7.8%	10.5%	8.1%
Customer service score (1 to 5 with 5 being excellent)				
APX	3.4	3.9	4.1	

The above figures are for the most recent financial year and illustrate the metrics used by APX. Equivalent monthly figures are produced for each of the monthly partner meetings which review practice performance.

The staff are remunerated based on their grade, with non-partners obtaining a bonus of up to 10% of basic salary based on their line managers' annual review. The partners receive a fixed salary with a share of profit which depends on their contractual responsibilities within the partnership.

The managing partner of APX is dissatisfied with the existing performance management system, as she is not convinced that it is helping to achieve the long-term goal of expanding and ultimately floating the business on the national stock exchange. Therefore, she has asked you to consider the impact of applying Fitzgerald and Moon's building block approach to performance management in the practice.

In addition, the marketing manager at APX believes that the firm as a whole doesn't pay enough attention to customer service. At the last management meeting he said that, in his opinion, the customer service score(*) was the most important figures out of the performance metrics currently used by APX, and he said he felt it was no coincidence that the area of the business with the highest customer service score had also performed best financially.

[* Customer service scores reflect ratings given by customers in relation to the level of service they feel they have received from APX.]

Required

(a) Briefly describe Fitzgerald and Moon's building block model of performance management. **(4 marks)**

(b) Evaluate the existing performance management system at APX by applying the building block model.

(8 marks)

(c) Explain the main improvements the introduction of a building block approach to performance management could provide, and suggest specific improvements to the existing system of performance measures at APX in light of the introduction of the building block model. **(8 marks)**

(d) Briefly evaluate the marketing manager's statement about the customer service score. **(5 marks)**

(Total = 25 marks)

55 Robust Laptops (APM 12/10, amended) 49 mins

Robust Laptops Co (RL) makes laptop computers for use in dangerous environments. The company's main customers are organisations like oil companies and the military that require a laptop that can survive rough handling in transport to a site and can be made to their unique requirements.

The company started as a basic laptop manufacturer but its competitors grew much larger and RL had to find a niche market where its small size would not hinder its ability to compete. It is now considered one of the best quality producers in this sector.

RL had the same finance director for many years who preferred to develop its systems organically. However, due to a fall in profitability, a new chief executive officer (CEO) and a new chief financial officer (CFO) have been appointed. The CEO wishes to review RL's financial control systems in order to get better information with which to tackle the profit issue.

The CEO wants to begin by thinking about the pricing of the laptops to ensure that selling expensive products at the wrong price is not compromising profit margins. The laptops are individually specified by customers for each order and pricing has been on a production cost plus basis with a mark-up of 45%. The company uses an absorption costing system based on labour hours in order to calculate the production cost per unit.

The main control system used within the company is the annual budget. It is set before the start of the financial year and variances are monitored and acted upon by line managers.

More generally, the CEO is concerned about the performance information which is provided in the monthly board papers. The board papers contain a high level summary of financial information, comparing performance against budget for revenue, costs and profit. They also report RL's KPIs which are: profit, profit margin, free cashflow and return on capital employed.

Although the CEO acknowledges that the fall in profitability is a concern for RL, he believes that the company's performance measurement systems should not focus solely on financial information. Instead, he wants RL to identify its objectives and its critical success factors, and then link its KPIs to them.

Financial and other information for Robust Laptops

Data for the year ended 30 September 20X1

		Total
Volume (units)	23,800	
		$'000
Direct variable costs		
Material		40,650
Labour		3,879
Packaging and transport		2,118
Subtotal		46,647
Overhead costs		
Customer service		7,735
Purchasing and receiving		2,451
Inventory management		1,467
Administration of production		2,537
Subtotal		14,190
Total		60,837

Labour time per unit	3 hours
Data collected for the year	
No of minutes on call to customer	899,600
No of purchase orders raised	21,400
No of components used in production	618,800

Order 11784

Units ordered	16
Direct costs for this order:	$
Material	27,328
Labour	2,608
Packaging and transport	1,424

Other activities relating to this order:	
No of minutes on call to customer	1,104
No of purchase orders raised	64
No of components used in production	512
Administration of production (absorbed as general overhead)	3 Labour hours per unit

Required

(a) Evaluate of the current method of costing against an Activity Based Costing (ABC) system. You should provide illustrative calculations using the information provided on the costs for 20X1 and for Order 11784. Briefly state what action management might take in the light of your results with respect to this order.

(16 marks)

(b) With reference to RL, explain the link between objectives, critical success factors and KPIs, and why it is important to consider non-financial performance information as well as financial information. **(9 marks)**

(Total = 25 marks)

56 SFS (APM 6/10, amended) 49 mins

The Spare for Ships Company (SFS) has a specialist machining facility which serves the shipbuilding components market. The current job-costing system has two categories of direct cost (direct materials and direct manufacturing labour) and a single indirect cost pool (manufacturing overhead which is allocated on the basis of direct labour hours). The indirect cost allocation rate of the existing job-costing system is $120 per direct manufacturing labour-hour.

Recently, the Visibility Consultancy Partnership (VCP) proposed the use of an activity-based approach to redefine the job-costing system of SFS. VCP made a recommendation to retain the two direct cost categories. However, VCP further recommended the replacement of the single indirect-cost pool with five indirect-cost pools.

Each of the five indirect-cost pools represents an activity area at the manufacturing premises of SFS. Each activity area has its own supervisor who is responsible for his/her operating budget.

Relevant data are as follows:

Activity area	Cost driver used as allocation base	Cost allocation rate ($)
Materials handling	Number of components	0.50
Lathe work	Number of cuts	0.70
Milling	Number of machine hours	24.00
Grinding	Number of components	1.50
Inspection	Number of units inspected	20.00

SFS has recently invested in 'state of the art' IT systems which have the capability to automatically collate all of the data necessary for budgeting in each of the five activity areas.

The management accountant of SFS calculated the manufacturing cost per unit of two representative jobs under the two costing systems as follows:

	$ Job order 973	$ Job order 974
Current costing system	1,172.00	620.00
Activity-based costing system	1,612.00	588.89

Required

(a) Compare the cost figures per unit for Job order 973 and Job order 974 calculated by the management accountant and explain the reasons for, and potential consequences of, the differences in the job cost estimates produced under the two costing systems. **(8 marks)**

(b) 'The application of Activity Based Management (ABM) requires that the management of SFS focus on each of the following:

(i) Operational ABM
(ii) Strategic ABM
(iii) The implicit value of an activity'

Required

Critically appraise the above statement and explain the risks attaching to the use of ABM. **(8 marks)**

SFS manufactures and sells a range of products. It is not dominant in the market in which it operates and, as a result, it has to accept the market price for each of its products. The company is keen to ensure that it continues to compete and earn satisfactory profit at each stage throughout a product's life cycle.

Required

(c)   Explain how SFS could use Target Costing and Kaizen Costing to improve its future performance.

Your answer should include an explanation of the differences between Target Costing and Kaizen Costing.

(9 marks)

(Total = 25 marks)

57 LOL cards (APM 12/10, amended)   49 mins

LOL Co is a chain of shops selling cards and gifts throughout its country. It has been listed on the stock exchange for 10 years and enjoys a fairly high profile in the retail sector of the national economy. You have been asked by the chief executive officer (CEO) to advise the company on value-based management (VBM), as a different approach to performance management. The CEO has read about this method as a way of focusing on shareholder interests and in the current tough economic climate, she thinks that it may be a useful development for LOL.

The company has traditionally used earnings per share (EPS) growth and share price in order to assess performance. The changes being proposed are considered significant and the CEO wants to be briefed on the implications of the new analysis and also how to convince both the board and the major investors of the benefits.

Financial data for LOL

	20X9 $m	20Y0 $m
Profit before interest and tax	50.7	43.5
Interest paid	4.0	7.8
Profit after interest and tax	35.0	26.8
Average number of shares in issue (millions)	160	160
Capital employed at the end of the year was	(in $m)	
20X8	99.2	
20X9	104.1	
20Y0	97.8	

LOL aims for a capital structure of 50:50 debt to equity.

Cost of capital were

	20X9	20Y0
Equity	12.70%	15.30%
Debt (post-tax cost)	4.20%	3.90%

Corporation tax is at the rate of 25%.

Stock market information

	20X9	20Y0
Stock market all-share index	2,225.4	1,448.9
Retailing sector index	1,225.6	907.1
LOL (average share price) ($)	12.20	10.70

The fall in profits can, in part at least, be attributed to an increase in costs. The CFO has advised that LOL needs to focus on cost reduction rather than cost containment. She proposes to achieve this through the introduction of activity based management.

Required

(a)   Explain to the CEO what value-based management involves and how it can be used to focus the company on shareholder interests.   **(4 marks)**

(b)   Perform an assessment of the financial performance of LOL using Economic Value Added (EVA™) and evaluate your results compared with those of earnings per share (EPS) growth and share price performance. You should state any assumptions made.   **(12 marks)**

(c)   Evaluate VBM measures against traditional profit based measures of performance.   **(3 marks)**

(d)   Discuss how activity based management (ABM) differs from traditional cost allocation systems, and how ABM seeks to achieve cost reduction.   **(6 marks)**

(Total = 25 marks)

58 BEG (APM 6/10, amended)   49 mins

The Better Electricals Group (BEG) which commenced trading ten years ago manufactures a range of high quality electrical appliances such as kettles, toasters and steam irons for domestic use which it sells to electrical stores in Voltland.

The directors consider that the existing product range could be extended to include industrial sized products such as high volume water boilers, high volume toasters and large steam irons for the hotel and catering industry. They recently commissioned a highly reputable market research organisation to undertake a market analysis which identified a number of significant competitors within the hotel and catering industry.

At a recent meeting of the board of directors, the marketing director proposed that BEG should make an application to gain 'platinum status' quality certification in respect of their industrial products from the Hotel and Catering Institute of Voltland in order to gain a strong competitive position. He then stressed the need to focus on increasing the effectiveness of all operations from product design to the provision of after sales services.

An analysis of financial and non-financial data relating to the application for 'platinum status' for each of the years 20X1, 20X2 and 20X3 is contained in the appendix.

The managing director of BEG recently returned from a seminar, the subject of which was 'The Use of Cost Targets'. She then requested the management accountant of BEG to prepare a statement of total costs for the application for platinum status for each of years 20X1, 20X2 and 20X3. She further asked that the statement detailed manufacturing cost targets and the costs of quality.

The management accountant produced the following statement of manufacturing cost targets and the costs of quality:

	20X1 Forecast $'000	20X2 Forecast $'000	20X3 Forecast $'000
Variable manufacturing costs	8,400	10,500	12,600
Fixed manufacturing costs	3,000	3,400	3,400
Prevention costs	4,200	2,100	1,320
Appraisal costs	800	700	700
Internal failure costs	2,500	1,800	1,200
External failure costs	3,100	2,000	980
Total costs	22,000	20,500	20,200

Required

(a)   Explain how the use of cost targets could be of assistance to BEG with regard to their application for platinum status. Your answer must include commentary on the items contained in the statement of manufacturing cost targets and the costs of quality prepared by the management accountant.   **(8 marks)**

(b)   Assess the forecasted performance of BEG for the period 20X1 to 20X3 with reference to the application for 'platinum status' quality certification under the following headings:

(i)   Financial performance and marketing
(ii)   External effectiveness
(iii)   Internal efficiency   **(12 marks)**

(c)   Briefly explain how the performance pyramid (Lynch and Cross) could help BEG gain its 'platinum status' quality certification.   **(5 marks)**

(Total = 25 marks)

Appendix
'Platinum status' quality certification application – Relevant statistics

	20X1 Forecast	20X2 Forecast	20X3 Forecast
Total market size ($m)	300	320	340
BEG – sales ($m)	24	30	36
BEG – total costs ($m)	22	20.5	20.2
BEG – sundry statistics:			
% of products achieving design quality standards and accepted without further rectification	92	95	99
Rectification claims from customers ($m)	0.96	0.75	0.1
Cost of after sales rectification service ($m)	1.8	1.05	0.8
% of sales meeting planned delivery dates	88.5	95.5	99.5
Average cycle time:			
customer enquiry to product delivery (days)	49	45	40
Product enquiries not taken up by customers (% of enquiries)	10.5	6	3
Idle capacity of manufacturing staff (%)	12	6	1.5

59 Turing (APM 6/14)   49 mins

Turing Aerodynamics (Turing) has formed a joint venture (JV) with Riemann Generators (Riemann) in order to design and manufacture high-performance wind turbines which generate electricity. The joint venture is called TandR with each party owning 50%. Turing will design and build the pylons, housing and turbine blades while Riemann will supply the generators to be fitted inside the housing.

Turing is a medium sized firm known for its blade design skills. It is owned by three venture capital firms (VCs) (each holding 30% of the shares), with the remaining 10% being given to management to motivate them. The VCs each have a large portfolio of business investments and accept that some of these investments may fail provided that some of their investments show large gains. Management is an ambitious group who enjoys the business and technical challenges of introducing new products.

On the other hand, Riemann is a large, family-owned company working in the highly competitive electricity generator sector. The shareholders of Riemann see the business as mature and want it to offer a stable, long-term return on capital. However, recently, Riemann had to seek emergency refinancing (debt and equity) due to its thin profit margins and tough competition, both of which are forecast to continue. As a result, Riemann's shareholders and management are concerned for the survival of the business and see TandR as a way to generate some additional cash flow. Unlike at Turing, the management of Riemann does not own significant shareholdings in the company which has preferred to pay fixed salaries.

TandR is run by a group of managers made up from each of the JV partners. They are currently faced with a decision about the design of the product. There are three design choices depending on the power which the wind turbines can generate (measured in megawatts [MW]):

Design	Description
8 MV	a large 8 MW unit
3 MW	a 3 MW unit
1 MW	a basic 1 MW unit

The engineering for the 1 MW and 3 MW units is well understood and so design is much simpler than for the 8 MW unit which would be world leading if completed.

The demand for the different types of units will depend on government subsidies of the electricity price charged by the electricity generating companies who will buy the wind turbines and the planning regulations for building such large structures. It is believed that there will be orders for either 1,000 or 1,500 or 2,000 units but there is no clear picture yet of which demand level is more likely than the others.

The estimated costs and prices for the units are:

Type	Variable cost per unit $m	Fixed costs $m	Price per unit $m
8 MW	10.4	7,500.0	20.8
3 MW	4.8	820.0	9.6
1 MW	1.15	360.0	4.6

Notes

1   The fixed costs cover the initial design, development and testing of the units.

2   The costs and prices are in real terms with the 8 MW unit likely to take more years to develop than the others.

Required

(a)   Assess the risk appetites of the two firms in the joint venture and provide a justified recommendation for each firm of an appropriate method of decision-making under uncertainty to assess the different types of wind turbines.
(9 marks)

(b)   Evaluate the choice of turbine designs types using your recommended methods from part (a) above.
(8 marks)

(c)   Discuss the problems encountered in managing performance in a joint venture such as TandR.   **(8 marks)**

(Total = 25 marks)

60 Callisto (APM 6/12, amended)   49 mins

Callisto Retail (Callisto) is an on-line reseller of local craft products related to the historic culture of the country of Callistan. The business started ten years ago as a hobby of two brothers, Jeff and George. The brothers produced humorous, short video clips about Callistan which were posted on their website and became highly popular. They decided to use the website to try to sell Callistan merchandise and good initial sales made them believe that they had a viable business idea.

Callisto has gone from strength to strength and now boasts sales of $120m per annum, selling anything related to Callistan. Callisto is still very much the brothers' family business. They have gathered around themselves a number of strategic partners into what Jeff describes as a virtual company. Callisto has the core functions of video clip production, finance and supplier relationship management. The rest of the functions of the organisation (warehousing, delivery and website development) are outsourced to strategic partners.

The brothers work from their family home in the rural North of Callistan while other Callisto employees work from their homes in the surrounding villages and towns. These employees are involved in video editing, system maintenance, handling customer complaints and communication with suppliers and outsourcers regarding inventory. The employees log in to Callisto's systems via the national internet infrastructure. The outsourced functions are handled by multinational companies of good reputation who are based around the world. The brothers have always been fascinated by information technology and so they depend on email and electronic data interchange to communicate with their product suppliers and outsourcing partners.

Recently, there have been emails from regular customers of the Callisto website complaining about slow or

non-delivery of orders that they have placed. George has commented that this represents a major threat to Callisto as the company operates on small profit margins, relying on volume to drive the business. He believes that sales growth will drive the profitability of the business due to its cost structure.

Jeff handles the management of outsourcing and has been reviewing the contracts that exist between Callisto and its strategic partner for warehousing and delivery, RLR Logistics. The current contract for warehousing and delivery is due for renewal in two months and currently, has the following service level agreements (SLAs):

(1)   RLR agree to receive and hold inventory from Callisto's product suppliers.

(2)   RLR agree to hold 14 days inventory of Callisto's products.

(3)   RLR agree to despatch from their warehouse any order passed from Callisto within three working days, inventory allowing.

(4)   RLR agree to deliver to customers anywhere in Callistan within two days of despatch.

Breaches in these SLAs incur financial penalties on a sliding scale depending on the number and severity of the problems. Each party to the contract collects their own data on performance and this has led to disagreements in the past over whether service levels have been achieved although no penalties have been triggered to date. The most common disagreement arises over inventory levels held by RLR with RLR claiming that it cannot be expected to deliver products that are late in arriving to inventory due to the product suppliers' production and delivery issues.

Required

(a)   Assess the difficulties of performance measurement and performance management in complex business structures such as Callisto, especially in respect of the performance of their employees and strategic partners.   **(17 marks)**

George has also been increasingly concerned about the length of time it is taking for customer complaints to be addressed, and the damage which delays in replying to customer complaints could have on Callisto's reputation. In this respect, he is also worried that Callisto's employees are not working as productively as they could be.

Consequently, he has designed a daily report which lists all the employees in alphabetical order, and then shows four columns of data for each employee:

(1)   How long they have been logged on to Callisto's system

(2)   How many videos they have edited

(3)   How many complaints they have handled

(4)   How many suppliers or outsourcers they have contacted

Required

(b)   Evaluate the usefulness of George's proposed report, and suggest ways the output report could be improved.   **(8 marks)**

(Total = 25 marks)

61 Coal Creek (APM 12/12, amended)   49 mins

Coal Creek Nursing Homes (CCNH) is a company operating residential care homes for the elderly in Geeland.

The residents at CCNH are those elderly people who can no longer care for themselves at home and whose family are unable to look after them. There are 784 homes with about 30,000 residents under the care of the company. There are about 42,500 staff, who range from head office staff, through the home managers, to the care staff and cleaners and caterers.

The company is a private company which aims to make a suitable return to its shareholders. It had revenues of $938m in the last year and is one of the largest providers of residential care places in Geeland.

The company is split into two divisions: General Care (GC) which handles ordinary elderly residents and Special Care (SC), which is a newer operation that handles residents who need intensive care and attention due to physical or mental ailments.

CCNH does not own its homes but rents them from a number of large commercial landlords. It has taken on a large number of new homes recently in order to cope with the expansion of SC, which has proved successful with 24% pa revenue growth over the last two years. GC is a mature business with little growth in a sector that is now fully supplied. GC has seen volumes and margins falling as price pressure comes from its main customers (public sector health organisations who contract out this part of their care provision).

A new chief executive officer (CEO) has just taken over at CCNH. She was appointed because the board of CCNH believed that the company was in difficulty. The previous CEO had been forced to leave following a scandal involving a number of the homes where residents' money had gone missing and their families had called in the police. The finance director and the operations director had also resigned, leaving the company without any experienced senior management.

The board have tasked the new CEO with ascertaining the current position of the business and identifying a strategy to address the issues that arise. The CEO wants to address the strategy, deciding whether to divest or retain elements of the business.

The CEO has come to you, as the most senior member of finance staff, for assistance with this task. The first area that she wants help on is the problem that the business is having with its landlords. The company struggled to meet its most recent rental payment, which the bank eventually agreed to cover through an increase to the overdraft, as CCNH had no ready cash. She is upset that the chosen strategic measures of performance (earnings per share growth and operating profit margin) did not identify the difficulties that the firm is now facing. One of the other directors had mentioned gearing problems but the CEO did not follow what this meant.

Also, the CEO has heard of qualitative models for predicting corporate failure and wants to apply one at CCNH. Obviously, she wants to know if CCNH exhibits any symptoms of failure.

You have been given the outline financial statements to help with this task (see Appendix below the Requirements).

Required

(a) Discuss why indicators of liquidity and gearing need to be considered in conjunction with profitability at CCNH. Illustrate your answer with suitable calculations. **(11 marks)**

(b) Explain one qualitative model for predicting corporate failure (such as Argenti) and comment on CCNH's position utilising this model. You are not expected to give scores, only to comment on the areas of weakness at CCNH. **(9 marks)**

(c) Advise the CEO why it is important to consider product portfolios when she determines her strategy for the business. **(5 marks)**

(Total = 25 marks)

Appendix:

Outline financial statements for CCNH for the year just ended

Summary Income Statements

	General Care $m	Special Care $m	Total $m
Revenue	685	253	938
Operating costs			
Homes payroll	397	139	536
running	86	24	110
Rents	193	64	257
Central costs	27	3	30
Operating profit	(18)	23	5
Interest			5
Profit before tax			0
Tax			0
Profit for the period			0

Statement of Financial Position

	General Care $m	Special Care $m	Total $m
Assets			
Non-current assets	244	87	331
Current assets	17	47	64
Total assets	261	134	395
Equity and Liabilities			
Share capital			165
Retained earnings reserve			24
Long-term borrowing			102
Current liabilities	76	28	104
Total equity and liabilities			395

[**Note**. A breakdown of the long-term financing into two divisions has not been possible.]

62 BPC (APM 12/07, amended)

49 mins

The directors of Blaina Packaging Co (BPC), a well-established manufacturer of cardboard boxes, are currently considering whether to enter the cardboard tube market. Cardboard tubes are purchased by customers whose products are wound around tubes of various sizes ranging from large tubes on which carpets are wound, to small tubes around which films and paper products are wound. The cardboard tubes are usually purchased in very large quantities by customers. On average, the cardboard tubes comprise between 1% and 2% of the total cost of the customers' finished product.

The directors have gathered the following information:

(1) The cardboard tubes are manufactured on machines which vary in size and speed. The lowest cost machine is priced at $30,000 and requires only one operative for its operation. A one-day training course is required in order that an unskilled person can then operate such a machine in an efficient and effective manner.

(2) The cardboard tubes are made from specially formulated paper which, at times during recent years, has been in short supply.

(3) At present, four major manufacturers of cardboard tubes have an aggregate market share of 80%. The current market leader has a 26% market share. The market shares of the other three major manufacturers, one of which is JOL Co, are equal in size. The product ranges offered by the four major manufacturers are similar in terms of size and quality. The market has grown by 2% per annum during recent years.

(4) A recent report on the activities of a foreign-based multinational company revealed that consideration was being given to expanding operations in their packaging division overseas. The division possesses large-scale automated machinery for the manufacture of cardboard tubes of any size.

(5) Another company, Plastic Tubes Co (PTC) produces a narrow, but increasing, range of plastic tubes which are capable of housing small products such as film and paper-based products. At present, these tubes are on average 30% more expensive than the equivalent sized cardboard tubes sold in the marketplace.

Required

(a) Using Porter's five forces model, assess the attractiveness of the option to enter the market for cardboard tubes as a performance improvement strategy for BPC. **(10 marks)**

(b) Discuss the limitations of Porter's five forces model as a technique for assessing how attractive an industry is to enter. **(5 marks)**

JOL Co was the market leader with a share of 30% three years ago. The managing director of JOL Co stated at a recent meeting of the board of directors that: 'our loss of market share during the last three years might lead to the end of JOL Co as an organisation and therefore we must address this issue immediately'.

Required

(c) Discuss the statement of the managing director of JOL Co and discuss six performance indicators, other than decreasing market share, which might indicate that JOL Co might fail as a corporate entity. **(10 marks)**

(Total = 25 marks)

63 RM Batteries (APM 12/10, amended)

49 mins

RM Batteries Co (RMB) is a manufacturer of battery packs. It has expanded rapidly in the last few years under the leadership of its autocratic chairman and chief executive officer, John Smith. Smith is relentlessly optimistic. He likes to get his own way and demands absolute loyalty from all his colleagues.

The company has developed a major new product over the last three years which has necessitated a large investment in new equipment. Smith has stated that this more efficient battery is critical to the future of the business as the company operates in a sector where customers expect constant innovation from their suppliers.

However, the recent share price performance has caused concern at board level and there has been comment in the financial press about the increased gearing and the strain that this expansion is putting on the company. The average share price has been $1·56 (20X8), $1·67 (20X9) and $1·34 (20Y0). There are 450 million shares in issue.

A relevant Z-score model for the industry sector is:

$$Z = 1.2X_1 + 1.4X_2 + 3.3X_3 + 0.6X_4 + X_5$$

Where

X_1 is working capital/total assets (WC/TA).

X_2 is retained earnings reserve/total assets (RE/TA).

X_3 is Profit before interest and tax/total assets (PBIT/TA).

X_4 is market value of equity/total long-term debt (MVE/total long-term debt).

X_5 is Revenue/total assets (Revenue/TA).

A score of more than 3 is considered safe and at below 1·8, the company is at risk of failure in the next two years.

The company's recent financial performance is summarised below:

Summary Income Statements

	20X8	20X9	20Y0
	$m	$m	$m
Revenue	1,460	1,560	1,915
Operating costs	1,153	1,279	1,724
Operating profit	307	281	191
Interest	35	74	95
Profit before tax	272	207	96
Tax	87	66	31
Profit for the period	185	141	65

Statements of Financial Position

	20X8	20X9	20Y0
	$m	$m	$m
Assets			
Non-current assets	1,120	1,778	2,115
Current assets	235	285	341
Total assets	1,355	2,063	2,456
Equity and liabilities			
Share capital	230	230	230
Retained earnings reserve	204	344	410
Long-term borrowings	465	991	1,261
Current liabilities	456	498	555
Total equity and liabilities	1,355	2,063	2,456

A junior analyst in the company has correctly prepared a spreadsheet calculating the Z-scores as follows:

		20X8	20X9	20Y0
Share price ($)		1.56	1.67	1.34
No of shares (millions)		450	450	450
Market value of equity ($M)		702	752	603
X_1	WC/TA	−0.163	−0.103	−0.087
X_2	RE/TA	0.151	0.167	0.167
X_3	PBIT/TA	0.227	0.136	0.078
X_4	MVE/Total long-term debt	1.510	0.758	0.478
X_5	Revenue/TA	1.077	0.756	0.780
	Z	2.746	1.770	1.452
Gearing [debt/equity]		107%	173%	197%

Required

(a)   Discuss the strengths and weaknesses of quantitative and qualitative models for predicting corporate failure.
(6 marks)

(b)   Comment on the results in the junior analyst's spreadsheet.
(5 marks)

(c)   Identify the qualitative problems that are apparent in the company's structure and performance and explain why these are relevant to possible failure.
(5 marks)

(d)   Critically assess the results of your analysis in parts (b) and (c) alongside details of RMB's recent financial performance and suggest additional data that should be acquired and how it could be used to assess RMB's financial health.
(4 marks)

RMB used a market skimming pricing strategy for its new product at the introduction stage in its lifecycle. However, John Smith now believes that the new product has moved into its growth phase, and he is concerned about how long it will be until the product becomes mature.

(e)   Explain the changes that are likely to occur at the maturity and decline stages of the product's life cycle in relation to its selling price and production costs.
(5 marks)

(Total = 25 marks)

64 NW Clothes   49 mins

NW Clothes Co (NWC) is a well-established clothes retailer in Nordland, with a number of shops across the country. In recent years, NWC, like many of the other clothes retailers in Nordland, has offered customers the opportunity to buy clothes online as well as by visiting its shops.

Tough economic conditions in Nordland in recent years have placed consumers' disposable income under increasing pressure, and value for money is becoming increasingly important in their purchasing decisions. At the same time, increases in commodity prices (particularly cotton prices) have led to an increase in NWC's costs.

An extract of some key figures from NWC's financial statements is given below:

	20X7 ($m)	20X9 ($m)
Revenue	230.0	232.0
Operating profit	40.0	36.0
Net cash flow from operations	25.5	26.7
Total debt	42.5	49.5

The latest market research figures that the value of total clothing sales increased by 4.5% between 20X7 – 20X9, with low cost stores and online sales being the major contributors to this growth. Internet sales increased by nearly 20% over the two years.

In 20X8 NWC had refurbished all of its stores because the Chief Executive felt that their dated look and feel was adversely affecting NWC's sales. The other directors felt the company should be focusing on increasing its online sales, but they Chief Executive dismissed their arguments claiming that the high street stores remained the core area of NWC's business.

There have been adverse comments in the financial press about the cost of the refurbishment programme, and the effect that it has had on NWC's gearing and interest payments. NWC drew down an additional $10 million loan in 20X8 to cover the cost of the programme, which has been budgeted to cost $9 million. It ended up costing just under $11 million.

The Directors are also concerned that about the downward trend in NWC's share price over the last three years. The average share price has been: $1.76 (20X7), $1.65 (20X8) and $1.42 (20X9).

At the latest annual general meeting, a number of shareholders expressed serious concerns about NWC's performance and some even questioned its future as an independent entity. The Chief Executive, however, said he remained bullish about the company's prospects, and highlighted that a new inventory management system had allowed NWC to reduce inventory holdings to less than 3% of revenue, and by switching some of its suppliers it would be able to reduce costs in the future.

The day after the general meeting, one of the national newspapers in Nordland published an article about the dramatic increase in the number of customer complaints about the poor quality of NWC garments they have bought recently. Another newspaper published a leaked report which suggested NWC is considering closing some of its shops, and it will not be renewing the leases for those shops when they become due for renewal next year.

Required

(a) With reference to NWC, discuss the importance of evaluating external factors as well as internal ones when predicting corporate failure.

(8 marks)

(b) Identify the problems that are apparent in NWC's structure and performance, and explain how they are relevant to possible failure.

(12 marks)

Following the concerns the shareholders raised at the annual general meeting about NWC's performance, the management accountant calculated the company's Z-score based on figures from the 20X9 financial statements. His calculations showed that NWC had a Z-score of 2.7.

Required

(c) Briefly discuss the implications of the accountant's calculations for NWC.

(5 marks)

(Total = 25 marks)

65 Culam Mining (APM 12/14)   49 mins

Culam Mining (Culam) is a mineral ore mining business in the country of Teeland. It owns and operates four mines. A mine takes on average two years to develop before it can produce ore and the revenue from the mine is split (25:75) between selling the ore under fixed price contracts over five years and selling on the spot market. The bulk of the business's production is exported. A mine has an average working life of about 20 years before all the profitable ore is extracted. It then takes a year to decommission the site and return the land to a useable form for agriculture or other developments.

Recently, one of Culam's foreign competitors surprised the market by becoming insolvent as a result of paying too much to acquire a competitor when the selling price of their minerals dipped as the world economy went into recession. As a result, the chief executive officer (CEO) wanted to know if this was likely to happen to Culam. She had read about the Altman Z-score as a way of predicting corporate failure and had a business analyst prepare a report calculating the Z-score for Culam. The report is summarised below:

Analyst's Report (extract)

The Altman Z-score model is:

$$Z = 1 \cdot 2X_1 + 1 \cdot 4X_2 + 3 \cdot 3X_3 + 0 \cdot 6X_4 + X_5$$

Another quantitative model (Q-score model) has been produced by academics working at Teeland's main university based on recent data from listed companies on the small Teeland stock exchange. It is:

$$Q = 1 \cdot 4X_1 + 3 \cdot 3X_3 + 0 \cdot 5X_4 + 1 \cdot 1X_5 + 1 \cdot 7X_6$$

Where for both models:

X_1 is working capital/total assets;
X_2 is retained earnings reserve/total assets;
X_3 is profit before interest and tax/total assets;
X_4 is market value of equity/total long-term debt (MVe/total long-term debt);
X_5 is revenue/total assets;
and
X_6 is current assets/current liabilities.

Using the most recent figures from Culam's financial statements (year ending September 2014), Culam's Altman Z-score is 3·5 and its score from the other model (Q) is 3·1.

For both models, a score of more than 3 (for Z or Q) is considered safe and at below 1·8, the company is at risk of failure in the next two years.

The analyst had done what was asked and calculated the score but had not explained what it meant or what action should be taken as a result. Therefore, the CEO has turned to you to help her to make sense of this work and for advice about how to use the information and how Culam should proceed into the future.

Required

(a) Evaluate both the result of the analyst's calculations and the appropriateness of these two models for Culam.

(10 marks)

(b) Explain the potential effects of a mine's lifecycle on Culam's Z-score and the company's probability of failure.

Note. You should ignore its effect on the Q-score. **(7 marks)**

(c) Give four detailed recommendations to reduce the probability of failure of Culam, providing suitable justifications for your advice. **(8 marks)**

(Total = 25 marks)

SECTION A QUESTIONS

Questions 66 to 77 are 50 mark questions which, like the Section A questions in the P5 exam, cover a range of topic areas.

66 Lopten (APM 12/13, amended)   98 mins

Lopten Industries is one of the largest, listed consumer durables manufacturers in the world, making washing machines, tumble dryers and dishwashers. It has recently expanded into Beeland which is a developing country where incomes have risen to the point where demand is increasing for Lopten's goods among the growing middle-class population.

Lopten believes in the economies of scale of large manufacturing sites with dispersed selling branches in the markets in which it operates. Therefore, it has entered the Beeland market by setting up a local sales force and supporting them with a national marketing campaign. The company is currently selling only two products in Beeland (both are types of washing machines):

- A basic product (called Cheerful) with functions which are comparable with the existing local competitors' output

- A premium product (called Posh) which has functions and features similar to Lopten's products in other developed countries

Both products are manufactured and imported from its regional manufacturing hub, which is in the neighbouring country of Kayland.

The competitive environment in Beeland is changing rapidly. The washing machine market used to be dominated by two large local manufacturers who make simple, cheap and reliable machines. There are two other major international manufacturers apart from Lopten. One of these has already opened a factory in Beeland and is producing machines similar to Cheerful to compete directly with the existing local producers. The government of Beeland has supported this new entrant with grants, as it is keen to encourage inward investment by foreign companies and the resulting expertise and employment which they provide. The other international competitor is now considering entering the Beeland market with more highly specified machines similar to Lopten's Posh brand.

Lopten's stated mission is to be the 'most successful manufacturer of its type of products in the world'. The board has set the following critical success factors (CSFs) for Lopten's Beeland operations:

1.   To obtain a dominant market presence

2.   To maximise profits within acceptable risk

3.   To maintain the brand image of Lopten for above average quality products

The board is considering using the following key performance indicators (KPIs) for each product: total profit, average sales price per unit, contribution per unit, market share, margin of safety, return on capital employed (ROCE), total quality costs and consumer awards won.

(**Note**. Margin of safety has been defined as [actual sales units – breakeven sales units]/actual sales units.)

The board has asked you as a consultant to assess its current performance measurement systems. They want a report which calculates the various indicators suggested above and then assesses how the key performance indicators address issues in the external environment. The report should assess the balance between planning and controlling represented by the KPIs as they want to ensure that these match what they should be doing at the strategic level in Lopten. Also, it should evaluate how the KPIs fit with the CSFs which have been selected. The data given in Appendix 1 has been collated for your use.

Finally, the board is considering two new marketing strategies going forward:

Plan A is to continue operations as at present allowing for 4% growth pa in volumes of both Cheerful and Posh.

Plan B is to dramatically reduce the marketing spend on Cheerful and to reallocate resources to focus the marketing on Posh. This is expected to lead to an anticipated growth in volume of 15% p.a. for Posh and flat sales for Cheerful.

The target operating profit for the Beeland operation in two years' time is set at $135m and the board wants an evaluation of these strategies in meeting that target.

Appendix 1

Beeland operation's information for the most recent financial year

	Cheerful	Posh	Total
Variable costs	$ per unit	$ per unit	
Materials	90	120	
Labour	60	80	
Overheads	40	50	
Distribution costs	45	45	
Quality costs	20	30	
Fixed costs	$m	$m	$m
Administration costs	18	18	36
Distribution costs	16	16	32
Quality costs	6	6	12
Marketing costs	80	80	160
	Cheerful	Posh	Total
Other data	$m	$m	$m
Revenue	448	308	756
Capital employed	326	250	576
	Units	Units	Units
Total market size (millions)	9.33	1.33	10.66
Beeland operation's sales (millions)	1.12	0.44	1.56

Notes

1 Cheerful has won one best buy award from the Beeland Consumer Association.

2 Posh has won four best buy awards from the Beeland Consumer Association.

3 The allocations of fixed costs are based on a recent activity-based costing exercise and are considered to be valid.

Required

Write a report to the board of Lopten which:

(i) Calculates the key performance indicators (KPIs) suggested by the board for the assessment of performance of the Beeland operations. **(11 marks)**

(ii) Uses PEST analysis to identify issues in the company's external environment and then evaluates the effectiveness of the suggested KPIs in addressing these issues. **(11 marks)**

(iii) Takes each critical success factor (CSF) in turn and evaluates how the suggested KPIs fit to the CSF given. **(10 marks)**

(iv) Assess the extent to which the suggested KPIs would be suitable for use in planning rather than controlling. **(5 marks)**

(v) Evaluates whether the two proposed marketing strategies will enable Lopten to achieve its operating profit target. **(9 marks)**

Professional marks will be awarded for the format, style and structure of the discussion of your answer. **(4 marks)**

Note. All figures are real for the purpose of this scenario so that inflation can be ignored. Also, round to the nearest $million as appropriate.

(Total = 50 marks)

67 Film Productions Co (APM 12/10, amended)   98 mins

Film Productions Co (FP) is a small international company producing films for cinema release and also for sale on DVD or to television companies. FP deals with all areas of the production from casting, directing and managing the artists to negotiating distribution deals with cinema chains and TV channels. The industry is driven by the tastes of its films' audience, which when accurately predicted can lead to high levels of profitability on a successful film.

FP was founded by three people 20 years ago. At that time, the company used a new technology which had been developed by one of the founders which improved the quality of computer generated imagery and 3-dimensional graphics in its films. The third person is Mr Z, who is the current CEO, who has a strong, dynamic, personality.

Mr Z has been the driving force behind the development and growth of the business to its present size of 350 employees. In the early years, with a charismatic leadership style, Mr Z was very proud of the fact that he knew all employees by their first names and considered everyone to be part of one big team. Everyone understood exactly what the company stood for and how things should be done. As the company has grown, Mr Z feels he is not in touch with newer members of staff and that they do not understand his, and the company's, values.

In addition, the technology used by FP is no longer considered innovative and there are a number of other competitors operating in exactly the same way.

The company produces films which it hopes will have mass appeal. The company makes around $200 million of sales each year equally split between a share of cinema takings, DVD sales and TV rights. FP has released 32 films in the past five years. Each film costs an average of $18 million and takes 12 months to produce from initial commissioning through to the final version. Production control is important in order to hit certain key holiday periods for releasing films at the cinema or on DVD.

The company's films have been moderately successful in winning industry awards although FP has never won any major award. Its aims have been primarily commercial with artistic considerations secondary. Recently, FP has been approached by two companies with requests to make promotional videos (for use as television adverts) for them, but FP turned the requests down because it did not have sufficient resources available to make the videos in the timescale required. However, Mr Z feels that making these promotional videos could be a useful way to supplement FP's income in future.

The company uses a top-down approach to strategy development with objectives leading to critical success factors (CSFs) which must then be measured using performance indicators. Currently, the company has identified a number of critical success factors. The two most important of these are viewed as:

(i)   Improve audience satisfaction
(ii)   Strengthen profitability in operations

At the request of the board, the chief executive officer (CEO) has been reviewing this system in particular the role of CSFs. Generally, the CEO is worried that the ones chosen so far fail to capture all the factors affecting the business and wants to understand all possible sources for CSFs and what it means to categorise them into monitoring and building factors.

These CSFs will need to be measured and there must be systems in place to perform that role. The existing information system of the company is based on a fairly basic accounting package. However, the CEO has been considering greater investment in these systems and making more use of the company's website in both driving forward the business' links to its audience and in collecting data on them.

The CEO is planning a report to the board of Film Productions and has asked you to help by drafting certain sections of this report.

Required

You are required to draft the sections of the CEO's report answering the following questions:

(a) Explain the difference between the following two types of CSF: monitoring and building, using examples appropriate to FP. **(4 marks)**

(b) Identify information that FP could use to set its CSFs and explain how it could be used giving two examples that would be appropriate to FP. **(6 marks)**

(c) Explain why it is important for FP to measure non-financial performance indicators as well as financial ones. **(5 marks)**

(d) For each of the two critical success factors given in the question, identify two performance indicators (PIs) that could support measurement of their achievement and explain why each PI is relevant to the CSF. **(10 marks)**

(e) Discuss the implications of your chosen PIs for the design and use of the company's website, its management information system and its executive information system. **(11 marks)**

Professional marks will be awarded for the style and structure of your sections of the report. **(4 marks)**

Despite having a clear set of strategic objectives the company does not have a mission statement. The CEO feels that this should be remedied as a matter of urgency.

(f) Discuss the issues which FP should consider when creating an appropriate mission statement. **(10 marks)**

(Total = 50 marks)

68 Mackerel (APM Pilot Paper) 98 mins

Mackerel Contracting (Mackerel) is a listed defence contractor working mainly for its domestic government in Zedland.

You are a consultant brought in to advise Mackerel on a number of issues facing the company. The board need a report from you:

- Outlining the external factors affecting the profitability of a potential new contract and how these factors can be built in to the choice of the design budget which is ultimately set

- Advising on a proposed change to the company's information systems, and

- Advising on suitable performance measures for Mackerel.

Firstly, Mackerel is currently considering tendering for a contract to design and develop a new armoured personnel vehicle (APV) for the army to protect its soldiers during transport around a battlefield. The invitation to tender from the government specifies that the APV should take two years to develop and test, and be delivered for a full cost to Mackerel of no more than $70,000 per unit at current prices. Normally, government contracts are approximately priced on a cost plus basis with Mackerel aiming to make a 19% mark-up.

At the last briefing meeting, the institutional shareholders of Mackerel expressed worry about the volatility of the company's earnings (currently a $20·4m operating profit per annum) especially during the economic downturn which is affecting Zedland at present. They are also concerned by cuts in government expenditure resulting from this recession. The Zedland minister for procurement has declared 'In the current difficult economic conditions, we are preparing a wide ranging review of all defence contracts with a view to deciding on what is desirable within the overall priorities for Zedland and what is possible within our budget.' The government procurement manager has indicated that the government would be willing to commit to purchase 500 APVs within the price limit set but with the possibility of increasing this to 750 or 1,000 depending on defence commitments. In the invitation to tender document, the government has stated it will pay a fixed sum of $7.5m towards development and then a 19% mark-up on budgeted variable costs.

Mackerel's risk management committee (RMC) is considering how much to spend on design and development. It has three proposals from the engineering team: a basic package at $7.5m (which will satisfy the original contract specifications) and two other improved design packages. The design packages will have different total fixed costs but are structured to give the same variable cost per unit. It is believed that the improved design packages will increase the chances of gaining a larger government order but it has been very difficult to ascertain the relevant probabilities of different order volumes. The RMC need a full appraisal of the situation using all suitable methods.

The risk manager has gathered information on the APV contract which is contained in Appendix A. She has identified that a major uncertainty in pricing the vehicle is the price of steel, as each APV requires 9·4 tonnes of steel. However, she has been successful in negotiating a fixed price contract for all the steel that might be required at $1,214 per tonne. The risk manager has tried to estimate the effect of choosing different design packages but is unsure of how to proceed to evaluate the different options.

Secondly, the Board is also considering a change to the information systems at Mackerel. The existing systems are based in the individual functions (production, sales, service, finance and human resources). Currently, reports are submitted by each function and then integrated at head office into the board papers which form the main strategic information system of the company. The board are considering the implementation of a new system based on an integrated, single database that would be accessible at any of the company's five sites. The company network would be upgraded to allow real-time input and update of the database. The database would support a detailed management information system and a high-level executive information system.

Finally, the chief executive office (CEO) of Mackerel believes that this new information system will provide the opportunity for a change in how performance is evaluated within the company. The company's mission is to maximise shareholder wealth and, currently, the board use total shareholder return (TSR) as an overall corporate measure of performance. The CEO has asked you to consider the general impact of the new information system, and also, how profit-based measures such as return on capital employed (ROCE) compare to newer measures such as economic value added (EVA™) with regard to meeting the overall goals of Mackerel and its external measure of performance.

Appendix A

Budgeted cost for APV

Variable cost per unit

	$
Steel	11,412 (9·4 tonnes at contracted prices)
Engine/transmission	9,500
Electronics	8,450
Other	4,810
Labour	13,800

Design and development (fixed total)	$
Package	
Type 1	7,500,000
Type 2	8,750,000
Type 3	10,000,000

Risk manager's assessment of likely government order:

		Probability	
Demand	Type 1	Type 2	Type 3
500	85%	25%	20%
750	10%	50%	50%
1,000	5%	25%	30%

Required

Write a report to the board of Mackerel to:

(i) Analyse the risks facing the management of Mackerel and discuss how the management team's attitude to risk might affect their response. **(9 marks)**

(ii) Evaluate the APV project using metrics and methods for decision-making under risk and uncertainty, and assess the suitability of the different methods used. **(19 marks)**

(iii) Recommend an appropriate choice of method of assessing the project and, therefore, a course of action for the APV contract. **(3 marks)**

(iv) Evaluate the potential impact of the introduction of the new executive information system on operational information gathering and strategic decision-making at Mackerel. **(8 marks)**

(v) Assess how profit-based measures such as return on capital employed (ROCE) compare to newer measures such as economic value added (EVA™) given Mackerel's overall goals. **(7 marks)**

Professional marks will be awarded for the format, style and structure of the discussion of your answer. **(4 marks)**

(Total = 50 marks)

69 TSC (APM 12/08, amended)　　　　　　　　98 mins

The Sentinel Company (TSC) offers a range of door-to-door express delivery services. The company operates using a network of depots and distribution centres throughout the country of Nickland. The following information is available:

(1) Each depot is solely responsible for all customers within a specified area. It collects goods from customers within its own area for delivery both within the specific area covered by the depot and elsewhere in Nickland.

(2) Collections made by a depot for delivery outside its own area are forwarded to the depots from which the deliveries will be made to the customers.

(3) Each depot must therefore integrate its deliveries to customers to include:
   (i) Goods that it has collected within its own area
   (ii) Goods that are transferred to it from depots within other areas for delivery to customers in its area

(4) Each depot earns revenue based on the invoiced value of all consignments collected from customers in its area, regardless of the location of the ultimate distribution depot.

(5) Depot costs comprise all of its own operating costs plus an allocated share of all company costs including centralised administration services and distribution centre costs.

(6) Bonuses for the management team and all employees at each depot are payable quarterly. The bonus is based on the achievement of a series of target values by each depot.

(7) Internal benchmarking is used at TSC in order to provide sets of absolute standards that all depots are expected to attain.

(8) (a) The Appendix shows the target values and the actual values achieved for each of a sample group of four depots situated in Donatellotown (D), Leonardotown (L), Michaelangelotown (M), and Raphaeltown (R).

   (b) The target values focus on three areas:
      (i) Depot revenue and profitability
      (ii) Customer care and service delivery
      (iii) Credit control and administrative efficiency

   (c) The bonus is based on a points system, which is also used as a guide to the operational effectiveness at each depot. One point is allocated where the target value for each item in the Appendix is either achieved or exceeded, and a zero score where the target is not achieved.

Appendix

Target and actual value statistics for Donatellotown (D), Leonardotown (L), Michaelangelotown (M), and Raphaeltown (R) for the year ended 31 October 20X8

Revenue and Profit Statistics:

	Revenue (1)		Profit (2)	
	Target	Actual	Target	Actual
	$m	$m	$m	$m
Company overall	200	240	30	32
Selected depots:				
D	16	15	2·4	2·3
L	14	18	2·1	2·4
M	12	14	1·8	2·2
R	18	22	2·7	2·8

Note. For the purpose of calculation of each depot's points it is essential that actual profit as a percentage of actual revenue must exceed the target profit (%).

Customer Care & Service Delivery Statistics:

	Target		Actual		
Selected Depots:		D	L	M	R
	%	%	%	%	%
Measure (% of total):					
(3) Late collection of consignments	2·0	1·9	2·1	1·8	2·4
(4) Misdirected consignments	4·0	4·2	3·9	3·3	5·1
(5) Delayed response to complaints	1·0	0·7	0·9	0·8	1·2
(6) Delays due to vehicle breakdown	1·0	1·1	1·4	0·3	2·0
Measure (% of revenue):					
(7) Lost items	1·0	0·6	0·9	0·8	1·9
(8) Damaged items	2·0	1·5	2·4	1·5	1·8

Credit Control & Administration Efficiency Statistics:

	Target	D	L	M	R
(9) Average receivable weeks	5·5	5·8	4·9	5·1	6·2
(10) Receivables in excess of 60 days (% of total)	5%	?	?	?	?
(11) Invoice queries (% of total)	5%	1·1%	1·4%	0·8%	2·7%
(12) Credit notes as a % of revenue	0·5%	?	?	?	?

Other information:

	D	L	M	R
	$'000	$'000	$'000	$'000
Aged Debtor (receivables) analysis (extract):				
Less than 30 days	1,300	1,500	1,180	2,000
31–60 days	321	133	153	552
Value of credit notes raised during the period ($000)	45	36	28	132

Note. TSC operates all year round.

Required

(a)   Prepare a report for the directors of TSC which:

   (i)   Presents a summary table which shows the points gained (or forfeited) by each depot. The points table should facilitate the ranking of each depot against the others for each of the 12 measures provided in the Appendix.   **(9 marks)**

   (ii)   Evaluates the relative performance of the four depots as indicated by the analysis in the summary table prepared in (i).   **(5 marks)**

   (iii) Assesses TSC in terms of financial performance, competitiveness, service quality, resource utilisation, flexibility and innovation and discusses the interrelationships between these terms, incorporating examples from within TSC.   **(10 marks)**

   (iv)   Critiques the performance measurement system at TSC.   **(6 marks)**

Professional marks will be awarded for the format, style and structure of the discussion of your report.   **(4 marks)**

A central feature of the performance measurement system at TSC is the widespread use of league tables that display each depot's performance relative to one another.

Historically, these league tables were prepared manually by the management accountant, but TSC has now introduced a new IT software system which produces them automatically. The new software system also enables operational managers to view key performance information themselves, something again was something they historically relied on the management accountant to provide them with.

When the new software was introduced, the management accountant asked the financial director how the software would affect her job, because she was considered that there would no longer be a role for her at TSC. However, the finance director reassured the management accountant there she still had an important role to play at TSC, although her new role would be more akin to that of a business partner for the operations than that of a traditional management accountant. In addition, the finance director highlighted the need for TSC to monitor developments in the industry and the performance of its competitors more closely that it had done previously. He said that he felt TSC's management information has historically been too inward looking, and hoped the management accountant would be able to help his address this issue.

Required

(b)   Evaluate the potential benefits and problems associated with the use of 'league tables' as a means of measuring performance.   **(6 marks)**

(c)   With reference to the developments at TSC, discuss the reasons suggested by Burns and Scapens as to why the role of the management accountant has changed over time, and assess the on-going contribution that the management accountant can make at TSC.   **(10 marks)**

(Total = 50 marks)

70 Lincoln & Lincoln (APM 12/12, amended)   98 mins

Lincoln & Lincoln Advertising (LLA) is an advertising agency based in Veeland, which is a large well-developed country considered to be one of the wealthiest in the world. LLA operates out of three regional offices (North, East and West) with its head office functions based in the East offices. The business offers a wide range of advertising services:

Strategic: Advising on an overall advertising campaign (mix of advertising channels and overall themes);

Buying: Advising and buying advertising space (on television, radio, websites and in newspapers and magazines); and

Creative: Designing and producing specific adverts for the customers' use.

The company is one of the three largest agencies in Veeland with many years of experience and many awards won. Competition in advertising is fierce, as advertising spending by businesses has suffered recently during a general economic downturn. Most new business is won in tender competitions between different advertising agencies.

Veeland is a large country with considerable diversity of markets, economic conditions and fashions across its regions. As a result, the regional offices have developed with a considerable amount of decision-making autonomy. This also reflects the temperament of the key creative employees of the firm who have a strong attachment to their campaign ideas and take great personal pride in their success. The individualism of the key employees also comes from the way that LLA has grown. The business has been built through acquisition of small, local businesses in each of the three regions. Each of these acquisitions has been consolidated into the appropriate regional office.

You have been recruited in to LLA in order to take up the newly created post of senior management accountant. Your recruitment caused some concern amongst the board but was championed by the chief executive officer (CEO) as 'necessary to stay ahead of the game'. The board have asked that you prove yourself and also give a fresh perspective on LLA by providing them with a report. Initially, you have been asked to provide an assessment of the current financial position of the three regional offices. The most recent management accounts are in Appendix 1. The basic assessment calculations have already been accurately completed by one of the junior staff and the results are in Appendix 2.

As part of the briefing for this exercise, you attended part of a recent board meeting where you were told that the board want your views on the choice of net income as the performance measure for each of the regional offices. They want you to suggest other measures and why they are appropriate for each office. The CEO has advised you that you may want to use different key measures for each office, rather than have a 'one-size fits all policy'. During the board's discussion, issues around controllability and responsibility accounting appear to be the main concerns of the board. The CEO also stated that the board would not be interested in a long list of which numbers have gone up and which have gone down. They will want to be given a coherent picture of what is going on at each of the regional offices.

Finally, the CEO said, 'Well, if you are not completely tired out at the end of this little project then I'd also like you to comment on our remuneration policy at the regional offices including ideas based on your assessment of performance measures.' Later, the CEO gave you a note (see Appendix 3) describing these policies at LLA.

Shortly after the Board meeting, the Operations Director spoke to you and re-iterated the CEO's point about not producing a long and detailed commentary on individual performance metrics for the regional offices. He said, 'Over the last few months, I seem to have been getting more and more reports, with different sets of figures comparing different aspects of performance. But, if anything, the more reports I get, the harder I find it to assess how well the offices are actually performing. I know we need information about how the business is doing, but I'm not really a numbers man, so I wonder if these reports could be presented in a more accessible way.'

Required

Write a report to the board of LLA to:

(i)   Assess the recent performance of the three regional offices by interpreting the data given in Appendices 1 and 2.
                                                                                                    (10 marks)

(ii)   Explain the importance of external information when assessing the performance of the three regional offices.
                                                                                                    (5 marks)

(iii)   Evaluate the choice of net income as the performance measure for the regional offices and suggest other measures and why they are appropriate for each office.
                                                                                                    (10 marks)

(iv)   Evaluate the benefits to LLA of using different performance measures for each office rather than using the same performance measures for all three offices.
                                                                                                    (5 marks)

(v)   Using the information provided, evaluate LLA's remuneration policy, suggesting changes as appropriate.
                                                                                                    (10 marks)

(vi)   Discuss the potential problem of information overload at LLA, and suggest changes which could be made to its performance reports.
                                                                                                    (6 marks)

        Professional marks will be awarded for the format, style, structure and clarity of the discussion of your answer.
                                                                                                    (4 marks)

        Note. The Appendices referred to in the scenario follow these requirements.

                                                                                                    (Total = 50 marks)

Appendix 1: LLA financial data

The figures are drawn from the regional offices' management accounts for year to September 20X2.

	North $m	East $m	West $m
Revenue	151	523	467
Cost of sales	45	147	159
Staff costs	53	194	145
Other costs	27	86	67
Operating profit	26	96	96
Allocated head office costs	6	31	16
Net income	20	65	80
Net cash flow in year	24	86	46
Current assets	22	82	119
Current liabilities	10	35	31
Capital expenditure	3	10.2	23.8
Capital employed	39	121	112

Notes

1 East office data is for the regional office only. It excludes any costs of the head office function based there other than the allocated costs listed.

2 Notional cost of capital at LLA is 9%.

3 Current assets contains only accounts receivable for each office.

Appendix 2: Basic calculations

[These can be assumed to be calculated correctly.]

		Change on year		Margins		
		Sep X2	Sep X1	Sep X2	Sep X1	Sep X0
Revenue						
	North	−1.9%	−1.3%			
	East	1.0%	1.0%			
	West	8.9%	8.1%			
Cost of sales						
	North			29.8%	29.9%	30.1%
	East			28.1%	29.0%	30.0%
	West			34.0%	31.9%	30.0%
Staff costs						
	North			35.1%	35.1%	35.3%
	East			37.1%	37.1%	37.0%
	West			31.0%	31.0%	31.0%
Operating profit						
	North	−7.1%	0.0%	17.2%	18.2%	17.9%
	East	7.9%	8.5%	18.4%	17.2%	16.0%
	West	5.5%	4.6%	20.6%	21.2%	21.9%
Net Income						
	North	−4.8%	−4.5%	13.2%	13.6%	14.1%
	East	12.1%	13.7%	12.4%	11.2%	9.9%
	West	6.7%	5.6%	17.1%	17.5%	17.9%

Notes

1 Other costs and allocated head office costs are fixed.
2 Margins are calculated as a percentage of revenue.

		Sep X2	Sep X1	Sep X0
Current ratio				
	North	2.2	2.3	2.1
	East	2.3	2.3	2.4
	West	3.8	2.9	2.4
Receivable days				
	North	53	55	54
	East	57	58	59
	West	93	68	55
ROCE	(based on operating profit)			
	North	67%	88%	117%
	East	79%	90%	103%
	West	86%	106%	140%
	(based on net income)			
	North	51%	66%	92%
	East	54%	59%	64%
	West	71%	87%	115%
Residual income ($m's)	(based on operating profit)			
	North	22.5	25.1	25.8
	East	85.1	80.1	74.8
	West	85.9	83.3	81.4
	(based on net income)			
	North	16.5	18.1	19.8
	East	54.1	49.1	43.8
	West	69.9	67.3	65.4

Appendix 3:

Note on remuneration from the CEO:

There are broadly five grades of staff at each regional office. The following is an outline of their remuneration packages. (The head office staff are treated separately and are not part of this exercise.)

Senior management

All staff at this level are paid a basic fixed salary, which reflects industry norms over the last few years, plus a bonus dependent on the net income of their office.

Creative staff

The 'creatives' are on individual packages which reflect the market rates in order to recruit them at the time that they were recruited. Some are fixed salary and some have a fixed element plus a bonus based on their office's revenues.

Buying staff

The buyers are paid a fixed salary plus a bonus based on the prices for advertising space that they negotiate compared to the budgeted cost of space. The budget is set by the finance team at head office based on previous years' experience and their forecast for supply and demand in the year in question.

Account management staff

Account management handles relationships with clients and also develops new clients. They are paid a fixed market-based salary.

Administration staff

These staff are paid the market rate for their jobs as a fixed salary based on hours worked.

71 BEC (APM 12/09, amended)   98 mins

The Benjamin Education College (BEC), which is partially government funded, is a well-established provider of professional courses for students of accounting, law and marketing in the country of Brightland.

Its mission statement states that the college 'is committed to providing high quality education to all students'. BEC provides education to private fee-paying students as well as to students who are funded by the government.

The Jackson Business Centre (JBC) which commenced trading during 20X4 is also a provider of professional courses for students of accounting, law and marketing in the country of Brightland. It is a privately owned college and all its students are responsible for the payment of their own fees.

Relevant operating data for BEC and JBC for the year ended 30 November 20X9 are as follows:

(1)   Both BEC and JBC offer a range of courses in accounting, law and marketing on a twice per annum basis.
(2)   Fees (budget and actual) payable to BEC and JBC in respect of each student who enrolled for a course:

	BEC Privately funded students	BEC Government funded students	JBC Privately funded students
Course type:	$	$	$
Accounting	1,200	900	1,000
Law	1,000	750	1,200
Marketing	800	600	1,200

(3)   Salary costs per staff member were payable as follows:

	BEC Budget	BEC Actual	JBC Actual
	$	$	$
Lecturer	50,000	52,000	55,000
Administrative	20,000	20,800	22,000

(4) Budgeted costs for the year based on 8,000 students per annum for BEC were as follows:

	$	Variable cost (%)	Fixed cost (%)
Tuition materials	720,000	100	–
Catering	100,000	80	20
Cleaning	40,000	25	75
Other operating costs	600,000	20	80
Depreciation	40,000	–	100

Variable costs vary according to the number of students attending courses at BEC.

(5) Actual costs (other than salary costs) incurred during the year:

	BEC	JBC
	$	$
Tuition materials	741,600	730,000
Catering	95,680	110,000
Cleaning	40,950	40,000
Other operating costs (including costs of freelance staff)	646,800	645,000
Depreciation	40,000	60,000

(6) The management of JBC is considering introducing on-line tuition support by its lecturing staff.

(7) Both BEC and JBC operated a policy which aimed to employ 60 lecturers throughout the year.

(8) The appendix below shows budget and actual statistics for BEC and actual statistics for JBC.

Appendix

Sundry statistics for the year ended 30 November 20X9

	BEC Budget	BEC Actual	JBC Actual
Number of students:			
Accounting	3,600	3,800	4,000
Law	1,500	1,400	1,560
Marketing	1,800	2,000	2,000
Student mix (%) for each course type:			
Privately funded	80	70	100
Government funded	20	30	
Number of enquiries received:			
Accounting	4,800	4,750	5,000
Law	2,000	2,800	2,000
Marketing	2,400	2,500	2,400
Number of lecturers employed throughout the year:	60	60	60
Number of lecturers recruited during the year:			
Accounting	2	6	1
Law	1	3	–
Marketing	1	3	–
Number of administrative staff employed throughout the year	10	10	8
Number of administrative staff recruited during the year	2	8	–
Number of times freelance lecturing staff were used	–	–	20
Number of new courses under development	–	–	4

Required

(a)   The senior management team of BEC has asked you, as management accountant, to prepare a report providing them with the following:

(i)   A statement which shows actual and budgeted income statements of BEC and an actual income statement for JBC in respect of the year ended 30 November 20X9 on a comparable basis.

(10 marks)

(ii)   An assessment of the performance of BEC and JBC using both financial and non-financial measures based on the information contained in the question. You should identify other measures of performance which you consider relevant to BEC.   **(10 marks)**

(iii)   A discussion of the issues that might restrict the extent to which a performance measurement system is accepted and supported by management and employees.   **(6 marks)**

Professional marks will be awarded in this question for appropriateness of format, style and structure of the report.   **(4 marks)**

'Total reward package'

JBC experiences difficulty in recruiting staff even though it pays comparable salaries to rival colleges in Brightland. Senior managers do not feel that there are problems with either staff morale or the external image of the company. The Director of Strategy explains that although JBC offers a number of benefits to its employees beyond basic pay, this is not made explicit enough either internally or externally.

The Director has so far identified a good pension scheme, flexible working hours, personal insurance cover at reduced rates, and a subsidised canteen. The Director has also found that employees feel that the 'work-life balance' (between professional and personal life) is a distinguishing feature of being an JBC employee. It is the Director's view that all the benefits which are available to staff should be examined and a 'total reward package' approach should be introduced. This would draw together all the financial and non-financial benefits (including working practices, and development opportunities) into an integrated package, and employees would then be able to select which benefits they want to receive from the package. The Director has proposed that the 'total reward' scheme should be open to all employees.

Performance appraisal system

JBC has operated a formal performance appraisal system, supported by standardised procedures and paperwork, for a number of years. The system has clear organisational objectives, which are based on staff development and improved performance, rather than being a basis for pay reviews or paying individual annual bonuses. However, the scheme is not well regarded by either managers or staff and its objectives are not being met.

Senior managers complain about the amount of time that is taken up holding appraisal interviews and then completing the necessary paperwork afterwards.

Exit interviews are conducted whenever someone leaves JBC, and a review of a sample of recorded comments indicates staff feelings on the scheme very clearly: 'appraisal is just a paper exercise', 'a joke', 'a waste of time and effort'.

Required

(b)   (i)   Discuss the potential advantages and disadvantages for JBC of developing a 'total reward package' approach.   **(10 marks)**

(ii)   Discuss the possible reasons why the objectives of the formal appraisal system are not being met.   **(10 marks)**

(Total = 50 marks)

72 HFG (APM 6/08, amended)

The Health and Fitness Group (HFG), which is privately owned, operates three centres in the country of Mayland. Each centre offers dietary plans and fitness programmes to clients under the supervision of dieticians and fitness trainers. Residential accommodation is also available at each centre. The centres are located in the towns of Ayetown, Beetown and Ceetown.

The following information is available:

(1) Summary financial data for HFG in respect of the year ended 31 May 20X8.

	Ayetown $'000	Beetown $'000	Ceetown $'000	Total $'000
Revenue:				
Fees received	1,800	2,100	4,500	8,400
Variable costs	(468)	(567)	(1,395)	(2,430)
Contribution	1,332	1,533	3,105	5,970
Fixed costs	(936)	(1,092)	(2,402)	(4,430)
Operating profit	396	441	703	1,540
Interest costs on long-term debt at 10%				(180)
Profit before tax				1,360
Income tax expense				(408)
Profit for the year				952

Average book values for 20X8:

	Ayetown $'000	Beetown $'000	Ceetown $'000	Total $'000
Assets				
Non-current assets	1,000	2,500	3,300	6,800
Current assets	800	900	1,000	2,700
Total assets	1,800	3,400	4,300	9,500
Equity and liabilities				
Share capital				2,500
Retained earnings				4,400
Total equity				6,900
Non-current liabilities				
Long-term borrowings				1,800
Total non-current liabilities				1,800
Current liabilities	80	240	480	800
Total current liabilities	80	240	480	800
Total liabilities				2,600
Total equity and liabilities				9,500

(2) HFG defines Residual Income (RI) for each centre as operating profit minus a required rate of return of 12% of the total assets of each centre.

(3) At present HFG does not allocate the long-term borrowings of the group to the three separate centres.

(4) Each centre faces similar risks.

(5) Tax is payable at a rate of 30%.

(6) The market value of the equity capital of HFG is $9 million. The cost of equity of HFG is 15%.

(7) The market value of the long-term borrowings of HFG is equal to the book value.

(8) The directors are concerned about the return on investment (ROI) generated by the Beetown centre and they are considering using sensitivity analysis in order to show how a target ROI of 20% might be achieved.

(9) The marketing director stated at a recent board meeting that 'The Group's success depends on the quality of service provided to our clients. In my opinion, we need only to concern ourselves with the number of complaints received from clients during each period as this is the most important performance measure for our business. The number of complaints received from clients is a perfect performance measure. As long as the number of complaints received from clients is not increasing from period to period, then we can be confident about our future prospects'.

Required

(a) The directors of HFG have asked you, as management accountant, to prepare a report providing them with explanations as to the following:

   (i) Which of the three centres is the most 'successful'? Your report should include a commentary on return on investment (ROI), residual income (RI), and economic value added (EVA) as measures of financial performance. Detailed calculations regarding each of these three measures must be included as part of your report.

   Note. A maximum of seven marks is available for detailed calculations.   **(14 marks)**

   (ii) The percentage change in revenue, total costs and net assets during the year ended 31 May 20X8 that would have been required in order to have achieved a target ROI of 20% by the Beetown centre. Your answer should consider each of these three variables in isolation. State any assumptions that you make.   **(6 marks)**

   (iii) Whether or not you agree with the statement of the marketing director in note (9) above. **(5 marks)**

   Professional marks for appropriateness of format, style and structure of the report.   **(4 marks)**

(b) The Superior Fitness Co (SFC), which is well established in Mayland, operates nine centres. Each of SFC's centres is similar in size to those of HFG. SFC also provides dietary plans and fitness programmes to its clients. The directors of HFG have decided that they wish to benchmark the performance of HFG with that of SFC.

Required

   Discuss the problems that the directors of HFG might experience in their wish to benchmark the performance of HFG with the performance of SFC, and recommend how such problems might be successfully addressed.   **(7 marks)**

The managers of each of HFG's three centres are paid a basic salary which is broadly in line with the industry average, but they are also eligible for an annual bonus of up to 15% of their salary. The level of bonus awarded depends on the manager's performance against a range of financial and non-financial objectives. However, in order for the manager to qualify for a bonus in any year, the operating profit for their centre has to at least achieve its budgeted level.

The manager of the Ceetown centre has only recently been appointed, but he is unhappy about the bonus scheme.

In particular, he believes the budget for 20X9 is unachievable. Because there was only an interim manager at the Ceetown centre during the budgeting process, the budget was set by the senior management team, without any discussion with the interim manager or the staff at Ceetown. The 20X9 budget set a target for fees received of $5.0 million, and a contribution of $1.575 million.

However, not only is Mayland currently in a recession, but a competitor has recently opened a new fitness centre in Ceetown and has been offering promotional discounts.

The manager pointed out that because HFG's policy does not allow him any discretion over the price of memberships or fitness programmes, he has seen a decrease in client numbers since the rival centre opened, even though he has not received any complaints about the quality of service or the programmes available at his centre.

The manager has suggested that he thinks he should be entitled to a bonus according to how well he has performed against his personal objectives, regardless of whether or not his centre achieves its budgeted profit.

Required

(c) Assess the appropriateness of HFG's current bonus scheme in relation to the manager at Ceetown.
                                                                                                (6 marks)

(d) Evaluate the manager's suggestion that he should be entitled to a bonus, and suggest alternative improvements to the reward system and HFG.   **(8 marks)**

                                                                                        (Total = 50 marks)

73 SBC (APM 6/10, amended)

98 mins

The Superior Business Consultancy (SBC) which is based in Jayland provides clients with consultancy services in Advertising, Recruitment and IT Support. SBC commenced trading on 1 July 20X3 and has grown steadily since then.

The following information, together with that contained in the Appendix at the end of the question, is available:

(1) Three types of consultants are employed by SBC on a full-time basis. These are:

Advertising consultants who provide advice regarding advertising and promotional activities
Recruitment consultants who provide advice regarding recruitment and selection of staff, and
IT consultants who provide advice regarding the selection of business software and technical support.

(2) During the year ended 31 May 20Y0, each full-time consultant was budgeted to work on 200 days. All consultations undertaken by consultants of SBC had a duration of one day.

(3) During their 200 working days per annum, full-time consultants undertake some consultations on a 'no-fee' basis. Such consultations are regarded as Business Development Activity (BDA) by the management of SBC.

(4) SBC also engages the services of subcontract consultants who provide clients with consultancy services in the categories of Advertising, Recruitment and IT Support. All of the subcontract consultants have worked for SBC for at least three years.

(5) During recent years the directors of SBC have become increasingly concerned that SBC's systems are inadequate for the measurement of performance. This concern was further increased after they each read a book entitled *'How to improve business performance measurement'*.

Required

(a) Prepare a report for the directors of SBC which:

    (i) Discusses the importance of non-financial performance indicators (NFPIs) and evaluates, giving examples, how a 'balanced scorecard' approach may be used to improve performance within SBC.

        (13 marks)

    (ii) Contains a calculation of the actual average cost per chargeable consultation for both full-time consultants and separately for subcontract consultants in respect of each of the three categories of consultancy services during the year ended 31 May 20Y0. **(7 marks)**

    (iii) Suggests reasons for the trends shown by the figures contained in the appendix. **(5 marks)**

    (iv) Discusses the potential benefits and potential problems which might arise as a consequence of employing subcontract consultants within SBC. **(6 marks)**

    Professional marks will be awarded for appropriateness of format, style and structure of the report.

    (4 marks)

After receiving your report, one of the directors expressed concern that SBC's information systems will not be able to provide the range of non-financial information which would be needed for a balanced scorecard. The director suggested that it would be better for SBC for focus on those areas of performance it can measure easily rather than incurring additional costs to include data about additional areas of performance in its information systems.

Required

(b) Briefly evaluate the director's statement about which areas of performance SBC should measure. **(5 marks)**

Currently SBC pays all its consultants a fixed salary. However, some of the IT consultants are unhappy that their salaries are lower than those earned by the other types of consultant. Recently four of SBC's longest-serving IT consultants resigned to go and work for rival consultancies. All of them said that the reward packages available had played a significant part in their decisions.

The directors are worried about the prospect of more consultants leaving SBC and joining rival consultancies. As a result, the directors are reviewing SBC's reward packages. The directors are aware that all the major software providers in Jayland pay a commission to consultancy firms if the firm recommends their software to a client. Currently, this commission is payable to SBC as a whole, but the directors are considering whether it should be paid to individual consultants. They are also considering a proposal under which the IT consultants would receive a lower basic salary, but would then be entitled to receive any commissions earned from the software providers.

Required

(c) Evaluate the directors' proposal to revise the way in which SBC's IT consultants are paid. **(10 marks)**

(Total = 50 marks)

Appendix
SBC – Relevant actual and forecast statistics

	20Y0 Actual	20Y1 Forecast	20Y2 Forecast
Number of full-time consultants by category:			
Advertising	20	20	20
Recruitment	30	25	20
IT Support	50	50	50
Salaries per full-time consultant ($):			
Advertising	40,000	40,800	40,800
Recruitment	35,000	35,700	35,700
IT Support	30,000	30,600	30,600
Number of chargeable consultations (total demand):			
Advertising	4,200	4,100	4,000
Recruitment	6,250	5,750	5,000
IT Support	10,250	10,500	10,000
Per cent of chargeable days spent on Business Development Activity (%):			
Advertising	7	8	10
Recruitment	22	22	25
IT Support	12	13	14
Cost per consultation undertaken by subcontract consultants ($):			
Advertising	300		
Recruitment	220		
IT Support	200		
Other operating costs ($000):			
Full-time consultants	1,075	1,050	1,270
Subcontract consultants	125	270	182

74 Kolmog Hotels (APM 6/13)   98 mins

Kolmog Hotels is a large, listed chain of branded hotels in Ostland. Its stated mission is: 'to become the No. 1 hotel chain in Ostland, building the strength of the Kolmog brand by consistently delighting customers, investing in employees, delivering innovative products/services and continuously improving performance'. The subsidiary aims of the company are to maximise shareholder value, create a culture of pride in the brand and strengthen the brand loyalty of all stakeholders.

The hotels in the Kolmog chain include a diverse range of buildings and locations serving different customer groups: large conference venues, city centre business hotels and country house hotels for holidays. For reporting purposes, the company has divided itself into the four geographical regions of Ostland, as can be seen in a recent example of the strategic performance report for the company used by the board for their annual review (see Appendix 1). At the operational level, each hotel manager is given an individual budget for their hotel, prepared in the finance department, and is judged by performance against budgeted profit.

Kolmog is planning a strategic change to its current business model. The board has decided to sell many of the hotels in the chain and then rent them back. This is consistent with many other hotel companies who are focusing on the management of their hotels rather than managing a large, property portfolio of hotels.

In order to assist this strategic change, the Chief Executive Officer (CEO) is considering introducing the balanced scorecard (BSC) across Kolmog. He has tasked you, as a management accountant in the head office, with reviewing the preliminary work done on the development of the scorecard in order to ensure that it is consistent with the goal of meeting the strategic objectives of the company by tying operational and strategic performance measurement into a coherent framework.

The CEO is worried that the BSC might be perceived within the organisation as a management accounting technique that has been derived from the manufacturing sector. In order to assess its use at Kolmog, he has asked you to explain the characteristics that differentiate service businesses from manufacturing ones.

Senior executives at the head office of Kolmog have drawn up a preliminary list of perspectives and metrics as an outline of the balanced scorecard in Table 1:

Table 1: Performance metrics

Key strategic perspective	Metric
Strategic financial performance	Financial performance benchmarked to Kolmog's main competitors (share price and return on capital employed)
Customer satisfaction	Customer satisfaction survey scores
Hotel performance against budget	Variance analysis for each hotel
Employee satisfaction	Staff turnover

The history of rewards at Kolmog has not been good, with only 1% of staff receiving their maximum possible bonus in previous years, and 75% of staff receiving no bonus. This has led to many complaints that targets set for the reward system are too challenging.

Under a new performance reward system, employee targets are to be derived from the above BSC strategic measures depending on the employee's area of responsibility. The new system is for hotel managers to be given challenging targets based on their hotel's performance against budgeted profit, industry wide staff turnover and the company's average customer satisfaction scores. The hotel managers will then get up to 30% of their basic salary as a bonus, based on their regional manager's assessment of their performance against these targets. The CEO wants you to use Fitzgerald and Moon's building block model to assess the new system. He is happy with the dimensions of performance but wants your comments on the standards and rewards being applied here.

Appendix 1

Strategic performance report for review
Kolmog Hotels Year to 31 Mar 20X3

	East Region $m	West Region $m	North Region $m	South Region $m	Total $m	Total 20X2 $m	As % of revenue for 20X3
Revenue	235	244	313	193	985	926	
Cost of sales	28	30	37	21	116	110	11.78%
Gross profit	207	214	276	172	869	816	
Staff costs	61	65	78	54	258	245	26.19%
Other operating costs							
hotels	68	70	97	54	289	270	29.34%
head office					158	150	16.04%
Operating profit	78	79	101	64	164	151	16.60%
Financing costs					78	73	7.92%
Profit before tax					86	78	8.73%

	20X3	20X2	Growth Year on Year
Capital employed	$1,132m	$1,065m	6·29%
EPS	$1·36	$1·27	7·09%
Share price	$12·34	$11·76	4·93%
ROCE	14·49%	14·18%	

Required

Write a report to the CEO to:

(i) Explain the characteristics that differentiate service businesses from manufacturing ones, using Kolmog to illustrate your points. **(5 marks)**

(ii) Evaluate the current strategic performance report and the choice of performance metrics used (Appendix 1). **(8 marks)**

(iii) Evaluate the outline balanced scorecard (Table 1) at Kolmog, suggesting suitable improvements. **(12 marks)**

(iv) Describe the difficulties in implementing and using the balanced scorecard at Kolmog. **(7 marks)**

(v) Explain the purpose of setting targets which are challenging, and evaluate the standards and rewards for the hotel managers' performance reward system as requested by the CEO. **(14 marks)**

Professional marks will be awarded for the format, style and structure of the discussion of your answer.

(4 marks)

(Total = 50 marks)

75 Cantor (APM 6/14)   98 mins

Cantor Group (Cantor) is a listed company with two subsidiaries, both involved in food and drink retailing in the small country of Deeland. Its mission is 'to maximise shareholder value through supplying good value food and drink in appealing environments for our customers'.

Cantor Cafes (Cafes) is the original operating company for the group and is a chain of 115 cafes specialising in different coffee drinks but also serving some simple food dishes. Cafes has been running successfully for 15 years and has reached the limit of its expansion as the cafe market is now considered to be saturated with competition. Further growth will occur only as the opportunity to obtain profitable, new sites is presented, although such opportunities are not expected to be significant over the next few years.

Cantor Juicey (Juicey) was started by the Cantor Group two years ago. Now, it is made up of 15 juice bars which serve a variety of blended fruit juice drinks and health snacks. The products served by Juicey have benefited from an increased awareness in Deeland of the need to eat and drink healthily. Cantor Group expects to increase the rate of property acquisition in order to feed the rapid growth of this business, intending to open 25 outlets per year for the next four years.

Cantor Group organises its two subsidiaries in a similar way, as they are involved in similar areas of business. There is one exception to this, namely in the arrangements over the properties from which the subsidiaries operate. Cafes rent their properties on the open market on standard commercial terms with a five-year lease at a fixed rental payable quarterly in advance. Juicey, on the other hand, has made a single arrangement with a large commercial landlord for all of its properties. Juicey has agreed that the rent for its sites is a percentage of the revenue generated at each site. Juicey believes that it can continue its expansion by obtaining more sites from this landlord under the same terms.

The board of Cantor is reviewing their performance reporting systems and would like your evaluation of the current report given in Appendix 1. This report contains information for both of the subsidiaries and the group and is used by all three boards. The CEO has advised you that the board does not require an evaluation of Cantor's performance. However, the CEO does want you to consider the cost structures at Cantor and advise on the implications of the mix of fixed and variable elements in the key cost areas of staff and property for performance management.

At a recent shareholder meeting of Cantor, one of the large shareholders expressed concern that the group lacks focus and suggested the introduction of value-based management (VBM) using economic value added (EVA™) as the measure of value. Cantor's CEO has asked you, their strategic management accountant, to give the board more information on the implications of this suggestion. She has asked you to do an example calculation of the EVA™ for the Group using the current data (Appendices 1 and 2) and explain how the shareholders might view the result. Next, the board needs to have the VBM system explained and evaluated to be able to make a decision about its use at Cantor.

Finally, the board is considering amending the mission statement to include more information on the ethical values of the company. The area being considered for inclusion in the overall mission is on the treatment of employees as it is felt that they should share in the progress and profitability of Cantor since a happy working environment will help them to better serve the customers.

The proposed new mission statement would read:

'To maximise shareholder value and to provide a fair deal to our employees by supplying good value food and drink in appealing environments for our customers.'

The CEO has asked you to consider how the Group's performance in the area regarding employees could be measured using the current management information at Cantor. You have obtained additional information from the management information system to assist with this task, given in Appendix 3.

Appendix 1

Cantor Group

	Year to 31 March						Costs and profit as a % of revenue	
	Cafes	Cafes	Juicey	Juicey	Group	Group		
	Budget 20X4 $	Actual 20X4 $	Budget 20X4 $	Actual 20X4 $	Budget 20X4 $	Actual 20X4 $	Group	Industry average
Revenue								
Drink	47,437,500	46,521,000	5,130,000	5,398,000	52,567,500	51,919,000		
Food	15,812,500	15,913,000	570,000	582,000	16,382,500	16,495,000		
Total	**63,250,000**	**62,434,000**	**5,700,000**	**5,980,000**	**68,950,000**	**68,414,000**		
Cost of sales								
Drink	12,808,125	12,560,670	1,385,100	1,457,460	14,193,225	14,018,130		
Food	3,478,750	3,500,860	125,400	128,040	3,604,150	3,628,900		
Total	**16,286,875**	**16,061,530**	**1,510,500**	**1,585,500**	**17,797,375**	**17,647,030**	25·8%	
Gross profit	**46,963,125**	**46,372,470**	**4,189,500**	**4,394,500**	**51,152,625**	**50,766,970**	74·2%	72·8%
Staff costs	**16,128,750**	**15,920,670**	**1,453,500**	**1,524,900**	**20,082,250**	**21,345,000**	31·2%	30·9%
Other operating costs								
Rent	2,875,000	2,875,000	342,000	358,800	3,929,000	3,945,800		
Local property tax	920,000	920,000	60,000	60,000	980,000	980,000		
Insurance	276,000	282,000	18,000	18,400	294,000	300,400		
Utilities	874,000	861,000	61,500	62,900	935,500	923,900		
Marketing	6,957,500	6,888,000	627,000	750,000	7,584,500	7,638,000	11·2%	10·0%
Depreciation	4,427,500	4,427,500	353,400	353,400	4,780,900	4,780,900		
Total	**16,330,000**	**16,253,500**	**1,461,900**	**1,603,500**	**18,503,900**	**18,569,000**	27·1%	
Operating profit	**14,504,375**	**14,198,300**	**1,274,100**	**1,266,100**	**12,566,475**	**10,852,970**	15·9%	15·3%
Finance costs						798,000	801,000	
Group profit before tax						**11,768,475**	**10,051,970**	14·7%	
Tax						2,942,119	2,512,993	
Group profit after tax						**8,826,356**	**7,538,977**	11·0%	

Appendix 2

Additionally, you have discovered the following data about the group for the financial year:

1	Debt/Equity	30·0%
2	Cost of equity	15·7%
3	Tax rate	25·0%
4	Group ROCE	19·0%
5	Group capital employed: $53,400,000 at period start and $58,500,000 at period end.	
6	Pre-tax cost of debt	6·5%
7	There has been $2·1m of tax paid in the year.	
8	It is estimated that half of the marketing spend of $7·638m is building the Cantor brand long term.	
9	It is further estimated that there has been the same level of annual spending on long-term brand building in the years leading up to 20X4.	

Appendix 3

Additional management information

	Cafes	Juicey	Group
No of employees			
At year start	1,495	96	1,611
Leavers	146	15	161
Joiners	152	35	187
At year end	1,501	116	1,637

Note. Group numbers include Cafes, Juicey and head office numbers

Required

Write a report to the CEO of Cantor to:

(i)   Evaluate the current performance report in Appendix 1.   **(15 marks)**

(ii) Assess the balance of fixed and variable elements of the CEO's two key costs in each of the two subsidiaries and the impact which this may have on performance management of these costs.

   Note. Detailed calculations are not required.   **(6 marks)**

(iii) Evaluate the economic value added (EVA™) of Cantor Group, justifying any assumptions made.   **(9 marks)**

(iv) Explain how value-based management (VBM) could be implemented at Cantor and evaluate its potential impact on the group.   **(10 marks)**

(v)   Using the information in the appendices, provide justified recommendations for suitable performance measures to reflect the proposed change in the company's mission statement.   **(6 marks)**

Professional marks will be awarded for the format, style and structure of the discussion of your answer.   **(4 marks)**

(**Total = 50 marks**)

76 Boltzman Machines (APM 12/14, amended)   98 mins

Boltzman Machines (Boltzman) is a listed, multinational engineering business. Its mission is 'to maximise shareholder value through engineering excellence'.

Boltzman has two divisions, one manufacturing aerospace parts and the other automotive parts. The company is known for innovation and it allows its managers much autonomy to run their own divisions and projects. However, there has been recent criticism at a shareholders' meeting of the executive management for not listening to shareholders' concerns and allowing this autonomy to run out of control.

Therefore, the board at Boltzman has been reviewing a number of aspects of the way performance is controlled and managed in the business. However, there are a number of initiatives already running within the company, which the board feels may help to address the shareholders' concerns.

The initiatives which are running at present are:

(1)   An analysis of stakeholder influence at Boltzman leading to suitable strategic performance measures.

(2)   A benchmarking exercise of the performance measures from Initiative 1 with Boltzman's main competitor, General Machines.

(3)   The introduction of quality initiatives bringing lean production methods to Boltzman.

(4)   The introduction of a balanced scorecard performance measurement system.

The CEO has asked for your views on the impact these initiative could have on performance management within the company.

First, a stakeholder analysis has been completed by one of Boltzman's managers (in Appendix 1) but she has gone on holiday and has not written up a commentary of her results. Therefore, the CEO wants you to take the information in Appendix 1 and explain the results and evaluate the suggested performance measures. The CEO has asked that you do not, at this stage, suggest long lists of additional indicators.

Second, the CEO wants you to use these suggested measures to benchmark the performance of Boltzman against General Machines. The CEO stated, 'Make sure that you calculate the measures given in Appendix 1. You should also add two justified measures of your own using the data provided. However, restrict yourself to these seven measures and don't drown us with detail about individual business units.' A junior analyst has gathered data to use in the benchmarking exercise in Appendix 2.

Third, the company has stated that one of its strategic aims is to be the highest quality supplier in the market place. In order to achieve this, the head of the aerospace division has already started a project to implement just-in-time (JIT) manufacturing. An extract of his email proposing this change is given in Appendix 3. The CEO feels that there are some important elements hinted at but not developed in this email. In particular, the CEO wants you to explain the problems of moving to JIT manufacturing.

Finally, the CEO feels it is important that the company's performance is measured across a range of non-financial areas as well as financial ones. He believes that the balanced scorecard would provide a good choice, but has asked you to evaluate its suitability in the light of the shareholders' criticism, and the other initiatives currently in progress at Boltzman.

Required

Prepare a report to the board of Boltzman to:

(a)   Briefly justify appropriate management approaches to each of the stakeholders and, based on this analysis, evaluate the appropriateness of the performance measures suggested in Appendix 1.   **(14 marks)**

(b)   Benchmark Boltzman against General Machines as suggested by the CEO, evaluating the approach to benchmarking used.   **(16 marks)**

(c)   Explain the problems which will accompany a move towards just-in-time manufacturing at Boltzman.

(7 marks)

(d)   Assess the suitability of using the balanced scorecard as a performance measurement system at Boltzman, as requested by the CEO.

(9 marks)

Professional marks will be awarded for the format, style and structure of the discussion of your answer.

(4 marks)

(Total = 50 marks)

Appendix 1

Key stakeholders	Level of interest	Level of power
Shareholders	Low – institutions have delegated management to the board and are only interested in financial returns	High – ability to vote out existing management
Employees	Medium – in a high skill industry employees are interested in the new opportunities which the market can present	Low – although there is a group of key employees in product development whose skills must not be lost
Customers	Medium – some of the parts supplied by Boltzman are unique and specifically designed for the customer	High – as there are few major players in the aerospace and automotive businesses, the loss of a customer would have a significant impact on Boltzman
Suppliers	Medium – Boltzman is one of the large customers to many of the company's suppliers	Low – the suppliers are generally bulk component producers and there is significant competition for Boltzman's business

Suggested performance measures:

- Return on capital employed
- Economic value added
- Revenue growth
- Average pay per employee
- Net profit margin

Appendix 2

The figures are drawn from the financial statements for the year to September 20X4.

	Boltzman $m 20X4	General Machines $m 20X4
Revenue	23,943	25,695
Cost of sales	18,078	20,605
Other costs	2,958	3,208
Operating profit	2,907	1,882
Financing costs	291	316
Tax	663	718
Net income	1,953	848

	Boltzman $m 20X3	Boltzman $m 20X4	General Machines $m 20X3	General Machines $m 20X4
Non-current assets	16,335	16,988	17,716	17,893
Current assets	10,618	11,043	11,515	11,630
	26,953	28,031	29,231	29,523
Equity	8,984	9,961	9,744	10,083
Non-current liabilities	9,801	9,739	10,629	10,405
Current liabilities	8,168	8,331	8,858	9,035
	26,953	28,031	29,231	29,523

		Boltzman 20X4	General Machines 20X4
Notes:			
No of employees		86,620	93,940
Staff costs	($m)	4,731	4,913
Revenue for 20X3	($m)	22,506	25,438
Product development costs	($m)	2,684	2,630

No. of top 10 biggest potential customers where
the business has top tier supplier status

	Boltzman 20X4	General Machines 20X4
Aerospace	6	6
Automotive	7	8

A suitable cost of capital for both companies is 11%.

The tax rate is 28%.

Appendix 3

Extract of Head of Aerospace's email on his quality initiative:

In order to improve the quality and profitability of our products, we intend to begin by introducing a lean approach to manufacturing.

The first step in our move to lean manufacturing will be the introduction of JIT manufacturing. Although this will be a difficult process, the financial rewards in reduced working capital required and a de-cluttering of the workplace should be significant. We will have to consider how this change impacts up and down our supply chain with customers and suppliers.

77 Merkland Sportswear (APM, 6/15)   98 mins

Merkland Sportswear (MS) is the market leader in sportswear in Ceeland, selling a variety of sportswear products under its own well-known brand. It is primarily a product development and marketing business as it contracts out all of its manufacturing to third parties around the world and it mostly sells its products through third-party retailers. It has only one store which is located in the capital city of Ceeland. The purpose of this store is to act as a centre for its marketing activities and to be a tangible representation of the MS brand. However, the main marketing activity for MS is the recruitment and promotion of star sports men and women as MS brand ambassadors. MS tries to have the most well-known sports star in each of the 10 most popular sports in Ceeland as an ambassador.

You are a performance management advisor to MS, brought into the company by the chief executive officer (CEO) to help the board with a number of issues. The first area which the board of MS requires your input is in a review of the existing performance dashboard for MS (Appendix 1). The dashboard is deliberately kept focused as it is for board use and the CEO has indicated that the three performance headings of 'financial, design and brand' will be kept at this time. The board has accepted that there may need to be up to two metrics for each of 'brand' and 'design' but they want to keep the number of financial metrics at three.

The mission statement of the business is designed to be broadly appealing. It is 'to inspire Ceelanders to compete'. From a business perspective, the aims are more focused, MS aims to grow as a business and to maximise shareholder wealth. The CEO further clarified the broad strategy to achieve these aims saying, 'We want to inspire competition not just in our customers but also within the company, to seek our greatest competitive advantage. We will achieve this by creating innovative products which provide reduced risk of injury and enhanced sporting performance supported by the best marketing operation in Ceeland.'

In order to assist in providing more detailed strategies to achieve these aims, the board has instituted a review of the competitive position of MS by commissioning a SWOT analysis (Appendix 2).

The CEO has asked that your first task be a review of the current dashboard metrics (Appendix 1). You should then review the SWOT analysis to suggest changes to the dashboard metrics within the constraints which the CEO has outlined.

Also, you are given details on a recent new development in the market. Nush Sportswear, one of the major competitors of MS, has recently suffered a scandal which has been widely reported. An investigative reporter discovered that one of the suppliers who manufactured sports shoes for Nush had been using child labour. The country in which the manufacturer worked had rules prohibiting child labour, but enforcement was very weak. This story has been widely covered in the media and has led to consumer boycotts and a review by the Ceeland business regulator into Nush's sourcing policies. It has been discovered that this is common practice in the sports footwear business where manufacturing is outsourced to such countries.

MS' shareholders have reacted with alarm to the potential damage that this could do to MS' brand. They have asked the board to consider changing their policy of outsourcing footwear manufacture. The board is considering two alternative responses:

1. Review and ensure that all outsourced footwear manufacture complies with appropriate employment terms and conditions (where necessary manufacturing would move to third-party companies in countries with appropriate regulation and enforcement); or

2. Create a manufacturing operation for MS in order to have full control of operations.

In response 1, the review of existing third-party manufacturers is being performed by a team from the procurement department. They have also considered the impact of moving all footwear sourcing to more strictly regulated environments. The results of this investigation are given in Appendix 3 and the board wants an evaluation of the qualitative and quantitative impact of this response.

In response 2, the board is considering setting up a factory for the manufacture of all MS footwear. They want to understand the impact of this on MS' existing performance metrics. First, they need a forecast of the profit from the factory as there are three distinct economic scenarios under which it might operate (see Appendix 4 for details).

Second, the board wants to know how the new factory will impact on the existing performance dashboard. However, since the probabilities of these economic scenarios are under debate, the board has said that they want this work to be independent of the results of the profit calculation from Appendix 4. Therefore, the board wants you to use an estimate of $103m profit before interest and tax from the new factory to evaluate the impact of the new factory on the dashboard. (This estimate is before product development and marketing costs as it only represents the manufacturing operation at the factory.)

Finally, the consultant who did the SWOT analysis has mentioned to the board that if they are thinking of reviewing their existing strategies, then they should consider using the value chain to secure competitive advantage. The CEO thinks that you should assess the implications of using the value chain for the performance management of MS. (An outline of the value chain is given in Appendix 5.)

Required

Write a report to the board of MS to:

(i) Assess the existing five metrics (Appendix 1). Using the SWOT analysis in Appendix 2, make suggestions for improvements within the constraints outlined by the CEO.

Note. You should ignore the impact of the Nush scandal in this part of the question. **(16 marks)**

(ii) Using the data in Appendix 3, assess the qualitative and quantitative impact on performance management at MS of response 1. **(8 marks)**

(iii) Calculate the expected operating profit of the new factory and evaluate the use of this method of decision-making under risk. **(6 marks)**

(iv) Using 2015 figures as a base, evaluate the impact of the new factory on the values and choice of metrics in the existing dashboard. **(10 marks)**

(v) Explain the implications of using the value chain for performance management at MS. **(6 marks)**

Professional marks will be awarded for the format, style and structure of the discussion of your answer. **(4 marks)**

(50 marks)

Appendix 1

MS performance dashboard

Report for the year to March 2015

	20X5	20X4	20X3	Change 20X5/20X4 %
Financial				
Revenue ($m)	273	238	209	14.7%
Operating profit ($m)	71	60	54	18.3%
ROCE	41.7%	37.5%	36.0%	11.2%
Design				
Design awards won	2	2	1	0.0%
Brand				
Awareness	64%	63%	59%	1.6%

Notes.

Design awards are national clothing design awards which address both the look and technology in a product. Brand awareness is the percentage of those sampled who could identify the company's logo and can name at least one of its products.

Appendix 2

SWOT (completed before the Nush scandal was reported)

S:	W:
– High market share – Excellent brand awareness – Strong revenue growth (compared to industry average of 11%) – Supply chain management	– Loss of a key brand ambassador (who was injured when he tripped over the laces of his MS boots) – Weak IT expertise
O:	T:
– New products in the market for new sports (such as those being introduced at each World Championships)	– Growth of social media as main marketing channel

Appendix 3

Procurement review of new outsourced footwear manufacturers

Currently, MS buys 2 million pairs of shoes at an average of $21 per unit (a pair of shoes) and we assume an average selling price of $75. Cost per unit will increase by 10%. Additionally, there will be a need to perform annual audits of these suppliers which will cost $0.5m.

The change of policy will be marketed as sustaining the values of MS. The MS ethics code states 'We will play fair and source our goods responsibly.' This marketing will cost $0.8m p.a. but it is hoped that this will produce a gain in market share. However, the increase in sales cannot be estimated at this time as competitors are making similar moves. The reviewer commented, 'It would be helpful to know how many units we would need to sell in order to cover these increased costs so this can be used as a marketing target.'

Appendix 4

New factory

The data collected on the new factory depends on three possible economic scenarios in response to MS' change in sourcing policy:

	Bad	Medium	Good
Probability	30%	60%	10%
Units manufactured ('000s)	1,800	2,000	2,200
Variable costs per unit ($)	21	22	23
Fixed costs ($'000s)	2,500		

Capital required	$'000
Building and equipping	36,000
Working capital	11,000

Notes

One unit is one pair of shoes.
Assume all units made are sold.
Assume an average selling price of $75.
The total Ceeland market for this type of shoe is estimated as 6.25m p.a.

Appendix 5

Value chain analysis

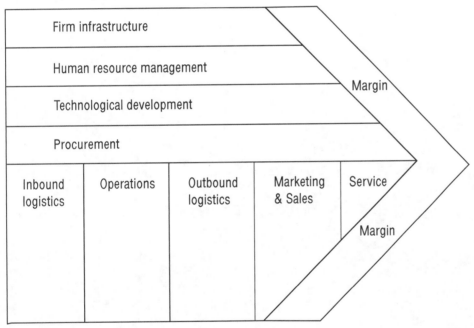

Answers

1 AB Electronics

Text reference. Strategic management accounting issues are discussed in Chapter 1 of the Study Text. Attitudes to risk are discussed in Chapter 6.

Top tips.

For part (a), think about the features of strategic management accounting which distinguish it from 'traditional' management accounting: for example, a focus on external factors, and on non-financial information as well as on internally generated financial information. How could these features be useful to AB for managing the performance of the trading company?

Part (b). Although there are likely to be financial implications of withdrawing from Asia (eg the liability to the local entrepreneur) you should not have focused solely on this in your answer. There are also likely to be non-financial implications: for example, what will be the impact on AB's reputation?

Moreover, if AB withdraws from Asia, are there any alternative markets it can move into to generate replacement sales and growth? Remember, the shareholders want increased growth and profitability, and the company has declared a strategic aim to expand internationally.

In this respect, it is important for AB to consider both the short-term cost implications and the longer-term organisational issues, and the discussion in your answer should reflect this.

Part (c). The scenario highlights that the Board take a relatively cautious approach to risk, while the institutional shareholders appear to be less risk averse. How might this affect the way the two parties respond to different opportunities?

(a)   **Strategic management accounting** – Unlike 'traditional' management accounting which looks primarily at internally generated financial information, strategic management accounting looks at information which relates to **external factors**, and it looks at **non-financial** as well as financial information.

Competitors' costs – For example, as well as looking at the trading company's own operating costs and margins, strategic management accounting would also encourage AB to look at competitors' costs. This will help focus attention on the need to control the trading company's costs if it is going to compete successfully with its competitors. For example, why are the trading company's wage costs proportionally so much higher than its competitors' costs?

Given the nature of IEC's product (standardised electrical components) cost efficiency is likely to be an important factor in the trading company's competitiveness. There is likely to be little scope for differentiation as a competitive strategy.

Market growth – Strategic management accounting will also encourage AB to look at market size and growth, and the trading company's share of the market. The scenario highlights that the downturn in economic conditions has slowed the growth demand for electronic components as a whole, which could intensify competition in the market. Instead of market growth being a source of increased sales, the trading company will now have to increase its market share in order to increase its sales.

Although the scenario mentions the presence of competitors, it does not give any indication of the number of competitors or their size relative to the trading company. However, these factors could both affect the trading company's ability to compete successfully in the market.

In this respect, strategic management accounting's **external focus** is very important: AB needs to understand the market environment in Asia in order to analyse the trading company's current performance, and then to evaluate future strategies for the company.

Analysis of current performance – Strategic management accounting can contribute to the trading company's success by **monitoring its performance** and results compared to its competitors, and then assessing whether its current strategy appears to be working successfully or not.

For example, the trading company's revised forecast suggests that its profit for 20X1 is now expected to be 20% lower than had originally been expected. Some of this shortfall may be due to an over-optimistic budget, since the trading company is still a relatively new entrant to the Asian market. However, it could also be an indication that the trading company has not been able to sustain its initial success and break into the market as successfully as it had hoped. Therefore it will be useful to compare the company's performance against its competitors, for example to see the extent to which their revenues and profits are growing or falling.

If it appears the trading company is performing relatively worse than its competitors, then AB should consider how it could revise its strategy to help improve the company's performance.

Forecasting – Strategic management accounting can also be used to help forecast performance.

AB's forecasts should not look solely at the trading company's own performance but should also look at competitors' performance and market trends in general. For example, how realistic is the level of forecast sales growth in the context of a slowdown in the market?

Equally, economic intelligence suggests that wage inflation is going to continue increasing over the next two years. However, the reason the trading company's wage costs are currently much higher than its competitors' may be that it is paying above the market rates. In which case, it may be able to offer lower annual wage increases than many of its competitors who are currently paying lower wage rates. If not, the trading company will need to review its staffing model and its labour productivity, and try to reduce its wage costs relative to its competitors.

(b)   **Sales potential** – Despite the trading company not seeming to be as profitable as had hoped, it is still generating a profit for AB (with its 50% share of the company's profit expected to be around $800,000 in 20Y1). It is not clear how much AB has invested in the company is, or what its target rate of return is on any investments.

Although the local entrepreneur has invested $500,000, it is likely that AB has invested more, given the level of profit the company is generating.

Therefore, before deciding whether to withdraw, AB needs to consider how profitable it expects the trading company to be in the future, and equally whether it feels it could invest its capital more profitably elsewhere.

Impact of environmental factors – The trading company's performance appears to have been adversely affected by **economic factors** (economic slowdown) and **political factors** (protectionism) in the external environment. However, it is not clear the respective impact that these two factors have had on the trading company's performance, nor the impact that other factors have had on its performance.

Long term or short term impact – Although economic conditions have worsened at the moment, they should improve again in the future, at which point AB might expect demand to increase again. Therefore the protectionist policies introduced by some of the Asian countries may be a more significant factor, if they are expected to remain in place for the longer term.

Alternative business structures – Although AB is considering withdrawing from the trading company this need not mean it withdraws from Asia completely. Although the trading company does not seem to have been as profitable as it had hoped, AB should consider whether it stops selling its products in Asia altogether or whether it needs to find an alternative channel. For example, if there is still a market for IEC's products in Asia, it could consider using Asian sales agents to act on its behalf.

Strength of competition – However, AB should also consider the strength of **competitive rivalry** within the Asian markets, because this will affect its profitability, both in the short term and the longer term. Alongside this, AB could also consider factors such as the **threat of new entrants**, and the **bargaining power of customers** which could also affect its profitability.

Exit barriers – AB and the local entrepreneur both have 50% shares in the trading company. If AB withdraws, the local entrepreneur will have to decide whether he wants to acquire AB's share and try to maintain the trading company himself, or whether the company should cease trading. If the company ceases trading, AB will be liable to pay the entrepreneur C$500,000. This exit payment could affect AB's decision of whether to withdraw or not.

Wider implications – The trading company seems to have been AB's first significant venture into Asia. If AB withdraws from the venture within about three years of establishing it, this could be damaging for its reputation. This could be problematic either if AB wants to continue selling its products through sales agents, or if, in future, it wants to re-establish a joint venture company.

(As we have noted earlier, although market conditions have worsened at the moment, they should improve again in future at which point AB might look to expand into Asia again. But if AB has a poor reputation in Asia, local businesses will be reluctant to become venture partners with it.)

Business portfolio – Moreover, before withdrawing from the Asian company, AB should critically assess the growth prospects of its current European and American markets. If there are limited growth opportunities in these market (for example, because they are **more mature** than the overseas markets), the Board might be advised to persevere with looking at expansion into new overseas markets.

Fit with strategic aims – AB has stated in its annual report that it wants to develop its international presence by expanding into overseas markets. Establishing the trading company in Asia is a way of helping to achieve this aim. By contrast, withdrawing from the Asian market would seem contradictory to this aim, and to the shareholders' wishes for increased growth and profitability.

(c)   AB's board has traditionally taken a 'relatively cautious approach' to providing strategic direction for the company which suggests that they are likely to be relatively averse to taking risks and cautious when dealing with uncertainty. By contrast, if the institutional shareholders are looking for the company to achieve increased growth and profitability, they may be prepared for it to take higher risks in order to achieve this.

This difference in the amount of risk which the different groups are prepared to accept could influence the way they look at possible new opportunities.

Risk averse – For example, if the Board are essentially risk averse they could make decisions based on the worst outcome that could occur, and will try to minimise the effect that this could have on AB. This suggests that they might adopt a 'maximin' approach to decisions they take in the context of strategic planning.

Risk seekers – By contrast, the institutional shareholders might prefer the directors to evaluate strategic options in terms of the best outcome which could occur, and seek the one which maximises the benefit for AB, regardless of how small the chance that this outcome will actually occur. This would entail the the directors adopting a 'maximax' approach to decisions in strategic planning instead of a 'maximin' approach.

In this respect, the Board and the shareholders could come to different conclusions about what course of action to take in relation to strategic options (for example, around how AB should grow or expand).

Risk and return – When looking at potential new opportunities, AB should also set a target return which compensates for risk. Again, the difference in attitude to risk between the Board and the shareholders could mean that the Board will want higher level of return to compensate for the perceived risk involved than the shareholders would want. This might, therefore, lead to the directors rejecting possible opportunities which the shareholders would have been keen for them to accept.

2 Megasnack

Text reference. The scope for potential conflict between strategic business plans and localised decisions is covered in Chapter 1 of the BPP Study Text.

Top tips.

Part (a). A key issue here is whether the KPIs are aligned with Megasnack's targets and strategy (both financial and corporate) and can therefore help the company achieve its strategy, or whether the KPIs could also be encouraging any of the 'incidents' outlined in the scenario.

In answering **part (b)**, explain the problem fully and clearly, making reference to the details given in the scenario. Do not assume that some of the points are so obvious that there is no need to describe them. There is a risk of failing to state the obvious and so losing marks that could be fairly easily earned.

Nevertheless, make sure that you 'use' the details given in the scenario (for example, by explaining how they illustrate the reasons for conflict) rather than simply copying out the problems and incidents described in the scenario.

Part (c) calls for judgement about the measures that might be taken to reduce the scope for conflict and the risk that incidents will occur. Consequently, your view may differ from the solution that is suggested here, and your points could be equally valid. However, you should avoid the temptation to give an answer that is over-simplistic – such as suggesting that 'management should do their jobs better' or that head office should 'tell' the outlet managers what to do.

(a) **Revenue per store** – An important element of Megasnack's financial strategy is achieving sales growth. In this respect, measuring revenue is important, so revenue per outlet seems a sensible performance indicator to use; although it may be more useful to measure 'revenue growth' over time rather than a simple 'revenue per outlet' figure.

However, managers' actions leading to incident 1 (offering special discounts and deals) could possibly be an unintended consequence of a KPI based on revenue per outlet. For example, if revenue figures are running below budget for certain outlets, the managers of those outlets may decide to offer special discounts and deals in order to try to boost revenues.

In this respect, if Megasnack does not already do so, it may also need to measure gross profit margin (%) per outlet as well as a simple revenue figure – because offering special discounts and deals is likely to reduce the gross profit margin an outlet will earn.

Perhaps more importantly, though, managers' behaviour in offering special discounts and deals is not consistent with Megasnack's overall strategy based on conformity. Again, therefore it will be important for Megasnack to have additional controls which ensure conformity, in addition to the revenue KPI.

Staff costs – Staff costs are likely to be a significant cost at Megasnack so it is important to monitor them. Equally, the numbers and quality of staff employed in Megasnack's outlets could play an important part in determining if Megasnack meets customer needs and expectations better than its rivals. For example, Megasnack needs to ensure if has enough staff on duty at any time to ensure that customers do not have to wait a long time for their meals. Equally, however, it will be inefficient for Megasnack to be over-staffed, particularly during less busy times of the day.

Crucially, the measure Megasnack uses is a relative one. It does not simply measure 'staff costs per outlet' but measures staff costs as a **proportion of revenue**. Therefore, outlets could improve their performance against the indicator by increasing revenue as well as by reducing staff costs. In this way, the measure appears designed to strike a balance between revenue and staffing levels.

However, incident 2 could still be seen as an unintended consequence of the KPI. If managers are looking to reduce wage costs in their outlet they could cut training or take on untrained staff as a means of doing so. Such actions are likely to reduce customer service levels and so are not congruent with Megasnack's strategy. Again, however, if revenue falls as a result of falling customer service levels, this will be picked up by the KPI, by virtue of it being a relative measure (staff costs as a percentage of revenue).

(b) **Conflict of interest** – A conflict between the strategic aims of an organisation and local decision-making can be explained largely by a conflict of interests. The strategic aims of a company are often decided by senior management but responsibility for operations is delegated to local management.

(i) Strategic objectives are usually **long-term** in nature, but at the same time local managers are given **short-term** performance targets, and may be rewarded with incentive bonuses for achieving or exceeding those targets. Even if there is no bonus payments system, local managers may be put under pressure by head office to achieve their budget targets. The short-term targets may not be fully consistent with strategic aims, but will nevertheless be given priority by local managers wanting to earn a bonus.

(ii) Head office strategy is concerned with the objectives of the organisation as a whole. Local managers may have a much more narrow view, and shown concern for the performance of their local operation. For example, if a rival fast food outlet is taking business by offering discounts or other incentives to customers, it is natural to expect local managers in Megasnack's outlets to want to respond with counter-initiatives of their own – regardless of head office policy.

(iii)   Local managers may also want to exercise their own authority to make decisions, even if this sometimes means ignoring head office guidance or instructions.

The difference between head office strategy and local decision-making is evident in some of the incidents at Megasnack. Local managers have taken their own initiative to improve the performance of their outlet, for example by offering price discounts as a means of increasing sales. At a local level price discounts or similar measures may 'work', but they are not consistent with the broader policy of standardisation of products and service, and consistency in meeting customer expectations. If different outlets offer different discounts customers will no longer know what price they should expect to pay for their meals when they visit different outlets.

Short term focus – In many organisations, management have traditionally been expected to focus on financial performance, and this had led to them focussing on measures to cut costs, improve productivity or increase sales and profit margins. A typical response by local management to short-term cost pressures is to cut discretionary costs, such as the cost of training staff, without considering the consequences for performance standards of inadequate training.

Local focus – The focus of local managers on the concerns of their own area of operations can sometimes result in a misguided belief that what seems best for the local operation must also be best for the organisation as a whole. This may be the reason why some food pre-preparation centres were reluctant to the demand for more output. The centre managers may have considered product quality to be the overriding concern for the company, when the concern should have been on finding ways of meeting the higher demand without compromising on quality – which is a different perception of the problem.

The suggestions provided so far about the reasons for a conflict between corporate and local decision-making have assumed that the problem lies mainly with the local managers. In some respects, however, the problem may originate at the corporate centre (head office).

(iv)   Head office may set long-term strategic performance targets and short-term 'budget' **targets that are not consistent with each other**. For example, if the long term strategic plans are aimed at business growth, it would be inconsistent not to also expect some costs to increase in order to facilitate revenue growth. If targets are inconsistent, the incentive for local managers to take short-term decisions (in this example, by cutting costs) may actually be encouraged by head office.

(v)   **Head office may not communicate all of its policies sufficiently well**. The manager at the outlet which disposed of food in a way which contravened Megasnack's health and environmental policies may not have deliberately breached company policy. It is possible that he or she didn't understand the policy properly (although this doesn't excuse the local manager for disposing of food in a way which was contrary to health and safety laws.)

(vi)   To some extent there may also be **lack of clarity in the company's policy** on delegation of decision-making. It is surprising that the outlets in one country should have sold additional products, given the importance Megasnack places on the standardisation of its menu. This should raise a question about why the outlet managers considered that they had the authority to take this initiative, and whether head office had not made it clear to them that the menu should remain fixed.

(c)   **Problem recognition** – The first essential step has been taken to deal with the problem, namely that senior managers have now recognised that a problem exists. They should try to establish the reasons for conflicts between strategy and local short-term decision-making in order to identify suitable measures to take.

Strategy review – Senior management should review the company's strategies, and re-assess whether these are appropriate for and consistent with its long-term objectives. The current strategy is to provide a consistent standard product and service that meets customer expectations no matter which outlet they visit. This strategy has been used by other fast food chains, and may well be appropriate. However, Megasnack's management may wish to consider the implications of current strategy for flexibility and innovation. Some local decision-making by outlet managers may have been prompted by the lack of flexibility in the company's strategy.

Range of performance targets – It is appropriate for head office management to establish shorter-term targets for local managers, but these should be consistent with the strategic objectives of the company.

Instead of rewarding local managers for achieving financial targets, a balanced scorecard approach may be introduced, in which non-financial and strategy-related performance is also rewarded. Key performance indicators for strategic objectives should be established and reported regularly to local management. For example, if outlet managers are rewarded for providing training to staff, this will give them an incentive to provide the training rather than to cut training costs in order to meet financial performance targets.

Improved communication – Head office should also communicate its strategies, and what they are intended to achieve, throughout the management structure of the company. At Megasnack, this would mean communicating not only the company's strategies for consistency of products and service, but also (possibly in a corporate code of ethics) company policy on employee relations, health and safety, and environmental protection. The benefits of standardisation and consistency should also be stressed, in terms of meeting customer expectations, brand or corporate image, and the effectiveness of global advertising.

Business monitoring – Finally, head office should establish procedures for monitoring compliance with strategic business plans. This may require the establishment of an **internal audit team** or team of inspectors to carry out checks on local outlets, (for example, health and safety checks, or price checks). These teams should report apparent inconsistencies between local operations and corporate policy, and Megasnack also needs to establish policies and procedures for following up on these reports.

Although it may be impossible to eliminate a conflict of interest between long-term strategy and short-term opportunism entirely, a recognition of the problem and a willingness to look for solutions, by both head office and local managers, would go some way to keeping the problem under control.

3 Ganymede

Text reference. Benchmarking is discussed in Chapter 1 of the BPP Study Text. Public Sector League Tables are discussed in Chapter 11.

Top tips.

Part (a). A useful approach to this requirement would be to think through, in order, the stages involved in a benchmarking process. This should help you identify which stages Ganymede has already undertaken and which it still needs to undertake. To answer this question well you need to know the stages involved in a benchmarking process, but don't simply list the stages in general terms. Make sure you consider specifically which stages Ganymede has undertaken, and which are still required.

Part (b). Note that the focus of your evaluation here should be Ganymede's position, not on benchmarking's usefulness for assessing Ganymede's position.

However, the fact that the question requirement says 'as far as possible' should serve as an indicator that some details which would help you evaluate Ganymede's position may be missing from the information provided. In this case, you should highlight the additional information which would help you evaluate Ganymede's position more fully.

Part (c). You are asked to evaluate the usefulness of the league tables from the students' perspective. So, you should consider how they might be useful to students in making a decision about where to study; but, perhaps more importantly, you should also consider the drawbacks or limitations in the league tables, or why they may not be helpful to students in making their decisions about where to study.

Examining team's comments. Part (b) ought to have been a relatively straightforward analysis of the data given in the scenario. However, candidates displayed a disappointing lack of judgement over what constitutes useful advice in this scenario and failed to use the drivers highlighted in the scenario to calculate suitable relative measures.

		Marks
(a)	For each relevant point on the progress of the benchmarking exercise – 1 mark	
	Note. Only 2 marks in total are available for identifying the stages of the benchmarking process in general terms	7
	Total for part (a) – Up to 7 marks	

(b)	Calculation of performance indicators using appropriate drivers – 1 mark each	Up to 6	
	Commenting on the results – 1 mark per relevant point	Up to 6	
	Total for part (b) – Up to 10 marks		10

(c)	Potential benefits of proposed league tables – 1 mark each	Up to 3	
	Limitations of proposed league tables – 1 mark each	Up to 7	
	Total for part (b) – Up to 8 marks		8

Total = 25

(a) Benchmarking exercises can be described using seven stages, and we will use these stages to assess the progress of GU's current benchmarking exercise.

Actions that have been undertaken

(i) Set objectives and determine the area to benchmark.

The underlying objective of the exercise is to improve efficiency, and the area being benchmarked has been identified as the administrative costs incurred in relation to teaching and research.

(ii) Identify key performance drivers and indicators.

It is important that the benchmarking exercise focuses on performance areas which are crucial to Ganymede's success.

Three key drivers of costs have revenues have been identified (research contract values supported; student numbers; and staff numbers). Key performance indicators can be derived from these; for example, costs per student.

However, although the drivers have already been set, the driver 'staff numbers' could be improved by distinguishing between teaching staff and administrative staff.

(iii) Select organisations to study and benchmark against.

The chancellor has asked the administrator to benchmark Ganymede's performance against the other two large universities in Teeland (AU and BU), and the government has endorsed this proposal.

However, the exercise as it stands will not compare GU's performance against any of the five smaller universities in Teeland, nor against any foreign universities.

This could be a weakness in the proposed exercise, because the universities which are excluded could provide examples of best practice which GU could lead from if they had been included.

(iv)   Measure performance for own organisation and the other organisations involved in the exercise

Information about GU, AU and BU's administrative costs for the most recent academic year has been collected.

The step has been made easier by the government insisting that all three universities co-operate and supply information to each other.

Actions still required

(v)   Compare performance.

This is the stage that the exercise has currently reached. The results of the performance comparison are given in part (b).

(vi)   Design and implement improvement programme.

The results of the performance comparison should help identify which areas GU needs to improve.

For those aspects of performance where GU is lagging behind one (or both) of the other universities it should send a member of staff to the university which is performing best to identify what that university is doing differently to GU which is leading to the difference in performance levels.

In turn, that staff member should devise a programme to introduce improvements at GU and implementing the best practices which have been identified at the other universities.

(vii)   Monitor improvement.

Whilst implementing the improvement programme should help GU improve its performance, there is no guarantee how successful it will be and how much improvement it will actually deliver. Therefore, management should monitor GU's performance once the programme has been implemented to see if it achieves its goals or if further improvements will still be necessary.

> At the end of the programme, GU's management should also consider a post-project review, to consider any lessons which have been learned from the project and which could be useful for any subsequent projects.

(b)   Results from the benchmarking exercise:

	GU ($)	AU (S)	BU ($)
Research (Cost per $000 of contract value supported)			
Contract management	78	87	97
Laboratory	226	257	281
Teaching facilities management (Cost per student)	951	1,197	920
Student support services (Cost per student)	71	89	73

	GU ($)	AU (S)	BU ($)
Other support services			
(Cost per staff member)			
Teachers' support services	506	532	544
Accounting	204	204	197
Human resources	156	156	191
IT management	817	803	737
General services	2,153	2,088	2,286

Research categories

GU has the lowest costs relative to the value of the research contracts supported, and it has also earned the highest value contracts. This may suggest that the government monitors factors such as cost control when deciding where to allocate its costs, in which case it is important that GU continues to maintain its good practice in this area, particularly if the other universities will be looking to improve their performance to bring its closer to GU's performance.

Teaching facilities management & Student support services

AU spends significantly more per student on its teaching facilities and student support than the other two universities. AU also has significantly fewer students than the other two universities.

We might expect that AU's higher spending on teaching facilities and student support would make it more attractive to students than the other two universities, leading to higher student numbers. At face value, the benchmarked figures would suggest that student enrolment is not significantly influenced by these factors though. However, the lower student numbers at AU may also reflect that it can accommodate fewer students than the other two universities; or even that it only wants to accommodate a smaller number of students and therefore sets harder entry requirements than the other two.

Therefore, it might also be useful to compare the number of applications each university receives relative to the number of places it has available. Equally, it might also be useful to compare factors such as student drop out rates, pass rates, and students' success rates in gaining employment after they graduate, to assess whether there is a correlation between these and the more expensive teaching environment at AU.

However, these quality measures are not currently reflected in the benchmarking exercise.

Other support services

Human Resources – BU's human resource costs per staff member are 22% higher than the other two universities, despite BU having the highest number of staff to spread its HR costs. In this respect, it appears that BU may have more HR staff, or more-highly-paid HR staff than it needs, whereas GU's model appears more efficient.

Teachers' support services – BU also appears to provide more support services for its staff than the other two universities. The difference between BU and AU is not significant, but GU's costs are around 7% lower per staff member than BU's.

However, it is not clear exactly what costs are included in this category so it is difficult to determine whether the figures suggest that GU is more efficient in the provision of these services, or whether it offers less support services to its teachers than BU.

IT management – By contrast to their respective positions for HR and Teachers' support services, GU spends considerably more (around 11%) on IT management than BU. However, this may be due to the subjects being taught. For example, if GU is more oriented to science and technology-based subjects this is likely to mean it will need greater computing resources than if it was more oriented to arts and humanities.

However, if the difference in IT management costs cannot be explained by variations in the subjects taught, then GU (and to a slightly lesser extent, AU) need to consider how BU appears to have been able to control its IT costs more effectively than them. For example, has BU outsourced any of its IT services rather than managing them all in house?

> **Accounting services** – All three universities cost control appears broadly the same here. BU has achieved a small advantage (3.5%) over the other two, but there is nothing significant here.
>
> **General services** – Again, there appears to be relatively little variation between the three universities here, although AU appears to have slightly lower costs than GU, which, in turn, is has slightly lower costs than BU.

General point

Although we have identified some variations between GU's performance and that of the other two universities, it is important to exercise a degree of caution when looking at these comparisons. We have no information about the mix of the subjects being taught or researched at the different universities, but this mix could have an impact on their performance statistics. Equally, we do not have any information about the relative locations of the three universities. For example, if one of the universities is a region which is economically more prosperous than the other two, then that university's staff costs are automatically likely to be higher than the other two's, as a result of the geographical variation in salary weightings rather than any internal factors.

(c)   The league tables will provide students with some additional information which could help them compare different universities before deciding which ones to apply to.

Academic and non-academic criteria – The measures chosen seem to recognise the importance of non-academic factors as well as academic ones. For example, if students are strongly dissatisfied with the university facilities this may lead to them not completing their courses, as would the fact that the course content is not what they had hoped it would be.

Equally, the prospects of finding work after graduating is likely to be something which is important to students, so the inclusion of this measure in the league tables could be valuable to them.

However, some of the other measures included in the table may be less important to students when choosing where to study:

Research or tuition – The value of research funding secured by each university may give some indication of the quality of the academic staff it employs, and how highly the university is regarded in the academic and research community. However, a potential student may be more interested in the quality of tuition they will receive than the amount of research the university carries out.

If a university prioritises research above teaching, this would improve its ranking in this element of the league table, but may actually be disadvantageous to the student; if the tutors are more concerned with their research than their students.

Choice of measures – In addition, there are a number of other possible measures which the tables do not include, yet which would be valuable for students. For example, information about spending on academic services, and the ratio of students to academic staff might be more useful to students than information about research funding. Equally, information about entry requirements is also likely to be useful to prospective students.

Aggregate measures – However, perhaps the biggest weakness in the league tables is that they look at aggregate figures, rather than figures for particular departments for example.

However, the quality of the particular course they want to study is likely to be a very important factor for a student when choosing where to study. A university which performs relatively poorly overall in the league tables may be a centre of excellence in a particular subject; while conversely a university which performs well overall might have poor departments for certain subjects.

By only considering overall figures, there is a danger that the league tables will obscure variation within them.

Importantly, also, the league tables do not give any indication of the numbers of students taking different courses, but this could also affect the results. For example, if there is a shortage of engineering graduates in Teeland, and a University has a large engineering department, this might lead to the proportion of its graduates in employment being higher than a University with only a small engineering department.

Trends – It is not clear from the scenario how frequently the ministry envisages the league tables should be produced. However, when looking at any figures in the tables, students should consider whether the figures for a single period are representative, or whether the need to look at an average or a trend over a longer period of time. For example, the numbers of students gaining first class or 2:1 degrees could vary from one year to the next, so looking at one year in isolation may not give an accurate picture of the university's overall performance in this respect.

Unintended consequences – Another potential disadvantage of introducing league tables focusing on only a small number of measures is that they will encourage the universities to focus on their performance in those areas potentially at the detriment of other areas. For example, if there is a focus on ensuring that the proportion of students achieving first class and 2:1 degrees is as high as possible, there could be a danger that a university makes its entry requirements more demanding, with the result that less students overall come to the university. The league tables do not show entry requirements, which could be a useful measure for students to consider when choosing which universities to apply to.

Equally, there could be a danger that universities could inflate results (for example, by uplifting marks so that students obtain 2:1 degrees instead of 2:2 degress) to improve the university's place in the league tables.

---

4 Wheeler

Text reference. Strategic management accounting is discussed in Chapter 1 of the BPP Study Text, as is benchmarking. Kaizen costing is discussed in Chapter 13.

Top tips. The best approach to written questions like this one is to prepare an answer plan, making clear what your paragraph headings will be and adding bullet points for the facts and examples you intend to include. Break down the requirements of the question and identify which elements of your answer will come from knowledge and which will come from the scenario.

Note the way parts (a) and (b) are linked. In part (a) you need to identify the problems with the reports which Wheeler currently produces, and then in part (b) you need to suggest how its information could be improved. So, as far as possible, your answer to part (b) should include suggestions for how to deal with the problems identified in part (a).

Although part (c) is only worth 5 marks, note that there are still, in effect, two parts to it: first, explain the concept of benchmarking (in general terms); and then, second, explain how it could be applied to information for strategic planning (specifically in the context of Wheeler).

Part (d) picks up on a specific issue in Wheeler's current system – that it uses a standing costing approach. The key point to note here the distinction between cost reduction (in Kaizen costing) and cost control (in traditional approaches).

Marks

(a)	List of criticisms (1 mark each max 5 marks)		5
(b)	Suggestions of improvements (1 mark each)	up to 5	
	New information (financial and non-financial)	up to 5	
			10
(c)	Explanation and application of benchmarking		5
(d)	Description of Kaizen costing – 1 mark per relevant point	up to 3	
	Comparison of Kaizen costing vs standard costing – 1 mark per point	up to 3	
			5
			Total = 25

(a) Management accounting information should help managers of a business to exercise their functions of **planning**, **decision making** and **control**. Criticisms of management accounting information are that it is not relevant for many of these tasks in that it is historical and lacks external focus. Particular criticisms of the information currently provided are these.

(i) **Backward looking.** It is primarily historical, although the budgets probably contain a forecasting element. Strategic plans are future orientated. They also deal with uncertainties.

(ii) **Not relevant to decisions.** It is more concerned with allocating costs than taking decisions. Presumably Wheeler Ltd has an absorption costing system. This is inadequate for strategic planning, where a knowledge of competitors' costs can be important.

(iii) **It appears almost entirely financial.** Other performance indicators provide a valuable insight into the business. For example, it might be useful to know the value of the business turned away, or the number of new customers acquired by advertising in the magazine.

(iv) Jobs appear to be priced on a **cost-plus basis**. The firm is turning away customers; perhaps it is pricing its work too cheaply. A small firm in a competitive industry can price according to the market.

(v) **The existing standard costing system is not appropriate for this type of production.** Different jobs require different, unique machinery configurations, and the cost of set-up times does not seem to be dealt with in the accounting system. This indicates that an approach such as **activity based costing** would give a better idea as to real costs and real profits.

(vi) No **competitor information** is offered.

(vii) **Customer information** is skimpy. Customers now require larger orders. The firm should understand why.

That said, the reports are **timely**, **accurate** and **comprehensive**.

(b) **How to improve accounting information at Wheeler**

(i) **New costing system.** The current costing system should be reviewed, to ensure it captures costs in an appropriate way. Some of the insights of ABC, in identifying the real costs of each job, may be useful here. Costs would include set-up times for each order, administration costs and machine usage. Any product/job profitability analyses would therefore be more accurate.

(ii) **Non-financial information** relating to costs could include quality information (eg on a TQM basis) such as wastage, reject rates and so forth. Statistical process control measures can be incorporated in management reports.

(iii) **The standard costing system can be used for strategic purposes.** For example, it can show trade-offs between using higher quality materials or more labour. Rather than use standard costing only to reconcile actual with budgeted costs, it can be used for decision-making purposes (for example, to take account of different materials prices, different mixes of materials, future costs).

(iv) **Marketing information.** At present, the firm has no marketing department. In an ideal world, marketing information would also be included in management reports.

   (1) **The firm's market share**, if it is possible to assess it accurately and if it is a relevant indicator, can be provided

   (2) **Customer profitability**. Such information can probably be provided from within the accounting system, which could be adapted to job costing where necessary. Segmentation analyses can be applied to identify the groups of customers which are worth most to Wheeler.

   (3) **The cost of lost business**. The firm should estimate revenues it has sacrificed by turning away larger orders. This can then be input into a model to see whether investment in new capacity would be worthwhile. At present the firm cannot use all its capacity; would expansion, just to win a few larger orders, make this problem even worse?

   (4) **Repeat business** from satisfied customers and the value of such business.

   (5) If it did **marketing research** it might find new customers for its small scale engineering business.

(v) **Competitor information** should be provided as a matter of course. The company needs to be aware of its own advantages in relation to competitors, with a view to pricing.

(c) **Benchmarking**

Benchmarking provides a means of identifying how well areas of an organisation are performing, by comparing their performance to that of other areas or of other organisations.

The hope is that benchmarking will then lead to an improvement in performance in those areas which are currently underperforming.

Types of benchmarking include the following:

(i) **Internal benchmarking** – Comparing one operating unit with another within the same industry.

(ii) **Functional benchmarking** – Internal functions are compared with those of the best external practitioner of these functions, regardless of the industry they are in.

(iii) **Competitive benchmarking** – Information is gathered about direct competitors, such that performance can be compared against these competitors.

Possible areas of performance which could be benchmarked include:

(i) **Speed of new product development** (Japanese firms had expertise in this area, which European and American firms tried to copy)

(ii) **Productivity** (for example, number of cars per worker per year)

(iii) **Quality** (for example, rejected parts per million)

(iv) **Service** (for example, delivery dates)

Benchmarking can be applied to Wheeler's **strategic information** in the following ways.

(i) The company can fairly easily benchmark its **prices** against those of **competitors** as the necessary information should be available.

(ii) It can benchmark **quality and waste**.

(iii) Wheeler might find a firm of a similar size, but dealing with different markets, with which to enter an **alliance**, where information is jointly shared.

(iv) It can benchmark **productivity and efficiency**.

(d) **Kaizen costing** – Traditional costing systems, such as Wheeler's current system, focus on **cost control**. By contrast, Kaizen costing systems focus on **cost reduction**.

Kaizen costing involves a process of **continuous improvement** in which the costs of producing a product are constantly reduced over the product's life.

Functional analysis is applied at the design stage of a new product, and a **target cost for each function** is set. The functional target costs are added together and the total becomes the **product target cost**.

Once the product has been in production for a year, the actual cost of the first year becomes the starting point for further cost reduction in the second year, and so on into subsequent years.

Impact of Kaizen approach at Wheeler

Kaizen costing vs Standard costing – Wheeler currently applies a standard costing system, and the focus of its variance reports is on **cost control** rather than **cost reduction**.

However, because Kaizen focuses on continuous improvement and cost reduction, standard costs have much less value for monitoring performance because they are fixed over the relevant period. However, the nature of Kaizen costing means that the 'standard' costs themselves should be reduced over time. Therefore when Wheeler sets its cost budgets, it will need to factor these target reductions into its budgets.

However, the impact of introducing Kaizen costing at Wheeler could be significant. Whereas standard costing doesn't provide any motivation to improve performance levels, the whole focus of Kaizen costing is on cost reduction and performance improvement.

5 BPL Leisure

Text reference. The changing role of management accountants in organisations is discussed in Chapter 1 of the Study text.

Top tip.

Part (a). You should have realised from the scenario that the Operations Director has been characterized as having a very 'traditional' view of the management accountant's role, while the Marketing Director has a more modern, 'hybrid' perspective. This contrast underpins part (a) of the question.

However, in reality, organizations are unlikely to be polarised so extremely into 'traditional' and 'modern' views. Hence, in **part (b)** you need to evaluate the results of the study cited by the HR director. How far do the results suggest that the management accountant's role in an organisation has shifted to a business partner role, or how far do the results suggest that the traditional view of a management accountant's role is still applicable?

Part (c). Burns & Scapens (who are specifically referred to in the P5 Study Guide) state there are three main forces for changes in the role of the management accountant. These are changes in technology, management structure and competition. In this question, you need to focus specifically on technology, and competition, and then link them to the scenario which has been described at BPL.

Part (d). The scenario provides you with information about market growth and relative market share, so you should be able to identify the hotel division's position on the BCG matrix relatively easily. However, you then also need to consider whether the proposal to sell the division seems sensible. Does it fit with the strategy recommended by the BCG matrix? But also, what other factors should BPL consider before making any decision to sell the division?

(a)   **Traditional vs hybrid view** – The Operations Director appears to have a very 'traditional' view of management accounting and the role of the management accountant within an organisation. He seems accounting as a mechanism to help **control performance**, but is insistent that the management accountant should not be allowed to get involved with any operational aspects of the business.

By contrast, the Marketing Director appears to view the management accountant as being more integrated into the business, which is characteristic of the modern model of the **hybrid accountant**.

In this modern model, the management accountant is closely involved in **decision support** and **providing advice** throughout the business, applying their specialist technical knowledge as necessary. This appears to be what the Marketing Director wants when he asserts that it is very important that the accountant be involved in any discussions about the division's performance and strategy.

Strategic management accounting – The Marketing Director also appears to have a more strategic view of management accounting information than the Operations Director, recognising the contribution it could make to planning and future performance.

By contrast, the Operations Director appears to have a very traditional view of management accounting information:

Financial vs non-financial information – The Operations Director appears to be only concerned with aspects of financial performance. However, as frameworks such as the balanced scorecard have indicated, it is also important to consider non-financial aspects of performance.

Historical vs forward-looking orientation – The Operations Director also only appears to be concerned with information about performance to date, rather than any forecast information about the division's future performance, and the potential profitability of any new strategies. Although the Marketing Director doesn't specifically **forecast** or assess how much **value** any new strategies could generate, these could well be reasons why he wants the accountant involved in the discussions about the division's future performance.

(b) **Business Partner roles** – Two of the five aspects of the management accountants' work (identifying profit improvements, and strategic financial planning) can be seen as business partner roles. This suggests that there is an increasing demand for management accountants to become more integrated into the operations of a business, rather than remaining detached from them.

Traditional roles – However, while two of the five aspects are business partner roles, the remaining three are aspects associated with the traditional management accountant's role. And, perhaps more significantly, these three were the **most highly ranked activities** in the study which the HR Director is referring to, which suggests they remain central to the role.

Supplementing not replacing – Consequently, it seems that while aspects of the new role type are important, they are perhaps better viewed as supplementing rather than replacing traditional roles. For example, the study showed that the 'preparation and interpretation of management accounting information' remained the most important aspect of the management accountant's role.

Hybrid view – In this respect, the study findings appear to support the hybrid model, in which the accountant has both accounting knowledge and an understanding of the operations and commercial processes of an organisation.

Context – It is not clear from the scenario which organisations had formed the basis for the study the HR Director referred to. However, the extent of change in the management accountants' role is likely to vary among different organisations.

In particular, it is likely that the uptake of the new role type will be higher in larger organisations than in small ones. Larger organisations are likely to have greater capacity to implement change than smaller organisations, through resource availability, supporting investment in new technology, and restructuring. It is perhaps not a surprise that the Marketing Director at BPL has joined from a much larger organisation (the market leader), meaning that he values the 'newer' aspects of the management accountant's role more highly than the existing staff at BPL.

(c) **Technology**

Self-sufficiency of operational staff – The new IT software will reduce the demands on accountants to produce and monitor information, because operational staff can now generate this information and therefore monitor their own performance.

In addition, this also means the Directors should all be aware of how well the division is performing before the management accounts are produced. Therefore, the significance of the management accounts will also be reduced.

Adding value – However, the reduced demands to produce and monitor information will enable the accountant's expertise to be deployed in roles that deliver greater value to BPL. For example, if the directors are evaluating different strategic options, the management accountant could play a vital role in assessing the relevant costs and projected benefits of each option, and therefore in determining which option looks like it will add most value to the business.

Risk of downsizing – However, it could also be argued that if it takes less time to carry out core accounting tasks roles then the number of accountants required across BPL as a whole could be reducing, potentially leading to a downsizing of the finance function.

Competitive environment

External vs internal focus – BPL is operating in a very competitive environment, and the hotel division, in particular, is performing very poorly. However, the intensity of competitive environment means that it is very important for BPL to analyse its competitors and their strategies, as well as considering its own financial performance and strategies.

The Operations Director's remarks seem to suggest that BPL has traditionally adopted an internal, financial perspective for analysing its own performance. There is a danger that such an approach could lead to short-term measures designed to improve the division's profits, but which overlook its future earning capacity and strategic position in the hotel industry as a whole.

Commercial orientation – In this respect, the management accountant's role needs to become more strategic; looking at the wider, long-term commercial implications of any strategies, not just short-term profits.

However, given that the division's economic circumstances seem to be deteriorating in the short term, monitoring and turning around short-term profits will also remain very important. This again suggests that the accountant's role could usefully combine traditional elements (such as cost control) with newer elements (such as identifying strategic profit improvements).

(d) **Low relative market share** – The Accountant's figures show that the Hotels division has a very low relative market share. Based on the current year's figures its relative market share is only 0.08 (135 / 1,620), although it should not be a surprise that BPL only has a low market share considering it is only a medium-sized company and there are some very large multinational companies competing in the European hotel market.

Low market growth – Market growth in the hotels sector also appears to be low, around 2% per year.

Dog – This means the hotels division should be classified as a dog. This suggests that BPL should either be looking to 'divest' or 'hold' the division, although the more common strategy for dealing with dogs is to divest them. This would appear to support the proposal to sell the hotel division.

Contribution to company – However, this does not mean the BPL should automatically sell its hotels division. Although its operating profit and revenues are falling, it still made $6.5 million profit this year, and is forecast to make over $ 5 million next year.

We do not know how much revenue or profit BPL generates as a whole, but the directors should consider the relative contribution the hotels divisions makes to the group before making any decision to sell. Given that BPL is a 'hotel and leisure' company, it seems likely that the hotels business is central to its corporate strategy, so the directors should consider the impact that any disposal will have on the BPL's overall strategic objectives.

Equally, given that BPL's revenues and profits are falling overall, they need to consider how any decision to sell the hotels division will strengthen the company's strategic position overall; for example, will BPL be able to use the proceeds from the disposal to invest in a more lucrative area of the leisure industry?

Impact on portfolio – Also, before making any decision about the sale, BPL should consider if there are any strategic benefits from retaining the hotel division in the company. For example, does it complement any of BPL's other divisions, such that customers who use the hotel division also use BPL's other divisions and if BPL sold the hotels division it could lose the related revenues from the other divisions.

6 Mentons

Text reference. The changing role of the management accountant, as outlined by Burns and Scapens, is covered in Chapter 1 of the BPP Study text.

Top tips. The central theme of the question is an analysis of the views of Burns and Scapens about the changing role of the management accountant (or 'hybrid accountant'). However, you should also comment in part (a) on the reasons why the relevance and value of traditional management accounting came into question.

Part (b). Burns and Scapens stated that there are three main forces for change in the role of the management accountant: changes in technology; management structure; and competition. You should use these as the framework for your answer, and think how they have affected the developments at Mentons.

Part (c). Despite the CEO's doubts, the management team will still need information about the company's performance. Think about the way the accountant – particularly in a 'hybrid' accountant role – could provide valuable information for the company.

(a)   It is assumed that the 'traditional' methods of management accounting are principally budgeting and budgetary control, standard costing and variance analysis, and absorption costing.

   (i)   **Budgeting** is still a widely-used planning method. Budgets usually cover a financial year, but this is arguably its weakness, since plans should cover a period that is relevant to the objectives of the organisation rather than an arbitrary 12-month period.

   (ii)   In addition, the environment in which firms operate is becoming increasingly uncertain and dynamic, which means that budgets are likely to be a less reliable measure of performance than they would be in a predictable and static environment.

   (iii)   On the other hand, budgets do still help to link operational plans to financial reporting.

   (iv)   Just as budgeting is still a relevant activity, the regular comparison of actual performance against the plan is also relevant. It may be argued that financial comparisons are not necessarily sufficient by themsleves, because they do not consider **non-financial aspects of performance** such as quality. Even so, comparisons of actual and expected spending and income are useful for management control purposes.

   (v)   **Standard costing**, on the other hand, has lost much of its relevance. Fewer manufacturing companies now than in the past produce standardised production-line products. In response to competitive pressures, many companies have become more **flexible** and willing to **adapt products** to specific customer requirements, or to innovate and offer a wider range of products. This has happened at Mentons, which now produces a wider range of products and appears to **innovate continually** in order to remain competitive. However, continuous innovation and changing products mean that the usefulness of standard costing is severely reduced.

   (vi)   Equally, if Mentons strives for continuous improvement, its focus will be on cost reduction rather monitoring performance against a standard cost.

   (vii)   **Absorption costing** has also lost much of its relevance (even though activity-based costing may offer an alternative and more useful approach to the analysis of overhead costs). In manufacturing businesses, labour costs are a smaller proportion of total production costs than they were in the past, and a costing system that apportions overhead costs on the basis of labour time is inappropriate. Some manufacturing companies apply lean manufacturing concepts to their operations: lean concepts include just-in-time purchasing and manufacturing (manufacturing to order and not for inventory), and minimising inventories. One of the few purposes of absorption costing is to obtain a value for work-in-progress and finished goods. When inventories are minimal, an absorption costing system is much too elaborate and costly for this purpose, and its costs exceed its benefits. Simpler methods of inventory valuation can be applied.

         In order to remain useful, management accounting methods have therefore had to change.

(b)   Burns and Scapens suggested the role of the management accountant in organisation has changed, even though the underlying function of the management accountant – to provide useful information to management – has not changed.

         Burns and Scapens suggested three main reasons for the changes in management accounting:

   (i)   **Technology and IT systems** – In the past, **IT systems** were often centralised and offered limited in-line access, such that management accountants had better access to files and information than operational managers.

With developments in IT systems and networks, many organisations have systems that offer access to a much larger number of (authorised) individuals. Operational managers therefore have the same access to much of the information that management accountants have access to, and so management accountants are no longer in a position to 'control' information provision.

The management accountant's value is to prepare useful reports or provide useful information that other managers are not producing themselves, but the accountants often rely on data that has been input to the system by other departments, not the accounts department.

This change has occurred at Mentons. The company now has an integrated IT system and it is probable that operations departments are now responsible for much of the data input. If so, Mentons' management accountants will now be users rather than controllers of accounting data in the system.

(ii) **Management structure** – Burns and Scapens also suggested that **changes in management structure** within organisations have contributed to a change in the role of the management accountant.

Shifts in responsibility – As we noted in the previous point, information technology has developed to the point where operational managers are able to access information on-line and even to prepare information (such as forecasts) themselves. Authority is often delegated, and operational managers are made responsible for preparing their own budgets – something which, historically, was the function of the management accountant. By using available IT software, line managers are now able to **produce their own budgets** and budget control reports or other performance measures.

Therefore, the role of the management accountant has changed so that they now focus on producing information (and analysing the information) that local managers do not produce themselves. For example, the management accountant can give senior management a broader view of the business' performance, by linking financial outcomes with the strategic consequences of the activities which have been undertaken.

This change in responsibility structure has also occurred at Mentons. Authority for operational decisions has largely been delegated to local management and it is probable that the role of the management accountant at each production site has changed as a consequence. However, the management accountant's role in providing senior management with a broader view of the business does not appear to have been recognised at Mentons, which may be why the CEO does not think they can add any value to the business.

(iii) **Competitive environment** – The third reason given by Burns and Scapens for changes in the nature of management accounting was **competition.**

In many markets there has been an increase in competition as a result of the internationalisation of the markets, and so companies have often needed to become more innovative to survive. Competitive advantage is a key to success and survival. In order to compete, management needs to respond to changes in the competitive environment and to consider strategy over the longer term as well as short-term profit. As a result, the need for management information has expanded beyond being solely financial information such that it now includes to **external (competition) information** as well as information that is relevant to **strategy and the long-term** (including non-financial issues).

Management accountants have had to respond to this significant change by providing information from a wider range of sources that includes non-financial as well as financial aspects. Equally, management accountant may need to look at external information, for example either analysing changes in market share, or benchmarking their company's performance against competitors' performance.

This change in the competitive environment is evident at Mentons, where competition from European firms has increased and where Mentons has responded by competing successfully in Europe. Again, however, it is not clear how the performance measures which Mentons monitor have changed to reflect the company's need to respond to competition.

Burns and Scapens suggested that the management accountant must now have a better understanding of **operational matters** as well as costing and other financial matters, and they must work closely with operational management. They suggested that the term 'hybrid accountant' may be more appropriate than 'management accountant'. With the growing importance of competition and strategy, the term 'strategic management accounting' is also sometimes used.

(c) The CEO at Mentons may well be correct to identify that traditional management accounting methods are no longer relevant to the needs of management in the company. However, as Burns and Scapens argued, management accounting has remained valuable to companies because the role of the management accountant has changed from its 'traditional' role into a more strategic role that remains useful and relevant. However, if such a change has not happened at Mentons, then the CEO's claim that the management accountants are not providing value for money would be correct.

Mentons currently has six management accountants, one at each production centre and two at head office. This may be an excessive number, but there is insufficient data to make a judgement on this point.

There are several ways in which management accountants (or 'hybrid accountants') should add value by providing information, either at production site level or at head office.

(i) Mentons' senior management need consolidated performance information for the four production sites, and one of the management accountants' responsibilities should be to provide senior management with the information they need for this purpose. The management accountant can also provide a link between local management and head office, through communications between the local and head office accounting functions.

(ii) Management accountants may have the responsibility for **providing information about competition and markets**, and for providing strategic non-financial as well as financial information; for example, by providing information about Menton's market share or market growth figures. There is no reason why this information function should necessarily be undertaken by accountants, but management accountants should be specialist information providers and may fulfil the function better than anyone else.

It is also the reason why Burns and Scapens commented on the need for the management accountant to become a 'hybrid accountant', with a better knowledge of operational matters and closer integration with operational management.

(iii) There are some specialised aspects of information analysis for which training and experience may help. This is evident **in capital investment appraisal**, and decisions about whether or not to make new capital investments. Standard software can be used to compute a net present value, but specialist knowledge may be required to identify relevant costs and to assess the impact of inflation, risk and uncertainty, (including perhaps) foreign exchange and taxation on the investment.

Overall, management accountants should still be able to make a positive contribution to management at Mentons, through their role as providers and analysers of information. However, to remain valuable their role (as indicated by Burns and Scapens) has had to change, such that they become more involved in providing advice and supporting decision-making in relation to operational aspects of the business, rather than having a role which was solely focussed on controlling financial performance.

Hybrid accountants – The concept of the hybrid accountant reflects the modern model of the accountant's role in a company. The hybrid accountant is someone who has both accounting knowledge and a detailed understanding of the operating functions or commercial processes of their company. So, while the hybrid accountant is part of the finance function, he or she is also increasingly integrated into the operations of the business – in effect spending the majority of their time as a business analyst or an internal consultant for the operating division they work with.

Currently it appears that Mentons still have a traditional, old-fashioned view of the role of the management accountant in a company. However, it is likely that the accountants would make a more valuable contribution to Mentons through adopting a 'hybrid' accountant role, rather than continuing in the traditional role which they currently seem to have.

7 CFD

Text reference. Mission statements, CSFs and the relationship between CSFs and performance metrics are discussed in Chapter 2 of the BPP Study Text. The concept of value for money is discussed in Chapter 11, and non-financial performance indicators are covered in Chapter 12.

Top tips. Part (a) (i) draws on your knowledge of mission statements and their benefits and drawbacks. Begin with a definition. We use Mintzberg's version which nicely contains the elements of a mission. You aren't asked to refer to the scenario which makes it a bit easier as you are just writing down what you know. We have listed thirteen benefits and failings, and ACCA's official answer contained the same number. These are all short one line points so, in this case, the examination team appears to expect many, but brief, responses. The marking scheme gives six marks in total.

In **part (a) (ii)** think about what value for money (VFM) means. Does CFD provide this for its customers? Will the new initiative mean CFD is still providing VFM?

Part (b) (i) is a test of knowledge; so you should define what CSFs and KPIs are, and then explain how they relate to each other. The key point here is that an KPIs need to be used to help an organisation measure how well it is performing in relation to its CSFs.

Part (b) (ii) needs to be related back to CSF; so make sure the three critical success factors you discuss are appropriate for for CFD. Think about which performance requirements are critical to its success and how are these measured.

Quality of service is important in a service business. In **part (c)** think about what you would want to see in terms of quality if you had a pet and wanted to send it to CFD.

Marking scheme

				Marks
(a)	(i)	Purpose	2	
		Potential benefits	3	
		Failings	3	
				8
	(ii)	Changed circumstances Up to 2	2	
		Conclusion Up to 2	2	
				4
(b)	(i)	Definition of CSFs	1	
		Definition of KPIs	1	
		Relationship between CSFs and KPIs	2	
				4
	(ii)	For each CSF discussed – 1 mark	3	
		For KPI highlighted for each CSF – 1 mark	3	
				6
(c)		Performance measures 3 × 1	3	3
			Total =	25

(a)   (i)   **Purpose, potential benefits and potential problems of mission statements**

Purpose

Mission describes the organisation's **basic** function in society, in terms of the products and services it produces for its clients (Mintzberg). Organisations often write down their mission in a mission statement. A **mission statement** should be **brief, flexible and distinctive**, placing an emphasis on serving the customers. It often **refers to key stakeholder groups** including employees and shareholders. The mission statement should make it clear to employees their **contribution** towards attaining the mission. It should also **remain the same** unless the mission changes.

Potential benefits of mission statements include:

- A written, public statement of the reason for the organisation's existence.

- Allied to this, communicate a clear image of what the organisation is to customers and other stakeholders.

- Also help in resolving conflicts between stakeholder groups over what the organisation stands for.

- Identify key cultural values to employees.

- Aid strategy by helping businesses define their nature, services and products and competences.

- Guide policies and standards of behaviour by managers and employees by stating business principles such as social responsibility and anti-discrimination.

- State ways of competing, for instance on price or innovation.

Potential problems of mission statements include:

- Vague statements which don't explain what the business is for or how it intends to achieve its aims.

- Jargon which obscures what the meaning of the statement is.

- Failure to be flexible and open ended as the mission will probably change over time as the business changes.

- Being unrealistic in its aims.

- Not taking account of external factors.

- Inconsistency between the elements of the mission.

(ii) **Appropriateness of the mission statement for CFD**

Value for money is providing a service in a way which is economical, efficient and effective, and so CFD's mission statement would appear to have accorded with its overall mission (as it has operated on a profit-making basis)., and would remain appropriate as long as CFD continued offering its original services, When it decided to open a homeless sanctuary for strays, its mission and services changed and so it needs to recast the mission to include some element capturing the new charitable activity. When CFD decided to undertake this non-profit-making activity, this meant its new aims would not necessarily be profit-making and therefore could not deliver value for money.

(b) (i) **Critical success factors** (CSFs) are the key factors and processes which enable an organisation to achieve its objectives and thereby achieve future success. In effect, CSFs highlight the areas in which it is crucial for an organisation to perform well in order for it to be successful.

CSFs and KPIs – However, once an organisation has identified its CSFs, it needs to know how well it is performing in relation to them. Simply identifying the areas where an organisation needs to perform well does not guarantee that it will do so. Therefore it needs to measure how well it is performing in these areas. This is done by using key performance indicators (KPIs).

Key performance indicators – KPIs are the **measures** which indicate whether or not CSFs are being achieved, and how well the organisation is performing. This idea of measurement is vital for KPIs. KPIs must be measurable, because otherwise an organisation will not be able to measure whether or not its CSFs are being achieved.

(ii)   CFD is a service business and so its CSFs are likely to relate to the services it offers, and in particular to the features of those services which are valued by its customers.

- Maintaining a high standard of cleanliness of accommodation for the dogs at CFD.

  If prospective clients come to visit CFD's kennels and they look dirty and untidy, it is unlikely that the owners will want their pets to stay at CFD.

  A performance indicator which could be used to measure cleanliness could be the number of cleans made per day or week of the dog kennels and common areas.

- Guaranteed safety of the dogs whilst in CFD's care.

  Again, owners are not going to want to use CFD to care for their dogs unless they feel confidents their dogs will be well looked after.

  This could be measured by the number of accidents over a given period.

- An excellent health record. This means no or minimal breakout of infections which would damage the reputation of the business. This could become particularly important if CSF does start accommodating homeless dogs, because if any of the homeless dogs have got infections or diseases it will need to ensure that none of these get transmitted to the pets in its care.

  This could be measured by the number of dogs that fall ill during their time at CFD.

(c)   **Three quantitative non-financial performance measures to assess quality of service**

- **Service availability** may be measured by the number or percentage of owners able to book their dogs in on preferred dates and times.
- **Care taken of the dogs and the quality of the service experience** will be measured in return bookings and possibly word of mouth referral.
- **Prompt and reliable collection and return of dogs to their owners.** This is a key element of the service offered. This could be measured by logs of delivery and return of dogs safely and within the time promised.

8 ZTC Communications

Text reference. The performance hierarchy (objectives, CSFs, and KPIs) is discussed in Chapter 2 of the BPP Studt Text. The impact which stakeholders could have on an organisation is considered in Chapter 5, while the impact of the external environment on an organisation's performnance is considered in Chapter 6.

Top tips. Neither the scenario nor any of the requirements make use of the word 'stakeholder', but it should spring to your mind as soon as you begin thinking about this question. ZTC has some very important new stakeholder groups to consider and their interests will be the main formative influence on what the company sets out to do. Stakeholders will be a major consideration for both part (b) and part (c).

(a)

Top tips. Two models which are useful for analysing the external environment are PEST analysis and Porter's five forces. The external environment is a source of opportunities and threats for an organisation, so, in effect, this question is asking about how opportunities and threats could affect ZTC's performance.

Opportunities and threats – ZTC needs to ensure that it understand the ways in which it is affected by the environment in which it operates. In this context, it needs to consider the wider environmental factors (which could be highlighted by 'PEST' analysis) as well as any factors which relate more specifically to the telecommunications industry (which could be highlighted using Porter's Five Forces model as a guide).

The most significant recent environmental influence on ZTC's performance is likely to have come from a **political factor** – the deregulation of the telecommunications market in Zeeland.

Impact of deregulation – Historically, ZTC held a monopoly position in the telecommunications market in Zeeland. However, now that the market has been deregulated, ZTC's market share is likely to be eroded when new competitors enter the market. Consequently, it seems likely that ZTC will suffer a fall in revenue, at least in the short term until it identifies alternative markets which it could enter as well.

New entrants – It is not clear how many competitors have entered the market so far, but another threat ZTC needs to be aware of is the threat of additional new entrants entering the telecommunications market in Zeeland in future, and potentially reducing its market share further.

> **Telephone networks** – It is likely that ZTC's monopoly was of the fixed line network in Zeeland, rather than mobile telecommunications networks as well. However, it is also likely ZTC will face competition from mobile phone companies.
>
> In this respect, developments in technology (for example, 4G networks) could also boost the performance of mobile phone companies, and thereby increase the level of competition ZTC is facing.

Overall market growth – The scenario does not indicate whether the telecommunications market overall in Zeeland is growing, or if it is, how high the growth rate is.

However, this will also have an effect on ZTC's performance. For example, if the market is growing rapidly, this could help reduce the impact on ZTC's revenues of its market share declining.

Similarly, if the **global market** is growing significantly, this could provide opportunities for revenue growth. It appears that one of the government's motives behind the deregulation was to make ZTC more competitively internationally, and so the state of the global market is likely to be important for its future performance.

Customer bargaining power – Another consequence of the deregulation is that customers in Zeeland now have increased bargaining power in relation to ZTC. Previously, as ZTC was the sole supplier, customers had little or no bargaining power over it. However, now that there is increased choice in the market, customers' bargaining power has increased significantly, because if ZTC's tariffs are not competitive against other providers, or its standards of customer service are poor, customers will be able to switch to one of the competitors in the market.

> **Employees** – The deregulation of the market could also affect ZTC's relationship with its employees. In effect, it could increase their bargaining power as suppliers. Previously, telecommunications engineers in Zeeland could only work for ZTC; but it is likely that in future there will be a choice of companies they could work for. Therefore, ZTC will need to ensure that its rewards package is competitive so that it retains its best staff.

(b)

> **Top tips.** It is necessary to deploy a little knowledge of the public sector in order to answer this requirement properly. Simply saying what the new objectives should be will not be enough: it is necessary to think in terms of change and this implies some consideration of what the company's objectives were before privatisation.
>
> Don't overlook the demands of corporate governance; this is about both what is to be done and also how it should be done.
>
> The solution below adopts a stakeholder approach. An alternative approach would be to make a series of points related to the primacy of profit in a commercial firm compared to a state monopoly, the need to hold market share at home, the need to gain sales revenues by expanding product range and providing services abroad, and the need to protect its share price by good corporate governance and adequate communication with investors.

As a state monopoly, ZTC's role was expressed in terms of its service to the nation of Zeeland as a whole. Its focus was on the public sector aspirations of **efficiency, effectiveness and economy**, but it was not subject to market discipline and its finances were controlled by government. The lack of market input and the highly technical nature of its operations make it likely that its main operational concern was **engineering competence**, rather than customer interests. However, the government, as principal stakeholder, imposed requirements around performance and service levels to be achieved.

Shareholders as new stakeholders

ZTC now has a new and important class of stakeholder in the form of its shareholders. They will have firm ideas about their requirements in the form of growth, earnings and dividends.

Importance of customers

The company faces a de-regulated market where competition will intensify. It will need to pay great attention to the views and needs of its customers; they are a stakeholder group that is likely to wield far more influence than previously, since they will be able to choose new suppliers when new providers of telecommunications services enter the market following its deregulation.

Impact on objectives

These influences will affect objectives at all levels in the organisation and will require a significant realignment of attitudes. In particular, there will be pressure to reduce costs; to develop new and attractive products; and to improve customer service, particularly in the matter of installing new equipment and dealing with faults.

The respective requirements of shareholders and customers also highlight a potential conflict which will need to be addressed by the directors when setting the company's objectives.

Shareholders will want to maximise profitability which may be achieved by raising prices. But customers will seek the lowest price they can get.

Although the government is no longer the main external stakeholder, it will still be interested in ZTC's performance. The company will continue to make a large contribution to the economy of Zeeland as a major employer and taxpayer; it also has the potential to develop as a major centre of technological excellence.

While the government will step back from direct involvement in the running of ZTC, it is likely that it will retain an interest in its overall success, and possibly a closer involvement in such matters as the promotion of technological development and overseas expansion, which if successful could increase ZTC's tax liability to the government.

Corporate governance

A final influence on the strategic objectives of the privatised company will arise in the field of corporate governance. As a quoted company, ZTC will be subject to the normal regulations and codes of practice laid down by its quoting stock exchange. It may also be subject to special government regulation designed to prevent it from using its size and current dominant position to discourage competitors. These influences are also likely to have a marked effect on the directors' attitudes and practices.

Overall, the objectives of ZTC will need to change to focus on profitability and shareholder reward, as well as customer satisfaction which becomes increasingly important in a deregulated market. Alongside this, the directors will need to ensure the business' controls and governance are adequate to comply with its new regulatory requirements.

(c)

> **Top tips.** You must think carefully here. First, note that you are not being asked for a mission statement: the objectives you select must be strategic (long term, not short term), but they can be very specifically aimed at particular aspects of strategy. Approaching the problem from the stakeholder angle would be a good way to proceed here, but make sure you explain why the objective is appropriate to ZTC.
>
> The second important point is that the objectives you provide must be SMART.
>
> However, note (c) is only worth four marks so do not spend too long on this requirement.

Objective 1

To achieve an average of 5% annual growth in share valuation for the next five years or until competitors achieve a total of 25% market share.

This objective is relevant to the concerns of shareholders. It is specific, measurable and time-bound. It is also realistic, in that it acknowledges that the company's existing privileged position is likely to be damaged by the entry of competitors into its markets.

Objective 2

To create, within twelve months, an affordable and humane restructuring plan that will reduce staff costs by 20% and to implement the plan over the following three years without provoking a major labour dispute.

This objective addresses the continuing strategic need for cost efficiency to allow ZTC to compete effectively in a deregulated market. It recognises the need to balance that need against the interests of the existing employees and the practical difficulties of implementing a headcount reduction.

(d)

> **Top tips.** Although the question requirement doesn't specify that the CSFs you recommend need to relate to the objectives you have identified in part (c), it seems sensible to identify CSFs that link to these objectives. However, make sure you identify CSFs and not KPIs (which are the measures ZTC could then use to assess how well it is performing against its CSFs).
>
> Also, before you recommend your TWO CSFs you need to explain briefly the link between objectives and CSFs in general terms.

Once an organisation has established its objectives, it needs to identify the key factors and processes that will enable it to achieve those objectives. These key factors are its critical success factors. In effect, the CSFs are the building blocks which will enable an organisation to implement its mission and thereby achieve future success.

In an effective organisation, the factors that are crucial to success will influence all aspects of its operations, especially those relating to people. For example, if a company identifies excellent customer service as a CSF, then its recruitment process, training, appraisal and reward systems should all be geared towards promoting customer-service skills in its staff.

However, once an organisation has identified its CSFs, it also needs to know whether it is delivering on them. This is done by using KPIs, which measure how well the organisation is performing against its CSFs. The KPIs are the hard data which tells the organisation how well it is performing.

The change in ZTC's circumstances and the increased competition for market share highlights the importance of delivering value to customers. Therefore two appropriate CSFs for ZTC could be:

Customer satisfaction – ZTC must be able to keep its existing client base happy. ZTC's share price will affected, in part at least, by the company's financial performance, and the number of customers ZTC retains will have a significant influence on this. Ensuring customers are satisfied with the products and service which ZTC offers them will be vital in ensuring they remain ZTC's customers rather than switching to one of its rivals.

Competitive prices – Now that the market has been deregulated, ZTC faces competition from national and international rivals. This suggests that customers will have a relatively high degree of choice for what appears to be a fairly undifferentiated product (telephone services). Therefore the ability to compete on price will be important to ZTC's success.

9 Stayzee Hotels

(a)   **Performance measures for the Shepham hotel**

	Per day		Per year	
	20X4	20X1	20X4	20X1
Number of rooms occupied	141	117	51,465	42,705
Revenue	9,165	10,530	3,345,225	3,843,450
Service costs	846	995	308,790	362,993
Promotion & marketing costs	458	790	167,261	288,259
Other operating costs (*balancing figure*)	6,963	7,724	2,541,342	2,819,384
Net profit margin	9.8%	9.7%	9.8%	9.7%
Net profit (*EBIT*)	898	1,021	327,832	372,815
Total assets (*EBIT/ROI*)			2,927,072	3,389,224

Long-term objectives – Stayzee's long-term objectives are focused around growth: increasing market share in its home country and then expanding into neighbouring countries.

However, in order to achieve this, it will be important for the reputation of Stayzee's hotels (for high quality accommodation and service) to be maintained.

Manager's focus – The example of the Shepham hotel illustrates that managers could be driven by shorter-term goals, such as achieving their annual bonuses. The figures illustrate that occupancy rates and net profit margin in the Shepham hotel have increased between 20X1 – 20X4, meaning that the new manager is more likely to receive a bonus than the previous one.

Sacrificing long-term objectives – However, the ways in which the manager has increased occupancy rates and the net profit margin (%) do not appear to be aligned with Stayzee's longer term objectives.

Occupancy rates – The manager appears to have increased occupancy rates by significantly discounting the price of the rooms. Although discounting the price of the rooms may increase occupancy in the short term, if it leads to the hotel being perceived more like a budget hotel than a high quality hotel, this could be detrimental to Stayzee's brand and reputation in the longer term. In turn, this could hamper Stayzee's expansion plans.

Cuttting costs – The way the manager appears to have maintained the Shepham hotel's net profit margin (despite the discounted room rates) is by reducing the hotel's running costs. Again, however, this is a short-term approach, which could be detrimental in the longer-term – both to the individual hotel and to the Stayzee group as a whole.

Customer feedback already suggests that the reduction in the amount spent on servicing and cleaning the guest rooms has led to them becoming dirty. More generally, the overall reduction in operating costs is likely to have contributed to the decline in customer service; for example, if the number of staff has been reduced.

Postponing capital expenditure – The reduction in the value of total assets suggests that the manager has restricted the amount of capital invested on fixtures and fittings; for example, in relation to buying new beds or mattresses for the rooms to replace ones which are getting worn out. Again, customer feedback suggests this lack of expenditure will be damaging to the hotel in the longer term, because guests will not want to stay there again.

Marketing and promotions – The manager also appears to have significantly reduced the amount of expenditure on marketing and promotion. Again, it seems that this has been driven by his desire to boost net profit margins in the short term. However, a failure to promote the hotel is likely to lead to a fall in the number of guests in the longer term, and therefore is not consistent with Stayzee's objectives for growth.

'What gets measured, gets done' – The decisions taken by the manager of the Shepham hotel seem to illustrate the phrase that 'What gets measured, gets done.' The manager knows that his bonus depends on occupancy rates, and net profit margin, and he appears to have focused solely on these aspects of performance. However, while the results for both of these measures have increased under the current manager compared to the old manager, the hotel's performance in other crucial areas (like customer satisfaction) appears to have deteriorated significantly.

Manager's autonomy – The manager's focus on selected aspects of short-term performance highlights a **lack of goal congruence** between his objectives and those of the Stayzee group as a whole.

The scope for conflict between managers focusing on short-term performance and the group's overall objectives is increased by the relative autonomy given to the individual hotel managers. For example, there do not appear to be any restrictions on the extent to which managers can adjust room rates. Therefore, a manager has the scope to alter the market position of his hotel by charging room rates which would normally be expected in a budget hotel rather than a high quality hotel.

(b) **Competitive strategy** – As we noted in part (a), Stayzee appears to be competing on the basis of the **high quality** of its accommodation facilities, and the high quality of the service it offers its guests. In this respect, it appears to be pursuing a **differentiation** strategy, based on quality.

Therefore, ensuring that guests receive the quality of accommodation and service which they expect from a stay in a Stayzee hotel is likely to be a **critical success factor** for the group.

Quality measures – However, none of Stayzee's performance indicators appear to measure quality, or customers' perception of the quality of their visit to the hotels. For example, Stayzee does not appear to measure **customer satisfaction ratings**. Yet these could be a valuable way of monitoring how well the hotels are delivering the levels of quality which customers expect. Moreover, it appears that at least some of Stayzee's guests are willing to provide such ratings because they are already doing so through online review sites such as TripAdvisor.

Focus on cost – By contrast, two of the six performance indicators focus specifically on costs: the servicing costs for rooms; and advertising and promotion costs.

A focus on cost might initially appear to be more suitable for a cost leadership strategy. However, companies which pursue differentiation strategies still need to monitor and control their costs. It is not clear what the cost figures in Stayzee's performance indicators are compared against, but, for example, if the costs for room servicing were compared against a target cost per room, this could still be a valuable indicator for a firm pursuing a differentiation strategy.

Maximising profits – Whichever competitive strategy it pursuing, Stayzee will do so with the aim of maximising its profits. In this respect, a potential weakness in the performance indicators is that they only look at net profit margin, without any reference to the net profit figure. As the figures for Shepham illustrate, the net profit margin increased slightly from 20X1 to 20X4, although the net profit actually fell by 12%. In this respect, it could be useful to also include the actual net profit figure (or an indication of how the net profit compares to prior year) as well as the margin.

Similarly, the current indicators do not make it easy to see how revenue has actually changed. For the Shepham hotel, although occupancy rates have increased, the greater than proportional reduction in room rates mean that total revenue has fallen. In this respect, a performance indicator showing revenue per available room could also be useful.

Return on investment – It seems likely that Stayzee will need to upgrade the fixtures and fittings in its hotels regularly to ensure it maintains the high quality of accommodation which its guests expect. However, including 'Return on investment' as a key performance indicator may discourage managers from doing so; because the increase in the cost of assets will lead to a fall in return on investment, even if EBIT remains constant from one year to the next.

Market growth – A key part of Stayzee's strategic plan is to expand its market share. In order to monitor how well it is achieving this, Stayzee needs to measure its revenues (or the number of rooms booked) in comparison to the total for its country. However, because the current performance indicators focus solely on internal measures of performance, they cannot provide any insight as to how well Stayzee is performing relative to the rest of the hotel sector.

Occupancy rates – It is possible that Stayzee could be using occupancy rates to help measure its growth. If its hotels regularly have empty rooms, one way in which Stayzee could increase its market share is by ensuring it fills all its hotels to maximum capacity. In effect, this could be seen as a market penetration strategy.

Nonetheless, because occupancy rates are only an internal measure of performance, they still don't give any insight into how they are affecting Stayzee's market share.

10 Drinks Group

Text reference. Different approaches to budgeting are discussed in Chapter 3 of the BPP Study Text.

Top tips.

Part (a). A sensible approach to this question might be to think about the benefits and drawbacks of incremental budgeting in general terms, and then think how these would affect its suitability for each of the different divisions. For example, the scenario identifies that F is growing quite rapidly, so how would this affect the suitability of incremental budgeting in F?

The question specifically asks about its suitability at 'each division' so it is important that you deal with the different divisions in turn, although the similarities between S and H mean you could look at them together.

Part (b). Up to 6 out of the 8 marks available here were for calculations, so this part of the question should have offered you some easy marks. However, it is important you apply the information given in the scenario correctly; for example, noting that administrative costs are fixed, although cost of sales and distribution costs are variable.

Also, remember that because you now have actual figures for Quarter 1 of the current year, the rolling budget should include budgeted figures for Quarter 1 of the next year.

Finally, note that not all the marks in this part of the question are available for calculations; so you still need to comment on the potential benefits (or drawbacks) of using rolling budgets for F.

Part (c). One of the key issues highlighted in the scenario is that the managers of the manufacturing divisions are very doubtful about the value which M adds. Therefore, to try to remove these doubts, the approach to budgeting in M needs to be one which challenges and justifies any proposed expenditure before it is approved. On this basis, zero-based budgeting would seem to be appropriate.

Part (d). The context of this question is the contrast between top-down budgeting (with little participation) and bottom-up budgeting (which involves much greater participation).

However, a useful way to approach this part of the question could be to think how the degree of participation changes in the different types of budget you have considered in parts (a), (b) and (c).

DG's current (incremental) approach appears to be essentially a top-down process with little participation from the divisions. This could provide your analysis of the current level of participation (and if DG decides to retain incremental budgeting in the S and H divisions, a top-down approach could remain appropriate there).

But could DG successfully introduce rolling budgets or zero-based budgeting (in F and M respectively) without having a greater degree of involvement from divisional managers? Consequently, what level of participation will be appropriate at DG in the future?

Examining team's comments. Candidates are reminded that budgeting is a core topic, and candidates will be expected to know the relative merits of different methods of budgeting, and how to apply them in a scenario.

In part (a), some candidates seemed to assume that because incremental budgeting was being questioned it must be flawed for all the divisions, and they then sought reasons to justify this well. This is a poor approach to any question, however, because it pre-judges the outcome without any consideration of the evidence given in the scenario. In this case, incremental budgeting would actually be appropriate at the stable H and S divisions.

Candidates generally performed well in part (b) although many did not bother to prepare the new quarter's figures which keep the budget rolling forward. As a result they missed out on some easy marks.

In general, part (c) was answered poorly, and candidates were unable to identify the relevant circumstances at M (such as the project-based nature of marketing activity) which suggest possible budgeting methods.

For part (d) most candidates identified the current level of participation in the budgeting process, although some candidates assumed that the current process was all top-down – ignoring the fact that division managers have input into growth estimates. The best candidates realised that, as different budget methods would be appropriate for the different divisions, the level of participation in each division would also vary, depending on the budget method.

Marking scheme

		Marks
(a)	Evaluation of the advantages and disadvantages of incremental budgeting in general – 1 mark per relevant point	Up to 5
	Recommendations about the suitability of incremental budgeting in S and H division – 1 mark per relevant point	Up to 3
	Discussion about the suitability of incremental budgeting for F – 1 mark per relevant point	Up to 3
	Discussion about the suitability of incremental budgeting for M – 1 mark per relevant point	Up to 3
		8

(b)	Explanation of the rolling budget process – 1 mark per relevant point	Up to 2	
	Calculations (up to 6 marks in total for calculations):		
	Actual figures in Q1	1	
	Revenue; Cost of Sales; Distribution costs; Administration costs; Operating profit – 1 mark for correct figures for each line in the budget	Up to 4	
	Budgeted figures for Q1 in the next year	1	
	Comments on the use of rolling budgets at F – 1 mark per relevant point	Up to 3	
			8
(c)	Recommendation of an appropriate method (1 mark), plus 1 mark per valid point justifying the choice of method	3	3
(d)	Explanation of top-down vs bottom-up budgeting – 1 mark per relevant point	Up to 2	
	Evaluation of use of bottom-up control at DG, and its impact on current processes	Up to 6	
			6
		Total =	25

(a) **Incremental budgeting**

Advantages

Not too time-consuming – DG currently uses incremental budgets. One of the main advantages of incremental budgets is that they are relatively quick and easy to prepare. This is a general advantage at DG given the time constraints which the finance department is currently experiencing in relation to the Information Systems implementation.

Stable environment – Incremental budgets are also appropriate for stable environments, where current or historic figures can provide a reliable basis for projecting future figures, and where only small changes are required to those figures.

Disadvantages

Accepts inefficiencies – A major problem with incremental budgets is that, by their nature, they reinforce existing practices. The fact that the FD has identified that the most promising area for performance improvement lies in better internal control practices suggests that there are inefficiencies in DG's current processes, which are likely to be reflected in its current figures. However, by basing future years' budget on the current figures, these inefficiencies will be perpetuated rather than challenged. Consequently, for example, DG may miss opportunities to make cost savings.

Can encourage spending – Similarly, managers may feel they have to spend the full amount of their current year's budget in order to preserve the same level of budget next year, even though the expenditure may not actually be required at the moment. Once again, such an approach could lead to DG's costs being unnecessarily high.

H and S divisions

Stable markets – Both H and S divisions are in stable markets. The fact that sales growth is unlikely suggests that incremental budgeting could be appropriate for them.

Moreover, such an approach would fit with the managers' preference for maintaining existing practices rather than changing them.

Margin improvements – Because H and S have limited opportunities to increase revenues, in order to increase their profitability they will need to improve their margins. However, incremental budgeting will not be suitable to help them do this.

In order to improve their margins, the divisions will need to challenge and reduce their costs. However, by basing future budgets on current figures, an incremental approach will not provide the stimulus for continuous improvement which is required.

F division

Rapid growth – F's rate of growth means an incremental approach is unlikely to be suitable for it. Its rapid growth means that budgets based on current results will quickly become out of date.

The customer complaints and the managers' complaints could both be symptoms of the constraints which incremental budgets have placed on the business. For example, the complaints about late deliveries and poor quality could result from F trying to satisfy rapidly increasing demand and in the face of budgetary constraints – which mean it either doesn't have sufficient capacity to keep pace with demand or it has to use poorer quality materials in order to reduce material costs.

The managers' complaints pick up on this point further. If the cost budgets have been set in line with current levels of demand, they are unlikely to be sufficient to cope with the higher levels of demand.

M division

Justifying costs – The managers of the manufacturing divisions are sceptical of the need for a marketing department and using an incremental budget will not do anything to change their opinion of this.

The current budgetary approach at M (simply adding a percentage to the current year's expenditure) doesn't require M to justify its spending. Until it does this, however, it seems unlikely that M will be able to change the other division's perceptions of it.

Perhaps more importantly though, simply adding a percentage to the current year's spend could lead to unjustified expenditure. For example, if the marketing division commits some expenditure this year on the basis that it is currently within budget rather than the expenditure will add value for DG, next year's budget will be uplifted from the higher figure. Under such circumstances, the budget will continuously be higher than it needs to be. Again, this would justify the other managers' scepticism about the amount of value M adds to the company.

(b) Under a rolling budget, another accounting period is added to the budget when the most recent one finishes. The budget is then recalculated using the actual data from the most recent period as a basis.

Because Fizzy (F) division's budget is based on a quarterly basis, the rolling budget will include actual figures for Quarter 1 of the current year, and then forecasts for Quarters 2 – 4 of the current year, along with Quarter 1 of the following year.

Based on the assumption that cost of sales and distribution costs increase in line with sales, and that administration costs remain fixed as in the original budget, F's rolling budget would be as follows:

	Q1	Q2	Q3	Q4	**TOTAL**	Q1
	$'000	$'000	$'000	$'000	**$'000**	$'000
	Actual	Forecast	Forecast	Forecast	**Forecast**	Forecast
Revenue	17,932	18,470	19,024	19,595	**75,021**	20,183
Cost of sales	(9,863)	(10,159)	(10,464)	(10,778)	**(41,264)**	(11,101)
Gross profit	8,069	8,311	8,560	8,817	**33,757**	9,082
Distribution costs	(1,614)	(1,662)	(1,712)	(1,764)	**(6,752)**	(1,817)
Administration costs	(4,214)	(4,214)	(4,214)	(4,214)	**(16,856)**	(4,214)
Operating profit	2,241	2,435	2,634	2,840	**10,149**	3,051

As we noted in part (a), F is growing rapidly, and the rolling budget gives F's managers the scope to increase their variable costs to reflect that growth, rather than being constrained by the original budget.

As a result, F should be better able to sustain its growth, and the level of complaints about late deliveries and poor quality (which could otherwise jeopardise its growth) should be reduced.

Moreover, the rolling budget should provide managers with more realistic targets against which to compare actual performance. In this way, the rolling budget provides a more effective control mechanism than an annual budget, which could potentially be disregarded as being out of date.

It is likely that additional resources in the finance department will be required to prepare rolling budgets, because updated budgets will need to be prepared each quarter rather than on an annual basis as they currently are. However, the benefits which F's managers would derive from having rolling budgets should outweigh the additional costs incurred to prepare them.

(c) **Justifying expenditure** – The scepticism from the managers of the manufacturing divisions about the need for a marketing department (M), in conjunction with the Board's requirement that M's costs should be carefully controlled, suggests that an incremental budget may not provide a robust enough framework for M.

Zero based budgeting – By contrast, a zero-based budgeting approach may be appropriate, and this is the approach recommended for M.

As each marketing campaign is run as an individual project, it seems more appropriate M to budget for the campaigns on a project-by-project basis. A zero-based budget approach would provide a suitable framework for doing this, with the cost of each campaign having to be justified at the start before the campaign is approved.

Under a zero-based budget, M would need to justify every cost which is required for a specific marketing campaign. If a cost element cannot be justified, then no resources will be allocated to it in the budget.

Tighter control – Such an approach should also appease the managers of the manufacturing divisions because it will mean that marketing expenditure is being much more tightly controlled.

(d) **Top-down budgeting**

In a top-down budgeting environment, budget figures are essentially imposed on operational managers and other budget holders by senior management. Operational managers have very little participation in the budgeting process.

Limited participation – The divisional managers at DG do appear to have some input into the budget process because they discuss the market growth estimates with the head office finance managers before the budgets are prepared.

However, the budgeting process still appears essentially top-down, and this appears to be causing resentment about the divisional managers – particularly the F managers who want to be less controlled by constraints "imposed" by the Board.

Bottom-up control

In contrast to top-down budgeting, a bottom-up approach would allow divisional managers **much greater participation** in preparing and setting their own budgets.

This would appear to be the approach which the F managers want, because their greater participation in setting the budgets should mean they feel "less controlled" by the Board.

Improved motivation – If the divisional managers have a greater sense of ownership of the budgets, this should also increase their motivation to achieve the budget targets.

Accountability – Equally, if managers are going to be held accountable for their performance against budget targets, it seems fair that they should have some input into setting those targets; for example, so that they think they are realistic.

Improved decision-making – Moreover, the divisional managers at DG should have a more detailed knowledge of their markets than the Board. Therefore, by allowing the managers to participate in the budgeting process, the quality of decision-making and budgeting may also be improved. In this respect, a bottom-up approach would benefit DG as a whole, not just the divisional managers.

Similarly, if the divisional managers do more of the work to prepare the budgets, this means the budgeting process is less onerous for the senior management team, which allows them more time to spend on other matters.

BPP
LEARNING MEDIA

Levels of participation

Overall control – At DG, the budget system in each business is the main method of central control. Therefore the Board needs to ensure that the budgets remain in line with overall corporate objectives, and are not too easily achieved.

Consequently, it appears that an approach which combines aspects of both top-down and bottom-up budgeting would appear to be most appropriate for DG.

It is important that the managers are involved in the budget-setting process, because their own personal targets are set around achieving the relevant budget numbers.

Equally, however, it is important that head office should also be involved, to ensure that the budgets fit with DG's overall strategic objectives and that budget targets remaining challenging.

Also, it is debatable how far the managers of H and S division will voluntarily drive down costs without close monitoring from the head office. In this respect, the Board may decide that the control which is imposed by a top-down approach is still required in relation to these two divisions, and therefore the level of participation for these two divisions will be lower than for the other two divisions.

Rolling budgets – If DG introduces rolling budgets for F, the process of preparing these budgets should be delegated to the divisional managers. On the one hand this is due to the resource constraints within the finance department, but on the other it is because the divisional managers should be more aware of changes in the market which need to be reflected in the updated figures. However, senior finance staff should still review the budgets, and the underlying assumptions behind them, to ensure they seem reasonable.

Zero-based budgeting – If M adopts zero-based budgeting, divisional managers will have a crucial role to play in the budgeting process, because they will need to assess what activities and expenditure are required to support each campaign.

11 Godel

Text reference: Different approaches to budgeting and different types of budget variance are discussed in Chapter 3 of the BPP Study Text. (The 'PRIME' mnemonic for summarising the purposes of budgets is covered in Chapter 1.)

Top tips.

Part (a). It is important that you focus specifically on the planning and operational variances here rather than discussing the variances shown in the operating statement more generally. As such, the figures you need to be looking are those shown in the 'Detailed variances' at the bottom of the operating statement.

Part (b). The requirement here is to 'evaluate' the budgeting system. An 'evaluation' should include both the advantage and the disadvantages of the system. As the examining team's comments (below) indicate, if you are asked to evaluate something, it is important that you give a balanced argument – and don't focus only on the advantages or the disadvantages.

One possible way of approaching this requirement would be to use 'PRIME' as a framework for your answer, and to evaluate how well the budget reflects the elements of 'PRIME' - planning, responsibility, motivating, evaluating performance. (This is the approach we have used in our suggested solution.)

Part (c). Note the verb here is also 'evaluate' – so, you need to consider what the potential benefits from moving to a bottom-up approach might be, but also what factors may limit those benefits or make it an unsuitable approach.

Importantly, you need to think not only about the context of the scenario here (for example, Godel's command-and-control management style), but also your evaluation of the current approach to budgeting – in part (b). If Godel is going to change its approach to budgeting, it will only be worth doing so if the new approach helps to address the problems with its current system. But does it?

There is an important general point to note here. Just because the FD has proposed a change in the approach, this doesn't necessarily mean the change is appropriate.

Marking scheme

		Marks

(a) Definitions of planning and operational variances – 1 mark

Advice about planning and operational elements of total variable cost variances – up to 3 marks

Advice about planning and operational elements of sales price variance – up to 3 marks

Total for part (a): up to 6

6

(b) Benefits of budgeting for Godel – 1 mark per relevant point – up to a maximum of 6

Points could include:

- Planning and co-ordination – meeting overall strategy
- Responsibility
- Integration
- Motivation
- Evaluation of performance

Problems with budgeting at Godel – 1 mark per relevant point – up to a maximum of 6

Points could include:

- Time-consuming and unnecessary
- Lack of recognition of planning failures
- Insufficient planning and operational analysis
- Impedes continuous improvement

Total for part (b): up to 12

12

(c) Description of bottom-up budgeting – up to 2 marks

Evaluation of appropriateness of bottom-up budgeting for Godel - up to 6 marks

Total for part (c): up to 7

7

Total = 25

(a) **Planning variances** result from the assumptions or standards used in the original budget setting process not being accurate. For example, if the original budget assumed that sales prices would be increased by 2%, but market conditions have meant that sales prices could only be increased by 1%, the resulting sales price variance should be treated as a planning variance.

In effect, a planning variance is the difference between the original budget and the budget as it would have been revised with the benefit of hindsight.

Operational variances, in effect, are the differences between this 'revised' budget, and actual performance. Operational variances result from the decisions of operational managers, rather than issues with the original budget-setting process.

Variable cost variance

The total variable cost variance considers a number of costs together, and so it is unlikely that any gains or problems highlighted by it can be attributed to one individual. As such, the variable cost variance has little use for Godel, although highlighting the total variance could, in turn, identify the need for more detailed analysis to identify the specific causes of the variance.

The $20,680 favourable planning variance suggests that the standard costs have been set too high, and therefore most of the apparent cost improvements are due to this. Compared to the planning variance, the operational variance is very low ($580) which suggests that the operational managers have had little impact in driving down costs in the month.

Sales price variance

The sales price variance indicates the extent to which sales prices were incorrectly estimated in the budget (planning variances) and how effective the sales managers have been in negotiating higher prices with customers (operational variances).

The adverse planning variance ($15,600) suggests that the original budget was too optimistic in the initial price it set for Godel's sweets. However, the favourable operational variance ($6,640) suggests that the sales managers have been quite successful in their price negotiations with customers, although not successful enough to overcome the advsere planning variance.

The initial price-setting process should be examined, to identify why prices were budgeted too high. For example, Godel's market intelligence about the prices being set by competitors, or the commercial situation of its customers (the supermarkets) may have been faulty.

(b)   **Cost control** – Godel's competitive strategy is based on it being a cost leader, and therefore it will be very important for the company to control its costs effectively.

The budgeting system provides a mechanism for monitoring costs, and overall it seems that Godel is being successful in controlling its costs – as its total costs show a favourable variance.

Planning - More generally, budgets can be used to help communicate and co-ordinate all the management activities within Godel towards its overall strategic plan – minimising costs, and winning supermarkets' business.

Responsibility – The budget can also help to attribute responsibility for performance, and to identify which managers are responsible for which costs. For example, the favourable material usage variance indicates that fewer raw materials were required than planned, which suggests the production manager has been able to reduce waste and/or improve the efficiency of the production process.

Motivation – Although the managers do not appreciate the time taken by the budgeting process, the standard costs and assumptions being used in the budget are nonetheless discussed with them before being included in the budgets. The fact that the managers have the chance to participate in the budget process should help to motivate them to achieve the budget figures set.

In particular, it is important that managers are given the chance to identify any areas of the budget which they think are not realistic or achievable – otherwise the budget will become demotivating to the managers and their teams.

The CEO's feeling that there is no dysfunctional behaviour at Godel, and that all the managers are working in the best interests of the company, suggests that the budgeting system is not damaging motivation, even if it is not necessarily doing anything to enhance it.

Evaluation – Budgets assist performance evaluation by identifying variances which can then be analysed and investigated. This is particularly important for areas where actual performance is adverse to budget, to enable corrective action to be taken to improve future performance.

At Godel, sales are under-performing the budget both in terms of volume and price. However, more favourably, labour costs are considerably under budget – with the favourable labour 'efficiency' variance suggesting that staff are working efficiently.

Problems with Godel's budgeting system

Although the top-down nature of Godel's budgeting system fits with the organisation's strategy and management style, nonetheless there are still several problems with it.

Time-consuming – The nature of Godel's business – in a mature market, and with little scope for innovation or new product development – suggests that budget-setting should not be a complex process. However, the managers' complaints that it is very time-consuming process.

The managers may be exaggerating here, and their complaints may be more of an indication of the fact that the budgets ultimately have limited value to them (because the operational variances are relatively small), and therefore they do not want to spend much time preparing them.

Nonetheless, there appears to be a danger that Godel's current budgeting system may have become more complicated than it needs to be.

Planning variances – The bulk of the variances at Godel relate to planning variances, rather than operational variances. This reinforces the suggestion that there is little point spending lots of time on the operational aspects of the budget, but, instead, more time could be spend analysing the external factors with a view to reducing the level of planning variances.

Responsibility – The fact that the operational managers are frequently asked to explain variances which are not their fault suggests that the distinction between operational and planning variances needs to be more extensive.

Currently, the analysis between operational and planning variance is quite limited in scope. However, for example, instead of only analysing the total cost variance into operational and planning variances, some of the main cost headings in the operating statement could also be analysed in this way, so that managers are only held responsible for the operational variances.

No incentive to reduce cost – Although the CEO does not believe the managers build slack into their budgets, the use of standard costing nevertheless does not provide any incentives for them to try to reduce costs further. Given Godel's strategy as a cost leader, it would be beneficial to it if the budget system encouraged a system of continuous improvements in relation to efficiency gains and cost reductions.

However, given the mature nature of the business, Godel's senior management may feel that it is unlikely there will be a need to update budgeted costs on a regular basis and that a review of them once a year is sufficient.

(c) **Bottom-up budgeting**

The FD's suggestion is a response to managers' complaints that the current varianaces are not their fault, and so it appears that the FD's intention is to make the managers more accountable for variances, and more motivated to achieve their budgets.

Typically, the arguments in favour of bottom-up budgeting are: that managers should be motivated to achieve their budgets if they have been involved in setting them; and that operational managers should have better knowledge than senior management of the conditions their business units face, meaning that the resulting budgets should be more realistic and achievable.

However, the nature of Godel's business and culture means that bottom-up budgeting may not be appropriate or beneficial.

Fit with culture – The operational managers already discuss the budget assumptions and standard costs, but do so without having the responsibility of producing the budget. Managers are therefore already involved in the budget-setting process, but in a way which fits with the 'command-and-control' management style at Godel. Moving to a bottom-up approach does not appear to fit with this style.

Resistance to change – The fact that many of Godel's employees have worked for the company for many years, could mean that they will be uncomfortable with the change. Equally, if the managers – like most of Godel's employees – like the straightforward nature of their work, they may resent the additional burden of having to prepare their own budgets. Conversely, however, some managers may welcome the change if they feel it will give them more control over their budgets.

Time-consuming – T If the managers have to produce the budgets themselves, this is likely to increase their complaints about the budget process being time-consuming. Similarly, the managers could complain that the increased amounts of time they have to spend preparing budgets is reducing the time they have available for other aspects of their roles.

Dysfunctional behaviour – As the CEO has noted, the current, top-down approach to budgeting means there is no dysfunctional behaviour, as represented by budget slack or excessive spending. However, bottom-up budgeting could increase the risk of dysfunctional behaviour as operational managers will focus on the individual concerns of their business area rather than Godel's overall corporate objectives. Equally, managers may create budgetary slack, and set targts which are too easy to achieve – although any targets which are obviously too easy should be challenged when the drafts budgets are reviewed centrally.

Contollability – Most importantly, perhaps, even though the managers have set the budgets, they are still likley to argue, justifiably, that some of the variances they have to explain are not their fault. The proposed changes do not address the weakness in the lack of distinction between operational and planning variances (which we highlighted in part (b)).

Godel's sales are dependent on the state of the general economy and competitive forces – factors which are outside the control of operational managers. Therefore, operational managers cannot be held responsible for variances resulting from unforeseen changes in the level of sales.

Therefore, reiterating the point made in part (b), rather than changing the way the budgets are prepared, a more useful improvement to Godel's performance management systems would be to distinguish the main cost variances into operational and planning variances.

12 Booxe

Text reference. Business process re-engineering is discussed in Chapter 4 of the BPP Study Text. Appraisals and human resource management more generally are discussed in Chapter 14.

Top tips.

Part (a) – Although the requirement here was to 'Assess the financial impact' of the project, the majority of the six marks available were for calculations, and should have proved relatively easy marks to score.

Perhaps the most obvious way to assess the impact of the project is through a cost benefit analysis – and this is the approach we have used in the suggested solution below. However, the marking guide indicated that using other methods – such as payback period or accounting rate of return would have been equally acceptable.

The crucial point to identify from the calculations is that the benefits significantly outweigh the costs over the life of the project (eight years), but you only need to write a couple of sentences after the calculations to explain this. There are only six marks in total for this part of the question – so there isn't time for a lengthy assessment of the project here.

Part (b) – Whereas part (a) of the question looked at the financial impact of the project, part (b) now looks at two non-financial impacts of it – on culture, and on Booxe's management information systems. And, note, to score well in this part of the question you have to discuss the impact of BPR on both of the areas required by the question: (i) culture, (ii) management information systems.

The scenario is also important in this question because it highlights that Booxe currently operates within a traditional, functional structure. However, BPR focuses on processes and process team rather than functional departments. This change will be central to the impact BPR has on culture at Booxe.

And it will also have important implications for the company's management information systems – for example, will performance reports structured around departments still be relevant in a process-oriented structure? And how might performance measures need to be redesigned to reflect the new approach?

Part (c) – A sensible approach to this part of the question would be to consider the purpose of an appraisal system, and then consider the issues in Booxe's appraisal system in the light of this, before suggesting possible solutions to them.

The reference in the last paragraph of the scenario to 'the appropriate balance between control and staff development' should have given you an indication of the points which needed to be considered here. Obtaining the right balance between control and development is one of the key issues in any appraisal process – but Booxe's current process appears to place very little emphasis on the 'control' aspect of appraisal.

Marking scheme

		Marks
(a)	Calculations: Up to 5 marks	
	Costs: Depreciation – 1 mark; Total cost – 1 mark	
	Savings: Warehousing – 1 mark; Purchasing – 1 mark	
	Net benefit: 1 mark	
	Comments: 1 mark for suitable comments on the calculations	
	Total for part (a): up to 6	6
(b)	Definition of BPR – 1 mark per relevant point – up to a maximum of 2	
	Analysis of the impact of BPR on culture at Booxe – 1 mark per relevant point – up to a maximum of 5	
	Analysis of the impact of BPR on management information systems/ accounting systems at Booxe – 1 mark per relevant point, up to a maximum of 5.	
	Total for part (b): up to 11	11
(c)	Definition of appraisal and the appraisal process – 1 mark per relevant point – up to a maximum of 2	
	For advice on the purpose of appraisal at Booxe – 1 mark per relevant point – up to a maximum of 4	
	For advice on the balance of control and development in the appraisal process – 1 mark per relevant point – up to a maximum of 4.	8
	Total for part (c): up to 8	
		Total = 25

(a) **Annual cost benefit of the new system**

		$
Benefits of new system (cost savings)		
Warehouse staff	10 × 25,000 × 50%	125,000
Purchasing staff	32,000 × 8.5/5	54,400
Annual costs of new system		
Depreciation - hardware	220,000 / 8 years	(27,500)
Depreciation - software	275,000 / 8 years	(34,375)
On-going servicing cost		(22,500)
Net benefit		95,025

The pilot BPR project will yield a benefit of $95,025 per year, meaning it is financially successful.

There are likely to be some other costs which are not included in this analysis, such as redundancy or retraining of the staff whose workload has been reduced, and the training costs for staff on the new system. However, given the figures involved, the project should still be beneficial even when these have been accounted for.

(b)   Business process re-engineering (BPR) is the fundamental rethinking and radical redesign of business processes to achieve dramatic improvements in critical contemporary measures of performance, such as cost, quality, service and speed.

Culture

Process teams – One of the key consequences of BPR for organisations is a shift from a functional structure to process teams, in order to achieve a more efficient delivery of products and services.

This will have a significnt impact on Booxe, since the company has historically been divided into functional departments. The pilot project has shown the effect that BPR could have on the warehousing and purchasing departments.

Skills – The change to a process approach may require employees to retrain in order to gain additional skills. One of the characteristics of BPR is that it leads to multi-skilling; but given Booxe's current (bureaucratic, traditional) culture, it is likely that staff will have specific roles, rather developing multiple skills.

Organisational hierarchy – BPR also leads to a flattening of organisational structures (from hierarchical to flat). Since processes become the work of the whole team, then similarly the team becomes responsible for managing the process.

Interdepartmental issues become matters the team resolves itself, rather than requiring managerial intervention. As a result, BPR means companies require less managerial input, and managers have less to do.

Although it is not clear which aspect of the cultural change required by the BPR project the warehouse manager was uncomfortable with, the risk that BPR would diminish their role could have played a part in the decision to take early retirement.

Change management – Nonetheless, the change required at Booxe – to shift from a well-established functional structure to a process-based structure – is likely to be a major change. Therefore, for it to be implemented successfully will require effective communication and leadership from senior management – for example, explaining the benefits of BPR to the staff, and over-coming any resistance they may have to it.

Management information systems

Performance measures – Performance measures under BPR must be built around processes rather than departments. This again is likely to require a significant change to Booxe's management information systems (assuming that Booxe's current accounting system reflects the functional structure of the organisation).

Focus on value adding – The aim of management information under BPR is to identify where value is being added in processes, so that activities where resources are employed without producing a valuable outcome can be eliminated.

Activity-based costing – As the CEO has suggested, activity-based costing (ABC) is often used to model the business processes as part of BPR. Again, however, the change to ABC from Booxe's traditional overhead absorption based on labour hours could be quite significant for the company's management information.

ABC will provide a more detailed method for allocating overheads, and in turn, should allow Booxe to calculate more accurate product costs, and determine the profitability of each product more accurately.

However, ABC will be more time-consuming to administer than Booxe's current basis of overhead absorption.

Performance reports – The change from functional departments to process teams will mean that financial reports also have to be re-designed around process teams.

Also, the variances to budget, used as control indicators, may also need to be revised following the introduction of the activity-based approach to overhead allocation.

(c) **Purpose of appraisal**

The overall purpose of appraisal is usually seen as the improvement of employees' performance, but appraisals can also be useful for assessing current performance; determining rewards; selecting people for promotion; and for identifying employees' training and development needs.

Control and staff development

The issue of finding an appropriate balance between control and staff development (which the CEO has identified) highlights one of the inherent problems with appraisals.

Judgement and control – One of the key purposes of appraisals is to assess how well employees have performed (against targets and objectives), with a view to determining pay increases and promotion. This reflects the judgement and control aspect of appraisal.

Development - One the other hand, the development aspect of appraisals focus on assessing employees' training and development needs; to support them, and to help them perform better in the future.

Booxe's appraisal system

Despite the issue of resolving the balance between control and development aspects, organisations need some kind of performance assessment for their staff.

However, appraisal systems are often criticised as being irrelevant to the organisation's work. And this may well be the case at Booxe.

The current system has become very informal, possibly due to the fact it is not taken very seriously be either the appraiser or the appraisee.

Control aspects - In order for the appraisal process to become relevant to Booxe's work, the control aspects need to be linked to the organisation's overall goals – such as driving down costs, to support the overall strategy of cost leadership.

Developemnt – However, the appraisal system also needs to be linked to the development of appropriate skills and greater motivation among the staff. (This could be particularly important if employees' jobs are re-designed following BPR.)

It is not clear whether Booxe's current appraisal system is linked to the employee rewards, but if the 'control' elements of appraisals are linked to a suitable reward system, this should help to increase performance in the company as staff strive to meet the performance targets set in their appraisals.

However, it is important that the appraisal process still reflects the culture and strategy of the company. Although Booxe has a strategy of cost leadership, there is also an appreciation of craft skills among the workforce. As such, the 'development' aspects of the appraisal process may be important for enabling staff to highlight new skills they want to learn. But equally the 'control' element of the appraisal process may be important for improving efficiency and controlling costs.

It seems likely that the general discussions about how to improve employees' efforts – which currently constitute Booxe's appraisal process – may be focussing more on the 'development' aspects of appraisal, rather than the 'control' element. However, it seems that the CEO may be looking to change this, by evaluating the balance between control and development in the process.

13 Business process re-engineering

Text reference. Business process re-engineering is covered in Chapter 4 of the Study Text.

Top tips.

Part (a). Hammer identified seven key principles of BPR, and these provide the answer to part (a). There is no requirement to link part (a) to the scenario; this is a test of knowledge only.

However, parts (b) and (c) should be linked to the scenario, with part (b) looking at the potential advantages of implementing BPR, while part (c) is looking at one of the perceived criticisms on BPR programmes.

The scenario has identified a number of issues with the way that FCI currently operates: for example, increasing errors, falling customer satisfaction, and inefficiencies resulting from the reliance on paper-based transactions. Therefore, it is likely that the directors will hope that the BPR exercise will improve FCI's performance in relation to a number of fundamental areas: cost, quality, service and speed.

Notice that the requirement for part (b) (ii) is to recommend performance **targets**. The scenario highlights, for example, that the number of complaints from customers is increasing, which should indicate the importance of monitoring the level of customer complaints. However, the question isn't simply asking you what FCI should measure, but rather to recommend suitable targets for those areas of performance it is measuring.

Part (c). The BPR exercise is also likely to reduce the number of paper-based transactions the staff have to deal with. How if this likely to affect staff morale and motivation? Will staff be pleased by the ways technology could help them in their work and reduce the amount of paperwork they have to do, or will they be concerned that the BPR programme will ultimately lead to job cuts?

(a) **Business process re-engineering**

Business process re-engineering (BPR) is the fundamental redesign of business processes to achieve dramatic improvements in key measures of performance such as cost, quality, service and speed.

There are seven principles of BPR:

(i) **Focus on customer-focused outcomes** – Processes should be designed to achieve a desired customer-focused outcome (for example, quality, service or speed) rather than being organised around existing tasks.

(ii) **People who use the output from a process should perform that process** – If the staff who use the output of a process are involved in the operation of that process, the risk of errors should be reduced and so should time delays in the process.

(iii) **Information processing should be included in the work which produces the information**. In other words, there shouldn't be a distinction between information **processing** and information **gathering**.

The development of online databases can be crucial here, allowing users to have access to real time information, thus minimising delays in response to queries.

(iv) **Geographically-dispersed resources should be treated as if they are centralised** – For example, there should be a centralised database of suppliers which all departments use, so that they benefit from the economies of scale achieved by the central negotiation of supply contracts.

(v) **Parallel activities should be linked rather than integrated** – As far as possible, activities should be processed in parallel rather than sequentially. If tasks are performed sequentially, bottlenecks and delays might arise while waiting for the output of a previous process.

(vi) People should be **self-managing** and exercise greater **autonomy** over their work – The traditional distinction between workers and managers should be abolished. BPR aims to allow decisions to be made as quickly as possible and as near to the end customer as possible. This allows increased responsiveness, and also empowers the individuals who make the decisions.

(vii) **Information should be captured once, and at source** – If information is transferred from one data source to another there is a risk of human error. If information is only input into a system once, and is input as early as possible, the risk of error is reduced, and consistent replies can be obtained in response for any queries about the information.

(b) (i) **Expected improvements**

More rapid information processing and error reduction – It appears that the processes at FCI haven't been updated to take advantage of the IT / IS systems that are widely available today. In particular, relying on a predominantly paper-based system makes FCI's processes much slower than they need to be, and it also increases the opportunity for error as information is manually recorded and then transferred between systems. A new database-led system would prevent the need for re-keying and transferring information, and so should reduce the scope for errors in the system.

This system will also mean that FCI has reliable, **up-to-date information** about its customers. Any details the sales staff or telephone operators obtain about a customer can be entered into the central database on a real time basis, and the system can then be continually updated for other staff to use.

Moreover, no **paper-based transfers of information** from one part of the organisation to another will be necessary. Again, this reduces delays and reduces the risk of errors occurring.

Improved database system – If FCI develops an electronic database which stores all customer data, this should enable staff to respond to telephone enquiries more quickly. For example, if a phone operator receives a call, they can access the database and gather the relevant information to help them deal with the customer enquiry straight away. This faster response time should lead to improved customer satisfaction.

Better support for sales staff – Having an electronic (or online) database and improved technology should also help the sales staff when they visit potential customers. If the sales staff can access the database remotely (from laptops) they can get details of policies and premiums while they are with the customer, and so could potentially make a decision about a policy application straight away without having to return to the office to check details or process paperwork. Customers have complained about the slowness of FCI's current process, so speeding up the process should directly address these complaints.

Increased staff motivation – Not only have customers complained about the current sales process, but FCI's sales staff have also complained about them. Staff motivation and job satisfaction are likely to suffer if the staff feel they are having to work with out-dated processes and technology. Therefore, providing the sales staff with more up-to-date technology will not only allow them to do their job more effectively but it should also improve their motivation to do so.

Moreover, customers are likely to have a more favourable impression of the sales staff if they provide a quick and efficient service. If this, in turn, leads to the sales staff making more sales it is likely to increase their motivation still further.

Organisation structure – BPR's principle of working back from a desired 'customer-focused outcome' will help FCI to find the most efficient and effective way of delivering that outcome. This is likely to lead to a change in FCI's organisation structure or the tasks that individual people do, to reduce the level of internal communication required in response to telephone enquiries.

The degree of communication required internally to respond to telephone enquiries suggest that FCI's organisation structure is quite inflexible, and everyone has quite narrowly defined areas of responsibility. The increased focus on the customer may lead to a greater flexibility, as FCI's business will be organised around outcomes rather than tasks.

Greater process flexibility and speed – The paper-based nature of FCI's current system means that tasks have to be done sequentially. However, one of the principles of BPR is that linked activities should be conducted in parallel rather than sequentially. In this case, if FCI improves its IT/IS systems, and stores customer details electronically, staff may be able to deal with different aspects of a customer transaction in parallel, thereby speeding up the transaction process.

(ii)   **Key business objectives** – It seems that reducing the time taken to process transactions and improving the quality of the paperwork issued are key business issues within FCI and so it is likely that it will have business objectives relating to these areas. Consequently, FCI should also have performance measures looking at these areas, in order to assess how well the re-engineered processes have helped to improve performance in relation to them.

Performance targets

% of transaction completed within a given time – The slow speed of the current process is a major source of complaints, therefore FCI should want to speed up the process. It may not be practical to measure (or monitor) how long FCI takes to complete each individual transaction, and some, more complex, policies may take longer to process than others. Therefore, a more useful target could be to ensure that a certain proportion of transactions that a completed within a given time.

Number of complaints about errors in paperwork reduced by x% – One of the key aims behind the BPR exercise is to help FCI reduce the number of errors in the paperwork which customers receives. Setting a target to reduce the number of complaints about errors should focus people's attention on addressing this issue.

(c)   **Perception of BPR programmes** – Although the main aim of BPR programmes is to increase business efficiency, there is often a perception that they end up simply being cost-cutting exercises. It is likely that this is a major reason behind the staff's concerns about the programme, with them being concerned that it could lead to **redundancies,** or could threaten their jobs and prospects within a company.

Change and uncertainty – Even if the programme doesn't lead to redundancy, the fact that it will result in the fundamental redesign of business processes is still likely to lead to **significant changes** which affect staff. For example, if may lead to new patterns of work, changes in people's roles or changes in the composition of work groups.

In this respect, people's uncertainty about how the programme could affect them is likely to make them concerned about it and may lead them to resist it. Resistance may be exacerbated because the out-of-date processes are likely to have been in place for some time and have therefore become ingrained in the staff.

14 BV Entertainments

Text reference. The characteristics of service organisations are covered in Chapter 4 of the BPP Study Text. The benefits of information systems providing instant access to data are covered in Chapter 8.

Top tips. Part (a): Although the requirement asks you to make reference to BVE in your answer, this should still be a relatively simple test of knowledge. If anything, the references to BVE should help you explain the characteristics identified by the requirement.

Part (b) deals with a specific item in the syllabus: assessing the changing needs of modern service-orientated businesses compared with the needs of traditional manufacturing systems. In this context, it is important to think how the nature of a 'service' differs from manufacturing production, and therefore how this affects the nature of performance management and control in each.

The key issues in part (c) are the quality and availability of information. The nature of the representatives' meetings with clients means that the representatives need to be able to find accurate, up-to-date information which they can use in their negotiations with the clients. If the representatives don't have this information, how can they agree any prices or deals with the clients?

(a) **Intangibility**

Unlike the outputs from a manufacturing organisation which are tangible, individual products which can easily be quantified or measured, the outputs of a service organisation are not tangible. For example, if one of BVE's clients visits a sporting event, they don't have anything tangible at the end of it in the way they would, for example, if they had bought a new piece of kitchen equipment.

In BVE, for example, not only is the service provided intangible, the performance of the service comprises many other intangible factors (such as the speed which customers are dealt with and the helpfulness of the staff) which will undoubtedly influence customers' perception of the service they have received.

Heterogeneity

Each 'service' provided by BVE is likely to be slightly different from all those that have already been provided or those that will be provided in the future, The exact 'service' that a customer receives each time they visit a theatre show or an opera, for example, will vary according to how well the performers perform on the night, the atmosphere created by the audience members, or how busy the venue is. By contrast, if a customer buys a manufactured product, they could expect that product to be the same every time they buy it.

Simultaneity

The production and consumption of a service occur at the same time, and therefore a service cannot be inspected for quality in advance and neither can it be returned if it was not what was required. For example, if one of BVE's clients books a package for a sporting event, they cannot guarantee in advance the quality of the sporting action they will see.

The concept of simultaneity also highlights the important of the interaction between the producer and the consumer in a service transaction. For example, a restaurant can produce a dinner, but for the dinner 'event' to take place it also needs diners to eat the meal. And this interaction with the consumer can play an important part in the outcome of a service transaction. For example, if two of BVE's clients order the same item from a restaurant menu, one might like it a lot, but another may not like it.

Perishability

Services are inherently perishable and cannot be stored for later use. For example, a given sporting event takes place at a given time and date. Therefore, unlike a piece of kitchen equipment which can be used repeatedly, a sports event can only ever be 'used' once; because after that it no longer exists.

(b) **Production costs** – In a traditional manufacturing company, the main focus of management accounting information is often on production costs. There will be a cost accounting system that records costs of production and provides a valuation for inventory. Annual plans are produced in the form of budgets, and where standard products are manufactured, there may be a standard costing system.

Manufacturing conditions are often relatively stable, which means that budget forecasts can often be produced by using the previous year's performance as a basis for planning the future. Control information for management is likely to be provided in the form of monthly variance reporting.

Basis of costing – However, while such information will be useful for DAS, it will be less useful for a service organisation like BVE. Although cost information is required about the services provided, there should be little if any requirement for inventory costs. This means that costing is more likely to be based on marginal costing than absorption costing.

Individual packages – Even more importantly, BVE does not provide standard services, and clients negotiate entertainment packages. Because services are non-standard and BVE needs to be flexible in its operations, BVE's accounting system must be able to **monitor the profitability of individual contracts** with clients.

Historical cost information may be of limited value for BVE, because services are non-standard. It is much more important for the IT system to provide information about current costs and expected costs. This will allow representatives to calculate the cost of packages that clients are requesting, quote prices and, where necessary, negotiate on the details.

Timeliness of information – In a traditional management accounting system, it may be sufficient to obtain control information about costs on a monthly basis. In BVE it is much more important to provide immediate access to information for all the company's representatives, as well as management. The IT system must be accessible and responsive.

Feed-forward control – Cash flow is important for BVE because it often has to make payments (for tickets or venue hire) well in advance of receiving payment from clients. BVE's information system must therefore be capable of providing feed-forward control information about cash flow, so that management can anticipate any future cash shortage and take measures to deal with the problem, for example by deferring some payments, asking some clients for deposits, or arranging for a sufficient overdraft facility with the company's bank.

Non-financial information – Given the nature of the services BVE offers, financial performance information should be supplemented by critical non-financial information, such as customer satisfaction and the quality or dependability of service delivery. BVE's accounting information system should therefore include non-financial elements.

BVE operates in a changeable and flexible business environment. A company such as DAS manufactures high-volume consumer products and operates in a more stable and predictable environment. The accounting systems in each company will differ substantially because of the different information needs of management in each business.

(c) An IT system that provides instant access to data about costs, prices and entertainment venues and resources should improve the effectiveness of the company's selling operations, which in turn should result in higher sales revenue and profits.

Timeliness of information – The most important quality of the information provided by the system is probably timeliness. There are two aspects to this:

The first is that information can be made available to sales representatives in meetings with the client, which will often be at a time that the client may be able to make a decision and agree to buy an entertainment package.

The second and more important aspect of timeliness is the **speed with which the information is made available**. Representatives will have immediate access to information about cost/prices and ticket available to make an instant price quotation for any type of package that the customer may want. Whenever some costs change, the new cost can be fed into the system and made immediately available for re-pricing of services and packages. The representative's sales message can be reinforced if the system also delivers visual information about possible venues and entertainment facilities.

The immediacy of the information provision should therefore encourage prompt decision-making by the customer, which should in turn result in more sales.

Costs and ticket availability – The IT system should also contribute to the longer-term performance of the company by giving representatives reliable information about costs/prices and ticket availability. The information should be more reliable than if it is provided by a manual information system or by a separate sales system, because it should be more up-to-date. Up-to-date reliable information should enable representatives to quote realistic prices and confirm the availability of tickets. Over time the company should develop a reputation for efficiency and reliability in this way.

Managing supply and demand – The system will also allow management to monitor the state of the business, for example by checking customer demand patters and by ensuring that quoted prices are sufficient to cover costs. It should also be possible to anticipate sporting events where the company will have too many tickets or too few tickets. By anticipating surpluses or shortages, measures can be taken to deal with the problem – reducing the price of entertainment packages to sell more tickets, or trying to acquire more tickets.

In summary, the IT system will become an integral part of the selling and management systems, and by improving the quality of information, it should improve the performance of the company.

15 EEE Chemical company

Text reference. Stakeholder analysis is covered in Chapter 5 of your BPP Study Text.

Top tips. This question is obviously built around Mendelow's work, but you need to be clear in your mind exactly what it is asking for. There is no part of any of the requirements that asks you to explain in detail what stakeholder analysis is, or what Mendelow's matrix is. This question requires the **application** of knowledge to the scenario described.

(a)

Top tips. Although you are not asked what 'stakeholder analysis' is, thinking about this would have helped you focus on what is relevant here and what is not.

However, note you were not required to identify or discuss any individual stakeholders in the part of the question. That was the requirement for (b), and should have been kept separate from this part of the question.

EEE's stakeholders are persons or groups with a legitimate interest in what EEE does.

Stakeholder analysis establishes who the organisation's stakeholders are and the various discrete categories which they fall into. These categories are determined by a combination of the nature and extent of their **interest** in the organisation, and the extent of their **power** to influence the organisation's behaviour.

Advantages of stakeholder analysis

(i) **Identify potential backers** of the proposal to develop the new extraction process. This will help the Board to approach them and gain their support.

(ii) **Identify potential opponents** who might try to block the proposal. The Board could then try to take action to reduce the resistance of opponents. However, if the Board feel that the opposition to the proposal is too strong they could decide to modify or abandon the proposal before money is wasted on it.

(iii) **Demonstrate good corporate governance.** As part of their commitments to corporate social responsibility, managers are increasingly being asked to consider the interests of a range of stakeholders groups and not just shareholders in their decision making. By considering the interests of a different stakeholder groups in its decision-making process, EEE can demonstrate it is taking its corporate social responsibility seriously.

If EEE does decide to proceed with the proposal, it will then also have to **manage the reactions** of the various groups, given that some will support the project while others will oppose it. Again though, it will be useful for EEE to have identified the levels of interest and power of the different stakeholder groups, because these factors will help to shape the way it manages different groups.

(b)

Top tips. To answer part (b) well you have to apply your knowledge of stakeholder mapping to the specific context of the **organisational decision**. Note that you are not simply asked to analyse the principal stakeholders of EEE as an organisation, but specifically in relation to the proposed investment in the new process.

The information provided in the scenario should have pointed you towards the principal stakeholders, and you should then have analysed them using the concepts of 'power' and 'interest' (from Mendelow's matrix).

However, it is vital to **think about the practical context** of the scenario. In particular, in this case, it is important to recognise the potential overlaps between groups of stakeholders - for example, many of the employees could also be local residents.

An analysis of EEE's stakeholder groups using *Mendelow's* criteria of power and influence is shown below.

Key players (high degree of both interest and influence)

(i) The **founding family** forms a majority of the board and holds 30% of the share capital; it therefore, collectively controls the company. Its members are likely to give strong support to adoption the new process since it will confer a definite competitive advantage.

(ii) If **local government** operates as in the UK, it will have extensive power to regulate industrial processes and developments. It will be very interested in EEE because it is a major element in the local economy and in the new process because of the complaints of the local residents. The council will therefore have mixed feelings about the new process.

(iii) EEE's **employees** depend on the company for their livelihood and make a major contribution to its success. They also control or influence 20% of the shares in the company. Their interest lies in the successful introduction of the new process, since the competitive advantage its gives should also be to their benefit in terms of job security and, possibly, pay.

Note. The **trade union representative** who is also a local councillor falls into two of these categories: like the council itself, he may have mixed motivations, to the extent that he suffers from a **conflict of interest** that he should formally declare to his fellow councillors.

Keep satisfied (low degree of interest, high degree of power)

The **institutional shareholders** control 20% of the share capital; the extent of their activity in relation to the running of the company is unknown, but is likely to be minor. They will probably be content if EEE continues to operate reasonably successfully. However, they have the capacity to become interested if a major and costly problem arises.

Keep informed (high degree of interest, low degree of power)

Local residents fall into two sub-categories. Both will be directly interested in the new process, but any influence they can bring to bear on the company will be mediated through intermediaries.

(a) The **affluent residents** that have complained can only have significant effect through the local council and, possibly, by a media campaign. The effectiveness of either route will depend on how well EEE manages its press and public relations. In addition, the ambivalence of the council already commented on will limit this group's power. However, this group could seek to cause problems for EEE in the future if they are antagonised and so EEE should treat them with respect.

(b) **Other local residents** may also be concerned about unpleasant odours, but many of them are likely to be connected to the company through the employment of a family member; this group is more likely to be sympathetic to the new process.

Minimal effort (low degree of interest and influence)

Although the remaining **shareholders** own 30% of the shares in total, they are unlikely to be particularly interested in the new process or, perhaps more importantly, to act as a single group.

(c)

The **economic advantages** of the new process are such that all of the key players are likely to agree that it is very desirable for EEE to adopt it on a large scale. However, the company cannot afford to ignore the feelings

of those local residents that object on grounds of amenity. People can be very resistant to changes affecting their home life, and **a campaign against the company** could, eventually, be very damaging.

The company should therefore adopt the process but should also take two important steps to safeguard its position.

First, it should be prepared to make a reasonable investment in developing the technology in a way that will **minimise the objectionable odours**. This might involve further chemical processing or filtering or merely something as simple as only using the process on days when the wind is in an appropriate direction. This will both reduce the potential for actual dispute and provide a basis for the second step, which is **careful PR management**.

EEE should ensure that its operations are presented in the best possible light, stressing the **economic benefits** to the area, and the company's efforts to be a good neighbour. This will assist the local council to take a positive view of the company and will discourage the formation of a **single-issue pressure group** by the objecting affluent residents.

EEE could also consider some more pro-active PR events such as sponsoring local events or facilities, to build up its image as a good neighbour.

16 PLX Refinery

Text reference. Environmental management accounting is covered in Chapter 5 of the Study Text.

Top tips. Although part (a) is only worth six marks there are still effectively two parts to the requirement. What cost categories could aid transparency in internal reporting? And, what cost categories could aid transparency in external reporting? Make sure you address both in your answer, and make sure you give examples, as you are instructed to do.

There are also two stages to answering part (b): 'explain' then 'evaluate'. However, don't just explain the two techniques (activity-based costing; and lifecycle view) in general terms; make sure you link them back to PLX's environmental and strategic performance.

Similarly, in your evaluation, make sure you look specifically at how the techniques could be useful in managing performance at PLX. And because you are 'evaluating' them, try to include some limitations in using them as well as the advantages of using them.

Also, note that requirement (b) asks you how the techniques can assist in managing environmental *and* strategic performance. So, for example, how might a better understanding of environmental costs affect strategic decision-making (as well as the more obvious issues of how might an understanding of environmental costs affect environmental performance)?

Part (c). The scenario tells us that PLX's performance measures currently focus mainly on financial performance, and its existing information systems also focus on financial performance. So how will they have to change in order to PLX to monitor its environmental performance? And what issues could this present? The scenario specifically mentions the government's goal to reduce carbon dioxide emissions, so this could be a useful example to link your answer to – for example, does PLX currently monitor its carbon dioxide emissions?

Part (d). The figures given in the scenario indicate that there are some significant environment costs associated with the project. Consequently, whether they are included in a project appraisal or not will have a significant impact on the perceived profitability of the project. In effect then, you could approach by asking: What are the potential problems with Kayplas' current costing approach? And then, how could a lifecycle costing approach help address these problems?

Marks

(a) Up to 2 marks for each cost area discussed – Up to a maximum of 6 marks
To score 2 marks, the discussion of each cost must include relevant examples, linked to the scenario.
Total: up to 6

6

(b) Up to 2 marks for explaining each technique, and explaining its link to environmental performance. Up to a maximum of 4 marks
Up to 2 marks for an evaluation of the techniques.
Total: up to 6

6

(c) For assessing the impact of environmental accounting on performance measurement at PLX – 1 mark per relevant point; up to 3
For assessing the impact of environmental accounting on information systesm – 1 mark per relevant point; up to 3
Total: up to 6

6

(d) Up to 2 marks for calculation of lifecycle costs.
Up to 2 marks for calculating the product profits of the two approaches

Up to 4 marks for discussing the potential improvements and issues identified by lifecycle costing.

7

Total: up to 7

Total = 25

(a) PLX will need to identify existing and new cost information which is relevant to understanding the environmental impact its operations have.

Operating costs – PLX's current management accounting system is already likely to record conventional costs such as raw material costs and energy costs. However, the costs of waste through inefficiency will not be recorded. If they were, however, this should encourage PLX's management to reduce the amount of waste generated by the company's processes.

Additionally, a number of environment-related costs (such as waste filtration) are currently classified within overheads, meaning that they are not very transparent to management. Similarly, the regulatory fines are also likely to be included within overheads. However, if all these environment-related costs were classified separately they would immediately be more visible to management.

Decommissioning costs – The profit forecast for Kayplas highlights that PLX incurs a number of significant costs at the end of a project, for example the costs of decommissioning equipment, or cleaning industrial sites once they stop being used.

These costs (because they are large) can have a significant impact on the shareholder value generated by a project, and can also make significant demands on PLX's cash resources. However, because they occur at the end of a project there is a danger that they will be given a lower priority if management focuses on short-term financial measures, such as annual profit.

Reporting on costs – As well as making the costs more visible to management, increasing the focus on environmental costs could also be beneficial to PLX from a public relations perspective. If PLX highlights these costs in its financial reports, and also highlights the actions it is taking to reduce to reduce its environmental impact, it can demonstrate to pressure groups and the regulator that it is taking its environmental responsibilities seriously.

Reputational costs – By contrast, if PLX is deemed not be taking its environmental responsibilities seriously, this could result in adverse publicity for the group, and ultimately could lead to consumer boycotts and lost revenues.

(b)   **Activity-based costing**

Traditional activity-based costing allocates costs to cost centres or cost drivers on the basis of the activities that caused the costs.

Environmental activity-based costing looks to distinguish between environment-related costs and environment-driven costs.

Environment-related costs are attributed specifically to an environmental cost centre, for example, waste filtration at PLX.

Environment-driven costs are not allocated to a specific environmental cost centre, but still relate to environmental drivers. For example, PLX may reduce the working life of some of the machinery in its refinery to reduce pollution levels in the later years of its working life. The increased annual depreciation charges that will result from this are environment-driven costs.

Applying activity-based costing in this way will help PLX identify and control environmental costs.

Lifecycle view

Lifecycle costing looks to record a product's costs and revenues across the whole of its life, rather than for a single year, or for a specific phase of its life (such as the production phase.)

This is important because it highlights the importance of costs incurred **prior** to production and those incurred *after* production ceases (for example, in PLX's case, the costs of decommissioning plant and equipment.) These costs can often be very large, and so could have a significant impact on the shareholder value generated by a project. As a result they may potentially influence the decision about whether or not to undertake a project.

Given the nature of PLX's business, it is very important that any investment appraisals capture all the costs generated over the whole lifecycle of a project – including decommissioning costs, which for the Kayplas project are estimated at $18million.

Evaluation

Costs – One of the major issues PLX would face if it chooses to introduce environmental activity-based costing is that it will need to collect significant additional amounts of information from the management accounting system, and there are likely to be costs involved in upgrading the system to be able to provide this.

Benefits – At the same time, while the techniques can help improve PLX's economic and environmental efficiency, it may be difficult to quantity the benefits which will accrue from using the techniques. Therefore, it may be difficult to justify introducing the techniques on the basis of a financial cost/benefit analysis.

Strategic benefits – However, perhaps the stronger case for using the new techniques is a non-financial one. PLX believes it will be strategically important to be at the forefront of environmental developments, and using the new techniques will demonstrate its commitment to this.

By demonstrating its commitment to environmental issues, PLX could improve its **public image**, appease the **pressure group** (Green Kayland) and reassure the **government** it is helping to improve its treatment of the environment.

(c)   **Performance metrics** – The focus of PLX's current performance measures are predominantly financial, suggesting there are few, if any, environmental performance metrics.

However, the increasing focus on the environmental impact of PLX's activities means that it should also identify some key environmental performance indicators, and measure its performance against them. Carbon dioxide emissions could be a particularly important metric, given the government's commitment to reducing it, and the threat of a tax on emissions being introduced in the future.

Unlike its current metrics, however, PLX will not be able to see how its environmental performance is directly contributing to its financial performance. For example, it will not be able to put monetary values on its CO_2 emissions figures – although if the government does introduce the proposed tax then PLX will be specifically able to identify the 'cost' of the eimssions.

Information systems – Similary, given that the focus of PLX's information systems is currently on producing financial performance measures, the addition of environmental performance information could involve significant changes – for example, PLX may need to modify its existing database structure, or add additional records.

However, before it can monitor its CO_2 emissions, PLX will have to start collecting data on the volume of emissions, which can then be recorded in its management information systems. As such, PLX will need to install measuring equipment to capture the relevant data, and then feed it back to the company's management information systems.

The measuring equipment could capture real-time data whch is uploaded automatically into the information systems. Having real-time environmental data could be particularly useful in detecting a potential problem in the refinery as early as possible (eg an unexpected increase in the level of CO_2 emissions), and thereby helping to minimise the environmental damage the problem causes.

(d) PLX's traditional performance measure of product profit for Kayplas suggests it will generate a profit of $41.5m over five years. However, this ignores the environmental costs (of waste filtration, and carbon dioxide exhaust extraction) as well as the cost of decommissioning at the end of the project.

By contrast, a lifecycle analysis would include all of these costs:

Kayplas product profit	$ million
Traditional view:	
Revenue:	149.4
Production, marketing & development costs	107.9
Product profit (over 5 yrs)	41.5
Profit margin	27.8%
Adjusted for environmental costs:	
Revenue	149.4
Production, marketing & development costs	107.9
Waste filtration	8.1
Carbon dioxide exhaust extraction	5.3
Decommissioning costs	18.0
	139.3
Revised product profit	10.1
Profit margin	6.8%

When the environmental costs are all included, the forecast profit margin on the Kayplas project is reduced from 27.8% to 6.8%, which makes it a much less attractive investment. Moreover, if the actual costs of decommissioning in five years' time are higher than the forecast ($18.0m) – for example, due to changes in environmental legislation in the next five years – then the profit margin will be reduced even further.

Importantly, also, lifecycle costing makes the post-production costs visible at the start of the project and in the design stage of the product. This should help PLX appreciate early in the project the need to minimise the costs of decommissioning. So, for example, they could investigate whether they could design any of the equipment to be used to produce Kayplas in such a way that it could also be used to produce Kayplas2.

17 GHG

(a) (i) **Strategic factors to consider**

The nature and extent of competition will need to be considered. If there is likely to be a lot of competition from other multinational hotel chains this will affect performance. Clearly if the hotel has less competition then this will make the prospect more attractive.

As the hotel will be some distance from other group hotels, it will have to be more self-sufficient and will require delegated management. The extent **to which local management** is employed depends on the expertise of local staff. It may be that initially the hotel uses seconded management until local managers are up to the required standard.

Local legislation is likely to affect the operation of the hotel. If Tomorrowland has strict pollution control laws or employment protection regulations these will affect how the hotel operates. There may be laws in place that require some local ownership or control in a foreign business and this may make the decision unattractive.

Political stability will be a significant factor in the group's decision to site a hotel in Tomorrowland. If Tomorrowland has a stable government the group could consider a long-term investment. However if there is instability and the possibility of civil war, the group should defer the decision.

(ii) **Economic factors to consider**

The stability of the local economy is important when deciding to invest in Tomorrowland. This is a developing country and if its economy grows very fast the hotel could benefit from this. If the economy is founded on tourism, it is highly dependent on the state of the economies in the home countries of tourists. Any recession in these countries could see the tourist industry suffer in Tomorrowland.

Taxation and fiscal policies will also affect the decision to set up in Tomorrowland. Clearly low corporate taxation or incentives such as reliefs for investors will make the decision to locate the hotel there more attractive.

Exchange rates will affect the cost of anything brought into the country and the cost of holidays taken by foreign tourists.

If there is a cheap, skilled local labour force this will make the decision to invest more attractive.

BPP
LEARNING MEDIA

Other factors you might have raised

(i) **Strategic factors**

(1) **Social and cultural constraints**

GHG needs to consider the local attitude toward international brands in Tomorrowland where it may not be seen favourably as an 'outsider'.

(2) There is also the **local attitude toward work and outside management** to take into account. GHG will have to understand what these are and consider how to work within or despite existing attitudes.

Communication

Language barriers are likely to exist and these must be addressed as early as possible to minimise any risks to GHG.

(ii) **Economic factors**

(1) **The availability** of resources, especially suitable building materials and local labour need to be planned for early on in the building programme.

(2) **Local and international legislation** will affect the planned hotel. For instance, local planning and licensing laws in alcohol impact on the siting of the hotel and how it operates.

(b) **Cultural differences and their impact on the performance of a local workforce**

(i) **Religious views.** If members of the workforce belong to a religion which forbids alcohol and certain foods, they may object to working in an environment that encourages alcohol and a wide range of foods. They may also regard the dress of tourists on holiday as immodest and see their behaviour as

(ii) **Attitude to authority.** It is possible that custom in Tomorrowland encourages long lunch breaks if the climate is hot during the height of the sun. This may conflict with construction timetables and hinder timely completion. When the hotel is open for operation this may remain an issue. Local workers may also regard management as having more authority and worthy of more respect than a 'western' employee would. This could help managers in issuing orders but may not encourage employees to be independent and think for themselves.

(c) **Strategic management accounting** – Unlike 'traditional' management accounting which looks primarily at internally generated financial information, strategic management accounting looks at information which relates to **external factors**, and it looks at **non-financial** as well as financial information.

Market growth – Strategic management accounting will encourage GHG to look at market size and growth, and the company's share of the market in Tomorrowland.

Strategic management accounting's **external focus** is very important: GHG needs to understand the market environment in Tomorrowland in order to analyse the trading company's current performance, and then to evaluate future strategies for the company.

External factors – Developing an understanding of the market conditions and the external environment will be particularly important for GHG since Tomorrowland is 3,000 kilometres away from GHG's next hotel. Therefore, GHG will need to build up its understanding of the local market in Tomorrowland. For example, if economic conditions in Tomorrowland are more favourable than in other countries, GHG might also be justified in expecting the hotel in Tomorrowland to perform better than hotels in other countries.

Analysis of current performance – Strategic management accounting can also contribute to GHG's success by monitoring the hotel's performance and results and **benchmarking** them against its competitors. GHG can then assess whether its current strategy appears to be working successfully or not. For example, GHG could consider its room occupancy rates or its revenue per available room compared to its competitors.

If it appears the company is performing relatively worse than its competitors, then GHG should consider how it could revise its strategy to help improve the company's performance.

18 CAP

Text reference. Financial performance measures are covered in Chapter 9 of the BPP Study Text. The impact of external factors (PEST factors) on an organisation's performance is considered in Chapter 6.

Top tips.

Part (a) asks you to **evaluate** financial performance. You need to comment on the performance of CAP and come to a conclusion on this performance based on the figures you have calculated. You will only earn minimal marks for just calculating measures. We have included a table in our answer to keep our workings neat and you can refer to the table in your answer. Just select a few measures, four or five will do. **The majority of the marks will be awarded for showing you can understand and comment on the measures.** The information in the question guides you toward what measures to use and hints at a year on year comparison. Look at **activity measures** such as the revenue or profit per park. These tell you about what the business is doing as well as how well it is doing.

What does the **P/E ratio** tell you about the future prospects of CAP perceived by the market? How **liquid** is the company? Is it in a good position to cover its liabilities? **Don't just write 'yes' or 'no' answers.** At this level you must be willing to argue and come to a conclusion using the data you have calculated to support your points. The examining team awards half of the marks here, for evaluation, to measures of margin and the remainder for dividend, liquidity and PE measures. We suggest up to half a page to answer this part including a table for the calculations of year on year measures.

Part (b) asks for a discussion on the proposed expansion using the environmental considerations. Use information in the scenario, and answer each of the three requirements separately.

Part (c). You should have realised from the scenario that the expansion into Robland would be the first time CAP has operated outside Lizland. So, in effect, the question is asking you to discuss the potential issues with performance management in a multinational organisation; for example, practical issues such as how Jody Cundy can control operations in a country 3,200 kilometres away, or how variations in the value of the 'Rob' could affect the performance which gets reported.

Examining team's comments. Most candidates used the scenario satisfactorily. Part (a) saw maximum marks for many candidates with very good evaluations of the financial performance, rather than simply providing calculations or ratio analysis.

Part (b) was mainly acceptable but a significant number of candidates assumed retained earnings were available to finance the redemption of the preference shares or the expansion planned.

Marking scheme

			Marks
(a)	Financial performance:		
	Margin	Up to 3	
	Dividend cover	1	
	Liquidity	1	
	Price earnings ratio	1	
			6
(b)	Issues:		
	Financial	Up to 5	
	Economic	Up to 5	
	Social	Up to 5	
	Maximum 14		14
(c)	For each difficulty discussed, and related to the scenario:		
	Up to 2 marks each	Up to 5	
	Maximum 5		5
		Total =	**25**

(a) Jody Cundy (JC) has correctly perceived a difficulty in maintaining profitability in the Lizland parks. Workings are given in the table below.

- Turnover has been falling since 20X7, in the latest year by 9.1% from 20X8. It is now $4.52m per park from $5.89m per park in 20X6.

- Profits have fallen from $60m in 20X6 to $40m in 20X6, or by 1/3 over three years. The average profit per park fell to $0.65m ($40m/62) in 20x9 from $1.07m ($60/56) in 20X6, a drop of 40%.

- Operating costs have also fallen, however, from $270m in 20X6 to $240m in 20X9, or by 11%.

- Despite this, net margins have suffered, falling from 18% in 20X6 to 14% in 20X9.

Before making a decision to move into Robland, JC should consider alternative options.

- He could review revenue sources in Lizland, from both existing sites and new ones, rather than expanding overseas at a huge cost of $120m.

- He may be able to squeeze more cost savings out of existing operations, given that operating costs have increased from 81. 8% of turnover to 85.7% from 20X6 to 20X9. This does depend on the level of variable cost against fixed costs, as fixed costs are more difficult to cut in the short term. The split between variable and fixed costs is unknown.

Workings

	20X6	20X7	20X8	20X9
Net profit margin %	60/330 = 18%	56/320 = 17.5%	52/308 = 16.9%	40/280 = 14.3%
Turnover per park ($m)	330/56 = 5.89	320/58 = 5.52	308/60 = 5.13	280/62 = 4.52
Net profit per park ($m)	60/56 = 1.07	56/58 = 0.97	52/60 = 0.87	40/62 = 0.65
% fall()/rise in turnover	((330-325)/325) × 100% = 1.5%	((320-330)/330) × 100% = (3.0)%	((308 − 320)/320) × 100% = (3.8)%	((280 − 308)/308) × 100% = (9.1)%
% fall()/rise in operating costs	–	((270 − 264)/270) × 100% = (2.2)%	((264 − 256)/264) × 100%= (3.0)%	((256 − 240)/256) × 100%= (6.25)%
Operating costs as % of turnover	(270/330) × 100% = 81.8%	(264/320) × 100%= 82.5%	(256/308) × 100% = 83.1%	(240/280) × 100% = 85.7%

Dividend cover of 1.5 ($(30m PAT – $9m pref shares div)/$14m dividend) for 20X9 is low and it may be difficult to keep up this level of dividend in future years if profits continue to fall.

Liquidity is also a concern as the bank balance of $10m at 30 November 20X9 is insufficient to meet trade and other payables due at that date of $15m.

The **low PE ratio** compared with industry average suggests the market has concerns over future prospects for CAP. The repayment of the redeemable preference shares may have caused this in part: CAP must find $110m in the next year but has only $120m in reserves at the latest year end.

(b) **Financial considerations**

JC will need to guarantee finance of $120m to fund the new parks, starting December 20X9. He also needs to fund the redemption of the preference shares, due in 20Y0, for $110m. Thus up to $230m needs to be found in the next year, though it is unlikely all of the parks will be built in 20X9. If construction costs can be staggered over several years then the immediate need for funds will be less, but inflation may mean final costs are more than $120m. There is only $122m of retained profits at 30 November 20X9.

JC will need to raise funds by loan or share issue if he is going to fund all of these obligations.

- **He is reluctant to lose control, however,** which he may do if he issues more shares. He must also consider how existing shareholders will see the expansion and if they will expect their level of dividend to be maintained. The company is already priced at a discount based on its PE ratio so shareholders regard the company as underperforming.

- **If he agrees a loan** then he may have to fulfil covenants relating to performance and will have to repay the loan and interest. Present trends in profitability may see lenders reluctant to lend unless the downward path ceases. However gearing is low and there is adequate security from net current assets ($30m) and non-current assets ($220m).
- A third possibility is for CAP to obtain some funding from the government in Robland given that he will be investing in the company, bringing in revenue and probably jobs and tourism.

Economic considerations

The market research indicated reasonable future prospects but gave no more detail on the economy of Robland. For instance, data on the size of the market, existing competition and structure of the economy would have been useful. JC should obtain more information on these factors as a minimum before he decides to invest in Robland.

Government policy may favour industry investment rather than investment in pleasure parks. On the other hand, Robland may favour tourism and incentives could be available for inward investment including low tax rates. **Given the size of the investment, CAP should be clear on how the government of Robland views the investment and what incentives are available for a major investment in their economy.**

Finally, **CAP needs to plan for exchange rate fluctuations** if it is going to remit funds. There may be problems with remitting profits if these are made in an unstable currency or one which may devalue against CAP's own currency leading to significant losses on exchange. CAP should therefore decide whether to hedge for any fluctuations between the Rob and CAP's own currency ($).

Social considerations

The market research indicated reasonable future prospects for investment in Robland. **If Robland is a developing country**, it may have little infrastructure and industry and these may take time to develop and the standard of living to rise. There will be few local consumers of pleasure activities if the consumers cannot afford entry. **If Robland is a mature economy**, with a high standard of living and ample leisure time, then the parks could do very well.

The research didn't comment on how the investment would be seen locally. For instance setting up parks in a country with strong religious laws may see locals reluctant to work in construction or be employed by the parks at certain times. Some countries have **traditions of afternoon rest** which would not suit an all-day amusement park. There may be **local customs governing how people in authority are respected and the role of women and minorities**. This affects the operation of the parks.

JC needs to seek local professional advice on these issues and others, including rates of pay and legal responsibilities in employment.

(c) **Impact of becoming an interarntional company**

Currently, CAP operates entirely within Lizland, so the expansion into Robland means that it will become an international company for the first time.

Performance measurement and performance management in an international company will bring different challenges compared to managing a company in a single country.

Performance comparisons – When assessing the performance of the forty Aqua Parks in Robland, CAP will need to allow for any differences in economic conditions between Robland and Lizland; for example, the potential impact of different inflation rates on revenue and cost figures, or the wider impacts of there being different economic growth rates in the two countries. If economic conditions in Lizland are different than in Robland, it may be unrealistic for CAP to compare the financial performance of the parks in the two countries on a like-for-like basis.

Any such differences in the economic conditions between Robland and Lizland could also make it harder to set reliable budgets for the Robland business, particularly in the early years of its operation, because there will be little (if any) comparative performance information to base budgets and performance targets on. Moreover, the distance between Robland and Lizland means that CAP may have imperfect knowledge and the market conditions in Robland.

Local management – It is not clear from the scenario who will be managing the new parks in Robland; for example, whether expatriate managers from Lizland will be used, or whether local managers from Robland will be used. In choosing which approach to take, CAP will need to consider practical issues such as **any language or cultural differences** between the two countries (which may mean it is preferable to use local managers).

On the other hand, CAP may prefer to use experienced managers from Lizland to ensure that its new operations in a similar way, and with similar standards of quality and customer service, than its existing operations.

Although Jody's statement that he always wants to control the business relates to its share capital, it may reflect a wider desire to keep tight controls over the business. In which case, Jody may prefer to use experienced managers to manage the new parks.

Geographical distance – Nonetheless, the distance between Robland and Lizland could make it harder for Jody to manage the new parks than it would be to manage the existing parks. In particular, it will be more time-consuming for Jody to visit the parks in person to see how they are operating.

Management accounting information – In this respect, it is likely that Jody will want the management information produced by the new parks to be in a similar format to the existing parks, to assist comparison between them and to see how CAP group as a whole is performing.

However, there may be differences in the accounting policies used in Robland compared to Lizland, which could mean that the results are not necessarily comparable. For example, if assets are valued differently in Robland compared to Lizland this could lead to difficulties in comparing performance using ROI or RI as performance measures.

---

19 FGH Telecom

Text reference. Stakeholder management is considered in Chapter 5 of the BPP Study Text, where environmental management accounting is also discussed. The impact that external factors can have on an organisation's performance is discussed in Chapter 6.

Top tips. Part (a) asks you to evaluate how well the environmental strategy is aligned to stakeholder interests. So it is important that you link the stakeholders' interests directly to the strategy, and don't just talk about stakeholders in generic terms. Also note that part (a) is only worth 5 marks, so don't spend too long on this part of the question.

Part (b) asks for an environmental assessment. You could use PEST/PESTEL as these provide a structured analysis. However, you then need to suggest suitable performance indicators for each factor. Remember, performance indicators need to be measurable. To score well, the performance indicators you suggest need to be well explained. So, for example, a vague reference to competitor reviews for instance is not sufficient, and would score few marks.

Part (c) asks for an evaluation of the data in the table. What categories could be used to summarise the data? Remember to refer to the company's stated goal and how it is a long term goal. The company is part-way though the period covered by the goal so do you think it is on target for reaching a 60% reduction by 20Y7? At this level you need to take an overall view of performance measurement so think about overall performance not just the detail.

In **part (d)** think of what factors affect the data – for instance, miles travelled using each form of transport.

Marks

(a)   Up to 2 marks for the interests of each stakeholder group evaluated in
       relation to the environmental strategy.
       Maximum of 5.

5

(b)   1 mark per factor identified as relevant for each section of the broad
       sections of the analysis (PEST or PESTEL sections are appropriate and
       competition could be an additional area considered).
       Up to 1 mark for each performance indicator relevant to the factors
       identified.
       Maximum of 8.

8

(c)   Up to 4 marks for analysis of basic data, commenting on overall picture
       and achievement of target.
       Up to 2 marks for simplifying data into broad categories and commenting
       Up to 4 marks for analysis of mix of methods of travel and commenting
       (Another acceptable categorisation could be related to fuel type: petrol,
       diesel and aviation – rail is problematic as it is a mix of diesel and
       electricity but reasonable assumptions will be acceptable.)
       Maximum of 9 marks.

9

(d)   1 mark per relevant point – up to 3 marks.

3

Total = 25

(a)   **Shareholders** – The tough economic environment, in conjunction with the competitive nature of the
       telecommunications sector, are likely to mean shareholders will be particularly concerned about the level of
       profits which FGH can maintain.

       The environmental strategy could be particularly useful for two reasons in this respect:
       •   It can save costs and increase efficiency through reducing resource usage
       •   It could lead to increased sales as a result of improved reputation amongst customers

       Government – Government has been calling for change from the business community in relation to
       environmental issues, and FGH have taken action which are designed to bring about these changes. If
       organisations (such as FGH) reduce their environmental footprints voluntarily, this will reduce the need for
       government to impose regulation and legislation in order to encourage better performance.

       Public – Like government, sections of the public have been calling for change from the business community
       in relation to environmental issues. If it can demonstrate that it has responded to these calls, FGH should be
       able to benefit from an improved reputation amongst customers and potential customers.

       Employees – Although it is not clear from the scenario whether FGH's employees prefer working at home to
       commuting into an office, it is likely that a number of them will. In which case, they will be pleased with the
       impact of the strategy on their day-to-day life, regardless of the environmental benefits of the strategy. If
       other employers prefer working in the office rather than working at home, they are likely to resent the new
       initiative. By contrast, the content of some employees' work may mean that they cannot work from home, in
       which case the homeworking initiative is unlikely to affect them, so they may have little interest in it at all.

       Similarly, it is not clear whether the employees prefer teleconferences to the travel required to attend regular
       meetings, but again, it is likely that at least some will be pleased with the reduced amount of travelling they
       have to do.

(b) **Regulation and legislation** – FGH's environmental strategy will be directly affected by increased regulation and legislation from government. These would include recycling targets for materials, and limits on emissions such as pollution and waste levels. Carbon levies may be an additional tax.

Performance indicators which FGH could use to monitor its progress include the cost of additional recycling, fines for failing to meet regulations and targets, and the cost of a carbon levy.

Economic factors – Economic factors which could affect FGH's strategy include the difficulty in obtain capital (through the debt or equity markets) as well as general factors such as inflation, interest rates and exchange rates.

The difficulties in raising capital through the debt or equity markets could be monitored through FGH's cost of capital. This could be particularly important if any environmental initiatives it is considering would require significant capital expenditure in order to implement.

The touch economic environment is also likely to mean that firms will find it difficult to maintain their profits, so any cost savings from reductions in energy use could be useful to help offset any fall in profits.

Social factors – The general public has an impact on FGH's environmental strategy as they use its products and are calling for reductions in emissions. So, for example, if FGH is known to be more environmentally friendly than other telecommunications providers, this may improve its brand image and may prompt consumers to switch to FGH in preference to other providers.

A suitable performance indicator could be to measure the perceived image of FGH by means of a customer survey.

Technological factors – Finally technological change will affect FGH's environmental strategy as it can adopt new technologies such as electric and hybrid cars, and new technologies for storing and capturing energy such as recharging solar cells which could be used in production.

Performance indicators would require the measurement of how new technologies affect existing emissions data.

(c) **Progress to date** – The company has set itself a target of reducing emissions by 60% of their 20X1 value by 20Y7 (16 years). In total it has been able to cut emissions by 38% in nine years from 20X1 to 20Y0 (106.6/172.6).

In just the last year (20X9 to 20Y0) it has cut emissions by 16% (106.6/127.5).

However, this optimistic rate may not necessarily continue as emissions become increasingly hard to cut when the easier targets have been met in the early years of the programme.

Modes of transport – The data used can be usefully summarised into road, rail and air and the individual measures included under each. Detail of the data is included in Appendix 1 below.

In summary, rail travel has seen a decrease of 63%, the largest across the categories, then road travel which as seen a reduction of 38% and the least in air travel which saw a decrease of only 16% over the nine years. Both the first two categories are decreasing at a rate well within the target of 60% as the falls already achieved are at least 38% with seven years to go. The problem with air transport may reflect increasing globalisation and the need to travel to meet clients and have meetings.

If the composition of the three types of transport are analysed in the base year of 20X1 and compared with 20Y0 it is clear that air travel has increased slightly from 6% to 8% of total travel whilst rail travel has fallen by the same amount which may explain part of its success in reducing emissions. However, the reason for this may be a change in the emissions technology relating to each category travelled rather than the number of miles travelled by each method.

Looking in detail at each category, the largest trend is a move from commercial petrol vehicles to commercial diesel vehicles whereby there are nil emissions in 20Y0 from petrol vehicles. This reduction is easier to achieve with the commercial fleet than the other types of car as there may be an element of choice exercised by employees in the other categories for instance company cars.

(d)   **Total distances travelled** – One key area that could be measured is the number of miles total distances travelled by employees so that the impact of the changes on employee behaviour can be monitored. This would allow the assessment of the home working scheme to see how far employees commute and the effect on this of working from home.

It would also allow FGH to measure how much travel is done by air and the effect of moving from travelling to meetings by air and alternatives such as teleconferencing.

The data could also be used to calculate the effect of switching transport by calculating average emissions per kilometre travelled.

Appendix 1

Measured in millions of kgs	20X1 Base year	20X9	20Y0	Change on base year
Commercial Fleet Diesel	105.4	77.7	70.1	–33%
Commercial Fleet Petrol	11.6	0.4	0.0	–100%
Company Car Diesel	15.1	14.5	12.0	–21%
Company Petrol	10.3	3.8	2.2	–79%
Other road travel (Diesel)	0.5	1.6	1.1	120%
Other road travel (Petrol)	3.1	0.5	0.3	–90%
Rail travel	9.2	9.6	3.4	–63%
Air Travel (short haul)	5.0	4.4	3.1	–38%
Air Travel (long haul)	5.1	7.1	5.4	6%
Hire Cars (Diesel)	0.6	1.8	2.9	383%
Hire Cars (Petrol)	6.7	6.1	6.1	–9%
Total	172.6	127.5	106.6	

	20X1 Base year	20X9	20Y0
Index	100%	74%	62%
Year on year change		–16%	

Simplifying categories

	20X1 Base year	20X9	20Y0	Change on base year
Road travel	153.3	106.4	94.7	–38%
Air travel	10.1	11.5	8.5	–16%
Rail travel	9.2	9.6	3.4	–63%
Total	172.6	127.5	106.6	–38%

Mix of travel methods in each year

	20X1 Base year	20X9	20Y0
Road travel	89%	83%	89%
Air travel	6%	9%	8%
Rail travel	5%	8%	3%

20 Stokeness

Text reference. Porter's five forces model is discussed in Chapters 1 and 6 of the BPP Study Text.

Top tips.

Part (a). Although this part of the question should offer some relatively easy marks (for analysing the impact the different forces could have on Stokeness) it is important that you realise that the requirement isn't only about the impact of the five forces. You also have to recommend a performance measure for each of the five forces.

This second element of the requirement (recommending new performance measures) requires careful thought. The performance measures need to measure the strength or impact of each of the **five forces** themselves, not primarily different aspects of Stokeness' own performance. So, for example, what would be a suitable measure to indicate the threat of new entrants?

Also, in relation to the first part of the requirement, note that you are asked about the impact of the five forces on **performance management** at Stokeness, not, for example, how the five forces could be used to assess the attractiveness of the industry. In other words, you should be thinking how the Stokeness could use an understanding of the five forces to improve its performance or develop its strategy, rather than simply identifying that a particular force is strong or weak.

Part (b). A key question here is 'Who are Stokeness' competitors?' Is it competing against all engine manufacturers (including manufacturers of petrol/diesel engines)? Is it competing against suppliers of all the alternative technologies? Or is it only competing against other fuel cell manufacturers?

These questions should highlight the problem Stokeness faces when measuring a market share: unless it has identified its market, how can it measure its share of that market?

Part (c). Even though this part of the question is only worth five marks, in effect there are still two different elements to it: the VCs risk appetite, and key issues in performance measurement at Stokeness.

Stokeness appears to be a technology start-up company, which suggests the VCs were prepared to accept a relatively high degree of risk by investing in it. Equally, they will expect returns from the company in the future. However, currently, Stokeness is still three years away from a commercial launch. So, for the moment, the key aspects of its performance relate to this pre-launch phase; for example, has Stokeness got sufficient cash to sustain it until it can begin to sell its products? If Stokeness runs out of money before it launches its fuel cells, then there is little chance of it generating any returns for the VCs in future.

Examining team's comments. Part (a) was generally well done, with candidates making good use of the information in the scenario to give useful performance management advice to Stokeness. However, many candidates appeared not to read the second part of the requirement fully: this asked for 'a *justified* recommendation of *one, new* performance measure for each of the five forces. Instead, they simply produced a list of performance measures for each area, often also including market share, meaning that they failed, in three different ways, to answer the question.

Part (b) was poorly answered. Many candidates chose to answer the question 'How do you measure market share' thereby completely missing the point of the question actually set. However, better candidates realised that the definition of market (and hence its size) depended on whether you were talking about hydrogen fuel cells, alternative energy power technologies, or any sort of power unit (including existing petrol/diesel engines).

Similarly, in part (c), many candidates wasted time listing the different possible risk appetites, despite these not being required by the question set. Candidates are reminded that it is vital to read the requirement carefully, and to answer the question asked – not an alternative question of their own creation.

Marks

(a) For each of Porter's five forces:

Up to 4 marks for performance management implications of the force, and justifying a suitable performance measure

Total: up to 16

16

(b) For each valid point made about the problems of defining Stokeness' markets - 1 mark per point

Total: up to 4

4

(c) For assessing the risk appetite of the VCs – 1 mark per valid point; up to 2 marks.

For assessing the VCs impact on performance measurement at Stokeness – 1 mark per valid point; up to 3 marks.

Total: up to 5

5

Total = 25

(a) **Threat of new entrants**

Barriers to entry – The threat of new entrants into the fuel cell market will be determined by the extent of the barriers to entry into the market. The barriers to entry appear to be high, given the technical skills and the length of time required to develop a viable product.

These barriers to entry will be strengthened further by the need to develop a relationship with the vehicle manufacturers who will be the customers for the fuel cells. Even if a potential new entrant develops a viable product, they will not be able to establish themselves in the market unless they can attract any buyers for their product.

Performance measure: Patented revenue – One of the ways in which technology firms can create a barrier to entry into their markets is by registering patents over new products or technologies. In this respect, Stokeness needs to ensure that it obtains patents for new cell designs or technology processes which could provide it with competitive advantage.

A suitable performance measure to use here would be the percentage of revenue which is generated from patented protects. This will indicate the degree to which Stokeness' patents will act as a barrier to entry.

> **Performance measure: Customer loyalty** – If vehicle manufacturers (customers) are committed to using Stokeness' cells on a long-term basis, this will make it harder for new entrants to join the market.
>
> To this end, it would be useful to measure customer loyalty by looking at the number (and value) of the long-term contracts Stokeness has to supply fuel cells to vehicle manufacturers.

Threat of substitutes

Alternative fuel sources – The existing petrol/diesel engines remain a substitute for Stokeness' products, especially as their manufacturers are reducing the level of carbon dioxide emissions from these engines. Equally, electrical batteries and compressed natural gas products could also be substitutes for the fuel cells.

The petrol/diesel engines still have a number of strengths in the market; in particular, they are the only fuel source for which there is an infrastructure in place which enable end users to refuel their vehicles easily.

Performance measure: Output – The level of threat from substitute products could be measured by analysing the power output of different types of power supply compared to the level of emissions they produce and the cost of producing the power.

The cost of creating different engine types and the price of the fuels required to run them are likely to be very significant in determining the extent to which different types of engine are considered viable by vehicle manufacturers.

Bargaining power of suppliers

Component elements – The membrane which is used to produce the fuel cells requires rare and expensive elements. As a result, the **suppliers' bargaining power is high**. Stokeness' ability to produce the fuel cells will depend on the price and availability of the elements required for the membrane.

In particular, if the supply of these elements is controlled by a small number of suppliers they will be in a particularly strong position to dictate the price of the elements.

Subcontractors – The engineering firms to which Stokeness has subcontracted the production of certain components for the fuel cell also have a high bargaining power because of the knowledge they have gained of Stokeness' products. In this respect, it is important that there is a non-disclosure agreement in place to protect any commercially sensitive details of the products.

The size of the two engineering firms relative to Stokeness is not clear from the scenario, but it is possible that one of them may also consider some kind of forward vertical integration if they feel that Stokeness' products are going to be commercially successful.

Performance measure: Switching cost – The power of the suppliers could be measured by estimating the cost involved in switching to an alternative supplier. This cost could include any penalty fees payable to the existing suppliers, as well as the opportunity cost of lost sales arising as a result of delays incurred in switching supplier. These delays could be quite significant, given the specialist nature of Stokeness product, which any new suppliers would have to understand, and tailor their processes to, before production could re-commence.

Performance measure: Proportion of cost – An alternative measure of the suppliers' bargaining power could be taken as the price of the suppliers' components in relation to the cost of the fuel cell as a whole. Such a measure can give an indication of the importance of the components to the overall fuel cell.

Bargaining power of customers

Large manufacturers – Stokeness' customers are manufacturers of large vehicles, such as buses and trucks. It is likely there will be only be relatively few of these companies, but they will be quite large, giving them significant bargaining power. Crucially, the manufacturers have a choice of what fuel source to use (for example, fuel cells or standard petrol/diesel engines), and before they agree to use Stokeness' cells they will need to be sure that the cells are compatible with the existing technologies used in the vehicles.

Switching costs – However, once customers have committed to using a particular type of power source, the cost of switching to an alternative source is likely to be high. This may reduce the bargaining power of customers, but only once Stokeness has secured them as customers. In this respect, the fact that Stokeness has a two-year lead over the other companies developing fuel cells could be a significant advantage to it, if it can secure some significant contracts before the competitors have developed their cells.

Given the relative size of Stokeness compared to the manufacturing companies, and the potential importance of the fuel cells in the engine production process, one of the manufacturers might try to acquire Stokeness. However, this might prove to be an attractive option for the venture capitalists, depending on the price offered.

Performance measure: Discounts requested – The level of discount which customers request would provide Stokeness with an indicator of how strong the customers perceive their bargaining power to be. If the customers feel that Stokeness' fuel cells will provide them with a significant competitive advantage, then they will be less likely to press hard for a discount.

> **Performance measure: Switching costs** – The costs which a manufacturer would incur to switch from one power source to another could also be used as an indicator of the strength of the bargaining power of customers. The higher these costs are, the less likely a customer will want to switch power source, thereby reducing their bargaining power. Although Stokeness is unlikely to be able to calculate this figure exactly, it should nonetheless be able to make an estimate of it.
>
> **Number of alternative suppliers** – The number of alternative suppliers which customers could choose from could also affect the customers' bargaining power.

Competitive rivalry

Development advantage – As Stokeness has a two-year lead over the other companies developing fuel cells, the level of existing competition from these companies currently seems low. If Stokeness patents any key technologies it develops, this should help sustain its competitive advantage over its direct competitors.

Moreover, if Stokeness is able to secure contracts with some of the vehicle manufacturers before the other companies have developed their products, this will make it harder for the competitors to break into the market. In turn, this could help reduce the level of competitive rivalry in the industry in the future.

Performance measure: Launch date – Once Stokeness and then the competitors have launched their products, it will be possible to measure the strength of competitive rivalry by analysing market share. Until that point, however, there isn't a 'market' to analyse. Instead, the time until the commercial launch date of a viable fuel cell is a key performance measure. Although it may be difficult to obtain exact information about competitors' expected launch dates, Stokeness should try to monitor these alongside its own.

This measure highlights the importance of avoiding any over-runs in the development process, and in delivering a commercially viable product as soon as possible, thereby maintaining Stokeness' competitive advantage over the other companies which are also developing fuel cells.

(b) **Market definition**

The problem of defining the market is a particular issue for Stokeness because there could be some significant variations in the extent of that market.

Overall large vehicle market – In the broadest terms, Stokeness makes power supplies for large commercial vehicles such as buses and trucks. Therefore, its market share could be seen as the number of commercial vehicles powered by Stokeness' fuel cells as a proportion of the total number of commercial vehicles.

However, such a broad definition would include vehicles powered by standard petrol/diesel engines in the overall market, many of which were produced before Stokeness was even formed. If Stokeness wants to measure its share of the entire market on a more comparable basis, it may be preferable to focus on new vehicles only – that is, the proportion of the new vehicles manufactured each year which are powered by Stokeness cells.

Fuel cells – At the other extreme, Stokeness could define its market purely as the market for fuel cells, and therefore measure its performance against other fuel cell makers.

Alternative engine technologies – In between these two extremes, Stokeness might consider itself to be competing in the market for alternative engine technologies (for example, electrical batteries, compressed natural gas).

Because these three markets are so different in size, Stokeness will need to define which one it sees as most important to measure its performance in, so that it can set appropriate market share targets.

(c) **Technology start-up** – Stokeness seems to be a technology start-up company, which suggests that it is a risky company for external investors to invest in. Equally, however, it offers the prospect for high returns if its fuel cell technologies prove successful. Therefore, it appears that the venture capitalists (VCs) are risk-seeking by investing in Stokeness.

However, it appears that the VCs have tried to moderate the level of risk to some degree by placing commercially-experienced managers into the business to assist the engineers who founded it. Moreover, because the VCs now have some of their own employees on the management team, this will give them a high degree of influence at Stokeness.

Medium/long-term returns – Given that Stokeness is still three years away from the commercial launch of its cells, the VCs will not begin to see any returns from their investment until the medium to long-term. However, the VCs could use net present value calculations, based on projected returns, as a performance measure in this respect.

Cash flow and cash control – In the shorter term, it is vital that Stokeness does not run out of cash while it is still developing its product (and hence not yet generating any revenue from it). Consequently, monitoring actual expenditure against budget and cash outflows will be key performance measures, to ensure that spending is kept under control.

Development targets – Stokeness needs to measure key non-financial aspects of performance as well as financial ones. Crucially, the point at which Stokeness can start selling a commercially viable product and therefore start acquiring customers will have a significant impact on its cash flow and NPV calculations. If the launch of the product falls behind schedule, this will increase the risk of the company running out of cash.

Therefore, it will be important for Stokeness to measure operational progress against key milestones: for example, completing successful test runs of the product.

Customer acquisition – Equally it will be important for Stokeness to sign contracts with customers, in order to secure revenue. Therefore, performance measures showing the number of definite customers signed-up and the number of potential leads would also be useful.

21 Handra

Text reference. The difference between strategic and operational information is discussed in Chapter 1 of the BPP study text. Performance management information systems are covered in Chapter 7. The importance of monitoring non-financial aspects of performance as well as financial is discussed in Chapter 12.

Top tips. Part (a) may seem relatively straightforward, although you need to provide sensible examples of the different types of information that may apply to Handra.

Part (b) should also be relatively straightforward. The scenario has highlighted that the quality, reliability and functional features of Handra's equipment are important to customers, so it is important for Handra to monitor how well it is performing in these areas. But cost control and profitability are also important, so it cannot afford to overlook them.

Part (c) may need some careful thought. One sensible approach might be to consider what the objectives of management accounting (and management accounting information) are, and then consider whether the current management accounting system at Handra provides the appropriate information. Part (a) could be a useful link here, by encouraging you to think whether the current system provides information which is suitable for the different levels of the hierarchy (strategic; tactical and operational).

Part (d) also picks up on this idea. If more responsibility is being delegated to the employees, they will need operational information to be able to assess their performance. But does Handra's current system provide any (operational) information which would be useful to the employees working on the factory floor?

(a)   Strategic, tactical and management information are classifications of information that distinguish the purposes for which that information is used. The classifications can also be used to distinguish the type of information that is used at different levels in an organisation with a hierarchical management structure.

Strategic information – Strategic information is used for strategic decision-making. It often relates to long-term objectives and performance, and to matters that are external to the organisation.

For Handra, relevant strategic information would include information about competitors in the market. It appears that a competitor may be in financial difficulty; it may be useful for Handra to know more about this and the reasons why the competitor may be in difficulty. It would also be useful to have information about how rival organisations may respond to any competitive initiative by Handra.

The management of Handra would also benefit from strategic information about technological developments in the industry, the possibility of rising water and energy prices, or even the possibility of government action to discourage excessive energy use by business organisations.

Tactical information – Tactical information is generally associated with planning and control activities within the framework of annual budgets or plans. It is information to help management make decisions for planning, or for monitoring actual performance against the budget expectation, and also to manage spending and efficiency within the organisation.

Tactical information can include both non-financial and financial information. Examples of tactical information include budgets, variance reports for control purposes, efficiency and capacity ratios, and summary information about quality failures (re-working of faulty items and items returned under warranty) and on-time deliveries.

Operational information – Operational information is information provided to management, supervisors and other employees at a day-to-day operational level. It is usually detailed information and much of it is non-financial in nature. It is needed to help individuals to do their day-to-day work.

Examples of operational information include detailed information about throughput times, machine failures and downtime, bottlenecks, complaints, quantities of rejected items and so on.

Information systems should provide sufficient relevant information for decision-making at all levels and for all management an operational purposes within the organisation. When information is not sufficient, there is a much greater risk of inappropriate decision-making by management.

(b) **Importance of non-financial measures** – The quality and reliability of the equipment that Handra produces could both potentially be critical success factors for Handra because they are likely to be important in customers' buying decisions.

By performing well in these areas, Handra should be better placed to sustain its financial performance than if it performs badly in them. For example, if it provides its customers with high quality, reliable equipment, this should ensure a high level of customer retention, which should in turn help it maintain its revenues.

In this way, there would seem to be a strong link between non-financial performance and financial performance.

Importance of financial measures – However, it is also important that Handra continues to monitor its financial performance, because there is no guarantee that favourable non-financial performance will necessarily translate into favourable financial performance. For example, although Handra's equipment may be very reliable, if it is significantly more expensive than competitors', customers may choose to buy the competitors' equipment instead.

Also, the directors have already highlighted the importance of reducing costs in order to improve profitability. This identifies the importance of monitoring financial performance, in order to assess how successfully Handra is reducing its costs and improving profitability.

Combination of measures – Handra's profit margins are known to be low, as a result of the intense competition in the market. This reinforces the need to monitor aspects of its financial performance (such as costs and margins). However, it is equally important to monitor whether sales and market share are increasing or decreasing in this competitive market, and how Handra is performing in relation to the other critical success factors which will affect customers buying decisions.

Efficiency measures – Handra's costs and margins are also likely to be affected, at least to some extent, by operational efficiency. Measures of efficiency (such as machine utilisation or capacity utilisation usage, for example) could be seen as non-financial performance measures, but they are also closely related to financial performance.

(c) **Focus on tactical information** – The cost and management accounting system of Hydra appears to provide information about product costs, including standard costs, and also monthly variance analysis reports. This should help management to prepare budgets and then control performance at a tactical level by providing comparisons between actual and standard or budgeted costs. The system presumably also produces estimates of cash flows for the purposes of DCF analysis, because a decision was taken not to invest because the rate of return was insufficient.

Lack of strategic information – Management accounting should provide information to assist and support decision-making by management. Information is needed at a strategic as well as a tactical level. Much strategic information is forward-looking and long-term in nature, whereas budgetary control variance reports are historical and most budgets do not plan beyond the next financial year.

Strategic management accounting information should also include non-financial as well as financial information, such as information about customer needs and customer satisfaction, competitive advantage and product differentiation. It seems that Handra does not have a management accounting system that provides strategic information, and the current system is therefore incompatible with the purposes of management accounting.

Focus on cost – The current management accounting information system appears to focus exclusively on cost. Competition is strong and profit margins are low; therefore it is appropriate to consider costs and cost control. However, customer buying decisions are influenced by **quality** and **product design** considerations and it is therefore appropriate to provide management information about these aspects of performance as well as cost. A lack of information about these matters indicates a weakness in the information system.

Investment decisions – The decision against investing in the new machines may also indicate a weakness in the current management accounting system. The decision was presumably based on estimates of net present value or IRR, but the possible future rises in water and energy costs may have been omitted from the assessment. In retrospect, if the costs of water and energy increase significantly, the decision not to invest in the machinery may turn out to be a bad one. At the very least, the board should have considered this issue when it made the decision about the investment. If it failed to do so, this would suggest a weakness in the current management accounting information.

The management accountant of Handra is unwise to be satisfied with the current management accounting system. By failing to provide non-financial information and strategic information, it is not fulfilling the purpose of management accounting, to support well-considered decision-making.

(d) If employees in the manufacturing units are empowered, and given some authority to take decisions affecting production operations, they will need information to help them to make decisions and to provide them with feedback about the effects of their decisions. Much more information will have to be made available to them, although much of this information will probably be operational (and so non-financial) in nature.

Budgetary control information is unlikely to be of much value, unless the employees are involved in setting standards and budgets, because they will not accept responsibility for plans and targets with which they have not been involved.

It may also be necessary to provide an information system in which information can be exchanged between employees in different areas of manufacturing operations, with horizontal rather than vertical information flows.

22 TREN engine components

Text reference. Lean manufacturing and lean information systems are covered in Chapter 7 of the BPP Study Text for P5.

Top tips. This question focuses on one specific part of the P5 syllabus: "Evaluate whether the management information systems are lean and the value of the information that they provide."

To answer the question, it is necessary to identify the requirements of a lean information system (part (a)) and then to discuss why the existing 'traditional' management accounting system at TREN may fail to do this (part (b)).

Having established the difference between the two types of system, you then need (part (c)) to identify the changes which are needed to convert TREN's 'traditional' systems into 'lean' systems.

Note that there is no requirement to link your answer to part (a) directly to the scenario. However, your answers to parts (b) and (c) do need to be linked directly to the scenario.

(a) A lean information system should provide value to the users of the system. Key principles are the **elimination of waste, speed of information flow,** and **clarity.**

Elimination of waste – A lean system seeks to eliminate all waste. In an information system, waste is created by errors in the information, which means that incorrect information is used and wrong decisions may be taken. Alternatively the information has to be corrected when the error is identified, and this results in a cost of correction. Correcting errors does not add value, because the error should not have occurred, and correcting errors is wasted effort.

Efficiency in the flow of information – A lean manufacturing system is one in which there is an efficient flow of items though the manufacturing process. In a lean information system, there should be an efficient flow of information. Information should be available to individuals when they need it, and there should not be unnecessary delays in providing it or making it available.

While efficiency in the flow of information means that information should be available when it is needed, it should not be provided before it is needed. Information should be available 'just in time'. This is the concept of **pulling items** through the system rather than pushing them through. If information is provided before individuals are ready to use it, it does not have value.

Clarity is also an element of lean information. Information must be clear to the people who use it and should therefore be presented in a form that they can understand and use. If information is presented in a form that is difficult to understand, it will be difficult to use. Unless it is used for its intended purposes, information has no value.

Together, the elimination of waste, efficiency of information flow, and clarity of information are qualities of an information system that give value to the information that the system produces.

Reasons why lean principles may not lead to improvements in productivity and profitability

In many situations, an organisation supposedly using lean principles has not experienced the improvements in productivity and profitability expected. It is difficult to know whether this is due to shortcomings in the lean philosophy or whether the techniques involved are being **interpreted and applied correctly**.

Change in approach – To be successful, lean techniques should be seen and treated as outward signs of a more **fundamental approach** to operations and quality. However, many organisations seem to treat the techniques as the end itself – they have a mistaken belief that simply putting structures and mechanisms (eg quality circles) in place will improve efficiency and quality. Sustainable differences require a change in thinking and in culture – which are difficult to achieve.

Cost-cutting exercise – Lean production is often viewed as a simple cost-cutting exercise rather than a fundamental commitment to eliminating waste and adding value. Many companies use lean manufacturing to improve quality and reduce costs. But the benefits most businesses realise are only a fraction of what could be achieved if these strategies were applied in conjunction with the aim of creating a workplace with real organisation and order, and with an engaged workforce who take pride in their work.

(b) There are several reasons why TREN's current management accounting system does not fulfil the requirements of a lean information system.

Errors – There are many errors in data capture for the cost accounting system. Errors represent waste in the system, by providing incorrect information about costs, or requiring correction when the errors are found. Errors also reduce the confidence of users in the information that the system provides.

'Push' system – Monthly variance reports are provided but not until two months after the end of the month. There are two weaknesses in this reporting system. The first is the delay in making information available if required. The information about performance is being held by accountants and is not made available to the managers who can use it.

The second problem is that the information is pushed out to management in the form of monthly variance reports, when it would be more appropriate to make the information available when management want to use it for monitoring and control purposes. The information system is dictating how and when the information should be used, whereas management should be doing this.

Not encouraging lean manufacturing – More fundamentally, it can be argued that traditional cost and management accounting methods provide managers with inappropriate information that encourages the wrong sorts of management for an organisation that uses lean manufacturing methods. A key feature of lean manufacturing is the elimination of inventory, because holding inventory is wasteful. Absorption costing, however, encourages manufacturing at full capacity, even if this means manufacturing items that are not yet needed by customers, so that inventory will build up. This is because high volumes of production reduce the unit costs of manufacture by spreading overhead costs over a larger volume of output.

Variance reporting of efficiency also encourages greater volumes of output, because greater efficiency means faster production. When the work force is paid a fixed wage or salary, attempts to improve efficiency will result in greater production quantities, and a build-up of inventory.

The current reporting systems therefore encourage managers to control operations in a way that is inconsistent with lean manufacturing.

(c) **Error reduction** – To create a lean management accounting system, waste must be eliminated and information flow improved. The causes of the data errors in data capture are not known. The problem may be the use of manual documentation for recording costs, or errors in input by inadequately trained staff. Methods of recording costs should be investigated, and the target should be to eliminate input errors entirely.

Flows of information – The flow of information must be improved, so that up-to-date information is available to management when they want it. The speed of entering data into the accounting system should be reviewed, and the aim should be to minimise the delay between recording data and inputting it into the accounting system. Automated methods of monitoring inventory movement or recording labour times may be considered.

User access to information – The accounting system should also allow managers on-line access to information about costs, so that they can obtain and use the information they need at a time that they need it. This should apply to senior management as well as to management at the operational level.

Cost allocation – The information provided by the accounting system should be reviewed, and absorption costing should be abandoned. There may be some value in using activity-based management to monitor and control overhead costs, but the most important requirement should be to value inventory at direct materials' cost. This means that there will be no incentive to produce at high capacity volumes or operate at unnecessary levels of efficiency. Favourable capacity and efficiency variances will not affect inventory costs and so will not improve management performance.

Performance measures – Different items of information should be provided for performance measurement purposes. Traditional performance measurement methods for materials – price and usage variances – should be used to control materials costs. For labour, however, non-financial measures of performance may be appropriate, such as production cycle times of throughput times and the ratio of idle time to active time for the work force. The company is considering JIT purchasing for its main suppliers: if so, a suitable measure of performance may be the order-to-delivery cycle time for purchase orders.

In a lean information system, information should have a practical use and support the aims of management. The management accounting system should be changed so that it provides value – a practical purpose, with no waste, rapid information flow and clarity of meaning.

23 KLP divisions

(a) **Responsibility accounting** is accounting in way that makes managers responsible and accountable for performance that they are in a position to control. In the case of investment centres, a responsibility accounting system should make divisional managers responsible and accountable for sales revenues, costs, profit and return on investment, for aspects of performance within their area of control.

Controllable and non-controllable costs

For the new performance reporting system at KLP, divisional managers should be made accountable for the costs within their control, but they should not be made accountable for apportioned head office overhead costs. An appropriate reporting system may therefore distinguish between controllable and non-controllable (apportioned) fixed costs, as follows:

Divisional performance	$
Sales	X
Variable costs	(X)
Contribution	X
Directly attributable divisional fixed costs	(X)
Controllable profit	X
Apportioned general overheads	(X)
Net profit	X

The profit performance of divisional managers should be based on the controllable profit.

Manufacturing costs last year were 53% of sales revenue, but sales and distribution costs (17% of sales revenue) were also quite high. The responsibility accounting system should ensure that sales and distribution costs for which each division is directly responsible are included within the variable costs or directly attributable fixed costs of each division.

In the same way, the assets that are accounted for as divisional assets should be assets over which the divisional managers have some control. This may be difficult in practice, especially when a division occupies a building that is shared with staff from other divisions or head office staff.

Learning curve

The design of a responsibility accounting system should also recognise the implications of the learning curve in one division, and its potential impact on transfer pricing arrangements.

The existence of a learning curve in one division means that expected average production times will get shorter as new products are produced in (cumulatively) larger quantities. The division should therefore benefit from improving efficiency but these improvements will come 'naturally' and should not be attributed to effective management. The reporting system should therefore be capable of including the expected learning curve effect when setting performance targets for the division and comparing actual costs and production times with expectation. The divisional manager should not be credited with the efficiency improvements that come from the learning curve.

Transfer prices

When investment centres transfer goods or services between each other, the transfers add to the revenue and profits of the transferring division and add to the costs of the receiving division. This creates potential for disagreements about what the transfer prices should be. Since there is no external market for most transferred items, transfer prices for these items at cost plus would seem to be appropriate. However, the transfer prices should be fixed periodically at a negotiated price based on expected cost plus a profit margin. Actual cost plus should not be used for transfer pricing, because inefficiencies and overspending in the transferring division would be passed on and charged to the receiving division in the transfer price. This would be inconsistent with the principle of responsibility accounting.

(b)   It should be assumed that if divisional managers are rewarded on the basis of the performance of their division, they will be motivated to optimise the performance by which they are rewarded. They will be much less concerned about aspects of performance that do not affect their reward.

Short vs long term performance

The board currently believes that divisional managers should be rewarded on the basis of financial performance only – profitability and return on investment. It is likely that rewards would also be based on annual financial performance rather than longer-term financial performance. This would be inappropriate, because long-term performance is an important consideration, and non-financial aspects of performance as well as short-term financial measures will affect longer-term performance. The new performance reporting system should be designed in a way that motivates divisional managers to recognise the longer-term aspects of performance.

Financial and non-financial performance

An appropriate performance reporting system may therefore be one based on a balanced scorecard of performance targets, with annual bonuses based on the achievement of non-financial as well as financial targets. A balanced scorecard would include performance measures from customer, internal efficiency and innovation and learning perspectives.

Goal congruence – Performance measures could still include short-term performance measures. For investment centres, an important aspect of performance is financial return on investment. The performance measurement system should encourage managers to make capital investment decisions that are in the best interests of the company. Ignoring issues such as risk, investment decisions should be taken if they will be expected to achieve a positive net present value.

However, if divisional performance is based on accounting return on investment, there will be a possibility that divisional managers will choose not to make new investments because, in the early years of the investment, the effect will be to reduce the division's ROI. The performance reporting system should therefore be designed in a way that encourages desirable capital investment. The use of residual income, or even economic value added (EVA™), should therefore be considered as alternatives to ROI as measures of short-term financial performance.

(c)   There are three broad categories of control mechanism which KLP might use to cope with the problem of organisational control: action control; personnel control; and results control.

Action control

The aim of action controls is to ensure that only those actions which are desirable occur, and actions which are undesirable do not occur.

Action accountability involves defining actions that are acceptable or unacceptable, observing the actions and then rewarding acceptable (or punishing unacceptable) actions. In this way, action accountability sets limits on employee behaviour. For example, setting budgets for different categories of expenditure in each division makes the divisional managers accountable if they exceed the budget limit, such that they have to explain or justify their actions.

Personnel control

The aim of personnel controls is to help employees do a good job, by ensuring they have the capabilities and the resources needed to do that job. This is through appropriate recruitment and selection (finding the right people to do a specified job); training and job design (where job design includes making sure that jobs are not too complex, onerous or badly designed so that employees do not know what is expected of them); and providing the necessary resources for people to do their jobs.

Cultural control – These represent a set of values or social norms that are shared by members of an organisation and influence their actions. The Board of KLP could introduce codes of conduct, or group based rewards schemes, such as annual bonuses based on how well staff perform against objectives (rather than simply based on profitability and return on investment).

Results control

The focus of results control is on collecting and reporting information about the outcomes of work effort. The key value of results controls for KLP would be to identify deviations from desired performance measures (eg variances to budget) and then allow corrective actions to be taken to try to improve performance.

24 Racer deliveries

Text reference. Recording and processing methods, including the recoding of qualitative information, is covered in Chapter 8 of the BPP study text. Issues around interpreting qualitative data are covered in Chapter 12.

Top tips. Performance measurement systems need to provide information of a qualitative nature to management, although quantitative measures should be used even for qualitative issues, where this is achievable.

Qualitative aspects of performance can be particularly useful in service businesses, and this appears to be the case here. However, the question is whether these qualitative factors do actually contribute to RACER's competitive advantage, or whether the directors have just assumed they have.

In part (a) you need to identify what aspects of performance are perceived to contribute to RACER's competitive advantage, and then think how qualitative information could help assess the impact they are actually having on the company's performance.

In part (b) you then need to think about the practical problems associated with trying to capture qualitative information. It is often subjective, so how can it be measured?

Part (c) picks up on this point. The surveys which the management accountant will could enable RACER to quantity qualitative data, but are there any potential issues with such a process? For example, will all customers give the same level of service the same score?

(a)   The board of directors of RACER believes that its competitive advantage is based on **reputation, brand recognition, reliability, experience and personalised service** by its call centre staff. This belief appears to have made the directors decide that RACER should not copy its rivals and introduce an automated ordering system, even though this may be less expensive to operate.

Information for decision-making – The directors would probably benefit from information about these aspects of the company's service, because their views currently seem to be based on opinion rather than firm evidence. In this respect, it seems probable that the board is basing decisions about the company's future strategy on its views of RACER's competitive advantage, rather than any firm evidence.

If the directors believe that these qualitative aspects of performance are the reason why RACER is successful in the market, they will probably base the company's future strategy on preserving the factors that create this advantage. Therefore it would be valuable to obtain information about whether these qualitative aspects of performance really do create value for RACER; for example, by establishing whether they affect customer's choice of which delivery service to use.

Competitive advantage – If qualitative aspects of performance are strategically significant, then it is also important that Information about them is reported regularly so that the board can monitor any change in circumstances that might create a threat to competitive advantage.

The most significant qualitative aspects of performance that appear to be significant for RACER may be those that have been identified by the board.

(i) **Brand recognition** – The board believe that RACER has a good reputation for service and that it benefits from strong brand recognition. Information about the strength of the company's reputation and brand recognition by customers would help the company to develop its marketing strategies. For example an advertising campaign might promote the brand name and image.

(ii) **Service reliability** – The board believes that the company's reputation is based largely on its service reliability. Reliability probably means on-time collections and deliveries, or possibly speed of delivery. Information about on-time services and speed of services would help management to monitor this aspect of performance, and try to ensure that the service standard is maintained.

(iii) **Customer service** – The board also believes that customers value the experience and personal service of its call centre operators. As a result, it has taken the important decision to retain a personal calls system for customer orders, when rival companies have chosen to cut costs and use automated voice recognition ordering systems. Information about the value of this service to customers would enable the board to confirm their view – or prove it wrong.

(iv) **Customer needs** – Information about the quality of the telephone ordering service and reliability of service are important only if they are significant to customers. RACER does not seem to have obtained reliable information about customer needs and whether RACER's services are meeting them sufficiently well. Information about how much extra customers would be willing to pay for additional features in the service would also be of value.

(b) One of the distinctions between qualitative and quantitative information is that it can be harder to measure qualitative information and qualitative aspects of performance. For quantifiable aspects of performance, it is possible to set specific targets for achievement; whereas often qualitative aspects targets can only be expressed in more general terms. When targets are not measurable and performance is not measured, it can be difficult to assess whether the targets are being achieved.

There is a risk that monitoring qualitative aspects of performance can become self-delusional.

Management may decide that actual performance is what they would like it to be, not necessarily what it actually is. Strength of reputation is one such qualitative aspect of performance. Others may be employee loyalty, team spirit and quality of strategic leadership.

Since qualitative information is not currently measured at RACER, there are problems in gathering and analysing information, and in accessing and retrieving qualitative information that is held on file. The information provided by a reporting system may also be of limited value, because management may not know what to do about it.

Information must have a purpose, but qualitative information may not be sufficiently specific and its purpose may therefore be unclear.

It may be argued that qualitative information may be of value for strategic planning rather than performance management and control. Information about the strengths and weaknesses of the company, and about threats and opportunities in the industry and the business environment, may be largely qualitatively in nature, but this information is used to assess strategic options and make strategic choices.

SWOT analysis, however, is unlikely to be made part of a regular performance reporting system for management.

The importance of non-financial information is now widely recognised: much qualitative information is non-financial in nature, but many aspects of non-financial performance can be measured quantitatively.

If RACER's board wants to obtain information of a qualitative nature, an appropriate approach may be to convert as many qualitative aspects of performance as possible into quantifiable aspects. Customer satisfaction, for example and aspects of service quality may be measured by means of regular customer surveys or market research surveys.

(c) **Quantifying data** – The surveys which the management accountant has suggested will provide RACER with a means of converting qualitative data into quantitative data. RACER's performance in key areas of the business such as service quality or customer satisfaction can then be recorded and monitored, by looking at the scores it receives for them, and for example, taking an average score for a given period. For example, this could be useful for quantifying the impact on customer service of introducing the automated calling system, and in turn allowing the directors to assess how successful the new system has been.

Subjectivity – One of the major problems in interpreting qualitative data is that it based on people's opinions and judgements, and is therefore it is subjective. For example, the quality of service which one of RACER's customers might rate as 'Excellent' (and score '5') another customer might simply rate as 'Average' (and score '3').

Equally, when people complete surveys there is a tendency to score towards the middle. In general, respondents are likely to feel more comfortable selecting scores in the range 2 – 4, rather than using the extremes of 1 or 5.

Trends – Because of this subjectivity, the surveys may be more useful for looking at trends in RACER's performance rather than looking at one-off performance. For example, RACER could monitor how their average score for customer service varies over a period of time, as an indication of whether customer service is improving, remaining at much the same level, or getting worse over time.

Equally, if there are significant variations in the scores over time, this should prompt the Directors to investigate the reasons for these variations.

25 Forion Electronics

Text reference. Enterprise Resource Planning Systems (ERPS) are discussed in Chapter 8 of the BPP Study Text. Non-financial performance indicators are discussed in Chapter 12.

Top tips.

Part (a). As is the case with a number of P5 questions, note that there are two elements to this requirement: first, you need to discuss the integration of information systems in an ERPS; then, second, you need to discuss how the ERPS at Forion may affect performance management issues there.

The first element doesn't specifically require any application to Forion. However, you could use the issues which Forion is facing, and the different departments mentioned in the scenario, to illustrate the way an ERPS could integrate information from different systems.

The marking guide indicates that six out of the 10 marks for this requirement are available for the second element – discussing how the ERPS can affect the performance management issues at Forion.

Even if you didn't know much about an ERPS, you should have been able to identify how deficiencies in the information sharing between departments could lead to the problems identified in the scenario. There are six marks available for three problems; so two marks per problem. If, for each problem, you provide a brief discussion of the likely causes of each problem, and then indicate how better information sharing could help to avoid that problem, this should help you earn the majority of the marks available for this part of the requirement.

Part (b). An important factor to consider here is the relationship between Forion and BAS. BAS is a supplier to Forion, and Forion has chosen BAS because of its reputation for quality and new product development. This suggests Forion consider these aspects of performance to be important (and Forion has previously identified it needs to have high-visibility, durable screens in order to be competitive – so visibility and durability could be considered as aspects of 'quality').

A useful way to answer the question would be to consider how well the performance measures chosen allow Forion to assess BAS's performance in the areas which it has identified as important.

In this respect, don't just think about the aspects of performance selected, but also think about the practicalities of measuring the performance. How easy will it be to measure whether or not BAS achieves the desired levels of performance?

Part (c). Note that the question requires you to make two separate comparisons: financial vs non-financial data; and internal vs external data. Also, it is important that you discuss the issues specifically in the context of the service level agreement between Forion and BAS. For example, will BAS be happy to use internal performance data prepared by Forion given that it (BAS) could be liable for a financial penalty if it fails to achieve the target performance levels?

Examining team's comments (for part (c)) – Evaluating the reliability of data has been a common topic in part exams, yet candidates answers to this question were unexpectedly poor. Many candidates seemed unaware of what constitutes internal and external sources, and – surprisingly – many considered audited, financial data to be amongst the least reliable source. In addition, many candidates discussed the type of information that both parties to the alliance would need, without discussing its reliability (which is what the requirement actually asked for).

Marking scheme

		Marks
(a)	For general description of an ERPS and how it integrates information: 1 mark per relevant point – up to 5 marks	
	For specific discussion of the impact an ERPS could have on the problems at Forion: 1 mark per relevant point – up to 6 marks:	
	Total for part (a): up to 10	10
(b)	For relevant points about the usefulness of the three areas for measuring performance – 1 mark per point	
	Note. In order to score a clear pass, all three issues must be addressed	
	Total for part (b): up to 12	8
(c)	For relevant points about the relative reliability about the different types of data – 1 mark per point	
	Note. In order to score a clear pass, both issues (financial/non-financial; and internal/external must be addressed	
	Total for part (c): up to 7	7
		Total = 25

(a)   An Enterprise Resource Planning System (ERPS) is a software system which supports and automates the business processes in an organisation. An ERPS can assist in identifying and planning the resources needed to perform many different activities in different departments across the whole organisation – including inventorying management, manufacturing, distribution, invoicing and accounting. An ERPS can incorporate support functions such as human resource management and marketing.

As such, an ERPS enables the performance information from all departments that are involved in operations or production to be integrated into one system, thereby assisting the flow of information between the departments and across the organisation as a whole. Integrating performance information in this way would seem very useful to Forion, given the problems it has encountered to date.

As well as improving the flow of information between the department in an organisation, ERPSs can also help to improve linkages with outside stakeholders – for example, by incorporating customer relationship management (CRM) and supply chain management (SCM) software.

Again, this would seem very useful to Forion, given the high number of customer and supplier relationships it has to manage.

The impact of an ERPS on performance management issues at Forion

Information sharing – The board has suggested that a number of the performance management problems at Forion arise from poor communication and information sharing between departments; not least because each of the departments has its own information system rather than having an integrated system across the organisation as a whole.

As such, by providing an integrated system which assists the flow of information between departments, an ERPS could help to solve the three problems identified.

Amount of subcomponents ordered – This reflects a problem with the information being shared between the purchasing department (which orders the subcomponents) and the manufacturing department (which uses them). If the purchasing department has incorrect or out-of-date information, this will lead to it ordering the wrong amount of subcomponents, which in turn means that Forion's inventory handling and storing costs will be higher than they need to be.

However, if Forion had an ERPS, information from the manufacturing department would automatically be shared with the purchasing department, meaning the purchasing department should be able identify the quantities of subcomponents to order more accurately.

Stock-outs or obsolescence –Both of these problems arise from the amount of goods being manufactured not reflecting the expected level of orders. Although the marketing department may produce good sales forecasts, if these forecasts are not shared with the manufacturing department, it will not know what quantities of different goods it needs to make. If it produces too few, this will lead to stock-outs (and a loss of potential revenue); while obsolescence results from producing too many units of a good which cannot then be sold. (The risk of obsolescence could be a particular concern for Forion as a manufacturer of electronic goods.)

If the marketing department's forecasts were captured in an ERPS, they would be available to the manufacturing department when it was setting its production plans.

Lack of delivery vehicles – The delivery schedule needs to incorporate sales information (customers' orders) and manufacturing information (when goods will be available).

If the warehouse department only becomes aware of a customer order after it has scheduled all its delivery vehicles this would help to explain why there seem to be insufficient vehicles to meet customer deadlines. Similarly, if there are delays in manufacturing which the warehouse department isn't aware of, this could mean that goods can't be included in their scheduled delivery, and will require an additional delivery and an extra vehicle to fulfil the customer order.

By linking the manufacturing schedule, customer orders, and the delivery schedule, Forion should be able to schedule its deliveries as efficiently as possible, to make best use of its delivery fleet.

Equally, though, by having greater visibility over orders and the manufacturing schedule, the delivery department should be able to identify in advance any times when it will not have sufficient vehicles of its own to fulfil all the orders required. Knowing this, it can then make arrangements for a third-party logistics company to deliver the order in time to meet the customer's deadline.

(b)   **Usefulness of performance areas**

The three performance areas selected (quality of manufacturing; timeliness of delivery; technical upgrades) all seem appropriate. The 'quality' area derives from underlying logic behind the alliance – Forion's need for high-visibility, durable screens; timeliness of delivery will be important for the smooth operation of the production process; and the ability to make technical upgrades is likely to be critical in a rapidly changing market – such as the market for smartphones.

Quality of manufacturing – BAS's strong reputation suggests the number of faults should be low. Nonetheless, as screen manufacturing is a key part of the assembly process, and having high quality screens is likely to be a critical success factor for the phone overall, it will be important to meaure performance in this area.

There could also be significant costs involved in remedying any faults with the screens. If the faults are identified during internal inspection, the time taken to fix them will delay delivery. If the faults are identified by customers, Forion will incur the cost of repairing – or replacing – the faulty phone. Customers' dissatisfaction with faulty items may also mean they are less likely to buy a Forion smartphone again in the future.

Time of delivery – The screen is a key component of the phone so delays to shipments could cause significant disruption to the production process if Forion is trying to use a just-in-time (JIT) production process. Conversely, if Forion holds inventory 'just-in-case', then concerns about delayed shipments could lead to it holding higher levels of inventory than it might wish to.

If Forion wants to use a JIT production process, then implementing the ERPS, and giving BAS access to the system could be very useful. For example, this would give BAS greater visibility around when screens are needed and in what quantity.

Technical upgrades – Whilst upgrades are likely to be important in keeping Forion's phone competitive, it will be difficult to measure BAS's performance against the metric as it is currently defined. For example, there is no timescale in which BAS needs to provide the upgrade, and deciding when the market demands an upgrade could be subjective.

If performance in this area cannot be measured effectively, BAS could pay less attention to it. Although, in theory, building financial penalties into the agreement is appropriate, Forion may not be able to apply them if it cannot measure whether or not BAS has achieved the target levels of performance.

Moreover, as Forion selected BAS as its strategic partner due its strong reputation for quality of manufacturing and new product development, it is suprising that both of these acknowledged strengths are being measured, rather than any areas of potential weakness.

(c) **Reliability of financial vs non-financial data**

The requirement to produce annual accounts, and to have them audited, means that there should be robust controls in place around the production of financial data. Although non-financial data will be useful to management in controlling the business, it may not be subject to the same scrutiny and controls as financial data.

Similarly, financial data will be quantitative and objective, whereas non-financial data can sometimes be subjective. For example, an issue with a phone screen which some customers may report as a fault, other customers may not report.

Although the subjectivity of non-financial data can sometimes make it difficult to measure, this does not appear to be a problem in this context. The fault rates and the number of shipments overdue should be relatively easy to measure.

Internal vs external sources

Forion is likely to place greater reliance on its own data rather than external data (for example, as provided by BAS in relation to shipments supplied). As such, Forion is likely to use its own warehouse records to determine the number of shipments which are overdue, although this means that Forion will need to have sufficient controls in place to ensure that expected and actual delivery times are recorded accurately.

However, if both parties place greater reliance on their own data than the other party's data, this could be a source of problems for the alliance; for example, if the number of shipments BAS believe to be late differs from the number Forion believe to be late. This could be a particular issue here, given the financial penalties relating to performance.

In this case, it may be useful for both parties to have the right to inspect (audit) each other's data to confirm the reliability of that data.

26 Quark Healthcare

Text reference. Radio-frequency identification devices (RFID tags) are discussed in Chapter 8 of the BPP Study Text. Lean systems are discussed in Chapter 7.

Top tips.

For part (a), it is very important that you think about the impact of the RFID system specifically in the context of the areas highlighted by the CFO: (i) the costs and benefits associated with producing information from the system; (ii) the impact of the system on the nature of the information supplied; (iii) changes to performance management reporting; and (iv) how the new information could be used to improve control at the hospitals.

To this end, it would be sensible to use each of the CFO's suggestions as headings in your answer, to make sure you cover all of them.

The 'control' issues and their impact on performance should be relatively easy to identify from the scenario – for example, staff are unable to find equipment because it hasn't been replaced after being used, and as a result patient care is delayed while staff waste time trying to find the equipment.

However, the marking guide indicates that only 6 out of the 12 marks for this requirement are available for internal control issues. So, don't spend too long on this one area at the expense of the other areas.

Nonetheless, the problems staff face in finding equipment and drugs provide a link between parts (a) and (b) of the question. One of the key principles of 'lean' systems is the removal of waste and non value-adding activities. Time spent looking for equipment or drugs clearly doesn't provide add any value to hospital patients. Similarly, 'lean' systems aim to promote efficiency.

So a sensible way to approach this requirement will be to evaluate how far the RFID system can reduce waste and improve efficiency at the hospital.

Part (c). The scenario highlights that an earlier system which the hospital had tried to introduce has not been fully implemented due to complaints from the medical staff. The medical staff are clearly key stakeholders at the hospital and so if they oppose a new system it is unlikely to be successful.

This provides the context to the first part of the requirement: how the medical staff's attitudes will influence the design and implementation of the system.

However, note that there are effectively two parts to the requirement, with the second looking at issues around responsibility and accountability.

How far can the system make staff responsible One of the key issues here, though, is how the system can promote accountability given the 'strict social order' among the staff. For example, can a nurse be responsible for a piece of equipment being in the wrong place if it has been moved by a doctor?

Marking scheme

		Marks

(a) Costs and benefits associated with producing the information from the RFID system – 1 mark per relevant point up to a maximum of 3 marks
Impact of the RFID system on the nature of the information supplied – 1 mark per relevant point up to a maximum of 3 marks

Changes to performance reporting resulting from the implementation of the new system – 1 mark per relevant point up to a maximum of 3 marks

Use of information from the new RFID system to improve control at the hospitals – 1 mark per relevant point up to a maximum of 6 marks

Total for part (a): up to 12   12

(b)   Definition of lean systems – up to a maximum of 2

Analysis of the impact of the RFID system on the management of the
hospital – 1 mark per relevant point, up to a maximum of 7

(Within this 7 marks, up to 2 marks are available for definition of the five
S's of lean)

Total for part (b): up to 7   7

(c)   Evaluation of how the attitude of medical staff will influence the design of
the new system – 1 mark per relevant point, up to a maximum of 4

Evaluation of how the system might be used to promote responsibility and
accountability – 1 mark per relevant point, up to a maximum of 4

Total for part (c): up to 6   6

                                                                                  Total = 25

(a)   **Costs and benefits of the system**

Cost – There is likely to be considerable cost associated with the hardware and software needed to establish
the RFID system. A significant amount of time may also be required to tag the equipment and drugs which
are to be included in the system.

However, the costs should be compared to the benefits which will accrue from the system:

Efficiency savings – Hospital staff will save time because they will no longer have to search for items once
those items have been tagged.

Patient care – Improvements in patient care as a result of hospital staff being able to find equipment or
drugs immediately rather than having to search for them.

Impact of the nature of the information supplied

Non-financial information – Although the information being supplied about Quark's equipment and
inventory is non-financial (relating to the location and quantity of equipment and drugs in Quark's hospitals)
it should already be included in the hospital's information systems.

Timeliness and accuracy – However, the major impact of the new system should come from the
improvements it can provide to the timeliness and accuracy of the information being recorded. The RFID
tags will update information on a **real-time basis**. Moreover, because movements are **recorded
automatically** the problem of the register not correctly reflecting the physical location of an asset will be
overcome.

Batches of drugs – However, the quality of the information provided by the RFID tags may be less reliable
for the drugs which are delivered in a single packaged batch. If a tag is applied to a batch as a whole when it
is delivered to the hospital, then the information provided by the tag will no longer be reliable once the batch
is opened and drugs are used from it. Instead, there will still be a need for the hospital to physically count
the quantities of these drugs actually held in inventory, rather than relying on the RFID information alone.

Performance management reporting

Weekly physical checks – Under its existing systems, Quark has to make weekly physical checks of the
drugs held in inventory in order to update its records on the basis of those checks. However, the information
provided by the RFID tags should mean that inventory records can be updated on a real-time basis, rather
than being dependent on these weekly checks.

Access to information – The fact that the RFID information will be available on terminals throughout the
hospitals should also help the speed with which staff can locate items of inventory or equipment. The ease
and speed with which staff can search the information will depend on the number of terminals which are

installed. It would also be useful for relevant staff to receive training on how to search for information on the terminals.

Improved control

Control over drugs – Quark's existing accounting systems aim to avoid theft and obsolescence of equipment and drugs. RFID tags should improve controls over security by providing greater transparency about the location of assets. For example, the tags will make it easy for staff to check that all the high-value drugs are stored in secure locations, thereby reducing the risk of them being stolen.

Reduced obsolescence – Additionally, the information available about the date drugs were delivered should help staff identify the order in which different batches of a drug should be used to prevent obsolescence and wastage.

Tagging equipment – We have already noted that tagging items of equipment will allow staff to find them more quickly and thereby provide faster service to patients. However, the RFID tags will also enable the hospitals' management teams to ensure that pieces of equipment are replaced and locked away in secure areas once they have been used. This again should help reduce the risk of theft, but perhaps equally importantly staff should be reminded of the importance of replacing items after they have been used, and of storing them in useful locations. This also links to the ideas of 'lean' systems which the CFO is interested in.

(b) **Lean systems**

Removal of waste – The aim of 'lean' systems is to minimise the amount of resources (including time) which are consumed by the activities of an organisation. A key element of this comes from identifying and eliminating all non-value-adding activities. In this context, 'lean' also involves the systematic elimination of waste.

In relation to information systems, waste arises from difficulties in accessing and retrieving information, or from having to correct inaccurate information. This kind of 'waste' has clearly been an issue for Quark – for example, where staff have had to waste time looking for equipment or drugs which have not been not stored in the correct place. Such activity is clearly not value-adding; rather it detracts from the value (care) which Quark can offer to its patients.

Improved efficiency – By contrast to this, the goal of a 'lean' operating system is to get the right things to the right place at the right time. In the context of Quark, this could mean enabling staff to know where equipment is so that it can be made available in the right place when it is needed by patients. Consequently, introducing the RFID system should help the operations management at the hospitals become leaner.

'Lean' systems can also have wider cultural implications which could be beneficial at the hospitals; in particular in relation to changing attitudes towards 'waste' and 'inefficiency'. The instances of equipment lying unused in one area of the hospital while being searched for in another area (to the detriment of patient care) would seem to be symptomatic of waste and inefficiency in the hospitals.

5 S's – Lean principles are often characterised through 5 S's, which could usefully be introduced at Quark:

Structurise – Identify the things which are most important and introduce order where possible. At Quark this could mean identifying the optimal locations for storing equipment, on the basis of where it is used most frequently.

Systemise – Arrange essential items in order so that they can be quickly and easily accessed. The RFID system will make it easier for staff to locate the equipment and drugs they need.

Sanitise – Keep the working environment clean. Be tidy, and avoid clutter. Although the RFID system should help staff to find drugs and equipment more easily, there is a danger that staff may think that this reduces the need for them to replace them after use, or to keep stocks of drugs tidy and in order.

Standardise – Make cleaning and checking a routine. For example, the RFID information could be used by managed to check that equipment is replaced after use; and staff could even be monitored on the extent to which they keep their sections of the hospitals tidy.

Self-discipline – Sustain via motivation; for example, by reporting on performance. The system could produce exception reports highlighting pieces of equipment which had not been returned to a secure store once they were no longer being used. Corrective action can then be taken to return the equipment to an appropriate store area.

Impact of the RFID system

In some organisations, 5'S' has become a cleaning and housekeeping exercise only, and the underlying philosophy behind the concept has been lost. If this happens, then RFID's ability to make the management system leaner will be reduced. However, if the RFID information system is seen as an important part of quality management at the hospitals, then its impact should be more beneficial.

(c)   **Key stakeholders** – The **medical staff** are likely to be key stakeholders in the hospitals, so their attitude to the new system is likely to be very important. If they resist the system, then its implementation is unlikely to be successful, as appears to have been the case with the new method for recording drugs administered to patients.

In this respect, it will be important to consult the medical staff over the design and implementation of the RFID system. Not only does consulting them recognise their position as key stakeholders, but also it gives them the opportunity to ensure the system is designed in a way which provides them with the information they need.

Improvements to patient care – Crucially, consulting the medical staff about the design of the system should help encourage them to accept it rather than to resist it. Equally, it will be important that medical staff realise that the primary purpose of the system is to enable equipment and drugs to be found more easily - thereby improving patient care – rather than as a piece of bureaucracy. If the medical staff realise the benefits of the system, they should be more willing to accept it.

Usability – The user-friendliness and ease of use of the new system will also influence how successfully it will be implemented.

Again, this highlights the importance of consulting the medical staff, to ensure that the system is designed in a way which makes it easy for them to use. Some of the complaints from the nurses and specialist doctors about the new method of drug administration may have been caused by the system proving difficult or time-consuming to use.

Responsibility and accountability

The RFID system will provide much greater transparency as to where equipment or drugs are actually being stored, and can provide management with the information to control how well staff are looking after the hospitals' assets. However, in itself, the system cannot promote responsibility or accountability.

Quark will also need to identify who is responsible for ensuring assets are held in the right place at the right time. For example, responsibility schedules could be introduced for each department or ward identifying which assets the nurses are responsible for and which the doctors are responsible for.

Quark's management should only hold people accountable for assets being in the right place if those people have control over how and where those assets are used. For example, can a nurse be held accountable for equipment being in the wrong place if a doctor has moved it? Crucially, if nurses start being criticised for items not being stored in the correct place when those items have been moved by a specialist doctor, this is likely to demotivate the nurses, and could also create resentment between the nurses and the doctors.

27 Bluefin School

Top tips.

Part (a). There are two different issues to consider in this question: (i) what are the controls over data and information that make it useful for decision-making and control; (ii) what security procedures are needed to protect that data itself. You need to address both of these issues to score well in this requirement, and to link it to the specific context of Bluefin School.

Part (b). The verb requirement here is to 'evaluate' the information so you need to consider how useful or valuable it is to the Board. In your evaluation you should try to consider both the advantages and disadvantages of the pack's current format, even though you should have realised that there are rather more disadvantages than advantages!

Part (c). The scenario identifies that some departmental heads use graphs to present information while others use tables and figures. When presenting information, it is important that the method chosen helps the audience understand the information, so you need to consider how the different methods of presenting information could help the Board understand departmental performance most effectively.

Part (d). Here again, as you are asked to 'evaluate' you should try to consider the potential advantages and disadvantages of the suggested improvements. Also, note there are two potential aspects of the improvements you should consider: (i) the introduction of the unified database; (ii) the internet connection.

Marking scheme

		Marks
(a)	For each relevant point discussed in relation to controls and security procedures – 1 mark each. Up to a maximum of 9.	9
(b)	Positive aspects of the pack – 1 mark each, Up to a maximum of 2	
	Problems of information overload – Up to 2 marks	
	Problems of information being confusing and unexplained – Up to 2 marks	
	Pack failing to cover overall objectives – Up to 2 marks	
	Maximum for part (b) – 6 marks	6
(c)	For each different way discussed – 1 mark each	
	Usefulness of the different methods of presenting information (and potential drawbacks of them) – 1 mark each	
	Maximum for part (c) – 5 marks	5
(d)	Benefits of suggested improvements – 1 mark per relevant point, Up to 4	
	Problems with suggested improvement – 1 mark per relevant point, Up to 3	
	Maximum for part (d) – 5 marks	5

Total = 25

(a) **Controls**

Comparisons – An important control over management information which is prepared on a decentralised basis by different departments (as at Bluefin school) is that it is prepared in a way that enables the **performance of the different departments** to be compared. For example, at Bluefin School, the information should allow the governors to analyse the performance of each department in the school by comparing performance in key areas (such as exam pass rates.)

Standard templates and definitions – However, the fact that the department heads are using different approaches to reporting information and are presenting their performance information in different formats will make it much harder for the governors to compare performance in this way. To overcome this problem, all the departments could be asked to present their results in a standard template, and using **standard approaches for reporting performance** (for example, presenting both pass rates and average marks.

Costs vs benefits – Another important control is that the cost of producing the reports does not outweigh the benefits of producing them. However, in practice this is likely to be hard to monitor. At Bluefin, the costs of the reports are likely to come from the cost of the **heads of departments' time** spent producing them, and they may not by themselves have any direct quantifiable (or financial) benefit. However, the reports will be necessary to satisfy key stakeholders (such as the government) that performance within the school is being adequately managed.

Management information used – However, any benefits from producing the reports will only accrue if the reports are actually used by the governors. In this respect, an important control is monitoring (for example, by reviewing meeting minutes) that the departmental results are discussed at the board meetings, and actions taken to investigate any unexpected variances in performance between departments.

Security measures

Back ups – Data and information needs to be backed up on a regular basis to prevent it being lost. The decentralised nature of the information system at Bluefin means that each department will be responsible for backing up its own data. This could be seen as a risk, because some departments may be less reliable in backing up their information than others.

Protecting confidential information – Bluefin's management information contains two types of sensitive or confidential information: information about **individuals' exam performance**, and information about the **school's income and expenditure**. The school needs to ensure that it has adequate security procedures to ensure that this information is **not accessed by unauthorised people**.

The decentralised nature of the school's information systems **is** likely to make it harder to ensure controls are maintained, for example because of the number of PCs containing confidential information.

Password controls – However, a properly applied system of password controls could help ensure the security of this information. For example, Bluefin should have a policy that all passwords should be changed regularly, and the passwords for logging on to any PCs should not be written on, or near, the relevant PC.

Safeguarding memory sticks – Bluefin also needs to consider the security procedures required to manage the risks associated with information being passed to the administration office on memory sticks. For example, the **memory stick could be lost or stolen**; and this should be addressed by a copy of the final departmental report being **saved on the departmental PC** before it is transferred on the memory stick. Then any data on the memory stick should be **encrypted** before being passed to the administration office.

A further risk associated with the memory sticks is that they could transfer viruses between different PCs. To protect against this, Bluefin should ensure that **up-to-date anti-virus software** is installed on all its PCs, and all memory sticks are scanned for viruses before any data from them is loaded onto a PC.

(b) **Benefits of pack**

Highlights financial and educational performance – The pack addresses the two of the key areas of the school's performance (financial and educational performance) and does provide the governors with data about performance in both of these areas. This data should help the governors to assess the quality of the teaching and financial management in the school.

Problems with pack

Information overload – However, the contents of the pack appear too detailed for their audience (who are selected from the local community and parents, rather than being academic or financial experts).

The governors only review their pack once a year, and so it would seem more appropriate for the information in the pack to be a summary of the school's performance, rather than the detailed information currently presented.

For example, if the governors are presented with 11 departmental reports similar to that from the mathematics department it will be difficult for them to identify any key trends or variances in performance. Similarly, rather than presenting the governors with a detailed income and expenditure statement, it may be more appropriate to present them with a summary of the key financial highlights.

In addition, the financial information currently only focuses on the school's income and expenditure. However, it would be useful to also show a summary of the school's assets, in a statement of financial position. For example, it would be useful to understand the school's cash position before making a decision about the proposed IT improvements.

Lack of narrative – The governors' pack does not appear to contain any narrative explaining any of the data provided in the detailed reports. For example, it would be useful if the departmental reports also included a short narrative explaining any significant factors which have affected the class averages provided. Although the previous years' figures are provided as a basis for comparison, this does not help to explain any variations in performance between the two years.

Limited performance measures – The pack only addresses the financial and educational performance of the school, but the school's ethos also highlights the importance of promoting 'citizenship and self-confidence among the pupils.' However, there does not appear to be any analysis or measurement of how well Bluefin is achieving this. Admittedly, it may be difficult to measure the pupil's self-confidence objectively, but some measures of citizenship could be included in the pack; for example, the number of hours which pupils spend working on community projects.

Lack of external comparisons – Finally, the pack only focuses on Bluefin's own performance, although it would also be appropriate to include some external comparisons of the school's performance. In this respect, benchmark data (for example, comparing Bluefin's exam performance against that of other schools in the area) could also be provided, in addition to the current, internal performance information.

(c)   The information may be presented in a written format, or as a **table, graph** or **chart.**

The use of charts, graphs and tables can often present information in a way which is easier for users to understand. In particular, charts or graphs can be effective ways of communicating information, and may focus the board's attention on key aspects of departmental performance. In this way, using graphs or charts could be more effective than presenting too much information in tables.

However, it is important to remember that the usefulness of different types of chart or graph (for example, pie charts, bar graphs and line charts) depends on the sort of information being communicated. Therefore, it is important to select the most suitable type of chart or graph in any given situation:

Pie charts – are useful in reflecting percentage or other proportional relationships; in this instance they may have limited use.

Bar charts (or column charts) – are useful for making comparisons between two or more items when absolute amounts are being presented instead of proportional or percentage figures. They may be used, for example, to provide a valuable visual representation of average marks over time and between departments.

Line charts (or similar scatter plots) – are most useful for presenting a trend (or a combination of trends) over a period of time and can be used to show trends, for example, in average marks.

However, it is important that there are not too many charts or graphs in the report. If too many charts are used, they are likely to lose their effectiveness, because the reader will be likely to end up ignoring some of them.

There also needs to be consistency in the ways that the information is presented to allow the board to make easy and fair comparisons between the departments and over time.

(d)   **Benefits of having a unified database**

The improvements will result in all of Bluefin's performance information being stored in a single database, which all the departments and the administration office can access. This should not only prevent any unnecessary duplication of files, but should also reduce storage requirements on account of all the data being unified in one database.

Transfer of information – Having a single database will significantly increase the ease with which information can be transferred between the departments and the office, and will reduce the risk of data (currently transferred on memory sticks) being lost.

Control over data and security – Storing all the data on one network rather than having local repositories in each department should also improve control over the data. For example, all the data can be backed up centrally, rather than relying on each department to back up its own data. Equally, standard templates for the department reports can be created on the network, which the department heads then fill in, thereby ensuring consistency in the way information is presented between departments.

Data sharing – Under the new system, Bluefin's computers will be linked to the internet, which will make it easier to submit information to key stakeholders, such as the government or the governors. The internet connection may also mean that Bluefin can share data with other schools more easily, which could help in benchmarking performance between the schools.

Limitations of new system

Risks to data and security – Whilst there could be benefits from opening the school network to the internet, there are also risks to doing so: it will provide additional opportunities for the spread of viruses, and could make any information on the network vulnerable to hackers.

Equally, if all the school's data is stored in one place, it would mean the consequences of a system failure would be greater, because potentially all the data could be lost. However, backing up data regularly should reduce the impact of this risk.

Underlying usability of information – While the new system may address some of the current problems with the control and security of the data, simply improving the information systems by themselves will not solve the problem of information overload in the governors' pack.

28 Great National Trains

Text reference. Performnace management in not-for-profit organisations is discussed in Chapter 11 of the BPP Study Text. Integrated reporting, and the management accountant's role in providing information for integrated reports, are discussed in Chapter 8.

Top tips.

Part (a): Although the context of this question is the issues faced when setting and measuring objectives in a public sector organisation as opposed to a commercial organisation, the requirement is to discuss the difficulties faced specifically by GNT, rather than the difficulties faced by public sector organisations in general.

The difficulties GNT faces may be the same as those faced by public sector organisations in general (for example, multiple stakeholders, with conflicting objectives; the prevalence of qualitative objectives) to score well in this question you need to relate the difficulties specifically to the problem of setting and measuring objectives in GNT.

Also, note that you have to consider the difficulties in two different contexts: the difficulties of **setting** objectives; and then the difficulties of **measuring** performance against those objectives.

The reference to measuring performance against objectives could have highlighted the idea of 'SMART' objectives. For example, are GNT's (qualitative) objectives specific enough to measure; are they time-bound... and consequently, how effectively can they be measured?

Part (b): In effect, this requirement is asking you about the elements which should be included in an integrated report. The scenario tells you that GNT's current report focuses largely on financial and operational performance for the last year only, meaning that there is little information about GNT's wider strategy or future outlook. However, these are key elements of an integrated report.

Part (c): The focus of this question isn't the integrated report as such, but the role of the management accountant in producing information for the report. What additional information (if any) would be required to produce an integrated report, and what potential difficulties could the management accountant face in providing that information?

(a) **Setting objectives**

Range of stakeholders – As a public sector organisation, GNT Railways has a wide range of stakeholders, including: government, passengers, freight companies, the rail regulator, and society as a whole (for example in relation to carbon emissions). The three subsidiary companies (Passenger, Freight, Track) could also be viewed as stakeholders of GNT.

However, the different stakeholder groups have different expectations of GNT, which in turn means that GNT has multiple objectives to achieve.

Prioritising objectives – Unlike commercial organisations, which have an underlying objective to be profitable and to deliver value for their shareholders, as a public sector organisation, GNT does not have a single defining objective of this kind.

The number of elements in GNT's current strategic objectives highlights the potential difficulties of identifying which elements of performance are most important: reliability, punctuality, safety, cost effectiveness, or environmental impact.

Conflicting interests – Moreover, the nature of these objectives means that GNT may inevitably not be able to achieve all of them, because some of them could be mutually exclusive. For example, GNT might be able to improve reliability and safety, and possibly also to reduce its environmental impact, by investing in new trains, but such a major investment would have significant cost implications, and therefore may not be viewed as being cost effective.

This again highlights the difficulty GNT faces in trying to satisfy the needs of different stakeholder groups. For example, the decision to reduce the number of passenger services on (less profitable) rural routes appears to be driven by a need for cost effectiveness, but reducing the level of services has a detrimental impact on local residents for whom the rail service provided a vital means of transport.

To complicate matters further for GNT, in some cases single stakeholder groups may have multiple interests in the railway. This increases the difficulty GNT has in prioritising its objectives. For example, while supermarkets are clearly concerned by the environmental impact of their supply chains, the reliability and punctuality of freight deliveries are likely to be equally, if not more, important to them. If GNT's key stakeholders have different interests in this way, then its own goals and objectives have to address these different aspects of performance.

Subsidiary company objectives – The interests of the different groups of external stakeholders also create difficulties for GNT in managing the performance of its subsidiary companies. Reliability and punctuality are clearly issues for both passenger and freight trains and so need to be reflected in the objectives and KPIs for both subsidiaries.

However, as passenger services generate more revenue than freight services (50% vs 40% of total revenue) this suggests that greater focus will be given to ensuring passenger services run on time than freight services. Equally, though, the suitability of a KPI measuring punctuality of freight services could be reduced if freight trains are delayed as a result of having to wait for passenger trains to use a section of track in preference to them.

Tutorial note. *Additional point about conflicting interests and objectives*

IF GNT focuses primarily on its passenger services, and ensuring that these are on time, there is a danger that freight services get overlooked within its portfolio. However, given that demand for freight services has been increasing in recent years – due to congestion on the roads – freight services could be a source of growth for GNT. Therefore, it could face a dilemma around how to achieve growth in its freight services alongside maintaining punctuality levels for its passenger services.

Measuring objectives

SMART objectives – Effective objectives should be 'SMART' – specific, measurable, attainable, relevant and time-bound.

GNT's overall strategic objective does not exhibit a number of these characteristics. For example, instead of 'continuing to reduce' its level of carbon emissions, GNT's objective would be more specific and measureable if it sought to 'reduce carbon emissions by 5% each year'.

Selecting performance measures – For GNT's performance measurement system to be effective, the aspects of performance which are measured (the KPIs) should be linked directly to GNT's critical success factors, and, in turn, to its overall strategic and financial objectives.

However, the difficulties we have identified in relation to setting objectives could also create difficulties in terms of performance measurement.

In particular, if GNT is struggling to decide what its performance priorities are, it may end up measuring performance in too many areas (rather than concentrating only on the **key** performance indicators). If GNT's managers and the Board become overloaded with information, this could actually reduce their ability to assess GNT's performance and make strategic decisions effectively.

Objectives and controllability – It appears that there is only a single strategic objective for GNT as a whole, rather than there being strategic objectives for the three subsidiary companies as well. However, each of the individual companies has its own KPIs.

This situation could create problems in relation to controllability. For example, one of Freight's KPI's is the proportion of trains arriving at their destination on time. However, if there is a signal failure (Track's responsibility), Freight's punctuality performance will suffer, even though the cause of any delays is outside its control. Equally, as we have already mentioned, freight trains could be delayed by passenger trains, if they are given priority on the rail network.

Stakeholder influence – There could also be a danger that the aspects of its performance which GNT chooses to prioritise will be influenced disproportionately by interests of the stakeholders which hold the greatest power. For example, if GNT considers the government to be its most important stakeholder, it could focus on the objectives and performance measures which are most important to the government, potentially at the expense of the interests of other stakeholders such as customers, or its staff.

This kind of prioritisation of objectives could create problems for GNT though. For example, a focus on cost effectiveness (to please the Government) may lead to under-investment in new trains. But as GNT's trains (particularly its diesel engines) become increasingly old and unreliable, customers may feel their objectives are not being met. In turn this could lead to them seeking alternative modes transport and GNT losing customers as a result.

This situation again reflects the problems associated with identifying GNT's key strategic objectives. GNT's performance measures need to be selected to help ensure it meets its key performance objectives. However, if GNT has a number of (potentially conflicting) performance objectives, then the process of selecting performance measures also becomes much more difficult.

Measurement vs management – Whilst GNT can measure factors such as punctuality or safety, these measures by themselves provide relatively little insight into the factors determining performance levels. For example, Freight train's punctuality figures could be affected by a number of different factors. Similarly, assessing the safety of the rail network in GNT is likely to be far more complex than simply measuring the number of signals passed at danger.

Therefore while individual aspects of performance can be measured, a range of factors all need to be considered before any actions are taken to improve individual aspects of performance.

(b) **Context of performance reporting** – In an integrated report, GNT will still report on its financial and operational performance, as it currently does, but the report should make clear to readers the extent to which GNT has achieved its strategic objectives. For example, as well as reporting its KPIs for punctuality, the report should highlight the extent to which GNT has achieved its objectives in relation to the reliability and punctuality of its services.

Importantly, in an integrated report, GNT will also report on social and environmental aspects of its performance. Currently, there appears to be little emphasis in GNT's performance management and reporting on the way it manages and develops its 'human capital' (staff). However, as human capital is one of the six categories of capital identified within the integrated reporting framework, this should encourage GNT to evaluate the contribution of its people to its performance.

Impacts on different categories of capital – More generally, performance reporting within an integrated report should explain the outcomes of an organisation's performance in terms of six categories of capital: financial; manufactured; intellectual; human; social and relationship; and natural. Using these six categories could provide GNT with a framework for analysing its performance; for example, 'manufactured' capital could relate to track work and station upgrades, while 'social and relationship' capital could relate to improving customer satisfaction or customer loyalty.

However, the 'integrated' nature of the reporting also means that in its report GNT should highlight the interrelatedness and dependencies between different factors which affect its ability to create value over time. For example, investing in new engines (manufactured capital) should help to improve performance reliability and reduce pollution (natural capital), but these benefits will come at the financial cost of acquiring the new engines.

Importantly though, one of the key aims of integrated reporting is to reflect the longer-term consequences of the decisions organisations make, in order that they make more sustainable decisions. So, in its integrated report, GNT would be able to highlight the longer term benefits of investing in the new engines.

Future strategy and outlook – The current annual report appears to focus on GNT's financial and operational performance in the last year. In this respect, it is a backward-looking report. However, an integrated report would provide greater focus on future strategy and outlook.

In an integrated report, GNT would provide not only a summary of past performance but also a summary of how the organisation's strategy, governance and performance can lead to the creation of value in the future – in both the short- and the long term. For example, how the investment in new trains or new tracks can help GNT provide an improved service to its customers.

Opportunities and risk – By focusing on its own financial and operational performance, there is a danger that GNT's current report may become inward-looking. However, in an integrated report it would also highlight the opportunities and risks which affect its ability to create value, and how it is dealing with them. Although GNT has a monopoly over rail services in Pecoland, it competes directly against road transport for both passenger and freight services. So, for example, GNT should use its integrated report to explain how it plans to use increasing road congestion as an opportunity to promote rail travel as a substitute for road travel.

Equally, however, GNT needs to consider the risks and threats to its business model. Even though the current Minister of Transport and the Rail Regulator oppose privatisation, this could change if a new government was elected in Pecoland. However, one way to increase GNT's resilience to any threat of privatisation is to demonstrate the value it currently creates, and thereby to highlight to any future governments that keeping the rail network under national control remains the best way to create value from it.

(c) **Amount of information** – The Board's scepticism towards integrated reporting appears, at least in part, to come from their concerns about the extra cost and effort involved in producing an integrated report.

However, integrated reporting does not necessarily entail producing **more** information, and one of the potential benefits of integrated reporting is that it encourages organisations to produce shorter, more streamlined communications, rather than longer reports.

Instead of focusing on the quantity of information provided, the focus in integrated reporting is more about changing the way information is presented.

For example, instead of presenting information about GNT's commercial, social and environmental performance in distinct 'siloes,' integrated reporting would seek to highlight the connections between these different elements. In this way integrated reporting aims to provide stakeholders with a more holistic understanding of an organisation and its performance.

Therefore, rather than requiring the management accountant to prepare lots more information, the change to integrated reporting may be more likely to require the management accountant (and members of GNT's senior management) to consider how different performance measures and indicators relate to each other.

Stakeholder interests – However, integrated reporting also seeks to respond to stakeholder interests by providing them with the information they want about the performance and direction of an organisation. As we have seen in part (a), there are a number of stakeholders with an interest in GNT, and if each of them want information about different aspects of performance, there is danger that this could end up creating information overload in the report.

As part of its preparations for producing an integrated report, GNT could introduce a stakeholder engagement process with key stakeholders to identify what they want to know about the performance and direction of the organisation.

Additionally, the management accountant (in conjunction with the management team at GNT) will need to decide what data is most appropriate to collect, as well as what data it is possible to collect given the management information systems currently in operation at GNT.

Type of information

Reporting or focusing on strategy – An important theme in successfully applying integrated reporting is that it is not simply about reporting for its own sake, but that the information being reported needs to focus on an organisation's core strategy.

From the examples given in the scenario, it seems that the KPIs which GNT already monitors are linked to its key objectives. If this is the case, then again integrated reporting should not require the Group management accountant to produce additional performance measures. However, rather than simply preparing the figures the management accountant would be expected to highlight the significance of the figures, and how they are affecting GNT's ability to create value.

Non-financial KPIs – Another important benefit of integrated reporting is that it helps organisations to make clearer links between financial and non-financial performance.

By focusing on value generation in its broadest sense (rather than, for example, narrower goals of revenue generation) integrated reporting will also encourage organisations to review the set of performance measures they use. One of the main consequences of integrated reporting is likely to be the increased use of non-financial data to gain a clearer picture of an organisation and its performance.

In this case, however, it seems that a number of GNT's KPIs are already non-financial, suggesting that GNT already appreciates the link between non-financial and financial performance. This again suggests that introducing integrated reporting may not require the introduction of many additional KPIs; although some may be required in relation to 'human capital' if this is not already covered by any of the existing KPIs.

Issues

Nonetheless, the increased importance on non-financial information could produce a number of issues for the Group management accountant:

- Can GNT's current management information systems supply the full range of non-financial data which stakeholders would wish to see in an integrated report?

- If the data cannot be obtained from GNT's current systems, how can the management accountant obtain the information?

- More generally, can non-financial information be gathered and verified within financial reporting timelines?

- How can the accountant ensure the information is reliable and, more generally, what assurance is there over non-financial data in the report? (Non-financial data is typically not audited in the same way that financial data is; but if stakeholders are going to rely on this data, then GNT should consider obtaining some kind of 'assurance' over the data.)

Integrated reporting is not yet mandatory, and there are currently no standard formats for producing integrated reports. Therefore a significant practical issue the accountant will face when producing GNT's first integrated report will be decide what information to include in the report and how to present it.

If the management accountant has to develop and produce the integrated report in addition to his or her existing work, this means the accountant will have less time available for that existing work. As a result, there is a danger management reports could be delayed, or the quality of them could be reduced – particularly in the short term, following the introduction of integrated reporting.

29 Amal

Text reference. Big Data is discussed in Chapter 8 of the BPP Study Text.

Top tips.

Part (a). Note that there are effectively two parts to this requirement: (i) choosing and calculating appropriate performance indicators, and then (ii) commenting on the indicators you have calculated.

The context of the scenario could also be important here. Amal and Kayland Air both appear to be pursuing differentiation strategies, whereas Cheapo Air is a budget airline.

The requirement doesn't specify how many performance indicators you should analyse. The key point here is perhaps not the quantity of indicators you calculate, but making sure they are relevant.

We have chosen four in our answer below. However, this is not an exhaustive selection. If you have made other relevant calculations, and then commented on them, you would have got credit for this.

A sensible approach here is to select indicators which relate to Amal's key business issues (eg fuel costs), identify the key drivers behind them (eg fuel cost per seat kilometre) and then provide a short commentary showing how the indicator links to the companies' strategies and the issues mentioned in the scenario.

Part (b). There are four areas for you to exaplin here, and eight marks available, so two marks per area. This means you are not expected to write in-depth about any of the areas. However, make sure you explain how the areas could be used to help Amal's performance, rather than explaining what the benefits of Big Data are.

In effect, the key areas from the conference already identify the benefits of Big Data, so you need to think practically here, and assess Amal could use them.

Part (c). Although the question doesn't ask you to discuss the characterisitcs of Big Data – and so you can't pass the requirement just by doing this – thinking about the characteristics should nonetheless help you identify the potential implications Big Data could have for an organisation's information systems. For example, what implication could the 'volume' characteristic have for the capacity of an organisation's information systems?

Examining team's comments for part (a). The overall quality of the commentary which candidates provide in relation to numerical results they have calculated remains a concern. Simply putting the numbers which have been calculated into a sentence isn't an analysis of the figures. For example, saying 'Amal has a higher profit margin than either Kayland or Cheapo' doesn't add any value to a reader (who has already seen the calculations which show this). Consequently, such a statement will not score any marks.

However, good answers used the numerical work as an opportunity to show they have understood the scenario; for example, by commenting that Amal's higher profit was not surprising given that Amal is a 'premium airline.'

		Marks
(a)	Calculations – up to 6 marks 1 mark for each meaningful indicator selected 2 marks for load factor or similar measure of capacity utilisation Commentary – 1 mark per relevant point, up to 7 marks Total – up to 12 marks	12
(b)	For explaining how Big Data could improce performance in each of the four key areas identified – up to 2 marks per area Total – up to 8 marks	8
(c)	For identifiying potential implications of Big Data on Amal's management information systems – 1 mark per relevant point Total – up to 5 marks	5
		Total = 25

(a) The following performance indicators could be used to analyse the three airlines:

	Amal	**Kayland**	**Cheapo**
Operating profit margin	630/5,430	54/7,350	127/2,170
	11.6%	0.7%	5.9%
Capacity utilisation (load factor)	79,619/100,654	82,554/105,974	40,973/46,934
	79.1%	77.9%	87.3%
Revenue/staff member ($000s)	5,430 m/32,501	7,350 m/56,065	2,170 m/5,372
	167	131	404
Fuel cost/seat kilometre ($)	1,480 m/100,654 m	1,823 m/105,974 m	535 m/46,934 m
	0.015	0.017	0.011

Operating margin – Amal has the highest operating margin of the three airlines (11.6%), which suggests it is being run efficiently overall. We might expect Amal to achieve a relatively high margin because it appears to be pursuing a **differentiation strategy**. However, Kayland, which appears to be pursuing a similar strategy, generates an operating profit margin of less than 1%.

Capacity utilisation – By showing, on average, how full each airline's aircraft are this indicator shows how well the airlines are using their asset base (ie their aircraft). Amal and Kayland's performance is similar in this respect, but Cheapo's is significantly better. This is likely to be because Cheapo (a low cost airline) is pursuing a **cost leadership** strategy. Amal might consider reducing its prices to try to improve capacity utilisation, but it needs to do so in the context of its overall strategy. If it reduces prices too much, it may end up compromising the quality and service it offers to passengers, but these elements are crucial to its strategy as a differentiator.

Revenue per staff member – This is an important measure in the context of the recent disputes over working conditions and pay. Amal's staff appear to be performing better than Kayland's, which in turn might strengthen their claims for a pay rise.

The comparison between Amal and Cheapo's performance for this measure may be less meaningful. Cheapo **outsources** many of its activities, meaning its staff numbers will be significantly lower than Amal which carries out the corresponding activities **in-house**.

Fuel costs – The board's interest in new fuel-efficient aircraft indicates that reducing fuel costs is an important concern for Amal. Again, Cheapo appears to be controlling its fuel costs better than Amal or Kayland. This might be because it has more **fuel-efficient planes**, which would support the board's argument for Amal investing in new aircraft. However, Cheapo may have negotiated more favourable fuel contracts with its suppliers, or be using lower grade fuel.

> **Tutorial note.** It is important to use fuel cost per *seat* kilometre as the performance indicator here rather than fuel cost per **passenger** kilometre, because we are looking to monitor the fuel efficiency of the aircraft, rather than the airline's ability to fill their aircraft with passengers.

(b) Amal's business strategy as a premium airline, coupled with the difficult trading conditions, mean that it is increasingly important for the company to provide its customers with the best services and experiences possible, so that they choose to fly with Amal in preference to another carrier. Increasing the data it holds about customers, and potential customers should help Amal's management make better decisions, and thereby should help the company ahieve this.

Detecting key trends – Analysing conversations on social media could help Amal identify potential trends in customer demand; for example, if there are major events taking place in a particular place, or if certain resorts are increasing (or decreasing) in popularity as holiday destinations. Being able to forecast demand more accurately – and almost in 'real time' – could help Amal boost revenue, through applying **dynamic pricing**. For example, Amal could keep prices high on flights which are going to be popular, but could reduce prices on flights which look like they are going to have a lower capacity utilisation in order to try to boost demand for those flights.

Customer selection process – One of the key issues here is for airlines to understand the reason why potential customers have not completed their transaction – for example, this could be due to price, seat availability, difficulties in the booking process itself. In this respect, if Amal was able to capture data about the stage in the booking process which causes potential customers to abandon their booking, it could then look at ways to tackle the problem – for example, if there was a confusing user interface on the Amal website this could be amended to make booking easier. Equally, applying the 'velocity' aspect of Big Data, if a customer abandons a transaction, and Amal already has their contact details, the customer could immediately be sent an incentive to try to encourage them to complete the purchase.

In-flight sales – Amal currently offers a standard selection of in-flight products across all its flights. However, the amount of products Amal sells (and therefore the amount of in-flight revenue ancillary revenue Amal generates) is likely to depend on how well the products offered meet customer needs. By analysing the purchasing patterns of different passengers (or different types of passengers) on different routes, Amal could customise the range of products it offers on different flights, to focus on the products which are most likely appeal to the passengers on a particular flight.

Customer satisfaction – In the same way that conversations on social media could help to identify trends in demand, they could also help to indicate how satisfied customers are (or aren't) with their flights and the service they receive from Amal. However, although knowing whether customers are satisfied or not is useful, perhaps the greater value will come from identifying any factors which are reducing satisfaction levels so that Amal can then address the causes of any problems and take steps to improve its performance in those areas.

(c) Big Data is typically characterised by a range of 'V' characteristis – volume, variety, velocity, and veracity.

Capacity - The potential benefits to Amal of Big Data will come from the useful information they can extract from large amounts of data. However, the 'volume' and the 'variety' of the data could also require increased information systems capacity in order to capture and store the data correctly. If the data is not stored correctly, this will undermine its veracity – its integrity and reliability as a basis for making deciisons.

The fact that a number of IT staff are already working on the website upgrade project could be a problem here, if it means that there aren't sufficient staff available to increase the information system capacity to the degree required for Big Data.

Analytical tools - As well as having the capacity to store Big Data, Amal will also need the right analytical tools and technologies to be able to analyse it, because it is too large and unstructured to be analysed through traditional means. Again, the lack of available IT staff could present problems here.

Data overload – A more general concern to beware of is the difference between data and information. Management decisions need to be based relevant information, not raw data. Therefore, by itself, increasing the volume of data available to Amal would not necessarily provide managers with better information for decision-making. Here again, Amal would need analysts with the experience and expertise to be able to extract meaning from the captured data, but it seems unlikely that any such staff will currenty be available,

Similarly, if the volume and variety of the data means that Amal's current information systems are not able to process it, the 'velocity' aspect of Big Data will be undermined. If IT teams or business anlaysts become burdened with increasing requests for ad hoc analysis and one-off reports (because the systems cannot process the data automatically), the information and analysis from Big Data will not be available for decision-makers as quickly as they might want.

30 NCL

Text reference. Issues surrounding reward schemes and human resource management are discussed in Chapter 14 of the BPP Study Text. Financial performance measures are discussed in Chapter 9. Social and ethical issues are considered in Chapter 5.

Top tips.

Part (a). The scenario suggests that NCL's management incentive plan may lead to a lack of goal congruence between individual divisions and the company as a result of the way the annual bonus payments are calculated. This should remind you that the benefits of reward schemes arise when the promote behaviour which is beneficial for an organisation, but they can be problematic when poorly designed performance measures promote behaviour which is not beneficial for the organisation. Although you do not have to link your answer for Part (a) to the scenario, you may find it useful to use the potential issues with NCL's reward scheme as an illustration.

In **Part (b),** note that two of the projects had a life of four years, one had a life of three years, and that capital employed is based on the average during the year. Depreciation is on a straight-line basis. So the capital employed at the end of year 1 will be the value of the investment less one year's depreciation on a straight-line basis.

Your comments for part (b) should also pick up on the ideas about short-term decision making and lack of goal congruence from part (a). Here, however, your answer must be specifically linked to the scenario.

Part (c). Note that you are not asked to describe how residual income should be calculated, but, in effect, to discuss whether it is a superior measure of performance to ROI.

Part (d). There are two elements to this requirement. One is the calculation; the second is the discussion around the non-financial issues involved – for example, public opinion/reputational risk, corporate social responsibility issues, and NCL's moral obligation to clear up the pollution it creates.

(a)   **Benefits for the organisation**

Align goals – The aim of a well-designed reward scheme should be to encourage behaviour which supports the organisation's strategy and helps it to achieve its goals. A reward scheme can help do this by **aligning employees' goals with those of the organisation**.

Provide incentives – A reward scheme should also provide an incentive to achieve a good level of performance, and the existence of a reward scheme can help to both attract, and retain, employees who are making favourable contributions to the running of the organisation.

Potential drawbacks for the organisation

Poorly designed measures – Whilst a well-designed reward scheme can benefit an organisation, reward schemes can also be detrimental if the performance measures used are poorly designed, or unrealistic performance targets are set. In particular, problems can arise if the performance measures used in reward schemes encourage behaviour and actions which are not aligned with the organisation's goals.

Two particular issues which could arise in this context are **short-term decision making** and **increased risk-taking**. For example, if managers know that their bonuses depend on annual profit targets being reached, they may be encouraged to undertake risky projects which might be profitable in the short-term (and therefore increase the bonus), but may not be beneficial to their organisation in the longer term.

Lack of goal congruence – The situation at NCL highlights the potential dangers of poorly designed performance measures. The nature of the management scheme means that divisional managers will only support new investments which generate a favourable ROI during their first two years. However, this means they are likely reject schemes which would generate value for NCL overall, but don't have a favourable ROI in their first two years. In this way, the reward scheme could lead to a lack of goal congruence between the IOA division and the company as a whole.

(b) Divisional management's decision making will be influenced by the fact that their **annual bonus payments** are calculated with reference to **ROI** earned during the **first two years** of an investment. We therefore need to look at ROI of the three projects in Years 1 and 2.

		North	East	South
Year 1	Cashflow	6,000	11,500	12,000
	Depreciation:			
	24,000/4 years	(6,000)		(6,000)
	24,000/3 years		(8,000)	
	Profit	0	3,500	6,000
	Average capital:			
	(24,000 + 18,000)/2	21,000		21,000
	(24,000 + 16,000)/2		20,000	
	ROI (profit ÷ average capital) × 100%)	**0**	**17.5%**	**28.6%**
Year 2	Cashflow	8,000	11,500	10,000
	Depreciation:			
	24,000/4 years	(6,000)		(6,000)
	24,000/3 years		(8,000)	
	Profit	2,000	3,500	4,000
	Average capital:			
	(18,000 + 12,000)/2	15,000		15,000
	(16,000 + 8,000)/2		12,000	
	ROI	**13.3%**	**29.2%**	**26.7%**

The management of the IOA division will prefer to **invest in the South project** as it has by far the highest return on investment in year 1 and an ROI only marginally lower than that of the East project in year 2 and so will result in higher bonus payments for them in years 1 and 2. They will not look further than this to consider the whole life of each project. This reflects a **short-term** focus that is at odds with the view of the board of directors of NCL. As the latter's objective is the maximisation of shareholder wealth over the longer term, the board is likely to choose the North project as this has the highest calculated NPV.

The **incentive plan** motivates management to adopt a **short-term focus** which is detrimental to the organisation as a whole and leads to a **lack of goal congruence** and **dysfunctional decision making**.

The **attitude to risk** of the directors of NCL will have an impact, however. The East project has a life of three years (compared with four for North and South projects) which means that the cash flow estimates associated with it are less subject to uncertainty.

(c) An alternative way of measuring the performance of an investment centre, instead of using ROI, is residual income (RI) and its use as a basis for a performance measurement system has a number of **advantages**.

Residual income is a measure of the centre's profits after deducting a notional or imputed interest cost. The imputed cost of capital might be the organisation's cost of borrowing or its weighted average cost of capital. Residual income **increases for investments earning above the cost of capital**, so if it is used as a basis for performance measurement it will **result** in **projects** being undertaken that will increase shareholder value. It also allows **different costs of capital** to be applied to investments with different risk characteristics so it is a **more flexible measure than ROI**.

However using net book value at the start of each year, and depreciating on a straight line basis to a nil residual value, **tends to distort project returns in the early years** of a project's life. RI also cannot be used to make comparisons between investment centres as it is an **absolute** measure of performance. Finally, RI **does not relate the size of a centre's income to the size of the investment** other than indirectly through the interest charge.

(d) **West project**

	Cashflow	Discount factor	Discounted cash flow
	$m	12%	$'000
Year 0	(12)	1.000	(12,000)
Years 1–4	5	3.037	15,185
NPV			3,185

NCL needs to consider whether it is strategically appropriate to then spend a further $4 million in Year 4 on redressing the environmental damage caused by the project.

Environmental repair

	$'000
NPV as calculated	3,185
Year 4 expenditure ($2 million × 0.636)	(1,272)
NPV	1,913
Further expenditure ($2 million × 0.636)	(1,272)
NPV	641

Depending upon how **socially responsible** the board of NCL is and whether they think they have a **moral obligation** to clear up their **own pollution**, it could find the NPV of the West project reduced from $1,913,000 (after the minimum required cleanup expenditure) to $641,000. Polluted water will create substantial **negative public opinion** and publicity for the company, and it may find its future activities limited, or at least subjected to intense scrutiny, if **pressure groups** target the company and make it difficult to undertake similar projects in the future. Being seen as a socially responsible company will promote local goodwill and could bring greater long-term benefits.

31 Landual Lamps

Text reference: Transfer pricing is covered in Chapter 10 of the BPP Study Text.

Top tips.

Part (a). As the requirement asks you to 'evaluate' the current system of transfer pricing, it might be useful to start by considering what the aims of transfer pricing are. Then, having identified the aims, you can then evaluate how well Landual's current transfer pricing system fits with those aims.

Does the current system promote goal congruence between the individual divisions and the company as a whole?

Does the current system enable the performance of the individual divisions to be measured fairly?

The distinction between the markets available for the two types of component is important: there is a readily available external market for electrical components, while there is no external market for housing components. Therefore a market-based transfer price could be appropriate for the electrical components and a cost-based transfer price could be appropriate for the housing components.

But is it fair to include transport, marketing and bad debt cost in the transfer price for electrical components?

And is it fair that the price of housing components should be at cost only, with no mark-up? On the other hand, should the transfer price for housing components be based on actual production costs or budgeted production costs?

An important part of your 'evaluation' should be what impact these possible changes to the current transfer pricing systems could have on divisional performance. You should demonstrate this through the 'illustrative calculations' the requirement asks for.

Part (b). The change being proposed is to include variable production costs only (rather total production costs) in the transfer price for housing components. The illustrative calculations here should be relatively simple, but a key issue is what impact the changes have on the profitability of the two divisions. Does the revised position accurately reflect the value added to Landual as a company by the different divisions?

Part (c). The requirement here asks you to evaluate the impact of the changes on the profit in the divisions as well as on the company as a whole. So you need to look at the impact of the changes on four different elements: the new housing components division; the new electrical components division, the assembly division, and Landual Lamps overall.

Again, you need to calculate the divisional profits under the new structure, and then consider what benefits (or drawbacks) the changes might yield for the divisions, and for Landual Lamps overall.

The biggest change will see the housing components division change from a profit centre to a cost centre. Although the 'profit' in the housing division will fall significantly because it no longer has any revenue, what might be the benefits of making this change? Remember, the housing components are only sold internally anyway.

Examining team's comments. This question was generally poorly answered with weak (often no) efforts at handling the quantification issues – recalculating the current transfer price; and calculating the impact of the two proposed changes on the various entities in the scenario. As a result, this meant candidates often had very little to say in evaluating or giving advice in the narrative parts of their answers.

For example, in part (b) if the (simple) quantification work was not done, candidates could not see that the proposed change will lead to lower profits in the division which provides the key competitive advantage of the company.

As a general point, during their revision candidates would be advised to consider the impacts that strategic changes – such as designation of cost, profit and investment centres – would have on the performance management of divisions or departments within a company.

(a)   *Electrical components*

Evaluation of the basic policy to use market-based transfer price – Up to 2 marks

For comments on adjusting market price to exclude additional costs (of transport, marketing & bad debts) – 1 mark

For calculating the impact on divisional profits of adjusting market price – 1 mark

Housing components

Evaluation of the basic policy to use cost-based transfer price – Up to 2 marks

For comments about including a mark-up on cost in the transfer price – Up to 2 marks

For comments about the merit of using actual or budgeted costs as the basis of the transfer price – Up to 2 marks

For calculating the impact on divisional profits of including a mark-up, and of using budgeted costs – Up to 2 marks

Total: Up to 10

10

(b)   For calculating the new revenue figure for the components division – 1 mark

For calculating the revised profit figures for each entity – 1 mark each

For comments on the impact of the changes – 1 mark per valid point; Up to 4 marks

Total: up to 6

6

(c)   For calculating new profit figures for each entity (Housing, Electrical, Assembly, Landual) – 1 mark per entity – Up to 4 marks

For evaluating the impact of the changes on the profit in the divisions and for Landual overall – 1 mark per valid point – Up to 7 marks

Total: up to 9

9

Total = 25

(a)   **Aim of transfer pricing** – The aim of transfer pricing is to ensure goal congruence between the divisions of an organisation and the organisation as a whole, by ensuring that the performance of the divisions is measured fairly and is not distorted by any internal transfers.

A good transfer pricing system will also maintain a level of managerial autonomy for the managers of the different divisions in an organisation.

Electrical components

Market-based transfer price – As there is already an external market for electrical components, it seems appropriate to use a market-based transfer price for electrical components. The assembly division can choose either to buy components from an external supplier or to source them internally from the components division, depending on the respective prices charged by the two sources.

Under the current system, the components division generates a contribution of $383k to head office costs from the sale of electrical components: $1,557k - $804k - $370k. Given the generic nature of the components, we would not expect the contribution to profit to be very high, so this figure seems reasonable.

Adjustments to market price – However, the assembly division could legitimately argue that the transfer price charged by the electrical components division should be lower than the open market price, because transferring the components internally doesn't incur transport or marketing costs in the way that an external sale would. Also, there is no risk of bad debt. Therefore, the $269, 000 in respect of these costs should be deducted in order to get an adjusted market price.

If these adjustments are made, then the contribution to head office costs from electrical components within the components division falls to $114k [$383k - $269k].

Housing components

Actual production costs – The transfer prices for housing components are based on actual production costs. Again, this seems appropriate because these components are designed specifically for Landual's products, so there is no external market for them.

However, because the price set for the housing components only covers the actual *production* costs, the proceeds from the sales of the housing components will not make any contribution towards the allocated head office costs.

As a result, since the housing components account for 84% of the division's total sales by revenue [$8,204/$9,761] it will be very difficult for the components division ever to earn a significant profit.

Since the housing components make a significant contribution to Landual's competitive advantage, it would seem fair if they are rewarded with greater divisional profit than they currently get. Therefore rather than selling the components at cost, Landual could consider a transfer price which includes a mark-up on actual production costs. This would also re-distribute the divisional profit between the assembly and components division.

If a mark-up of 25% (for example) were applied to the total actual production costs of the housing components ($8,204k) this would generate additional profit of $2,051k for the components division. If this mark-up were applied, the components division would then show a profit of $1,973k, while the assembly division would only show a profit of $668k.

Actual vs budget costs – Because the components division uses actual production costs rather than budgeted costs as the basis for its transfer price, there is no incentive for the components division to control or reduce its costs, because it knows it will recover any additional costs through the price charged to the assembly division. By contrast, if budgeted productions were used as the basis for the transfer price, the cost of any adverse variance would continue to be borne by the components division.

The current system, based on actual production costs, may be part of the reason behind the $575,000 adverse cost of sales variance in the components division for the last year.

Revised divisional reports

The divisional reports could be adjusted to reflect these points:

- Costs relating to transport, marketing and bad debts are no longer included in the transfer price of electrical components: $1,557 – $269k = $1,288k

- Transfer price for housing is now based on budgeted cost, with a mark-up for 25%:

    ($6,902 – $575k) + $1,302 = 7,629 + 25% mark-up = $9,536

		Components	Assembly
Sales	Electrical	1,288	
	Housing	9,536	
	Sub-total	10,824	15,794
Cost of Sales	Electrical	804	1,288
	Housing	6,902	9,536
	Sub-total	7,706	10,824
Fixed production costs			
	Electrical	370	
	Housing	1,302	
	Sub-total	1,672	1,268
Allocated head office costs		461	2,046
Profit		985	1,656

(b) **Variable costs basis**

The proposal will reduce the revenue of the components division (and correspondingly the cost of sales of the assembly division) by the fixed production costs relating to housing components: $1,302k. There will be no change to the company's overall profit as a result of the change.

This change further tilts the balance in the relative profitability of the two divisions towards the assembly division.

Given that the housing components are specifically designed for Landual's products, and therefore could be a source of significant competitive advantage, the proposed change doesn't seem particularly appropriate. The component division adds significant value to Landual's overall product, but the change seems to be emphasising the importance of the assembly division to the company.

If the results are balanced too heavily in favour of the assembly division, this will understate the importance of the work done by the components division, and could demotivate its staff. This would be a mistake given the intricate nature of the work.

Despite these concerns, the decision to use variable costs as a basis for transfer pricing (rather than total costs) is not necessarily a bad one. The clarity gained by using only variable costs may help Landual to set the optimal prices and profits for its products.

> **Note.** The following solution shows the full data for the two divisions under the revised basis. However, you did not need to show these figures in full to earn the marks available here (for the new revenue figure for the components division, and for the revised profits figures for both divisions.)

		Components	Assembly
Sales	Electrical	1,557	
	Housing	6,902	
	Sub-total	8,459	15,794
Cost of Sales	Electrical	804	1,557
	Housing	6,902	6,902
	Sub-total	7,706	8,459
Fixed production costs			
	(No changes)	1,672	1,268
Allocated head office costs		461	2,046
Profit/(loss)		**(1,380)**	**4,021**

(c)   **Housing division**

Cost centre – Under the proposed changes, the housing division will be a cost centre only.

Given that the housing division only sells its (bespoke) products to the assembly division, and therefore the difficulty of determining a fair revenue figure for its work, is seems more appropriate to treat the housing division as a cost centre rather than a profit centre. Treating the division as a cost centre is better aligned with the ideas of responsibility accounting.

Moreover, because the focus of the division will now be on cost control, this should help avoid adverse cost of sales variances like the one incurred in the last year. The performance measures and reward packages in the division will also need to be re-designed to reinforce the focus on costs.

In addition, the change in status could enable a greater focus on the quality of the division's output, which will be important given the key role which the housing components play in Landual's overall manufacturing process.

In this respect, it is important that the change from being a profit centre to becoming a cost centre is not seen as downgrading the status of the division. If it is, such a perception will demotivate the divisional managers, and any fall in morale is also likely to filter through the staff.

Electrical division

Under the proposed new divisional structure, the electrical division will make a profit of $335k (see Working at the end of the answer).

As the electrical components are generic and could easily be obtained externally, it is appropriate to continue treating the electrical division as a profit centre. Under this basis, Landual has the information it needs to decide whether to 'make or buy' the electrical components for its lamps.

The current figures, showing that the electrical division is making a contribution to head office costs, suggest that the electrical division should continue to supply components to the assembly division.

Assembly division

The changes do not directly affect the assembly division. However, being able to see the electrical division's results more clearly will allow the managers of the assembly division to ensure that the electrical division remains competitive (compared to any external suppliers which could provide the components instead).

Landual Lamps

The changes have no direct effect on the company's reported profit. However, if the changes help to improve cost control (in the Housing division) and reinforce the need for competitiveness (in the electrical division), they should help to improve the company's profits in the future.

Working: Revised profits for each of the divisions, and for the company as a whole.

Allocated head office costs for the Components Division have been re-allocated between the Housing and Electrical Components Divisions in proportion to their cost of sales.

	Housing $'000	Electrical $'000	Assembly $'000	Landual
Sales			15,794	15,794
Electrical		1,557		
Housing				
Cost of Sales				
Electrical		804	1,557	804
Housing	6,902		8,204	6,902
Fixed production costs			1,268	1,268
Electrical		370		370
Housing	1,302			1,302
Allocated Head Office costs (apportioned in line with CoS)	413	48	2,046	2,507
Profit/(Loss)	-8,617	335	2,719	2,641

32 Alpha Division

Text reference. Financial performance measures (including RI, NPV and EVA) are considered in Chapter 9 of the BPP Study Text.

Top tips. In part (a) (i) you must adjust the cash flows for the depreciation charge when you calculate residual income (RI) as this is a profit measure.

Part (ii) is asking for a commentary on the controllability of costs and how these are used to evaluate performance. It has elements of transfer pricing too so think about how transfer prices can be fairly charged between divisions or whether they are imposed. We have drafted a table as part of the notes to this answer showing you the key points to put in your answer. The table picks out the three profit measures, divisional profit and economic performance, for the five items on the list. Don't use the table in your answer though – it is part of your workings when you are planning out your answer.

Part (b) primarily tests your knowledge of how to calculate EVA. You need to read the question carefully to pick out the elements needed for the WACC calculation. You will also need to update the capital employed figure brought forward to calculate the capital charge. Make sure you state the assumptions made in part (b) (i) so it is clear where figures come from. Although it is always a good idea to state any assumptions you make when answering a question, it is particularly important to do so here since the requirement specifically asks you to 'State clearly any assumptions that you make'.

For tutorial purposes we have listed four potential disadvantages you could have included in part (b) (ii) but you are only asked for three, and so should onlyhave included three in your answer. Note, however, that you are asked for disadvantages of EVA, not the advantages of using it.

Easy marks. Part (a) (i) calculating RI should have been a source of easy marks

Examining team's comments. A large number of candidates did not attempt all parts of this question. Marks in part (a) were either very good or very poor. A number of candidates earned maximum marks in part (b) (i) but others made no attempt at this at all. Many candidates gave the **advantages** of EVA, not the **disadvantages** as asked for in part (b)(ii).

				Marks
(a)	(i)	Calculations of RI	3	
		Comments (on merit)	3	
				6
	(ii)	For each of measures 1 to 3 including reference to managerial/economic performance and illustrative items given the question and to illustrative items given in the question	3 × 3	Up to 8
(b)	(i)	Adjusted profit after tax	3	
		Adjusted capital employed	3	
		WACC	1	
		EVA	1	
		Comment	1	Up to 8
	(ii)	Disadvantages of EVA	3 × 1	3
			Total =	25

(a) (i) **Residual income for the proposed investment and comments on the short-term and long-term decision views of management on the viability of the proposed investment**

	Yr 1 $m	Yr 2 $m	Yr 3 $m
Net operating cash inflows	12.5	18.5	27.0
Depreciation	(15.0)	(15.0)	(15.0)
Profit or (loss)	(2.5)	3.5	12.0
Less imputed interest (w)	(4.5)	(3.0)	(1.5)
Residual income	(7.0)	0.5	10.5

Working

Imputed interest at a cost of capital at 10% as follows:

Y1 10% × $45m = $4.5m
Y2 10% × $(45 – 15) m = $3m
Y3 10% × $(45 – 15 –15) m = $1.5m

Comments

If management take a long-term view and use NPV as their measurement of project success the investment will go ahead as it has a positive NPV of $1.937m at a 10% cost of capital. However if they use RI as their measure, then the project will only be successful from year 2 onward and make income of $4m overall. As the **bonus scheme** is based on short-term performance evaluation the negative RI in year 1 may sway management away from taking on the investment if they use RI as their measure. This short-term focus may lead to the rejection of investments that take a while to become profitable which may not be in the long-term interests of Alpha.

(ii) **Divisional profit measures**

Notes to the answer

This question clearly needs more detail than many students expect. Before the answer is written, it needs planning as follows:

Profit measure	Divisional management	Illustration	Divisional economic	Illustration
1	Contribution is controllable - fair	As it contains **(i)** Even if it contains **(ii)**	Not the whole picture	As missing fixed and other costs
2	Profit is controllable	**(iii)** are fixed costs that are controllable **unless** decision made before new manager appointed		**(iii)** are the sorts of items that are fixed that should be included in divisional profit assessment
3	Can't be used	**(v)** is not controlled by manager	Shows economic contribution of division to group	Assume **(v)** will not be incurred by group if division closed down

This leaves (iv) – where can I use this? Depreciation is a fixed cost – is it controllable by managers?

This is affected by two factors:

Controllability of asset acquisitions and disposals by managers – could be head office decision

Depreciation policy may be a head office decision

The measurement of divisional performance is a sensitive area for managers who are concerned with the control they have over the performance they are measured by and especially where it is tied into their bonus scheme. Managers would prefer to be measured only in areas where they have a **direct control** over the revenues and costs.

(1) **Variable short run contribution margin**
The use of such a measure can be deemed unacceptable by divisional managers if it includes revenue and costs from inter-divisional transfers. Transfer prices are unpopular where they are imposed rather than negotiated. However an adjusted market price uses the external selling price and adjusts this for savings on packaging and delivery costs for instance. This means that the price is more likely to be acceptable to the divisions involved. Sales to customers outside the Delta group would be at market price. However a central sales force may negotiate the sales rather than the division so they may have less discretion than would appear over these revenues.

(2) **Controllable profit**
This measure is calculated by deducting controllable fixed costs from the variable short run contribution margin. These costs are likely to include **labour or equipment rental costs that are fixed in the short term. These costs can be controlled to some extent by divisional management** who may be able to influence working practices affecting productivity and therefore efficiency in the use of labour and equipment. They may also be able to negotiate separately agreements for equipment though it is unlikely that they would have much control over wage negotiation or the hiring of suitable employees. **Depreciation** may be controllable to the extent that the division has some control over the purchasing of non-current assets.

(3) **Divisional profit**
This is controllable profit less non-controllable avoidable costs. **Head office staff costs** such as finance staff are **largely unavoidable and cannot be controlled by the division** unless through a service level agreement which is an annual negotiation. **Depreciation** may be seen as unavoidable and not controlled by the division if the charge is centrally imposed and relates to assets acquired centrally rather than at divisional level. The divisional profit figure is useful in evaluating the economic performance of the division in that it represents the contribution made by Alpha Division towards the overall profitability of the Delta Group.

(b) (i) **EVA of the Gamma Group 20X6 and 20X7**

	20X6 $m	20X7 $m
Profit for the period (after tax)	67	82
Add		
Goodwill amortised	5	5
Non-cash expenses	12	12
Interest expense (W1)	4.2	4.2
Adjusted profit	88.20	103.20
Adjusted capital employed		
Capital employed b/f	279	340
Non-capitalised leases	16	16
Non-cash expenses	-	12
Goodwill (W2)	45	50
Adjusted capital employed	340	418
Calculation of EVA		
Adjusted profit	88.2	103.20
Less capital charge (W3)	(39.1)	(52.25)
EVA	49.1	50.95

Workings

1 Interest expense = Interest payable × (1 – tax rate) = $6m × 0.7 = $4.2m

2 Goodwill

   20X6: Amount brought forward from 20X5 = $45m

   20X7: $45m b/f at start of 20X6 + charge to revenue during 20X6 of $5m = $50m.

3 Capital charge

   Step 1 Calculate the WACC.

   20X6

Equity	16% × 50% =	8%
Debt	10% × 70% × 50% =	3.5%
		11.5%

   20X7

Equity	18% × 50% =	9%
Debt	10% × 70% × 50% =	3.5%
		12.5%

   Remember to adjust the cost of debt for the tax rate.

   Step 2 Apply the WACC to the capital employed to get the capital charge

   20X6 capital charge = 11.5% × $340m = $39.1m

   20X7 capital charge = 12.5% × $418m = $52.25m

Assumptions made

EVA is based on economic profit which requires a series of adjustments to be made to the accounting profits of $67m and $82m.

Depreciation is usually adjusted so that the accounting depreciation is added back and an adjustment made based on the wear and tear of assets. In this case (note 8) economic depreciation is stated to be the same as accounting and tax depreciation and so no further adjustments are needed.

Lease charges are usually added back in the calculation of NOPAT but note 2 states that the leases were not amortised so no adjustment has been made.

EVA is based on economic profit which approximates to cash flow so any **non-cash costs** (note 10) are added back to the accounting profit and capital employed. Although we are told there were non-cash expenses of $12m in 20X6 and 20X7 we don't know whether there were any in 20X5. Therefore the capital employed figure for 20X6 (based on the figure brought forward from 20X5) has not been adjusted. However, the capital employed figure for 20X7 has been adjusted, to reflect the non-cash expenses added back in 20X6.

Interest costs are added back when calculating NOPAT as they are charged as part of the capital charge. Interest costs of $6m less tax at 30% (see note 9) have been adjusted. The net of tax adjustment reflects the fact that the post tax profit is used as the starting point for the NOPAT calculation.

The replacement cost of net assets is used in the calculation of the capital charge. This usually requires adjustment to the NBV of assets to their replacement cost. There are no replacement costs given for the assets in the statements of financial position at the start of 20X6 and so the **capital employed** figure of $279m is used as a starting point to calculate replacement costs.

The book values of assets need to be adjusted for capitalised costs. Therefore the non-capitalised leases are added back. EVA also adjusts the asset figure for **investments for the future.** This would include goodwill of $45m which needs to be adjusted as noted above.

Comments on the Group's performance

The EVA measures are positive which show increases in the real wealth of Gamma Group based on economic values.

(ii) Three disadvantages of using EVA in measuring financial performance:

1 EVA tends to focus on **short-term performance** rather than looking at the long term.

2 EVA depends on **historical data**, which may be a limited guide to the future. The accounting adjustments made to this data may not be completely eliminated by the adjustments made by EVA.

3 EVA requires a large number of adjustments to be made to accounting information, and the number of adjustments required can make EVA difficult (and time-consuming) to use.

Additional answer

4 EVA is not easily used to **compare different organisations** or divisions as it is not a ratio and can be distorted by size.

---

33 Stillwater Services

Text reference. EVA is discussed in Chapter 9 of the BPP Study Text. Stakeholder management and the potential impact of stakeholders on performance are discussed in Chapter 5.

Top tips.

Part (a). Up to 10 of the marks available in Part (a) are for calculations. There should be some relatively easy marks here (for example, for identifying the adjustments to operating profit), even if you don't get all of the figures correct.

A few months before the exam which included this question, a technical article was published on ACCA's website – 'Economic value added versus profit-based measures of performance.' This article explained the adjustments to operation profit which are required in EVA, as well as the logic behind them. Candidates who had read (and understood) this article should have been well-placed to tackle this question. This highlights the importance of reading relevant technical articles on ACCA's website as part of your preparation for your exams.

One particular point to note in relation to the EVA calculation itself: Remember that your calculations for capital employed figure need to be based on the published accounts figure at the start of 20X2, not at the end of it.

However, also note that the question requirement isn't simply to calculate EVA; you should also have used the EVA figure you have calculated to evaluate SS's performance. In other words, how well is it creating value for its shareholders?

Part (b). The reference in the requirement to 'analysing the potential influence' of different stakeholder groups should have suggested that Mendelow's ideas of power and interest could be relevant here. However, perhaps more importantly, the reference to 'managing different stakeholder groups' should have also alerted you to the potential conflict of interests between different groups. In particular, how are the regulator's interests likely to differ from shareholder's interests, and how do these differences affect SS's directors?

Part (c). As in part (a), this part of the question combines calculations with a discussion related to the figures you have calculated. Crucially, though, you must make sure your ROCE calculations relate solely to the Regulated parts of SS's business.

Also it is vitally important that you recognised that the ROCE target of 6% is the *upper* limit that SS can achieve on its regulated business, not a minimum target it is trying to achieve.

This is very important because the presence of this target means that SS has very little scope to increase its profits from regulated business. So, in terms of performance management for SS as a whole, what implications does this have for the role of unregulated business in increasing the company's profits?

Examining team's comments. The calculation of EVA was discussed in a technical article on ACCA's website, and had clearly been well prepared by many candidates who scored most of the calculation marks available in Part (a). The calculations of NOPAT could be done by starting from PAT, or from Operating Profit and both approaches gained credit. The weakest area of the calculations was the adjustments to capital employed.

Most candidates realised the need to comment on the figures they had calculated and gave a summary sentence. However, many candidates did not offer any broader comment on the key assumptions in the EVA method, or the limitations of the method. This could be seen as a failure to appreciate the need to 'evaluate' performance using EVA, rather than simply to 'calculate' performance.

Part (c) was generally poorly answered, with many candidates not appearing to realise that the ROCE target was an upper limit on the company. Few candidates spotted that the constraints on the regulated side of the business would mean that the unregulated side would be the engine of growth for SS, while the regulated side could act as a cash cow.

Marking scheme

		Marks
(a)	Adjustments to operating profit:	
	Non-cash items	0.5
	Accounting depreciation	1
	Doubtful debts	1
	Research and development	1
	Interest	0.5
	Tax (cash amount paid; tax on interest)	Up to 2
	Capital employed figure:	
	Capital employed (per accounts) at start of year	0.5
	Provision for doubtful debts	1
	Other non-cash items	1
	WACC	1
	EVA	1
	Note. *Maximum 10 marks available for calculations*	10
	Comments about SS's performance, consistent with EVA calculation –	
	1 mark per relevant point	Up to 3

13

			Marks

(b) Analysis of different interest and power of each stakeholder group – up to 2 marks each ... Up to 6

Identifying potential conflicts between interests of regulator and shareholders ... <u>1</u>

               5

(c) *Calculations*:

ROCE (on regulated business only) ... 1

Maximum regulated operating profit allowed ... 1

Operating margins (regulated vs non-regulated business) ... 1

Other relevant calculations ... 1

Commentary:

On calculations – 1 mark per relevant point ... Up to 2

On performance management of regulated areas of SS – 1 mark per relevant point ... Up to 2

On performance management of unregulated areas of SS – 1 mark per relevant point ... <u>Up to 2</u>

             <u>7</u>

Total = <u>25</u>

(a)

	$m	$m	Comments
Operating profit		68.00	
Add back			
Depreciation	59.00		
Doubtful debts	2.00		
Research and development	12.00		
Other non-cash items	7.00		
		80.00	
Less			
Economic depreciation		-83.00	
Tax		-9.00	Cash amount only
Tax adjustment on finance charges		-5.75	$23m × 25%
NOPAT		**50.25**	

		$m	Notes
Capital employed		637.00	Based on figure b/f at start of 20X2
Add back			
Provision for doubtful debts	2.50		(see working)
Other non-cash items	6.00		Non-cash items in 20X1
		8.50	
		645.50	

WACC:

	$m	Notes
Equity: 40% × 16%	6.4%	
Debt: 60% × 5% × (1 – 25%)	2.3%	
	8.7%	

EVA:

NOPAT – (Capital employed × WACC)

50.25 – (645.5 × 0.087)   **–5.91**

No adjustment for depreciation required at the start of 20X2.

Working:	$m
Provision for doubtful debts at end of 20X2	4.5
Movement in year	–2
Provision at start of year	2.5

Negative EVA – SS's negative EVA figure for 20X2 suggests that, instead of creating wealth for its shareholders, it is actually destroying value. More specifically, the value which SS is generating (NOPAT) is not sufficient to cover the economic cost of the capital it has employed to generate that value.

Such a position is not sustainable in the long run, and will lead to dissatisfaction amongst SS's shareholders. SS could look to address this issue either by increasing its net operating profit; or by reducing its cost of capital; or through a combination of both.

Net operating profit after tax (NOPAT) – SS's current NOPAT of $50.25m leaves it with a negative EVA of $5.91m. At the current cost of capital, SS would need to increase its NOPAT to $56.16m to break even on EVA.

Cost of capital – Alternatively, SS would break even on EVA, with its current level of NOPAT, if its weighted average cost of capital was 7.8%. ($645.5m × 7.8% = $50.3m). In this respect, SS's current cost of equity (16%) appears high, particularly given the highly regulated nature of the industry. Moreover, given that 80% of SS's sales (for water and sewage services) are for services which are necessities for everyday life, there is relatively little risk that demand will fall. Again, this suggests that SS's cost of equity should be lower than it currently is.

> **Asset base** – SS could also look to reduce its asset base by selling under-utilised assets. If it could reduce the amount of capital employs without any significant reduction in its NOPAT, this could help its EVA break even or become positive.

(b) **Regulator**

Interest – The regulator is likely to have a high interest in SS. Although the regulator will only be interested in SS's regulated services, these still constitute 80% of its total revenue. The regulator's interest is in controlling the prices SS charges, and the returns in generates.

Power – The regulator also has a high level of power to influence SS's performance. Not only does the regulator set the level of pre-tax ROCE which SS is allowed to generate, but it also the power to impose significant fines if SS exceeds this figure.

Shareholders

Interest – Although the shareholders will be interested in the wealth which SS creates for them, they will be less interested in the day-to-day business of the company and the operational decisions taken within it. (They have delegated authority for these to SS's management). Therefore, shareholders' interest in performance management at SS is likely to be lower than that of both the regulator and SS's management.

However, shareholders' interests are likely to differ from those of the regulator. Whereas the regulator is interested in controlling profits, the shareholders are likely to want SS to maximise the profits and earnings it generates.

Power – It is not clear how SS's shares are distributed, but this could determine the level of power the shareholders have. If SS's shares are owned primarily by institutional investors they are likely to have more power than if the shares are held by a large number private investors. For example, institutional investors will have more voting power than individuals, and so could look to replace SS's management if they felt the company was under-performing.

It seems that SS's shareholders have at least a moderate level of power since the board are trying to drive performance for the shareholders' benefit.

Management

Interest – SS's management have a high level of interest in the company's performance, because if the company is unsuccessful their jobs will come under threat. However, SS's management also have to ensure that the conflicting interests of the regulator and the company's shareholders are managed successfully.

Power – The management team also have a relatively high level of power because they dictate the strategies which the company will pursue. However, the presence of a strong regulator means that the management team's power is less than it would be in an unregulated market, because, for example, performance levels in SS's regulated services have to comply with the parameters imposed by the regulator.

(c)   Target ROCE: 6%

Operating profit from Regulated business: $46.0 m

Average capital employed: (779.0m + 761.0m)/2 = $770.0m

ROCE: 5.97%

Alternative calculation:

The Examining team's answer uses capital employed at the end of 20X2, rather than average capital employed during the year.

Under this basis ROCE is: 46.0m / 779.0m = 5.90%.

Return within prescribed limit – The return which SS generates from its regulated business (5.97%) is within the limit set by the regulator (6.0%).

However, because SS's current return is so close to limit there is very little scope for it to increase the profitability of the regulated aspect of the business. The maximum operating profit that SS could generate in its regulated business is $46.2m ($770m × 6%).

Non-regulated activities – The constraints on the regulated business increase the importance of the non-regulated activities as a potential source of profit growth for the business.

Additionally, the operating profit margins which SS earns from non-regulated business are significantly higher than those from regulated business.

Regulated services: $46m/ $276m = 16.7%

Non-regulated services: $22m/$69m = 31.9%

Consequently, SS should be looking to expand its non-regulated business, as a source of profitable growth.

In effect, SS's regulated business could be seen as a 'cash cow.' SS should look to invest cash generated by its regulated business to help support the expansion of its non-regulated business (either through organic growth or through acquisition).

Cost control – The regulator's primary concern appears to be that SS doesn't increase its prices unjustifiably. If SS has little scope to increase prices, then in order to maintain its profits it needs to ensure that its costs do not increase significantly either.

Therefore, controlling costs will be a key element of performance management within the regulated part of the business. On the one head this highlights the importance of variance analysis (comparing actual costs to budget), but on the other hand it also suggests the importance of identifying potential cost savings (for example, through efficiency improvements).

> **Lack of investment** – The target level of 6% is lower than SS's weighted average cost of capital (of 8.47%; see part (a)). If SS uses WACC as a discount rate for decision-making, then it would be reluctant to invest in the regulated part of the business at all.
>
> The infrastructure in the regulated side of the business is likely to suffer as a result. This could have an adverse effect on other aspects of SS's performance. For example, if SS has increasing problems with burst water mains due to lack of investment in its infrastructure, this could lead to an increase in repair costs, and also a decline in customer service if customers' water supplies are disrupted.

Growth – By contrast, the focus of performance measures for the non-regulated services should be on revenue and profit growth. For example, SS should look to set targets for revenue growth or market share growth. However, it is equally important for SS to set targets for profit margins, to ensure that it doesn't sacrifice profitability in search of revenue growth.

34 Seatown

Text references. Performance measurement in not-for-profit organisations is covered in Chapter 11. Service level agreements are covered in Chapter 16.

Top tips. It's probably best in both parts of the question to list the information required when you make each point. You need to think about what performance measures are relevant, also whether performance can be compared or benchmarked with other departments or councils.

Note in (a) that measures of efficiency need to take into account time taken and distance covered. Your answer needed to recognise that it isn't just a question of measuring quantity of rubbish picked up. Public reaction to litter remaining on the beach has to be taken into account. Thus although the tractor sweeping may not pick up much litter, it is justified if it picks up the litter that would concern the public.

Part (c). It will be important for the council to ensure that the quality of the beach cleaning is maintained if it uses an outsource partner instead of providing the cleaning services itself. A service level agreement will be an important tool which it can use to measure and monitor the outsource partner's performance. However, don't forget that it is also important that the outsource partner knows the council's expectations of it; so think how the service level agreement can assist with this as well.

(a) **Economy**

Costs of labour

Controlling labour costs will be an important element of economy. The council needs to **break labour costs down** for sweeping the sands and emptying the bins. To judge whether the costs are being limited sufficiently, the council will need to **compare actual costs with benchmarks**. These include **comparing actual costs with budget**, with **costs of previous years**, with **comparable costs** for the other areas of the council's activities and **costs incurred by other councils** responsible for beaches. The council's management will need to investigate fluctuations from any of the expected benchmarks.

The council's **management accounting data** should provide most of the information required, assuming that a proper system of budgeting is in place. It should be possible to obtain labour cost information from other councils.

Costs of machinery

Similar comparisons for labour costs should be made for machinery costs such as **vehicle running costs**. The analysis made will need to take into account the cost drivers such as the **number of tractors** and the **number of vehicle miles covered.**

As well as **management accounting cost information and budgets, details of vehicle miles covered** will also need to be maintained.

Efficiency

Efficient use of labour and machines

The council needs to find out how resources are being used. It needs to know **how much time** is being spent **sweeping the sands** and how **frequently bins are being emptied.** The actual frequency of emptying bins should be **compared with the standards** the council set, to review whether bins are being **emptied more frequently** than required or whether the schedule for emptying bins is unrealistic.

It would also be helpful to have **more detail** about how much time is being spent on different areas. Some beaches may be more problematic to clean because of **obstacles** such as rocks. The time and costs spent on these beaches could be reduced by limiting access to them to popular times of the year. To judge efficiency fairly though, the council will also need to take into account the **area of different beaches and the number of litter bins.**

Employees will need to maintain **detailed records of the time spent on each beach** and **when they empty the litter bins**. It will also be important to keep the permanent data, the areas covered by cleaning and the number of litter bins, up-to-date.

(b) **Quantity of refuse collected**

The council will need to ascertain how much refuse has been collected. Again it will be helpful if the **refuse collected from sweeping** can be recorded separately from the **refuse collected from bins**, in order to judge both activities fairly. When quantities are reviewed over time, it will be useful to see how much the litter generated is **proportionate to the number of visitors**. The Council should also try to identify whether **other seasonal variations** have a **significant influence** (visitors being less likely to consume food and hence drop food litter during the autumn and winter, and also fewer refreshment kiosks being open during these seasons). The council will need to assess whether more staff resources are needed at the busiest times of the year to keep the litter under control.

Records kept will therefore need to include the quantity of litter disposed of each week. There are various ways in which the number of visitors can be estimated, including **number of users of tourist information centres, car park records** and **estimates based on physical space occupied** by each beach user.

Quantity of refuse not collected

As well as assessing how much litter has been collected, the council needs to have an idea of whether all litter has been **collected from the beach** (or how long litter remains on the beach before it is collected). Complaints or feedback from beach users will give indications. Management also needs to consider whether litter bins have been **emptied frequently enough** to avoid overflowing. It should be possible to compare records of how frequently litter bins have been emptied compared with the **standards** set by the council. Management should investigate if bins are being emptied less frequently than required by standards.

The council should maintain records of complaints it has received about **litter, ratings made by external parties** and other indications of problems, for example adverse media comment or injuries caused by litter left on the beach. The council should also try to **collect feedback systematically throughout the year from visitors,** for example through issuing questionnaires in tourist information centres.

Spot checks of beaches after sweeping and of bins, particularly during the busiest seasons of the year, by internal audit will also provide evidence of whether litter is being collected thoroughly and promptly. Spot checks of beaches will need to distinguish between different types of litter. Larger items, or items that could cause injury, will be of most concern. This will also help determine whether the standard frequency for emptying bins is appropriate and whether the frequency should vary at different times of the year.

(c) It seems likely that the internal audit department believes that a commercial cleaning company (the outsourced partner) could provide the beach cleaning work more cheaply than the in-house cleaning department currently does.

However, as the cleanliness of the town's beaches is a major factor in its success as a family holiday destination, it cannot afford for the **quality** of the cleaning to fall as a result of the outsourcing.

In particular, the council will need to be confident that if it outsources the cleaning contract the frequency and quality of cleaning will be maintained at their current levels. The service level agreement should help to ensure this is the case.

Define work to be done – The service level agreement will specify the different cleaning tasks which the outsource partner needs to carry out: including sweeping and skimming the beaches, and emptying the litter bins.

Setting standards for services – As well as defining the work to be done, the agreement should help define performance standards. For example, the council knows that litter bins need to be emptied regularly, and so the service level agreement could either define how frequently the bins need to be cleaned, or else it could define that the bins need to be emptied within a certain time limit after they become full.

Measuring performance – The service level agreement will also help the council monitor whether the outsource partner is performing to the standards it requires. In order to measure whether the partner is meeting the council's requirements, these requirements first have to be established. As we have noted, they are established in the service level agreement.

Dispute resolution – If the council subsequently has any concerns or disputes with the outsource partner about the frequency and quality of the cleaning work being carried out, the service level agreement should help resolve them, by identifying what the partner has agreed to do.

35 Essland Police Forces

Text reference. The use of league tables in relation to measuring public sector performance is discussed in Chapter 11 of the BPP Study Text.

Top tips.

Part (a). It is vital that you read the requirement very carefully before starting to answer this requirement.

In particular, note the following:

- You are asked to evaluate the **method** of calculating and measuring the Force Scores, not to evaluate the performance of the different Forces based on their Force Scores.

- You need to evaluate how useful the league tables are in improving the performance of the police forces in the context of achieving the Department of the Interior's aims and goals.

The scenario reiterates this first point, with the reference to the CEO's comment: 'I'm not interested in the performance… I'm interested in the method of assessment.'

Nonetheless, the statistics provided in Appendix 1 are very important to the question; for example, for indicating other measures which could potentially be included; eg number of police force employees per head of population.

In relation to this second point (about the usefulness of the tables) a key question is: how well do the variables included in the tables relate to the Department's overall aim (achieving value for money) rather being linked to the Department's goals?

Part (b). Although the majority of requirements in P5 require you to apply your knowledge specifically to a scenario, the first part of this requirement asks you to discuss the merits of league tables in general terms.

However, the second part of the requirement then links directly back to the scenario. The CEO has raised concerns about how staff will respond to the introduction of the league tables, and has also raised concerns about how appropriate it will be to transfer league tables from the schools sector into the police forces. Are these concerns valid? For example, will the league tables lead to police forces focusing only on the measures of performance included in the league tables at the expense of other aspects of performance?

In terms of structuring your answer, it could be useful to use the main points of the CEO's concerns as headings for your answer and then address them in turn.

Marking scheme

Marks

(a) Evaluating the appropriateness of variables used in the context of achieving the overall aim of the Department of the Interior – 1 mark per relevant point – up to a maximum of 3 marks

Evaluating the appropriateness of variables used in the context of achieving the detailed goals of the Department of the Interior – 1 mark per relevant point – up to a maximum of 5 marks

For relevant comments on other indicators which could be included in the tables – up to a maximum of 2 marks

Evaluating the allocation of the weightings across the different forces – 1 mark per relevant point – up to a maximum of 4 marks

Up to 2 marks for other relevant points

Total for part (a): up to 14   **14**

(b) General evaluation of league tables – 1 mark per relevant point – up to a maximum of 4 marks

Comments on employees' attitude to the introduction of the system – up to a maximum of 2 marks

Impact of the league tables on employee behaviour and their sense of accountability – 1 mark per relevant point – up to a maximum of 5 marks

Appropriateness of using league tables from schools in relation to the police forces – 1 mark per relevant point – up to a maximum of 2 marks

Total for part (b): up to 11   **11**

Total = 25

(a) **Choice of variables selected**

The variables used to measure the Force Score should be aligned to the aims and goals of the police forces. At the highest level, the two main aims of the police forces are: to provide a **value for money** service, and to ensure the **security** of the community.

Detailed goals – However, the detailed goals of the department focus primarily on crime, justice and community support without providing any more detail about the economy, efficiency or effectiveness (value for money) of the policing service.

Choice of 'Ranks' – In turn, the four 'Ranks' used to calculate the Force Score appear to be derived from the detailed goals, rather than the overall aims.

Goal	'Rank' indicator used
Tackling the underlying causes of crime	Rank 1 – number of reported crimes
Bringing perpetrators to justice	Rank 2 – proportion of reported crimes solved
Providing protection and support for individuals and communities	Rank 3 – user satisfaction score (for service offered by police forces)
Responsiveness, accessibility and community engagement	Rank 4 – responsiveness (to calls). Rank 3 – User satisfaction will also reflect responsiveness, accessibility and engagement more generally

The indicators selected don't measure all aspects of the goals exactly, but they provide a reasonable coverage of them. For example, one way to reduce the number of reported crimes would be to tackle the underlying causes of crime so that fewer crimes are committed.

Nonetheless, the 'ranks' could still be improved. For example, the number of public meetings between the police and the local community could be used to measure the level of community engagement.

Value for money

More importantly, however, because the goals focus on tackling crime and promoting community safety, the Ranks also focus on these aspects of performance rather than the degree of value for money achieved by the police services. For example, whereas the current Rank 2 is based on the solution rate for crimes, it might also be useful to measure the number of crimes solved per police force employee in order to assess the efficiency of the police service.

The data which the police forces already keep (Appendix 1 in the scenario) would be suitable for calculating some value for money performance measures. For example, using the data already available, the following additional 'Rank' scores could be calculated:

	C	D	E	F
Number of police per 10,000 population	49.6	48.9	50.0	52.7
Cost of police force per head of population ($)	323.2	331.1	336.5	340.0
Number of crimes solved per police force employee	5.0	5.2	5.4	4.2

Weightings used

Another potential issue with the current system is that it assigns the same weighting to each of the four ranks. This approach has the benefit of simplicity, but it also presumes that each aspect of performance is equally important to the performance of the force. In practice, this may not be the case, but no explanation is given to justify the weightings used.

Importantly, however, the weightings used could affect the overall ranking of the forces in the league table. Currently, Force F is top ranked, while Force C is bottom ranked. However, if for example, user satisfaction was given greater weighting than the other factors, this would be likely to mean that Force E became top ranked.

Equally, as we noted earlier, if value for money measures were included, the rankings would also change – particularly because Force F performs worst in relation to this area.

Therefore the Department faces a trade-off between preserving the simplicity of the calculations and including additional factors and prescribing different weightings to different factors.

Additional point:

Impact of using ranks – The difference between the best and worst performing forces in relation to call handling is only 3 percentage points (94% vs 91%), whereas the equivalent difference for user satisfaction is 12 percentage points (80% vs 68%). However, both of these performance spreads generate a difference of 0.75 in the forces' scores. In this way, the ranking system currently being applied doesn't take into account the degree of variation in performance between the different forces for any of the measures.

(b)   **Merits of league tables in performance management**

Benchmarks – By providing a single performance summary, league tables can provide a useful way of benchmarking performance between not-for-organisations. Moreover, because they are not directly competing with each other, not-for-profit organisations should be more willing to exchange data than commercial organisations, thereby making it easier to carry out a benchmarking exercise.

Benchmarking performance in this way could help identify areas of best practice among the police forces, and could help to motivate poorer performers to improve their performance levels to bring them closer to the best performers.

Limited comparisons – In effect, benchmarking and league tables are both relative measures of performance – comparing the performance of an organisation against other similar organisations. However, there could still be other organisations (not included in the benchmarking exercise) which are performing better.

In this case, although Force F performs best at call handling (with 94% calls answered within 10 seconds) this figure may still be relatively low compared the performance of the other emergency services (fire, ambulance) in Essland or compared to police forces in other countries.

To overcome this issue, the league tables could try to include figures for comparable organisations (in particular, foreign police forces). However, it could be difficult to find the comparable data necessary to calculate a force score for a foreign police force (as opposed to benchmarking individual elements of performance).

Factors affecting performance – One of the main issues with league tables is that while they can highlight variations in performance, they do not take account of any factors leading to those variations in performance. For example, the number of reported crimes per 10,000 of population could reflect the social and economic conditions of a region.

Controllability and motivation – Perhaps even more importantly, the police forces do not have the power to affect the external environment, such as economic conditions. Therefore, if the police forces feel their performance is being judged on factors they cannot control, introducing the league tables could serve to demotivate, rather than motivate, the forces.

As the CEO has pointed out, the police forces have strong union representation. Therefore if the forces resist or resent the introduction of the league tables, with the backing of their unions, the forces could potentially discredit the league tables, and possibly even the way the Department of the Interior manages the forces.

Measure fixation – Another potential issue with league tables is that they could lead to the police forces concentrating on those aspects of performance which are included in the tables at the expense of others. The notion that 'what gets measured, gets done' would seem to be appropriate here.

In particular, the league tables do not currently include any measures linked to the value for money provided by the forces. Therefore, the league tables could lead the police forces to overlook this aspect of the Department's aims, because they are focusing solely on the aspects of safety and security being measured in the league tables. So, for example, the police forces could recruit additional staff to answer phone calls (and improve their call handling score) but it is debatable how much value for money this would provide overall.

Use of league tables from the schools sector – Although the introduction of school league table may have been successfully applied in Essland's schools, there are some significant differences between schools and police forces which may make the use of league tables less appropriate for the police forces.

Users of the league tables – In particular, parents in Essland have a choice about which school their children attend, so they can use information about the relative performance of different schools to help them make that choice. However, residents cannot choose which police force is responsible for their safety and security – unless they relocate to a different area of the country. Therefore, whereas the school league tables can help users (parents) in their decision-making, the police force league tables do not have an equivalent benefit for the residents of their regions.

Number of measures included – Additionally, the school league tables are entirely based on a single measure of performance (exam results) whereas the 'Force score' tries to include a wider range of factors.

However, as we have already noted, this then raises questions about which factors should be included in the tables, and whether all the factors being considered are equally important.

36 Beeshire Local Authority

Text reference. The issues surrounding performance measurement in public sector organisations are discussed in Chapter 11 of the BPP Study Text. Non-financial performance indicators are discussed in Chapter 12.

Top tips.

Part (a). A useful start point for understanding the importance of non-financial indicators in public sector organisations will be to think about the goals and objectives of those organisations, and how they differ from commercial organisations.

The first paragraph of the scenario provides some very useful pointers here. We are told the goal for BLA's waste management department is 'to maintain Beeshire as a safe, clean and environmentally friendly place', and also that the department does not charge residents or businesses for most of its services.

If it doesn't charge for its services it can't possibly make a profit, which therefore rules out any profit-based performance measures. Nonetheless, the scenario tells us, BLA has so far 'focused on financial measures of performance' rather than, for example, quality of service. Does such an approach seem consistent with the department's goals, or might looking at non-financial performance indicators be more constructive?

Part (b). There are several different elements in the requirement, so it is important that you cover all of them to score the marks available in this part of the question.

In effect, the requirement can be broken down into three parts: (i) explain how value for money provision should be assessed; (ii) by suggesting (and justifying) suitable performance indicators; and then (iii) calculating performance in relation to those indicators.

Value for money is typically measured in terms of the three 'E's: economy, efficiency, and effectiveness. So a useful approach to this requirement would be to explain the Es first, and look at each one in turn to suggest suitable performance indicators for it. The requirement to 'calculate justified performance indicators using the information in the scenario' should have been a reminder that the indicators you suggest need to be specifically relevant to the scenario, rather than being generic measures of economy, efficiency or effectiveness.

Part (c). In the same way that a useful approach to part (a) was to think how public sector organisations differ from commercial ones, a useful starting point for this requirement would be to think how qualitative factors of performance differ from quantitative ones. What are the key characteristics of qualitative data?

The key characteristic of qualitative data is that it is subjective (based on peoples' opinions). Once you identify this point, the difficulties of measuring it should become easier to identify.

However, note you aren't only asked to discuss the difficulties of measuring qualitative performance you also need to suggest appropriate solutions to help BLA overcome the difficulties associated with measuring qualitative performance.

Marking scheme

Marks

(a) General discussion of the usefulness of non-financial indicators in public sector
     organisations – up to 4 marks

     For identifying examples relevant to BLA – up to 4 marks:

     Total for part (a): up to 6   6

(b)   General description of VFM (economy, efficiency, effectiveness) – up to 3 marks

For discussing each heading (economy; efficiency; effectiveness) in relation to BLA –
1 mark per relevant point – up to 12 marks

Total for part (b): up to 12   12

(c)   For identifying difficulties of measuring qualitative factors of performance –
1 mark per valid difficulty identified

For suggesting appropriate solutions for BLA – 1 mark per relevant point

Total for part (c): up to 7   7

Total = 25

(a)   Unlike commercial organisations which have an underlying objective to maximise the profits they generate for their shareholders, it is often much harder to define the objectives of public sector organisations.

Multiple objectives – The waste department's goal identifies three potential objectives: cleanliness, safety, and environmental friendliness. As such, its performance indicators will need to measure how well it is performing in these three areas. However, as none of the areas are financial, non-financial performance indicators – such as survey scores for how clear residents or tourists feel the area is – are likely to be more relevant than financial ones.

Lack of profit measure – The goal also highlights that generating a profit is not a priority for the department in the way it is for commercial organisations. The chief executive's desire to keep costs under control suggests that financial performance measures (focusing on costs) will still be important. However, if BLA focuses too much on cutting costs (for example, by reducing the frequency of waste collections), this could be detrimental to the primary goal of maintaining cleanliness and safety. As such, BLA needs a range of performance indicators, linked to how clean, safe and environmentally friendly the area is.

Difficulty in selecting financial measures – As with many public sector organisations, the results (output) from the waste department's services are non-financial: for example, clean streets, a safe environment. Therefore it will be difficult to find any financial indicators which measure the outputs of the department's services in any meaningful way.

Consequently, in any assessment of the department's services it will be difficult to introduce any direct comparison between cost (financial) and benefits (non-financial). In addition, it could be difficult to define the cost unit against which to measure the department's performance. For example, should BLA be measuring the cost per tonne of waste collected, or the cost per household?

(b)   **Value for money**

The extent to which BLA provides value for money services should be assessed in relation to:

Economy – the extent to which services of an acceptable quality are provided at the cheapest cost possible

Efficiency – the way BLA's services are organised, to ensure that the department maximises the benefits and ouptuts it obtains from its resources

Effectiveness – the extent to which the waste services department's activities achieve its goals.

Possible performance indicators at BLA

Economy

BLA's staff costs account for 44% of its total costs, and so the extent to which BLA controls its staff costs will have a significant impact on the economy of its services.

The average salary for BLA's waste collection staff is $31,429 compared to the national average of $29,825. The fact that BLA's average salary exceeds the national average suggests its services are not being provided as economically as they could be. However, this may reflect the fact that Beeshire is a wealthy area, so wage levels in general may be higher there than in other parts of the country. Equally, though, by paying above the national average for staff, BLA may be able to recruit more experienced or higher quality staff. As a result, this could improve its efficiency.

Another significant cost driver for BLA is likely to be its fleet of vehicles. Therefore, it could also measure economy in relation to the costs it pays for its vehicles, their fuel and their maintenance.

Efficiency

Benchmarking the performance of BLA's waste collections against the national figures indicates that BLA is relatively efficient:

	BLA	Nationally
Tonnes of waste collected per member of staff	629	583
Cost per tonne of waste collected ($)	114	123
Staff cost per tonne of waste collected ($)	50	51

This supports the point we made earlier: that although BLA's average salary is above the national average, BLA benefits from the greater efficiency of its staff.

Effectiveness

Effectiveness needs to be measured against a variety of aspects, linked to the need for waste collection:

Public health concerns – The fact that waste is only collected every 14 days (compared to the national average of 12 days) could suggest that BLA is less effective in maintaining public health. However, the level of public health concerns could also be measured by the number of complaints about vermin or other problems related to waste. If the level of complaints BLA receives is in line with national average (or below it) there would seem to be little reason to increase the frequency of the collections it carries out.

Clean and attractive streets – Finding a way to measure the cleanliness of BLA's streets could be difficult, because 'cleanliness' is inherently subjective, and therefore difficult to quantify. However, BLA could use the number of complaints it receives from residents or businesses as an indirect measure. If the number of complaints is relatively low, this would suggest that the cleanliness of the streets is being maintained at an acceptable level.

Increased recycling – The government has set a target of 40% of all waste to be recycled, therefore BLA needs to measure the percentage of its total waste it recycles. It currently recycles 43% of all waste collected (950,000 / 2.2m). As such, BLA has already achieved the target level, and the proportion of waste it recycles is above the national average (41%).

Nonetheless, as the government is planning to increase the levy charged on landfill, it will be important for BLA to ensure the proportion of waste that it recycles is as high as possible. As such, this remains an important indicator to monitor.

(c) **Difficulties of measuring qualitative performance**

Subjectivity – One of the main problems in measuring qualitative performance is that is based on people's opinions and judgements and therefore is subjective. For example, people's assessment about what constitutes an acceptable level of cleanliness in BLA's streets may be differ, and but this in turn could affect the degree to which the areas streets are perceived to be 'clean'.

Equally, as Seeland is currently in a long recession, some people may prefer that waste be collected less frequently to allow the local government to save money, instead of, for example, increasing local taxes to pay for more frequent collections. In this case, people's priorities could dictate their willingness to complain about uncollected waste or the frequency of collections.

The fact that the underlying data is qualitative rather than quantitative can, in itself, create problems for measurement. For example, if the waste management department receives a phone call from a resident complaining that some uncollected waste is 'disgusting', it will be difficult for the department to gauge whether this is a more serious or less serious problem than the uncollected waste described by another resident as 'foul'.

Currently, BLA records the number of complaints it receives, but there is no indication of the seriousness of these complaints – possibly due to the subjective nature of the data involved.

Scoring – One way of addressing the problem of subjectivity could be to try to make the data quantitative. For example, the waste management department could introduce a scoring system to judge how satisfied residents are with the cleanliness of their streeets. The scoring system could ask residents to rate cleanliness on a scale from 1 to 5, with '1' signifying 'Very satisfied' and '5' signifying 'Very dissatisfied'.

However, scoring systems are still subjective, because the level of cleanliness which one person grades as 'Very satisfactory' may only be deemed 'Satisfactory' by another person. In general, there is also a tendency to score towards the middle in this type of scoring system: people feel more comfortable selecting scores in the range '2' to '4', rather than using the extreme scores of '1' or '5'.

Trends – One way to reduce the subjectivity in non-financial performance measures is by looking at trends over time rather than one-off metrics – for example, monitoring trends in the average scores for cleanliness.

Although individual scores will still be subjective, looking at average scores over time can help to overcome this subjectivity and highlight changes in quality or satisfaction. For example, if the residents are surveyed about the cleanliness of BLA annually, and the average score declines from one year to the next, this should provide a good indication that the quality of the waste collection services is declining.

37 CFE coffee shops

Chapter references. Branding is discussed in Chapter 12 of the BPP Study Text.

Top tips.

Part (a). The marketing director's proposal is that CFE should introduce a loyalty card scheme in order to improve customer loyalty and strengthen CFE's brand. The key question, however, is what impact this customer loyalty or brand awareness will actually have on CFE's performance?

Notice that you are asked to 'evaluate' the importance of brand awareness so you need to think of its potential benefits for CFE's business performance, but you should also think whether there are any potential limitations on its impact.

Part (b). The success (or failure) of the Finance Director's plan is likely to depend on customers' reactions to it. So it is important that CFE understands its customers and their buying decisions. This highlights the importance of looking at CFE as an open system, and how its activities and decisions are affected by the external environment.

Part (c). The scenario has identified that some of the managers think CFE would be able to increase its profits if it stopped using 'Fair Trade' coffee. Clearly this argument has some merits. However, you also need to consider the counter arguments. Are there any potential benefits to CFE from being seen as a socially responsible company?

(a)   **Competitive market** – The high number of branded coffee shops in Teeland suggests that the market there is likely to be competitive, because customers will have a high degree of choice about where to buy their coffee. In this respect, branding, and the loyalty card scheme, could be valuable to CFE if it encourages customers to keep returning to CFE shops to buy their coffee rather than going to rival shops.

Customer loyalty – By creating customer loyalty a strong brand identity is a way of increasing or maintaining sales; for example, by improving customer retention rates and encouraging repeat purchases. This is the logic behind the loyalty cards being proposed by the marketing director.

However, whilst increasing sales will allow CFE to increase its profits overall, it may not, by itself, have as much impact as the Marketing Director might hope.

Importantly, CFE currently generates more revenue per shop than the market leader, although its profit margins are significantly lower.

Comparison of financial performance

	CFE	Market leader
Revenue per shop ($'000)	1,434.5	1,384.6
Gross margin (%)	64.5%	68.9%
Gross margin per shop ($'000)	925.0	953.8
Operating profit margin (%)	9.77%	12.50%

In this respect, it seems that CFE's cost structure and its product mix may have a greater impact on performance than brand awareness. For example, CFE makes the highest profit margins on coffee sales, so if it could sell relatively more coffee drinks compared to food and snacks this would improve its profit margins. The loyalty card scheme could help here, by encouraging customers to buy hot drinks so that they qualify for their free drink. (Obviously, though, margins will then be reduced by the 'free' seventh drink.)

Product mix

	Coffee	Other drinks	Food & snacks
% of total revenue	34.0%	9.7%	56.3%
Gross margin (%) earned per product	80.7%	52.4%	56.8%

However, although there appear to be more important factors affecting CFE's performance than its company profile, branding could still have a positive impact on its performance.

Brand awareness – Brand awareness would be an indicator of CFE's position in the coffee shop market, and would indicate whether customers or potential customers do actually differentiate CFE from its customers, for example as offering higher quality products and service. If customers don't associate CFE's products as being higher quality than the competitors, then the money spent on higher quality ingredients and service staff is effectively being wasted.

Quality and trust – One of the key attributes of a successful brand is that it conveys a sense of quality and trust to potential customers, thereby encouraging them to buy the product or service in question in preference to a rival product.

Quality seems to be very important to CFE: it uses high quality ingredients for its food and drinks, and seeks to ensure customer receive a high standard of service (by paying its staff wages above the industry average).

Differentiation – In this respect, CFE appears to be trying to differentiate itself from its competitors on grounds of quality. If it can ensure that its brand becomes synonymous with quality, then this will help CFE compete successfully with other branded coffee shops.

Premium price – Branding messages are usually qualitative rather than focusing, and therefore reduce the importance of price differentials between a product and its rivals. This could be very important for CFE. Customers do not appear to be price sensitive, yet CFE is charging broadly the same prices as its competitors.

If CFE is able to strengthen its brand, by focusing on quality and service, this may in turn allow it charge a higher price for its products. This could be crucial for CFE's profitability, because it could allow CFE to reverse the current situation in which its gross margin percentages are lower than its competitors'.

(b) **Demand for the product** – When deciding whether or not to increase the price of its coffee products, CFE needs to consider what impact the changes in price are likely to have on customer demand for them. Therefore market research will be important to assess how demand (and consequently revenue) will be affected by any change in price.

It seems that CFE's customers are not particularly price sensitive, which should increase the chances of the Finance Director's proposal. However, CFE should still research their reaction to any change before implementing it.

In this respect, it would also be useful for CFE to gauge the strength of any brand loyalty towards it.

Amount of increase – Equally, market research will give CFE an insight into what price customers are willing to pay for their coffee. CFE's competitive strategy (of differentiation based around quality) might enable it to charge higher prices than its customers to an extent and still retain its customers. However, if CFE increases its prices too much, it is unlikely that the customers will remain loyal to it, even if it offers higher quality coffee and service that its competitors.

Competitors' pricing policies – Currently, CFE's are largely the same as those charged by the multi-national competitors. However, these competitors might also be planning to change their prices. For example, if CFE's competitors increases their prices, that could give CFE greater scope to increase its prices.

Competitors' plans – Currently, CFE seems to serve a higher proportion of 'Fair Trade' products than its competitors, and this might help it justify its higher prices. However, if its competitors are also planning to use more 'Fair Trade' coffee, or increase the quality of other ingredients, this would reduce the basis of differentiation between CFE and its competitors. In this respect, any insights which CFE could gain into its competitors' plans before it changed its prices would be useful.

Input prices – The Finance Director's suggestion is designed to help CFE increase margins. However, if the price of coffee beans rises, it might need to increase prices in order to maintain its current margins.

Equally, if costs such as the rents CFE has to pay for its premises rise, these may also increase the pressure on CFE to increase its prices in order to maintain its profit margins.

(c) **Social responsibility** – The directors have been keen to stress that CFE is a socially responsible company, and their commitment to using Fair Trade suppliers is a way that they can demonstrate this. Acting responsibly, and being seen to act responsibly, can help CFE build trust with consumers, and enhance the image of its brand.

Fair Trade marketing – As well as demonstrating their social responsibility, using fair trade brands can also provide CFE with a marketing opportunity.

An increasing number of customers care about how suppliers in the developing world are treated, and wish to support them by buying fair trade brands. Therefore, by positioning and promoting itself in support of fair trade brands, CFE may be able to **attract ethical consumers** away from its rivals if they do not offer similar brands. In this way, Fair Trade marketing could allow CFE another point of **differentiation** from some of its competitors.

Cost and Price premiums – Because Fair Trade brands pay their suppliers an agreed 'fair' price, which is slightly higher than other coffee growers often receive, the cost to CFE of using Fair Trade will be slightly higher than if it used non-Fair Trade coffee.

Normally fair trade brands are normally sold at a slight **price premium** to reflect this cost differential.

It is not clear from the scenario whether all the major branded coffee shops sell Fair Trade coffee. However, if they are not, and CFE is selling its coffee at the same price as theirs, then CFE's margins will be slightly lower. This may the point that the regional managers are making when they suggest that CFE could increase its profitability if it stopped using Fair Trade coffee.

Nonetheless, CFE still earns a **gross margin of 80%** on its coffee sales, which suggests that the increase in profitability if CFE's shops stopped selling Fair Trade coffee might not be as significant as the regional managers might think. Moreover, the adverse public relations impact of discontinuing sales of Fair Trade coffee may outweigh the short-term cost savings from doing so.

Economic responsibilities – However, it is important not to overlook the fact that ultimately CFE exists to make a profit for its shareholders, so this is also a vital part of its social responsibility. It is not clear whether the directors are also the shareholders, but if they are not then they need to balance their **ethical** and **philanthropic responsibilities** with their **economic responsibilities to the shareholders**.

In this respect, they do need to consider what effect selling Fair Trade is having on CFE's profitability, but they need to do so in the context of considering the marketing opportunities and benefits to the brand image of being seen as a socially responsible company.

38 Herman Swan & Co

Top tips.

Part (a). In effect, the requirement for part (c) should have given you some useful context for part (a). If brand loyalty (and presumably, therefore, also customer retention) are important issues for HS, then HS needs to measure how well it is performing in these areas.

Similarly, the scenario also highlights that quality is a critical success factor for HS. And in this respect, the link between CSFs and KPIs is a very important aspect of this requirement. HS needs to have performance measures to gauge how well it is achieving its CSFs. But can it do this by measuring financial performance alone?

Part (b). Although part (b) is presented as a single requirement (for 12 marks) there are, in effect, three components to it:

(i)   Describe the changes in the role of the management accountant
(ii)   Explain what is driving these changes at HS
(iii) Justify why the changes are appropriate to HS

However, a sensible way to tackle this question would be to deal with the first two components together. In other words: take each of the changes identified by Burns and Scapens, describe the changes in general terms, and then consider whether the conditions which promote the changes are present at HS. You can then give a short justification of whether the changes as a whole are appropriate after you have looked at each of the changes in turn.

Crucially, though, to score well in this question you must link the factors driving the changes specifically to HS, rather than simply discussing Burns and Scapens' factors in general terms.

Part (c). Here again, it is vital to break down the components of the requirement very carefully. You are asked to discuss the impact of both brand loyalty **and** brand awareness on the business, and you are asked to do so from the customer perspective **and** the internal business process perspective. Finally, you are asked to evaluate suitable measures for brand loyalty and awareness.

Given that there are only 8 marks available for part (c) in total, though, it should be clear that you shouldn't spend too long on any single aspect of the requirement. However, it is important that you distinguish between brand loyalty and brand awareness. Brand awareness is primarily relevant to attracting **new** customers, while the main benefits of brand loyalty relate to the retention of **existing** customers.

Examining team's comments. This question was based on a company which makes fashionable clothes and leather goods. Although this question was the least popular of the Section B questions, those candidates who tackled it clearly grasped the nature of the business featured in the scenario and typically did well in the scenario-related comments and illustrations.

In part (b), most candidates demonstrated a broad grasp of the issues addressed by Burns and Scapens, and candidates did well trying to weave these in to the specific circumstances at HS. However, few candidates appeared to be able to remember the detail of Burns and Scapens' report, and so their analysis often missed out on one of the three factors mentioned in the report (technology, management structure, and competition).

In part (c), most candidates were able to discuss brand loyalty from a customer perspective and suggest suitable measures, but fewer were able to distinguish the internal process perspective, even though they had realised that quality was a key part of the product offering. Similarly, only the better candidates successfully differentiated between customer loyalty and awareness. However, by doing so, these candidates distinguished themselves from the rest.

Marks

(a) Identifying the need for performance measures to support critical success factors, and
the non-financial aspect of CSFs – up to 3 marks
For illustrating CSFs and performance measures specifically in the context of HS – up to
3 marks
Total for part (a): Up to 5 marks

5

(b) Describing Burns and Scapens' view of the overall change – up to 2 marks
Up to 3 marks for identifying each of the three factors driving change (technology;
management structure; competition) and illustrating them in the context of HS – up to 9
marks across the three factors
For justifying why the changes are appropriate at HS, and what the benefits of them are
for HS – up to 3 marks.
Total for part (b): Up to 12 marks

12

(c) Describing brand loyalty and brand awareness – up to 2 marks
Discussing the impact of brand loyalty and brand awareness on the business – up to 6
marks
[**Note**. To score well in this part of the question, your discussion needs to include both
the customer perspective and the internal business perspective.]
Evaluating measures of brand loyalty and brand awareness – up to 4 marks
Total for part (c): Up to 8 marks

<u>8</u>

Total = <u>25</u>

(a) **Critical success factors** – Historically, performance measures have tended to focus mainly on aspects of an
organisation's financial performance. This may appear sensible as financial performance indicators play an
important role in allowing organisations to **measure** success.

However, organisations also need to monitor the aspects of performance which **ensure** success. These
aspects which ensure success are an organisation's critical success factors (CSFs).

Crucially, CSFs are often **non-financial in nature**:

Quality – For example, it appears that HS's continuing success is dependent on it continuing to product high
quality clothes. The company has built a strong reputation for quality, and the high quality of its clothes
enables HS to charge high prices for them.

Brand loyalty – The competition HS faces has been intensifying for more than 10 years, and therefore issues
of brand loyalty and brand awareness are likely to become increasingly important for it. The strength of HS's
brand is likely to play in important role in the company's ability to maintain (or even grow) its market share.

In this respect, ensuring it produces high quality clothes, and ensuring that it develops brand loyalty and
brand awareness are likely to be CSFs for HS.

Performance measures – Once HS has identified its CSFs, it then has to develop performance indicators
(KPIs) to measure how well it is actually performing in these key areas of the business. If HS's performance
is below target in relation to key areas, then performance will need to be improved in order for HS to remain
competitive in an increasingly competitive environment.

Because the CSFs are non-financial, it follows that the KPIs used to measure them are also non-financial. For
example, HS could use indicators such as the number of garments returned to help measure the quality of
its clothes.

Longer term objectives – Another reason why non-financial aspects of performance are becoming increasingly important is that they tend to have less of a short-term focus than financial performance measures.

Financial performance measurement systems often focus on annual, or short-term, performance against financial targets. However, these may not be directly linked to an organisation's longer-term objectives. For example, financial performance measures do not assess how well an organisation is meeting customer-related objectives.

However, non-financial objectives (such as achieving customer loyalty or brand loyalty) may be vital in sustaining profitability, competitiveness and other longer-term strategic goals.

(b)   **Financial control role** – The traditional view of accounting is as a mechanism for control, and therefore the focus of the management accountant's role has traditionally been on financial control within an organisation.

In this traditional model, it was felt that management accountants needed to remain independent from operational managers, in order for accountants to be able to judge performance objectively and then report on it to senior management.

Business support role – However, Burns and Scapens' studies found that the primary purpose of management accounting has now changed from financial control to business support. The management accountant's role has also had to change accordingly.

In particular, instead of remaining detached from operating divisions, management accountants now need an understanding of these divisions and the commercial issues they are facing, so that, in effect, accountants can provide an internal consultancy service to the divisions.

Hybrid accountant – Burns and Scapens characterise the management accountant's new role as being that of a hybrid accountant. As such, an accountant is no longer simply a financial or numbers specialist, but also needs an understanding of the operating functions and commercial processes of their organisation. The accountant acts as a source of **business support and advice** for operational managers.

Accordingly, management accountants have become increasingly involved with the operations of their business, rather than working in a separate 'accounting department.'

Burns and Scapens state that there are three main forces for change in the role of the management accountant: changes in technology, management structure and competition.

Technology

In recent decades there have been major changes in the quality and quantity of information technology (IT) resources available in organisations.

Historically, the management accountant was one of the few people in an organisation who had access to the IT system and the information generated, because the outputs from the IT system were usually used to prepare financial reports to management. Data input was strictly controlled, and only a few people were allowed to enter data onto the IT system.

Impact of MIS – Now, however, management information systems (MIS) allow users across an organisation to run reports, providing them with the type of analysis once only provided by the management accountant. Therefore, rather than having exclusive access to information, the management accountant is simply another user of the system, in the same way that operational managers are.

This force for change is evident at HS, because the new management information system has increased the data available to all managers throughout the business.

Management structure

Changes in management structure have also affected the role of the management accountant in organisations.

Responsibility for budgeting – One of the main changes in organisations has been a shift in the responsibility for budgeting. Instead of budgets being produced by head office, and imposed on operational managers, operational managers now have greater responsibility for producing their own budgets.

This force for change is also evident at HS. The SBU managers have taken on greater responsibility for budgeting, whereas this had previously been carried out by the finance team at head office.

The increased autonomy given to the operational managers in organisations also means they have increased responsibility for managing the performance of their operations; for example, by monitoring actual performance against key financial and non-financial performance indicators, and producing revised forecasts based on current performance and trading conditions.

Producing reports – Consequently, whereas in the traditional model, the management accountant was the only person who produced performance reports for senior management, now operational managers will also be producing them.

Therefore, the nature of the reports produced by the management accountant will need to change. For example, the accountant's reports may have to try to highlight the financial consequences of the information presented in the operational reports, or may have to illustrate how operational performance is affecting the organisation's progress towards achieving its strategic goals.

Competition

Strategic focus – Burns and Scapens' project found that the management accountant's role had an increasingly commercial orientation. This change reflected organisations' own needs to respond to competition and deploy a more strategic focus to help achieve, and maintain, competitive advantage.

Traditionally, management accountants focused largely on the 'bottom line' profit figure. However, this focus on profit has subsequently been associated with a **short-term approach** to performance management.

A commercial and strategic orientation recognises the importance of an organisation's future earning capacity as well as its profit in the current period. Therefore, management accountants need to look at a wider range of performance measures to try to capture **longer-term trends** in performance and future profitability, as well as reporting on current profits.

This strategic orientation also encourages management accountants to assess an organisation's performance in the context of its wider **external environment**.

Competitive position at HS – Competition and the competitive environment is having a significant impact on the role of the management accountant at HS.

HS sells its goods across the world and its main goal is to grow the business organically for the next generation of the family. This highlights that HS isn't solely interested in short term performance, but also has longer-term goals.

However, HS is also faced with increasing competition in its markets, and it needs to be aware of the threat from large brands which will try to dominate markets using economies of scale to their competitive advantage. Therefore, HS needs to be flexible and innovative in its response to larger competitors, but will also need to ensure it maintains the high quality of its products which could help it differentiate itself from these competitors.

Appropriateness of the changes at HS

The three main forces for change in the management accountant's role (changes in technology; management structure and competition) are all present at HS.

The changes in organisational structure (leading to SBU managers taking more responsibility for budgeting) would appear to fit particularly well with the concept of the accountant as an internal consultant. For example, the accountant could work with the operational managers to identify ways of improving how the new MIS is used, and tailoring the reports it produces to the managers' particular needs.

Equally, the accountant can play an important role in ensuring that the aspects of operational performance which the SBU managers measure are properly aligned to, and support, HS' overall strategic goals and objectives.

(c)   **Brand identity** helps to convey information about the quality or price of a product or service to customers. A strong brand identity can help create customer loyalty to the brand, thereby improving customer retention rates and encouraging repeat purchases, which in turn can be a means of increasing or maintaining sales.

Brand loyalty results in a consumer consistently buying the same brand within a product class, rather than buying a range of different brands. Again, this loyalty helps to maintain sales.

Brand awareness is an indicator of the strength of a product or organisation's position in the market place, and in customer's minds. Whereas brand loyalty helps to retain existing customers, brand awareness is important for attracting new customers and thereby generating new revenues.

Customer perspective

Competitive advantage – From the customer perspective, HS's brand is part of its competitive advantage. Customers are attracted to HS by its history and the family story which goes behind its products. In particular, customers are willing to pay high prices because they identify with the company's values, and because HS's brand signifies a high quality of manufacturing. In this respect, branding acts as a form of product differentiation which can make it possible for HS to charge premium prices for a luxury product.

Brand loyalty – In this respect, customers' loyalty to the HS brand can help compensate for the price differential between HS's products and those of its global competitors who benefit from economies of scale.

Equally, since HS's family story is an important part of its brand, the company will need to ensure that this story is maintained, and customers remain aware of it.

Brand awareness – However, because HS is competing against global brands, awareness of HS's brand among the public at large may be lower than awareness of some of the competitor brands. This highlights the importance of marketing expenditure within HS to increase public awareness of its brand.

Marketing and promotion – While HS needs to promote itself in order to maintain brand awareness, it must also ensure that its marketing campaigns are tailored to places and media which fit with its brand story, for example by sponsoring public events attended by stylish or high income people.

However, as well as any regular marketing expenditure (reminder advertising) required to maintain HS's brand in general, it may also need one-off marketing campaigns, for example linked to the launch of specific new products.

Performance measurement – The management accountant could have an important role in monitoring the effectiveness of HS's marketing spend; for example, by trying to identify any relationships between marketing and sales growth. In particular, it could be useful to identify which marketing channels are most effective for different campaigns.

A measure such as return on marketing expenditure could be useful here: looking at the incremental revenues which are generated following different marketing campaigns.

Market segmentation – In this respect, it will also be important for HS to identify the different markets in which it operates, so that these can be segmented appropriately (for example, by age, gender, income or lifestyle), and then marketing campaigns can be specifically targeted, based on the target market, and the products or product ranges being promoted.

Internal business perspective

Quality – In order to sustain the reputation of its brand, HS needs to ensure that it maintains the high quality of both its **manufacturing** and also its **retailing** operations.

Quality in production – Since the HS brand promotes the idea of high quality, customers will be disappointed if the products they buy do not live up to their expectations. In this respect, **quality assurance** and **quality control** will be very important for HS. Therefore, it could be useful for the management accountant to monitor the expenditure incurred in relation to preventing or detecting faulty goods in the production process. However, it will equally be important to monitor the level of customer complaints about goods which do not meet their quality standards.

Retail quality – The quality of the service customers receive in HS's shops will also shape their perception of the brand. In this respect, the amount of **training** given to staff will need to be high in order to ensure a high quality of service is offered to customers in HS's shops. In addition, there may need to be high **capital costs** in order to fit out the retail premises to the standards expected of a premium brand such as HS.

Brand loyalty – If customers continue to receive high quality goods and high quality service from HS (which meet, or even exceed their expectations), they are more likely to remain loyal to HS than if they receive products and service which do not meet their expectations.

Suitable measures

> **Tutorial note.** The marking guide indicates that there are up to 4 marks available for evaluating suitable measures for brand loyalty and awareness.
>
> The solution below includes a range of possible measures which you could have referred to in this context, but you would not have needed to include all of them to score the 4 marks available.

Brand loyalty

Retention rates – Brand loyalty can be measured through customer retention rates and the level of repeat purchases by customers. We would expect there to be a correlation between brand loyalty and the level of repeat purchases: the higher the proportion of HS's customers who make repeat purchases from it, the stronger the loyalty to the HS brand would appear to be.

Price elasticity of demand – Another way of measuring brand loyalty could also be to measure price elasticity of demand. If HS's customers continue to buy its products despite an increase in price, this would suggest they are loyal to the HS brand. A brand's ability to increase prices with only a relatively small reduction in demand is one of the key benefits of brand loyalty.

Profit margins – Another benefit of branding is that it could help HS charge premium prices for its products, thereby enabling it to earn higher profits than if products had to be sold at a lower price. In this respect, it would be useful to measure the profit margins HS can earn, and compare these to other companies who make similar products to HS but who don't have such a strong brand.

Brand awareness

Market share – A relatively crude way of trying to gauge customers' awareness of HS's brand would be to measure the market share that HS enjoys. If HS's market share is increasing, this should suggest that customers' awareness of the brand is also increasing.

Brand awareness surveys – A more detailed way of assessing brand awareness would be through brand awareness surveys; for example, HS could test whether customers can correctly associate the brand associated with its logos or products.

Such an exercise could be particularly useful in assessing the impact that an advertising campaign has had on brand awareness. However, given the segmentation of HS's markets, it will be important for HS to test its brand awareness in different markets.

39 Navier Aerials

> **Text reference.** Activity-based costing in relation to cost reduction is covered in Chapter 15 of the BPP Study Text. Quality management is covered in Chapter 13.
>
> **Top tips.**
>
> **Part (a).** In order to evaluate the impact of using activity-based costing, compared to the existing costing system, we need to know what difference there is between the cost allocations under the two systems. Accordingly, you need to do the calculations before you can begin to evaluate the impact of any change.
>
> Note the cost allocations should be 'per dish' not 'per order'.
>
> Once you have done the calculations, you then need to compare the allocations under the two systems. For example, are the cost allocations similar under the two systems, or are there any significant differences? How accurate is the FD's assumption that the cost of the additional customer care for specialised dishes is $100 per dish?
>
> Remember that ABC costing is likely to be more time-consuming the current method. So are the cost allocations sufficiently different under the two methods to justify the extra work involved in applying the ABC method?

Part (b). Make sure you read the requirement for part (b) very carefully. Although the issues of cost reduction and quality management in the customer care department are important, the key element in the requirement relates to how **information** about the activities can be used and improved.

So, for example, whilst reducing the number of customer complaints could reduce complaint handling costs, Navier needs to know what the main reasons for customer complaints are in order for it to tackle the causes of those complaints. If Navier doesn't have any information about why customers are complaining, how can it decide what changes need to be made to its current processes?

Examining team's comments. This question was generally answered poorly, with weak efforts at handling the quantification of the two costing systems, compounded by lack of knowledge about quality issues.

Part (a) required candidates to use the partially completed calculations in the question to work out cost per dish (using the two methods for allocating overheads), and then to consider the implications of the results. Many candidates seemed perplexed that the calculations were not more difficult; and yet commonly failed to do them accurately.

At the P5 level, candidates will often be presented with data which has already been prepared (by a more junior accountant) and then be asked to complete or to assess/interpret the work done. However, candidates seemed ill-prepared for this kind of task, and for evaluating the impact of activity-based costing on overhead absorption systems.

The scenario presented a situation which candidates could easily come across in real life. The finance director has estimated the impact of different product types, and candidates were then required to do the work more accurately and comment on the results. A key question posed here – which few candidates identified was: is the effort required to generate a more accurate overhead allocation worth the effort?

Candidates should be wary of simply **assuming** that the newer, more complex method (in this case, ABC) is the best solution in practice.

Part (b) moved from the performance measurement aspect of the scenario into the performance management implications. The question required an assessment of the information available about each of the activities, and how that information can be used – or improved – in order to help reduce cost and improve quality.

Unfortunately, most candidates displayed a weak grasp of quality cost issues, and also failed to prioritise their work towards the major cost areas of 'handling enquiries and prepared quotes' and 'complaints handling.'

Marking scheme

Marks

(a) Calculating the number of dishes – 1 mark

Calculating the standard absorption cost per dish – 1 mark

Calculating costs to be allocated to each dish using activity-based costing; 1 mark per type of dish – up to 2 marks

For comments on the consequences of using the current costing system – 1 mark per valid point, up to 4 marks

For comment on the impact of using activity-based costing – 1 mark per valid point, up to 7 marks

Total: up to 13

13

(a) **Current absorption costing** – Under the current costing system, the total costs of the customer care (CC)
department are allocated to each dish by dividing total departmental costs by the total number of dishes.
Under this basis, the cost of customer care per dish is $8.03. This cost is then added to the other costs
incurred in the production of the dishes (such as material and labour) to obtain a total cost per dish.

Specialised dishes – The FD adds an additional $100 per specialised dish to cover the cost of customer
care in relation to these dishes. However, because the total costs of the customer care department have
already been absorbed in the $8.03 charge, this additional charge means that CC costs will be over-
absorbed. (Assuming that Navier manufactures 1,600 specialised dishes per year, the CC cost over-
absorbed will be $160,000.)

ABC costing

As Navier produces two different types of product, which use different amounts of the customer care
department's resources, applying ABC costing will enable overhead costs to be allocated to the different
products more accurately.

The activity-based analysis (see Working: Costs per dish) shows that the costs of customer care per
standard dish should be $6.22, instead of $8.03. As a result, the profit per dish will be higher under the
activity-based costing system than under the current system.

Under the activity-based system, the CC costs attributed to each specialised dish are $106.05. It should not
be a surprise that the costs attributed to the specialised dishes are so much higher than for the standard
dishes because of the disproportionate amount of time spent handling enquiries, preparing quotes and
dealing with complaints in relation to specialised dish orders.

Working: Costs per dish

Standard absorption cost per dish

		$
Total cost of customer care department		707,000
Number of dishes (16,000 x 5.5)	88,000	
Standard absorption cost per dish		8.03
Finance director's adjusted cost per specialised dish		108.03

Activity-based costs

	All orders	Standard	Specialised
Total costs ($)	707,000	537,320	169,680
Average dishes per order		6	1
Number of orders	16,000	14,400	1,600
Total number of dishes ($)		86,400	1,600
ABC absorption cost per dish ($)		**6.22**	**106.05**

The difference between the allocated CC costs of specialised and standard dishes under the activity-based system is $99.83 ($106.05 – $6.22). The appears to justify the finance director's estimate, under the current system, of adding $100 to the CC costs of a standard dish in order to find the costs of a specialised dish.

However, the fact that the absorption costs of both standard and specialised dishes are lower under the ABC system than under the current system again suggests that costs are being over-absorbed under the current system. (No adjustment is being made to the basic figure of $8.03 to reflect the additional $100 costs being allocated to the specialised dishes.)

Evaluation of ABC analysis

Value adding activities – ABC analysis enables Navier to identify the activities which are driving the higher costs of the specialised dishes.

Given the CEO's wish to be able to identify non-value-added activities, further analysis could then be undertaken to determine whether customers value the additional customer care work associated with their bespoke dishes (and therefore whether the additional costs of almost $100 per dish add value or not). If there are any processes which do not add value for the customers, these should be removed or redesigned.

Cost benefit analysis – Although the ABC exercise has enabled costs to be allocated to the two types of product more accurately, it is debatable whether the extra effort involved in calculating the activity-based costs is worthwhile. The FD appears to have been able to estimate the costs to be allocated to the products reasonably accurately before any ABC analysis was undertaken.

If the current absorption calculations are adjusted to correct for the over-absorption in relation to the specialised dishes, then the costs to be allocated per dish (see working below) would be very similar to those proposed under the activity-based costing system.

		$
Total cost of customer care department		707,000
Costs attributable to specialised dishes		(160,000)
General costs to apportion		547,000
Number of dishes (16,000 × 5.5)	88,000	
Standard absorption cost per dish		**6.22**
Finance director's adjusted cost per specialised dish		**106.22**

(b) **Cost activities**

The main cost activities in the CC department are pre-sales (handling enquiries and preparing quotes: $282,800) and post-sale (handling customer complaints: $176,750). Together, these activities account for 65% of the total cost of the department.

Sales enquiries – The pre-sale work is vital for converting customer enquiries into firm orders. Currently just under 46% of all enquiries are converted into actual orders (16,000/35,000). Given the importance of pre-sale activities for the CC department, it would be useful to know how effectively the department converts enquiries into orders compared to other similar departments.

In this respect, some kind of benchmarking exercise could be very useful. Navier could try to benchmark its enquiries-to-orders ratio against its competitors (competitor benchmarking), although its competitors may not publish this information as they may consider it to be commercially sensitive. Alternatively, Navier could monitor the number of enquiries and its own conversion rate of enquiries to orders over time (historical benchmarking).

Complaints handling – Complaints handling should be seen as a non-value-adding activity. Whilst dealing effectively with customer complaints is important from a relationship management perspective, it doesn't in itself add any value to the product which customers buy from Navier. Instead, complaint handling is only required where the products or service customers receive do not meet the standard they expect.

Quality management – In this respect, reducing complaint handling costs could be linked to quality management. If the quality of Navier's products is improved, this should reduce the number of customer complaints, and in turn the level of customer handling costs.

Currently, there are 3,200 complaints per year in respect of 16,000 orders. Although there could be more than one complaint in relation to a single dish, this level of complaints suggests that there is a complaint in relation to approximately 20% of Navier's total orders, which seems quite a high proportion. Moreover, the level of customer complaints (**external failure costs**) suggests that there is scope for Navier to improve its internal controls so that problems can either be prevented or else detected before they reach the customer.

In order to reduce the number of complaints, Navier needs to identify what is causing them. There could be a number of different issues which lead to complaints. Some of the complaints may relate to the CC department, while others are likely to result from the manufacturing process.

If the CC doesn't understand a customer's order correctly, the instructions it passes on to the manufacturing and installation teams are also likely to be incorrect.

Equally, although the instructions were correct, there could be problems with the work undertaken by the manufacturing and installation teams. It is not clear what level of supervision and inspection is in place, but it is possible that this needs to be increased in order to prevent and detect quality issues. In this respect, it may be beneficial for Navier to increase the level of inspection and detection costs, in order to reduce the level of non-conformance costs which would otherwise result if a dish does not meet the customers' expected standards.

Financial information – The other activities in the CC department (such as credit checks and order processing) are administrative, and the financial information systems can provide some measures of their quality. The quality of order processing can be measured by reference to the number of invoice disputes or the value of credit notes issued. Equally, the effectiveness of Navier's credit checks can be assessed by measuring the level of bad debts incurred.

40 TAW

Text reference. Chapter 13 of the BPP Study Text covers costs of quality.

Top tips. This question is split into two fairly even parts which you must answer in order as the analysis in part(a) will help with your answer to part (b). Read the requirements in part (a) carefully and draw up your answer to show % of turnover, and total cost of quality. The examining team's answer shows percentages for **each cost** but the question only asks for each **cost heading**. By all means do this if you have time. We also show whole percentages as the question doesn't state you must calculate these to a certain number of places. The question requirement only asks you to comment on the inclusion of opportunity costs, but ACCA's suggested solution actually also includes the costs in the answer. They should be easy enough to calculate though.

Part (b) wants you to work out the costs of each option and the savings from adopting the option. The savings come from avoiding the costs of non-conformance associated with poor quality.

Part (c) – Don't just explain what Kaizen principles are here; but make sure you explain how they could be used by TAW in the way the question asks.

Examining team's comments. This was the least popular of the option questions. However some answers were excellent and earned very high marks. Poorer answers revealed confusion over what the cost categories meant. Some poorer answers to part (b) had poorly laid-out, incorrect calculations.

(a)   **Cost analysis**

	Year ended 31 May 20X8 $'000	$'000	% of turnover
Prevention costs			
Training (Note 3)	180		
Design engineering (Notes 1 and 2) 48,000 × $96	4,608		
Process engineering(Notes 1 and 2) 54,000 × $70	3,780	8,568	2
Appraisal costs			
Inspection (Notes 1 and 2) 288,000 × $50	14,400		
Product testing (Note 3)	72	14,472	4
Internal failure costs			
Rework (Notes 1 and 2) 2,100 × $4,800	10,080	10,080	3
External failure costs			
Repairs (Notes 1 and 2) 2,700 × $(4,600 + 240 +280)	13,824	13,824	4
Total cost of quality		46,944	
Opportunity costs – lost contribution (Note 4)		12,960	4
Total cost of quality		59,904	17

Opportunity cost is the contribution associated with the loss of potential sales arising out of a poor public perception of quality. The estimate of lost sales is 4% of turnover. These are not ordinarily included in the four standard categories of quality cost but could be classified as external failure costs.

Quality cost statements frequently omit costs that result from poor quality but are difficult to estimate. These **opportunity costs** include:

- Profit from lost sales
- Lost production
- Lower prices as a consequence of poor quality

(b)   **Financial consequences of options for improving quality**

Option 1

Costs	Description	$'000
Prevention cost	Physical inspections 10,000 × $50	500.0
Savings		
Internal failure cost	Variable costs of rework 720 × $1,920	1,382.4
External failure cost	**Variable cost** of customer support 600 × $96	57.6
	Transportation 600 × $210	126.0
	Warranty repair 600 × $1,700	1,020.0
Extra sales (contribution)	300 × $7,200	2,160.0
		4,746.0
Net saving		4,246.0

Option 2

		$'000
Costs		
Prevention cost	Redesign cases 2,000 × $96	192.0
	Process engineering 5,000 × $70	350.0
Savings		
Internal failure cost	Variable costs of rework 960 × $1,920	1,843.2
External failure cost	**Variable cost** of customer support 840 × $96	80.6
	Transportation 840 × $210	176.4
	Warranty repair 840 × $1,700	1,428.0
Extra sales (contribution)	360 × $7,200	2,592.0
		6,120.2
Net saving		5,578.2

Option 2 has a larger estimated net saving at $5,578,200 and should be chosen as this is $1,332,200 more than the estimate for Option 1 ($4,246,000).

(c) **Kaizen** – Kaizen principles are built around the theory of gradual, continuous improvement and focus on obtaining small incremental cost reductions during the production phase of the product life cycle.

Cost reduction – Although the directors have suggested that TAW will be unable to save any of the fixed costs of interenal and external failure, they have also indicated that it could be possible for TAW to achieve improvements in quality.

Consequently, it may be possible for the improvements in quality to reduce the level of variable costs resulting from quality issues at TAW (for example, as a result of a reduction in the number of items needing to be reworked).

Moreover, because Kaizen focuses on the idea of continuous improvement, it could also lead to an on-going reduction in the cost of quality issues from one year to the next.

41 Thebe

Text reference. Quality issues and Six Sigma are considered in Chapter 13 of the BPP Study Text.

Top tips.

Part (a). The scenario highlighted that customer service is likely to be key to helping the business grow. However, the absence of any non-financial information in the performance report presented to the Board suggests that the Board aren't monitoring customer service levels.

You should have identified that this seems odd, given the importance of customer service to the business' success. But, if the non-financial performance information was included in the performance report alongside financial information, this would help redress the balance.

Parts (b) and (c) of this question provide a good illustration of why it is important to read all the requirements before starting to answer a question.

In **Part (b)** of the question you are asked to discuss the general ways in which Six Sigma could help improve quality. You shouldn't spend time discussing *how* Six Sigma is implemented in this part of the question, but rather how does the process of implementing Six Sigma (in general terms) improve the quality of performance in an organisation

The reason why shouldn't discuss how Six Sigma is implemented in part (b) becomes clear when you look at part (c) of the requirement: to explain and illustrate how the DMAIC method could be applied at Thebe.

Part (c). A sensible approach to this question would be to use 'DMAIC' as the framework of your answer, and then to work through each of the elements (Define, Measure etc) in turn.

However, note that you aren't asked simply to explain DMAIC in general terms, but to illustrate how it could be applied specifically at Thebe, so make sure you include examples of issues from the scenario.

Marking scheme

		Marks
(a)	1 mark per relevant point up to 2 marks for each benefit of non-financial performance measures evaluated	
	Up to 8 marks	8
(b)	1 mark per relevant point up to 2 marks for each way Six Sigma can improve performance	
	Up to 8 marks	8
(c)	Up to 3 marks for each stage of the DMAIC process; being 1 mark for a general description and 2 marks for application to the scenario.	
	Up to 9 marks	9
		Total = 25

(a) **Importance of non-financial measures** – The CEO has identified that customer service is crucial in growing the business, and differentiating it from competitors (such as FayTel) which suggests that providing excellent customer service is a critical success factor for Thebe.

By performing well in this area of the business, Thebe should be better placed to perform well financially than if it offers poor customer service.

In this case, there would seem to be a clear link between non-financial performance and financial performance. However, if the board are not aware of how well Thebe is performing in key operational (non-financial) areas of the business they may not notice performance issues which could subsequently have an impact on Thebe's financial performance.

What gets measured gets done – Thebe's employees and line managers are likely to pay more attention to those areas of the business in which performance is being measured, compared to those areas of which are not being measured.

Similarly, there is a danger that what doesn't get measured, might not get done. The focus of the board meetings, on financial performance, suggests that this might be prioritised over non-financial aspects of performance.

However, the fact that the CEO has championed the project to improve billing accuracy suggests that he believes it is important. In turn, however, this suggests Thebe should be measuring its performance in relation to billing accuracy – for example, through measuring the number of complaints it receives from customers who are complaining that they have been billed incorrectly.

Information for decision-making and control – The current position suggests that it could be difficult for the board to know how to improve Thebe's performance, if they do not have adequate information about its current performance. Although the CEO is aware that all telephone businesses (including Thebe) have problems in relation to applying incorrect tariffs, it seems unlikely that he will have any actual information about how Thebe is performing in this area of the business.

Again, having this information would have been useful before deciding to undertake the project to improve the quality and accuracy of billing – both to decide whether the project was necessary, and also to see how much impact the project has on the quality of Thebe's billing.

Linkages – However, directors will need to be careful which non-financial measures they choose to monitor, and in particular how the non-financial measures link to Thebe's financial performance. For example, there will be little value in monitoring aspects of operational performance which add little value to Thebe's financial performance. Indeed, the CEO may find that, ultimately, customers choose their telephone provider based on price rather than the quality of customer service they receive.

In this respect, it is also important that the Directors continue to monitor financial performance as well as non-financial performance, because there is no guarantee that favourable performance in customer service or other non-financial areas will necessarily translate into favourable financial performance. For example, even though Thebe may provide its customers with accurate bills, and may provide a very high level of customer service, its revenues may still fall if FayTel introduces new tariffs so that customers can get a cheaper phone service by switching to them.

Despite the increased importance of non-financial performance measures, the ultimate measure of Thebe's performance will be how well it generates financial value for its owners.

(b)   **Focus on the customer** – One of the key aspects of Six Sigma methodology is that it requires organisations to have a genuine focus on the customer. Thebe's CEO has clearly identified that customer service is crucial to the success of the business, and so the project to improve customers' bills is an important element of this.

Importance of facts and data – Another important element of Six Sigma is that it highlights that decisions should be taken on the basis of facts and data, rather than intuition, and this in turn highlights the importance of performance measurement.

This is evident at Thebe in the way that data has been sourced from customer feedback. This data could relate, for example, to the number of customer complaints, or to customer satisfaction ratings.

Business process improvement – One of the key themes in Six Sigma is that processes are the key to success. Therefore implementing Six Sigma will encourage Thebe to identify which processes (and which activities within a process) are critical to its success, so that it can then focus on understanding those process and improving them where necessary.

Involvement of management – When an organisation commits to Six Sigma, it will normally appoint an implementation leader and a steering committee at a senior level, to oversee the implementation. By involving management in this way it highlights a business' commitment to improving quality; as appears to be the case at Thebe where the CEO is championing the project to improve service quality.

Increased profile of quality issues – Six Sigma project teams are made up of staff experienced in the process under review. By involving team members in the project, they will realise the importance of quality issues, and improve their knowledge of quality management.

The nature of Six Sigma **project leadership** means that managers should learn from working with layers of trained experts. For example line managers who are be 'Green Belts' helping to lead a Six Sigma project can learn from 'Master Black Belts'.

Collaboration – Another key theme in Six Sigma projects is the need for collaboration between staff from across different departments or divisions within an organisation. In this way, Six Sigma implementation highlights the importance of the whole organisation focusing on quality, not just individual departments. For example, the project team at Thebe brings together line managers from all three business units, as well as from the billing department.

(c)   **Define customer requirements/Define the problem**

Customers underlying requirement is that they are billed accurately, and if they aren't this could lead either to delayed revenue (while the customers dispute their bills) or lost revenue (if customers switch to an alternative provider).

However, the organisational structure at Thebe highlights that this project also needs to focus on complaint handling as well as billing itself, and in this respect customer requirements may need to be defined further. It is likely that there will be is a minimum acceptable level of service (for example, that billing errors are corrected), but Thebe should identify ways which its customers feel would improve its service above that minimum level: for example, in relation to how quickly any complaints are responded to; or by offering some form of compensation as a goodwill gesture.

Measure existing performance

The CEO's customer service project has highlighted two key areas of focus: the accuracy of customer's bills, and the handling of complaints.

Accordingly, Thebe needs information to assess how well it is performing in both of these areas; so it needs to measure its performance in both areas. For example, Thebe could measure the number of customer complaints per million bills issued, or the average time it takes to resolve a customer complaint fully. (Measures such as that looking at the number of complaints links directly to Six Sigma methodology which identified that there should be less than six defects per million.)

However, when selecting the aspects of performance to measure, it is important that Thebe focuses on those areas where improvement will be valued by the customer, rather than, for example, areas which are easy to measure.

Analyse the existing process

In part (a) we identified that the Six Sigma methodology highlights the importance of facts and data, rather than intuition. This stage of the DMAIC process focuses on collecting the data, which can then be analysed to identify the root causes of problems in Thebe's existing processes.

Thebe can then focus its improvements towards those issues which lead to the most problems (complaints). If a relatively small number of problems give rise to the majority of complaints, then this will highlight the importance of tackling the causes of those problems as the most urgent priority. For example, if a large proportion of customer complaints relate to the length of time it takes Thebe to issue revised bills, then it will be important to analyse what factors are slowing down the process.

Improve the process

Once the causes of problems have been analysed, Thebe should then be able to identify potential changes which could be made to improve performance in these areas of its business. For example, in relation to the time taken to reissue corrected bills, Thebe may need to consider whether it needs more staff to be authorised to make changes to bills.

However, before any specific improvements are recommended it will be important for Thebe to check that they are feasible; for example, that they will not be prohibitively expensive to implement, and that Thebe has the resources necessarily to implement them.

Control the process

Once the improvements have been implemented, the line managers (and the board) need to continue monitor performance to ensure that the benefits from reduced complaints and improved customer satisfaction are maintained.

At an operational level, Thebe can do this by continuing to monitor complaint numbers – perhaps by means of exception reporting, so that managers are only alerted of a potential issue if the number of complaints increases above a specified threshold level.

However, Thebe can also measure its success in relation to customer service levels more generally in relation to customer retention rates or the churn rate (the percentage of existing customers lost each year.)

If the company has successfully improved its performance in those areas which customers value as important, then the number of customers who switch to another service provider should be reduced. This in turn will mean that a greater proportion of the new customers which Thebe acquires will contribute to growing the business rather than replacing lapsed existing customers.

42 There 4 U

Marking scheme

			Marks
(a)	Comments (on merit):		
	Explanation of process – DMAIC	8	
	Explanation of different grades of leadership (Black Belt etc)	3	11
(b)	Application of DMAIC to analyse and address problems	14	14
			Total = 25

(a) **Describe the Six sigma methodology for the improvement of an existing process**

Six Sigma is a rigorous operating methodology designed to ingrain a culture of excellence, responsiveness and accountability in the organisation. It aims to deliver defect-free products or services at a level of 99.9997 percent so only 3 per million errors or faults would arise. It has been applied in a variety of functions from service centres to manufacturing plants.

Six Sigma uses programmes to analyse processes continually for defects. Statistical techniques are used to work out what improvements are needed to minimise defects. These programmes also collect customer feedback.

There are five consecutive steps involved in improving processes. **A project team** would be set up to run all five steps from defining the problem to implementing and measuring outcomes.

Step 1	**Define**. The team would identify the customer's requirements, and clarify the problem and set goals.
Step 2	**Measure**. Decide what needs to be measured, where information can be gathered. The team would analyse the current process to see what is causing the problem(s) and concentrate on the main causes to start with.
Step 3	**Analyse**. The team would develop hypotheses, identify the key variables and root causes.
Step 4	**Improve**. The team can now work on generating solutions and implementing them to remove the problem. This is achieved by modifying existing processes or developing new ones. Costs and benefits would be quantified at this step.
Step 5	**Control**. The team would devise new controls for monitoring to ensure continued high-quality performance. The controls should reveal whether the new processes are delivering the desired improvements.

Leadership grades

Staff involved in the **leadership of projects** may possess varying grades of qualification in Six Sigma.

Master Black Belts are in-house consultants in Six Sigma and spend all of their time on it. They are especially skilled in the statistical techniques involved and will contribute to several projects simultaneously.

Black Belts also spend all of their time on Six Sigma and lead specific projects.

Green Belts also lead projects. They are managers who retain other job responsibilities alongside Six Sigma.

(b) **Analysis and improvement to processes at T4UC using Six Sigma methodology.**

Step 1	**Define**. Customers want a twenty-four hour hotline, and right-first-time servicing. Neither is available at present. They also want, engineers who turn up when they are supposed to, with the correct parts (not arriving after the engineer has left). Finally they want consistent and standard service so engineers take the same time to do the same job.
	In **quantifiable terms**, the problems are that the customer satisfaction rating is lower than the industry average and alleged market leader. Remedial visits are higher than industry average or market leader. The number of contracted clients has fallen from 20X7 to 20X8 and the number of recommendations has fallen year on year since the business began. The number of product support issues resolved by telephone has fallen since 20X7 and the number of visits to contracted clients has risen since the business began (this is despite a fall in the number of contracted clients and suggests a number of repeat visits).
Step 2	**Measure**. T4UC needs to measure customer satisfaction, number of visits, problems resolved by telephone, number of clients gained by recommendation and remedial visits. Much of the data is already available from the customer survey undertaken by Ken or from benchmarking data. The data could be supplemented by collecting information on times taken to answer telephones, qualifications and backgrounds of the best engineers for future recruitment, reason why engineers fail to turn up, reasons for repeat visits and efficiency of manufacturers who send parts direct to customers.
Step 3	**Analyse**. T4UC can then start to develop hypotheses on the causes of these problems. Possible reasons for the problems identified so far include:

- **Staff utilisation as the key measure of profitability**. This would be at the expense of quality of service if staff are solely measured on their utilisation.
- **Unavailability of the contact centre at weekends**. This is cited as a problem by customers who wanted weekend service.

- **Reliability of service**. Why are remedial visits necessary? Is this down to engineer training and/or problems with delivery?
- **Consistency of service**. Why is it that there is so much variety in the time taken and the necessity for repeat visits.

Step 4   **Improve**. Once problems have been identified T4UC can look at removing the problems. Ideas include:

- **Measuring profitability using more than just staff utilisation**. T4UC could consider looking at the number of repeat visits per engineer and how long each engineer takes on each visit. They could also consider employing more engineers who might solve some of the problems such as unavailability and remedial visits being necessary. As the data obtained shows, T4UC engineers have more clients per engineer than their competitors. This would probably support further recruitment especially with some of the problems fed back by clients on availability and consistency of service.
- **Ensuring the call centre is fully staffed especially at the weekends when many clients call.**
- **Training all engineers to the same high standard** to ensure a consistent service is provided to all clients. Engineers could specialise so that they become experts in certain machinery or be trained across all machinery.
- **Ensuring parts are available** by managing stock and relationships with suppliers.

Step 5   **Control**. T4UC then needs to measure these areas on an ongoing basis to ensure improvements are sustained.

It is important that T4UC continues to monitor the relevant problems variables during the course of its routine performance measurement. In particular, it should monitor the number of clients, client recommendations, the proportion of remedial visits requirement, the level of weekend accessibility, staff training, stock availability and overall customer satisfaction.

T4UC should aim to exceed industry average scores on **remedial visits** and **customer satisfaction rating** and should try to attain similar results to those achieved by Appliances R us.

43 SSH

Text reference. Financial performance meaures are considered in Chapter 9 of the BPP Study Text. Ethical issues are considered in Chapter 5. Quality issues are discussed in Chapter 13, and the importance of non-financial performance indicators is considered in Chapter 12.

Top tips. Part (a). Set out your table using the headings suggested in the question – results for two years for the two divisions plus the combined results. You will want to think about comparisons year on year and between the divisions. Consider what performance measures might be appropriate for the operations as opposed to the group company. You will need to comment on your calculations as the question asks you to 'assess' which means to 'determine the strengths/weaknesses/importance/significance/ability to contribute'. For fourteen marks aim for around seven relevant calculations and commentary plus three marks for suggesting what else you need to be able to assess the financial performance.

In **part (b)** think why the operations manager is pushing for delivery at all costs. What does this suggest in terms of problems with performance? Are his statements ethical?

In **part (c)** the requirement may throw you – what is meant by quality software? Try to think broadly about what makes software fit for use. Are there any industry standards? Do quality costs come into this?

Whereas part (a) of the requirement looked at financial performance, **part (d)** is looking at non-financial performance–specifically aspects of quality. Having a mixture of non-financial and financial measures is important in real life to enable organisations to have a more balanced view of performance measurement. You don't need to write much here though because there is only half a mark available per measure. However, it is important to note that you are asked for the performance measures themselves, not for aspects of performance or performance criteria which could be measured.

Examining team's comments. Many candidates provided quantitative ratios or commentary but not both. In many cases, answers to Part (a) were brief suggesting candidates did not recognise that 14 marks were available. Parts (b) and (c) answers were generally reasonable.

Part (d) provided some confusion as poorer answers suggested **performance criteria** eg responsiveness, rather than **performance measures** (see the suggested answer for examples).

(a) **Financial performance of SSH and the two operations**

	Bonlandia 20X8	Karendia 20X8	Combined 20X8	Bonlandia 20X7	Karendia 20X7	Combined 20X7
Revenue growth %	4.3	40.0	8.8			
EBITDA (W1)			$2,760,000			2,450,000
Gross margin %	36.6	14.7	33.0	37.1	(12.5)	30.9
Net margin %	17.5	(12.4)	7.8	19.3	(37.5)	6.6
ROCE % (W2)			16.7			15.8
Debt/equity %			43.7			57.7
Asset turnover (W3)	1.3	1.4	1.3	1.27	1.53	1.3

Workings

	20X8 $'000	20X7 $'000
1 EBITDA		
Revenue	17,400	16,000
Costs	11,648	11,050
	5,752	4,950
Marketing	2,992	2,500
EBITDA	2,760	2,450
2 ROCE		
EBITDA	2,760	2,450
Depreciation and amortisation	560	500
PBIT	2,200	1,950
Capital employed	13,150	12,300
ROCE %	16.7	15.8

BPP
LEARNING MEDIA

Note. The ACCA's suggested solutions used PBIT/(total assets) in their calculation of ROCE. Either method is acceptable.

3. Asset turnover

The ACCA's suggested solutions used revenue/non-current assets in their calculation to arrive at a non-current asset turnover ratio. We use revenue/(total assets – current liabilities). Either method is acceptable.

Revenue growth

Both operations and the combined company have grown from 20X7 to 20X8. Karendia has grown by 40% by comparison but it starts from a smaller base.

EBITDA

EBITDA has improved from 20X7 to 20X8 by $310,000. This is due solely to the $1,400,000 improvement in revenue as total costs have increased in the year.

Gross margin

Combined has improved from 30.9% to 33% year on year solely from the improvement in revenue as costs have all risen but less than the growth in revenue. Bonlandia has seen a fall in its gross margin but Karendia has seen its gross margin turn from a negative figure to a positive 14.7% due to $800,000 extra revenue.

Net margin

This has improved for Combined and Karendia but fallen for Bonlandia. Karendia still remains a loss maker but the loss margin has shrunk as the growth in revenues has outstripped the increase in costs in the year. Bonlandia has seen an absolute fall in net profit by $152,000. Karendia continues to make a loss but has reduced this from $750,000 to $348,000. This suggests Karendia should look at controlling its costs even though this is only the second year of operation. Overall profit has improved by $300,000 or 29%. Interest has fallen due to the fall in the tense of long term debt. Increased marketing could be one of the factors that has led to increased turnover.

The increase in costs in Bonlandia ($752,000) above those in Karendia ($398,000) reflects difficult operating conditions or poor cost controls.

ROCE

The percentage has improved from 15.8 to 16.7% as the percentage growth in PBIT has outstripped that of the capital employed in the business. The reason is mainly revenue growth. Total assets have increased by $1,350,000 whilst short-term debt has only gone up by $500,000.

Debt to equity

Share capital and reserves have increased by $1,350,000, which is the profit for the period, but long-term debt has fallen by $500,000, so the gearing ratio will fall.

Asset turnover

This has declined for Karendia as revenue has grown faster than capital employed (total assets less current liabilities). It has remained broadly the same for the other two.

Additional information needed to make a comparison

Intergroup transfers of software between Bonlandia and Karendia need to be split out and eliminated on consolidation or else there will be a double counting of transactions. Figures for payables and receivables would be needed for a detailed look at the cash cycle. The level of inventories would be useful to enable a calculation of liquidity ratios such as the current ratio. It would also be useful to have comparatives going back some years so that trends can be revealed.

(b)   **The statements of the operational manager of Bonlandia**

The operations manager's first statement reveals he is fixated on achieving installation by the deadline irrespective of whether all software problems have been fixed. This is an example of **measure fixation**: he is determined to attain a specific performance indicator whatever it takes. The problem is that a large 40% of his basic salary bonus is based on this one activity. It affects SSH's ultimate performance as fixing software problems after installation may be expensive and clients may not make repeat purchases if they are unhappy with the service and software they received. It may also have a detrimental effect on their business performance.

It also results in a bonus being paid where the intention was to award timely and correct installation of software but because of the way the bonus is framed, it is being awarded for timely installation. This also sends out messages to staff that certain behaviours are more important than others even if they are not beneficial in the long run.

His second statement strays into the unethical: he is effectively stating if customers might complain they have no choice but to keep the software once installed.

This is clearly not good, fair business practice and does not set a good example for his staff in the way they might behave in business.

(c) **Criteria for software to be considered quality software**

Quality software should be **software fit for the purpose it is designed for.** It should comply with the user specification, be tested prior to implementation, and signed over to the client only once all tests have been completed satisfactorily and it is operational.

There may be **industry standards for software, such as ISO9000 quality standards,** which govern the quality of software development and installation.

Quality costs can also be considered as these consider the costs of building in quality in the process of manufacture against testing for faults prior to shipping out or waiting for warranty claims to be invoked.

Shipping on time can also be a quality measure though of course the product shipped needs to be a product fit for the user.

(d) **Six performance measures to assess quality of service** (only six asked for)

On-time delivery of software. This does however have the problem that it may not be error free and is indeed one of the measures easily achieved by the operation!

The **correct installation of software** to the satisfaction of the client including a sign-off of systems testing. This builds in a quality element.

Number of complaints received. This is an external failure cost.

Number of return visits to **fix software problems. The number of complaints is a measure of** external failure.

Competence of staff in providing training to client.

Client feedback on installation and training for using the software.

The responsiveness of staff to client enquiries.

The availability of staff to meet clients' emergency needs.

44 Albacore

Text reference. Controllability and accountability are discussed in Chapters 3, 7 and 14 of the Study Text. Performance management styles are discussed in Chapter 14.

Top tips.

Part (a). The scenario identifies that the budget in Albacore is imposed by the corporate centre and a number of costs are also controlled centrally. However, in terms of assessing a shop manager's performance, is it fair to assess them on factors they cannot control?

The current branch information measures the shop's performance, rather than the manager's performance. How would the branch information for the Tunny branch be different if it only included factors the manager could control? This should suggest the improvements you could make to the report in relation to the second part of the requirement – drafting an improved report.

Importantly, though, note that part (a) is **not** asking you to assess the performance of the branch manager; it is asking you to assess the **suitability of the information** as a means of appraising the shop manager's performance.

Marking scheme

Marks

(a) Calculation and discussion of operation and planning variances – 1 mark per point, up to a maximum of 4

Discussion of other variances – 1 mark per point, up to 2

For highlighting the importance of measuring controllable costs – 1 mark

Revised performance report distinguishing controllable and non-controllable costs – 1 mark

For highlighting the importance of controllable profit as a measure of the manager's performance – 1 mark

Total: up to 8 for suitability of existing report

Alternative report – highlighting controllable costs, controllable profit – Up to 3

Comments on report – including controllability, realistic budgets – 1 mark per point, up to 3

Total: up to 5 for alternative report and justifications for changes

Total: up to 13

13

(b) Analysis of performance management styles – 1 mark per relevant point, up to a maximum of 6

Evaluation of performance appraisal system – 1 mark per relevant point, up to a maximum of 6

Total: up to 12

$\frac{12}{\underline{25}}$

Total = 25

(a) **Accountability** – The managers should only be held responsible for those aspects of performance they can control. However, the branch information does not appear to distinguish between the factors that the shop managers can control and those they can't, which suggests the information is unsuitable for assessing the mangers' performance.

Budgets – If one measure of the manager's performance is comparing actual performance against budget, then it is important that the budgets are realistic and achievable.

The fall of 12% in sales across the industry as a whole suggests that the original shop budget (showing the same figures as the previous year) was unrealistic.

Although the shop shows an overall gross margin variance of $17,340 (adverse) based on the original budget, this can more usefully be split into **planning** and **operational** variances as follows:

		$	
Planning variance			
Original sales	(1)	266,000	
Revenue variance due to economic conditions (12%)	(2)	31,920	(A)
Gross profit variance (Gross margin 60%)		**19,152**	(A)
Operational variance			
Actual sales		237,100	
Revised budgeted sales	(1)-(2)	234,080	
		3,020	(F)
Operational variance (Gross margin 60%)		**1,812**	(F)

The operational variance more accurately reflects the shop manager's work in promoting sales, and here we can see that the manager's efforts have actually reduced the fall in gross profit by $1,812. The overall gross profit variance (of $17,340 adverse) comprises an adverse planning variance of $19,152 partially offset by a favourable operational variance of $1,812.

Discounting – One area where the managers have a degree of autonomy is in setting prices; for example, it is possible they could reduce the sales price of particular titles to boost sales of those titles. This is therefore an aspect of the manager's performance which could be measured, for example, by looking at the sales price and volume for individual product lines, and then looking at the impact of any promotions on gross profit.

The figures for the Tunny branch suggest that the manager has not made use of the discounting authority though. The actual gross margin achieved for the year has remained constant with the budget (60%) but discounting would have led to a reduction in the margin %.

Controllable and non-controllable costs – A number of non-controllable costs are currently included in the manager's performance assessment. In particular, the shop manager will have very little scope to control **property costs**, as the shop heating, lighting and rental contracts will all be managed by the central purchasing department. The shop managers may have some control over the amount of heat and light that are used in their shops, but the manager don't have any control over the unit prices paid for them.

Similarly the managers can't control their own wages. However, it is reasonable to classify the **part-time staff costs as controllable**. The managers manage the staffing for their shops, and so they could save on part-time staff costs by working longer hours themselves.

Consequently, a fairer way of assessing the shop managers' performance would be to distinguish costs into two groups: controllable (marketing; part-time staff) and non-controllable (managers' wages; property costs).

Controllable profit – Following on from this, a controllable profit could then be shown as well as the overall shop profit. The shop manager's performance should then be assessed on the controllable profit performance of their shop only.

If we apply this logic to Tunny Branch, then instead of shop manager facing an adverse variance of $12,840, she would have achieved a positive variance of $6,312, and would therefore have been entitled to a bonus, because she has actually been performing well in difficult economic circumstances.

Improved report

The revised report should split costs into two groups as we have suggested above (controllable, and non-controllable) to show the controllable profit as well as the shop's overall profit. In addition, it would be useful to analyse variances into operational (controllable) and planning (non-controllable) variances, because this enables a greater understanding of the causes of the variances.

Revised performance report
Tunny branch: Year to Sept 20X1

		Budget	Actual	Variance	Planning variance	Operational variance
Sales		266,000	237,100	(28,900)		
Cost of sales		106,400	94,840	11,560		
Gross profit		159,600	142,260	(17,340)	(19,152)	1,812
Controllable costs						
Marketing		12,000	11,500	500		
Staff costs	Part time staff	38,000	34,000	4,000		
Controllable profit		109,600	96,760	(12,840)	(19,152)	6,312
Non-controllable costs:						
Staff costs	Manager	27,000	27,000	–		
Property costs		26,600	26,600	–		
Shop profit		56,000	43,160	(12,840)		

The report now highlights that if the gross profit planning variance ($19,152) is added back to the controllable profit (of -$12,840), the manager would have achieved a positive variance in her controllable profit of $6,312.

(b)   **Budget-constrained style**

The performance management style at Albacore seems to be **budget-constrained style,** in which the predominant focus is a short term one, centred around achieving the budget set.

This style can be seen in the way the shop managers' performance is primarily evaluated on their ability to meet the budgets set, even though the general economic conditions mean that the budgets are no longer realistic or achievable.

Job-related tension – One of the characteristics of the budget-constrained style is that it leads to job-related tensions and poor relations between staff and the managers. This appears to be case at Albacore, where the shop managers have complained about the way they are managed and their remuneration.

Performance manipulation – The budget-constrained style can often motivate staff to manipulate performance reports to try to make it look as if they have achieved their budget targets. However, given the centralised nature of control at Albacore, it seems unlikely that any such performance manipulation would be possible at shop level.

Alternative performance management styles

Profit-conscious style – In contrast to the short-termist nature of a budget-constrained style, under a profit-conscious style, a manager's performance is evaluated in relation to their ability to increase the general **effectiveness of their business unit** in relation to the organisation's **long-term purposes**.

It is possible that such a style could be suitable for Albacore, given the management team's aim of running the business in order to maximise profits. However, the long-term perspective may be at odds with the venture capitalist's likely requirements.

Non-accounting style – Budget information is relatively unimportant in performance evaluation, and other non-financial factors are deemed to be more important.

Performance appraisal system

Reflects budget-constrained style – The performance appraisal system at Albacore reflects the budget constrained management style in the business.

Lack of discussion and negotiation – The shop managers appear to have little or no opportunity to influence their shops' budgets; they are simply presented to the managers at their annual appraisals.

Despite this, the bonus criteria appear to be rigidly enforced. If the Tunny branch manager's experience is representative of the other managers, it appears that the failure to achieve budget has led to no bonus being paid at all.

This is despite the shop still being profitable (making an operating profit of $43,160), and the manager's **controllable profits actually being higher than budget** (see part (a)).

This total lack of discussion and flexibility in the appraisal system, along with the apparent lack of appreciation of the managers' efforts in difficult economic conditions, is likely to **demotivate them**, and this appears to be the case, with the managers (justifiably) calling the current system unfair.

Improvements to the reward system

Focus on controllable aspects of performance – As we have noted in part (a), the reward system should distinguish between the **manager's performance** and the **shop's performance**.

If the managers feel that they are being judged on aspects of performance they can control, this should help to **motivate them**, and hopefully as a result also improve their performance.

However, given that Albacore's aim is to maximise profits, it is still important to monitor the shop's performance overall as well as the manager's profits. One possible solution might be to base part of the manager's bonus on their own performance (controllable profit) while another part of it could be determined by the shop's performance overall.

Stepped bonuses – Although the current bonus is 'up to 30% of basic salary' it is not clear how this is calculated. The current system seems to have an 'all or nothing' approach under which managers get a bonus if their shop achieves budget, and they don't if it doesn't.

One way this system could be improved is by introducing a graded system. For example, the amount of bonus the managers get will be determined by actual profit as a % of budget, with the bonus amount increasing above certain trigger levels. For example, above 90% of budget = 3% bonus; above 95% of budget = 6% bonus; above 100% = 9% etc.

Budgets agreed – Rather than the annual budget being determined centrally and then imposed on the shop managers, the managers should be involved in setting the budgets. The managers could be aware of factors that will affect the performance of their shops that central management are not aware of. Such a process may lead to more realistic budget targets being set for the shop, and in doing so increase the managers' motivation.

Nonetheless, it may still be necessary for the senior management team to adjust the budgets overall, to bring them in line with the Albacore's overall financial objectives or any performance expectations the venture capitalist may have.

Non-financial factors – Finally, the reward system could recognise longer-term and non-financial factors in the manager's performance. For example, they could be rewarded for innovative marketing ideas and staff development (eg part-time staff from their branch who progress to become managers in other branches).

45 Elegant Hotels

Text reference. Reward schemes and reward management are discussed in chapter 14 of the BPP Study Text and the DMAIC methodology is covered in Chapter 13.

Top tips. This should be a relatively straightforward question, and the first part in particular should not present many difficulties. The reward scheme is clearly in conflict with the strategy of the hotel and causing it to fail. There are lots of opportunities for quoting directly from the scenario to reinforce the points you make. As long as you refer back to the scenario and justify your arguments, you should be able to score highly.

Part (b) should also be straightforward if you are familiar with the DMAIC methodology. If you have not learnt the methodology, however, it would be very difficult to score any points here. This is not the first time that this has been examined and is a simple model to learn. If you know the model, you should be able to score highly in this question.

BPP
LEARNING MEDIA

(a)   Up to 1 mark for each relevant point up to a maximum of 15 marks   15

(b)   Up to 1 mark for an appropriate description of each of the 5 stages and up to 1 mark for its
      application to Elegant Hotels   10

      Total = 25

(a)   The main focus of the managers' reward scheme is on room occupancy rates. Therefore, the managers are
      concerned with simply filling rooms rather than looking at other aspects of performance.

      They are using a variety of ways to fill rooms, but these are proving damaging to the hotel:

      Broker sales

      Elegant advertises on online brokerage sites such as lastsecondhotels.com. These sites allow customers to
      compare prices, so in order to attract guests Elegant has to offer low prices. The quote on the website
      stating that it is a 'Value for money hotel' indicates they are doing this. This suggests Elegant will now be
      making a lower profit margin than it historically did as a mid-market hotel.

      Customer comments on the lastsecondhotels.com are also likely to encourage potential guests to wait until
      the last minute to book, to get bargains. If occupancy looks like it will be low, managers will reduce rates as
      illustrated by the quote 'very easy to get rooms at half the advertised rate.' Again, this puts downward
      pressure on the hotels' profit margin.

      In addition to the lowering of prices, Elegant will also have to pay a commission for guests who have come
      to them via the brokerage website. This further reduce the profit margin it earns.

      Group sales

      Another way Elegant has been increasing occupancy rates is through offering packages for school groups.
      However, again the profit margins on these will be lower than those earned when the hotel catered for mid-
      market guests.

      The use of the hotels by school parties along with the fact that a large percentage of its bookings are now
      received through lastsecondhotels.com. has led to a shift in customer perceptions. Elegant are now viewed
      as a budget hotel rather than a mid-market hotel which has historically been its market position. The
      presence of school groups may deter mid-market, higher value customers.

      Manipulation of rates

      Because the bonus is based on a percentage occupancy rate, the managers have an incentive to reduce the
      number of beds available for use, as well as get bookings for the rooms. Some managers are declaring
      rooms unfit for use. If the rooms are not unfit for use, this means the managers are artificially increasing
      their bonus while not generating any revenue by having guests staying in the room.

      Cutting costs

      Because room rates are being offered at a discount, managers need to cut costs even more to make a profit
      on. There is evidence that costs are being cut in a number of areas:

      - **Cheap ingredients**: Customer feedback on the website noted that the restaurant food was poor
        quality, suggesting managers are trying to reduce costs by using cheaper ingredients in the
        restaurant.

      - **Repairs and maintenance**: Customer feedback on the website also noted that 'The bath was cracked
        and the windows were dirty.' So it appears that managers are saving money but not arranging repairs
        when they are needed and by reducing how often the hotels are cleaned.

- **Low capital investment**: Guests have commented that there were no internet connections in the rooms or public areas. This suggests that managers have preferred to save money rather than investing in their hotels. This illustrates a short term focus because it will deter guests in the future.

- **No investment in staff**: Guests have also commented that the staff were not very helpful and were uncommunicative. Again, this suggests that either costs have been cut either by hiring cheap, less competent staff, or by not giving staff proper training when they join the hotel. Either way, measures that have been designed to save costs are leading to a decline in the service being offered to customers.

- **High prices on ancillary services**: The scheme is also leading to inconsistencies in the hotel's strategic approach. Whilst managers are trying to cut costs in a number of areas, they are trying to boost profit by charging high prices on food. This has led to a reduction in demand as guests on cheap, last minute deals are less likely to want to dine in the restaurant, than the guest Elegant traditionally catered for. This is evidenced by the quote "Cheap, but don't eat there. The price for breakfast was extortionate."

The conflict between the high prices charged for meals and the poor quality food offered is indicative of a confused strategy.

Ultimately, measures to cut cost have led to a decline in levels of customer service and perception of the hotel. However, this is unlikely to change as there is no incentive in the bonus scheme to improve customer service.

The management reward scheme has entirely the wrong focus and has led to a severe decline in the reputation and performance of the hotels. Rather than rewarding occupancy rates, the scheme should focus on customer service, quality and providing a good experience for its customers.

(b)
> **Top tips.** The 'define' in the DMAIC methodology relates to defining **customer requirements** not defining performance measures as some candidates suggested.

The main problem with Elegant hotels is that is has lost focus of what its customers want, and even of who its customers are. The reward scheme is in conflict with the strategy a successful hotel chain should have and its reputation and profit have suffered as a result.

Implementation of the DMAIC methodology would help Elegant focus on the needs of its customers and could assist them meet those needs as follows:

Define customer requirements

Elegant should first define who their customers are, and then what they want (ie internet access, peace and quiet, helpful staff, good food etc). Elegant currently pay little attention to what their customers want, despite the feedback on the website, and would benefit greatly from doing so.

Measure existing performance

Elegant do not currently measure customer satisfaction and instead measure performance based on occupancy rates. They have to define new ways of measuring performance based specifically on the customer requirements defined above, perhaps using feedback questionnaires and re-book rates. They then need to use this to find out how well they are currently performing.

Analyse the existing performance

The analysis should involve identifying the gap between current and target levels of performance. Root causes of problems should be identified along with opportunities for improvement.

Improve the process

Design solutions for correcting existing problems and preventing others, with the aim of meeting and exceeding target performance. The improvements should be clearly defined, explained and managed. Improvements Elegant could make might include refurbishing guest rooms, installing internet connections and providing staff with customer service training.

Control the new process

Measures have to be put in place to keep the new processes on track and prevent people slipping into old habits. This could be done using new systems and structures that support the process as well as providing training to staff. Elegant will obviously also amend its reward scheme to better reflect the targets of the hotel chain for example rewards could be based on customer satisfaction scores.

46 Equiguard

Study reference. Reward management and reward schemes are covered in Chapter 14 of the BPP Study Text.

Top tips. The scenario provides a lot of useful information for part (a) – particularly in Table 1 which emphasises the way Equiguard's current reward management scheme focuses only base pay rather than performance pay or indirect pay.

The quotes from the survey of engineers leaving the company also reinforce this point. Equiguard's current reward system is not motivating its engineers to high levels of performance. Safequipe and Guarantor's reward systems offer their engineers a better balance between base pay, performance pay and indirect pay that Equiguard's system does, and this balance is reflected in Safequipe and Guarantor having lower staff turnover rates.

The requirement for part (b) even gives you a clue as to one of the deficiencies of the current scheme. The fact that the HR Director wants to introduce a bonus scheme highlights the fact the current system has no such performance based scheme!

The answer below uses a freeform approach based on the points highlighted by the scenario. However you could alternatively have used the ideas about reward objectives and reward options from Bratton's reward management model as a framework for your answer, and against which to assess Equiguard's scheme:

Reward objectives – recruitment and retention; motivation; compliance.

Reward options – base pay; performance pay; indirect pay.

Note that in part (b) you need to comment on the limitations of two different measures: (i) the proposals for the team based bonus, and (ii) the proposals for an individual bonus.

Technical article. Also, note there is an article in the Technical Articles for P5 on ACCA's website about reward schemes and their effect on an organisation's performance and employees' behaviour (*'Reward schemes for employees and management'*). You are strongly advised to read this article as part of your preparation for your exam.

(a) **Impact of the reward management scheme on staff turnover**

The engineers at Equiguard are very important workers to the company. Their motivation, their commitment and their proficiency in undertaking repair work are all critical success factors for Equiguard, because they will influence how customers perceive the company, and therefore whether they will renew their warranties rather than moving to a competitor.

Equiguard's high labour turnover suggests its engineers are not as motivated and committed to the company as they could be, and this is a significant problem.

High labour turnover is also a problem because of the costs incurred in training newly recruited engineers – about $6,000 each – in additional to the costs of advertising jobs and arranging interviews.

Consequently, the extent to which the current reward management scheme contributes to this high labour turnover among Equiguard's engineers suggests there are a number of problems with the scheme.

Too much focus on base pay – Equiguard's rewards scheme focuses on base pay, with little attention being given to performance pay or indirect pay. The focus on basic pay is unlikely to encourage motivation among skilled staff, like the engineers. Although Equiguard's basic pay is higher than its competitors, it has a higher staff turnover rate than its competitors. This suggests that base pay alone is not an effective reward.

Lack of performance related pay – Safequipe and Guarantor both offer their engineers performance related pay. This is likely to act as a motivating factor for their engineers; knowing that they can gain extra pay by virtue of doing their jobs well. By contrast, Equiguard's engineers have no such incentive. An exit interview with one of the engineers reinforces this point, 'The real problem is that the pay structure does not differentiate between good, average and poor performers. This is really de-motivating.'

The HR director has recognised this weakness in the current reward management scheme, which is why he has suggested two new performance related pay measures.

Current scheme does not promote organisational goals – The lack of performance related pay means there is little incentive for the engineers to do a good job. Given the key role the engineers play in the success of the company, this is a major business risk. If customers do not feel they are getting a good service from Equiguard, they are unlikely to renew their warranties. Again, one of the exit interviews stresses the problem here. 'There is no point in doing a good job, because you get paid no more than [for] doing an ordinary one. Average work is tolerated here'.

Absence of profit share scheme – Overall organisational performance can be supported through profit sharing schemes, provided individual's goals are properly aligned to corporate objectives.

If employees benefit from the profitability of their company, then they have an incentive to try to maximise that profitability. Both Safequipe and Guarantor offer a profit sharing scheme for their engineers, but Equiguard does not. This is likely to reinforce the attitude among Equiguard staff that there is no point trying to do a good job, because they will get no benefit from doing so.

Levels of indirect pay – Indirect pay (or benefits) such as pension plans or private health care can form a valuable part of an organisation's total rewards package.

Two measures which could indicate Equiguard's approach to indirect pay are the number of days holiday staff are offered per year, and the average amount of training they are given. In both of these measures, Equiguard performs worse than its competitors.

Low average training spend – The relatively low amount which Equiguard spends on training is a particular concern. It suggests that Equiguard views training as a cost rather than as an investment in human capital.

One of the exit interviews highlights the impression this view is giving to the staff. 'This is the first place I have worked where learning new skills is not encouraged.' Equiguard seems to view training as a risk, thinking that once staff gain new skills they will inevitably leave. Ironically, however, the lack of opportunities for training and development seems to be one of the reasons which is prompting staff to leave.

(b) **General problems**

Ability of employees to influence performance measures – The key logic behind performance related pay is that the incentive of an increased income will motivate employees to improve their performance. However, if the employees cannot influence the performance targets they are being measured against then performance relate pay will not be a motivating factor for them. Unfortunately, it seems that the performance targets the HR director is proposing are largely outside the scope of the employee's influence.

Goal congruence – Performance measures should be designed so that individual's goals are aligned with organisational goals. If a scheme encourages employees to work in a way that maximises their individual income, but in doing so reduces the performance or profitability of their organisation as a whole, this will be a problem for the organisation. The HR director's focus on speed may create problems in this respect.

Limitations of proposed team-based bonus scheme

Response time measures outside employees' control – The HR director has proposed that the bonus should be based on the **time taken between the customer request for a repair being logged and the date of the engineer attending** to fix the problem. This correctly reflects the fact that customers value quick response times, but it overlooks that the measure is influenced by factors outside the control of the team.

The date an engineer can attend to fix the problem **depends on the availability of an engineer**. This could be influenced by the **number of engineers Equiguard chooses to employ**, rather than necessarily the efficiency of the engineers.

Customers can dictate visit dates – Also, Equiguard's policy is to schedule visits 'at the earliest possible time **convenient to the customer**.' However, if domestic customers are out at work and cannot immediately take time off to be at home for a service visit, this 'convenient time' may be quite a long way in the future. However, the team cannot control this timescale, making it an unsuitable basis for a performance measure.

Limitations of proposed individual bonus scheme

The individual bonus will be based on the average time taken for an engineer to fix a fault once they have arrived at the customer's premises. The HR director's logic for this is that company values quick response time because it increases business efficiency.

To an extent, the engineer can control the time taken to fix a fault, but there are still some significant problems with this measure.

Repair time depends on the complexity of the problem – An engineer called out to fix a complex problem will inevitability taken longer than an engineer who has to fix a simple problem. This measure would therefore penalise engineers working on complicated problems, which ironically could be the most important jobs for Equiguard to do well.

Trade off between speed and quality – The performance measure might encourage engineers to perform a **quick fix** (to get the job signed off) rather than to sort the underlying problem properly.

Consequently, the **measure could actually increase the volume of repairs** Equiguard has to undertake, whereas the business model is based on the need to minimise calls and repairs.

In respect, the HR Director's proposal would create a **problem with goal congruence**. By performing low-quality, quick fixes, individual engineers can boost their own incomes, but in doing so they will damage the profitability of the company as a whole.

Inaccurate job reporting – The measure could also encourage engineers to misrepresent the time they actually spent on a job. The bonuses are based on the time taken to **fix a fault once the engineer has arrived at the customer's premises**, so if an engineer claims it took longer to get to a client than it did the engineer can **artificially reduce the time reported against the job**. Again, the measure is promoting behaviour which is unhelpful for the company as a whole. For example, if customers' warranty fees are calculated according to the time taken to fix faults, if this time is understated then Equiguard could be charging a warranty which is too low, and therefore will be restricting its profits.

Focus only on time – As well as these specific issues around goal congruence, the HR Director's proposals suffer through focussing exclusively on time. Whilst speed is important to the customer (and so is an important performance measure), the proposals would benefit by including other measures which address quality, skills, or training. The lack of focus on quality and training are key issues behind the current high staff turnover, yet these proposals do not do anything to address this.

47 ENT Entertainments

Text reference. The BCG matrix is discussed in Chapter 1 of the Study Text. Management styles are discussed in Chapter 14.

Top tips. In effect, part (a) contains two requirements, although it is only worth 7 marks. First (i) you need to perform a BCG analysis of ENT's business, and then (ii) you need to use your BCG matrix to evaluate the company's performance. How is the balance of ENT's portfolio affecting its performance?

Note that the 'growth' axis on the matrix refers to the growth of the market sector and not the growth of the division itself (see Examining team's comment below).

Whereas the focus in Part (a) was is on ENT's performance, the focus in Part (b) is on the BCG analysis itself. An important part of the P5 paper is highlighting the advantages or disadvantages of different models which could be used in performance management. In this requirement you needed to highlight how the BCG could be useful for helping ENT to manage its performance, but also the weaknesses of the BCG matrix in this context.

Part (c) (i): You should have drawn on your analysis from part (a) to help you with part (c) (i). The BCG analysis has highlighted that some divisions offer growth or growth prospects for ENT, while the focus in other divisions should be on controlling costs. These different aims require a different style of management; but the bonus scheme (for all the divisions) is linked to performance against the cost budget, so there appears to be a lack of alignment here.

Part (c) (ii) picks up on the idea that some divisions are focusing on growth and some on cost control, because this is likely to mean that different management styles are required in the different divisions.

Examining team's comment. Many candidates did not appear to know that the growth element of the BCG analysis referred to the growth of the market sector and either ignored this element or calculated the growth of the division instead.

(a)

Division	Market growth (%)			
	20X1	*20X2*	*20X3*	*Average of annual growth rates (20X0-X3)*
Restaurants	1.0	1.0	–	0.67
Cafes	9.0	11.0	9.0	9.66
Bars	(2.0)	(3.0)	(3.0)	(2.67)
Dance Clubs	6.0	5.9	9.0	7.01

Market share (%)			
	ENT market share	*Market leader*	*Relative market share*
Restaurants	0.50	3.00	0.17
Cafes	1.01	3.00	0.34
Bars	3.50	3.00	1.17
Dance Clubs	10.99	15.00	0.73

BCG analysis and evaluation of performance

Restaurants division – This division has a low market share of a market sector with low growth, making it a **dog** in the BCG classification. The restaurant division therefore looks a likely candidate for **divestment**, unless it has any links with any of the other divisions in ENT's business.

Cafes division – The cafes division also has a relatively low market share, but it is operating in a market sector with high growth. It should therefore be classified as a **question mark**.

The market sector is already showing good growth, but it currently seems quite fragmented. There could be additional opportunities for ENT to grow by acquiring some rival businesses. Alternatively, if ENT does not want to invest in this way, it might consider selling its café division to another business looking to consolidate in the sector.

Bars division – The bars division is the market leader (high market share) in a market which has low (actually, negative) growth. This should be classified as a **cash cow**.

The Bars division is currently ENT's largest division, and it contributed about 55% of the group's total revenue in 20X0. The current decline in the bars market should therefore be a concern for ENT, given the Bars division's role as a 'cash cow' in the group. ENT is likely to want to use the Bars division to generate cash for the other businesses in its portfolio, but if the Bars market starts declining in time this may limit the division's ability to generate cash for the rest of the group.

Importance of controlling costs – The fact that the bars sector seems to be in the mature stage of its lifecycle also highlights the importance of controlling costs. The degree of profit growth ENT will be able to generate through increasing revenues seems limited, so instead it could look at reducing costs as a means of increasing profitability.

Dance clubs – The dance clubs division has a moderately high market share (although still less than 1) in a market with reasonably high growth. This should currently be classified as a **question mark** as ENT is not yet the market leader in the sector, but it has the potential to become a star if it can achieve market leadership.

Its market share is already relatively close to the market leader's share, so with continued investment the division could grow to become the leader. The performance of this division is likely to be crucial to ENT's longer term success, particularly if the performance of some ENT's more mature businesses continues to decline.

(b) **Context for performance** – The BCG provides a useful context in which to assess the performance of the different divisions. For example, it illustrates to management that they shouldn't expect the bars division to grow at the same rate as the clubs division, due to the underlying differences in the growth rates of the two sectors.

Management approach – Equally, identifying the differences in the growth potential of the different divisions identifies that different styles of management will be appropriate for the different divisions. For example, the clubs division may require capital investments to enable it to sustain its rate of growth, but the focus in the bars division (in a more mature business sector) should be on cost control.

Help set performance metrics – By helping to set expectations and approach in this way, managers can then also tailor their performance management systems and metrics to reflect the different contexts of each of the divisions. So, the metrics for the high growth divisions (cafes, and clubs) should be based on profit or return on investment, while the metrics for the low growth divisions (bars, and restaurants) should be focused on maintaining margins, cash control and cash generation.

Limitations of BCG approach

Problems of definition – Although we have identified that the BCG matrix can be useful for providing a context for performance management, its usefulness is limited by its simplicity. For example, a business unit is only considered to have a high market share if its relative market share is greater than 1. By definition, however, this means that only the market leader can have a high market share, and therefore also there can only be one star or cash cow in each market sector.

Overlooks possible synergies – Another issue which arises from the simplicity of the model is that it treats business units in isolation, and in doing so can overlook possible synergies between them. For example, some of ENT's bars and restaurants may be linked to its clubs, such that customers may go for a drink or a meal and then go on to a club afterwards. However, if in time the restaurants and later some of the bars are divested then this link between the business units will be lost.

Defining the market sector – Another potential issue with using the BCG matrix comes from defining market sectors themselves. For example, the bars division has launched a new wine bar format which appears to have been successful. This suggests it has been growing, although the rest of the bar division has actually had negative growth. However, this raises an issue of whether the wine bar format should be treated as a separate sub-section (and as a problem child which is given the support and investment needed to grow) or whether it should be subject to cost control in the same way that the rest of the bars division is.

Portfolio analysis not performance management – It is also important to remember that the BCG matrix was designed for analysing a product portfolio, not as a performance management system. Therefore, while it can act help determine the appropriate performance management approach for a business, it is not in itself a performance management system.

(c) (i) **Focus on cost budgets** – The bonus element (50%) of the remuneration package is based on divisional performance against cost budget. As a result, divisional managers are likely to focus on controlling costs. Such an approach may be appropriate in the bars and restaurants divisions, but is unlikely to be suitable for the faster-growing divisions (cafes and clubs).

In the cafes and clubs divisions, ENT should be looking to encourage growth, but the current remuneration package is unlikely to do this. As a result, there is likely to be a lack of **goal congruence**, between the divisional managers and the ENT overall.

Short term performance – In a similar way, the focus on controlling costs may also lead to divisional managers taking a short term view of performance. Again, it may actually be more beneficial for some of the divisions to spend now (for example, on marketing) in order to increase revenues and profits in the future.

Use of EVA – There also appears to be an inconsistency between this focus cost budgets and the use of EVA as the measure of divisional performance. The underlying logic behind EVA will be to try to **maximize the wealth of ENT's shareholder** – which is the company's objective – but this is not necessarily the same as controlling costs.

Importantly, EVA specifically identifies that some costs which are treated as expenses in the financial statements (for example, advertising costs) should actually be considered as investments for the future.

Therefore, rather than basing the bonus element of the managers' reward package on achieving cost budgets, ENT may be better advised to base the bonus element on achieving target EVA figures. In this way, the reward system at divisional level will reflect the **company's overall objective**.

(ii)　**Context** – The fact that some of ENT's divisions should be focusing on growth (cafes, clubs) while others (bars, restaurants) need to focus on cost control suggests that different management styles may be appropriate for the different divisions.

Budget-constrained style – Under a budget-constrained style, a manager's performance is primarily assessed by his ability to meet the budget on a short-term basis, particularly in relation to ensuring that actual costs do not exceed budgeted costs. 50% of the bonus elements at ENT are based on achieving the cost budget numbers set by the board, which suggests that ENT may be using a budget-constrained style.

A budget-constrained style can be appropriate in a business where it is important to keep costs under control, which suggests that it may be appropriate to use this style in the bars or restaurants divisions. However, it is less likely to be appropriate for the cafes or clubs divisions.

Moreover, the budget-constrained style often leads to poor relationships between managers and subordinates, and also encourages the manipulation and misreporting of information, so ENT needs to be aware of these potential problems.

Profit-conscious style – Under a profit-conscious style, a manager's performance is evaluated more in terms of long-term performance, and the ability to generate future growth, rather than short-term performance and cost control.

This style is likely to be appropriate for the cafes or clubs divisions at ENT. However, the current bonus structure suggests that this style is not being used, which could suggest that not only do ENT's remuneration packages need revising but also that the management styles need reviewing too.

48 Beach foods

Text reference. Financial performance measures – including Economic Value Added (EVA), ROI and RI are discussed in Chapters 9 and 10 of the BPP Study Text. Control and management styles are discussed in Chapter 14.

Top tips.

Part (a). Note the requirement here is to 'Assess the use of...' so you should focus on the potential advantages and disadvantages of using EVA as a performance measure, rather than, for example, describing how EVA would be calculated, or detailing the different adjustments which might be required to calculate it. In this respect, it is important to note (from the second paragraph of the scenario) that Beach already uses EVA, so we can assume that Beach's management accountants already know how to calculate it.

Part (b). The need to evaluate management's performance as well as the division's performance should have prompted you to think about issues of controllability. For example, if Baby's managers cannot control the R&D costs which are recharged to the department, is it fair to include them in an assessment of the manager's performance.

The reference to 'the assumptions made' also relates to the profit figure being used to assess performance – again, recognising the difference between divisional and managerial performance. Crucially though, your 'assumptions' should relate to the level of profit to include, not the cost of capital figure to use. The cost of capital figures used must be that for the division (11%), not the one for Beach as a whole (7.5%).

Part (c). Note the requirement here is that you recommend suitable styles, rather than discussing or evaluating different styles. Also, note that you need to recommend a suitable way to control each division (cost/profit/investment centre) as well as recommending a suitable management style (budget-constrained, profit-conscious and non-accounting). In both case, the options to choose from were identified in the scenario – control styles in the third paragraph, and management styles in the fourth.

Importantly, the requirement asks for recommendations for **each** division, so you need to cover all three divisions – Baby, Chocolate and R&D – not just the two operating divisions (Baby, and Chocolate).

Examining team's comments on part (c): This part was poorly answered as many candidates clearly did not know the criteria for the choice of responsibility centre, even though the centre headings to choose from were given in the scenario. Such a lack of knowledge continues to surprise the examining team.

Lengthy descriptions of the three management styles were not helpful here either, as candidates were expected, instead, to demonstrate their understanding of the styles by applying it to the scenario.

Marking scheme

		Marks

(a) For relevant points assessing the use of EVA as a divisional performance measure – 1 mark per point

Total for part (a): up to 8   8

(b) Calculations:

For applying the correct method to calculate RI – 1 mark
For applying the correct method to calculate ROI – 1 mark

For correct calculation of both RI and ROI based on different profit figures (controllable profit, profit after R&D, divisional profit) – 1 mark per profit figure used; up to a maximum of 4 marks

Comments: 1 mark per relevant comment up to a maximum of 4 marks

Total for part (b): up to 7   7

(c) Up to 4 marks for valid recommendations for any one division

All recommendations must be justified within the answer to gain credit
High marks within the answer for any divisions can only be scored by discussing both the type of centre and the management style which would be appropriate

Total for part (c): up to 10   <u>10</u>

Total = <u>25</u>

(a) **EVA as a divisional performance measure**

Advantages

Maximising wealth – Beach's overall objective is to maximise the family's wealth through their shareholding – in effect, to maximise shareholder wealth.

One of the main benefits of EVA as a performance measure (rather than profit-based measures such as ROI) is that it is a value-based approach, and therefore it will be aligned to the overall objective of maximising shareholder wealth.

Goal congruence – Moreover, using EVA as a divisional measure will help to ensure that decisions taken at divisional level support the best interests of Beach as a whole, rather than just the individual division.

The **other advantages of EVA** are:

- It gives an absolute measure of performance, and so shows the overall contribution the divisions make to the company

- The basic test of performance is simple. If a division has a positive EVA, then it is generating a return above that required by the providers of finance. (ROI requires a target level to be set, usually based on benchmarking to the industry sector).

- The adjustments required when calculating NOPAT mean that it is closer to cash flows than traditional accounting profits are, and also mean that EVA is less subject to choices in accounting policies.

- EVA encourages investment in the future (for example, in advertising and development) by adding back these costs to profit in the performance period and treating them like capital expenditure. This will reduce the temptation for dysfunctional, short-termist decision-making, which could otherwise be a problem where the capital employed figure from the financial statements is used in ROI and RI. This is likely to be particularly appropriate at Beach where R&D is significant.

Disadvantages

However, EVA does also have some disadvantages. Some of these are also disadvantages of ROI and RI, and some are specific to EVA.

All three measures are dependent on historical data and so have limited use in forecasting future performance.

The directors' complaint that EVA is complicated to understand appears reasonable, because of the number of adjustments which need to be made to the information from Beach's financial statements. By contrast, ROI and RI are derived from headline information in the financial statements which would be more familiar to the board. A related issue here would be the time and cost involved for Beach's management accountant in calculating the division's EVA.

EVA (like RI) uses a charge for the capital employed in the division. EVA uses the weighted-average cost of capital (WACC) for the company as a whole, which may not reflect the risks of the manufacturing divisions. Also, as an unlisted business, WACC may be difficult to estimate. By contrast, RI uses a notional cost of capital based on the risk of the divisions – although this will also be subject to an element of judgement and estimate.

Unlike ROI (which gives a percentage measure, rather than an absolute measure) EVA will not help to assess relative divisional managerial performance at Beach if the divisions are of different sizes.

(b) **ROI and RI**

A key consideration when calculating either ROI or RI for Baby is what profit figure to use for the calculations.

The data in Appendix 1 suggests three potential profit figures, which could be used for assessing the performance of Baby as a division, and its manager:

Controllable profit – The only costs included in controllable profit are those under the direct control of the division manager (ie the divisional operating costs of $121m).

R&D costs recharged – Although the divisional manager cannot influence the costs of the R&D division, Baby's divisional revenue includes the profit which results from new products and ideas generated by the R&D division. Therefore, in order to match costs with revenues more fairly, a proportion of the R&D division's costs should be included in Baby's profit figure.

Divisional profit – The division's performance (as distinct from the manager's performance) should take account of all relevant costs, including Baby's share of the head office management fees. As such the divisional profit ($60m) would be appropriate figure to use in this respect.

Performance analysis

Regardless of which profit figure is chosen, Baby seems to be performing relatively well though. Baby's EVA is positive ($35m) and its RI is also positive.

In terms of ROI, the return based on divisional profit (14.2%) is lower than that ROI for similar entities (20%), but the return based on controllable profit, or profit after R&D is higher than the benchmark figure. However, we do not know which profit figures were used in the benchmark figure, which means we cannot tell whether Baby's ROI figure is above or below the average achieved by similar entities.

	Controllable profit	Profit after R&D	Divisional profit
ROI			
Profit ($m)	99	88	60
Capital employed ($m)	424	424	424
ROI	**23.3%**	**20.8%**	**14.2%**
RI			
Profit	99	88	60
Cost of capital			
(424 x 11%)	46.6	46.6	46.6
RI	**52.4**	**41.4**	**13.4**

(c) **Management styles for the divisions**

Baby division

Responsibility centre – Baby's position as the star in Beach's portfolio, coupled with the fact it is developing and introducing new products, means that the division's focus should be on growth rather than cost control.

As such, it might seem appropriate for Baby to be treated as an investment centre, giving its managers autonomy to develop their business as they see fit.

However, it is not clear whether the divisional managers have the authority to make capital investment decisions or whether these are taken by head office. (Chocolate had to get approval from head office to upgrade its production line.)

If the authority for investment decisions remains with head office, then Baby should be treated as a **profit centre**, and managed according to its ability to generate profit.

Management style – A profit-conscious style focuses on longer-term performance and objectives (such as growth) whereas a budget-constrained style focuses on short-term performance and cost control.

Therefore, given the nature of Baby's market – and the market's rapid growth - the profit-conscious style would seem more appropriate for Baby.

However, elements of a non-accounting style (such as new product development) may also be appropriate.

Given the costs associated with new products and rapid growth (such as the publicity campaign Baby ran to support its new product launch), we recommend that a **non-accounting style** is applied initially.

However, once the market sector begins to mature, then given Baby's strong market share its focus should shift to optimising its profits – at which point, a profit-conscious management style should be adopted.

Chocolate division

Responsibility centre – As the Chocolate division is the cash cow in the portfolio, Beach needs it to generate the profits and cash necessary to support Baby's growth.

However, as a cash cow, and operating in a market with limited growth opportunities, Chocolate is unlikely to receive much investment. As such, it would seem appropriate to treat Chocolate as a profit centre.

Nonetheless, it appears that Chocolate does still makes some capital expenditure (for example, the upgrade to its main production line). As such it could be appropriate to treat Chocolate as an **investment centre**, so that its managers have the autonomy to take these decisions, rather than having to wait for head office to approve them.

Management style – Because it is operating in a mature market with limited growth opportunities, cost control is likely to be crucial in maintaining Chocolate's profitability. As such, a **budget-constrained style** will be the most appropriate management style for Chocolate.

R&D division

Responsibility centre – The R&D division does not generate any revenue in its own right, and therefore should be treated as a cost centre.

Nonetheless, it is important that the contribution the division makes to the group (through the overall profit generated by the products it develops) is not overlooked. The complaints which Baby's managers make about the recharge suggests they are only thinking about the costs rather than the revenue which the new products have generated for them.

As such, whilst Beach should continue to treat the R&D division as a cost centre for control purposes, it would also be useful to **monitor the profit generated by each new product** over its lifecycle, to demonstrate the division's value to the group as a whole.

Management style – As the R&D division is a cost centre, it might seem appropriate to apply a budget-constrained management style.

However, it is important that potentially profitable developments are not rejected simply to keep the division's costs within a fixed budget – and there is a danger this could be the case under a budget-constrained management style.

Therefore, elements of a non-accounting style might also be appropriate – with a focus on the number of new product ideas being generated, and the market reaction to new products being developed.

As such, it may be necessary to adopt a management style which combines some elements of the **budget-constrained style** with others from the **non-accounting style**.

49 Pharmaceutical Technologies

Text reference. The balanced scorecard is discussed in Chapter 13 of the BPP Study Text.

Top tips.

For part (a), you should be asking 'how well with the proposed measures help PT deliver its objectives and, in turn, its corporate strategy?' The scenario provided you with considerable detail about objectives and measures, and you should have used it to help answer this requirement.

Part (b). Note there are two distinct parts to this requirement. The first is a pure test of knowledge: describing a method for analysing stakeholder. Mendelow's matrix seems the obvious choice here.

However, don't spend too long on this part of the requirement (**briefly** describe...), because the second part of the requirement is more substantial: analyse the influence of four different external stakeholders on the regulator. Note that the question refers to stakeholders who could influence the regulator (not PT). Although some of the stakeholder groups identified by the working group (eg doctors, patients) could also be stakeholders of the regulator, it is important that you analyse their influence in relation to the regulator.

However, as there are only 8 marks available for part (b) in total you should only give a relatively brief analysis of each stakeholder's influence on the regulator – highlighting what power they have, and how interested they will be to exert that power.

In part (c), you need to establish how BDR differs from PT, because this will affect how the scorecard is applied in both organizations. In effect, the requirement is asking how the application of the scorecard would vary in a private sector organisation (PT) compared to a public sector one. To score well here, you need to make a comparison between the two, rather than simply talking about the application of the scorecard at one or other of them.

Marks

(a) 1 mark per relevant point – up to a maximum of 10
Relevant points include:
Evaluation of whether each of the measures suggested cover the perspective intended
Consideration of whether there are other suitable measures
Discussion of linkages between the measures and the company objectives
Discussion of the difficulty of collection appropriate data, and ranking the measures.
Total: up to 10

10

(b) Description of suitable method of stakeholder analysis - 1 mark per point – up to a maximum of 2
Analysis of the power and interest of each stakeholder – 1 mark for power, and 1 mark for influence of each stakeholder – Up to a maximum of 8.
Total: up to 8

8

(c) 1 mark per relevant difference between the application of the scorecard at BDR and PT.
Differences must be clearly linked to the scenario to score the marks available.

Total: up to 7

7

Total = 25

(a) **Financial measures**

Existing indicators – The two financial performance measures proposed for the scorecard (share price and earnings per share) are the same two which are PT's current measures of performance of performance. So in this respect, introducing the scorecard will not change the way strategic performance is measured. However, as well as simply measuring earnings per share PT could also consider measuring growth in EPS.

Link to shareholder value – Share price and earnings per share are both appropriate measures to use, given the overall objective of enhancing shareholder wealth. However, measures such as economic value added (EVA) or shareholder value added may actually be better long-term measures for enhancing shareholder wealth.

Liquidity – Although it is important to look at earnings and profits, PT should not overlook the importance of cash flow and liquidity, which will be essential to its survival. Therefore it could also include a measure relating to its cash flows in its scorecard.

Customer perspective

Type of customer – PT has two different types of customer: users (health care providers and patients) and the people who fund the drug use (insurance companies or government). The measure currently proposed seems to focus mainly on the end users. However, their concerns may not always be same as those who are paying for a course of treatment. For example, the health care providers and patients are likely to focus primarily on how effective the product is as a cure. However, the funding bodies will also be interested in the cost of the treatment.

Recognise cost – Therefore, PT should consider a measure looking at the cost of its drugs; for example, comparing the cost of its drugs against similar alternative drugs offered by rival manufacturers.

Internal business processes

Efficiency of drug development – One of the objectives from the medium term strategy is to improve the efficiency of drug development. Performance measures designed to improve the standard of design and testing, and to reduce the time to gain regulatory approval should help achieve this objective.

These measures also help support the financial objectives. If PT can reduce the time it takes to get new drugs approved by the regulator, it will also be able to be start selling those drugs more quickly, thereby increasing sales and earnings.

Learning and growth

Innovation – The third of the objectives from the medium term strategy highlights the importance of innovation in the drug approval process. The measures in the learning and growth perspective of the scorecard should therefore directly PT achieve this objective.

Ranking of measures – We are not told anything about the relative importance or ranking of any of the measures in the scorecard, but it is debatable whether the number of training days attended is the main measure of learning and growth. Reducing the time to market of new products, and increasing the percentage of drugs that gain final approval are likely to be more directly strategically important.

Measurement issues

Although the measures suggested seem largely appropriate in relation to PT's objectives, the management will also need to consider how practical it will to collect data for some of the non-financial measures. For example, an assessment of whether PT has exceeded industry-standard on design and testing is likely to be subjective, unless there are industry-wide quality audits which formally assess companies against a common set of criteria.

Conversely, measures should not be chosen because they are easy to measure. The number of training days undertaken by staff will be easy to measure by staff. However, there may be a danger that staff will simply end up going on training days simply to achieve a target number of days. Training will only be valuable to PT and its staff if it is relevant and appropriate for the people attending.

(b) **Stakeholder influence**

Power and interest – A stakeholder's influence over an organisation can be analysed in relation to the stakeholder's power and interest, using Mendelow's matrix.

Power identifies the extent to which a stakeholder (or group of stakeholders) has the power to influence a decision or situation.

The level of interest reflects the likelihood that a stakeholder will exercise their power in relation to any given decision or situation.

Four key stakeholders of BDR are: the drug companies being test, the government, healthcare providers, and patients.

Drug companies

Interest – The drug companies are likely to have a **high interest** in BDR, because it makes the final judgement about whether a product can be sold in the country. Without approval from BDR, the drug companies will not have any products to sell.

Power – However, the drug companies will have **little power** to influence BDR. BDR's responsibility is to the public and to public health, rather than to the drug companies. Therefore, BDR needs to be (and be seen to be) independent from the drug companies.

Government

Power – The government has **high power** because it appoints the board of trustees and also directly funds BDR.

Interest – The government will have a keen interest in public health overall, but their direct interest in BDR is likely to be **relatively low**. The government has appointed the trustees to manage BDR on its behalf, so unless there is a specific financial or medical scandal which requires it to do so, the government is unlikely to intervene in any decision-making at BDR.

Doctors and healthcare providers

Interest – The healthcare providers will have a **high level of interest** in the approval process, because they will want to be confident that any new drugs approved are safe for use. However, they will also have an interest in BDR's role in encouraging the development of beneficial new drugs. These new drugs could help them treat patients and diseases that they would not otherwise be able to treat as effectively.

Power – Nonetheless, the healthcare providers are only likely to have low power of the approval process because BDR is an independent regulator. However, one way doctors and healthcare providers may be able to exert some power is through lobbying the government.

Patients

Interest – In the same way that healthcare providers will **high level of interest in** the process that may lead to the approval of new drugs, so will patients. They will want to be reassured that any drugs approved are safe, but equally they will have an interest in potential new cures being available on the market quickly.

Power – Similarly, in the same way that healthcare providers only have **low power**, so patients also only have low power over any decisions made at BDR.

(c) **Differences in objectives** – BDR's objectives are less explicitly financial than PT's, not least because it does not have any shareholders. Therefore the emphasis the balanced scorecard places on non-financial performance will be relevant for BDR.

Stakeholder structure – BDR is a public sector organisation, while PT is a commercial organisation, which means that the government is a much more important stakeholder for BDR than for PT. It is likely that this will need to be reflected in BDR's scorecard, with there being a political dimension to measuring performance.

Complexity of the scorecards – BDR's scorecard is likely to be quite complex, because it needs to reflect the diverse nature of its stakeholders and their interests. For example, on the one hand, drug companies will be keen for new drugs to be approved as quickly as possible, while healthcare providers and patients will be most interested in the risk-benefit profile of any potential new drugs. Equally, the government will want effective drugs and treatments to be available for patients, but in terms of paying health care providers the government may not be willing to pay for drugs it considers to be too expensive.

In this respect, the **customer perspective** of BDR's scorecard is likely to be crucial, because in effect, the drug companies, health care providers and patients are all BDR's customers. In PT's scorecard the relative significance of the four perspectives is likely to be more equal. The financial perspective will be very important for satisfying shareholders, while the internal business processes and learning and growth perspectives will be crucial in developing and manufacturing the new drugs effectively. Process and innovation are likely to be less directly important in BDR because it doesn't develop 'products' of its own.

Selecting performance measures – However, the nature of BDR's work means that it will be quite hard to measure how well it is performance against its objectives. For example, determining whether a medicine has an 'acceptable balance of benefit and risk' will involve a degree of judgement and selectivity, and it is likely to be difficult to set a quantifiable performance measure to determine whether this objective is being achieved.

Potential conflicts – Of BDR's three objectives, the easiest to set quantifiable measures for is likely to be 'encouraging new beneficial product development' because a performance measure could be set around the number of new products developed. However, there is a danger that imposing quantifiable measures in this way may have unintended consequences. For example, it may lead to new drugs being introduced even if the new product is not a significant improvement on an existing drug.

50 Victoria-Yeeland logistics

Text reference. The balanced scorecard is discussed in Chapter 15 of the BPP Study Text. Reward systems and reward management are discussed in Chapter 14.

Top tips.

Part (a). One of the key arguments in favour of multi-dimensional performance measurement systems (such as the balanced scorecard) is that an organisation's financial performance ultimately reflects it performance in key non-financial areas.

This is the broad context of part (a) of this question, but read the requirement very carefully: it does not ask about the impact that success in the customer perspective will have on Victoria's financial position in general terms. Rather it asks specifically about the impact that success in the customer perspective will have on the three financial metrics identified in Appendix 1. Therefore, your answer must also focus specifically on the impact that achieving the success factors in the customer perspective is likely to have on Victoria's ROCE, profit margin and revenue growth.

Part (b). As the marking guide indicates, there are two marks available for each metric you recommend: one for calculating a suitable metric; and one for justifying why you have chosen it. Therefore, as is so often the case in P5, requirement is not simply about calculation. Justifying the metric you have chosen is equally as important as the calculation.

Note, also, that there is a second part to the requirement – a discussion about the problems of using customer complaints as a performance measure. For example, can Victoria be sure that all customer complaints are valid?

Part (c). The requirement asks you to advise on 'the reward management issues outlined by the CFO.' The context for this requirement is provided by the last paragraph in the scenario, but crucially you need to recognise that there are two sets of issues here: one relating to the senior management bonus scheme, and one relating to the operational managers' bonus scheme.

As the marking guide indicates, you can only score up to five marks for advising on the issues with either scheme, so it is vital to analyse both schemes in order to score well on this requirement.

The fact that the shareholders have been complaining about the senior management's bonus should be a clue that agency theory is an issue here – is the scheme designed with shareholder's best interests in mind, or management's?

Similarly, in relation to the operational managers' scheme, the fact that the scenario identifies a change to the way that bonus targets are set should prompt you to question whether these changes are appropriate.

Examining team's comments. Many candidates used the building block model as a template for their answer but failed to go further than a generic response – around the need for standards to be fair, achievable and owned, and for rewards to be clear, motivational and controllable. In order for answers based around the model to score well, candidates needed to show how each aspect could be applied to the specific scenarios at Victoria.

Candidates seemed unwilling to say that employees (either senior management or operational managers) may be unhappy but this need not be an issue for Victoria, as there will usually be a conflict of interest between employees and the company/shareholders. Good answers identified and discussed how to address this issue fairly. However, simply stating that employees should set their own targets is not a practical solution, nor one which is commercially valuable to Victoria.

Marks

(a) For relevant points discussing the linkage between customer perspective and the financial perspective – 1 mark each

Note. Answers must discuss all three financial metrics in order to score the full 5 marks

Total for part (a): up to 5 — 5

(b) Each suitable performance measurement recommended – up to 2 marks (for each of four perspectives; so up to 8 marks in total)
(1 mark for calculating a suitable metric; 1 mark for justifying the choice of metric).

For discussing the problems of using customer complaints as a performance measure – up to 4 marks

Total for part (b): up to 11 — 11

(c) For relevant points relating to issues in the senior management reward system – 1 mark each, up to a maximum of 5
For relevant points relating to the operational managers' bonus scheme – 1 mark per relevant point, up to a maximum of 5

Total for part (c): up to 9 — 9

Total = 25

(a) **Links between customer perspective and financial perspective**

The success factors identified for the customer perspective should help Victoria to increase customer satisfaction. Since the delivery business in Yeeland appears to be very competitive, increasing (or, at least, maintaining) customer satisfaction levels is likely to be crucial to Victoria's financial success.

Revenue growth – Since the market is saturated, in order to increase its revenues Victoria will need to win new customers (from its competitors) whilst retaining its existing customers. Victoria's reputation for delivering packages quickly, safely and on time is likely to be crucial in helping it attract business from competitors.

In addition to increasing its customer numbers, Victoria could also consider increasing its selling prices as a means of increasing revenue. In effect, Victoria could look to differentiate itself from its competitors, by virtue of its service quality, and could then charge premium prices for its service. The success factors linked to the customer perspective are ones in which Victoria will need to out-perform its competitors in order to pursue a differentiation strategy successfully.

Profit margin – Charging premium prices should provide a direct way of increasing profit margins.

Alternatively, increasing customer numbers should enable Victoria to benefit from economies of scale, which in turn could improve profit margins by reducing unit costs. For example, if Victoria can increase its capacity utilisation (the number of packages on each delivery lorry) the amount of fixed costs apportioned to each package on that lorry will be lower.

Return on capital employed – As the ways of increasing revenue and profit margins will not require any additional capital expenditure, then any increases in operating profit should also increase Victoria's return on capital employed.

(b) **Ability to meet customers' transport needs**

This success factor can be measured by the proportion of customer requests which Victoria is able to undertake.

$$\frac{\text{Total number of packages transported}}{\text{Total number of customer transport requests}}$$

$$\frac{548,000}{610,000} = 89.8\%$$

Ability to deliver packages quickly

This measure needs to take account how far packages have to travel as well as how long it takes them to get to their destinations. Therefore, a suitable measure will be one which measures **time taken per kilometre**, (rather than one which measures time taken per journey).

$$\frac{\text{Total package minutes}}{\text{Total package kilometres}}$$

$$\frac{131,520,000}{65,760,000} = 2.0$$

Ability to deliver packages on time

This measure needs to reflect the proportion of packages which are delivered within the time window given to the customer.

$$\frac{\text{Deliveries within agreed window}}{\text{Total number of packages transported}}$$

$$\frac{(548,000 - 21,920)}{548,000} = 96\%$$

Ability to deliver packages safely

This measure needs to reflect the number of packages delivered undamaged as a proportion of the total number of packages transported.

$$\frac{\text{Deliveries with no reported damage}}{\text{Total number of packages transported}}$$

$$\frac{(548,000 - 8,220)}{548,000} = 98.5\%$$

Problems of using customer complaints as a basis for performance measurement

Victoria delivers packages to a large number of different customers, and they could respond to problems with their delivery in different ways. This means it will be difficult for Victoria to get an accurate picture of the number of deliveries which were damaged or late.

Problems under-stated – Some customers may not bother to report that a package has been delivered late or was damaged. However, due to the inconvenience caused by the lateness or damage they will use one of Victoria's competitors to deliver their packages in future.

In such cases, the performance measure gives a misleading impression that Victoria is performing better than it is. And given the importance of customer retention in Yeeland's competitive market, this could have very significant consequences on Victoria's revenue performance in the longer term.

If Victoria recorded its own delivery performance it could take direct action to try to retain customers who have suffered from late or damaged packages. For example, acknowledging the problem at the point of delivery, it could offer to discount the next order for a customer whose package is delivered late.

Problems over-stated – In contrast to customer who do not report valid complaints, others may report unjustified complaints in the hope of obtaining a refund or a credit against future orders. Currently, the measures simply record the number of complaints received, even though some of these may not be valid.

In this respect, it would be better to measure the number of refunds or discounts given (as an indicator of the number of valid complaints) rather than simply recording the total number of complaints.

(c)   **Senior managers' reward system**

Assuming that the members of the senior management team are all on the board, the potential problem here is that senior management could be deciding their own bonuses.

Agency issues – As such, there is a danger that the reward system will favour the managers' interests, rather than those of Victoria's shareholders. For example, if the targets used to determine managers' bonuses are easy to achieve, this will maximise the chances of managers receiving bonuses. This would justify the shareholders complaints that the bonuses are not suitable – because, they are not supporting Victoria's objective of maximising shareholder wealth.

The introduction of the balanced scorecard (BSC) should help to align the senior management's objectives with those of the shareholders, particularly in relation to the financial perspective. However, the financial measures suggested for the BSC do not directly address shareholder wealth, because they are essentially still based around profitability rather than value-based management.

Controllability – The fact that the market is saturated, and dominated by two international companies, will constrain managements' ability to grow revenue. Similarly, fuel prices – which management cannot control – will be a significant influence on profit margin. This again suggests these may not be the most appropriate measures to use when assessing management's performance.

Operational managers' reward system

Choice of measures – Although the senior managers assess the operational managers' performance, it is not clear what measures are used as the basis of this assessment. The measures of performance against which operational managers are assessed should be aligned to Victoria's overall objectives.

However, the measures should also relate to the aspects of performance that the operational managers can influence (and therefore will typically come from the 'customer' and 'business' perspectives in the Scorecard).

Setting own bonus targets – The suggestion that the operational managers should be involved in setting their own bonus targets does not seem appropriate however. In the same way that senior management shouldn't set their own performance targets, neither should operational managers.

Although it could be beneficial to explain the **target setting process** to the manager, this should not be confused with the idea of letting managers set their own targets. Targets should still be set by a higher level of management, and should be set at a level which is stretching but achievable.

The target set should then be explained to the managers so that they understand what they have to do in order to earn their bonus.

51 Graviton

Text reference. The Performance Pyramid is discussed in Chapter 15 of the BPP Study Text. Problems of performance measurement are discussed in Chapter 14.

Top tips.

Part (a). The scenario identifies that the CEO is 'unhappy with the current performance measurement system', and that there are 'major gaps in the current list of key metrics used'. Equally, the evidence from the press reports suggests that Graviton is being successful in some areas, whilst performing less well in other areas.

A sensible approach to this question might be to think how far these variations in Graviton's current performance reflect the areas which are monitored by Graviton's current performance measures; and then to think how far the weaknesses in the current system could be addressed by using the performance pyramid.

Crucially, however, note that the requirement asks you to evaluate Graviton's performance measurement **system**, not its current performance. You will not earn any marks for discussing Graviton's performance as such.

Part (b). The issues listed by the board (myopia, gaming, ossification) are three of the problems listed by Berry, Broadbent and Ottley in relation to the use of performance measures.

If you were aware of Berry, Broadbent and Ottley's list, then identifying the problems at Graviton should have been relatively straight-forward, because evidence of them is fairly clearly illustrated by the scenario.

A sensible way to approach this part of the requirement would be to take each of the three problems in turn; provide a short definition of the problem; assess whether they apply to Graviton; and then suggest possible solutions for the problem.

There are 10 marks available for this part of the question, so if you describe each problem (1 mark each) and then make a couple of relevant points applying each problem to Graviton (2 marks per problem) this would enable you to score almost all the marks available.

If you weren't familiar with Berry, Broadbent and Ottley's terminologies, you are likely to have struggled with this part of the question. Nonetheless, you should have realised that the issues at Factories 1 and 2 had been included in the scenario for a reason. Therefore, even if you didn't know what myopia, gaming and ossification were, the scenario should have given you a clue that these issues were linked to problems with the company's performance measures, and so you should have been able to suggest appropriate performance management solutions to them.

Marks

(a) General description of performance pyramid (including diagram of the model) – up to 3 marks

All the remaining marks must have specific relevance to Graviton:

Current issues at Graviton where current performance measurement system leads to tunnel vision and focus on selected aspects of performance only – 1 mark per relevant point, up to maximum of 5 marks

Linking performance metrics to the company's vision – 1 mark per relevant point, up to a maximum of 4 marks

Using performance pyramid to identify ways Graviton's current performance measures could be improved: Market satisfaction; financial performance; customer satisfaction; flexibility; productivity; quality; delivery; cycle time; waste – 1 mark per relevant point, up to a maximum of 6 marks.

Total for part (a): up to 15   **15**

(b) Clear definition of each term – 1 mark per term, up to a maximum of 3

For assessing whether the problems apply at Graviton, and for suggesting appropriate solutions – 1 mark per relevant point, up to a maximum of 3 for each problem

Total for part (b): up to 10   **10**

Total = 25

(a) **Performance Pyramid** – The logic of the performance pyramid is that although organisations operate at different levels (for example, strategic and operational) those levels need to support each other in achieving business objectives. The structure of the pyramid seeks to highlight the links between the day-to-day operational performance and overall strategic performance.

Graviton's current performance measurement system

The aim of Graviton's current performance measurement system (to provide a list of measures at strategic, tactical and operational levels of management) seems to be consistent with the logic of the performance pyramid (to link strategic and operational performance drivers).

However, the CEO's concern that there are gaps in the current list of metrics could also be linked to a concern that the current performance measurement system at Graviton is concentrating attention on certain aspects of performance to the detriment of other aspects of performance.

Tunnel vision – Although this is not one of the problems listed by the board executives, the focus on selected measurements, at the expense of others, characterises the problem of tunnel vision in performance measurement systems.

For example, Graviton's recent results might suggest that the focus of the company's attention has been on revenue growth rather than profitability, which could help to explain why revenue has risen considerably more rapidly than operating profit in the last year. In such a case, the problem could be addressed by including performance metrics relating to operating costs or profit margins.

More generally, one way to prevent tunnel vision being a problem for an organisation is to ensure that the dimensions of performance being measured are comprehensive, and include metrics relating to all the critical success factors in the organisation. Importantly also, this means that performance measures shouldn't focus narrowly on financial indicators, but should also address the range of processes and driving forces which guide an organisation's ability to achieve its strategic objectives.

This recognition of the importance of focusing on the range of processes and activities which shape an organisation's ability to achieve its strategic objectives is one the key characteristics of the performance pyramid.

Moreover, the pyramid does not focus purely on financial objectives, but includes a range of objectives of **external effectiveness and internal efficiency**. Lynch and Cross propose that these elements of effectiveness and efficiency are the key driving forces on which company objectives are based.

The pyramid diagram highlights the way the performance of operational and business processes underpins an organisation's financial performance:

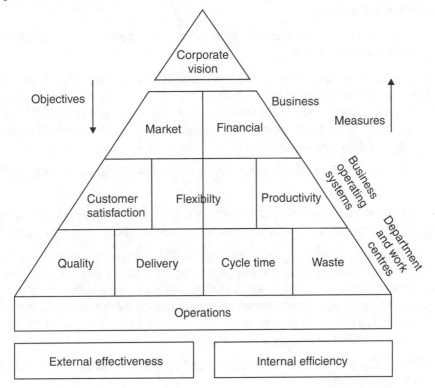

Corporate vision

Shareholder wealth – Graviton's overall objective is to maximise shareholder wealth; and therefore it seems surprising that the performance measures do not include **total shareholder return** (thereby recognising the importance of dividends and share price growth).

It is possible that Graviton is using ROCE as an overall measure of productivity and performance, but given the company's objective refers specifically to maximising 'shareholder wealth' then a performance measure focusing speciifically on shareholder return would be more appropriate.

Moreover, the absence of a dividend measure in may also explain why Graviton's dividend growth has not been strong – leading to criticism from the institutional investors.

Focus on changing market trends – Graviton's business aim is to satisfy changing market trends, and it seeks to do this by maintaining flexibility in production and close control across the supply chain. The elements of 'flexibility' and 'productivity' are included at the business operating system level in the performance pyramid, but it seems that they are higher level objectives at Graviton.

Flexibility – The measure of the average time for bringing new designs to market in Graviton's performance measurement system supports the importance of flexibility in its operations.

However, the current performance system does not measure the company's ability to replenish successful product lines, and therfore to take advantage of consumer demand. Whilst it is important for Graviton to introduce new designs quickly, it is equally important for the product availability of different clothes to reflect levels of demand.

Production control – Equally, however, it is important to maintain the quality of the production process. The criticisms from customers about the durability of Graviton's clothes may suggest there are issues relating to the controls in place in the production process.

The current performance measures do not indluce any measures around production quality or durability.

The apparent lack of focus on the production process could also help to explain why operating profits are increasingly significantly less than revenue. If Graviton's cost controls in the production processs are weak, this would lead to falling operating profit margins.

Market and financial performance

The pyramid suggests that the two key drivers for obtaining overall corporate vision are **satisfying the market** and **performing well financially**.

Financial performance measures – Although Graviton's performance dashboard includes figures for revenues and profits, it doesn't show figures for profit margins. And despite profit increasingly slightly from 20X1 to 20X3, the operating profit margin has fallen from 21.8% to 18.6% over this period. This again suggests that there could be issues with rising costs or weak cost control, but the current performance measure system doesn't draw attention to this.

Alternatively, there could be a danger that Graviton has sacrificed profitability in order to achieve revenue growth.

Productivity – The pyramid also suggests that productivity is a key driver in obtaining financial objectives, and the nature of Graviton's market means that production efficiency is likely to very important.

The measure of 'Deliveries on time' could be seen as linked to this; but it seems unlikely to be the most important indicator to measure productivity. Given the nature of the clothing industry, a measure of waste or obsolescence (such as inventory write-offs) would seem to be more instructive. One of the keys to Graviton's success will be getting the right clothes to the right place at the right time. If it is too slow in producing clothes, and its designs become obsolete before it has had a chance to sell them, this could have a significant impact on Graviton's operating profit margins.

Market satisfaction – The performace pyramid suggests that customer satisfaction and flexibility are crucial in achieving market satisfaction.

We have already noted that Graviton uses 'time to market' as a measure for its ability to introduce new products in response to changing market trends, suggesting that it already considers this aspect of flexibiliyt is important in achieved its corproate objectives.

Customer satisfaction – Although the current performance measures do not directly measure customer satisfaction, revenue growth could be seen, indirectly, as an indicator of customer satisfaction levels. If customers are not satisfied with the products they have bought from Graviton in the past, they are unlikely to make any repeat purchases.

Quality – In this respect, customer criticism over the durability of Graviton's clothes should be seen as a concern, because if these concerns remain they could hinder the company's sales and revenue in the future.

Alternatively, though, we could question how much customers value durability a in fast-changing industry. If customers are regularly buying new clothes to keep up with the changes in fashion, how important will durability actually be in their decision about which clothes to buy?

In this respect, it would be useful for Graviton to estabish how important the issue of durability is in customer's decision-making process. If it is significant, then it would be useful for Graviton to include a related metric (such as the number of customer complaints) in its performance measures.

Design awards – Although the current performance measures don't specifically look refer to product quality, the number of design awards could also be seen, indirectly, as an indicator of quality – and possibly also of customer satisfaction. Graviton's clothes would be unlikely to be nominated for awards if they are felt to be of poor quality or if customers are critical of them.

Again however, measuring the number of design awards is not the most obvious way of measuring quality or customer satisfaction (both of which are highlighted in the performance pyramid as drivers of external effectiveness).

(b) **Myopia**

Myopia relates to the problems caused by short-termist decisions leading to the neglect of longer-term objectives.

This currently appears to be an issue at Factory Site 2, where the factory appears reluctant to invest in any new machinery in order to preserve its excellent return on capital employed.

However, the failure to invest in the new machinery has led to a significant adverse variance in the cost of repairs and maintenance. It also seems likely that Site 2's production is less efficient than it would otherwise be if it had invested in some new machinery.

The use of ROCE as one of the metrics in the performance measurement systems (and in particular annual ROCE figures) could be one of the main reasons for myopia within Graviton; and specifically at Factory Site 2. One solution for this specific issue would be to include a performance measure for production efficiency (eg number of breakdowns or repairs required) at each of the Factory Sites.

More generally, Graviton could address the issue of myopia by measuring performance over a longer time period than a single accounting period.

Gaming

The problem of 'gaming' relates to the deliberate distortion of a performance measure in order to secure some kind of strategic advantage.

There is clear evidence of gaming at Factory Site 1, where the manager is manipulating revenue and profit figures (by delaying invoicing) in order to achieve profit targets.

It is not clear whether Graviton has an internal audit department, but if it does one specific action which could be taken is a review of the invoicing procedures, or a review of period end cut-offs, to try to prevent such manipulation recurring.

More generally, the probem of gaming also appears to have been driven by the desire to achieve short-term (annual) performance targets. So, as with the proposed soluton to myopia, one solution would be to reward performance over a longer time period than a single accounting period. For example, the factory manager's profit targets could be set as an average figure over a number of periods, rather than having single targets for individual periods.

> Additionally, behaviour such as the factory manager's could be addressed by promoting a culture of honesty within the organisation. It is not clear whether Graviton currently has a corporate Code of Ethics, but a Code of this sort could be useful for highlighting the standards of behaviour which are expected in the company.

Ossification

The problem of 'ossification' relates to an unwillingness to change a performance measure system once it has been set up. Ossification is likely to be a particular problem when the current system appears to be showing adequate results – because this situation could be hiding issues which could be highlighted if different measures were being monitored.

Ossification appears to be a problem at Graviton, where the board are sceptical of change have argued that the business' good performance means there is no justification for changing the performance measurement system.

The CEO will have to convince the board that Graviton's current good performance has been achieved despite the current performance measurement system rather than because of it. More specifically, the CEO will need to highlight how the gaps in the current list of key metrics will lead to longer-term difficulties in achieving Graviton's overall objective to maximise shareholder wealth.

Once again, recognising the importance of longer-term performance is likely to address this problem. For example, the remuneration and incentive plans for Graviton's executives and board members could be linked to the longer-term, sustainable performance of the company, rather than to its historical results, or to its results in the short term.

52 Bettaserve

> **Text references.** The performance pyramid is discussed in Chapter 15 of the BPP Study Text.
>
> **Top tips.** The question includes phrases that should tell you that it is asking you about the **performance pyramid**. For instance, reference is made to **external effectiveness** and **internal efficiency**, which are both aspects of the model. Part (a) wants you to apply your knowledge of the model to the scenario so you must refer to the statistics in Schedule 1.
>
> In part (b) you are being asked to **discuss the model** as a whole, that is, how it represents a view of organisational performance in an organisation. Note, although the requirement tells you that a diagram may be used to illustrate the links, drawing the diagram alone will not be sufficient to pass the requirement. As the question requirement suggests, you also need to provide 'relevant discussion' about the importance of the inter-relationships and the hierarchy between different the measures in the performance pyramid.

(a)　(i)　**Corporate vision**

The question alludes to a view of business taken by Lynch and Cross, in whose 'performance pyramid' corporate vision is what defines the following:

(1)　The **markets** in which an organisation will compete (such as a new market for an existing range of services)

(2)　The **bases** upon which it will compete (such as a 'gold standard' focus for an existing range of services)

For the 'gold standard' proposal Bettaserve's **market** has been defined both in terms of its key **competitors** and the **customers** with whom it can co-operate.

Bettaserve intend to compete on the following **bases**:

(1)　Offering **tailored** services that meet the **specific** design and quality requirements of customers

(2) **Improving** the services offered and enhancing **flexibility continuously**

(3) Providing effective after-sales service

(ii) **Market satisfaction** and **financial measures** are objectives set at the corporate level. Market satisfaction would cover objectives set for growth in markets. Financial objectives would relate to improved revenues, margins and profitability.

The data in the schedule suggests a growth in **total market size** of 8% from 20X7 to 20X9. Bettaserve's **share of this market** is anticipated to increase from 12.5% to 15.4% over this period. So Bettaserve is expecting to enjoy an increased share of an expanding market.

Profits (sales less total costs) are projected to grow by $13m in the period covered and net margins from 6% to 37.25%. This improvement in margins comes about partly from a fall in the costs of rectification and paying out on rectification claims. Bettaserve is therefore anticipating a fall in certain **costs of quality**, particularly external costs that impact on their reputation with customers.

(iii) Quality and delivery are operational activities that affect customer satisfaction and hence **external effectiveness**.

In terms of marketing, the proposal will be successful if customers are satisfied, and if customers are satisfied there will be high levels of customer satisfaction.

Quality measures in the schedule cover **rectification costs**, which are costs of quality. These external costs are expected to fall over the three years. Thus rectification claims are projected to fall from $0.9m to $0.2m, which is a drop of 78%, and cost for after sales rectification is expected to fall by $1m. Services not requiring further rectification should increase from 95% to 98% in the period, which shows an improvement in the quality of services to customers.

Delivery effectiveness is measured by how long it takes the customer to get the goods or services ordered. Sales attaining the planned completion date are projected to increase from 90% to 99% in the period covered.

(iv) In **financial terms** the proposal can be successful if productivity is high.

Relevant measures, therefore, include **average cycle time**, which is anticipated to fall from 6 to 5 weeks over the period covered, and **idle capacity**, which is a measure of waste and is expected to fall from 10% to 2% from 20X7 to 20X9.

Appraisal and prevention costs, which are internal quality costs related to processes and incurred before products and services go to the customer, are expected to fall or remain constant in total.

(b) **Performance pyramid**

The **performance pyramid** derives from the idea that an organisation operates at different levels, each of which has different concerns, which should nevertheless support each other in achieving business objectives. The pyramid therefore links the overall strategic view of management with day to day operations.

It includes a range of **objectives** for both **external effectiveness** (such as related to customer satisfaction) and **internal efficiency** (such as related to productivity), which are achieved through measures at the various levels. So for Bettaserve, the attainment of market satisfaction and financial objectives are immediately linked to the achievement of customer satisfaction and productivity and so on further down the hierarchy. Each level relates to that above and below it and all are dependant on each other for success.

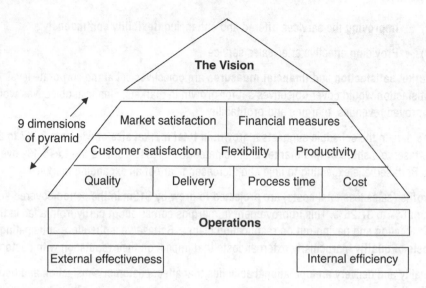

(i) At **corporate level**, financial and market objectives are set.

(ii) At **strategic business unit** level, strategies are developed to achieve these financial and market objectives.

    (1) **Customer satisfaction** is defined as meeting customer expectations.

    (2) **Flexibility** indicates responsiveness of the business operating system as a whole.

    (3) **Productivity** refers to the management of resources such as labour and time.

(iii) These in turn are supported by more specific **operational** criteria at departmental level.

    (1) **Quality** of the product or service, consistency of product and fit for the purpose.

    (2) **Delivery** of the product or service (the method of distribution, its speed and ease of management).

    (3) **Process time** of all processes from cash collection to order processing to recruitment.

    (4) **Cost**, meaning the elimination of all non value added activities.

The pyramid highlights the **links** running between the **vision for the company** and **functional objectives**. For example, a reduction in process time should lead to increased productivity and hence improved financial performance.

53 Cod

Text reference. The performance hierarchy (linking mission, objectives, and KPIs) is discussed in Chapter 2 of the BPP Study Text. The performance pyramid is covered in Chapter 15.

Top tips.

Part (a). The Board's concerns (identified in the fourth paragraph of the scenario) should provide you with some context for this requirement. In effect, the Board are highlighting that because the KPIs are not integrated with the mission statement, the mission has become seen as little more than a public relations exercise.

Crucially, though, the key part to this requirement is the relationship between the KPIs and the mission statement, so you should not spend a long time discussing the characteristics of mission statements or KPIs in isolation.

Equally, you are asked to make reference to Cod's mission statement, so make sure you do. Again, this should help you identify some of the reasons for the Board's concern – because the mission identifies a number of aspects of performance, none of which are then measured by the KPIs.

In effect, **part (b)** then asks you to explain how the performance pyramid can help to address some of the weaknesses in Cod's KPIs which you should have identified when answering part (a): for example, the absence of any non-financial measures alongside the financial ones, and the need to create an integrated hierarchy of performance measures throughout the organisation.

Although you need to link your answer to the scenario, this question is essentially about the benefits of the performance pyramid as a performance measurement system though.

It is important that you read the requirement to **part (c)** very carefully because there are three sub-requirements within it: (i) use the performance pyramid to evaluate Cod's current performance management sytem; (ii) apply the performance pyramid to suggest additional KPIs, and (iii) apply the performance pyramid to suggest a set of operational performance measures for Cod.

For part (ii) you need to think how Cod's existing additional performance information could be used to monitor Customer Satisfaction, Flexibility and Productivity (the business unit level criteria in the pyramid). Then for part (iii) you need to think how the information could be used to monitor Quality, Delivery, Process Time and Waste (the operational criteria in the pyramid).

Remember, however, that the focus of this question (in parts (b) and (c)) is on evaluating the performance *systems* at Cod, not on evaluating Cod's performance as an organisation.

Marking scheme

		Marks
(a)	For describing mission and KPIs – ½ mark each	
	For discussing the importance of the linkages between KPIs and mission statement (with suitable references to Cod) – 1 mark for each relevant point, up to a maximum of 5 marks	
	Maximum for part (a)	6
(b)	Diagram illustrating the performance pyramid – Up to 2 marks	
	For explanation of how the pyramid can help Cod reach its goal of a coherent set of performance measures – 1 mark for each relevant point, up to a maximum of 4	
	Maximum for part (b)	6
(c)	Describe performance drivers (customer satisfaction; flexibility; productivity) – ½ mark per point, Up to 1 ½	
	Assessment of current system – Up to 2 marks	
	New KPIs suggested – 1 mark per KPI, Up to a maximum of 4 marks	
	Operational measures suggested – 1 mark per measure, Up to a maximum of 6 marks	
	[**Note**. To score all 6 marks available, all FOUR areas of the operational level of the pyramid must be addressed.]	
	Maximum for part (c)	13
		Total = 25

(a) An organisation's mission statement reflects its underlying purposes. By doing so, the mission statement can also help to identify the aspects of performance which the organisation considers to be important in helping it to achieve its corporate vision, and therefore which need to be measured and managed.

Cod's mission statement identifies a number of areas which are important for its competitive success: competitive pricing, high quality, excellent customer service, product development (innovation) and staff training.

However, while the mission statement identifies areas which are important, the way they are presented is too high level and open-ended for the board to be able to measure Cod's actual performance against them. Therefore, the mission statement needs to be translated into more specific objectives and targets against which performance can be measured.

As their name suggests, KPIs should focus on factors which are central to a company's success or failure. Critically, however Cod's current KPIs focus solely on financial performance, meaning there is no obvious alignment between them are the key aspects of performance identified in the mission statement. For example, despite the mission statement identifying quality, customer service and product development as important to Cod, none of the KPIs reflect this. Consequently, at a strategic level, Cod is not measuring how well it is is performing in any of the areas which the mission has suggested are important.

In turn, this lack of integration between the KPIs and the mission statement might also explain why the employees view the mission statement as being merely a public relations exercise.Since none of the elements of the mission statement are measured – via the KPIs – this could lead to a perception amongst the staff that these elements are not actually very important after all. Equally, the perception could be that the only elements of performance which management are really interested in are the financial measures (profit, cashflow and ROCE).

The importance of KPIs being aligned to the mission statement is also reinforced by the adage 'What gets measured, gets done.' If the aspects of performance in the mission statement are those which are important for Cod, then in order to ensure that employees focus on them, then those aspects of performance also need to be reflected in the KPIs and related performance targets.

(b)   Lynch and Cross's performance pyramid stems from an acknowledgement that traditional performance measures based on financial indicators such as profitability, cash flow and return on capital employed do not address the driving forces that guide an organisation's ability to achieve its strategic objectives. This appears to be the problem with Cod's current performance measures.

Range of objectives – By contrast, instead of focusing purely on financial objectives, the pyramid focuses on a range of objectives for both **external effectiveness** (eg customer satisfaction) and **internal efficiency** (eg flexibility and productivity).

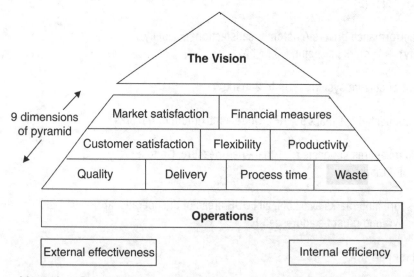

Performance hierarchy – The pyramid also highlights the way that different levels in an organisation support each other and relate to each other. This will allow Cod to develop a coherent set of objectives which are derived from the overall corporate vision.

The nine dimensions of the pyramid link strategic objectives (market satisfaction; financial measures) to operational objectives (quality, delivery, process time and waste) through the themes of external effectiveness and internal efficiency.

Linkages and support – In order for Cod to develop a coherent set of performance measures it is important the objectives and measures at each level of the organisation (strategic, tactical and operational) support each other. The performance pyramid highlights the importance of these linkages between the different levels of the organisation, and the overall link between Cod's vision and mission and its day-to-day operations.

Appreciating these linkages will help Cod devise a coherent set of performance measures. For example, increasing quality, should increase customer satisfaction, and in turn increase Cod's market share.

(c) **Customer satisfaction, flexibility and productivity** – The performance pyramid suggests that the strategies developed to achieve an organisation's financial and market objective should focus on three key driving forces: customer satisfaction, flexibility and productivity.

Currently, Cod's KPIs do not address any of these three areas, although the performance information already available means that Cod could develop non-financial KPIs for each of the three areas (see below).

It could be argued that some of these non-financial measures are more appropriate to the tactical and operational levels of the management hierarchy rather than the strategic (board) level. However, the existing performance information does not appear to be linked to the current KPIs, which suggests the board is right to be concerned about the current KPI system.

Additional KPIs

Customer satisfaction

Complaints – Customer satisfaction levels could be measured by the % of orders which with complaints against them.

	20X1	20X0
Orders with a complaint	138	123
Number of orders	2,560	2,449
% with complaint	5.4%	5.0%

Preferred supplier status – The number of customers who have awarded a preferred supplier status could also be seen as an indicator of customer satisfaction

	20X1	20X0
Preferential supplier status	14	12
Number of customers	24	24
% preferred status	58.3%	50.0%

Flexibility

Products launched – The number of new products launched in a year can be seen as an indicator of innovation.

Productivity

Quality costs – Failure costs (internal + external) can act as an indicator of inefficient production. Failure costs have increased from $3.46 million in 20X0 to $4.35 million in 20X1.

Operational performance measures

The operational performance measures suggested by the pyramid will relate to the four areas of quality, delivery, process time and waste.

Quality

Failure costs – Cod's additional performance information already shows **failure costs** and these could be used as a measure for quality. However, they would be improved as measures if actual costs were compared to budgeted costs.

Customer complaint numbers could also be used as a measure for quality, in particular those relating to product quality. However, there could be problems with using the information as it stands because there is no indication about the seriousness of the complaint or the consequences of it (for example, discounts or refunds offered.)

Equally, the number of complaints being classified as 'Other' is also a concern. These need to be broken down into further subcategories to help identify the causes of the complaint more accurately, and therefore identify which aspects of operational performance need improving.

Delivery

Customer complaint numbers – It is important for Cod to become (and remain) a preferred supplier for as many manufacturers as possible. Customer satisfaction is vital to achieving this, so again customer complaint numbers will be important here. If complains relating to produce quality are used as a measure of quality, then complaints relating to late delivery and customer service can be used a measures of delivery.

Staff measures – The number of **training days** and the number of **vacant posts** could also be used as measures relating to delivery. An increase in the number of training days should help improve quality and delivery, while posts remaining vacant is likely to have a detrimental impact on them. However, Cod's current performance information on training days could be improved by comparing them to benchmarking, for example, to see how they compare to competitor organisations.

Process time

The performance information which Cod currently collects does not appear to be useful for measuring process time. It is possible that the number of **new products** being developed in a year could give an indication of the time to market. However, the performance measure would be improved if Cod specifically measured the **time to market** for each new product developed, and possibly then also compared this to an industry benchmark.

Waste

The current performance information does not appear to be useful for measuring waste in production. Variance analysis (comparing actual performance to budget) of **idle time** for employees and **materials usage** would be instructive measures here.

54 APX Accountancy

Text reference. The building block model is discussed in Chapter 15 of the Study Text.

Top tips. Part (a) is a pure test of knowledge. You are simply asked to describe Fitzgerald and Moon's model; you do not need to apply it to the scenario.

However, in parts (b) and (c) you do need to apply your knowledge o f the model to the scenario.

It is vital that you read the requirement for part (b) carefully and answer the question set. You are asked to evaluate APX's performance *management system*, not APX's performance.

Notice also the link between parts (b) and (c). In part (b) you need to evaluate the existing system, and then in part (c) you need to explain and suggest improvements. Therefore, you should not have suggested any improvements while you were answering part (b); but should have saved these for part (c) instead.

Part (d) – At one level, the marketing manager seems to be highlighting the importance of non-financial performance measures, which seems reasonable. However, he also seems to have overlooked the environmental factors which have contributed to the relative financial performance of the different service areas. Has the Business Advisory division really performed best financially because it has the highest customer service score, or because the business advisory sector had a growth year across the industry as a whole.

Examining team's comments. It was sad to note how many candidates did not even know the names of the three building blocks. This demonstrated inadequate preparation for the examination.

Better candidates had read the full requirement to the question before beginning their answers, and so held back from offering improvements to the faults recognized in part (b) until their answers to part (c) of the question.

(a) **Performance measurement in service businesses** – Fitzgerald and Moon's building block model aims to provide a framework to improve performance measurement in service businesses.

The model suggests that performance systems should be based on three concepts: dimensions, standards, and rewards.

Dimensions – The model identifies six dimensions (competitive performance, financial performance, quality of service, flexibility and resource utilization and innovation) and suggests that the performance measures companies choose should focus on these six areas.

The model also suggests that the dimensions can be divided into two sets: **results** (competitive performance, and financial performance) and **determinants** (the other four). The logic here is that controlling and improving performance in respect of the determinants will then lead to improved results.

Standards – This aspect of the model relates to the targets which are chosen to be measured. Here, the model highlights three key properties which performance measures (standards or targets) should possess: **ownership, achievability** and **fairness.**

Rewards – Finally, the model also highlights the properties which reward schemes need to possess in order to encourage staff to work towards the performance standards set. Again, there are three key properties: **clarity, controllability** and **motivation**. The reward system needs to help motivate staff, and in order to achieve this, staff need to be clear about the goals they are working towards, and feel that the rewards are related to areas of responsibility that they can control.

(b) The current performance management system appears to be based primarily on financial performance, and so does not focus on a number of the determinants highlighted by the building block model.

Dimensions

Results – The current system does allow **financial** and **competitive performance** to be measured. The figures for **revenue growth** and **profit margin** can be used to measure APX's financial performance, while the data on accounting industry revenue can be used to calculate **market share**.

Determinants – However, the management information collected provides less opportunity to measure the determinants of performance. The customer service score could be used as an indicator of the quality of service offered, but there appears no information on which to measure flexibility and resource utilization and innovation.

Standards

Measuring competitive performance – The industry figures will allow APX to monitor its market share, and its revenue growth relative the industry as a whole, but they only look at revenue rather than profit. Therefore, it does not look as if APX can measure its profit margin against the industry as a whole.

Consequently, any standards for profitability will have to be **set internally**; for example APX could measure the profitability of each of its business streams. However, this could raise issues in relation to **achievability** and **fairness**. Given that Emland is currently in a recession, it is perhaps to be expected that the growth and margins in the audit businesses will be lower than those which the business advisory division, so the fact that this is the case does not necessarily tell us anything about how the relative performance of the divisions.

The scenario does not tell us anything about the target scores for customer service or how these are set, so we cannot comment on this aspect of the standards.

Reward system

Clarity – Non-partners receive a bonus based on their line managers' annual review, but the scenario does not indicate what aspects of their performance staff are judged on in this review. If they are not clear what their performance is being judged on, or if the judgement is perceived to be too subjective, this may serve to demotivate staff.

Controllability – APX's performance management system appears to focus predominantly on financial indicators, which may suggest that financial measures are used as the basis for the annual review. Again though, this could be a cause for concern, because non-partners have relatively limited scope to influence revenue or profit margins.

Divisional or group wide performance – There may be similar issues of controllability in relation to the partners' reward system. The partners currently receive a share of profit, but it is not clear if this profit-share is based on APX's profit as a whole or the profit for their area of the business. If the partners feel their rewards are being based on measures they cannot control, this is likely to adversely affect their motivation. For example, if partners' rewards are based on group profits, then partners in the audit division may not maximize their own performance if they know that they will benefit (regardless of their own division's performance) from the favourable performance of the business advisory services division.

(c) **Cover all dimensions of performance** – One of the key improvements a building block system can make to performance management is ensuring that all the key dimensions of successful performance are measured.

At APX, this will mean considering the importance of flexibility, resource utilization and innovation to the firm's success and then developing performance measures for these dimensions.

Flexibility – Flexibility is likely to be important for APX in terms of the scheduling of its work (to meet client deadlines), and in this respect, flexibility is also likely to have an impact on customer satisfaction. Accordingly, APX could introduce a performance measure looking at the percentage of jobs delivered on time.

Resource utilization – APX's key resource is its staff, so it would seem very important to measure staff utilization rates. One way of doing this would be to measure the percentage of chargeable hours worked as a percentage of total working hours, and such a measure would provide APX with information about the productivity of its staff. Moreover, if this measure were recorded on a monthly basis it would highlight periods when the business is busy and when it is less busy. The partners could then try to win new clients who need work done in APX's less busy periods.

Innovation – Innovation could be useful for improving APX's internal systems and working practices, but its impact is likely to be greater in relation to the new services APX can develop for its clients. In this case, it may be useful to have a performance measure which looks at the percentage of revenue earned from new customer initiatives.

Standards and rewards

Although the introduction of additional measures which cover the non-financial dimensions of successful performance is perhaps the biggest improvement the building block approach could make to APX, there are also **issues with the way standards are currently set.**

To address this, APX needs to ensure that the measures chosen (and performance targets set) are **achievable** and **fair**. In turn, this should encourage the staff to try to achieve the performance targets.

Similarly, the current rewards system should also be reviewed to ensure that it serves to **motivate partners and staff**. For example, if this is not already the case, an element of the partners profit share should be based on the profitability of the work from their divisions, rather than it all being based on APX's profitability overall.

Equally, it may also be beneficial to given the non-partners their own targets or objectives for the year, because then the line managers have some more clearly defined objectives to assess their staff against in the annual review process.

(d) **Top tip.** The measure being commented on is customer service, not customer satisfaction. You may have been tempted to discuss the potential trade-off between financial and non-financial performance measures – by suggesting that APX might be able to increase customer satisfaction by reducing its prices, and thereby also reducing its profit margins.

However, we have focused specifically on the customer service score, rather than customer satisfaction more generally, and so we have not included this more general argument in our suggested solution below.

Importance of customer service – Customer service is undoubtedly important for a service firm like APX, because if the service it offers its customers is poor they may look for other advisors.

It is not clear what factors contribute to the customer service scores which customers give, but the quality of the advice which APX gives its clients is likely to be an important factor in its on-going success, so this aspect of customer service is important to measure.

Reasons for scores – However, the inherent nature of the services provided could also contribute to the customer service scores, and so, in this respect, the marketing managers' statement could be misleading.

APX's clients have to have an audit, and they may almost resent this if they perceive the audit brings them little value. So the fact that the audit gets the lowest customer service score may reflect this rather than the quality of APX's audit staff.

External environment – However, perhaps more importantly, the marketing manager seems to be attributing the business advisory division's favourable performance to its customer service score alone, without considering the environmental factors which have also affected its performance. The current recession in Emland has led to an increase in demand for business advisory services across the industry as a whole. It seems likely that APX's performance reflects this more than its customer service scores.

Equally, the marketing manager's implication that the customer service score is a more important performance metric than financial measures is also mis-guided. Whilst it is important that APX considers non-financial aspects of performance, it should not do so at the expense of financial performance measures. Instead, APX's performance evaluation needs to consider both financial and non-financial performance measures.

55 Robust Laptops

Text reference. Activity based costing is discussed in Chapter 15 of the BPP Study Text in the context of Activity based management. Critical success factors and key performance indicators are discussed in Chapter 2, while the importance of non-financial performance measures is discussed in Chapter 12.

Top tips. In **part (a)** look at the verb requirement here: it asks for an *evaluation* of the existing method and an ABC system. So you need to consider the respective benefits and limitations of the current method and the ABC method, specifically in relation to Robust Laptops. What features of Robust Laptops would make the method suitable or not? The calculations you are also asked to provide should help you identify the issues here.

However, note that as well as evaluating the two methods, you then need to advise management what action they might take. Try to be practical here though. For example, if the ABC method suggests that the price of the laptops is too low, can Robust simply raise its prices as it wishes?

Part (b). Much of this part of the question is a test of knowledge. Although you need to relate your answer to Robust, a key issue here is the point that CSFs identify the key processes which an organisation needs to perform in order to be successful, and KPIs are the measures which are used to assess whether or not it is achieving this.

As is often the case with the requirements in P5 questions, note that there are two elements to this requirement: first, explaining the links between objectives, CSFs and KPIs; second, explaining the importance of non-financial performance information as well as financial. However, answering the first element should help you answer the second element. If most of an organisation's CSFs are non-financial, what implications will this have for the performance information the organisation needs to measure whether or not it is achieving its CSFs?

Marks

(a) General discussion of the two methods – 1 mark per point up to 4 marks.
Discussion of illustrative calculations – 1 mark per point up to 3 marks.
Further action to undertake – up to 2 marks
Conclusion on system of costing – 1 mark
Maximum of 9 marks

Workings:
Absorption cost
Cost per unit – 1 mark
Price per unit – 1 mark
ABC cost
Driver rates – 2 marks
Cost per unit – 1 mark
Price per unit – 1 mark
Difference between prices – 1 mark
Ignore minor rounding differences provided the candidate has used a reasonable level of detail.
Maximum of 7 marks for workings

Maximum of 16 marks for part (a)
16

(b) Explaining what objectives, CSFs and KPIs are – 1 mark each (max: 3)
Explaining the links between them, with reference to Robust – 1 mark per relevant point; up to 4 marks
Explaining the importance of non-financial as well as financial performance information – 1 mark per point; up to 3 marks
Maximum for part (b): 9 marks
9

Total = 25

(a) **Evaluation of the current method of costing against an ABC system**

The costing system is important at RL because it is not only a method of reporting activities in the business, but it also sets the prices that customers pay, and therefore it affects competitiveness.

The traditional system of absorption costing allocates overhead costs to products based on production activity (labour hours in RL's case). Absorption costing suits traditional production environments with few activities and fairly low overheads.

ABC is an alternative method for allocating overheads, intended to reflect the different activities that lead to costs being incurred. The principles benefit of ABC is that identifying and monitoring cost-generating activities leads to more accurate cost control. As such, ABC may be a more appropriate method of allocating overheads than absorption costing when overheads form a large proportion of an organisation's costs.

At RL, overheads comprise 23% of the total costs, meaning they overheads are a significant proportion of the total, although they are not dominant. ABC is most often used in manufacturing where production is typified by small batches and where there is significant tailoring of products to meet customer specifications. This is the case at RL.

We can use order 11784 to assess the impact of introducing ABC. Under the current absorption costing system, the cost per unit would be $2,556 and the price would be $3,706 as there is a mark up of 45%. Under an ABC system, the units would be costed at $3,194 and the mark-up would mean the price is $4,631. This represents an increase of 25% on the current figures. The overhead allocated to the order by the traditional absorption costing method is $596, while ABC allocates $1,234 per unit sold on the order.

Absorption costing cost and price per unit	Current method standard costing	ABC cost and price per unit	Difference	%
Costs		Costs		
Direct	1,959.96	1,960.00		
Overhead allocated (14,190,000/(23,800×3)	596.22			
Customer service		593.28		
Purchasing and receiving		458.13		
Stock management		75.86		
Administration of production	–	106.60		
Total cost	**2,556.18**	**3,193.87**		
Mark-up (45%)	1,150.28	1,437.24		
Price	**3,706.46**	**4,631.11**	924.65	24.9

	Total of cost activity $'000	No of driver units	Cost per driver unit $
No of minutes on call to customer	7,735	899,600	8.60
No of purchase orders raised	2,451	21,400	114.53
No of components used in production	1,467	618,800	2.37
Administration of production (absorbed as general overhead)	2,537	71,400	35.53

	Driver units on order	Cost allocated to order $	Cost per unit on order (16 orders) $
No of minutes on call to customer	1,104	9,492	593.28
No of purchase orders raised	64	7,330	458.19
No of components used in production	512	1,214	75.86
Administration of production (absorbed as general overhead)	48	1,706	106.60
			1,233.93

This difference in costs indicates that there is currently a significant under-pricing of the order. ABC has identified that the major components of the overhead are the time spent discussing the order, and the number of purchase orders that subsequently have to be raised. RL's management should review these two areas of activity to see if they can be made more efficient. If not, then management need to consider whether orders such as this should be repriced.

However, before increasing the price, RL's management need to assess the impact that any increase in price will have on customers and RL's competitive position. It seems unlikely that customers will accept a 25% increase in price, which is what the calculations are suggesting should be the case.

A change to an ABC system may be warranted as an ABC system would provide valuable extra costing data particularly on product costs and prices that could assist in profitability. However, ABC systems can be time consuming, in terms of collecting the volume of data needed and the systems needed to support this. So a cost-benefit analysis would need to be done between the additional costs of putting in such a system and the extra value of the data produced.

(b)   **Objectives** – An organisation's objectives are the operational goals it is trying to achieve. For example, RL could set a financial objective to increase operating profit by 5% in the next year, or it could set an objective of ensuring that its market share remains constant over the next year.

Equally, one of RL's objectives could be to ensure that it keeps pace with technological developments, and incorporates these into its laptops in order to maintain their reputation for quality.

Critical success factors – Once RL has established its objectives, it needs to identify the key factors and processes which will enable it to achieve them – its critical success factors (CSFs). In effect, the CSFs are the building blocks which will enable RL to be successful in the future.

Although the prices RL charges for its laptops are likely to affect the quantity it sells and the profits it makes, the factors which will determine its future success extend across all aspects of its operations, not simply pricing and costing. For example, innovation in product design could be important in improving the durability of RL's laptops in rough conditions.

This also highlights that performance measures need to reflect what matters to RL's customers, because to be successful RL needs to perform well in those activities which matter most to its customers – for example, meeting the individual specifications required by each customer.

Key Performance Indicators – Once RL has identified what its CSFs are, it also needs to know whether it is achieving them. This is done by using KPIs, which measure how well it is performing against its CSFs. In effect, RL's CSFs will indicate what it needs to do to be successful, and its KPIs are the means of measuring whether these CSFs are being achieved or not.

For example, RL could select the number of repeat orders it receives as a measure of how well it is meeting customer requirements. If its computers don't survive rough handling, and don't meet the customers' requirements, it is unlikely the customer will make future orders from it.

Importance of non-financial information – Although, ultimately, RL's performance will be measured in terms of its financial results, financial performance indicators typically *measure* success, rather than helping to *ensure* it. By contrast, many of the factors which ensure success (the CSFs) will be non-financial in nature – such as quality, or flexibility in meeting customer specifications. If these variables are important elements in RL achieving its strategy successfully, then it follows that the company should also measure its performance in relation to them.

Although the CEO has not specifically mentioned the idea of introducing a multi-dimensional performance measurement system (such as a balanced scorecard), such a system would highlight the linkages between non-financial and financial performance in the way he is suggesting.

56 SFS

Chapter references. Activity-based management is discussed in Chapter 15 of the BPP Study Text. Japanese business practices and management accounting techniques, including target costing and kaizen costing, are discussed in Chapter 13.

Top tips. In **part (a)** start by comparing the recharges using the two methods and what the differences are. Think about how the increase or decrease would affect decisions on whether to continue with the jobs, design issues and whether margins could be preserved.

Parts (b)(i) to (iii) are more tricky as they want you to relate what you know about ABM and ABC to the decisions made at different levels of the organisation. Implicit value refers to the non-financial value of an activity such as reputation.

Part (c). A sensible way to approach this question would be to think what the aims of Target Costing and Kaizen Costing are, and then think how SFA could use them to improve its future performance (in effect, by reducing its costs).

Examining team's comments. Overall answers were mixed. Many candidates seemed unprepared for (a) despite comparisons between costing methods and performance measurement being fundamental in this paper. Better answers showed how different answers can be arrived at using the two methods and how there were cost implications for instance in the design of products using the two methods.

Part (b) saw a wide spread of marks. Better candidates related the general definitions of operational and strategic ABM to the company.

(a) **Compare cost figures for two jobs**

Under the current costing system, Job 973 is charged $1,172 which implies 9.77 direct labour hours are spent on this job. Job 974 receives a lower charge of $620 or 5.17 direct labour hours. The ABC system building up a recharge based on activity areas results in a higher recharge to Job 973 of $1,612, or a 38% increase but a lower recharge to Job 974 of $588.89, or a 5% decrease. Assuming the data for the activity is accurate, and these are representative jobs, then this shows previous recharges may have considerably over or underestimated the true activity and therefore costs involved in manufacturing jobs.

Often it is found when activity-based costing is implemented that low-volume products see an increase in reported costs (because it is no longer based on direct labour hours) whilst high-volume products see a decrease. The reasons for the differences arise from the underlying processes or activities that comprise the manufacture. Each job consumes differing amounts of the five activity areas. Clearly direct labour hours may have once been a suitable measure but the five activity areas identified reveal a lot more goes into the manufacture than man hours and this should be a broader measure of actual resources consumed in manufacture.

However this is only a starting point. The managers responsible for the jobs will have to look at the resources consumed (the activity areas) and decide whether the jobs are worth continuing, whether they may need to negotiate costs with the departments making the recharges or indeed whether they need to increase their own recharges or prices charged to maintain margins. However this may affect customer demand too.

The manager responsible for Job 973 would probably prefer to retain direct labour hours but this may not be possible as the organisation is going over to ABC recharges. Product design is also a consideration where at the design stage consideration can be given to the processes going into the manufacture for instance the number of components required or number of cuts needed in the process. The data available from the ABC system is more detailed and credible than just using labour hours for product design purposes.

(b) **Explain the risks attaching to the use of ABM**

ABM sees the business as a set of linked activities which ultimately add value to the customer. The business should be managed based on the activities that make it up.

Operational ABM is using ABC to identify activities which add value to products and those which don't. It takes decisions at the operational level. The latter activities should be reduced. Products and services that take up more activity time than others should be reviewed with the aim of reducing the time required. Operational ABM is about 'doing things right'.

Strategic ABM uses ABC information at a strategic level using it to decide on which products to develop and which activities to use. It looks at profitability analysis deciding on which products or customers are the most profitable. Strategic ABM is about 'doing the right things'.

The implicit value of an activity refers to the value in the product not necessarily captured by financial analysis. It can be quality of service or a particular design feature. If this is reduced as an outcome of an ABC review customers may see a fall in value and stop buying the service.

ABM can lead to bad decisions where it doesn't show the complete context of a decision. For instance, operational ABM will not capture quality issues such as pleasant service. Strategic ABM will not identify intangibles that could be important in making decisions on products and activities.

(c) **Target costing**

Target costing is a costing system that can be used when a company (such as SFA) is unable to dictate a selling price and is forced to accept the prevailing market selling price for a product.

After the specification of the product is completed, SFA will determine the price that the market is prepared to pay for the product (this may be by considering similar products already available or by carrying out market research). SFA then would subtract a target profit from the selling price to determine its cost target. If the expected cost of the product already meets the target cost over its lifecycle, including any expected cost reductions, then production can commence. If the expected cost exceeds the target cost then major changes are introduced to reduce costs so that the target cost is achieved. If SFA cannot achieve the target cost then the product will be abandoned.

Kaizen costing

Kaizen costing has been used by some Japanese firms for over twenty years and is now widely used in the electronics and automobile industries. 'Kaizen' translates as continuous improvement.

Functional analysis is applied at the design stage of a new product, and a target cost for each function is set.

The functional target costs are added together and the total becomes the product target cost. Once the product has been in production for a year, the actual cost of the first year becomes the starting point for further cost reduction. It is this process of continuous improvement, encouraging constant reductions by tightening the 'standards', that is known as kaizen costing.

SFA could apply Kaizen costing as follows. The previous year's actual production cost serves as the cost base for the current year's production cost. A reduction rate and a reduction amount are set. Actual performance is compared to the Kaizen goals throughout the year and variances are monitored. At the end of the current year, the current actual cost becomes the cost base for the next year. New (lower) Kaizen goals are set and the whole process starts again.

Differences

One of the main differences between the two methods is that target costing is applied before production commences, but Kaizen costing is applied after production has started.

Another difference is that target costing requires significant changes to be made, but Kaizen costing involves making a number of small improvements to the whole process as part of continuous improvement.

57 LOL cards

Text reference. Value based management is discussed in Chapter 15 of the BPP Study Text.

Top tips. In **part (a)** you need to explain what value based management (VBM) is and how it focuses on shareholder wealth maximisation. You need to explain what performance measure is used in a VBM approach and how it is set throughout the organisation.

In **part (b)** you need to use the EVA calculation to make calculations and critically compare these with other measures of shareholder performance.

Part (c) requires an evaluation so be critical of the merits and drawbacks of EVA and the other measures you refer to. Remember to state any assumptions you make as you are using a model.

Part (d). A useful approach to this question might be to compare and contrast traditional approaches to cost containment with activity based management and cost reduction. There is no requirement to link this part of the question to the scenario, so it should just be a test of knowledge.

		Marks
(a)	Up to 2 marks on the explanation of VBM and then up to 2 marks on how it aids focus in the management process (Maximum 4)	4
(b)	Workings: NOPAT 1 Capital employed 1 Cost of capital 1 EVA™ 1 Assumptions 0·5 each up to a maximum of 1·5 EPS 1 Share price 3 x 0·5 Comments: 1 mark per reasonable point up to 2 on EPS and share price and 2 on EVA. Total 12	12
(c)	1 mark for each relevant point made up to a maximum of 3.	3
(d)	1 mark for each relevant point made up to a maximum of 6.	6
	Total = 25	

(a) **What value-based management (VBM) involves and how it can focus the company on shareholder interests**

The VBM approach starts with the primary objective of the business as shareholder wealth maximisation and develops a performance approach based on this. At the strategic level the primary measure of performance is economic value added (EVA) because this EVA is equivalent to discounted cash flow in the long term which is a widely used method of valuing shares by equity analysts.

EVA is used as the sole measure of performance by management and even throughout the organisation (at strategic, tactical and operational levels) thereby avoiding the conflict between multiple objectives and resulting measures. The variables within EVA that drive performance such as PBIT can be used by management to achieve value-based targets set down from the strategic value-based goal.

(b) **An assessment of the financial performance of LOL using EVA. Evaluate this against EPS and share price performance**

EPS has fallen by 23.4% (21.88 in 20X9 ($35m/$160m) compared with 16.75% in 20Y0 ($26.8m/$160m)) which suggests the company is not favoured by investors but the average share price has only fallen from $12.20 to $10.70 over the same period which doesn't suggest the company is out of favour as much. Indeed this is against a sector fall of 26% (907.1/1,225.6) over the same period and a main market index decline of 34.9% (1,448.90/2,225.40) thus inferring LOL has actually outperformed its sector and the main market.

The sector comparison is more relevant to LOL's performance as this includes only comparative companies. The view of the market that LOL is outperforming its sector is confirmed by the calculation of EVA. This remains positive at $22.6m in 20Y0 compared with $29.6m in 20X9. Calculations are in Appendix 1. Thus LOL continues to create value for shareholders even in difficult conditions.

(c) **Evaluate VBM against traditional profit based measures of performance**

Value measures take into account capital employed and the cost of capital and are therefore considered superior to profit measures which capture these less clearly. They are adjusted to take out accounting adjustments so they arrive at cash flow measures which are less affected by accounting adjustments. In the case of LOL the accounting and economic depreciation are assumed to be the same but may differ if additional information becomes available).

However EVA and other value-based measures are complex and unfamiliar to calculate and so may be off-putting to management used to profit measures. They also contain assumptions on CAPM (used to calculate the cost of capital) and data is historic and so may change in the future. For instance share values are calculated based on dividend flows in the future. However provided users are aware of the assumptions and become familiar with the process of calculating EVA it could be a useful measure.

EVA can be manipulated by choosing projects with low set up costs to massage the initial EVA figure which then falls in later years. It also fails to recognise the increase in shareholder wealth over the life of the project better captured by the use of net present value.

(d) **Traditional cost allocation systems**

Traditional costing systems, notably **absorption costing,** assume that all products **consume resources in proportion to their production volumes**. While this may be true for overheads such as power costs, it does not necessarily hold for all overheads, especially those connected with support services.

The amount of **overhead allocated** to individual products by absorption costing therefore bears **very little resemblance** to the **amount of overhead actually incurred** by the products and hence gives management **minimal understanding of the behaviour of overhead costs.** Consequently management also only have a limited ability to control/reduce overhead costs.

ABC/ABM approach

Activity based costing (ABC) attempts to overcome this problem by identifying the activities or transactions (**cost drivers**) which underlie an organisation's activities and which cause the incidence of the activity, and hence the cost of the activity (overheads) to increase. Costs can then be attributed to products according to the number of cost drivers they cause/consume using cost driver rates.

Activity based management (ABM) is the term given to those **management processes that use the information provided by an activity-based cost analysis to improve organisational profitability.**

ABM and cost reduction

Because ABM analyses costs on the basis of what causes them, rather than on the basis of type of expense/cost centre, it provides management with vital information on why costs are being incurred. If management can **reduce the incidence of the cost driver, they can reduce the associated cost.**

ABM involves a variety of **cost reduction techniques**.

(a) Ensuring activities are performed as efficiently as possible.
(b) Reducing or eliminating the need to perform activities that do not add value for customers.
(c) Improving the design of products.
(d) Developing better relationships with customers and suppliers.

In short, it aims to ensure that customer needs are met while fewer demands are made on organisational resources.

Appendix 1

(W1)
EVA calculations for the periods given are:

	20X9	20Y0
	$m	$m
Profit after interest and tax	35.0	26.8
Interest (net of tax at 25%)	3.0	5.9
Net operating profit after tax (NOPAT)	38.0	32.6
Capital employed (at year start)	99.2	104.1

Assumptions:

Economic and accounting depreciation are equivalent.

There are no non-cash expenses to adjust in the profit figure.

There are no operating leases to be capitalised.

There are no additional adjustments to make regarding goodwill.

Cost of capital

WACC = (%e × Ke) + (%d × Kd)

20X9	(50% × 12.7%) + (50% × 4.2%)	=	8.45%
20Y0	(50% × 15.3%) + (50% × 3.9%)	=	9.60%

EVA = NOPAT – (Capital employed × WACC)

20X9	38.0 – (99.2 × 8.45%)	=	29.6
20Y0	32.6 – (104.1 × 9.6%)	=	22.6

58 BEG

Chapter references. The performance pyramid is discussed in Chapter 15 of the BPP Study Text.

Top tips. In **part (a)** you are asked to comment on cost targets relating these to quality (the application for platinum status) and the four categories of quality cost.

Part (b)(i) to (iii) looks at the performance pyramid model which relates strategic management to daily operations. The three headings are taken from the pyramid and data for each can be found in the appendix.

Part (c) then looks at the benefits of the performance pyramid as a performance measurement model. However, don't just discuss the model in theoretical terms; make sure you link it back to the scenario. The references in the scenario are clear signposts to the different aspects of the pyramid, so make use of these in your answer.

Examining team's comments. Some candidates misread the question as being about target costing rather than the use of target costs to achieve the quality standard. Good answers showed that candidates were aware the numbers were forecasts and not historical basing their analyses on future activity. There was little awareness of how the cost categories affected each other, for instance the effect of spending on conformance costs, on non-conformance costs. In part (b), stronger candidates linked their analyses to the general headings whereas weaker candidates merely provided an analysis of trends without linking these to the headings and business objectives.

(a)   **Cost targets and platinum status**

BEG are aiming for platinum status and have been advised to focus on effectiveness in their services. This refers to operations meeting any objectives set. One way of measuring whether objectives have been achieved is through **quantitative measures** such as costs.

The managing director has asked for an analysis of **manufacturing cost targets** and **quality costs.** Cost targets have advantages in that they can be compared with competitors using benchmarking which then enables targets to be set based on market leaders. This does require the cost measures to be comparable or else like with like is not being measured. They can also be used as an internal comparative to monitor performance year on year and set stretch targets against which current profitability and hence return on investment is measured. The outcome of the comparison is that a gap may exist and BEG will need to act to close this gap.

The statement shows variable costs increasing 25% ($8.4m to $10.5m) from 20X1 to 20X2 and another 20% to 20X3 ($12.6m). Sales revenues are projected to increase by 50% over the total period from $24m to $36m so variable costs as a percentage of sales have remained stable at 35% and the increase here is down to volume. Fixed manufacturing costs are expected to increase 13% year on year to 20X2 and remain static at $3.4m thereafter.

Costs of quality are made up of **conformance costs (prevention costs and appraisal costs)** and **non-conformance costs (internal and external failure costs).** Internal and external failure costs are the difference or gap between current expected cost levels and cost targets regarding the application for platinum status for quality. **Internal failure costs** arise before the goods or services pass to the customer and are a failure to meet design quality standards. They include manufacturing flaws and incorrect processing of orders. **External failure costs** arise after sale and include warranty claims and costs of rectification. These can be compared to the manufacturing cost target in each year as a means of setting a projection. Internal failure costs are expected to fall from 21.9% (2,500/(8,400 + 3,000))of the cost target to 7.5% from 20X1 to 20X3. External failure costs are expected to decline from 27.2% of cost target to 6.1% from 20X1 to 20X3.

In a traditional manufacturing approach to quality, management spend more on conformance costs to reduce non-conformance costs but as costs of conformance are high, especially to secure zero defects, there is an acceptable level of defects. However in a **TQM system**, management would aim for zero defects and spend on conformance costs to reduce total quality costs over time. The emphasis is on getting things right first time and designing in quality.

BEG is projecting a decrease in all categories of quality cost over the three years which suggests a TQM approach is being taken. Prevention costs are the costs of management acting to achieve quality standards before and during manufacture and include the costs of training sales staff taking customer enquiries. These are predicted to fall by 50% in the first year from $4.2m to $1.32m by 20X3. Appraisal costs are incurred when ensuring compliance with quality standards and performance testing. These are projected to decrease by 12% from 20X1 to 20X2 and remain static to 20X3. These projections are quite ambitious and come on top of a reputation established for high quality. It would be useful for BEG to obtain some data on costs of quality from the competition in the hotel and catering industry to get a benchmark for what reasonable costs of quality are.

(b)   **Forecast performance of BEG**

The headings come from the performance pyramid a model that links the overall strategic view of management with day to day operations. The application for platinum status may be measured in financial and marketing terms.

(i)   **Financial performance and marketing**

BEG is aiming for an increase in sales of 50% to $36m from 20X1 to 20X3. This is allied to an overall fall in costs from $22m to $20.2m in the same period which can be attributed to the fall in costs of quality seen in the statement produced by the management accountant. The net margin has gone up from $2m or 8.33% to $15.8m or 43.89% over the three years but this large increase is due to the two trends just mentioned and is from a small base of $2m. The sales target is ambitious and may be unrealistic in a market with a number of significant competitors.

A less ambitious target of 8% rising to 11% is predicted for market share although the basis for this calculation is not stated especially as this is a new market for BEG. Presumably the data for the market share calculation and that of growth in the market from $300m to $340m is based on the market research analysis. Nonetheless the market does have a number of significant competitors although there is no quantification of their market shares such as a BCG analysis would illustrate.

(ii)   **External effectiveness**

This is measured through **customer satisfaction** for example. There are four measures that capture how satisfied customers are through measuring the quality of services provided and delivery. The external effectiveness of the business relies on all stages of the business cycle from design through to delivery and involving quality.

The first of the measures is the percentage of products accepted as meeting design **quality standards** without rectification. This appears to refer to the Institute's verification and it is predicted to rise from 92% to 99% over the three years to 20X3. This high quality standard aligns with the fall in the costs of quality suggesting a TQM approach to manufacture. Allied to this is a measure showing a fall in rectification claims from $0.96m to $0.1m over the period and another showing the cost of rectifying goods sold after sales decreasing from $1.8m to $0.8m.

These reveal that the business intends to build in quality before sale rather than relying on repairing goods sold (external failure costs).

Finally, a measure of sale service is projected to rise from 88.5% of sales meeting delivery dates to 99.5% doing so over the three years.

All of these measures are ambitious especially the first and last where the percentages are near 100% perfection. It would be useful to have comparatives in the industry if this data is available. Nonetheless these targets suggest a quality-led approach to manufacture which may be achieved by setting stretch targets.

(iii) **Internal efficiency**

This is captured through measures such as **productivity** and **flexibility**.

Productivity is the management of resources whilst flexibility is the responsiveness of the business as a whole. The average time from customer enquiry to product delivery is a measure of flexibility and is projected to fall from 49 days in 20X1 to 40 days in 20X3. This has added cashflow benefits as inventory is being converted to receivables and cash faster. A non-conversion rate of enquiries to sales (%) is planned to fall from 10.5% of all enquiries to 3% over the three years. The idle time measure and this measure are both productivity indicators and measures of waste. They also relate to costs of conformance preventing failure before it arises.

The final measure in this part is idle capacity of manufacturing staff which is also projected to fall, from 12% (which seems high) to 1.5%. However, this may mean that if any unanticipated changes in production arise the company may not be flexible enough to absorb these and may have to bring in outworkers. It would be a good idea to obtain comparable data on competitors if possible.

We don't know the precise standards required to obtain platinum status. Nonetheless, BEG is clearly setting ambitious targets for improvements in performance during the three years reviewed.

(c) **Performance pyramid**

The marketing director has stressed that BEG needs to focus on increasing the effectiveness of all operations as part of its application for platinum status.

The performance pyramid should encourage it to do this because it focuses on a range of objectives looking at both **external effectiveness** and **internal efficiency**. Of the areas which the directors mentions, product design will be addressed through looking at internal efficiency, while after sales services is likely to be addressed through looking at external effectiveness, specifically in relation to customer satisfaction.

Operational criteria – The statistics which are relevant for the Platinum Status application correspond to the operational criteria in the pyramid, which are: **quality, product delivery, process time** and **waste**. For example, the cost of rectification claims could be a reflection of quality; the percentage of sales meeting planned delivery dates will reflect the effectiveness of BEG's product delivery; while the idle capacity of staff is an indicator of waste.

Importance of processes – Using the pyramid will also highlight the importance of understanding the processes which drive BEG's costs and financial performance, rather than simply looking at costs and sales figures. However, the pyramid also highlights that BEG's business level strategies and day-to-day operations need to come together to enable it to achieve its financial objectives, such as increase sales by 50% over two years.

Developing strategies – The pyramid also highlights the way that different levels within an organisation support each other and relate to each other. BEG appears to have some fairly ambitious performance targets in relation to its application, and so it will be important that it develops a coherent set of objectives and performance measures across the organisation which will give it the best chance of being able to achieve those targets.

59 Turing

Text reference. Risk appetite and the different methods which can be used for decision-making under uncertainty are covered in Chapter 6 of the BPP Study Text. The issues involved in managing performance in joint ventures are discussed in Chapter 16.

Top tips.

Part (a). For each of the firms, you need to assess the risk appetite and then recommend a method of decision-making under uncertainty which is appropriate for that risk appetite.

The reference to 'uncertainty' was very important here, because it indicated that you should use techniques such as maximax and maximin, rather than expected values.

Note also that the requirement s to recommend an appropriate method for each firm. Therefore, you must make a clear recommendation, rather than evaluating the advantages and disadvantages of possible different methods for each firm. You will need to evaluate the appropriateness of different methods in order to decide which method is most suitable for each firm, but the final answer itself needs to be a recommendation.

When evaluating the method more appropriate for Riemann, a key point to note is the business' need to achieve a guaranteed minimum level of return, in order to aid the survival of the business. As such, this means that maximin should be chosen as the appropriate method, rather than minimax regret. However, the examining team indicated that students would be given some credit for suggesting minimax regret, because it is a risk averse solution (and therefore fits Riemann's risk appetite). However, minimax regret is not as clearly focused on obtaining a minimum level of return.

Part (b). Having identified in part (a) which method each firm would use, you now have to apply the methods in order to determine which turbine each one would choose to build.

The calculations in this part of the question should have been relatively relatively, and the marking guide indicates that you could have scored marks in part (b) for correct calculations of minimax reqret, even though it was not one of the methods which should have been recommended in part (a) – which were maximax and maximin.

Part (c). Parts (a) and (b) should have clearly identified one of the major problems facing the joint venture: that the different circumstances and risk appetites of the two venture partners is going to make it difficult for them to agree on strategic decisions. In this case, how do they decide which turbines to build, since Turing will want to build the 8 MW design, and Riemann will want to build the 3 MW design?

More generally, answering part (a) should also have helped you identify that the two firms are likely to have different cultures and management styles – which again could make it difficult for them to work together to manage the joint venture.

Examining team's comments. Part (a) of the question was generally well answered, and it was pleasing to note that most candidates understood that decision-making 'under uncertainty' is different from 'under risk' or else, they realised that the lack of information on probabilities meant that expected values were not appropriate here.

However, candidates should note that their answer needed to contain a single recommendation of the method for each firm to use, not a list of the available ones.

Part (b) was also well answered with many candidates scoring full marks. However, one point for future candidates to note is that the companies cannot choose to produce a certain number of units, as this is the uncertain factor. Therefore, conclusions such as 'Turing should make 2,000 units of the 8 MW in order to gain a profit of $13,300m' are misleading. Given the uncertainty inherent in the scenario, the appropriate conclusion here would be 'Turing should choose to make the 8 MW turbine, because this offers the highest potential maximum profit.'

Marks

(a) Turing

Assessment of risk appetite – 1 mark per relevant point up to a maximum of 3 marks

Method of decision-making – 1 mark for selecting an appropriate method (maximax); 1 mark for describing the method

Riemann

Assessment of risk appetite – 1 mak per relevant point up to a maximum of 3 marks

Method of decision-making – 1 mark for selecting an appropriate method (maximin); 1 mark for describing the method

Total for part (a): up to 9

9

(b) Calculations:

Variable costs – 2 marks

Total costs – 1 mark

Revenue – 2 marks

Profit – 1 mark

Maximax result – 1 mark

Maximin result – 1 mark

Conclusion – 1 mark

Total for part (b): up to 8

8

(c) For each relevant point (linked to the scenario) about potential problems in managing the joint venture – 1 mark

Potential points include: differences in goals and choice of performance measures between the venture partners; different risk appetites; differing time horizons for achieving results; deadlock in decision-making; different management styles, and cultural differences between the venture partners; information sharing; intellectual property.

Total for part (c): up to 8

8

Total = 25

(a) **Turing**

Risk appetite

The appetite for risk at Turing will be determined by the three venture capital firms (VCs), who collectively own 90% of the company.

Each of the VCs hold a large portfolio of investments, and are prepared for some of these to fail provided that others show large gains. As such, the VCs are **risk seekers**.

The other key stakeholders at Turing are the management team, who own the remaining 10% of the company. The fact the management have been given an equity stake in the business, coupled with their ambition and their enjoyment of the challenges of introducing new products, suggest that they will be comfortable with the high-risk approach taken by the VCs.

Turing's management are also likely to be attracted to projects which are innovative, such as the 8 MW unit. They enjoy the challenges of introducing new products, and are likely to be motivated by the prospect of developing a world-leading unit.

Method of decision-making

Maximax – The fact that both of Turing's key stakeholder groups (the VCs, and management) are prepared to accept high-risk approaches suggests that Turing will be a risk seeker. As such, the appropriate method of decision-making under certainty for it will be maximax.

Using the maximax approach, the design choice selected will be the one which offers the highest maximum profit possible, across any of the three demand scenarios.

Riemann

Risk appetite

The risk appetite at Riemann is likely to be determined largely by its investors – particularly as it has recently had to seek emergency refinancing.

Riemann's shareholders are concerned about the survival of the business, and its debt providers will also be concerned about its survival – and therefore its ability to repay any loans.

Riemann's management are also primarily concerned with the survival of the business. Although do not own any shares in the company, they will lose their jobs if the company collapses.

The fact that Riemann's shareholders and management both view TandR as a way to generate additional cash flow reinforces the fact that their primary concern is with identifying initiatives which can help secure the survival of the business.

The precarious nature of Riemann's current position suggests that all of its key stakeholders will be **risk averse**.

Equally, they are likely to favour projects which will start generating income soon. As such, the 8 MW unit – which takes two years longer to develop than the others – may be less attractive to Riemann, than the two units which can be developed more quickly.

Method of decision making

Maximin – Riemann's focus on the survival of the business means that a maximin approach to decision-making under uncertainty will be appropriate for it.

Using the maximin approach, the design selected will be the one which maximises the lowest profit which could be achieved across the three demand scenarios.

(b)   **Turbine design types**

Demand		1,000	1,500	2,000
Revenue		$m	$m	$m
8 MW	$20.8 per unit	20,800	31,200	41,600
3 MW	$9.6 per unit	9,600	14,400	19,200
1 MW	$4.6 per unit	4,600	6,900	9,200
Variable cost				
8 MW	$10.4 per unit	10,400	15,600	20,800
3 MW	$4.8 per unit	4,800	7,200	9,600
1 MW	$1.15 per unit	1,150	1,725	2,300

Fixed cost

8 MW	7,500	7,500	7,500
3 MW	820	820	820
1 MW	360	360	360

Profit				Max payoff	Min payoff
8 MW	2,900	8,100	13,300	**13,300**	2,900
3 MW	3,980	6,380	8,780	8,780	**3,980**
1 MW	3,090	4,815	6,540	6,540	3,090

Maximax = $13,300 earned by the 8 MW units

Maximan = $3,980 earned by the 3 MW units

Due to the differences in their preferred methods of decision-making under uncertainty, Turing and Riemann would choose to build different turbine design types. Riemann would choose to build the 8 MW units, while Riemann would choose to build the 3 MW units.

(c) **Problems of managing performance in a joint venture**

Decision-making – As we have seen in part (b), one of the main problems in a joint venture will be that of reaching a consensus between the venture partners when making strategic decisions.

This could be a particular problem for Tand R, given that both partners own 50% of the venture, and so it is difficult to prioritise the interests of one partner over those of the other.

Goals and objectives – As well as their differences in attitude to risk, it also appears that the venture partners have different goals and objectives for the venture. In this case, Riemann's primary goal from the venture is to generate additional cash flow in the short term. However, Turing appears to be more interested in the potential long-term returns which can be earned from designing and manufacturing the turbines. As such, it could be difficult for the venture partners to agree what TandR's goals and objectives should be.

Similarly, the venture partners could have different interests in relation to the performance measures they consider to be most important. Although Tand R could measure a variety of different indicators – including profit, growth and cash flows – Riemann is likely to prioritise cash flow measures and short-term performance indicators, while Turing is more likely to be interested in the growth and the longer-term prospects of the business, for example.

Management styles – In the same way that Turing and Riemann have different attitudes to risk, it is also likely that they will have different management styles and organisational cultures. This could cause problems at an operational level at TandR, since it is run by a group of managers from each of the JV partners – and therefore who may adopt different management styles.

Sharing capabilities and information – One of the problems, in general, with joint ventures is that they require the venture partners to share information, capabilities and intellectual property with each other. However, many of these elements may be commercially sensitive, and so the venture partners will be reluctant to share too much information about their own business with each other.

In this respect, establishing a climate of trust between the venture partners is likely to be important for the success of the JV. However, if the venture partners have very different cultures and management styles – as Turing and Riemann seem likely to – this trust could be harder to achieve.

Valuing the contribution of the venture partners – Another issue which arises from sharing information and capabilities relates to how the value of the different partners can be valued. It is likely that Turing's blade design skills will be a significant advantage for the venture, for example. However, it is likely to be difficult to measure the contribution that intangible assets (such as skills and competences) make to the venture in their own right.

Nonetheless, given that both partners hold a 50% stake in the venture, if one of them thinks they are contributing significantly more value to the venture than the other, this could quickly become a source of disagreement between the partners.

60 Callisto

Text reference. Performance management in complex business structures is discussed in Chapter 16 of the BPP Study Text. Management reports and the problem of information overload are discussed in Chapter 8.

Top tips.

Part (a). Note that the requirement distinguishes between performance **measurement** and performance **management** issues. Accordingly, you need to consider both in your answer.

Note also that the requirement highlights that Callisto deals with two different types of external partner: individual workers (employees working remotely) and strategic partners (which are multinational companies). The issues Callisto faces in managing the performance of a multinational company are likely to be very different to those involved in managing an individual worker.

Part (b). The key problem with George's report appears to be information overload, so in the first part of your answer you need to consider how this will affect the usefulness of the report.

In effect, in the second part you then need to suggest ways to reduce the amount of figures and data being presented on the report. However, note the requirement is asking about the output of the report – essentially its presentation – so make sure you focus on this, rather than suggesting amendments to the underlying aspects of performance being measured, or the frequency of the report. There may be problems with these too, but you are not asked to comment on them, so you should not spend time doing so.

Examining team's comment. Although part (a) was presented as a single requirement, candidates were correct to split it into areas such as the general impact of such a complex structure on the business as a whole, and then the impact on employee management and strategic partner management. However, the key to scoring well was making points which were relevant for Callisto – related to the difficulties of measuring and managing home-working employees and strategic outsourcing partners.

Marking scheme

			Marks
(a)	Up to 2 marks per relevant point relating to performance measurement –		
	Relevant points include (but are not limited to): Geographical distance; reliance on IT; difference between employees and strategic partners; technology solutions; use of service level agreements	Up to 9	
	1 mark per relevant point relating to performance management Employees – up to 4 marks Strategic partners up to 6 marks		
	Maximum marks relating to performance management	Up to 8	17
(b)	Evaluation of proposed report and issues of potential information overload – 1 mark per relevant point – Up to 5 Suggested ways of improving presentation – 1 mark per point – Up to 5 (**Note**. Improvements should only relate to the presentation of the report)		
	Total for part (b) – Up to 8 marks		8
			Total = 25

(a)   **Performance measurement issues**

Data collection – The main difficulties in performance measurement at Callisto are likely to arise from the fact that its employees do not work 'on site,' and also a number of key business functions have been outsourced. As a result, before it can begin to measure their performance, Callisto first has to collect the necessary performance data for its remote workers and outsource partners.

IT systems – Callisto needs to rely on information technology for collecting and handling data from its partners and remote workers. As far as possible, this data should be collected and monitored automatically, for example making use of electronic data interchange.

Given the likely number of remote workers and partners that Callisto uses, it is likely that it will need a large database for storing this performance information.

However, in order for the database to be automatically updated (with inputs from remote staff and suppliers), Callisto will need the systems which staff and suppliers use to be compatible with its system.

While Callisto can control the systems its employees use, it seems unlikely that it will be able to exert much, if any, influence over the systems its strategic partners (which are multinational companies) use.

Measuring employees' performance – Callisto's employees log in to its own systems via the internet. In this way, although the employees are not physically in the premises, Callisto is still able monitor aspects of their performance. For example, monitoring the number of hours employees are logged into the system gives an indication of the number of hours they have worked.

However, it is harder for Callisto to monitor the work the remote employees have actually done; for example, the number of videos they have edited, or the number of customer complaints they have resolved satisfactorily.

In this respect, it is important for Callisto to define its outputs clearly: for example, it should define the various steps which need to be completed for a video edit to be complete. If outputs are not defined in this way, there is scope for disputes between staff and managers about the amount of work they have done; for example, with staff claiming to have completed the editing on more videos than they actually have.

Strategic partners – Whereas Callisto's employees log on to its own systems, the strategic partners, such as RLR, will have their own systems. Therefore they will continue to use their systems rather than using Callisto's systems.

System reconciliations – As a result, there can be **discrepancies** between Callisto's systems and RLR's systems. Therefore, an added complication in the performance measurement process is that, before RLR's performance can be measured against the key SLAs, Callisto will first have to reconcile its inventory records with RLR's.

Lack of control – Without having any agreement over the figures, Callisto will not be able to enforce the SLAs. The disagreements with RLR illustrate this. For example, if an item is despatched late, it will be difficult for Callisto to prove that RLR has broken the service level agreement, if RLR argues that the item was not actually in stock when an order was placed, so that it couldn't be expected to despatch that item within three working days from when the order was placed.

The difficulty which Callisto faces is establishing whether RLR is responsible for the delay, or whether the product suppliers are responsible.

SLAs as controls – This lack of control over the SLAs is likely to be a significant problem for Callisto, because the SLAs represent its key control over the relationship with its strategic partners.

A potential solution would be for the partners to agree a standard reporting format for all data relating to the SLAs. This would then remove the need for the reconciliations Callisto currently has to carry out.

Performance management issues

Employee management – Because Callisto's employees work from home rather than at company premises, the brothers cannot monitor what the employees are doing in the same way as they could if everyone was working in the same place. For example, Jeff and George cannot monitor what hours their staff are working, or how productive they are being.

Equally, because Jeff and George have no direct contact with their staff, it is difficult for them to judge how motivated the staff are.

Reward schemes – Because the brothers cannot directly monitor or control how productive their employees are being, they need to ensure Callisto's reward scheme is designed such that it encourages productivity and motivation. One way to do this, would be link the reward scheme directly to achieving agreed outputs and targets for each employee.

Managing strategic partners

Reliance on partners – A key issue Callisto faces is that it is reliant on external partners (such as RLR Logistics) for the successful day-to-day operation of its business. The nature of Callisto's business structure means that some of the functions of which have been outsourced are business critical.

For example, if RLR decides not to renew its contract (when it is due for renewal in two months time) this could create major problems for Callisto. Equally, the reliability of partners such as RLR is vital, because Callisto's customer service reputation will be damaged if products are delivered late.

However, there is a danger that Callisto's reliance on strategic partners in this way strengthens the strategic partners' bargaining power in any negotiations with Callisto (because it is unlikely that Callisto will be able to replace a strategic partner immediately if it stopped working for Callisto).

Relationship management – However, the success of the relationship between Callisto and its strategic partners is likely to depend on establishing an atmosphere of trust between the parties. Currently, it appears the trust between the partners is limited; meaning, for example, that Callisto feels it has to reconcile performance data between RLR's figures and its own. However, such reconciliations do not ultimately add any value for Callisto, so they are a wasteful activity. Therefore, if Callisto was able to trust RLR's figures, this would be beneficial because the detailed reconciliations would no longer be required.

Pricing – Another issue which will have to be managed is how the agreements between Callisto and its strategic partners can be arranged so that they are motivating and profitable for both parties. George has already acknowledged that Callisto operates on small profit margins, so it needs to secure sales growth and high volumes of business in order to be profitable.

However, Callisto is dependent on partners such as RLR to deliver a good quality service to its customers. If the customers don't receive this, then Callisto's reputation is likely to be suffer, which in turn will reduce its ability to achieve the sales growth it needs (either by retaining existing customers or acquiring new ones.)

So Callisto needs to negotiate contracts which motivate the strategic partners to deliver the high quality it needs, whilst at the same time not being prohibitively expensive for it. Therefore, Callisto needs to ensure that the contracts are motivating and profitable for both parties.

(b) **Content**

Information overload – Whilst having a daily report will mean that George has up-to-date and timely information, there is a danger that its frequency will actually lead to **information overload**. In practice, George may find he doesn't have time to look through a detailed report each day. We do not know how many employees work for Callisto, but its turnover ($120m per annum) suggests there are likely to be quite a large number of employees. Therefore, George's report is likely to contain a large amount of data for him to look at each day.

There is a also a danger that if George spends too much time looking at detailed, daily reports he may overlook more strategic issues in the business, or higher level trends in performance.

Control – It is not clear from the scenario whether the employees will be told that George is monitoring their productivity. However, if the employees know that George is monitoring their productivity on a daily basis, then this could prompt any are not currently working as hard as they could to work harder. It seems likely that this is what George hopes will happen.

Usefulness of information – However, it is debatable how useful some of the measures George has chosen will be. For example, simply monitoring the number of complaints employees deal with doesn't reflect how long or complicated each complaint was. Equally, although an employee may have been logged on to the network this doesn't necessarily mean they have been working all the time they have been logged on.

The frequency of the reports could also be a problem in itself. If the reports looked at the average number of complaints employees dealt with in a month, this might be a fairer reflection of their activity than looking at a single day at a time.

Equally, it is not clear whether all the employees are expected to carry out all the tasks being monitored. For example, some may specialise in editing videos, while others concentrate on dealing with customer queries and complaints. However, this could mean that the report shows a large number of zeros in the columns for work the employees do not attend to.

Possible improvements

Sorting – If employees do have separate roles, George may find it more useful to produce separate reports for each role; for example, producing one report for video editors, and a separate one for customer service employees.

However, there are more fundamental ways in which George could improve the reports.

Exception reports – Instead of showing the performance of all employees, the report would only show results which are unusual or require attention; in other words, where an employee's figures are particularly high or particularly low.

Summaries and drill down reports – Alternatively, instead of showing performance for individual employees, the report could show totals in the first instance; for example, totals for the number of customer complaints dealt with, or the number of video edited.

If George was concerned about any of the summary totals, he could then 'drill down' into the total figure, to find out why it was lower (or higher) than he expected.

Charts and graphs – However, perhaps the most significant change would be showing performance graphically, rather than as columns of figures.

In this way, George could see not only the actual daily figures, but could also place them in context – for example, by comparing them to a rolling average, or to a target.

By using charts or graphs, George would be able to see how performance is changing over time, which is something he would not be able to do from the proposed numerical report.

61 Coal Creek

Text reference. The importance of considering indicators of liquidity and gearing as well as profitability is discussed in Chapter 9 of the BPP Study Text. Models for predicting corporate failure are discussed in Chapter 17.

Top tips.

Part (a). It is important you recognise that the main focus of this requirement is on the value of using different **indicators** rather than on CCNH's **performance** as such. In other words, you need to discuss why monitoring liquidity and gearing (in conjunction with profitability) is important; rather than simply discussing CCNH's liquidity and gearing positions. For example, why would it be useful for CCNH to monitor its ability to pay its liabilities when they become due (rather than simply: What is CCNH's working capital position?)

Also, although you are asked to 'illustrate your answer with suitable calculations' this does not mean that your answer should just become, in effect, a sequence of different ratios. The calculations should be used to *support* your answer, rather than **becoming** your answer in their own right.

In relation to gearing – remember that are two aspects of gearing: financial gearing, and operational gearing. The requirement doesn't limit you to dealing with one aspect or the other, and therefore you should have considered both in your answer. In CCNH's case, the question of monitoring the level of fixed costs compared to variable costs (operational gearing) seems to be particularly important.

Part (b). There are two aspects to this part of the requirement: (i) explain a qualitative model; and (ii) apply that model to the scenario in order to comment on CCNH's position.

However, note that 'explaining' the model doesn't simply mean listing the headings in the model; you need to explain why the different elements of the model could be useful for predicting corporate failure.

A sensible approach to part (b) of this question would be to illustrate each aspect of the model (in Argenti's case: defects, mistakes, and symptoms of failure) by referring to weaknesses at CCNH. In this way, you will ensure you address both aspects of the requirement: to explain the model, and to comment on CCHN's position.

The marking guide indicates that there are up to five marks available for describing the qualitative model, but up to six marks for using it to identify weakness in CCNH's position. Therefore, as so often in P5, there are potentially more marks available for applying a model to the scenario than for explaining the model itself.

Technical article. In the P5 Technical Articles section of ACCA's website there is an article called '*Business Failure*' which discusses different failure prediction models. If you haven't already done so, you are strongly advised to read this article to supplement your knowledge of this area of the syllabus.

Part (c). The scenario identifies that HC's revenue had grown significantly in the last two years. This could give you a clue that HC is in the growth phase of its life cycle. By contrast, GC is a mature business – with little scope for growth, and operating in a sector which is fully supplied. What implications does this have for the CEO's plans? Although the question requirement refers to 'product portfolios' rather than any specific model, the product life cycle model could be useful framework to apply here; given that CCNH's two divisions appear to be at different stages of their life cycles. The BCG matrix could also be useful, although the scenario does not give any specific details about the relative market shares of SC and GC. (However, we do know that CCNH is one of the largest providers of residential care places in Geeland.)

Examining teams's comments. Candidates still appear not to be reading question requirements carefully enough, with the result that they are not answering the requirements actually set. In part (a) of this question, instead of explaining why liquidity and gearing were important alongside profitability, many candidates chose to review of the **performance of the company** in the scenario, leaving the reader to draw their own conclusions about the relative importance of liquidity, gearing and profitability.

Moreover, although many candidates successfully dealt with issues around financial gearing, only a few addressed the operational gearing in the business. It appeared that candidates failed to identify the cost structures (fixed / variable) within CCNH although this ought to be a basic point in the financial assessment of a business by a management accountant.

In part (b) few candidates demonstrated a clear understanding of the issues in using a qualitative model, and the Argenti model in particular. Only a minority could explain defects, mistakes made, and symptoms of failure. Although many students could quote the headings from the model, few could explain what they referred to. The wiser candidates tried to cover this shortcoming by illustrating each heading with an example from CCNH, and it was pleasing to see that candidates managed to score reasonably well in this part of the question by identifying the specific issues at CCNH.

Marks

(a) Explaining liquidity, financial gearing and operational gearing – up to a maximum of 4 marks

For illustrating the importance of considering liquidity at CCNH – up to 4 marks

For illustrating the importance of considering financial gearing at CCNH – up to 2 marks

For illustrating the importance of considering operational gearing at CCNH – up to 4 marks

Total for part (a): Up to 11 marks

11

(b) For describing qualitative models (such as Argenti's A score model) and including examples of possible failure indicators – up to 5 marks

For identifying weaknesses at CCNH – 1 mark per relevant weakness identified; up to a maximum of 6 marks

Possible weaknesses include: culture of fraud in previous management; lack of senior management; poor cash flow planning; over-trading at SC; weak financial ratios; and inability to pay landlords.

Total for part (b): Up to 9 marks

9

(c) For discussing life cycle stage and strategic position of SC and implications of this – up to 2

For discussing life cycle stage and strategic position of GC and implications of this – up to 2

For discussing the implications of CCNH's portfolio on any future strategy – up to 3 marks

Total for part (c): Up to 5 marks

5

Total = 25

(a) **Profit-based measures** – It appears that CCNH's current performance measures (operating profit margin; earnings per share) are primarily focused on the amount of profit the business is generating.

However, these measures have not identified the problems which CCNH is now facing, even though these problems could potentially threaten the overall survival of the business. Profit-based measures can often be insufficient to highlight issues relating to an **organisation's survival**, either in the long term or the short term.

Liquidity

Liquidity – CCNH's liquidity relates to the level of funds it has readily available in order to pay its liabilities as they become due; for example, having sufficient cash to pay its rents, or to pay other suppliers.

CCNH struggled to meet its most recent rental payment, which suggests that it has liquidity problems.

CCNH's Liquidity – At the end of the year just ended, CCNH's current assets were $64m, but its current liabilities were $104m. Therefore, its current ratio was 0.62. The fact that this ratio is significantly less than 1 helps explains why CCNH is having trouble making payments (such as its rental payments) when they are due. CCNH's current liabilities are significantly greater than the funds it has available to pay them.

Furthermore, at the end of the year, CCNH has no ready cash.

> As CCNH is a service company rather than a manufacturing company, it is unlikely to hold a significant level of inventory. Therefore, given that CCNH has no ready cash, it seems likely that the vast majority of CCNH's current assets are receivables.
>
> **Receivable days** – The significance of receivables suggests that receivable days should be a key performance measure for CCNH. If it can collect the amounts it is owed from residents as quickly as possible, this should help increase the amount of funds it has available to pay for its liabilities.
>
> Currently, however, it appears that there may be problems collecting the amounts owed to SC. SC's receivable days are 68 [(47/253) × 365], compared to only 9 for GC [(17/685) × 365].

Gearing – Whilst liquidity issues can often be a problem in the short term, looking at gearing can highlight potential issues in the **longer term**. In this respect, monitoring gearing helps an organisation **measure risk**.

Gearing indicates the level of an organisation's fixed regular liabilities compared to the cash generators which will enable the organisation to cover its liabilities.

Financial gearing

Financial gearing – Financial gearing is measured by the ratio of debt to equity. Debt is a fixed liability for an organisation (for example, the annual interest payments which are due on loans), and equity is the capital equivalent which needs to generate the funds necessary to cover the liability (for example, to pay the interest due).

If the gearing ratio is high, this indicates that an organisation has to cover large fixed liabilities from only a small equity investment. As a result, the business could be at financial risk.

As well as looking at the gearing ratio itself, a second indicator which could be useful in relation to financial gearing is **interest cover**. Interest cover compares an organisation's profit before interest to the level of interest payable; again indicating whether it is generating sufficient returns to cover its fixed liabilities.

Gearing ratio – CCNH's debt [long term borrowings of $102m] is currently 54% of its equity [share capital + retained earnings: $189m]. A gearing ratio of 54% by itself should not be a particular cause for concern because it is relatively low.

Interest cover – CCNH's interest cover appears to be more of a concern though. Its operating profit was the same as the interest it had to pay for the year just ended, meaning that if its profit falls in future, CCNH may not be able to cover its interest payments.

CCNH appears still to have a relatively good relationship with its bank, since the bank agreed to increase CCNH's overdraft facility in order to enable it to make its most recent rental payments. However, if CCNH doesn't generate sufficient earnings to cover its interest payments this could be fatal for its relationship with its bank, and will also seriously damage its chances of receiving any further financing.

Operational gearing

Operational gearing – Operational gearing (or leverage) compares the ratio of fixed costs to variable costs in an organisation, by comparing contribution to profit with operating profit (PBIT). Operational gearing helps to identify the level of **business risk** in an organisation.

If an organisation has high operational gearing this suggests it also faces a high level of business risk. High operational gearing means that an organisation's fixed costs as a proportion of its total costs are also high. This is risky because, although variable costs will fall if revenue falls, fixed costs will not. Therefore, an organisation with a high level of operational gearing may find itself unable to cover its fixed costs if its revenue falls.

This inability to cover fixed costs could have been the type of gearing problems which the director was talking about at CCNH; because it seems likely that CCNH has a **high level of fixed costs**.

CCNH's rent payments are a fixed cost, and they alone take up 27% [$257m/$938m] of its revenue. In addition, it seems likely that the central costs and the costs of permanent staff in the care homes will be relatively fixed.

The danger for CCNH of having a high level of operational gearing is that if its revenues drop then it will quickly become loss-making, given that it was only just breaking even at the end of the last year. Again, this could have been the problem which the director was referring to.

Operational gearing ratio – If we treat rent costs, payroll costs and central costs as all being fixed (or relatively fixed), then the ratio between CCNH's fixed costs and variable costs (running costs) is 7.5:1 [536 + 257 + 30 = 823:110].

This ratio is very high, and so should also be viewed as a concern for CCNH.

In this respect, it is important for CCNH to see if it can change the nature of any of the costs within its business. In particular, it may be possible to use temporary or contract staff in its homes rather than permanent staff. Such a change would mean that staff costs effectively then become variable costs.

However, using temporary staff might also compromise the **quality of service** CCNH provides to its residents, which would not be acceptable.

(b) **Qualitative models of business failure** – Qualitative models of business failure look at a variety of qualitative and non-accounting factors to help identify the likelihood of corporate failure in organisations. These factors can include: the business environment (as exemplified by 'PEST' factors) the organisation's customer profile (for example, whether it is dependent on a small number of key customers); the level of management experience in the organisation; and whether the organisation has a history of qualified audit opinions.

Argenti's A score model – Argenti's A score model is a qualitative model which can be used to assess the risk of poor management causing corporate failure. The model looks at three different groups of indicators of poor management:

- Defects
- Management mistakes
- Symptoms of failure

These three groups are then further divided into a number of problem areas, and an 'A score' is obtained by assigning a score for each problem area. As such, Argenti's model attempts to quantify the causes of failure (defects; management mistakes) and the symptoms associated with failure.

'A scores' – The 'A score' model sets a maximum acceptable score of 25 overall. An 'A score' of greater than 25 indicates that an organisation is at risk of failing. However, the scores for each group of indicators are also important individually. In particular, if an organisation scores anything at all for 'symptoms' this immediately signifies that the organisation should be considered at risk of failing.

Defects

In Argenti's model, 'defects' are divided into 'management defects' and 'accounting defects'.

Management defects result from deficiencies in the senior management team: for example, a failure to separate the roles of chairman and CEO; having a passive board of directors; having a lack of experience and/or relevant skills among the senior management team; or having a management team with a poor record of responding to change in the business environment.

Lack of senior management – The fact that CCNH does not have any experienced senior management (following the recent departures of the CEO, finance director and the operations director) can be seen as a management defect for the Company.

Accounting defects – Examples of accounting defects could be a lack of budgets or budgetary control; a lack of cash flow planning, or and an absence of costing systems.

The fact that CCNH struggled to meet its most recent rent payments may suggest a lack of cash flow planning, particularly as CCNH had no cash available when the rent payments were due.

Management mistakes

If a company's management and accounting systems are weak, this could increase the chances of mistakes being made within the company. Argenti suggests that management mistakes should be analysed under three main headings: **high gearing; overtrading;** and **failure of major projects**.

As we saw in part (a), CCNH's financial gearing of 54% is actually relatively low, and so would not indicate a risk of failure. However, CCNH's high operational gearing should be viewed as more of a concern.

Moreover, SC's rapid growth, coupled with the apparent weaknesses in its credit control and receivables collection, may suggest that there has been some overtrading at SC. In turn, the weaknesses in SC's credit control (and the resulting high level of receivables) are straining the business' working capital.

Symptoms of failure

The logic of Argenti's model suggests that, over time, defects and/or management mistakes will lead to symptoms of failure emerging, at which point the prospect of corporate failure becomes more apparent.

These symptoms can be directly financial, such as poor ratios in the financial statements. However, evidence of creating accounting could also be a symptom of imminent corporate failure.

Equally, there can be non-financial symptoms of failure, such as high staff turnover, or declining market share.

CCNH's most recent financial statements show a number of symptoms of failure: CCNH made no profits in the last year, it has very low interest cover, and it has a very high operational gearing ratio. Moreover, the difficulty which CCNH faced in making its rental payments could be seen as an indication that failure is imminent.

In addition, the recent directors' resignations, coupled with and the police investigation of theft at CCNH could also be seen as symptoms of impending failure.

Overall position

Overall, it appears that CCNH's position is very weak, and it looks in serious danger of failing unless drastic action is taken to improve its performance.

(c) **Portfolio mix** – An organisation needs to plan the range of products (or services) it offers so that it has a mix of products at different stages in their life cycles: for example, products at the growth stage alongside established (mature) products generating cash. Planning ahead in this respect is a vital element of organisational survival.

Special Care (SC) division – SC appears to be growing rapidly, with revenue growth of 24% pa over the last two years. Therefore, it seems likely that SC is in the **growth stage** of its life cycle.

However, one of the characteristics of products in the growth stage of their life cycle is that capital investments are required in order to enable the business to expand in order to fulfill levels of demand. Consequently, the cash flows generated by products in the growth stage of their life cycle are lower than their profits.

This reiterates the importance of CCNH monitoring liquidity as well as profitability. However, in terms of the CEO's strategy, it also highlights the need to have a division within CCNH which generates sufficient cash to support SC's growth.

General Care (GC) division – GC appears to be a mature business, operating in a mature sector.

The lack of opportunities for growth in the sector is characteristic of a mature sector. Usually, however, mature products are able to generate healthy profits. Equally, because they require relatively low levels of investment, mature products are usually cash generators for a business.

Given that CCNH is one of the largest providers of residential care places in Geeland, we could suggest that the GC division could be classified as a **cash cow** using the BCG matrix.

However, the CEO needs to assess how well GC displays the usual characteristics of a cash cow. Rather than being a cash generator and earning good profits, GC made an operating loss for the last year.

Given that GC is coming under increasing price pressure from its main customers (the public sector health organisations), it appears that **cost control** is likely to be very important for GC, in order to preserve its margins.

SBUs in portfolio – The combination of a growing business unit (SC) with a mature one (GC) should be a relatively beneficial one for CCNH, because the company should be able to use the cash generated by GC to support SC's growth.

However, the CEO will need to assess whether GC is actually able to fulfil this cash generating role. In particular, the CEO needs to consider whether GC is in danger of moving from a mature business to a declining business, and therefore whether divestment is an appropriate strategy. Equally, however, the CEO needs to consider what impact divesting of GC would have on CCNH's business portfolio.

62 BPC

Text reference. Chapters 1 and 4 of the BPP Study Text consider Porter's Five forces model and how it can be applied in the performance management process. Chapter 17 discusses corporate failure.

Top tips. In **part (a)** BPC is assessing **its option to enter the cardboard tube market** so remember this when you use the five competitive forces to comment on the information in the question. If you have time, it is a good idea to write a little introduction explaining a model and your understanding of how a scenario can be appraised using that model. We have done this in two sentences.

Part (b). In P5 you should be prepared to explain the advantages and disadvantages of using different models, as well as being able to apply them to different scenarios. In this part of the requirement, there is no need to apply your answer to the scenario, but simply to demonstrate you are aware of the potential limitations of Porter's model.

Part (c) draws on your knowledge of predicting corporate failure though there is very little in the scenario to comment on. Make sure that you realise that the JOL Co in this part is that referred to in note (3) in part(a). Rather than labouring to apply your answer to the scenario, you may have to make general comments. You could use information from one of the writers in Chapter 15 and we have used Slatter's ideas. *Argenti's* A score is also good here as the variables are a good mix of financial and non-financial indicators.

Marking scheme

				Marks
(a)	Comments (on merit):			
	Each of the five forces	5×2	10	
	Conclusion		1	Maximum 10
(b)	Limitations – up to 2 marks for each limitation discussed		Up to 5	5
(c)	Comments (on merit)			
	Fall in market share significant		1	
	(with percentage 18%)		1	
	Indicators	6×1.5	9	Maximum 10
			Total =	25

(a) **Porter's five forces and the option to enter the cardboard tube market**

Porter's five forces model assesses **five competitive forces** that affect a firm's positioning in its market and ultimately its profitability.

BPC is considering whether it wants to enter the cardboard tube market. So using the model to assess the option to enter this market:

(i) **Threat of new entrants**. A new entrant such as BPC will bring **more competition** and **extra capacity**. The strength of this threat depends on the barriers to entry to the market such as high fixed costs or expertise in technology. It also depends on the response of the existing competition in the market. New machinery to make the tubes costs from $30,000 per machine, it only needs one operator and the expertise needed to operate it is fairly low as an operator only needs one day's training. This appears to be a high threat. Another threat would be the foreign multinational company which has the machinery to manufacture cardboard tubes.

(ii) **Threat of substitutes**. A substitute product is a good or service produced by another industry which satisfies the same customer needs. PTC has a range of plastic tubes that can be used to **house** small products. This use appears to be different from that of the manufacturers who use the tubing to **wind products around**. It is possible that the uses could be extended to satisfy some of the uses made of cardboard tubes. However the plastic tubes are at present an average of 30% more expensive than the cardboard tubes on offer.

(iii) **The bargaining power of customers**. Customers, who appear to be manufacturers, use the tubing for a variety of purposes and buy very large quantities. The customers seem to have some bargaining power in their purchasing as they buy in bulk, and may also be price sensitive as the tubing costs a tiny part of the total cost and they may wish it to remain so. The product is not likely to be specialised and so customers could switch suppliers readily. There are four main suppliers with similar ranges, so customers have some choice. This also appears to be a high threat.

(iv) **The bargaining power of suppliers**. Suppliers can drive up prices for goods and services supplied to the industry. Obviously a monopoly supplier with a **differentiated product** will have more influence than a range of small suppliers with a simple product. The tubes are made from a specialist paper that can be in short supply. So suppliers do have some influence. Again this is another high threat.

(v) **Rivalry amongst current industry competitors**. The intensity of competition within an industry will affect overall profitability. The industry has four main manufacturers with 80% share in total and between 18 and 26% share each. So the industry is fairly concentrated. There has been little market growth recently at 2% pa and the product is undifferentiated. Therefore the competition is likely to be quite strong for a shrinking market and a homogenous product. This therefore poses yet another high threat.

In summary, there are some good reasons for entering the market, which include **low entry barriers**, as the manufacture of the product is unspecialised (though this could be a threat once BPC has established itself in the market and wishes to keep out other competition). There is also a **small likelihood of substitution**. However the market is likely to be **very competitive** with a **high concentration of entrenched competitors and customers who have considerable buying power**.

On balance, the option to enter the market for cardboard tubes appears to be unattractive and BPC should consider alternative strategies for improving performance.

(b) **Limitations of the five forces model as a technique for assessing the attractiveness of an industry**

Problem of market definition – The aim of Porter's model is to identify the level of profits which can be sustained in an industry or market. However, it can sometimes be difficult to define exactly what the industry or market in question is – particularly for a large organisation, or one operating in a complex environment. Even in the BPC example, are cardboard tubes and plastic tubes in the same 'tube' market, or should they be distinguished on the basis of the different materials used?

This issue around market definition identifies a potential problem with Porter's model. The model is best used for analysing **simple market structures**, but analysis of the different forces can get very difficult in more complex industries with lots of interrelated segments or product groups.

Environmental change – Moreover, the model **assumes relatively static market structures**. However, this is often not the case in today's markets. For example, technological breakthroughs can change business models in relatively short timescales. Yet while the model can provide some useful analysis of the new market structure once it has emerged, it can only offer limited advice for any preventative measures.

The need for careful analysis is, perhaps, most important in the area of substitute products or services. It takes a particular alertness to discern potential substitutes in the early stages of their development.

Equally, while there may currently be strong barriers to entry into an industry, new technological developments could remove or severely reduce those barriers to entry.

Competition or co-operation? – It is also important to recognise that Porter's model is based on the idea of competition between firms. It assumes that companies try to achieve competitive advantages over other players in the markets as well as over suppliers or customers. With this focus, it does not really reflect the dynamic of approaches such as strategic alliances, electronic linking of information systems of all companies along a value chain, or in a virtual organization, in which the focus is primarily on collaboration rather than competition.

(c) **JOL Co and corporate failure**

JOL Co had a market-leading share of 30% just three years ago. The current market share is 18% (from part (a) note 3) so there has been a decline of 12% in 3 years. There are several performance indicators that

could be used to flag up corporate failure. These are both financial and non-financial indicators and could include:

(i) **Declining profitability**. JOL is losing market share in a slow growing market. It is very likely that profitability will be affected. If JOL starts to make losses it will become unviable to continue operating.

(ii) **Decreasing sales volume**. JOL has lost market share in a near static market and therefore it has lost sales.

(iii) **An increase in gearing**. JOL may well need to borrow if it is not earning sufficient revenue to fund operations and future growth. This is usually achieved through increasing its overdraft limit or long term debt which can eventually lead to lenders refusing further borrowing. High levels of debt or financial gearing create financial risk affecting the company and its stakeholders.

(iv) **Poor financial controls**. Organisations that lose control over costs and operations can fail spectacularly. Audit committees that do not exercise proper controls can fail to spot fraud or mismanagement.

(v) **Lack of planning**. The remark by the MD suggests that JOL has not done anything to date to stem the decline in market share. This shows a lack of planning by the board having let things drift for three years.

(vi) **Frequent changes in senior executives**. Mobility can be a sign of dissatisfaction with how the company is performing. The challenge of turning around a troubled company is outweighed by whether the company can be saved and the risk of being associated with a failed company.

63 RM Batteries

Text reference. Models for predicting corporate failure are discussed in Chapter 17 of the BPP Study Text.

Top tips. Part (a) asks for your knowledge of quantitative and qualitative models. However, note you are not asked to describe the different types of models themselves, but to discuss their strengths and weaknesses. In effect this question could be broken down into four elements: strengths of quantitative models; weaknesses of quantitative models; strengths of qualitative models; and weaknesses of qualitative models.

Part (b) requires you to review the data in the spreadsheet. Remember the analyst has correctly prepared the data so you don't need to evaluate it.

In **part (c)**, you need to use data from the question in conjunction with a suitable model. We use Argenti's A score model which has three categories–and data from the question is available for most of these.

Part (d) asks for a critical assessment. Do the models give a complete picture of RMB's position? Is it safe to conclude from the data you have already considered whether the company is failing? What else would you need to know and do you need compare the company with its market?

Part (e). This part of the question isn't looking at corporate failure, but looks at the wider issue of product life cycles as a whole. How do pricing and production strategies vary across the life cycle? One of the key issues here is the extent to which RMB may have to switch from a differentiation strategy to a cost leadership strategy as its product approaches maturity.

Easy marks. A good question if you are comfortable with quantitative and qualitative models but if you couldn't think of a suitable qualitative model you would miss out on five marks in part (c). Still there are plenty of marks available across four question parts.

		Marks
(a)	1 mark for each point made. Up to 3 for each type of model. Maximum of 6 marks	6
(b)	1 mark for each point made. Maximum of 5 marks	5
(c)	0·5 mark for identifying problem and up to 1 mark for explaining how this relates to corporate failure. Maximum of 5 marks	5
(d)	1 mark for each point explained. To score full marks some appreciation of the information not captured by parts (b) and (c) must be demonstrated. Maximum of 4 marks	4
(e)	1 mark for each point made in relation to selling prices – Up to 3 1 mark for each point made in relation to production costs – Up to 3	Up to 5

Total = 25

(a) **Strengths and weaknesses of quantitative and qualitative models for predicting corporate failure**

Quantitative methods such as the Z score use publicly available financial data to predict whether a firm is likely to fail in the two year period. The calculation is easy to make using the model but the calculation is only a probability not an absolute likelihood so it may need to be used with other data to make a more rounded assessment. It also only gives guidance below the danger level of 1.8 so other scores are difficult to interpret.

Furthermore the model is based on historical trading patterns of a specific group of companies so a change in trading patterns or a company that falls outside the industry grouping used may find the model inaccurate. There is also a danger that companies in trouble use creative accounting in calculating figures which means where these go into calculations they are unreliable.

Qualitative models attempt to 'fill in the gaps' that quantitative models leave by using in-depth questionnaires but again these have their flaws. For instance the Argenti A score uses fairly subjective categories to calculate an overall score. These are wide ranging but can be answered subjectively and be open to bias.

(b) **Comment on the results in the junior analyst's spreadsheet**

The Z score for RMB in 20Y0 is 1.45 which is below the danger level of 1.8 and so suggests a likelihood of insolvency in the next two years. It has fallen over the past three years between 2.746 and 1.45. During this period the variables making up the model have been mostly static or declining. Roughly half the decline in the Z score arises from variable X4 which has fallen from 1.510 to 0.478 or 68%. This represents the market value of equity to total long term debt. The bulk of the movement arises from a significant increase in long term borrowings from $465m to $1,261m because of the investment in new equipment. The average share price has fallen from $1.56 in 20X8 to $1.34 in 20Y0 or 14% in the last year though it would be useful to see if this is a general market trend and so a comparison with competitor share prices is advisable,

The other variable that has seen most decline is variable X3 (PBIT/TA) falling from 0.227 to 0.078 which reflects a sharp fall in profits ($ 185m to $65m) and an increase in total assets ($1,355m to $2,456m) thus the company has failed to extract profit from available assets. Maybe this will improve in future periods as revenue from the new investments is earned.

(c) **Qualitative problems in the company's structure and performance and why these are relevant to possible failure**

Using the Argenti A score model, the problems a company is experiencing may be broken down into three broad categories: defects, mistakes made and symptoms of failure. Looking at RMB, defects exhibited are a dominant chief executive officer, a failure to split the chief executive and chairman roles and passive senior management.

Mistakes made by RMB include a reliance on one large project to fuel growth, which is risky and relies on the success of the project. Overtrading as revenue rises is another mistake mainly funded by debt thus gearing has risen from 107% to 197% and interest cover has declined from 8.8 times to 2.0 times. This reliance on debt funding leads to a risk of failure to service debt payments.

Finally symptoms of failure. The information available doesn't reveal these yet but they typically include high turnover, low morale and creative accounting.

(d) **Assess the results of analysis in parts (b) and (c) and state what additional data should be obtained to assess the company's financial health**

The company is still profitable making $65m of profits in 20Y0. Its revenues are still growing (from $1,560m to $1,915m over the past year) but operating costs have increased by 50% from 20X8 to 20Y0 and interest charges have gone up by $60m over that period. Thus margins have suffered (falling from 21% to 10% operating margin over the period). It is likely at the early stage of the project that costs will be high and revenues low. So a longer term view needs to be taken before concluding the company is definitely failing.

However the decline in the margin needs further explanation looking at costs in detail and how these are being controlled.

Finally it would be useful to compare the fall in the share price with the movement in the market to assess whether this is a general trend or reflecting sentiment over RMB's prospects.

(e) **Selling price changes**

Maturity – Sales prices are likely to decrease significantly at the maturity stage. Competitors will have flooded the market with alternative products and RMB is likely to have to reduce its sales prices as a means of sustaining demand for its product and maintaining its market share.

Decline – At the decline stage, demand is likely to fall further, as the product becomes superseded by the next generation of 'new' products. Therefore, price will be lowered further in order to try to attract business sales. RMB may attempt to prolong the life of its product by reducing selling prices significantly at this stage, although such a decision may depend on whether RMB has developed a next generation product of its own.

Prices are also likely to be forced down by over-capacity in the industry. If the selling price becomes too low (so that the product becomes loss-making) RMB may decide to stop selling it.

Production cost changes

Total production costs are likely to change with unit sales over the course of the product life cycle. However, the more important changes for RMB will be how unit production costs vary of the life cycle.

Maturity – At the maturity stage, the growth in demand for the product will have slowed significantly. As we have already mentioned, price becomes more sensitive as firms compete with another to compete to increase their share of a static market.

In order to maximise profits, while defending market share, RMB will look to reduce its costs; for example, by automating and standardising production processes as far as possible.

Decline stage – RMB will need to continue to control costs at a low level during the decline phase, to try to retain a positive cash flow for as long as possible despite falling prices and falling demand.

However, as there is unlikely to be any investment in the machinery used to make the product, there could be an increase in costs due to machine breakdowns and inefficiencies.

64 NW Clothes

Text reference. Corporate failure models are discussed in Chapter 17 of the BPP P5 Study Text.

Top tips.

Part (a). One of the criticisms of corporate failure models (such as Argenti's A score model) is that they tend to focus on internal factors and internal indicators of performance. However, the external environment in which an organisation operates can also have a significant impact on the organisation's performance. Although you are not asked to you use any models here, PEST analysis could be a useful framework: how have economic, social and technological factors, for example, affected NWC's performance?

Part (b). You should have been able to identify a number of characteristics in the scenario which could be indicators of corporate failure. For example, falling profitability and declining quality could be **symptoms** of corporate decline, while an autocratic Chief Executive is a **defect**.

Importantly, you should address both financial and non-financial issues, and given pointers from part (a) you should also consider external factors (for example declining market share) as well as internal ones.

Many of the indicators in the scenario do not necessarily mean that NWC **will** fail, and you are not asked to predict whether you think NWC will fail or not. Rather, you need to identify the problems which could be relevant to failure.

Argenti's A score model could be a useful guide here, because a number of the problems identified in the scenario are listed as either symptoms, mistakes or defects in Argenti's model.

(a)   **Importance of environmental analysis** – Corporate failure prediction models (such as Argenti's A score) focus mainly on internal factors and indicators of performance. They do not incorporate environmental analysis (PEST analysis) or considerations about the performance of an industry as whole. However, these could also have an impact on the likelihood of corporate failure.

Economic factors – The tough economic conditions are likely to suppress demand for clothes, because consumers' disposable income is being placed under increasing pressure. Consumers are increasingly looking to get value from their purchases, and so if NWC's clothes are not perceived as offering good value for money, we can expect its trading performance to deteriorate further and low cost stores to continue to increase their market share.

Supplier costs – Another factor which is having an adverse impact on NWC's financial performance is the **inflation** in raw material costs. An internal analysis will highlight that NWC's profitability is likely to be decreasing (because it is under pressure not to increase prices too much), but external analysis can give add some insight into the reasons behind the decrease. If it is the case that NWC's margins are fundamentally robust, after adjusting for the increase in cotton prices, this could actually provide some reassurance that NWC is not failing.

Technology – Online sales have been one of the main reasons behind the increase in total clothing sales between 20X7 – 20X9. However, NWC's Chief Executive seems unprepared to accept the opportunities provided by the online market. If all of NWC's competitors develop their online sales more than NWC, this could further reduce NWC's market share.

Market share – Total clothing sales in Nordland increased by 4.5% between 20X7 – 20X9, but over the same period NWC's sales increased by less than 1%. This means that its market share is decreasing. Simply looking at NWC's sales in isolation would not highlight this point.

Context of decline – An important aspect to consider in relation to decline is whether an **industry** as a whole is declining or whether an **individual company** within that industry is underperforming. The fact that total clothing sales are continuing to increase despite the tough economic conditions suggests that the clothes retailing industry as a whole is not declining. Moreover, people will always need to wear clothes, so we could argue that the industry as a whole will never decline. Instead, individual brands and styles within it will grow and decline over time. This is perhaps the critical point to consider in relation to NWC: how well is it performing relative to other clothes retailers?

Causes of business failure – Nonetheless it is important to remember that firms often fail due to internal causes (such as poor leadership, weak controls, or inappropriate strategies) rather than external ones. So it is important to assess both internal and external causes when trying to predict business failure.

(b)   Argenti's A score model is based on the idea of a correlation between poor management and corporate failure. A number of the problems that NWC is currently experiencing are identified in Argenti's model, which suggests that they increase the risk that NWC suffering a business failure.

So, using the Argenti A score model, we can break down the problems NWC is experiencing into three broad categories: defects, mistakes made and symptoms of failure.

Management defects

Leadership – The Chief Executive appears **autocractic**. Despite all the other directors wanting to invest in developing NWC's online site, the Chief Executive over-ruled them in favour of the store refurbishment programme. In this respect, as well as the Chief Executive being autocratic, we can also suggest that the rest of the Board are weak which is equally much a problem for NWC.

Accounting defects

Poor budgetary control – The shop refurbishment programme was budgeted to cost $9 million, but ended up costing nearly $11 million; an over-spend of approximately 20%. It is not clear what the cause of the over-spend was, or if any action was taken to try and reduce this overspend once it became apparent. Nonetheless, the extent of the overspend suggests a significant weakness in NWC's budgetary control over a major project, and raises a concern that budgetary control could be equally weak across other aspects of company.

Mistakes

Store refurbishment – In the context of the growth of low cost stores, consumers' increasing focus on value for money, and the growth of online sales, it is debatable whether a major shop refurbishment programme was the best use of scarce funds.

Given the rapid rate of growth in the internet clothes market, it appears that NWC may have been better advised to invest in promoting its e-commerce facility.

Failure of a large project – It is not clear what impact the store refurbishment programme has had on sales on profitability, so it may not be justified to view it as a failure. However, if the leaked report is confirmed, this would suggest the shops are not proving as profitable as NWC had hoped.

Symptoms of trouble

Decrease in profitability – NWC's operating profit has fallen both in absolute terms and in percentage terms (from 17.4% to 15.5%) between 20X7 – 20X9. Given the context of rising cotton prices and a reduction in consumer confidence, this is perhaps not surprising, and should not by itself be taken as a sign that NWC is going to fail. However, in conjunction with the other factors we have identified, if NWC's profitability keeps falling then this is likely to be a symptom of trouble.

Falling market share – Although total clothing sales increased by 4.5% between 20X7 – 20X9, NWC's sales only increased 0.9%, meaning its share of the market has reduced. Again, this could only be a short term reduction, but if NWC's market share continues falling (particularly once the global economy picks up and consumer spending starts increasing again) then this should be seen as an increasing cause for concern.

Increasing debt – Total debt has increased from $42.5m to $49.5m between 20X7 – 20X9, leading to a fall in Beaver's ratio (cash flow from operations / total debt) from 0.6 to 0.54. However, the movement in the debt figure also includes the new loan of $10m drawn down to pay for the shop refurbishment, so by itself the increase should not be seen as a particular cause concern.

Moreover, a Beaver ratio figure of 0.54 also suggests that NMC is not in imminent danger of failing. Historically, organisations with a ratio above 0.4 have not failed within the next five years.

Declining quality – Perhaps the most worrying symptom for NWC is the increase in customer complaints about the poor quality of clothes they have bought recently. The Chief Executive's recent statement suggests that NWC has been looking to reduce costs by switching to cheaper suppliers. However, if NWC sacrifices too much quality in the effort to save money this could have significant adverse consequences for market share and profitability as customers stop buying from NWC.

Moreover, the switch to cheaper suppliers may be seen (rightly or wrongly) as an indication that NWC is struggling financially, and this could further reduce public and investor confidence in the company.

(c) **Grey area** – The Z-score model suggests that firms with a Z-score of 3.0 or higher are likely to be financially sound and so should be expected to survive, according to the financial data. By contrast, the model suggests that firms with a Z-score of 1.8 or lower are likely to fail and are heading for bankruptcy.

However, this leaves a 'grey area' between 1.8 – 3.0, for which the eventual failure or survival of a company cannot be predicted with certainty.

NWC's Z-score (of 2.7) falls within this 'grey area', which suggests that further investigation is likely to be required to assess whether the firm is financially sound or in danger of failing.

Although NWC's Z-score is towards the upper end of the 'grey area' – which suggests that it might be able to survive – the calculations reinforce the idea that the Chief Executive seems to have been too bullish in his assessment of NWC at the Annual General Meeting.

Context – The Z-score which the accountant has calculated is only valid for a single point in time. It doesn't indicate whether NWC's financial condition is improving or deteriorating. However, such information could be equally important in assessing the likelihood of corporate failure. For example, it would be useful if the accountant could calculate NWC's Z-scores over a range of years, because if the scores have fallen (and were previously over 3) this would suggest that NWC's financial condition is deteriorating, which should be a concern for the Directors.

Equally, it may be useful to for the management accountant to try to calculate Z-scores for any similar companies in Nordland. One of the limitations of the Z-score model is that it may not be appropriate to apply Z-scores uniformly to all companies across different industries, because financial ratios may vary in different industries. However, if NWC's Z-score was compared against that for another clothes retailer, this could provide a useful benchmark of NWC's position.

Overcoming distress – Importantly, though, even if the Z-scores suggest that NWC is in danger of failing, the Z-score model doesn't provide any suggestions or solution as to how the company could try to overcome its financial distress. Therefore while the accountant's figures may suggest there is a problem, by themselves they will not help NWC resolve that problem.

65 Culam Mining

Text reference. Corporate failure, and quantitative methods for predicting corporate failure, are discussed in Chapter 17 of the BPP Study Text.

Top tips.

Part (a). It is vital that you recognise that there are two parts to this requirement: (i) first you are asked to evaluate the results of the analyst's calculations; then (ii) you are asked to evaluate the appropriateness of the two models [Z-score and Q-score] for Culam.

The first part should be relatively simple (Culam's score is above the 'safety level' in both models), but there is also relatively little to say in the first part of the requirement. Therefore, the majority of the marks actually relate to the second part of the requirement.

Although the models suggest Culam can be considered safe, how reliable are they actually likely to be? For example, how closely does Culam – a mining company based in Teeland – resemble any of the companies Altman studied when he developed the Z-score model? Similarly, the scenario tells us that the Q-score model has been developed by studying the companies on the 'small Teeland stock exchange.' What is the significance of Teeland's stock exchange being small?

Part (b). A useful way to approach this part of the requirement could be to think about the different characteristics of a mine's lifecycle. The opening paragraph of the scenario identifies that a mine has three distinct stages in its lifecycle: development; production; then decommissioning.

What will the financial characteristics of each of these stages be? And how will these different characteristics affect the Z-score?

Part (c). The requirement here asks you to give **four, detailed** recommendations, and to justify how they will help reduce the probability of failure. The reference to 'detailed recommendations' should have been a clue that basic suggestions such as 'increase revenues' or 'reduce costs' were not to going to be sufficient to earn the marks available here.

The scenario should also have given you some pointers here. The first paragraph tells you that Culam's revenue is split 25:75 between fixed price contracts and sales on the spot market, and that most of the production is exported. Neither of these points was relevant to parts (a) or (b) of the question, suggesting they were relevant here. Do these circumstances present any risks to Culam? What could it do to reduce those risks?

Marking scheme

		Marks
(a)	For general interpretation of the calculations – 1 mark	
	For general description of how a quantitative model works – 1 mark per relevant point – up to a maximum of 4 marks	
	For relevant comments on the problems with the models, in relation to their use at Culam – up to a maximum of 9 marks	
	Total for part (a): up to 10	10
(b)	For general issues around lifecycles and the probability of failure – up to 2 marks	
	Description of a mine's lifecycle (development – production – decommissioning) – 1 mark	
	For explaining the impact of the lifecycle on Culam's Z-score – up to 6 marks	
	Total for part (b): up to 7	7
(c)	Up to 2 marks for each valid recommendation – 1 mark for the improvement being recommended and 1 mark for the justification – up to 8 marks	
	Possible recommendations include, but are not limited to: Increasing size of the business – portfolio effect Learn from the mistakes of others – avoid big project failures Use of fixed price contracts to avoid volatile commodity prices Use of foreign exchange hedging to avoid revenue volatility	
	Total for part (c): up to 8	8
		Total = 25

(a) **Results of the calculations**

In both calculations, Culam's score is greater than the score at which it is considered safe. Therefore, the models suggest that the company is not at risk of failing in the next two years. However, the models are only valid for a single point in time, and do not indicate whether Culam's financial condition is improving or deteriorating.

Moreover, Culam should not place too much confidence in these results because there are a number of factors which reduce how appropriate the models are for assessing its risk of failing.

Z-score

Quantitative models use financial ratios to predict the likelihood of business failure and bankruptcy. Altman's research (from which devised the Z-score) looked at a range of variables in relation to companies which failed and which didn't fail. From this, he identified that the five key indicators of the likely failure – or not –

of a company were: liquidity; profitability; efficiency; leverage and solvency. These characteristics are represented, in turn, by the five ratios used to calculate a company's Z-score.

The Z-score model enables analysts to identify companies which share the characteristics of ones which have previously failed, and are therefore at risk of failing themselves.

However, there are a number of factors which affect the reliability of the Z-score model, and three of these could significantly reduce its appropriateness for Culam.

Industry characteristics – The model will be most relevant for companies in similar industries and of similar size to the ones which Altman analysed in his initial research. Altman's data was primarily collected from the manufacturing sector, whereas Culam is a mining company. As such, it may not be appropriate to use the model without some modification to reflect the different financial characteristics of the mining companies compared to manufacturing companies – for example, their capital intensiveness.

Geographical location – The companies Altman studied were US companies, whereas Culam is based in Teeland. Apart from the fact it only has a small stock exchange, we do not know anything about the economy in Teeland, and therefore how similar or dissimilar it is to the US. However, if, for example, Culam is a developing country, this would reduce the relevance of comparisons based on the US.

Historical context – Altman's research was conducted in the late 1960s, and so the data used in his model is about 50 years old now. The global economy has changed significantly during that time, so it is debatable how relevant the original data is, generally, for companies today.

Q-score

Reliability of model – The Q-score model appears to overcome some of the limitations of the Z-score model – because it is based on recent data, and it relates to local (Teeland) companies rather than US ones.

However, Teeland's stock exchange is only small, which will reduce the sample size from which the academics developed their model. Perhaps more importantly, it is not clear how many companies in Teeland have failed recently; but if this number is small, this means the academics have derived their model from very limited data.

Industry characteristics – It is also not clear what the mix of companies listed on Teeland's stock exchange is. For example, if the majority of the companies listed on the stock exchange are manufacturing or service companies, then their financial characteristics may not be comparable with Culam's.

Therefore, neither the Z score nor the Q score are likely to provide a reliable indicator of Culam's risk of failing. Moreover, given the nature of Culam's business model, its survival could also depend on world commodity prices and foreign exchange rates. However, both models focus only on its internal financial characteristics, rather than looking at any external environmental factors.

(b) **Impact of mine's lifecycle on Z-score**

In total, a mine has a 'life' of 23 years: two for its initial development, 20 in production, and one for decommissioning.

Development phase – In the first two years, no revenue or profits will be generated, and the mine will require a large amount of capital investment. This investment, coupled with the underlying asset value of the mine and its ore, means that Culam's total assets will be increasing during this period.

X1, X2, X3 and X5 in the Z-score all use 'total assets' as their denominator, meaning that the Z-score will fall during this period, given the absence of any revenue or profit from the mine.

The weightings in the model mean that X3 (PBIT / total assets) has the greatest impact on the overall score; therefore the fact that the mine is not generating any profit during this period could lead to quite a significant reduction in Culam's Z-score.

Production phase – In this phase, the mine will be earning revenues, and hopefully will be profitable.

However, the asset value of the mine will begin to fall, as reserves of the ore begin to be extracted, and as the capital investment begins to be depreciated. Therefore, we would expect the Z-score to be higher during this period.

Decommissioning phase – In this final phase, there will be no revenues, although the value of Culam's assets will also be falling. As such, we could again expect a relatively low Z-score in this phase, although probably not as low as during the initial development phase (because the value of total assets will be lower now).

Lifecycle and probability of failure

Since Culam only owns four mines, the phase which any one mine has reached in its lifecycle could have a significant impact on the company's overall Z-score. For example, if two mines are being developed at the same time, then this is likely to lead to a significant reduction in the Z-score.

Although Culam will need to develop new mines to sustain its business as its existing mines reach the end of their lives, the capital investment required during the development phase will make significant demands on its financial resources. As such, the extent of the financial resources which Culam can call on over the life of the mines could be crucial in dictating its survival.

(c) **Recommendations for reducing the probability of failure**

Increase number of mines – As Culam currently only has four mines, the performance of any single mine will have a significant impact on the company's overall results. For example, if one of the mines proves much less profitable than had been expected, this could potentially threaten the future of the whole group.

If Culam increases the number of mines it owns, this will reduce its dependence on any single mine.

Effective due diligence – However, the recent demise of its competitor highlights that Culam must be careful not to pay too high a price for any new mines it acquires. As such, undertaking suitable due diligence and carrying out detailed risk analysis in advance of acquiring a new mine (or any other significant capital investment) should help reduce the probability of failure.

Securing long-term contracts – Currently, Culam sells 75% of its output on the spot market, and only 25% under long-term fixed price contracts. This mix makes Culam's revenues and cash inflows vulnerable to fluctuations in the commodity prices. However, if Culam increased the proportion of its output it sold under long-term contract this will provide greater certainty over its future revenues.

Hedging – Another way which Culam could look to reduce risk is by using hedging techniques to reduce the volatility of its revenues and cash flows. As Culam currently sells 75% of its ore on the spot market it could benefit from hedging against a fall in the market prices of its ores.

In addition, the bulk of Culam's production is exported. Assuming that many of Culam's customers will be large industrial companies, it is likely that they will want to use their own currency for buying the ores rather than local currency of Teeland. Therefore, Culam could be vulnerable to fluctuations in foreign exchange risks, since its revenues will be earned in foreign currencies while its costs will be denominated in the local currency of Teeland.

As such, hedging against foreign exchange rate risk could also help to reduce the risk of failure.

[Answers to the 50 mark Section A questions begin on the next page.]

66 Lopten

Marks

(i) Calculation of variable costs – 2 mark
Fixed costs – 1 mark each
Calculation of profit for each product – 1 mark
Average sales price per unit – 1 mark
Calculation of contribution per unit – 1 mark
Calculation of market share – 1 mark
Calculation of breakeven point – 1 mark
Margin of safety – 1 mark
Return on capital employed (ROCE) – 1 mark
Total quality costs – 1 mark
Total for part (i) – Up to 11 marks
11

(ii) PEST factors

For identifying relevant issues (political, economic, social
and technological) in the scenario – Up to 2 marks for each issue identified

For commenting on the relevance of the suggested KPIs to each issue –
Up to 2 marks per issue

Total for part (ii) – Up to 11 marks
11

(iii) For evaluating how well the KPIs fit with the CSF to obtain a dominant
market presence – Up to 4 marks
For evaluating how well the KPIs fit with the CSF to maximise profits
within acceptable risk – Up to 4 marks
For evaluating how well the KPIs fit with the CSF to maintain brand
image for above average quality products – Up to 4 marks
Total for part (iii) – Up to 10 marks
10

(iv) For each relevant point about the suitability of the KPIs for planning or
controlling – 1 mark per point

Total for part (iv) – Up to 5 marks
5

(v) For calculating contribution (1 mark) and profit (1 mark) for Plan A – Up
to 2 marks for calculations for Plan A
For calculating contribution (2 marks) and profit (1 mark) for Plan B –
Up to 3 marks for calculations for Plan B
For calculating difference in actual profits vs target profits under the two Plans – 1 mark
For relevant points evaluating whether the strategies will enable the
business to achieve its target profits – Up to 4 marks
Total for part (v) – Up to 9 marks
9

Professional marks – for style and structure of report – Up to 4 marks
4

Total = 50

Report

To: Board of Lopten Industries

From: Consultant

Date: [today's date]

Subject: Strategic performance and performance indicators

Introduction

This report calculates the KPIs suggested by the board for measuring Lopten's performance, and then evaluates the effectiveness of those KPIs in addressing issues in the company's external environment. The report also evaluates how well the KPIs measure performance in relation to Lopten's critical success factors. The report concludes by evaluating two marketing strategies which have been proposed, and their impact on Lopten's ability to achieve its target operating profit in two years' time.

(i) **Key performance indicators**

The Board has identified a number of key performance indicators (KPIs) which can be used to assess the performance of the Beeland operations.

These are shown below:

	Cheerful	Posh	
Total profit ($m)	42.4	45.0	See Appendix 1
Average sales price per unit ($)	400.0	700.0	
Contribution per unit ($)	145.0	375.0	
Market share (%)	12.0	33.1	
Margin of safety (%)	25.9	27.3	See Appendix 1
Return on Capital employed (%)	13.0	18.0	
Total quality costs ($m)	28.4	19.2	
Consumer awards won	1.0	4.0	

(ii) **Issues in Lopten's external environment**

Political factors

Government grants – The government has given grants to an international manufacturer (one of Lopten's competitors) which has opened a factory in Beeland. Lopten will not be eligible for any similar grants, however, because it manufactures its washing machines at its regional hub in Kayland and then imports them into Beeland – rather than manufacturing them in Beeland.

It will be difficult for the KPIs to measure the impact of the government grants directly. However, monitoring average sales price per unit of Lopten's machines (compared to the competitors' machines) could indicate whether the government grants have enabled the competitor to sell its machines more cheaply than Lopten can. Equally, if the government imposes any import tariffs on Lopten's machines this could adversely affect their average price compared to the price of the competitors' products.

Similarly, the market share KPI could also help Lopten assess whether the government's actions are influencing Lopten's market share (as a result of the competitor's washing machines becoming relatively cheaper than Lopten's products.)

Economic factors

Market growth – The growth of the middle-class, and rising incomes in Beeland, is leading to an increase in demand for Lopten's products.

The KPIs do not directly include any measure of sales growth rates (for example, by measuring annual sales increase compared to the prior year). However, measuring market share does provide an indicator of the rate at which sales of Lopten's washing machines are increasing relative to its competitors' sales.

Foreign exchange risk – Lopten's reported financial performance from its operations in Beeland could also be affected by movements in currency exchange rates between Beeland, Kayland and Lopten's own country. However, the KPIs do not reflect this foreign exchange risk.

Social factors

Customer tastes – As national income in Beeland continues to increase, it is likely that there will be increasing demand for premium products (such as Posh) relative to more basic products (such as Cheerful). This would justify the approach taken in the marketing Plan B to focus of Lopten's marketing resources onto Posh.

Again, a measure of the sales growth rates for the two products which would be useful for identifying changes in demand, but the KPIs do not currently provide this. However, the market share KPI could be useful for identifying how successful Lopten is in selling products – particularly Posh.

Technological factors

Developments in technology could affect Lopten in two ways:

New features – Technological developments could mean that Lopten needs to develop new features for its washing machines (for example, if competitors introduce new features into their machines.) However, this could be less of an issue in Beeland than developed countries, because Beeland's customers may not yet be as demanding as customers in more developed countries.

Moreover, as Lopten manufactures its products at a regional hub, and only sells them locally, it seems unlikely that the Beeland operation will have any impact on product development for the company as a whole. Therefore, although none of the KPIs address new product development, this seems to be reasonable.

Reduced costs – New technologies could also improve the efficiency of the manufacturing process for Lopten's existing products; for example, by increasing the levels of automation in the manufacturing process.

As such, this should help to reduce the cost of producing Lopten's washing machines. While any such cost reductions will be reflected in the contribution per unit KPI, the contribution figure is also affected by selling price.

Therefore, a more effective indicator to use in order to measure the impact which technological developments have had on the manufacturing process would be 'Manufacturing cost per unit'.

(iii) **Links between CSFs and KPIs**

Dominant market presence

Market share – The market share KPI provides an indication of Lopten's presence in the market, but in order to gauge whether or not it dominates the market, Lopten's market share also needs to be measured relative to its competitors. In this respect, a KPI of 'relative market share' (comparing Lopten's market share to that of the market leader) could be more suitable.

Growth strategies – One way in which Lopten could seek to increase market share is by reducing the price of its products in order to increase demand for them. However, this will also affect KPIs for average price per product.

It is important that Lopten doesn't discount the price of its washing machines too aggressively, to the extent that they no longer generate a contribution to profit. In this respect, the contribution per unit KPI will be valuable in ensuring that a balance is maintained between profitability and increasing market share.

Maximise profits within acceptable risk

Profit for each product – The amount of profit earned for each product is one of Lopten's KPIs, so this should encourage a focus on profits. Although the KPI only show profit for a single period, monitoring this profit figure over a number of periods will highlight trends in the level of profit being earned.

Contribution per unit – The contribution per unit KPI can also be used to monitor how effectively Lopten is controlling its variable costs relative to the price of its products. A focus on cost control in this way should also help to increase profits.

Return on capital employed (ROCE) – ROCE indicates how efficiently Lopten is using its capital in order to generate profits. As such, this KPI should also encourage profit maximisation, although there could be concerns that using ROCE as a profit measure encourages short-termist behaviour (for example, not investing in new capital projects even though such investment would be beneficial in the future).

Risk – The margin of safety provides an indication of the extent to which sales would have to fall before Lopten reaches a breakeven profit situation. In this way, the margin of safety could provide an indication of the level of risk relating to the marketing and pricing strategies of both types of washing machine.

Maintaining brand image for above average quality

Consumer Awards – The number of consumer awards won provides an indicator of the reputation of Lopten's products; because consumers are unlikely to nominate a product for an award if they are unsatisfied with the quality of the product.

Quality costs – The 'quality cost' KPI gives an indication of how much Lopten has spent on quality management, but, by itself, it doesn't given any insight into whether the quality of Lopten's products is 'above average.' For example, are there are customer reviews which could be used to rate the quality of Lopten's products against rival products?

In this respect, the KPIs might be improved by including a more specifically customer-focused indicator (for example, customer satisfaction ratings, or numbers of complaints) which could potentially also be benchmarked against competitors' products.

Finally, the need to 'maintain brand image' suggests a need for marketing activity. However, there are no KPIs which monitor the level or effectiveness of Lopten's marketing activities in Beeland.

(iv)   **KPIs and planning**

Forward looking – KPIs which are to be used for planning (rather than control) need to be forward-looking.

Control indicators – In general, financial performance measures tend to be backward-looking rather than forward-looking, in the sense that they are used to compare the actual performance achieved against some kind of budget or target. For example, KPIs for 'Contribution per unit' and 'ROCE' are more likely to be useful for controlling performance.

In order to monitor its control indicators effectively, though, Lopten should look to measure actual performance against budget or forecast. Currently, it appears to monitor actual performance only, with no reference to either a budget or to prior years. However, having some kind of benchmark against which to measure actual performance will help the Board to identify those areas where corrective action may be required to improve performance.

Planning indicators – By contrast to financial indicators, non-financial indicators can often be more appropriate as planning indicators.

Margin of safety – In Lopten's case, the margin of safety could be useful as a planning indicator. The margin of safety addresses the risk of making a loss going forward; although, at the moment, the size of the margin should reassure the Board that they can afford to take a reasonable degree of strategic risks without jeopardising the survival of the Beeland operation. For example, even if sales of both types of washing machines fell by 25%, Lopten would still make a contribution to profit from its operations in Beeland.

Consumer awards – The number of consumer awards won could also be useful as a planning indicator. Customers' perceptions of Lopten's products will shape the company's ability to increase sales in the future. For example, if Lopten can continue to win awards for 'Posh,' it could highlight this in any marketing material designed to boost sales of the product. Moreover, if Lopten can use its success in winning awards to illustrate the quality of its products, it could then use this as a factor which differentiates its washing machines from competitors' products. In turn this could be used to justify Lopten's washing machines being sold at a higher price than rival products.

Planning vs control – In general terms, planning activities tend to be high level, strategic activities, whereas control measures tends to be more appropriate at an operational level. In this respect, the mix of Lopten's KPIs seems rather unusual – because, although the KPIs are presented to the Board, there appears to be a greater focus on control indicators rather than planning indicators.

However, this issue could be address by modifying the indicators to include market share growth, for example, rather than simply market share. In this way, the Board could look use growth trends to help establish financial projections, rather than solely looking at their market share percentage at a given point in time.

(v) **Impact of marketing strategies**

Plan A

	Most recent $m	Year 1 $m	Year 2 $m
Contribution			
Cheerful	162.4	168.9	175.7
Posh	165.0	171.6	178.5
Fixed costs	240.0	240.0	240.0
Profit	**87.4**	**100.5**	**114.2**

Plan B

	Most recent $m	Year 1 $m	Year 2 $m
Contribution			
Cheerful	162.4	162.4	162.4
Posh	165.0	189.8	218.2
Fixed costs	240.0	240.0	240.0
Profit	**87.4**	**112.2**	**140.6**

The target operating profit in two years' time is $135 million. If the board pursues Plan A, Lopten's forecast operating profit will be approximately $21 million below the target at this point.

By contrast, if the board adopts Plan B the target profit figure could be achieved.

However, it would seem likely that there is more uncertainty around the figures used in Plan B than those in Plan A. In particular, Plan B assumes an annual growth rate of 15% in demand for Posh.

It is possible that the level of growth in the economy in Beeland can support this level of growth, because demand for premium products could be sustained by the continuing growth of the middle-class population in the country.

However, the prospects of achieving a growth rates of 15% per year are also likely to depend on the effectiveness of Lopten's marketing expenditure. In this respect, it is important to question how much impact any additional marketing expenditure will have. Lopten already spends $80m on marketing of Posh, and so it is debatable whether the additional marketing expenditure will generate proportionately more sales, or instead whether the effectiveness of the expenditure will be reduced by decreasing marginal returns.

In addition, the Board also needs to consider whether it is realistic to assume that sales of 'Cheerful' will remain constant – even if marketing expenditure on the product is reduced, as proposed in Plan B.

Conclusion

Lopten's current KPIs focus primarily on internal aspects of performance, rather than including a balance of internal and external factors. In addition, the link between the KPIs and Lopten's CSFs – particularly the need to obtain a dominant market presence – appears relatively weak.

Currently, the focus of the KPIs appears to be on control, rather than planning; whereas the board's focus should ideally really be more forward-looking. The Board should consider revising the KPIs used, in order to address these concerns.

The current marketing plan (Plan A) will not enable Lopten to achieve its profit target of $135 million in two years' time. Therefore the company could be advised to adopt Plan B, which has the potential to achieve this figure. However, Plan B assumes some fairly ambitious growth figures, so it will be important to assess how realistic these are before starting to implement the new marketing strategy.

Appendix 1

	Cheerful	*Posh*
Units sold (millions)	1.12	0.44
	$m	$m
Revenue	448.0	308.0
Variable costs		
Materials	100.8	52.8
Labour	67.2	35.2
Overheads	44.8	22.0
Distribution costs	50.4	19.8
Quality costs	22.4	13.2
Contribution	162.4	165.0
Fixed costs	18.0	18.0
Distribution costs	16.0	16.0
Quality costs	6.0	6.0
Marketing costs	80.0	80.0
Total fixed costs	120.0	120.0
Total profit	**42.4**	**45.0**

Margin of safety

	Cheerful	*Posh*
Contribution per unit ($)	145.0	375.0
Units sold (millions)	1.12	0.44
Breakeven sales (millions)	0.83	0.32
Margin of safety	**25.9%**	**27.3%**

67 Film Productions Co

Text reference. Critical success factors, key performance indicators, mission statements and objectives are all discussed in Chapter 2 of the BPP Study Text. The importance of non-financial performance indicators is discussed in Chapter 12.

Top tips.

Part (a). It is useful to start with an explanation of what critical success factors (CSF) are and setting them within the context of overall strategic management before defining the two types of CSF.

In **part (b)** you need to refer to internal information which would be available from the MIS for instance sales data. External information includes benchmarks and industry data. You then need to explain how this information would be used to set CSFs. Be clear that the question is testing CSFs and not KPIs.

Part (c). A useful start point to this question would be to think about the role performance indicators play in performance management – particularly the relationship between performance indicators and CSFs. Also make use of the information in the scenario. The scenario highlights the two CSFs which FP considers to be most important, so you should then ask what sorts of performance indicators would help to measure how well it is achieving those CSFs. Note, however, that the requirement doesn't simply ask why it is important to measure non-financial performance indicators; but why it is important to measure both non-financial and financial ones.

In **part (d)** you need to take the two CSF identified in the question and think of two performance indicators for each CSF that would measure their success. One is more externally focused and the other relates to internal financial and quantitative data. We have given more than two performance indicators for each CSF but you are only asked for two each which amounts to 2 ½ marks each.

Part (e) wants you to be a bit creative especially when you write about the website so think about websites you have visited and how they would collect data from visitors. You could take one of two approaches in answering this part. Either break it down into the three systems and write on the performance indicators under each or take your chosen performance indicators and talk about the implications of each KPI on the three systems.

Part (f). You are not asked to discuss mission statements in general terms here, but rather to discuss the specific issues FP would face when creating a mission statement.

A useful way of generating ideas for your answer might be to think of the advantages and disadvantages of mission statements. But remember, the question isn't asking for advantages and disadvantages as such. So you need to present your answer as the issues which FP's management needs to consider, rather than as a series of advantages or disadvantages of having a mission statement. For example, one of the perceived problems with mission statements is that they can be too general to have any real impact on employees' behaviour. So, the relevant issue which FP's management needs to consider is how to make the mission statement specific enough and relevant enough to FP's day-to-day activities to influence employees' behaviour.

		Marks
(a)	1 mark for general definition of a CSF. 2 marks each for a description of monitoring and building CSFs with examples appropriate to the scenario. Maximum of 4.	4
(b)	2 marks for the sources of information. 2 marks for each example including demonstration of why it is appropriate for FP. Maximum of 6.	6
(c)	1 mark for each relevant point discussing the importance of measuring a mixture of both non-financial and financial indicators. Maximum of 5.	5
(d)	2.5 marks for each suggested performance indicator with 0.5 for identification and 2 for discussion of use and relevance to FP. Maximum of 10.	10
	(Students may also discuss different margin measures such as operating and gross profit but these must be related to actual operations in order to gain much credit.)	
(e)	3 marks for each relevant information system indicating how it links to the performance indicators. Maximum of 11.	11
	Professional marks for the style and structure of the discussion in the answer 4 marks.	4
(f)	1 mark per relevant issue linked to creating a mission statement for FP. Maximum of 10.	10
		Total = 50

(a) **Difference between monitoring and building critical success factors (CSFs)**

A company needs to set CSF within the context of overall strategic management in order to achieve overall strategic objectives. CSF are the areas of business performance where it is essential the company must succeed to achieve its overall strategic objectives.

Monitoring CSFs are used to maintain existing operations for instance the use of comparatives between actual results and budgets or benchmarks in the industry.

Building CSFs look to the organisation's future and development. Examples include new products and markets. In the case of FP this may include new products launched into niche markets such as collectors of special editions for instance a director's cut (edit).

(b) **Information FP could use to set its CSFs and how this could be used**

FP would use information from internal and external sources to set its CSFs especially as monitoring CSFs might use benchmarks and building CSFs look at markets and products. Examples of external information include industry structure and the strategies of competitors if these are available. Information on sales markets is important and where production facilities are located for instance specialist facilities in the UK and likely sources of actors for instance India or Hollywood. Looking at sales markets, certainly targeted exposure of the product and company to the general film-going public is more likely to lead to success where going to see films depends on recommendation.

Internal sources of information include cost per film and production time for each film. Certainly important data includes the effectives of marketing campaigns and known patterns of sales for instance summer peaks for blockbusters and Christmas releases. These data can be used to forecast the likely market size and level of competition allowing for uncertainty by building in any probability as data cannot be forecast with accuracy. A CSF based on the quality of the forecast made would thus be appropriate.

(c)   **Importance of measuring non-financial indicators**

FP's performance indicators should be measures which enable the company's management to assess whether FP is achieving its CSFs or not. Therefore, its performance indicators need to be linked to its CSFs.

FP has identified that improving audience satisfaction is one of its most important CSFs, and this has a non-financial focus. Consequently, the performance indicators which will be relevant for measuring how well FP is improving audience satisfaction (which we will discuss in the next section) will also be non-financial.

However, the CSF of strengthening profitability in operations highlights that financial performance (profitability) is also important, meaning that FP also will also need performance indicators which assess how well it is performing financially.

Typically, financial performance indicators measure how successfully a company is performing, rather than ensuring its success. By contrast, non-financial performance indicators can help to ensure success. For example, if FP can improve audience satisfaction with its films (and more people want to watch) this should subsequently also be reflected in improved revenue and profits.

The second of FP's CSFs also reinforces this point. The profitability of FP's operations is likely to be determined by their effectiveness and efficiency. Therefore, measuring (and therefore improving) non-financial aspects of performance in relation to effectiveness and efficiency should in turn help to improve profitability (measured through financial indicators).

(d)   **Two performance indicators (PI) supporting measurement of the achievement of the CSF given and why each PI is relevant to the CSF**

Audience satisfaction

Performance indicators (PI) include:

Media response. Film critics give reviews and award scores for films seen that the public often use to assess whether it is worthwhile going to see a film. However critics may have different criteria than the general public when seeing a film and so this measure should be used with care.

Repeat viewings. Where films are shown on television it is possible to measure audience size and on repeat showings see if this has declined especially after the initial 'first to TV' showing. Customers who buy DVDs will also indicate the level of satisfaction with the intention to own a copy of the film after the film release.

Brand recognition. It is possible to use customer surveys to gauge awareness of the company name and its association with quality or other entertainment features such as particular actors and directors.

Awards won. Clearly major award ceremonies such as the BAFTAS and Oscars will guarantee greater success if the company wins awards and gets publicity so that the public wants to see the film. However the awards will also have more impact if they are voted on by the public giving a direct measure of approval.

Sales per film. The company's current release rate of 6.4 films per year (32 films over 5 years) and sales averaging $31.25m ($200m/6.4 films) can be measured against other data ain the industry that is industry averages or competitive companies. Trends should also be measured by type of film to gauge customer response over time to say action films.

Profitability in operations

Performance indicators include:

Costs. The internal performance measurement systems should be able to provide finer detail of costs for instance by 'employee' eg technicians and marketing staff or post production costs. These can be compared to other films made by the company or to industry data especially where this is a valid comparator.

Industry average margin. Benchmarking data can be used from relevant competitors to set a target margin. The comparator should be carefully chosen bearing in mind the average production budget in FP of $18m per film.

Time in production. This is driven to some extent by external customer demand and so some films may have to be pushed through at higher cost to meet market demand. This will affect costs and revenues thus the gross margin may vary from film to film. Other films taking longer may be cheaper to produce but revenue is further in the future. Again external relevant comparators are useful to see if the company is meeting industry standards.

(e) **Implications of chosen PI for the design and use of the company's website, management information system (MIS) and executive information system (EIS)**

Websites are useful sources of external data from visitors where audience surveys and comments are collected. Customers can view clips of current and production films and post comments and act as critics scoring films. Data on customers can be gathered (subject to data protection) and analysed giving valuable information on age, gender and location. Competitor websites may also be visited to obtain data especially published financial data.

A **MIS** collates data from the accounting information systems to give middle management data to control performance. Management can specify reports from customer purchases to reveal main customers eg cinemas and DVD sales and products that are selling well. Repeat viewings can be assessed from the number of times a customer appears as a purchaser. Financial data such as gross and net margin for each film and by customer allow targeted decision making and may feed into the performance reward system for production teams.

An **EIS** provides information to senior management summarising how well KPIs are being met and thus whether CSF are being met. The EIS can be interrogated in detail where more information on transactions is required. It draws on external information from the MIS and external data such as marketing and industry reports.

(f) **Impact on employees' behaviour** – One of the main reasons for FP to have a mission statement is to make its employees aware of its organisational culture. So the mission statement will need to illustrate FP's basic values and beliefs, to let the employees recognise the behaviours which are expected of them.

FP's culture and values are currently strongly **shaped by Mr Z's behaviour and ideas**. For example, the desire to know everyone's first names suggests an open culture and a friendly environment. But FP will need to ensure the values it encourages are **appropriate to the competitive environment**.

Impact of industry lifecycle – The fact that FP's technology is no longer innovative, and a number of other competitors are operating in the same way, suggests that the film industry has now reached the mature stage of its lifecycle. In turn this means that FP is likely to find itself facing increasing competitive pressure and the need to reduce costs. FP aim to create a mission statement that promotes behaviour which is consistent with this context. It may be that FP's management feel that maintaining the friendly working environment will help maintain staff motivation and therefore may help keep costs low.

However, the mission statement will need to make staff appreciate the need to **work efficiently in a competitive environment**, rather than simply being friendly with one another.

No experience of mission statements – FP, and its staff, have never had a mission statement before. Creating one for the first time could be an issue in itself, for both management and staff. It will take time and effort for management to develop the statement, so they need to feel the organisation will benefit from having it.

Equally, the staff will need to accept it and feel it is relevant to them. If they basically ignore it, its value will be significantly reduced.

Relevant to work – If the staff can't relate the statement to the work they do, it is unlikely to have any effect on their behaviour or the organisation. Consequently, FP needs ensure that the elements of its mission statement can be converted in everyday performance, and that staff will be able to apply them in their day-to-day work.

Equally, FP needs to ensure that its staff are aware how the mission statement applies to their everyday work. For example it should indicate how staff should treat each other, and how staff should treat customers, suppliers and other external stakeholders. One of the main criticism of mission statements is that they can be too general to have any impact what people do, so FP needs to avoid this problem.

Deliver competitive advantage – One of the key elements of a mission statement is to reflect an organisation's reason for existing.

FP's mission statement needs to reflect that it aims to produce commercially successful films that have a wide appeal.

Flexible to changing environment – However, mission statements also need to be flexible, and to be able to accommodate change.

If FP looks to introduce new ideas into the way it works, then the mission statement needs to be flexible enough to accommodate them. This might arise because of changes to the technological environment with the rise of the internet and broadband delivery of films.

Equally, the mission statement needs to be flexible enough to support FP's expansion into making promotional videos if it decides to pursue this line of business in future.

If the mission statement essentially forces FP to replicate what it is currently doing, rather than to look forward and develop, then it could be counter-productive in the long run.

Appropriate to competitive strategy – As FP aims to appeal to a mass market it might seek to compete not as a differentiator competing on quality but perhaps on cost as a least cost producer.

68 Mackerel

Text reference. Risk and uncertainty are considered in Chapter 6 of the BPP Study Text. Information systems are discussed in Chapter 7, while performance measures (including ROCE and EVA) are discussed in Chapter 9.

Top tips.

Part (i). Note that there are effectively two parts to this requirement: (a) analyse the risks facing the management committee; and (b) discuss how the management team's attitude to risk might affect their response. The scenario identifies a number of risks (eg earnings volatility, economic downturn, uncertainty over the size of the order) so these should help you get started.

The reference to 'attitude to risk' should also have prompted you to discuss different risk appetites: risk averse, risk seeking, and risk neutral. This is links parts (i) and (ii) of the question, because the management team will evaluate the project using different approaches depending on their attitudes to risk.

Part (ii) is a combination of calculations and then a critical analysis based around those calculations. As we have just noted, the relevant knowledge base here is the different approaches to decision-making which could be used: in this case, maximax, maximin, minimax regret and expected values. Remember, however that maximax, maximin, and minimax reget are calculated on **profits**, not expected values.

Step 1, in effect, is to calculate the profitability of the different packages at the different levels of demand, and then to work out which option Mackerel would choose using the four different approaches to decision-making.

Step 2 is to assess the suitability of the different methods for Mackerel: how appropriate are they given the management team's attitude to risk.

Remember, however, that you have been asked to write a report. Therefore any detailed calculations should be presented in Appendix at the end of the report, and referred to, rather than being included in the main body of the report.

Note. For tutorial purposes, our answers below have given full calculations. You may have found some short-cuts to avoid writing out the calculations in full, and ACCA's Examining team have has indicated that it was not necessary to write out all the calculations in full to obtain a good, correct answer.

Your evaluations in part (ii) then need to form the basis of your answer for **part (iii)**: the recommendation. Again, note, however, that you need to recommend two different things here: an appropriate choice of method, and a course of action.

Part (iv). Remember you are asked to evaluate the impact of the new information system at both an operational level, and a strategic level. And note you are asked to 'evaluate' the impact; so as well as considering its potential benefits you should also consider any limitations which would restrict those benefits.

Part (v). The scenario identifies that Mackerel's overall goal is to increase shareholder wealth, so in effect the question is asking how well ROCE or EVA will help Mackerel increase shareholder wealth. Note, you are not simply asked to compare ROCE and EVA as performance measures in general terms, but specifically in relation to the aim of increasing shareholder wealth.

Also, the question requirement highlights that ROCE and EVA are profit-based performance measures; how will this affect their usefulness in relation to increasing shareholder wealth?

Overall. Once again, remember that you have been asked to write a report, so make sure the style and structure of your answer, as a whole, is appropriate for a report.

Marking scheme

		Marks
(i)	Identifying appropriate metrics – 1 mark Identifying risk appetites (averse; seeking; neutral) – ½ mark each Identifying key stakeholders and risks – Up to 2 marks Discussion of risk appetite – Up to 3 marks Demand risk – 1 mark Cost overrun risk – Up to 2 marks Total for part (i) – Up to 9 marks	9
(ii)	Calculation of variable cost per unit – 1 mark Calculation of total cost under each package – Up to 2 marks Calculation of cost per unit for each package, and comparison to target figure – Up to 2 marks Calculation of total profits for each package – Up to 2 marks Description of different methods (maximax; maximin; minimax regret; expected values) – ½ mark each – Up to 2 marks Maximax: 1 mark for calculation; ½ mark for conclusion Maximin: 1 marks for calculation; ½ mark for conclusion Minimax regret: 2 marks for calculation; ½ mark for conclusion Expected values: 1½ marks for calculation; ½ mark for conclusion [Note. Workings rounded to thousands are acceptable] Evaluation of different methods – Up to 4 marks Total for part (ii) – Up to 19 marks	19
(iii)	Recommendation of method – Up to 2 marks Final recommendation on contract – 1 mark Any other relevant comments about risk reduction – 1 mark Total for part (iii) – Up to 3 marks	3
(iv)	Impact of new information system on information gathering – Up to 3 marks Benefits of new system for strategic decision-making – Up to 4 marks Potential problems of new system for strategic decision-making – Up to 3 marks Total for part (iv) – Up to 8 marks	8

(v) Comments on Total Shareholder Return (TSR) – Up to 2 marks
Comments on usefulness of ROCE (in relation to increasing TSR) – Up to 2 marks
Comment on usefulness of EVA (in relation to increasing TSR) – Up to 3 marks
Total for part (v) – Up to 7 marks   7

Professional marks – for style and structure of report – Up to 4 marks   <u>4</u>

                                                                  Total = <u>50</u>

Report

To: Board of Mackerel Consulting

From: Accountant

Date: December 20X1

Subject: APV contract, information systems and performance measurement

Introduction

The report assesses at the risks facing Mackerel in relation to the APV contract and the choice of which package to tender. The report also assesses how this decision will be influenced by the management team's attitude to risk.

(i) Analysis of risks facing the management team

Profit on contract

Mackerel is a commercial company, and therefore its ultimate objective will be to maximise the wealth it generates for its shareholders. In this context, one of the key performance measures for the APV project is the level of profit it can deliver for Mackerel.

Attitudes to risk

There is currently a significant degree of risk and uncertainty about the government contract, in relation to which APV to offer the likely orders to any vehicle. The amount of uncertainty the management team is prepared to accept will affect Mackerel's course of action for the APV project.

Risk seeking – Risk seekers will try to secure the best outcome and try to **maximise the benefit** this would have on their organisation, no matter how small the chance that this outcome will actually occur.

Risk neutral – Risk neutral decision makers are concerned with the **most likely outcome** in any situation.

Risk averse – Risk averse decision makers act on the assumption that the **worse outcome** will occur, and they try to minimise the effect this will have on their organisation.

It would seem sensible for Mackerel to evaluate the contract using different methods and then select the method which fits best with its objectives and risk appetite.

Earnings volatility

The institutional shareholders have expressed concern about the volatility of Mackerel's earnings. In this sense, it appears that the shareholders are **risk averse.** This may influence the management team's attitude to risk, but there are other factors which will also influence it.

Context of the contract

In this respect, it is important to think about the context of the government contract.

Economic conditions – The economic downturn in Zedland means that Mackerel is currently operating under difficult economic conditions. This increases the importance of winning the government contract, as does the fact that the contract is a major one for Mackerel.

Importance of the contract – The expected value of the contract is around $5 million (see Appendix 2), and Mackerel's current operating profit is $20.4 million per year.

Equally, the size of the contract should affect the risks Mackerel is prepared to take in connection with it. If such a large project were to fail, this could put the company's survival at risk.

Follow on contracts – Mackerel also needs to consider the APV contract in the context of the other work it does for the government. Winning the bid could lead to additional future work for Mackerel, so it may be more important to secure the bid than to maximise the profit on this single project alone.

Level of demand – Nonetheless there is still significant uncertainty about the project itself. The level of demand is uncertain, and this could have a major impact on the return Mackerel can earn from the project.

Cost overruns – The government is going to pay a fixed price for the contract, based on budgeted variable costs. If actual costs turn out to be higher than budgeted costs, this will again reduce the actual returns earned from the project.

Forecast price of steel – The price of steel could also have had a major impact on the profitability of the project. However, the risk manager appears to have removed this uncertainty by agreeing a fixed price for all the steel that might be required for the contract.

(ii) **Evaluation of the APV project**

As we have identified in part (i) of this report, it seems likely that the profitability of the contract will be an important performance measure in helping Mackerel maximise the value it creates for its shareholders.

Ideally, any decisions about the contract should be based on discounted future cashflows, but there is insufficient data available to calculate the cashflows. Therefore decisions about the project will be taken in relation to the profits it could generate for Mackerel.

Compliance with cost specifications

The first priority is to ensure that the cost to Mackerel of fulfilling the contract fall within the government's cost requirements (of $70,000 per unit).

The calculations in Appendix 2 indicate that the costs are within this limit:

	Demand		
	500	750	1000
Cost per unit ($)			
Package 1	62,972	57,972	55,472
Package 2	65,472	59,639	56,722
Package 3	67,972	61,305	57,972

Profits from design packages

The calculations in Appendix 2 also show that the profits for each package will vary significantly according to the different levels of demand:

	Demand		
	500	750	1000
Profit ($)			
Package 1	4,557,340	6,836,010	9,114,680
Package 2	3,307,340	5,586,010	7,864,680
Package 3	2,057,340	4,336,010	6,614,680

Methods for selecting a package

There are four possible approaches which Mackerel could use to select a package.

Three of these (maximax, maximin, and minimax regret) assume that there is insufficient information to estimate the likely level of demand for each package, and so are based on the profits which can be achieved under different demand scenarios. The calculations relating to each of these approaches are included in Appendix 1 of this report.

The fourth (expected values) tries try to incorporate the risk manager's assessment of the probabilities of the different demand levels into the decision about which package to offer (see Appendix 2).

Maximax

Risk seekers (decision-makers who aim to maximise the possible returns from the different scenarios) will use a maximax method to evaluate the different packages. If Mackerel adopts this approach, it would be advised to choose **Package 1**, which will have a maximax profit of $9.1 million (where demand is 1,000).

Maximin

Risk averse decision-makers (who seek to maximise the minimum possible returns from the different scenarios) will use a maximin method to evaluate the different packages. If Mackerel adopts this approach, it would still be advised to choose **Package 1**, which will have a maximin profit of $4.6 million (where demand is 500).

Regret

Pessimistic decision makers will focus on the amount of any profit they might lose in any scenario compared to the best choice at the same level of demand. In this way, they aim to minimise the maximum level of regret they could suffer under any demand scenario. If Mackerel adopts this type of **minimax regret** approach, it would still be advised to choose **Package 1**, because this will lead to zero regret at each level of demand.

The fact that all three methods indicate Package 1 as the preferred choice should not come as a surprise. Package 1 has significantly lower fixed costs than the other two packages, while the variable costs per unit are the same for each package and at all levels of demand.

Importantly, though, these three methods used so far do not take account of the probabilities attached to the different levels of demand for each package.

Expected values

A risk neutral manager will choose the option that yields the maximum expected value once the probabilities for each of the outcomes is factored into the decision-making process.

Probabilities – Mackerel's risk manager has tried to quantify the probabilities of the different levels of demand for each of the packages offered. These estimated probabilities allow the calculation of an expected profit for each design package (see Appendix 2).

Appendix 2 indicates that the maximum expected profit (of $5.6 million) can be earned if **Package 2** is chosen. This is because the improved design in Package 2 significantly increases the likelihood of securing a higher demand than for Package 1. Although Package 3 also has an improved design, the benefits of this in terms of expected demand do not outweigh the additional $1.25 million design and development costs incurred.

However, it is difficult to ascertain the relevant probabilities of different order volumes and so the management team need to recognise that the risk manager's estimates are likely to be subjective. Therefore the team should consider getting some other opinions on the probabilities before using them; for example, by consulting the sales team, or by referring back to any similar government tenders they have worked on in the past.

(iii) **Recommendations**

Method of assessing the project

The method chosen to assess the project needs to reflect the management team's **attitude to risk**. The context of risk averse shareholders, a difficult economic environment, and a major contract for the company, suggests that a low risk method will be appropriate here.

The use of expected values appears debatable here because they appear to be based only on one person's estimate. Instead, the **risk averse method of maximin** appears to be most appropriate here, and I recommend Mackerel use this method.

Course of action for the APV contract

Design package 1 should be chosen, because this carries the least risk for Mackerel and guarantees a profit of at least $4.6 million.

Although the expected values indicate that there could be the potential to earn an additional profit of $573k by choosing Package 2 in preference to Package 1, the level of uncertainty over the probability estimates does not justify such a decision in relation to a major contract such as this.

(iv) **New executive information system**

The new system will improve the availability of data (at operational level) and will help improve Mackerel's decision-making (at strategic level), but it will be important that the costs of the new system do not outweigh the potential benefits of the system. However, it will be much harder to quantify the benefits of the system compared to the costs.

Operational level

Immediate update – Once the new system is introduced, users will expect to be able to gather information about operational performance immediately, on a real-time basis. Whilst having this information on a real-time basis could help improve control over performance, there are also likely to be costs associated gathering the data.

Data entry – It is not clear how data is currently entered onto Mackerel's systems, but if users are going to be able to view data on a real-time basis, all transactions will need to be entered immediately, rather than, for example, on a batch basis. This could generate increased costs in relation to data processing and data entry, unless Mackerel already has a system of automated data input.

If Mackerel doesn't already have a system of automated data input, this would be an opportunity to automate the process, in order to maximise the benefits from real-time data availability.

Strategic decision-making

Summary information – The EIS should allow improved decision-making by presenting summary information relating to all the performance areas of the company, but with the option for senior managers to **drill-down** and get more detailed information about specific aspects of performance if they want to.

Consistency – Whereas summary data used to come from a range of different systems, it will now come from a single database, which should remove any inconsistencies within the data and the way it is structured. This could be a significant aid to decision-making, because it will enable managers to focus on analysing the data, rather than having to spend time reconciling different figures or reports prepared by different functions within Mackerel.

External information – However, the system should also be linked to external data sources to that managers do not focus solely on internal information at the expenses of what is happening in the wider business environment, and for example, the risk of any cut backs in government expenditure (which could have an impact on the number of APVs the government may buy).

However, including external information in the EIS will mean that Mackerel will need to include new data sources which again could increase the cost of the system.

Amount of information available – The new system will increase the amount of information which is available to managers, and the speed with which it is available to them. This will therefore increase the amount of analysis they could perform in relation to any strategic decisions.

However, if the level of information available is not controlled, managers could suffer from **information overload**. Therefore the new system will need to be structured so that managers only information which is necessary or appropriate to them.

Training – In order to gain the maximum benefit from the new system, managers will need to be trained how to use it, and this training should occur just before the system becomes available so that managers are able to use it immediately.

Performance measures

Shareholder wealth – Mackerel's mission is to maximise shareholder wealth, and total shareholder return is used as an overall performance measure to assess how well the company is achieving this.

Total shareholder return (TSR) is concerned with both the current performance of a business and its future performance. Current performance is likely to dictate current dividend payments, while expected future performance is likely to dictate share price.

ROCE – By contrast, profit-based performance measures focus on historical performance rather than potential future performance.

Whilst ROCE is a simple, commonly used measure of performance, it can be criticised as potentially be detrimental to future performance rather than enhancing it. Using ROCE as a performance measure can discourage investment in net assets, because such an investment will increase the level of capital employed and thereby reduce the ROCE figure (which is calculated as profit before interest and tax divided by capital employed).

Profit rather than cash – In addition, ROCE has the disadvantage of being based on profit rather than cash. Measures such as net present values (NPV) use cash flows, which are less subject to a company's accounting rules and policies, and so are more directly aligned with shareholder interests.

Overall, it is unclear whether ROCE will align with the overall performance measure of TSR, since TSR depends on share price and dividends paid rather than profit. In particular, given that share price is based on a long-term view of dividend prospects and future performance, it seems likely that short-term performance measures, such as profit-based measures, will have limited use in supporting TSR.

EVA

Calculating EVA involves a more complex calculation than calculating ROCE, because a number of adjustments are made to the accounting figures for profit and net assets.

Value-creating expenditure – However, these adjustments are intended to avoid the distortion of results by accounting policies, which we noted was one of the limitations of ROCE. In addition, EVA treats value-creating expenditure (such as marketing) as an investment rather than a cost, and so it can encourage appropriate capital expenditure rather than discouraging it in the way that ROCE does.

Shareholders' interests – In this way, EVA is more aligned with the shareholders' interests in future performance than ROCE is.

This should not be a surprise, because the logic behind the developed of EVA was that, if an organisation's primary objective is to maximise the wealth of its shareholders, then performance measures need to evaluate how well the organisation is achieving that objective.

However, EVA is still calculated based on historical data while shareholders will be focused on future performance. Therefore, although it is more directly aligned with the objective of increasing shareholder wealth than ROCE is, it still doesn't measure shareholders' expectations which are present in the share price.

Conclusion

Given the current risk appetites of key stakeholders, and the current volatility in the economic environment, it is recommended that Mackerel chooses design package 1 for the APV, because it carries the least risk.

The EIS provides an opportunity to improve the information for control and decision-making, but it is important that the costs of the new system are properly understood before it is finally approved.

EVA is more closely aligned to Mackerel's overall goal of increasing shareholder wealth than ROCE is. However, neither measure is a perfect match to the company's main performance measure of TSR, because they are based on historic performance information rather than expectations of future performance.

Appendix 1

Mark up per unit

	$
Variable cost per APV	
Steel (9.4 tonnes at $1,214 per tonne)	11,412
Engine/transmission	9,500
Electronics	8,450
Other	4,810
Labour	13,800
Total	47,972

Mark up @ 19%; $9,114.7

Payoff table

Demand	500	750	1000	Max payoff	Min payoff
Design package					
Type 1	4,557,350	6,836,025	9,114,700	9,114,700	4,557,350
Additional fixed costs	1,250,000	1,250,000	1,250,000		
Type 2	3,307,350	5,586,025	7,864,700	7,864,700	3,307,350
Additional fixed costs	1,250,000	1,250,000	1,250,000		
Type 3	2,057,350	4,336,025	6,614,700	6,614,700	2,057,350

Maximum of the maximum payoffs – Package 1	9,114,700	
Maximum of the minimum payoffs – Package 1		4,557,350

Regret table

Design package				Max regret
Type 1	0	0	0	0
Type 2	1,250,000	1,250,000	1,250,000	1,250,000
Type 3	2,500,000	2,500,000	2,500,000	2,500,000

Minimum of max regret - Package 1	0

Appendix 2

Demand	500	750	1000	
	$	$	$	
Variable cost (@ $47,972 each)	23,986,000	35,979,000	47,972,000	
Fixed cost				
Package 1	7,500,000	7,500,000	7,500,000	
Package 2	8,750,000	8,750,000	8,750,000	
Package 3	10,000,000	10,000,000	10,000,000	
Total cost				
Package 1	31,486,000	43,479,000	55,472,000	
Package 2	32,736,000	44,729,000	56,722,000	
Package 3	33,986,000	45,979,000	57,972,000	
Cost per unit				
Package 1	62,972	57,972	55,472	
Package 2	65,472	59,639	56,722	
Package 3	67,972	61,305	57,972	

Revenue
[$7.5 + (budgeted variable costs x 1.19)]

	500	750	1000	
	36,043,340	50,315,010	64,586,680	
Profit				
Package 1	4,557,340	6,836,010	9,114,680	
Package 2	3,307,340	5,586,010	7,864,680	
Package 3	2,057,340	4,336,010	6,614,680	

Expected profit

	500	750	1000	Total
Package 1				
Probability	85%	10%	5%	
Expected profit ($)	3,873,739	683,601	455,734	5,013,074
Package 2				
Probability	25%	50%	25%	
Expected profit ($)	826,835	2,793,005	1,966,170	5,586,010
Package 3				
Probability	20%	50%	30%	
Expected profit ($)	411,468	2,168,005	1,984,404	4,563,877

69 TSC

Marking scheme

					Marks
(a)	(i)	Revenue		0.5	
		Profit		0.5	
		Customer care and service		3	
		Credit control and administration efficiency		5	
					9
	(ii)	Overall comment on ranking		1	
		Analysis of each of the three sections in table		5	
			Max		5
	(iii)	Inter-relationship of dimensions/results/determinants		2	
		Definition/examples of financial performance and competitiveness as aspects of results	2 × 1.5	3	
		Definition/examples of determinants of quality, resource utilisation, flexibility and innovation	4 × 1.5	6	
			Max		10
	(iv)	Comments (on merit)		5	
			Max		6
		Note. Requirement (a) includes 4 professional marks			4
(b)		Benefits of league tables		4	
		Problems of league tables		4	
			Max		6

(c) General discussion of Burns & Scapens – up to 2   2

Impact of technology on role of accountant – up to 3   3

Impact of competitive environment on role of accountant –
up to 3   3

Discussion of role of 'hybrid' accountant – up to 2   2

Discussion of strategic management accounting – up to 2   2

Max   10

Total = 50

To:	Directors of TSC
From:	Management Accountant
Date:	5 December 20X8
Subject:	Performance of four depots for the year ended 31 October 20X8

This report will summarise the performance of the four sample depots chosen for review.

(a) (i) **Table showing the ranking of the four depots**

Measure Depot	1	2	3	4	5	6	7	8	9	10	11	12	Total
D	0	1	1	0	1	0	1	1	0	1	1	1	8
L	1	0	0	1	1	0	1	0	1	1	1	1	8
M	1	1	1	1	1	1	1	1	1	1	1	1	12
R	1	0	0	0	0	0	0	1	0	1	1	0	4

The table shows that M is the best performing depot based on the criteria chosen in the Appendix. M manages to attain the target on every performance measure. D and L come joint second with eight targets achieved each, although they achieve target on different measures. R is the worst performing depot with only four out of the 12 measures achieved.

Workings for measures 10 and 12 are shown in a separate Appendix at the end of this report.

Sample profit calculation (measure 2)

Actual results

Donatellotown = 2.3/15 = 15.3% (1 point)

Leonardotown = 2.4/18 = 13.3% (0 point)

(ii) **Relative performance of the depots**

1 **Measures 1 and 2 Revenue and profit**
M performed best overall with both measures achieved. None of the other depots attained both of these targets.

2 **Measures 3 to 8 Customer care and service delivery**
Again, M performed best overall, achieving all targets set. L achieved three measures, D, four and R only one. This suggests that R's performance needs to be looked at to find out why it has performed so poorly. The targets for 5, 7, and 8 were achieved by 3 out of the 4 depots. These were delayed response to complaints, lost items and damaged items. The measure achieved least, by M alone, was delays due to vehicle breakdown.

3 **Measures 9 to 12. Credit control and administration efficiency**
M and L achieved all four measures. D met three targets and R met two. Again, R's performance needs to be scrutinised and explanations sought for poor performance.

(iii) **Assessment of TSC using dimensions from the Building Blocks model**

The Building Blocks model of performance looks at several aspects of performance beyond the purely financial measures often used. It considers innovation for instance. The model also seeks to link the measures and shows how the performance in individual measures affects the other measures so they are interrelated. It looks at results (the financial and competitiveness measures) and determinants (other measures listed below).

1   **Financial performance**

This is measured by revenue and profitability. Overall, TSC exceeded target revenue and profit by 20% and 6.7% respectively. The four depots account for 30% of target revenue and profits but contributed 28.8% and 30.3% of actual revenue and profits for the company. The best performance overall came from L which exceeded target on both measures by the largest percentage (28.6% on revenue and 14.3% on profit). R remains the best performer on absolute revenue and profit although it performs so poorly on other measures. This suggests that it may not be making the necessary investment in service and quality to satisfy targets for these areas. All the depots excepting R met the target for credit notes (12).

2   **Competitiveness**

This is assessed in terms of sales growth, market share and growth in customers. We cannot measure year on year growth for revenue and profit as prior year data is not available but we can compare to targets set. So the depots should be compared to each other for financial competitiveness.

R, L and M have all seen growth in revenues compared with target on the year. D is the exception here and revenues are 6% under target.

3   **Service quality**

Service quality looks at reliability, courtesy and competence. Relevant measures are measures (3) to (8). M performs best across these measures and R achieves only one of them. If we compare the depots to the benchmark targets, M, L and D perform better than industry standard in at least three of the targets set.

4   **Resource utilisation**

This determinant considers productivity (how efficiently resources are being utilised). Resources would be people, vehicles and machinery used to sort and handle the parcels. The measures such as lost items, late collection and the other measures represented in (3) to (8) highlight possible problems with resource utilisation. An example of a measure revealing resource utilisation would be lost items as a percentage of revenue. All of the depots except R perform better than the target on this measure. Does this suggest R has a problem with its resources: numbers of people, machinery breakdowns and so on.

5   **Flexibility**

Flexibility has three aspects: speed of delivery, response to customer specification and coping with demand. Again measures (3) to (8) are the best indicators of how well TSC is performing on flexibility. The company may have a problem here as delays arise, deliveries are late and consignments are lost.

6   **Innovation**

Innovation looks at innovative ways of satisfying customer needs to gain competitive advantage. Individual innovations should be measured in terms of whether they bring improvements in the other dimensions. For TSC, innovation might include changes in delivery methods including staffing, machinery and vehicles to improve the time or ease of getting parcels to the depots.

Interrelationships between these dimensions.

The measures can be considered in terms of how they bring about improvements in the other dimensions. So innovations in delivery, briefly considered above, may lead to greater flexibility in the speed of delivery and response to customer demand. More efficient use of resources should result in better financial performance as costs are consumed at a lower rate.

(iv) A critique of the performance measurement system at TSC

1. It has internal benchmarks which are usually against the industry but **who are the industry comparators?**

2. Bonuses are awarded for attaining target but performance above target is not recognised. Therefore there is no incentive for staff to exceed their targets. An alternative would be for TSC to have a 'graded' system, so that staff receive a certain level of bonus if they reach their target, but a higher level if they exceed their target.

3. There is no weighting to assess **the relative importance of targets**. L and M achieve targets (9) and (10) but we don't know which has performed better or which of these are more important targets.

   As we do not know what TSC's objectives are, we cannot assess how these targets link to TSC's overall performance objectives or critical success factors.

4. The system includes **measures outside the control of the individual depots**. Allocated overheads are central overheads and distribution centre costs. It is unlikely that the central overheads are directly controllable by the depots. Revenue is credited to each depot based on the invoiced value of all consignments collected in its area. This is a matter of luck to some degree: so busy city-centre depots will earn more revenue than rural depots. The only controllable element would be the extent to which performance and reputation of the depot encourages or discourages new customers.

5. **The system does, however, use financial and non-financial performance measures** which is a more rounded approach to the assessment of performance than just financial measures.

Appendix showing how measures (10) and (12) were calculated

(10) Debtors (Receivables) over 60 days

	D	L	M	R
Revenue ($'000)	15,000	18,000	14,000	22,000
Debtor weeks	5.8	4.9	5.1	6.2
Total debtors ($'000) (Revenue x debtor weeks/52)	1,673	1,696	1,373	2,623
Aged debtors analysis up to 60 days ($'000)	(1,621)	(1,633)	(1,333)	(2,552)
Debtors > 60 days ($'000)	52	63	40	71
% of total debtors	3.1	3.7	2.9	2.7
Target %	5	5	5	5

(12) Credit notes as a % of revenue

	D	L	M	R
A. Value of credit notes raised ($'000)	45	36	28	132
B. Revenue ($'000)	15,000	18,000	14,000	22,000
A/B %	0.3	0.2	0.2	0.6
Target	0.5	0.5	0.5	0.5

(b) Benefits and problems in using league tables to measure performance

The table drawn up here for the four depots shows the relative performance of the four depots on the twelve measures chosen.

Benefits

A league table allows an easy way of making comparisons using a few indicators. **It is easy to read and understand the measures used in the table.**

The table uses **benchmarks** and we can assume best practice in these areas of performance.

It gives incentives for depots to perform better as **their performance is visible**.

Problems

A league table can be **oversimplified** as it represents a simplification of what might be complex measures.

How are the measures weighted and should some measures have more weight than others?

It leads **to fixation on the measures in the table** so that these are achieved at the expense of all others.

It can lead to **a sense of failure** for those at the bottom of the table.

(c) Burns and Scapens suggested three main reasons for the changes in the role of the management accountant: developments in technology and IT systems, changes in management structure and changes in the competitive environment.

There is no indication that there have been any changes in the management structure at TSC, but changes in the other two areas will have an impact on the management accountant's role.

Technology and IT systems – Historically, TSC's operational managers have relied on the management accountant to provide them with information because the accountant had better access to the information than them. However, the new software system will enable the operational managers to have access to much of the same information as the management accountant, so they no longer need the management accountant to prepare and provide it for them.

The management accountant may still be required to prepare some reports or provide information that other managers are not producing themselves, (especially in relation to consolidated reports, for example). However, in many cases the data the accountant uses for her reports will have come from the operations departments, and will have been processed automatically into the software system. Therefore the accountant is will now be a user of accounting data in the system, rather than the controller of it.

Competitive environment – Burns and Scapens also highlighted that management accountants' roles have shifted from financial accounting to a more commercial orientation as a consequence of organisations needing to respond to competition and also to deploy a more strategic focus.

The finance director's comments about the need to monitor the industry and TSC's competitors reinforces this point. However, perhaps more importantly, the finance director's criticism of TSC's management information as being too inward looking highlights that he wants the management information to become more strategic – for example, including external competitor and market information, as well as monitoring TSC's own internal performance information.

Equally, the need for TSC's management information to become more strategic highlights the need to focus on longer term issues and not simply short-term (annual) performance statistics.

In their original study, Burns and Scapens highlighted that one of the consequences of the increasingly competitive economic situation was that management accountant needed to provide information from a wider range of sources – including non-financial aspects as well as financial ones. However, the existing performance statistics at TSC (for example, around customer care and service delivery) shows that TSC already monitors some non-financial aspects of performance, so this element of the change is unlikely to affect the management accountant's role.

Management accountant's on-going contribution

Information about competitors and markets – As we have already noted, the finance director wants the management accountant to look at external information, for example, analysing market share data, or benchmarking TSC's performance against competitors' performance. In this respect, the management accountant's role could become more of a 'strategic management accounting' role.

Hybrid accountant – Burns and Scapens also highlighted that the 'modern' accountant's role should be that of a 'hybrid accountant.' This would mean that the management accountant will need an improved knowledge of operational matters, and should work more closely with the operational managers at TSC. For example, the management accountant should expect to become more involved in providing advice and helping operational managers make decisions in relation to operational aspects of the business, rather than seeing her role as being limited to controlling financial performance.

70 Lincoln & Lincoln

Text reference. Financial performance measures are discussed in Chapter 9 of the BPP Study Text. External influences on performance are considered in Chapter 6. Remuneration and HR management are discussed in Chapter 14. Information overload and performance reports are covered in Chapter 8.

Top tips.

Part (i). ACCA's Examining team have consistently stressed that P5 is about analysis and performance management, not simply calculation and performance measurement. Part (i) of this question highlights this point really clearly. The requirement asks you to 'Assess the recent performance of the three regional offices...'. Importantly, however, Appendix 2 (provided in the question) has already calculated a number of performance measures based on the financial data provided in Appendix 1. Therefore, the main focus of your answer needs to be on analysing the figures which have already been provided rather than doing additional calculations of your own.

Equally, did you note that the scenario highlighted that 'The Board would not be interested in a long list of which numbers have gone up and which have gone down'? This again should have highlighted that your answer should not have been a detailed commentary on individual figures from Appendices 1 and 2. Instead, you should have identified the key features in each office's performance and concentrated on them.

It is also important to think how you present your answer. Is it better to structure your answer under standard ratio headings (profitability; liquidity; investors' ratios) or will it be better to use the three offices as the framework for your answer, and analyse each office in turn? We have adopted the latter approach, and presented a short analysis of each office in turn. As there are significant differences between the performance of the three offices, we think it is sensible to make comments about each of them individually, as well as including a short summary comment about LLA as a whole.

When analysing the individual offices (using the data provided), you should try to identify the key areas of difference between them. For example, revenue has fallen slightly in the North, remained largely constant in the East, but grown quite rapidly in the West. Such distinctions will be important in part (iii) when you have to suggest appropriate measures for each office.

Part (ii). A key point to note here is that the information provided in the Appendices 1 and 2 only looks at internal performance measures. However, the scenario has identified that Veeland has considerable diversity in economic conditions across its regions. So, the relative performance of the different offices could be affected by these external factors as much as the efforts of the staff in the different offices. In effect, you should think about the importance of external information in relation to the benefits the Directors would gain from looking at external measures of performance alongside the existing internal ones.

Part (iii). The scenario highlights that 'issues around controllability and responsibility accounting appear to be the main concerns of the board.' In turn, the idea of controllability is very important in evaluating whether net income is an appropriate performance measure for the regional offices. The net income figure is shown after head office costs have been allocated to the offices, but do the regional offices have any control over the level of head office costs or how they are re-allocated?

However, note that there are effectively two elements to this part of the requirement: (i) evaluate the use of net income as a performance measure; (ii) suggest other measures which are appropriate for each office. As we noted in relation to part (i) earlier, it is important to identify the different issues which each office is facing, because the appropriateness of the measures will depend on how well they relate to these key issues.

Part (iv). In effect, this part of the question again relates to the diversity between the offices and the conditions they are operating in. For example, if one office is focusing on controlling costs and one office is focusing on growth should the performance measures in each office be tailored to reflect this? Importantly, note the verb requirement here is to 'evaluate' the benefits, so you shouldn't only consider what the benefits are, but whether there are any factors which restrict those benefits.

Part (v). Appendix 3 provides details of the remuneration packages for the five grades of staff in the regional office. A sensible approach to this question would be to work through each package in turn and identify which elements of the package are likely to be effective in motivating staff, and which will be less effective.

You should have noted that the question doesn't only ask you to evaluate LLA's current policy, but also to suggest changes as appropriate. This second part of the requirement should have alerted you to the fact that there are likely to be a number of problems with the current policy – which you should then look to address with the changes you have suggested. In effect, if your evaluation identifies a problem with an aspect of LLA's current policy, you should then try to suggest a change which could help overcome that problem.

Although there was no requirement to do so, you could have considered the 'Rewards' aspect of the Building Block model here as a framework for evaluating LLA's remuneration policy. How clear is the policy? How well does it motivate the different grades of staff? How far can the staff control the factors they are being measured against?

Part (vi). The final paragraph of the scenario provides the context for this part of the question. The Operations Director's comments (about the volume of reports making it harder for him to assess how well the offices are actually performing) should have been a clear indicator of the problem of information overload. Similarly, his reference to 'not being a numbers man' should have alerted you that he would appreciate performance reports with less numbers on them. So, for example, how else could performance information be presented?

Examining team's comments. The quality of numerical working, and commentary on results, remains an area of concern. In part (i), where an interpretation of numerical data was required, many candidates basically put into sentences the numbers which had been calculated. For example, simply saying 'North's net income has fallen while East and West's have risen' is not an 'interpretation' of the data, and so gained no marks as a comment.

Additionally, in parts (i) and (iii) candidates lost easy marks by not addressing their advice to the individual circumstances of the three offices, and offering instead generic comments for the whole company. The scenario gave much detail on the three offices and it should have been obvious that they each faced their own challenges which required a tailored response. The scenario even reiterated this point with the CEO's advice to avoid 'a one-size fits all policy.)

In part (iii) candidates who realised that non-financial indicators would be useful, and went on to make suggestions appropriate to LLA scored well. However, the many candidates who provided lengthy (rote-learned?) proposals of ROCE, EVA and RI in general terms scored few marks. These measures were of limited use in this scenario, because they did not address the issues in the different offices nor did they address the fact that LLA would be likely to have a large intangible asset base.

In part (v), many candidates assumed that all of the existing policies must be wrong and so made only negative comments. Candidates need to be aware that 'evaluate' means to give a balanced assessment – including both the positive and negative aspects of an issue.

Also, many candidates seem to be under the misapprehension that share schemes solve all issues relating to remuneration policies. Share schemes can address the alignment of interests between staff and shareholders, but they do not *necessarily* address the short-sighted nature of many bonus schemes.

Marking scheme

			Marks
(i)	Discussion of the overall performance of the offices	1	
	Evaluation of the performance measures used, and suggestions for improvements – 1 mark per valid point	2	
	Discussion of the individual performance of each office – 1 mark per relevant point	Up to 8	
			10
(ii)	Explanation of the impact external factors can have on the offices' performance – 1 mark per relevant point	Up to 2	
	Explanation of the potential benefits LLA could derive from including external information in its performance reports – 1 mark per relevant point	Up to 4	5

			Marks
(iii)	1 mark per each relevant point, either in relation to evaluating net income as a performance measure, or in relation to suggesting (and justifying) alternative measures.		
	To obtain a good mark, candidates must address the issue of controllability and responsibility.	<u>Up to 10</u>	10
(iv)	For each benefit discussed (specifically in relation to the context of LLA's regional offices) – 1 mark per relevant point	Up to 4	
	For discussing potential issues with using different performance measures in different offices – 1 mark per relevant point	<u>Up to 2</u>	5
(v)	1 mark per each relevant point, either in relation to evaluating the current remuneration package, or suggesting improvements to it	<u>Up to 10</u>	10
(vi)	Discussion of information overload – 1 mark per relevant point	Up to 2	
	Recommendations for possible improvements to LLA's performance reports – 1 mark per relevant point	<u>Up to 4</u>	6
	Professional marks for presentation, style and structure		<u>4</u>
		Total =	**50**

To: The Board

From: Senior Management Accountant

Date: [today]

Subject: Performance and performance management in the regional offices

This report assesses the performance of LLA's three regional offices, and looks at possible ways of measuring the performance of the offices in the light of the Board's concern about controllability and responsibility accounting.

The report also evaluates LLA's remuneration policy, and suggests some improvements which could be made to the current policy.

(i)   **Performance of the three regional offices**

   Overall performance

   All three offices generate a positive net income and a positive cash flow. Similarly, all three offices generate positive Residual Incomes (RI), and Returns on Capital Employed (ROCE) in excess of 50%.

   At a summary level, the figures suggest all three offices are doing well.

	North ($m)	East ($m)	West ($m)
Net Income	20	65	80
Net cash flow in year	24	86	46

   Performance measures

   However, indicators such as RI and ROCE are less effective for measuring performance in a service company, like LLA, than in a manufacturing company, due to the intangible nature of many of LLA's assets and the services it provides.

   By contrast, measures such as **customer satisfaction** and **customer retention** are likely to be very important for LLA. Given that competition is fierce, and likely to remain so as a result of the economic downturn, it will be important for LLA to retain as many of its existing customers as it can.

However, the data extracted from the management accounts (Appendices 1 & 2) concentrates solely on financial performance, so we cannot comment on the offices' performance in relation to these important non-financial performance indicators.

Financial performance of different offices

Nonetheless, within the financial position which is favourable overall, there are some noticeable variations in the performance and the growth prospects of the individual offices.

North Office

The North Office's revenues have declined slightly for the last two years; with revenue falling by 1.9% in the last year.

As a result, despite the North's cost of sales and wage costs remaining relatively constant as a proportion of revenue, its operating profit and net income have also both fallen in the last year.

The North Office now has the lowest operating profit margin (%) of the three offices.

East Office

The East Office currently appears to have only limited opportunities for growth, with revenue increasing 1% per year.

Importantly, although its revenues have only grown slightly, the East Office has enjoyed the fastest growth of the three offices in terms of operating profit and net income. Operating profit has increased around 8% per year for the last two years, reflecting the fact that the East office has managed to reduce its cost of sales over the same period.

Nonetheless, the East Office has the lowest net income margin (%) due to the level of head office costs which are allocated to it.

West Office

The West Office's revenue growth is significantly higher than the other two offices (8.9% in the last year). It also generates the highest operating profit margin (over 20%).

This combination of revenue growth and high margins may suggest that economic conditions in the West of Veeland are more favourable than in the other regions.

Capital expenditure – The West Office's capital expenditure is significantly greater than capital expenditure in the other two offices. This helps to explain the West Office's relatively low net cash flow, compared to the East Office. However, the level of capital expenditure appears consistent with an office which is growing.

Working capital management – The West Office's growth appears to have had an adverse impact on its working capital, with the increase in receivable days (up to 93 days) being a particular cause for concern. The increase in receivable days may also help explain the relatively low net cash flow.

(ii)   **External information**

Regional differences – There are noticeable differences in the revenue growth rates of LLA's three regional offices. However, it is currently not clear how far these are caused by the internal performance of the different offices, or the diverse economic conditions across Veeland.

For example, although the North Office's revenue has fallen slightly it is not clear whether this reflects an overall decline in advertising spending in the North of Veeland, or whether the North office has been less successful than its competitors in winning business. Conversely, it is not clear how far favourable economic conditions in the west of the country have contributed to the West office's ability to grow revenues while still maintaining a high margin.

As we will see later in this report, understanding the impact that **regional economic variations** is having on the offices performance could also be important in the context of **performance-related pay**.

Therefore, as well as looking at the offices' own revenue figures, it would also be useful to relate them to their respective advertising markets as a whole, to see how each office is performing relative to its competitors. In this respect, figures for **market growth** and **market share** could be particularly instructive.

Benchmarking performance – More generally, it could also be useful to benchmark the offices' performance in key aspects of performance against their competitors. For example, it could be useful for LLA to know the amount of revenue its offices generate per full time equivalent member of staff compared to its competitors.

Although it could be difficult to obtain reliable competitor information, if LLA is able to do this then such information could provide a valuable insight into its performance relative to its competitors. Equally importantly, it could help identify areas where LLA's performance needs to improve to help ensure it continues to be successful in a fiercely competitive market.

(iii) **Performance measures**

The discussions in the last meeting have indicated that issues around controllability and responsibility accounting are important for the Board.

Allocated costs – In this context, it is important to highlight that the net income for each division is stated after deducting the **share of head office costs** which are allocated to that division. However, the head office costs – and the share allocated to each department – are **outside the divisional manager's control**.

Therefore, net income is not an appropriate measure for analysing the divisional managers' performance. For example, the East Office has the lowest net income margin, but this is due, in part, to the fact it receives nearly 60% of the re-allocated Head Office costs.

Operating profit – In this respect, operating profit would be a better measure to use, because it more accurately reflects the performance of the each office itself, and doesn't include any costs which have been re-allocated from head office. Given the Board's concern around 'controllability,' it seems appropriate to exclude head office costs when measuring the performance of the regional managers, because head office costs, and the way they are allocated, are outside the managers' control.

However, it is important not to overlook head office costs altogether, because LLA needs to ensure that the operating profits generated by the regional offices are sufficient to cover the agency's head office costs. Therefore, while it may be appropriate to use operating profit to measure the regional managers' performance, it may still be appropriate to use net income to measure the offices' performance as a whole.

Service business – It is also important to remember that performance measures which look at income generated in relation to the amount of capital employed (such as ROCE and Residual income) are less relevant for LLA than they would be for a manufacturing business. For example, the level of tangible assets which LLA holds is likely to be significantly lower than for a manufacturing company with similar revenues to LLA.

However, of the two measures (ROCE and RI), RI has the advantage that LLA could apply different costs of capital for the different offices. This would seem appropriate given the apparent differences between the environment in which the West office is operating and the other two. The West's higher capital expenditure suggests it may be taking more risks (for example, if it is investing in new design technology) but equally there appears to be scope for higher returns in the West than the other regions.

Staff as key assets – In this respect, revenue growth could be a key measure for LLA. However, it is also crucial for LLA, as a service company, to recognise the importance of its staff as key assets and revenue drivers. Therefore, it would be appropriate to include some performance measures which relate staff costs to revenue; for example, staff costs as a percentage of revenue, or revenue generated per full time equivalent member of staff.

Alternative measures

The CEO has already suggested the idea of using different key measures of each office, and this seems appropriate given the different issues which each office is facing.

North – A key issue in the North would appear to be turning around the decline in revenue. Therefore, **revenue growth** would be an appropriate target for this office.

However, the North's revenue may be declining because the regional market as a whole is shrinking. Therefore, LLA should also look to measure **market share**, to gauge how well it is performing against other agencies in the region.

Whilst revenue growth is important for the North, it is also important that the office targets profitable growth. For example, the office could reduce prices in order to attract new customers, but if it reduces prices too far the new business it gains may not be profitable. Therefore, **operating profit margin (%)** would also be an appropriate measure to use here.

East – Although the East office's revenue appears stable, there appear to be limited opportunities for revenue growth. Therefore, the focus here should be on maximising profits by controlling costs as efficiently as possible. Therefore **operating profit margin** will be a key measure for the East office.

Importantly, whilst the East office has the lowest cost of sales, it has the highest staff costs (37% compared to 31% in the West). Therefore, a key performance measure for the East would seem to be **staff costs as a percentage of revenue**.

The East's staff costs may reflect economic differences between the regions; for example, if the East is the most affluent area of Veeland, the market rates paid to staff may be higher there than in other parts of the country. Here again, it could be useful to compare the East office's staff costs against those of other agencies in the region.

West – It is important that the West office continues to growth, and that it does so profitably, by achieving the best operating margins it can. Therefore, revenue growth and operating profit margin would both be appropriate measures to use here.

However, the key issue facing the West office appears to be working capital management. In particular, **receivable days** should be a key performance measure, because this figure needs to be reduced. Similarly, the West should monitor its **current ratio**, because the recent increase in this figure also reflects the increase in the level of receivables.

Operating profit

Overall, operating profit would appear to be the most important performance measure for the regional offices, with revenue growth as a subsidiary indicator. Individual measures (such as staff costs or receivable days) should then be tailored for each office to address the specific issues they are facing.

However, alongside these internal performance measures, it would also be appropriate to include some **external measures**. In particular, LLA should measure the **market share** of each of its office. This will help provide some context for LLA's own revenue growth figures.

(iv) Localised performance measures

Reflect local issues – We have already highlighted that the three offices appear to be facing different issues. Consequently, it is likely that the offices will have different goals and objectives. In particular, it appears that the West office should focus on growth, while the East office should focus on controlling costs.

Performance measures – The value of performance measures comes from them providing management with a means of assessing whether objectives are being met. In this context, if LLA's offices have different objectives then it also follows that they should also have different performance measures and key performance indicators.

What gets measured, gets done – The idea that 'what gets measured, gets done' could also be important here. For example, if the managers in the West office know that its performance is being measured in relation to how much it grows, this should give them greater incentive to focus on growth. Similarly, if the managers in the East office know that its performance is being measured in relation to how effectively costs are controlled, this should encourage them to focus on costs.

Goal congruence – However, despite the potential benefits of using some different performance measures for different offices, it is important that the local objectives and performance measures still support any overall objectives which LLA has. For example, if LLA has identified the quality of the service it provides its clients as a key success factor for the business as a whole, then it will be important that all of the offices measure their performance in this respect. Therefore, it may be appropriate for there to be some performance measures which are used across all three offices, while others are specifically chosen for individual offices.

Benchmarking – Similarly, if none of the performance measures used by the three offices are the same, then LLA will not be able to use any internal benchmarking to compare their performance. Again, this suggests it could be useful to have some performance measures which are common to all three offices, although the value of internal benchmarking could be reduced by the different economic circumstances under which the offices are operating.

(v)   **Remuneration policy**

Benchmarking to industry norms – LLA's underlying policy of paying market rates should help ensure that staff are broadly happy with their remuneration. However, because LLA's policy only matches the industry norm, it is unlikely to provide the agency with any competitive advantage over its rivals. For example, because the policy matches the industry norm (rather than exceeding the norm) the policy is unlikely to motivate staff to outperform their peers in other agencies.

Senior management – As we have already noted, the fact that the senior manager's basic salaries reflect industry norms should keep them amenable to working for the agency, but the bonus could help motivate their performance further.

Controllability – It is not clear what the net income of each office is measured against in order to determine the managers' bonuses (for example, against budget, or against prior year). Importantly, though, the net income of the office is likely to be affected by external conditions which the managers cannot control. For example, if the economic downturn worsens, this is likely to adversely affect the performance of an office compared to prior year.

However, these external factors do not appear to be taken into account when determining the bonus, which could serve to de-motivate managers. For example, if the economic conditions in the North are less favourable than the West, it will be harder for the North office to perform well than the West office, regardless of the efforts of the North office's own managers. Managers in the North could become de-motivated because they know they cannot achieve results as favourable as those in the West. Equally, though, managers in the West may work below their optimal level, thinking that the favourable external conditions will enable them to still get a bonus.

Moreover, because the bonus is dependent on net income, it could also be affected by the level of head office costs which are re-allocated to the manager's office.

This issue, and the potential impact of external factors, both highlight the importance of controllability, which the Board has already been discussing.

It is important that the managers' bonus (or at least part of it) is dependent on factors they can control. In this respect, it may be beneficial to base the bonus on operating profit rather than net income. However, it could also be worthwhile for LLA to try to benchmark the performance of each office against regional competitors, such that bonuses are dependent on the office's performance relative to its competitors. The potential problem with this approach, however, will be the difficult of obtaining detailed information about competitors' performance.

Creative staff – Because LLA offers packages which reflect the market norms, this should help it attract good quality 'creatives'. However, there appear to be two main problems with the current policy:

–   Some 'creatives' receive a fixed salary only, whilst some receive a salary and a bonus. Depending on the level of the bonus, this discrepancy could lead to resentment between staff on the different pay arrangements.

–   The bonus elements of the creatives' packages are based on their office's revenue, rather than its profit, for example. Therefore there is an incentive simply to introduce new ideas (because doing so will increase revenue) rather than to introduce new ideas which will also be cost effective to implement and therefore profitable.

The individual nature of the creative's work suggests it may be appropriate for them to continue to have individual packages to an extent. However, it would seem beneficial to standardise the overall structure; for example, so that the remuneration package for all the 'creatives' includes a fixed element plus a bonus element.

Equally, it is important that the factors used to determine the bonus are ones which the creatives can **control**, and ones which will **motivate** them towards achieving LLA's objectives. So, for example, two criteria which could be used to judge performance in relation to bonus entitlements could be: the number of tender competitions the creative wins; and the number of industry awards their campaigns win.

However, the detailed objectives for each creative (which the creatives will then be assessed against to determine their bonus entitlement) should be agreed between the creative and their line managers.

Buying staff – The idea to base the buyers' bonuses on the prices they pay for advertising space seems appropriate because the bonuses are thereby linked to the key aspect of their job.

However, the reliability of the budget as a basis for assessing performance could be a more problematic aspect of the bonus calculation. The budgets were set by the finance team, seemingly without any input from the buying staff or regional offices. However, as the finance team is based in the East office and may lack knowledge about local market conditions for the other two offices, the budget they have set may not be reliable or realistic.

In this respect there could be two ways to improve the fairness of the buyers' package: One would be to involve some of the senior buyers in the budgeting process. The other would be to increase the buyer's fixed salary, but reduce the bonus element of their package. Given that the budget may still be unreliable despite the involvement of the senior buyers, it may be wise for LLA to adopt the second of these options.

Account management – It seems surprising that the account managers' packages are based on a fixed salary alone, with no bonus element.

The competitive market environment in Veeland suggests it is likely that account management will become an increasingly important activity for LLA. Therefore, it would seem appropriate for account management staff to be eligible for bonuses in the same way that creative or buying staff are eligible for them.

Moreover, it would seem relatively simple to measure the performance of the account management staff against key metrics such as client retention rates and the value of new business won. Therefore, it would be appropriate for a relatively high proportion of their remuneration to be performance-related, rather than based on a fixed salary. Measures such as the number of clients and total client revenues could also be used to determine the level of bonus staff are entitled to.

Administration staff – The administration staff are likely to be the most junior grade of staff, so there may be less market pressure for them to receive bonuses compared to more senior or more specialist staff.

However, it may help to sustain motivation and loyalty among the administration staff if they were also eligible for a small bonus based either on the profitability of their office or even on the overall profitability of LLA as a firm.

It seems appropriate to base the administration staff's bonus on overall profitability, because, unlike buyers or account managers, for example, their roles are not directly linked to specific value activities within the business.

(vi)   **Information overload and management reports**

Information overload – The problem of information overload arises when senior management staff have difficulty understanding the issues in their business, or making decisions, due to the presence of too much information.

There seems to be a danger of this problem arising at LLA, if the increasing number of reports the directors receive makes it harder for them to assess how well the regional offices are actually performing.

Moreover, although the CEO has made it clear that the Board are not interested in receiving long lists of numbers, it seems to be the case that at least some of the reports LLA's Directors receive do comprise a lot of numbers.

Presentation of reports

In this respect, there are two key aspects of the reports which need to be addressed.

Level of detail – It is important that the reports produced for LLA's senior managers and directors do not contain unnecessary detail. If the current reports do contain too much detail, one possible improvement would be the introduction of **drill-down reports**.

These initially present information at a high level, but provide users with an option to 'drill down' and investigate specific aspects of performance in more detail. However, drill down reports enable users to dictate the level of detail and information presented, and can prevent them being overloaded with too much detail initially.

Graphs and charts – The second potential change to the reports relates to the way the information itself is presented. At the moment, the reports management receive seem to be purely numerical. However, in some cases it could be more instructive to use graphs and charts instead, to highlight key performance measures or trends in a more 'visual' manner.

In this context, LLA could consider whether it may be beneficial to introduce an **Executive dashboard**. In this way, numerical data would be supplemented by graphs and tables to illustrate how the business is performing.

Conclusion

The performance of the three regional offices is reasonably encouraging overall, although it will be important that the West office maximises the benefits from its growth opportunities, by managing its working capital effectively.

However, the current performance measure used for the regional offices (net income) is not suitable because it does not reflect the aspects of performance which regional managers can control. It would be more appropriate to use operating profit as the main performance measure for the regional offices.

Finally, there appears room for improvement in the performance-related elements of LLA's remuneration packages, and suggestions have been made as to how these could be applied for each grade of staff.

71 BEC

Text references. The importance of non-financial performance measures is covered in Chapter 12 of the BPP P5 Study Text, while multi-dimensional performance measurement models (such as the Building Blocks model) are discussed in Chapter 15. Reward and remuneration packages, and performance appraisals, are discussed in Chapter 14.

Top tips. Part (a) (i). The income statement needs a bit of care, and you only have 18 minutes to do the calculations and draw up the statement. The good news is you don't need to comment on it. We give the following guidance:

You will need to **flex the costs** for the BEC budget as note 4 states that variable costs vary according to student numbers.

Don't get confused over the number of lecturers to include in your staff costs. **Note 7 states both colleges aim to employ 60 lecturers in a year.**

The **freelancers are not included in staff costs** but included under other operating costs according to note 5.

There are lots of small, fiddly calculations in this part of the question. None of these are difficult but don't lose track of figures. We suggest **you keep separate workings for calculations** used in the income statement and refer to them.

You may round your figures to $'000 but there are some costs in the income statement, for instance $95,680, that will look odd as $95.68. So we suggest you do your workings in $ and include figures in the income statement in $. We have set out our workings in detail as a separate note which you would not normally include in a report but may form an appendix.

Finally, you may prepare the income statement separately when you are working through the question. However the question wants you to show this as a statement so you will need to include it as such in your report.

Part (a) (ii). You need to choose measures appropriate to **service organisations** which capture a wide range of performance outcomes. ACCA's suggested solutions used the **Building Blocks model** which is a good analysis of financial and non-financial measures and is tailored to the performance measurement of service businesses. There are **six dimensions** in the model, which works out at about one to two marks per dimension if you can make pertinent comments for each. The examining team do not award more marks for financial measures than others so don't spend a lot of time calculating ratios to illustrate your answer.

Part (a) (iii). Here you should be thinking about how performance measurement relates to motivation, accountability, and the ultimate aims of the organisation. There are six marks for this part and the examining team awarded one mark per comment. We have listed seven points to aid you in revision but you only need to make six.

Finally, remember to write this as a report. There are up to four professional marks available.

Part (b) (i). The 'total reward package' highlights the employee benefits which complement the base pay which staff earn. So, in effect, this part of the requirement is asking what the advantages and disadvantages to JBC are from having a reward scheme which uses employee benefits to complement the base pay which staff get.

Part (b) (ii). Although the requirement doesn't ask about the disadvantages of appraisal systems as such, it would be useful to think what some of these disadvantages can be. Then you can think whether any of these could apply to JBC; in which case, they could help explain why the objectives of the appraisal system are not being met.

To: Senior Management Team
From: Management Accountant
Date: Dec 20X9
Subject: Report on the performance of BEC against budget and compared with JBC for the year ended 30 November 20X9

This report contains the information you recently requested comparing the financial and non-financial performance of BEC and JBC.

(a) (i) **Statement of income statements – year ended 30 November 20X9**

Income statements	BEC Budget 20X9 $	BEC Actual 20X9 $	JBC Actual 20X9 $	Workings
Revenue				
Private				
Accounting	3,456,000	3,192,000	4,000,000	1
Law	1,200,000	980,000	1,872,000	2
Marketing	1,152,000	1,120,000	2,400,000	3
	5,808,000	5,292,000	8,272,000	
Government funded				
Accounting	648,000	1,026,000	0	4
Law	225,000	315,000	0	5
Marketing	216,000	360,000	0	6
	1,089,000	1,701,000		
Total revenue	6,897,000	6,993,000	8,272,000	
Costs				
Salaries - Lecturers	3,000,000	3,120,000	3,300,000	60 × $50,000 60 × $52,000 60 × $55,000
Salaries - Administrative staff	200,000	208,000	176,000	10 × $20,000 10 × $20,800 8 × $22,000
Tuition materials	648,000	741,600	730,000	BEC budget - $720,000 × 7,200 actual students/8,000 budget students

BPP LEARNING MEDIA

Income statements	BEC Budget 20X9 $	BEC Actual 20X9 $	JBC Actual 20X9 $	Workings
Catering	92,000	95,680	110,000	BEC budget – variable ($100,000 × 0.8 × 7,200/8,000) + fixed ($100,000 × 0.2)

Income statements	BEC Budget 20X9 $	BEC Actual 20X9 $	JBC Actual 20X9 $	Workings
Cleaning	39,000	40,950	40,000	BEC budget – variable ($40,000 × 0.25 × 7,200/8,000) + fixed ($40,000 × 0.75)
Other operating costs	588,000	646,800	645,000	BEC budget – variable ($600,000 × 0.20 × 7,200/8,000) + fixed ($600,000 × 0.80)
Depreciation	40,000	40,000	60,000	
Total costs	4,607,000	4,893,030	5,061,000	
Net profit	2,290,000	2,099,970	3,211,000	

Workings – to be shown in an Appendix to the Report

1. $3,600 × 0.8 × \$1,200 = \$3,456,000$
   $3,800 × 0.7 × \$1,200 = \$3,192,000$
   $4,000 × 1.0 × \$1,000 = \$4,000,000$

2. $1,500 × 0.8 × \$1,000 = \$1,200,000$
   $1,400 × 0.7 × \$1,000 = \$980,000$
   $1,560 × 1 × \$1,200 = \$1,872,000$

3. $1,800 × 0.8 × \$800 = \$1,152,000$
   $2,000 × 0.7 × \$800 = \$1,120,000$
   $2,000 × 1 × \$1,200 = \$2,400,000$

4. $3,600 × 0.2 × \$900 = \$648,000$
   $3,800 × 0.3 × \$900 = \$1,026,000$

5. $1,500 × 0.2 × \$750 = \$225,000$
   $1,400 × 0.3 × \$750 = \$315,000$

6. $1,800 × 0.2 × \$600 = \$216,000$
   $2,000 × 0.3 × \$600 = \$360,000$

(ii) **An assessment of the performance of BEC and JBC using financial and non-financial measures**

BEC and JBC are both **service businesses** which need to be measured on the service they provide to their customers – their students.

Financial performance measures consider costs and profits. The two colleges are not strictly comparable on revenues as one is privately owned and the two have different fee structures. It is therefore better to compare costs, which appear similar. A key measure is cost per student.

	BEC Budget 20X9	BEC Actual 20X9	JBC Actual 20X9
Total costs	$4,607,000	$4,893,030	$5,061,000
Students	6,900	7,200	7,560
Cost per student	$667.68	$679.59	$669.44

JBC has a lower cost per student than BEC actual but higher than that budgeted for BEC. BEC should review the reasons for the cost overrun, starting with the summary data in the income statement.

Management should continue to monitor cost per student over time and against comparable organisations, whether public or private.

Competitive performance considers sales growth and other measures of market performance. One measure is to compare the number of students signed up with the number of enquiries received, which gives the **take-up rate** for courses. The worst performing course is Law, where the actual take-up percentage for BEC was only 50%, compared with 75% budgeted and 78% for JBC. The rate for Marketing and Accounting was better than budget for BEC, but slightly below JBC for Marketing.

	BEC Budget 20X9	BEC Actual 20X9	JBC Actual 20X9
Accountancy			
Enrolled	3,600	3,800	4,000
Enquiries	4,800	4,750	5,000
Take up rate %	75	80	80
Law			
Enrolled	1,500	1,400	1,560
Enquiries	2,000	2,800	2,000
Take up rate %	75	50	78
Marketing			
Enrolled	1,800	2,000	2,000
Enquiries	2,400	2,500	2,400
Take up rate %	75	80	83

Quality of service. This looks at reliability, courtesy and competence, for example. Reliability and competence may be measured by pass rates. Students returning for future courses and word of mouth recommendation both signify student satisfaction at the quality of service they received. The organisations should, if not already doing so, ask students to complete assessments at the end of courses commenting on quality of teaching, support and materials. Internal reviews of staff and management should also capture service quality in other ways.

Flexibility measures the organisation's ability to deliver at the right speed, to customer requirements and to cope with changes in demand. For professional colleges, flexibility is reflected in the types and numbers of courses offered, and modes of delivery, for instance online or in the classroom. Another aspect of flexibility is colleges offering students the option to enter onto courses at different points and gain credits for different levels of achievement.

JBC employed freelancers during the year to support in-house lecturers, suggesting a more flexible approach to managing and providing courses and resource planning than BEC. JBC also considered offering on-line tuition to students.

Resource utilisation looks at how efficiently resources are being utilised. Resources in both organisation is mainly the staff. The key measure is staff to student ratios across courses and over time. Both BEC and JBC aim to employ 60 lecturers throughout the year. In 20x9, BEC recruited 12 lecturers to maintain the level of 60. This is 20% of the total and the reasons for this high turnover must be investigated. In comparison, JBC recruited only one new lecturer in 20x9. BEC also recruited eight new admin staff against two budgeted. The reason for this needs investigating.

Innovation measures the number and success of innovations offered. JBC is developing four new courses whilst BEC has none in progress.

(iii) **A discussion of the issues restricting the extent to which a performance measurement system is supported by management and employees**

Issues include:

1 How well managers and employees understand measures set and their relationship to the organisation's strategy

2 The reporting of results in ways that allow management to understand how well the organisation is progressing towards attaining overall strategy

3   How much say managers and employees have in setting targets for their own areas of responsibility and how equitable these are seen to be. This is the 'buy in' that is needed for the system to work well and to be supported.

4   Whether managers can be held accountable for performance in their divisions or whether this is outside their control

5   How and whether performance is linked to reward

6   Managers and employees 'owning' the performance outcomes and accepting any changes that are needed, given the outcomes

7   Appropriate training, education and leadership to support the introduction of and ongoing performance measurement process

Please contact me if you want any more information or clarification of the contents of this report.

Signed: Accountant

Date: Dec 20X9

(b)   (i)   The 'total reward package' comprises monetary and non-monetary motivators offered to staff. By proposing such a package, JBC is recognising that its staff are all different and some may not be motivated by money alone. The key principle is that employees can pick and choose what benefits they receive rather than everyone receiving the same. Employees can tailor their remuneration packages to suit their needs at any given time.

Advantages to JBC

Attract suitable potential employees

JBC operates in a competitive industry and must attract the highest quality staff to provide high standards of tuition to its students. However it is having problems attracting suitable applicants. By packaging all the benefits on offer and communicating it effectively in recruitment literature, JBC may help resolve this problem.

Improve staff motivation.

Pay is not always a motivator and therefore it is important to offer a range of benefits that meet a diverse range of motivational needs. For example, flexible working arrangements allows staff to maintain a healthy work life balance which will maintain interest and motivation in the job for a long period.

A number of other advantages of such schemes that are relevant to JBC.

They make a positive statement about the culture of the organisation.

Organisations that offer total reward packages are often seen as forward thinking and caring about the needs of their employees. This will not only further aid recruitment, but will boost the overall image of the organisation within the market place as it demonstrates an investment in its people.

The creation of a more inclusive rather than a 'them and us' attitude.

Staff morale and attitude may improve at all levels because the package of benefits is available to all rather than a select group of (possibly) senior employees.

Improved recruitment and retention as a result of employer branding.

Being seen as a good employer will further assist recruitment and retention of staff. Recruitment is improved as JBC may become considered as a 'good place to work' making it more competitive when attracting new staff. Retention is improved as employees find that their needs (financial and otherwise) are met so why would they want to move?

Disadvantages to JBC

It may not be a success

Whilst total reward packages have worked for many companies, there is no guarantee that JBC's scheme will also be a success. The company will run the risk of the scheme failing. Failure may cause problems such as loss of the company's image.

It may not solve the problem

It appears that the main reason for introducing the scheme is to solve the problem of poor recruitment. However, this problem may not be caused by a lack of a total reward package. It is possible that other causes such as choosing inappropriate recruitment methods are to blame. Therefore, introducing the scheme may not resolve the issue.

It may cause organisational stagnation

Staff may become 'too comfortable' and even complacent about their jobs. Employees with a satisfactory total reward package may not push themselves further as there would be few other benefits to be achieved.

Reduced staff turnover limits the amount of fresh blood being introduced into the organisation, resulting in fewer fresh ideas and reduced competition for higher status jobs.

It ignores other factors

The scheme ignores some other important factors concerning staff welfare and motivation. Those in highly stressful roles will still be stressed and employees working in under staffed departments may not be able to take full advantage of benefits such as flexitime.

Staff dissatisfaction

Not all staff will be happy with the benefits on offer and many may just prefer more money. Those who do not want the benefits on offer may feel left out and leave the organisation.

Cost

As the scheme is open to all employees, there could also be cost implications from offering it. JBC needs to consider whether the potential costs (for example, through employer pension contributions) justify the potential benefits in terms of staff motivation and retention.

(ii) There is only limited information available about JBC's appraisal system. However, it is clear that the organisation has taken a formal approach using standardised forms with clear objectives for staff development and performance improvements.

Problems with the system can be considered under two headings, firstly inherent problems with the design and implementation of the system, and secondly problems concerning its operation.

Design and implementation problems

The system may have been poorly designed in the first place. For example, it may be based on systems used by other organisations and no thought given to whether it is suitable for JBC.

The design of the system may have reflected the needs of the organisation at that time but is no longer relevant because the company has 'moved on'.

There may have been a lack of consultation and communication with senior managers when the system was being developed. They may view it as being imposed on them and therefore are not interested in making it work.

Appraisal schemes should provide **benefits** which justify the cost and effort put into them. Senior management comments such as 'a waste of time and effort' indicate that there is an imbalance between what is put into the scheme and what comes out; for example, whether or not any staff development needs which are identified during an appraisal are actually subsequently addressed.

This imbalance may have been caused by the system being put into place because senior management thought they should be seen to have an appraisal system, rather than it being a genuine method of improving staff development and performance.

Operational problems

Senior managers may have **insufficient time** to conduct the appraisal process properly. This may reduce the scheme into a form filling exercise just to meet HR requirements, missing the point of the scheme and its objectives.

The scheme focuses on staff development needs. This is likely to involve some **additional training costs,** and may also reduce the amount of time that academic staff are available for teaching (if they are attending training courses of their own). Therefore, managers may not see it as being in their interest to have their staff undergoing training. This, of course, is a short-sighted view, as properly structured training should improve JBC's performance in the long run. However, managers may not wish to wait for such benefits to materialise, preferring to focus on short-term issues and performance instead.

The scheme is **not linked to annual bonuses**. Employees are likely to act in a manner that maximises their bonus, which may be at odds with the objectives of the appraisal system.

Standard procedures indicate a **bureaucratic** or mechanical approach to appraisals. Senior mangers will be faced with a large volume of identical paperwork that needs to be processed in addition to their existing work load. There is likely to be a temptation to rush through the process with not much thought to the objectives just to get it done.

Appraisal schemes often involve **subjective judgements** and **opinions** by senior managers over their staff. There is a risk that employees are not assessed correctly or consistently meaning that some staff who do not require training are offered it whilst others that need help to improve their performance are not.

72 HFG

Text reference. Financial performance measures (including ROI, RI and EVA) are discussed in Chapter 9 of the BPP Study Text. The importance of non-financial performance indicators is discussed in Chapter 12. Reward schemes and human resource management are discussed in Chapter 14.

Top tips.

Part(a). The question is worth 29 marks including four marks for appropriate report presentation. There are only seven marks available in part(a)(i) for the calculations so you aren't expected to do more than brief calculations for each measure and each centre based on the simple data in the table in Note 1. This means the Examining team aren't testing anything tricky or complicated here. Your analysis and commentary on the figures is equally important as the calculations themselves, so remember to make comments on your figures.

Part (a) (ii) is trickier as you have to calculate the sensitivity of certain values in one of the centres. The simplest approach is to use simple formulae so look at what we've done below. Remember to state your assumptions here as they are asked for.

Part(a)(iii) is really asking you to consider non-financial and service measures of performance. This is a common theme in this exam so you should be prepared to state the pros and cons of financial and operational/service measures. Make sure you pick up the clues from the marketing director's statement too. He is clearly biased so you need to comment on his view based on your knowledge of performance measures. However don't just say he is wrong but try to say why and use 'professional language' as this is a report.

Part (b) moves on to look at **benchmarking** and asks you to consider how benchmarking can be successfully used given it does have possible problems. Remember why an organisation would use benchmarking which is to use external data to set its targets.

Part (c). The key issue here is controllability, and the importance of only judging the manager's performance on the basis of the results he can control. The scenario should have highlighted that a number of factors which led to the centre's actual results being below budget were outside the manager's control – so, is it appropriate to judge the manager's performance on them?

Part (d). You are asked to 'evaluate' the suggestion, so you shouldn't automatically assume that the manager deserves a bonus. Try to present a balanced argument, considering both the merits and drawbacks of his suggestion. For example, how will the owners feel if bonuses are being paid out when a centre's performance is below budget? Also, note the second part of the requirement: what alternative improvements could be made to the scheme. This again should suggest that the manager's suggestion isn't necessarily the only solution here.

			Marks	
(a)	(i)	ROI	1.5	
		RI	1.5	
		EVA	4	
		Comments	9	Up to 14
	(ii)	Comments (on merit):		
		% change in turnover, total costs, net assets 3×2	6	6
	(iii)	Comments (on merit):		
		Success/quality relationship	1	
		Number of complaints as performance measure	2	
		Reduce existing level of complaints	1	
		Other measures	2	Up to 5
		Professional marks		4
(b)		Comments (on merit):		
		Problems (up to 4)	4	
		Recommendations (up to 4)	4	Up to 7
(c)		Comments (on merit):		
		Accountability and controllability (up to 4)	4	
		Budget is not realistic/achievable (up to 4)	4	Up to 6
(d)		Comments (on merit):		
		Merits/drawbacks of manager's statement (up to 4)	4	
		Suggestions for improving the reward systems (up to 5)	5	Up to 8
				Total = 50

(a) **Report on the performance of HFG for the year ended 31 May 20X8**

To: Board of HFG

Date: June 20X8

Subject: Performance of three fitness centres and measures of performance for the year ended 31 May 20X8

This report has been prepared at the request of the board to explain performance in the three centres using a range of financial measures. The report will also comment on the recent statement by the marketing director on the use of measures to determine success in the Group.

(i) **Success of the centres**

The success of the three centres has been assessed using three **financial** measures. The table below ranks each centre under the three measures. Ayetown scores highest using ROI and EVA, Ceetown is the most successful if RI is used and Beetown performs poorly on all three performance measures. **So clearly 'success' depends on what measure is used. All of these measures are short-term too, and may encourage managers to only consider their immediate time horizon. This can lead to activity that maximises return in the short term but at the expense of future performance.**

Using ROI

Of particular note is that only Ayetown exceeds a target return of 20% for **ROI**, although this target may be for Beetown only. The other two centres fall below this but for reasons explained below, ROI is an imperfect measure and so their performance may well be distorted by how old their assets are or by their depreciation policy. The changes in revenue, total costs and net assets for Beetown to achieve the target rate are shown in (ii) below. There is an inevitable conflict between the group and the individual centres if group-wide decisions benefiting the group result in a decrease in the ROI in the centres.

Using RI

Both Ayetown and Ceetown have an **RI** of $180,000 or more compared with $33,000 for Beetown. However this success is for different reasons. Ayetown has a lower operating profit than Beetown but also smaller total assets. Ceetown has a higher operating profit and a higher value of total assets. It is noted below that RI is not a good measure for making comparisons between centres.

Using EVA

Finally, **EVA** as a measure shows that only Ayetown is creating wealth as its EVA is positive. The other two centres have capital charges which are greater than the cash flows arising (NOPAT). This means that they need to generate more operating profit on the same assets or invest in assets which make a higher return.

ROI, RI and EVA as measures of performance

Each measure attempts to define performance in a different way.

ROI

ROI compares income with the operational assets used to generate that income and is used for profit centres or investment centres. It can be easily understood by investors as the figures for PBIT and CE are clear from the financial statements. It can also compare investment centres which differ in absolute size.

However CE is open to manipulation as depreciation policy and replacement of fixed assets affect its value. So it may be difficult to compare centres where replacement polices are different or, say, the ages of assets affect repair costs and so profitability falls. ROI is therefore a short-term measure.

RI

RI is **a measure of a centre's profits after deducting a notional interest charge**. It highlights the finance charge associated with funding. Risk can be built into this by weighting the interest rate of higher-risk centres. However each of the fitness centres faces similar risks so this is not relevant. RI encourages managers to make decisions on investments where the investment will earn above the cost of capital.

Nonetheless RI does not allow comparisons between investment centres. It also doesn't relate the size of the investment to the income arising directly. This is a weakness compared with ROI. In common with ROI, RI tends to measure short-term performance.

EVA

EVA is an absolute performance measure and is similar to RI. However it generally uses the replacement cost of net assets in the calculation and adjusts profit to take out accounting adjustments such as depreciation and interest charges to reach an **economic profit** figure. It also takes account of taxation as the profit after tax is used when calculating NOPAT.

Advantages of EVA include less distortion by accounting policies as adjustments are stripped out and income more akin to cash flows is used. Maximising EVA also creates real wealth for shareholders. Thus managers are encouraged to make investments in say a development where the costs are capitalised under EVA and won't be penalised for doing so.

However there are flaws in using EVA and one of these is certainly the number of adjustments that may need to be made to get to EVA. EVA also cannot be used for direct comparison between investment centres so an allowance must be made for the **relative size** when making comparisons. EVA is still a relatively short-term measure and so managers focus on short-term performance.

Comparison between three centres using ROI, RI and EVA

	ROI (W1) 20X8 %	Ranking	RI (W2) 20X8 $'000	Ranking	EVA (W3) 20X8 $'000	Ranking
Centre						
Ayetown	23	1	180	2	42	1
Beetown	14	3	33	3	(123)	3
Ceetown	18	2	187	1	(30)	2

Workings

1 Calculation of ROI

	PBIT $'000	CE $'000	ROI %	Ranking
Ayetown	396	1,800 − 80 = 1,720	23	1
Beetown	441	3,400 − 240 = 3,160	14	3
Ceetown	703	4,300 − 480 = 3,820	18	2

> **Top tips.** The question gives PBIT for you to use. For each centre you will have to use net assets as your CE figure as Note 3 states that long-term borrowings are aggregated above centre level.

2 Calculation of RI

	PBIT $'000	Notional interest cost $'000	RI $'000	Ranking
Ayetown	396	1,800 × 0.12	180	2
Beetown	441	3400 × 0.12	33	3
Ceetown	703	4300 × 0.12	187	1

Use PBIT again and calculate the notional interest charge using the required rate of return given in Note 2 applied to total assets. Again keep things simple and state your outcome in $'000.

3 Calculation of EVA

	PBIT(A) $'000	PAT (B) $'000	CE (C) $'000	(Note 1)(D) WACC × CE	EVA=B−D $'000	Ranking
Ayetown	396	277	1,720	235.12	42	1
Beetown	441	309	3,160	431.97	(123)	3
Ceetown	703	492	3,820	522.19	(30)	2

Note. WACC is calculated for each centre as the market values of equity and long-term debt multiplied by the respective costs of debt and equity capital. The market value for debt is the same as the book value (note 7). Remember that the rate for debt is **after tax**.

Cost of equity = 15%
Cost of debt = 70% × 100% = 7%
Long-term borrowings (debt) = $1.8m
Equity = $9m (note 6)
$\therefore$ WACC = 9/(9 + 1.8) × 15% + 1.8/(9 + 1.8) × 7%
= 12.5% + 1.17% = 13.67%

(ii) **Changes needed for Beetown to achieve a target 20% ROI**

(All figures stated in $'000)

Current ROI   = 441/(3,400 − 240)   = 14%

If ROI is to increase to 20% then either the 441 revenue must increase or the (3,400 – 240) capital employed must decrease.

(1) **% change in revenue**

To achieve 20% ROI:

$0.20 = x/(3,400 - 240)$

$0.2 \times 3,160 = x$

$632 = x$

Contribution – fixed costs = operating profit

∴ required contribution = 632 + 1,092 = 1,724

Current C/S ratio = (1,533/2,100) × 100% = 73%

∴ required revenue = 1,724/0.73 = 2,362

∴ change in revenue required = ((2,362 – 2,100)/2,100 × 100)

= 12%

This **assumes that variable costs remain constant as a percentage of sales and fixed costs are fixed over the period.** At present Beetown offers dietary plans and fitness programmes and some accommodation. It may be possible to increase prices in some of these areas but this would have to be considered in tandem with customer sensitivity to changes in prices.

(2) **% change in total costs**

Current total costs   = 567 + 1,092 = 1,659
Therefore reduction in costs required   = (1,659 – 1,468) =191 or (191/1,659) × 100% = 12%

This can be analysed between fixed and variable costs:

If fixed costs remain constant over the period in question then required variable costs are $376,000 (1,468 – 1,092) variable costs. This is a decrease of 34% on the original level of variable costs. This also assumes that variable costs per unit are constant at all levels of normal provision. Costs could be reviewed using **value analysis** to see if there is any scope for reducing them without impairing the service offered.

(3) **% change in net assets**

To achieve 20% ROI:

$0.2 = 441/x$, where
X = required net assets
X = 441/0.2
= 2,205

Existing net assets = 3,160 (W1 above)

∴ required change

$$= \frac{(3,160 - 2,205)}{3,160}$$

= 30% decrease

This assumes that revenue remains constant as stated. Management must consider how they would achieve a reduction in the value of net assets. Clearly any reduction in facilities, including equipment and premises, could affect the quality of service offered. Using **value for money** criteria should allow them to consider the **effectiveness** of any service provided and streamline facilities.

(iii) **The marketing director's statement**

The marketing director's statement makes it clear that he only considers one measure of success, quality of service and that the organisation's future success is linked to this. He states in somewhat strong terms that this is 'the most important performance measure for our business' and is a 'perfect' performance measure. He also sees success provided the number of complaints from clients does not increase from period to period.

There are some reasons why the marketing director's statement should be interpreted with caution.

Firstly, **he only considers one measure of success**, which covers the quality of service provided. This is clearly an important measure as the group is in a service industry. However there are other measures that are important such as the financial measures calculated earlier. These measure financial health and are important to the owners as this is a privately owned business. Financial measures also satisfy external reporting obligations as businesses must report their performance annually.

Secondly **his focus on only one measure could be ignoring the full picture of the** *service* **being provided**. Therefore, complaints arising from long waiting times for facilities must be weighed up against the far more serious complaint of injury from badly maintained equipment or contamination from dirty showers.

Finally, **he measures success by the absolute number of complaints received**. This could be flawed if the base line is a high level of complaints. It also suggests that there is no reason to seek to decrease the number of complaints, whereas a reduction in complaints is probably a better target.

In conclusion, service measures are important and the customer attending the fitness centres here is clearly the main source of revenue. However, it would be better to look at customer service as part of a larger group of performance measures. A tool such as the **Balanced scorecard** would reflect the important customer measures that the marketing director wants to see but also measure other dimensions such as financial measures and business processes.

(b)   **Problems that may be experienced from benchmarking and how these may be overcome**

There are some fairly obvious problems that might arise with benchmarking.

(i)   It relies on accurate information on the comparator. This may be especially hard to obtain if it is not financial or quantitative.

(ii)   It can be difficult to decide which activities to benchmark.

(iii)   It implies that there is one best way of doing business.

(iv)   The benchmark may be out of date.

How might these problems be addressed?

(i)   The accuracy of information that is not in the public realm does depend on the relationship between the organisation and its comparator. If SFC can be persuaded of the mutual value of benchmarking then information should be of better quality.

(ii)   Deciding which activities to benchmark goes back to the setting of objectives and how activities cascade from these activities. If the organisation is clear where it wants to be and what it needs to do to get there then it should be clearer what performance it needs to measure.

(iii)   **The third problem may** be one that needs the organisation to think again about whether a **process is effective rather than merely efficient**. If this is so then it should consider other means of improving its processes. A good example would be amending the value chain to secure competitive advantage.

(iv)   **The final problem is strategic**. The organisation needs to be aware of developments in its environment that may be far reaching and will affect where it chooses to operate. Once it has made these decisions it can then review its activities and decide to benchmark them against the best comparator. So taking the ferry company mentioned earlier, if it decides to compete against the channel tunnel then it must benchmark activities accordingly.

Additional answer

(v)   The **value of the benchmarking exercise** needs to be compared to the cost of undertaking it. A cost-benefit analysis needs to be done therefore.

(vi)   **Ethical issues** may affect the exercise, including giving employees reassurance on jobs and working conditions. Management must be prepared to deal with these issues.

(c) **Accountability** – Managers should only be held responsible for those aspects of performance they can control.

In this case, it seems the manager has more discretion to influence non-financial aspects of performance (such as the quality of service provided to customers) than financial aspects of performance.

However, the manager's eligibility for a bonus payment depends on the operating profit of the centre as a whole. When assessing the manager's eligibility for a bonus, no distinction is made between the factors which the manager can control, and those which he can't.

In this case, the factors which have had the largest impact on the centre's performance – the economic downturn, the rival centre opening – are all likely to be outside the manager's control.

Furthermore, the manager's ability to control performance is reduced further by the fact that he has no discretion over pricing. This is likely to be a particular issue at Ceetown, because it prevented the manager offering discounts or special offers to try to match any deals being offered by the new competitor.

Controllability – However, it is not clear which aspects of financial performance, if any, the manager does have control over. In theory, a fairer way of assessing the centre manager's financial performance would be to distinguish controllable costs and profits from non-controllable. However, if all the financial decisions are taken by senior management, then none of the costs or profit will be controllable by the manager.

Budget – A second potential issue with the bonus scheme appears to the budget figures themselves. If the trigger point for whether the manager is eligible for a bonus payment is the centre' performance against budget, then it is important that the budget is realistic and achievable.

However, this does not appear to be the case at Ceetown.

It is not clear whether HFG's senior management team knew that the rival centre was going to be opening Ceetown when they prepared the budget, although it seems likely they should have been – for example, because the centre is likely to have needed to apply for planning permission (or something similar) before it could open.

Equally, a budget which shows an 11% growth in fees received seems very optimistic, given that Mayland is in recession.

On top of this, the contribution margin has increased slightly (from 31% to 31.5%).

Therefore, although we don't know how much operating profit the Ceetown centre is likely to make in 20X9, it seems likely that it will fall short of the operating profit, meaning that the manager will not quality for a bonus.

On this basis, the manager's dissatisfaction with the bonus scheme would appear to be justified – because, as he has suggested, the budgeted profit does appear to be unachievable.

(d) **Focus on controllable aspects of performance** – As we have noted in part (c), a reward system should try to distinguish between the centre's performance and the manager's performance.

In this case, it is not clear how much control the manager has over the centre's financial performance. Therefore this might support his argument that his performance should be judged against the non-financial aspects of performance (which he can control) rather than the financial aspects (which he can't control.)

Performance information – However, it is not clear what the manager's performance objectives are, and what performance information is recorded in relation to them.

It would seem likely that quality of customer service is an important success factor for HFG, and the number of customer complaints is one aspect of non-financial performance which is measured. It is not clear what the manager's other non-financial objectives are, and, more importantly, how performance against them is measured. If they are going to be used to determine the manager's bonus, then HFG will need to be able to record performance against target levels. However, if its reporting systems are primarily designed to monitor financial performance it may not currently record the necessary non-financial information.

Importance of financial performance – Also, it is important to remember that HFG is a commercial organisation, which measures 'success' in financial terms. Therefore, its reward system needs to operate in a way which is beneficial to both the company and the managers. In this respect, it remains important to monitor the centre's profits, because, for example, it would be detrimental to the owners if managers were paid their full 15% bonus each year, yet their centres consistently fell short of financial performance targets.

Stepped bonuses – In this respect, the bonus scheme could be adjusted to that the managers are entitled to an element of their bonus even if their centre falls short of its profit target. For example, the managers could be entitled to a proportion of their bonus, if their centre achieved, say, 90% of its profit target, and that proportion would increase if the centre achieves or exceeds its profit target.

Linkage between financial and non-financial performance – HFG may also need to reconsider what aspects of non-financial performance its managers are assessed. Ideally, the non-financial aspects of performance selected should be ones relating to the company's critical success factors, such that favourable performance in relation to them also helps support favourable financial performance. However, if the managers keep achieving their non-financial objectives but their centres keep failing to achieve their financial targets, then the relationship between the two may need to be re-examined.

Budgets agreed – However, perhaps the most important improvement is that rather than being determined by the senior management and then imposed on the centre managers, the managers should be involved in setting the budgets.

The managers could be aware of factors that will affect the performance of their centres that senior managers are not aware of (for example, activities and campaigns by rival centres). Such a process may lead to more realistic budget targets being set for the centres, and in doing so increase the managers' motivation.

Equally, if the managers have been involved in setting the budget, this should hopefully make them more motivated to achieve the budget.

Nonetheless, it may still be necessary for the senior management team to control the budgets overall, to bring them in line with the company's overall financial objectives or any performance expectations the owners may have. For example, whilst ensuring that budget targets are realistic, it will also be important for the senior management team to ensure that profit targets are not set too low, so that they remain challenging for the centre managers.

73 SBC

Chapter references. Non-financial performance indicators are discussed in Chapter 12, while the Balanced Scorecard is discussed in Chapter 15. Performance management and reward systems are discussed in Chapter 14.

Top tips. Remember the requirements asked for a report so make sure you present your answer as a report, and in a professional manner, to get the four marks available for this.

The main technical knowledge required in part (a) of this question is of the balanced scorecard and non-financial performance indicators (NFPI) in part (i). The rest of the question is looking for your ability to think widely about performance issues for instance in part (iv).

Part (i). A useful starting point for this question could be to think about the different perspectives of the scorecard, and how the non-financial elements contribute to it. This should help you identify why they are important.

Remember also SBC is a service company so performance measures capture the quality and 'SHIP' aspects of services. How do non-financial measures supplement financial ones and what benefits are there in using them in this respect? Why would SBC use the balanced scorecard to improve performance? The answer suggests it links ideas of customer service to activities in the organisation designed to achieve these and also financial measures capturing value for shareholders. Don't forget to give examples for each of the four perspectives using information in the scenario where possible.

Part (ii) wants you to calculate the average cost per chargeable consultation of the full-time consultants and the subcontractors. You need to work out the percentage of consultations that the subcontractors deal with. These are worked out from total demand less the time the fulltime consultants need to spend on business development and the 200 working days per consultant.

Part (iii) wants you to think about what the figures in the appendix reveal: is there a decline in demand, what about the numbers of consultants planned for over the next three years. What about the mix of full-time and subcontract consultants.

(a) **Report to the Directors**

To: The Directors

From: Management Accountant

Subject: The Balanced Scorecard

Date: June 20Y0

(i) **Importance of non-financial performance indicators (NFPI)**

NFPI are measures of performance based on non-financial information and are used in operating departments to monitor and control their activities without the need for accounting data. They can be gathered more readily by front line employees in their daily activities and reported at the end of an activity thus not relying on the accounting cycle of reporting. They are also lead indicators in so far as they give an indication of likely future performance. The types of data that NFPI report include employee data such as morale and training needs. They capture the quality side of manufacturing and service which is difficult to assess from financial measures. For instance inspection reports and warranty claims will report any issues with quality inside and outside the organisation.

Service quality is measured principally by qualitative measures as much of the experience of a service is based on an impression of that service.

They are less likely to be manipulated than traditional profit-related measures thereby avoiding short-termism whereby people modify their behaviour to suit the way performance is measured. In other words, what gets measured gets done.

However there is a risk of reporting too many NFPI which then blinds management to what is important to monitor. There is also a risk of becoming focused on operational measures and operational managers may lose sight of the overall strategy of the organisation. They are best combined with financial measures and ultimately the maximisation of profit (in for-profit organisations at least).

How a balanced scorecard approach may be used to improve performance in SBC

The balanced scorecard links financial and non-financial measures by focusing on four different perspectives. These are the **financial,** the **customer**, **internal business** and **innovation and learning**. The scorecard is built up from asking customers what they value and setting goals based on this. Then the other perspectives follow with the internal perspective considering what the organisation must do well to achieve customer objectives and the innovation and learning perspective looking at improving and creating future value. These all relate to the financial perspective which asks how the organisation creates value for shareholders.

For each of the four perspectives, goals need to be set and measures created to capture performance in achieving these goals. The scorecard is useful as it captures a wide range of data across the organisation. However it must be used with care as measures may conflict eg measuring revenue generation and also setting goals for business development work which is non-chargeable. Managers must be careful not to set too many measures such that important data gets lost. Non-financial managers may have difficulty interpreting financial measures but this is true of any performance measurement system.

Examples of measures for each perspective

Financial

This could be measured through consultancy fee income, revenue growth, trends in salary costs for full-time and subcontractors, gross margin on client accounts, EVA in relation to the budget.

Customer

SBC could use measures such as advice given on time, percentage of new customers, share of key customers, customer satisfaction ratings.

Internal business

Measures could include the time taken from introduction to actual consultation, percentage of client projects completed on time and within budget, number of consultations on business development days becoming client projects.

Innovation and learning

Measures could include number or percentage of new consultancy activities, consultation time spent on training and development

(ii) **Average cost per chargeable consultation 20Y0**

Fulltime Category	No of fulltime consultants	Salaries (per consultant) $	Total salaries $	Other operating costs $	Chargeable days (W1) fulltime	Actual average cost per chargeable consultation (W2) fulltime	Actual average cost per chargeable consultation (W3) subcontract
Advertising	20	40,000	800,000		3,720	277.55	
Recruitment	30	35,000	1,050,000		4,680	286.86	
IT	50	30,000	1,500,000		8,800	232.95	
				1,075,000			
Subcontract							
Advertising							335.71
Recruitment							255.71
IT							235.71

Workings

1   200 days × (1 − business development activity (BDA))% × number of consultants

	Working days pa per consultant	(1− BDA)%	Number of consultants	Chargeable days (based on 200 days) full-time	Chargeable days subcontract
Advertising	200	93	20	3,720	4,200 − 3,720 = 480
Recruitment	200	78	30	4,680	6,250 − 4,680 = 1,570
IT	200	88	50	8,800	10,250 − 8,800 = 1,450
Total chargeable days				17,200	

2   Actual average cost – full-time

		Apportioned other	Total	Chargeable	Actual average
	Salaries	operating costs	costs	days	cost $*
Advertising	800,000	1,075,000 × 3,720/17,200 = 232,500	1,032,500	3,720	277.55
Recruitment	1,050,000	1,075,000 × 4,680/17,200 = 292,500	1,342,500	4,680	286.86
IT	1,500,000	1,075,000 × 8,800/17,200 = 550,000	2,050,000	8,800	232.95

* Total costs/chargeable days

3   Actual average cost – subcontract

	Cost per consultation $	Chargeable days subcontract (W1)	Cost of sub- contractors $	Apportioned other operating costs	Total costs $	Actual average cost $*
Advertising	300	480	144,000	480/3,500 × 125,000 = 17,143	161,143	161,143/480 = 335.71
Recruitment	220	1,570	345,400	1,570/3,500 × 125,000 = 56,071	401,471	401,471/1,570 = 255.71
IT	200	1,450	290,000	1,450/3,500 × 125,000 = 51,786	341,786	341,786/1,450 = 235.71
Total chargeable days		3,500				

* Total costs/chargeable days

(iii)   Reasons for trends in the appendix

The percentage of chargeable days spent on business development activity has increased across all three types of consultancy. It has increased from 7 to 10% from 20Y0 to 20Y2 for advertising, by 3% to 25% in recruitment in that period and to 14% from 12% in IT. This suggests the company is looking to develop new business or offer more to its existing customers (eg free consultations).

However the activity of the business overall is predicted to decline as total chargeable consultations are projected to fall from a demand of 20,700 to 19,000 over 20Y0 to 20Y2 or 8%. The biggest fall is in recruitment, by 20%. This may well be the reason the number of consultants is also predicted to fall in this category by 10 to 20.

The business intends to increase salaries for full-time consultants over 20Y1 but thereafter they remain static. This may well reflect market conditions and the value attached to the consultants despite a fall in activity. It may also be cheaper to retain these full-time consultants than pay subcontractors to take up any shortfall in manpower. Nonetheless other operating costs for subcontractors is planned to double from 20Y0 to 20Y1, possibly to make up the shortfall in recruitment consultants.

(iv)   Potential benefits and problems of employing subcontractors in SBC

Benefits

Subcontractors may be drafted in when workloads are variable so they can be used to cover shortfalls in availability. This also avoids the risk of losing contracts because of unavailable staff.

They may cover areas where expertise is lacking and so the business can continue to provide a good service and not turn away work because of lack of expertise.

The flexibility inherent in drafting in subcontractors means contracts may be fulfilled without the expense of retaining full-time employees.

Problems

Subcontractors are not employees and so they may find it difficult to adapt to the culture and assumed knowledge that employees have and the operational standards offered by the full-time consultants. However training can overcome this.

They may be resented by the full-time consultants especially if they take on specialist work which other consultants may have wanted to do but for lack of training/expertise.

The two different pay scales used may lead to resentment among the full-time consultants and the subcontractors who will dislike the disparity in pay schemes. For instance, the full-time contractors may see the $200 -$300 per consultation paid to subcontractors as too high for the work done, damaging morale.

(b) **Performance and strategy** – An important issue in modern performance management is that of linking performance to strategy. In particular, this means that the focus of performance measures should be on those areas which are most important in enabling an organisation to achieve its strategic goals. However, there is no guarantee that the areas of performance which SBC can measure easily are necessarily those which will be most important in enabling it to achieve its strategic goals.

Selecting measures – If SBC decides to implement a balanced scorecard approach, one of the issues it will face is selecting which measures of performance to include. Again, however, when selecting measures it will be important for it to measure those aspects of performance which actually add value to an organisation, not simply those which are easy to measure.

This is the opposite of the approach the director is recommending – of selecting metrics which are easy to measure rather than choosing them because they relate to key processes or aspects which add value to the company.

Cost-benefit implications – However, the director is justified in highlighting the potential cost implications of implementing the Scorecard, because it seems there will be costs involved in measuring the performance of additional processes which are not currently included in SBC's performance information.

In this respect, it will be sensible for SBC to consider the costs and benefits of measuring additional aspects of performance. One of the qualities of good information is that it should not cost more to obtain than the benefit derived from having it.

The director is clearly concerned about the costs associated with the additional information SBC is looking to measure. However, in order to assess whether his concerns are justified or not, we would need to know how much benefit SBC is likely to get from measuring the additional areas of performance which are being proposed.

(c) **Staff retention** – It appears that SBC's current reward package for its IT consultants is not as competitive as that offered by some of its rivals. If this continues, then SBC's staff turnover could increase further, which is likely to be costly for SBC both in terms of having to recruit and train new staff, and also in terms of the loss of knowledge which occurs when consultants leave.

If the new proposal means that the overall value of the consultants' salary increases, then this could help to reduce staff turnover which should be beneficial to SBC.

Value of commissions – However, it is not clear what impact the proposed changes will have on the consultants' salaries. The scenario does not indicate how much lower the new basic salary will be than the consultants current salaries, nor does it indicate the size of the commissions received from the software companies.

It is possible that the proposal could actually end up reducing the consultants' salaries, which will have the opposite effect to what the directors are trying to achieve.

Impact on SBC's profits – Equally, however, the directors will need to ensure that the changes are not too generous in favour of the consultants because they are likely to reduce SBC's profit margins, for example because the commissions will no longer be income for the company. Moreover, if the commission system doesn't stimulate higher sales revenue, the effect of the commissions will be to reduce profits overall. Therefore, a key issue surrounding the acceptability of the proposal is whether it will result in higher revenues being generated.

Other consultants – The directors also need to consider how the other types of consultant will respond. Again, it is not clear how much communication there is between the three types of consultant, but advertising and recruitment consultants find out that the IT consultants have had their rewards schemes revised, they may want something similar themselves.

Risk to customers – When SBC's clients are looking to select a new software system, a key factor in their choice should be how well the system fits their requirements. Advice about the suitability of different systems is likely to be one of the key pieces of advice they want from the consultants. However, the new system could compromise the consultants' ability to give this advice impartially.

Under the current system, it appears that the consultants have no incentive to recommend one software supplier over another. However, under the proposed new system, consultants may be tempted to advise clients to buy the system which will earn them the highest amount of commission rather than the system which is necessarily best for the client.

Such practices could be damaging to SBC's reputation and future revenues. If clients install software systems, on SBC's advice, which do not meet their requirements effectively, then they are unlikely to use SBC in future.

Alternative bonus/reward scheme – It appears that the commission scheme is the only option which the directors have looked at so far. However, rather than only looking at one scheme, they should also consider whether there are any alternative schemes which may be more appropriate. For example, it is not clear whether SBC currently has any kind of performance related pay scheme, or bonus scheme; but a scheme which rewards consultants for their performance in relation to a range of targets, linked to SBC's overall objectives, may be more appropriate than the current proposal.

74 Kolmog Hotels

Text reference. The characteristics of service industries are highlighted in Chapter 4 of the BPP Study Text. The balanced scorecard and Fitzgerald and Moon's building block model are both discussed in Chapter 15.

Top tips.

Part (i). Although the requirement here asks you to 'explain' the characteristics, there are only five marks available for this part of the question. So you should keep your explanations relatively brief. There are five key characteristics which differentiate service businesses from manufacturing ones (and five marks available); meaning that there is only 1 mark available per characteristic. However, don't forget that you need to illustrate how the characteristics relate to Kolmog hotels. Don't just talk about the characteristics of service businesses in generic terms.

Part (ii) asks you to evaluate Kolmog's current strategic performance report. The word 'report' is crucial here. It is vital that you evaluate the **report** and the choice of metrics used in the report, rather than evaluating Kolmog's strategic **performance**.

The key issue to evaluate here is how well the performance report allows Kolmog to assess its performance against its mission. For example, does the report (or the metrics selected in it) help assess Kolmog's performance in relation to it becoming 'the No. 1 hotel chain in Ostland'?

Also think about the 'segmentation' of the report. For example, how useful is it to know how each of the four regions has performed, as opposed to how each type of hotel has performed?

Part (iii). One of the key problems with Kolmog's current performance report (which, hopefully, you identified during your evaluation in part (ii)) is that the report only includes financial metrics, rather than a range of metrics which can be used to measure performance in relation to the different elements of Kolmog's mission.

By contrast, the different perspectives included in the proposed balanced scorecard look at key aspects of non-financial performance as well as financial performance. This should be beneficial for Kolmog.

However, while the idea of introducing a balanced scorecard may be a good one, note that the question asks you to 'suggest suitable improvements' to the scorecard. So, are there any ways which the proposed metrics could be improved so that the aspects of performance being measured support the mission and objectives more effectively?

Part (iv). The requirement to part (iii) should immediately have highlighted that some of the measures originally proposed for the outline scorecard could be improved. In turn, this should have highlighted one of the main difficulties of implementing the scorecard: choosing what measures to actually include in it.

As Kolmog has not used the scorecard before, selecting appropriate measures and then educating the managers in how to interpret the reported results are likely to be significant challenges in relation to implementing the scorecard.

Part (v). The scenario highlights that 75% of Kolmog's staff have received no bonuses in previous years, and there have been many complaints that the targets are too challenging.

This suggests that the staff don't regard the bonus targets as achievable, and consequently the staff are not motivated to try to achieve them.

Achievability is one of the three key 'standards' identified in the building block model (along with ownership and fairness.) Similarly, motivation is one the three key aspects of 'rewards' identified in the model (along with clarity and controllability.)

The key issue in this part of the question is whether the new performance reward system fits with these standards and rewards any better than the old system appeared to. For example, will hotel managers feel they 'own' their performance targets if the budgets are imposed by head office?

Overall. Once again, remember that you have been asked to write a report, so make sure the style and structure of your answer, as a whole, is appropriate for a report. For example, a report should have a short introduction explaining the key issues to be discussed in it.

Examining team's comments. It was pleasing to note in part (ii) that there were fewer examples of candidates evaluating the performance of the company and many more evaluating the performance **report**, which was what was required by the question.

Most candidates handled part (iii) relatively well, but they could have scored more efficiently if they attended to the mission of the company, and how the scorecard would help the company achieve its mission.

However, part (iv) was answered very poorly, with many candidates choosing to discuss improvements required rather than the **difficulties** faced in implementing and using the BSC at Kolmog. It is vital to answer the question set!

In part (v), most candidates demonstrated good understanding of the use of 'stretch' targets and the reward system implications at Kolmog. However, there was weaker understanding of the 'standards' element from Fitzgerald and Moon's building block model.

Marking scheme

		Marks
(i)	Service industry characteristics – 1 mark per characteristic (intangibility; inseparability; variability (or heterogeneity); perishability; and no transfer of ownership.) Characteristics must be illustrated in relation to the hotel industry to score the full mark available for each characteristic.	
	Total for part (i) – Up to 5 marks	5
(ii)	For comments on how well the current report enables Kolmog to measure performance against its objectives – 1 mark per point; up to 6 marks For comments on the choice of measures used in the report – 1 mark per point; up to 6 marks	
	Total for part (ii) – Up to 8 marks	8

Marks

(iii) For comments on the outline balanced scorecard which has been proposed for Kolmog; evaluating current metrics and suggesting suitable improvements to the scorecard – 1 mark per point, up to 4 marks for each perspective of the scorecard.
Other relevant comments about the scorecard – 1 mark per point

Comments must be linked directly to the scorecard proposed for Kolmog, rather than being a generic description of the scorecard.

Total for part (iii) – Up to 12 marks ... 12

(iv) For difficulties in implementing and using the scorecard at Kolmog – 1 mark per point.

Again, to score the full marks available difficulties should be linked directly to implementing the scorecard at Kolmog.

Total for part (iv) – Up to 7 marks ... 7

(v) Explanation of the purpose of setting challenging targets – 1 mark per point; up to 3 marks. (To score the full 3 marks, the answer must be specifically relevant to Kolmog).
Standards – for explaining the criteria of ownership, achievability and fairness; 1 mark per standard; up to 3 marks.
Rewards – for explaining the criteria of clarity, motivation and controllability; 1 mark per reward; up to 3 marks.
For comments on the new reward system which has been proposed at Kolmog – 1 mark per point; up to 7 marks

Total for part (v) – Up to 14 marks ... 14

Professional marks – for report headings and introduction; clarity of report, and language used – Up to 4 marks

4

Total = 50

Report

To: CEO Kolmog Hotels

From: Accountant

Date: June 20X3

Subject: Performance measurement and targets at Kolmog Hotels

Introduction

This report explains the key characteristics which differentiate service businesses from manufacturing ones, and then evaluates the performance reports and measures which are being used to monitor Kolmog's performance. The report then evaluates the balanced scorecard which has been proposed for use at Kolmog, and describes the difficulties which could be associated with using the scorecard.

Finally, the report explains the purpose of setting challenging targets, and uses Fitzgerald and Moon's building block model to evaluate the standards and rewards which are applied to the managers' performance reward system at Kolmog.

(i) **Characteristics of service businesses**

There are five key characteristics of services that distinguish services from manufacturing.

(a) **Intangibility** – In contrast to manufactured goods which are tangible, physical products, services do not have any substantial material or physical aspects. When a customer books a room in one of Kolmog's hotels, they are not buying a physical product, rather they are buying their overnight accommodation in the hotel.

The fact that Kolmog isn't producing a physical product also helps to explain why its cost of sales (at around 12% of revenue) is much lower than equivalent figure would be for a manufacturing business.

(b) **Inseparability (or simultaneity)** – Whereas manufactured goods need to be produced before they can be consumed, services are created at the same time as they are consumed. For example, a guest's experience of one of Kolmog's hotels is formed during their stay in the hotel.

(c) **Variability (or heterogeneity)** – One of the key issues which service businesses face is ensuring consistency in the standard of their service. For example, it could be difficult for Kolmog to control the level of service provided to customers by the different hotels in the group, not least because the behaviour of individual staff working in a hotel on any given day will have a significant impact on the level of service which customers receive.

(d) **Perishability** – Services are innately perishable. If a room is unoccupied (unused) for a day, then the revenue which could have been earned from the room for that day can never be recovered. This explains why room occupancy rates are often used as key performance measures by hotel companies.

(e) **No transfer of ownership** – When a customer purchases a service, this does not result in a transfer of property to the customer. For example, when a customer buys a car, they become the owner of the car. However, when a guest books a stay at a hotel, they are only buying the right to stay at the hotel for a limited period of time; they do not own the hotel.

(ii) **Current strategic performance report**

Financial information only – The strategic performance report should help the board monitor how well Kolmog is performing in the light of its stated mission.

However, despite the mission highlighting non-financial aspects of performance, the performance report currently includes only financial information. As a result, the report does not provide any indicators of how well Kolmog is performing in relation to the non-financial elements of the mission, such as **customer satisfaction, employee development** or **product innovation**.

Shareholder value – The report covers the subsidiary aim of maximising shareholder value by providing figures for EPS, share price performance and ROCE, although total shareholder return and economic value added might be better measures than ROCE in this respect.

Importantly, however, maximising shareholder value is only a subsidiary aim, rather than a primary aim of the mission.

Key performance indicators – Hotels often have high levels of operational gearing because many of their costs (such as staff costs and property costs) are fixed. Consequently, their profit levels are likely to be sensitive to relatively small changes in revenue. As a result, hotel chains often view measures such as occupancy rates and revenue per available room as key performance indicators. Kolmog's performance report could be improved by including some key performance indicators like this – particularly indicators which are linked to revenue performance.

Market position – Perhaps the most important aspect of Kolmog's mission is the desire to 'become the No. 1 hotel chain in Ostland.' However, the report does not provide any indication as to how well the chain is performing in this respect, for example by measuring Kolmog's market share.

The absence of any external data is significant in this respect. Not only does it prevent the board from measuring overall market share, it also means they cannot benchmark Kolmog's performance in key performance areas against competitor hotels. For example, although the ratios of staff costs and hotel operating costs are useful, it would also be useful to know how these figures compare to the equivalent ratios for competitor hotels.

Segmental analysis – Although it is useful for the board to have information about how different segments of the chain are performing, breaking down the results into **geographical areas** may not be the most valuable basis of segmentation. For example, if the **mix of hotel types** varies significantly between each region, then simply comparing the performance of the four geographical regions may not be very instructive. In this respect, it may be more useful for the operating results to be broken down by hotel type (for example, conference venues, city centre business hotels, and country house hotels).

Budget figures – Although the individual hotel managers are judged by their hotel's performance against budget, the strategic performance report doesn't show any budget figures. This appears to be a significant weakness in the report. Including budget figures and variances in the report would enable the board to identify any significant deviations in actual performance compared to budget, and take corrective action where necessary.

(iii) **The balanced scorecard**

In general terms, the balanced scorecard is intended to help a company translate its mission into objectives and measures such that the measures are coherent with, and support, the overall mission. A company can also use the measures in its scorecard to inform its employees about the key drivers of success.

The balanced scorecard also highlights the importance of measuring both non-financial performance and financial performance. This could be particularly valuable to Kolmog, given the importance of the non-financial elements in its mission.

Although it may be easier for Kolmog to measure aspects of financial performance than non-financial performance, the long term success of the hotel chain is likely to depend on how it performs in key non-financial areas. Nevertheless, it remains important to measure financial performance, and the financial perspective of the scorecard highlights this.

Financial perspective

The financial perspective in the outline balanced scorecard focuses on measures of strategic financial performance: **share price** and **ROCE**. This fits with the overall objective of maximising shareholder value, although it would be useful to measure **dividend per share** as well as share price in order to **reflect total shareholder return.**

Operational gearing – Although ROCE is often used as a measure of overall performance, the change in Kolmog's business model may make it less suitable as a measure for the company. Once Kolmog has sold and rented back many of its hotels, the business will have a much lower capital base. However, its fixed costs (notably rental costs) will be much higher. Therefore, it may be more appropriate to include a measure such as **operational gearing** in the scorecard.

Revenue growth – It would also seem appropriate to include **revenue growth** as a measure, given Kolmog's stated intention to 'become the No. 1 hotel chain in Ostland.'

Customer perspective

Customer satisfaction survey scores – This measure seems to be appropriate because it is aligned to the mission and the aim of 'consistently delighting customers'.

Brand loyalty – However, measuring customer satisfaction alone does not provide any indication as to whether loyalty to Kolmog's brand is strengthening. In this respect, it would be also useful to measure the number (or proportion) of customers who are repeat customers, as opposed to customers who are staying in a Kolmog hotel for the first time.

Alternatively, it could be useful to measure the value of the revenues (or the proportion of the revenues) which are generated by returning customers, as distinct from customers who are staying in a Kolmog hotel for the first time.

It is not clear from the scenario whether Kolmog has any kind of loyalty card programme. If it does, then a measure based around the number (or value) of bookings from loyalty card customers could also be a useful measure in relation to brand loyalty.

Internal business perspective

Variance analysis – In the outline scorecard, variance analysis (comparing actual performance to budget) for each hotel has been proposed as a measure to support the internal business perspective.

Occupancy rates – In this respect, it will be important for the budgets to include non-financial performance indicators as well as financial ones. As we have already noted, room occupancy rates are a key factor in shaping a hotel's performance, and so should be monitored here alongside financial variances.

However, as we noted in relation to segmental analysis, it is also important to recognise that different business processes or elements of performance may be important in different types of hotel hotels. For example, city centre business hotels may be able to maintain reasonably consistent occupancy rates throughout the year, whereas occupancy rates in the country house hotels are likely to exhibit greater seasonality. Likewise, operating margins in the country house hotels may vary more during the year, because they will still be incurring fixed costs even in months when occupancy rates are low.

Therefore, it may be necessary to adapt the key scorecard measures being used for different types of hotel.

Internal benchmarking – Nonetheless, the performance of individual Kolmog hotels can be compared against others of the same type. Internal benchmarking in this way should enable Kolmog to identify which hotels are performing best, and in turn whether there any 'best practices' which can be shared between those hotels and others which are not performing so well.

In this way, knowledge sharing between different hotels may help Kolmog to 'continuously improve performance', which is one of the aims of its mission.

Innovation and learning perspective

The innovation and learning perspective of the scorecard should underpin this drive to continuously improve performance. Equally, the measures chosen in relation to the perspective should be ones which encourage the delivery 'of innovative products/services,' which again is an aspect of Kolmog's mission.

New products/services – There are not currently any measures proposed which relate to innovation or new products. A measure which could be appropriate here is a measure of the proportion of revenue which is generated from new products or services, for example, any new packages which might be offered by the country house hotels. However, as the hotel industry in general is now a fairly mature industry the scope to deliver innovative products and services may be relatively limited.

Employee satisfaction – As a service business, Kolmog's employees play a particularly important role in delivering customer satisfaction. If the staff in a hotel are happy and motivated this is likely to lead to guests in that hotel enjoying their stay more than if staff were grumpy and unhelpful. The performance metric of staff turnover could give an indication of how satisfied staff are with their jobs. In general, the higher staff turnover rates are, the less satisfied staff are likely to be with their jobs.

Alternatively, instead of using staff turnover as a surrogate for employee satisfaction, Kolmog could perhaps also introduce staff surveys in which staff satisfaction scores could be measured more directly.

> **No. 1 hotel chain in Ostland** – Whichever measures Kolmog finally chooses for its scorecard, it is important to remember the underlying emphasis of the stated mission is 'to become the No.1 hotel chain in Ostland'. Therefore, wherever possible, Kolmog should seek to benchmark its performance in all of the scorecard areas against its competitors, in order to identify whether or not it is actually achieving this 'No. 1' status.

(iv) **Implementing and using the balanced scorecard**
The balanced scorecard has not been used at Kolmog before, and therefore, as with any new framework, the company could face difficulties as it is introduced for the first time.

Selecting measures – In the previous section of this report we have suggested some alternative measures to the preliminary ones proposed by senior managers at head office. This highlights the first potential difficulty in using the scorecard: selecting which measures to include.

When deciding which measures are the most appropriate to include in Kolmog's scorecard, it is important to include measures which are related to key business processes and activities which add value to the company, not simply those that are easy to measure.

It is also important to remember the scorecard's role in translating strategic measures down to the operational level. So, for example, while there might be an overall measure focusing on customer satisfaction levels, at the operational level this may need to be broken down further into customer satisfaction on the service they received at reception, or the cleanliness and comfort of their room.

The innovation and learning perspective can often be the most difficult to measure directly. However, Kolmog appears to have worked round this problem by selecting measures relating to employee satisfaction.

Equally, it is important not to include too many measures. There is a danger that if the scorecard contains too many measures the impact of them will be reduced as a result of information overload.

Conflicting measures – Some measures in the scorecard may naturally conflict. For example, Kolmog may look to improve customer satisfaction scores by recruiting extra staff in some of its hotels. However, the costs of these staff could adversely affect financial performance in those hotels (at least in the short term).

The board may find it difficult to decide what combination of measures is likely to encourage the best results for Kolmog, but when making such decisions it will be important to look at how well each possible measure helps the company achieve its overall mission.

Interpretation – Even if Kolmog selects an appropriate set of measures for its scorecard they will ultimately only prove valuable to the company, if managers can interpret the results of the measures adequately, and use them to initiate appropriate actions to improve performance. If managers have difficulty analysing the figures, or interpreting what the figures are demonstrating, then it will be difficult for the managers to know what actions need to be taken in the light of the results being indicated by the scorecard.

Again, this also reinforces the importance of not including too many measures, in order to avoid information overload.

Management commitment – The scorecard is only likely to be effective if senior managers are committed to using it. If they revert to focusing solely on the financial measures they are used to, then the value of introducing additional (non-financial) measures will be reduced.

In this respect, the proposal to derive employees' targets for the performance reward system to the balanced scorecard seems sensible, because it encourages managers and staff to focus on all four perspectives of the scorecard.

(v) **Setting targets**

Challenging targets – When setting targets it is important to find a balance between ones which are too easy (and therefore don't require any effort to achieve) and ones which are too difficult (and are therefore demotivating because staff feel they are unachievable.)

In this respect, challenging – or **stretch** – targets provide a middle ground between targets which are too easy and those which are perceived to be unachievable.

This is the balance which Kolmog is trying to find with its new performance reward system.

Unachievable targets – The history of rewards at Kolmog suggests that, in the past, the targets set have been too difficult to achieve. The fact that 75% of staff have received no bonus in previous years suggests that the bonus scheme would not motivate staff because they would never expect to qualify for a bonus.

Standards

In their 'building block' model, Fitzgerald & Moon highlight that in order for performance measures to be effective, employees must view the measures as being **fair** and **achievable,** and the employees must take **ownership** of them.

Achievability – The fact that 75% of the staff have not received a bonus in previous years, suggests that Kolmog's reward scheme has historically not been an effective tool for motivating employees. If the staff feel the bonus targets are unachievable, they will only put in the minimum amount of effort they need to keep their jobs, rather than making any extra effort in the hope of receiving some extra reward as a result.

If the new targets are to be more effective in this respect, it is important that they are perceived to be more realistic to achieve.

Ownership – If the performance targets are based on budgets set by the finance department, this may also contribute to the sense of staff not accepting the targets and trying to achieve them. In particular, hotel managers' performance should only be judged against factors they can **control**. For example, if there is a downturn in market conditions, there is likely to be a downturn in revenue which managers cannot control.

Fairness – As we noted earlier in relation to segmental analysis, there are likely to be differences in the performance of different types of hotel. The concept of fairness suggests that targets should be adjusted for different types of hotel. For example, targets for city centre hotels should be comparable to each other, but may not be comparable to country house hotels.

Rewards

Rewards are the motivators which encourage employees to work towards the standards set. In order for rewards to be effective, they need to be clear, motivating and controllable.

Clarity – The employees need to be clear about the goals they are working towards.

Motivating – Employees need to be motivated to work towards the targets and in pursuit of the organisation's strategic objectives.

Controllability – Staff should not be held responsible for aspects of performance over which they have no control.

Issues with the proposed system

Ownership – The new system will propose that managers' targets are based on their hotel's performance against budgeted profit. However, if the budgets continue to be set by the head office finance department with no input from the managers, then there is likely to be a lack of ownership of the targets. Therefore, hotel managers should be involved in the budget setting process.

Fairness – Comparing staff turnover against an industry-wide standard may not be fair if managers cannot control staff wages. If wages are set centrally, and are not attractive compared to the wages offered by other hotel chains, staff turnover is likely to be high, and there will be little that managers can do to prevent this. A fairer measure would be to compare the staff turnover for individual hotels against other hotels of the same type within Kolmog.

Aligned to mission – Customer satisfaction is a controllable factor for hotel managers and therefore customer satisfaction scores should be an important element of performance assessment. However, given Kolmog's stated mission 'to become the No 1 hotel chain' it would be better to compare customer satisfaction scores against the scores achieved by Kolmog's competitors. The current proposal (to measure managers against the internal average) will not directly help Kolmog improve its performance against its competitors.

Clarity –The hotel managers' bonuses will be determined by their regional manager's assessment of their performance against the targets. In order for the reward system to be effective, the regional managers will need to explain the structure of the new scheme (for example, if there are different levels of bonus below the full 30%), and also the factors which will influence their assessment of the hotel managers' performance.

Ultimately, the success of the new scheme will depend on the extent to which it motivates staff and managers to help Kolmog achieve its mission. To do this, the targets will need to be stretching, but also to be perceived as achievable. In this respect, Kolmog should monitor the number of staff receiving bonuses to assess whether more staff are qualifying for some kind of bonus than under the old scheme.

75 Cantor

Text references. Performance reports are discussed in Chapter 8 of the BPP Study Text. Economic value added (EVA) is discussed in Chapter 9, and Value-based management (VBM) is discussed in Chapter 15.

Top tips.

Part (i). A crucial point to note here is that the requirement asks you to evaluate Cantor's performance *report*, not evaluate Cantor's *performance*.

There is a technical article for P5 on ACCA's website titled 'Reports for performance management' and this article suggests looking at four key aspects of a report to identify whether it is a good report or not: the purpose of the report; who the report is produced for; what information is needed; and, the layout of the report.

A sensible approach to this question would have been to use each of these four aspects as headings in your answer, and then to evaluate how well the report deals with each of them.

Purpose – The Examining team noted that candidates seemed reluctant to use the mission/strategy of the business to evaluate the report. A key issue in evaluating the report is whether it helps the Board understand how well Cantor is achieving its mission/strategy.

Audience – Has the report addressed the needs of its readers? In this case, a key point is that the report has three groups of readers (the main group board, and the boards of each of the two subsidiaries). This should have prompted you to think whether a single report can satisfy the needs of these different groups. For example, how much detail will the different groups need about different aspects of the business?

Technical article. Part (i) of this question is the subject of a two-part technical article on ACCA's website: *Improving your Paper P5 Answers (Parts 1 and 2.)*

In the article, a member of the P5 examining team highlights some of the errors which students made when answering the requirement to evaluate an organisation's current performance report. The article then goes on to demonstrate the sorts of points which candidates would have been expected to make in order to score well in this part of the question.

You are strongly advised to read this article as part of your preparation for the P5 exam.

Part (ii). The scenario has identified that the two key costs for review here are staff and property costs; and it also describes the rental arrangements of the two subsidiaries in detail.

Although this question is essentially about operating gearing, it is also important that you think about the different context of the two subsidiaries. Juicey's business appears more dynamic than Cafés', so what implications could this have for the appropriate balance of fixed and variable costs in each? Also, think about the nature of the costs involved. How can Cantor manage the balance between fixed and variable staff costs?

Part (iii). Make sure you note that the requirement here isn't simply to 'calculate' the economic value added (EVA) but to 'evaluate' it.

Equally, importantly, note that you weren't simply asked to state any assumptions you made when calculating EVA, but to 'justify' them.

Although this question was generally well-answered, with most candidates appearing to understand the adjustments to profit and capital employed that are required when calculating EVA, the examining team highlighted three areas where candidates struggled:

- When calculating WACC, many did not seem to be able to work out the weighting coefficients from the D/E.

- Many did not appreciate that the cost of debt needed an adjustment for it to be post-tax.

- The capital employed figure used for working out the cost of capital employed should be based on capital employed at the start of the year, not at the end of the year.

There are two articles about economic value added in the technical articles section of ACCA's website: Economic value added versus profit-based measures of performance – part 1 and part 2. You are advised to read them as part of your exam preparation if you have not already done so.

Part (iv) – There are two parts to this requirement: (i) explain how value-based management (VBM) could be implemented at Cantor and (ii) evaluate VBM's potential impact on the group.

One of the key elements of VBM is identifying the drivers which create value for an organisation, so that the organisation can then focus its performance management efforts on those drivers. This issue is also important in this requirement – because identifying Cantor's value drivers and performance targets linked to them will be a key part of implementing VBM at the organisation.

One follow-on question is then: how different are Cantor's performance metrics likely to be under VBM compared to its current performance measurement system? The degree of difference between them – and differences in the aspects of performance being measured – could be useful in evaluating the potential impact VBM could have.

Examining team's comments: The problem for the majority of candidates in part (iv) was a lack of knowledge, with many talking vaguely about value without an understanding of it, or of VBM, in the context of the scenario The fact that the question had just considered economic-value-added ought to have provided a memory jog, but there is little indication that it did. Some candidates although incorrectly appeared to think that VBM and ABM are the same thing.

Part (v) – It is important that you read the requirement very carefully here.

Firstly, note that the performance measures suggested need to relate to the proposed change in the mission statement ('to provide a fair deal to our employees') rather than to the mission statement as a whole. As such, performance measures looking at shareholder value or customer satisfaction were not relevant here.

Secondly, not that you are asked to use the information in the appendices as the source for the performance measures you recommend. So, for example, although employee satisfaction surveys might, in other circumstances, be a good way of finding out about employee satisfaction levels, they are not appropriate here, because they do not relate to the information in Appendix 3.

Finally, you need to justify why the measures you have recommended are suitable, rather than simply listing the measures.

Overall – As is the case with all of the Section A questions in P5, remember that you have been asked to write a report, so make sure the style and structure of your answer, as a whole, is appropriate for a report. Markers are looking for an introduction, suitable report headings, a logical structure, signposted by the use of sub-headings, and a clear, concise style.

The post examination report noted that a conclusion was not required for the four professional markets available in this question, but if candidates provided an appropriate, they were given credit for doing so.

Marks

(i) Each relevant point about Cantor's performance report – 1 mark
Points must be based on the scenario information, and must focus on
Cantor's performance report, rather than on its performance.

Possible relevant points include:
Assessment of whether the report supports Cantor's mission
Appropriateness of the level of detail provided for the three different
boards
Use of budgets
Use of industry averages
Lack of historical/trend information

Total for part (i) – Up to 15 marks 15

(ii) Each relevant point about the balance between fixed and variable costs in
each of the subsidiaries, and the impact this may have on managing
these costs – 1 mark

Total for part (ii) – Up to 6 marks 6

(iii) EVA calculation
Add back brand-building expenditure – 1mark
Taxation and loss tax relief on interest – 2marks
Capital employed – marketing – 1mark
WACC – 1mark
EVA result – 1mark

Brief evaluation of the EVA result – 1 mark
Assumptions made – identified and justified – up to 3 marks
Total for part (iii) – Up to 9 marks

9

(iv) For general description of VBM – up to 2 marks
Description of how VBM could be implemented at Cantor, and of what its
potential impact could be – 10 marks

Total for part (iv) – Up to 10 marks

10

(v) For calculations of suitable measures (eg average salaries; staff turnover
rates) – up to 3 marks
For each relevant point in justifying performance measures – 1 mark per
point

Total for part (v) – Up to 6 marks

6

Professional marks – for style and structure of report: introduction (1
mark); use of headings and suitable sub-headings (1 mark); clarity of
report, and of language used – Up to 4 marks

<u>4</u>

Total = <u>50</u>

Report

To: CEO

From: Strategic management accountant

Date: [today's date]

Subject: Performance reporting and value-based management at Cantor

Introduction

This report evaluates the current performance reports at Cantor, and the cost structures in the group.

It then calculates Cantor's economic value added (as an alternative measure of performance to the profit-based measures currently used in the performance reports) before evaluating the potential impact that value-based management could have at the group.

Finally, the report recommends some new performance measures to reflect the change in Cantor's mission statement.

(i) **Current performance report**

We can use four basic criteria to evaluate Cantor's current performance report:

Purpose – What the purpose of the report is, and whether it provides information which is relevant to Cantor's performance against its mission

Audience – Whether the report is appropriate for its audience and their requirements

Information – Whether the report provides information which is relevant for decision-making and control

Layout – Whether the report's layout is clear for its readers, and identifies the most important information.

Purpose

Performance against overall goals and objectives

One of the overall aims of Cantor's performance reports should be to enable the Board to identify how well the company is fulfilling its mission, and achieving its goals and objectives.

Cantor's mission statement identifies three key points:

- Maximising shareholder value
- Supplying good value food and drink
- Providing an appealing environment for customers

Shareholder value – The report currently only focuses on historic profits. It does not any future cash flows, economic value added, share price or dividends – all of which could provide an indication of shareholder value.

As such, the report does not directly measure shareholder value. This point has also been highlighted by one of Cantor's large shareholders who have suggested the introduction of economic value added (EVA) as the company's main measure of value. (We will return to this point later in this report).

One of the dangers of using annual profit as the main performance measure, is that it can lead to a focus on short-term performance. However, shareholders are likely to be interested in longer-term value creation as well as short-term performance.

Nonetheless, the comparison between budget and actual performance in the report is useful – both as a means of control, and also for giving some insight as to whether Cantor is performing in line with strategic targets.

Good value food and drink – Comparing Cantor's gross profit against the gross profit for the industry as a whole can give some indication of whether Cantor provides good value or not.

Cantor's gross profit margin is slightly higher than the industry average (74.2% vs 72.8%) which might suggest that the prices Cantor charges its customers are slightly higher than the industry average. However, the gross profit margin by itself is not a good indicator of whether Cantor is offering good value, because it doesn't provide any insight into the reasons behind the relative margins (for example, Cantor's costs of sales might be lower than its competitors) or the quality of the food and drink it is offering might be higher enabling it to can charge higher prices.

Another limitation of the report is that it does not provide any historical comparisons; although these could potentially give some insight into how attractive Cantor is to its customers. If Cantor is consistently able to increase its revenues over time, this could be seen as an indicator that it its customers feel it is providing them with good value.

Appealing environments for customers – It is difficult to measure the appeal of Cantor's cafés or juice bars from financial data alone (which is all the report provides). However, revenue growth gives some indication of customer satisfaction, because customers are unlikely to continue to use Cantor's premises if they are too unappealing.

Customer loyalty and price elasticity of demand could give a greater indication of the appeal Cantor's premises have for customers, but without surveying customers directly it will be difficult to assess the extent to which the environment has on their purchasing decisions, compared, for example, to the price and quality of the food and drink provided in them.

Audience

The same performance report is used by Cantor's main Group board, as well as the boards of the two subsidiaries. However, the information requirements of the subsidiary boards may be different to those of the Group board.

Main board – The main board is less likely to be interested in detailed figures, and so a summary of key performance measures for each of the subsidiaries may be more useful to them than, for example, the detailed information about operating costs currently provided.

Subsidiaries' boards – The report seems to treat the subsidiaries in the same way as the group, using profit and comparison to industry average margins and budgets as the main assessment tools. However, the different nature of Cafes and Juicey's business may make comparison to an overall industry average less meaningful.

Moreover, as the subsidiary boards are likely to be interested in more detailed performance issues than the main group board, it doesn't seem appropriate to only provide the subsidiary boards with the high-level overview which is produced for the group board.

For the subsidiaries, it would be useful to provide a more detailed breakdown of revenues and gross margins by product line, and by geographic region.

Similarly, it would be useful for the subsidiary boards to be provided with more detail about operating costs by geographic region so that they identify the profitability of different regions, and – if necessary, they may then need to drill down further to look at the profitability of individual outlets if some appear to be under-performing.

It seems that the measure being used to assess subsidiary performance is operating profit, which is appropriate as it contains the elements of performance controllable by the subsidiaries' managers. However, if the performance reports are only produced annually this would not appear appropriate for the needs of the subsidiary boards. They need more frequent information, to allow them to control their operations effectively.

Appropriate information for decision-making

The annual reporting period also reduces the report's usefulness as a basis of decision-making for the subsidiaries' boards.

In relation, to operational/tactical decision-making, the report would be more useful it provided greater detail for individual products or sites to assist the managers of the subsidiaries in their planning and control activities.

Conversely, at a strategic level, the report is likely to be more useful if it provided some external information – for example, competitor information – rather than focusing on internal financial information. Currently, the only external benchmarks provided are the industry average figures, but these may be less useful than figures for competitors who compete directly with Cantor in the same sectors of the market.

Also, for both boards, it would be useful to provide some historic information to help identify growth and trends. This is likely to be particularly important at Juicey, given the levels of growth it is currently enjoying.

Similarly, would be useful, for both boards, if the report included some non-financial KPIs in relation to the three key areas of Cantor's mission: shareholder value, product value and customer satisfaction with Cantor's sites.

The current focus (on financial performance only) only provides the boards with 'lagging' information on how well Cantor has performed, rather than providing them with any 'leading' indicators – and some insight into how well it will perform in future.

Layout

In terms of presentation, the data is clear and in a form which would be easily recognisable to those used to reading accounts. However, it could be useful to provide a short narrative commentary in conjunction with the report in order to highlight the key points highlighted by the figures – such as major deviations from the budget, or areas where Cantor is performing significantly better or worse than industry norms.

The report could also be made easier to read by rounding all figures to thousands and thus removing unnecessary detail.

(ii) Cost structures

The costs in each of the two subsidiaries include a mixture of fixed and variable costs. In general terms, higher fixed costs will constitute a higher level of risk to Cantor than variable costs. If Cantor's revenues fall, but level of fixed costs remains unchanged, then its operating gearing will increase.

In practice, however, it may not be possible to analyse costs simply into 'fixed' and 'variable' costs. Some will be partly fixed and partly variable.

Staff costs

Staff costs are likely to be part-fixed and part-variable. As these represent a significant part of the cost base, it will be necessary to establish what element is fixed (how many staff are the minimum required to run a site?) and what element is variable (how many staff can be used as needed when the sites are busy?).

This cost area will be managed through decisions over the balance of the numbers of permanent and casual staff, with casual staff being used to manage fluctuations in business. As such, this suggests that Juicey may need to use proportionately more casual staff than Cafes.

Property costs

The nature of the property costs is also different in the two subsidiaries:

Cafes – Rent is a fixed costs for Cafes – with fixed rental charges being payable quarterly in advance.

Juicey – Rent is a variable cost, being a percentage of revenue.

This structure appears appropriate to the nature of the different businesses. Cafes is a mature business whose revenues are likely to be relatively stable and predictable – meaning that there should be little risk of it not being able to cover its rental costs each month.

By contrast, Juicey is a relatively new business, but it is also rapidly growing, and therefore agreeing negotiating variable rental costs is more appropriate for it.

However, the percentage demanded will reflect the risk which the landlord is taking on the success of Juicey and so is likely to be higher than a fixed rent, such as that negotiated by Cafes. As Juicey becomes established, it may be worth considering beginning to move to negotiating fixed rental deals for Juicey in order to cut this cost.

This last point illustrates the dilemma which many businesses face in thinking about the balance of fixed and variable costs. Variable costs are more desirable as they do not threaten the survival of the business but they are often higher than a fixed cost deal.

(iii) Economic value added

	$	Notes
Operating profit	10,852,970	
Add back		
Brand building	3,819,000	50% of marketing expenditure
Less		
Taxation	(2,100,000)	Tax paid in year
Lost tax relief on interest	(200,250)	Finance costs @ 25%
NOPAT	**12,371,720**	
Capital employed	53,400,000	At start of 20X4
Brand building expenditure capitalised	3,819,000	Spending in previous years
Adjusted capital employed	57,219,000	
Cost of capital employed (@ 13.2%)	**(7,552,908)**	See Working for WACC calculation
EVA	**4,818,812**	NOPAT - Cost of capital employed

	$	Notes
Working		
Equity: 100/130 × 15.7%	12.1	
Debt: (30/130 × 6.5%) × (1-25%)	1.1	Adjusted for tax at 25%
WACC	13.2	

The EVA calculation suggests that the group's economic profits for the year (NOPAT) were significantly greater than its cost of capital – such that it was able to add $4.82 million to shareholder value over the year.

However, the EVA which has been has calculated is only an example, and it has made several simplifying assumptions which would need to be investigated in more detail if we started to use EVA as one of our main performance measures.

– **Depreciation** – We have not made any adjustments to the depreciation charge, which assumes that economic depreciation is the same as accounting depreciation. However, this may not be the case, in which case the depreciation charge in NOPAT would need to be adjusted to reflect economic depreciation.

– **Marketing and brand building** – We have estimated that half of the marketing spend relates to brand-building, but this figure may need to be investigated more closely.

More importantly, perhaps, although we have added back, the brand building expenditure in 2013 to adjust the figure for capital employed at the start of 20X4, we have not made any further adjustments for previous years. However, to calculate EVA properly, the total amount of the brand building expenditure in the years leading up to 20X4 should all be added back to capital employed.

Subsidiaries – As with the current profit measures in the performance report, if Cantor decides to use EVA, it may be useful to calculate EVA separately for the two subsidiaries as well as for the group. This will help to identify how much value each subsidiary is generating for the shareholders.

(iv) **Value-based management**

The premise behind Value-based management (VBM) is that the value of a company is measured by its discounted cash flows, and value is only created when the capital which companies invest generates returns which are greater than the cost of that capital.

Therefore, in contrast to Cantor's current approach to performance measurement which focuses on profits, VBM will encourage a focus on future cash flows, and the creation of value.

Importantly, given Cantor's mission, management decision-making under VBM focuses on what activities ('drivers') increase the value of a company – and create value for its shareholders.

The VBM approach also aligns strategic, operational and management processes so that they all work together to create value.

Understanding value drivers

Implementing VBM at Cantor will require that management understand the key value drivers which create value for the business.

Equally, VBM will also require management to establish processes which ensure that all business unit managers adopt value-based thinking when making decisions. For VBM to be effective, it will eventually have to involve every decision maker in the company.

Management processes and implementing VBM

There are four underlying management processes which govern the adoption of VBM (be it at group level, subsidiary level or operational level):

Step 1 - A strategy is developed to maximise value

Step 2 – Key value drivers are identified in relation to the strategy, and then performance targets (both short- and long-term) are defined for those value drivers

Step 3 – Action plans are drawn up to define the steps to be taken to achieve the performance targets

Step 4 – Performance measurement systems and incentive systems are set up to monitor performance against targets and to encourage employees to meet their goals.

Strategy development

Corporate level - Using VBM, Cantor's management will need to devise a corporate strategy which focuses specifically on maximising the overall value of the company – including acquiring or disposing of business units if appropriate. Currently, Cantor appears to be growing organically – with the growth of Juicey – but the board should consider whether this growth needs to be reinforced with external growth.

Subsidiary level – Similarly, the subsidiary boards will need to evaluate whether there are any alternative strategies for their businesses which could enable them to achieve competitive advantage and to create value.

Target setting

Once Cantor has agreed its strategies for maximising value, this will need to be translated into specific targets which can be used to manage performance at both strategic and operational levels. The targets should be based on key value drivers, and should include both financial and non-financial aspects of performance – so, for example, customers' rating of the appeal of Cantor's sites could be used as a target if this a key factor in maintaining customer satisfaction levels.

Impact of VBM at Cantor

Implementing VBM would require Cantor to introduce new performance measures based on the drivers, and the company's reward and incentive systems will need to focus on value creation and performance against value-driven targets.

Performance measures, targets and rewards will need to be developed at the group level, then at the subsidiary level and, finally, at the individual site level in order to ensure full co-ordination of the system across Cantor. In order to align the interests of employees and management with shareholder value – particularly in the longer term – the new reward system may include a share-based payment scheme.

The key benefits of VBM are the focus on value as opposed to profit, so reducing the tendency to make decisions which have positive short-term impact but may be detrimental in the long term. VBM thus will help to make Cantor more forward-looking.

However, a danger of the VBM exercise is that it becomes an exercise in valuing everything but changing nothing. It is important that the detailed operational issues of the organisation are addressed through the new measures/targets.

A further difficulty in implementation is that the measurement of the key value drivers can often involve non-financial indicators and these can represent a significant change for accounting-based management information systems.

(v)   **Performance measures – fair deal for employees**

The proposed change to the mission statement means that Cantor will need to find a way of measuring whether it provides a 'fair deal' to its employees. This will be inherently difficult to measure, due to the subjective nature of determining how Cantor treats its employees.

Staff turnover

However, the information about staff numbers and staff turnover given in Appendix 3 of Cantor's current Performance Report can provide some indication of employee satisfaction.

The figures indicate that the staff turnover rate for the Group as a whole was 9.9% for the last year, with staff turnover being significantly higher in Juicey (14.2%) than in Cafes (9.7%). Some of this difference may be due to the fact that Juicey is a much newer and more dynamic operation, and that it may have been employing staff on short-term or temporary contracts. However, the variation in rates should still be investigated, and Cantor's staff turnover rates should also be compared against competitors if possible. If Cantor's staff turnover rates are higher than its competitors, this could be an indication that employee satisfaction at Cantor is lower.

Staff turnover rates

	Cafes	Juicey	Group
Average number of employees in 20X4	1,498	106	1,624
Number of leavers	146	15	161
Staff turnover rate (%)	9.7%	14.2%	9.9%

> **Tutorial Note**. We have used the average number of employees across 20X4 to calculate staff turnover rates, but ACCA's marking guidance indicated that it was also acceptable to use year-end figures.

Average pay

The figures in Appendix 3 can also be used in conjunction with the staff from Appendix 1 to calculate the average wages Cantor pays to its staff:

	Cafes	Juicey	Head Office	Group
Average number of employees in 20X4	1,498	106	20	1,624
Staff costs ($ '000)	15,921	1,525	3,899	21,345
Average pay per employee	10,628	14,387	194,950	13,143

These figures could again be compared to competitors to indicate whether Cantor is offering its staff fair – or competitive – rates of pay. Benchmark information is not currently provided in the performance reports, although the fact that Cantor's staff costs as a proportion of revenue are slightly higher than the industry average (31.2% vs 30.9%) suggests Cantor offers its employees a reasonably fair deal.

However, the overall Group figures appear to be distorted by the salaries paid to Cantor's head office staff, and the averages wages earned by staff in the Cafes subsidiary earn are significantly lower than Group average of $13,143.

Conclusion

> **Tutorial Note**. ACCA's marking guidance indicated that you did not need to provide a conclusion for your report in order to score the Professional Marks available, although you would have earned additional credit if you did so.

Cantor's current performance report has a number of weaknesses – in particular that it does not provide an indication of how well the group is performing against the three aspects of its current mission. The report focuses on Cantor's profitability rather than shareholder value, but moving to a value-based management approach and introducing EVA as a performance measure could help to address this issue.

It would also be useful to produce separate reports for the main Board and for the subsidiaries' Boards, due to the differing information requirements.

76 Boltzman Machines

Text references. Stakeholder management is discussed in Chapter 5 of the BPP Study Text; benchmarking in Chapter 1, JIT is covered in Chapter 13 and the balanced scorecard is discussed in Chapter 15.

Top tips.

Part (a). Although the analysis of the different stakeholder groups in Appendix 1 indicates that Mendelow's matrix is the relevant framework for analysing the different stakeholder groups, you shouldn't spend time describing the matrix itself. Instead you need to use the aspects of the matrix (power; interest) as the basis for identifying how Boltzman should manage the different stakeholder groups; for example, by ensuring that any strategies it introduces are acceptable to key stakeholders.

In order to justify how Boltzman should manage the different stakeholder groups, you need to identify how important the different stakeholder groups are. However, you also need to consider the relative importance of the stakeholder groups in the second part of the requirement – evaluating the appropriateness of Boltzman's performance measures. In effect, the requirement is asking you to evaluate how far the measures relate to those aspects of performance which the stakeholders are most interested in.

Part (b). In P5, you need to be able to evaluate the approaches used to measure performance of an organisation, as well as being to evaluate the performance of the organisation itself. In part (b) of this question you need to do both.

First you need to benchmark Boltzman's performance against General Machines (ie how well is Boltzman performing) and then you need to evaluate competitive benchmarking as a type of benchmarking (ie how useful is competitive benchmarking as a way of measuring/managing Boltzman's performance? Might other types of benchmarking be more useful?).

When tackling the first part of the requirement, it is vital you do exactly what has been asked. You are asked to use the measures 'suggested by the CEO' (ie the five performance measures given in Appendix 1.) However, the instruction from the CEO (in the penultimate paragraph of the scenario says 'You should also add two justified measures of your own, using the data provided'. So, in total you need to include seven performance measures in the benchmarking exercise.

When choosing your two additional measures, it would be useful to think back to your stakeholder analysis and the assessment of Botlzman's current performance measures in part (a). For example, as far as possible Boltzman should try to benchmark the aspects of performance which are important for its competitive success.

EVA and development costs – When calculating economic value added, one of the potential adjustments needed to convert operating profit to NOPAT is adding back research and development costs which have been charged to the profit or loss account. In the notes for Appendix 2 there is a figure for 'Product development costs', but there is no specific indication whether these had been charged to the profit or loss account, or capitalised.

Given the level of Product development costs ($2,684m) compared to the total of 'Other costs' in the financial statements ($2,958m), and given the reference to 'development costs' only (rather than 'research and development') the Examining team's original assumption was that these development costs had been capitalised rather than charged to profit or loss. Therefore, no adjustment to operating profit would have been required when calculating NOPAT.

The suggested solution below has been produced on this basis. However, if candidates assumed development costs had been charged to profit and loss, and added it back when calculating NOPAT, they were given credit for doing so.

Part (c). Perhaps the most important word in the requirement for this part of the question is 'problems'. You are not being asked to explain what JIT is, or what the advantages of a move toward JIT manufacturing might be, but what the problems which accompany that move will be. Appendix 3 gives you some pointers here by mentioning the impacts on the supply chain with customers and suppliers.

For example, under a JIT system, Boltzman will carry very little inventory. But what problems could this cause if Boltzman can't predict customer demand accurately, or if its suppliers don't deliver components when they are scheduled to?

Part (d). The final paragraph in the scenario provides important context for this requirement: the CEO has asked for you to evaluate the suitability of the scorecard in the light of the shareholders' criticism, and the other initiatives currently in progress.

The link between this requirement and Initiative 1 (part (a) of the question requirements) could be particularly important in this respect. In part (a) you were asked to evaluate the performance measures which have currently been suggested, so one way of assessing the suitability of the balanced scorecard would be to assess the extent to which using it would improve Boltzman's performance measures, compared to the ones currently suggested.

Importantly though, this question requires an application of the scorecard to the scenario. You will score very few marks – if any – for simply describing the different perspectives of the scorecard.

Overall. Remember that you have been asked to write a report, so make sure the style and structure of your answer, as well as its tone, is appropriate for a report.

Marking scheme

		Marks
(a)	For analysing each of the four stakeholders, and identifying appropriate management approaches for each stakeholder – Up to 2 marks per stakeholder	
	For evaluating the appropriateness of the five performance indicators suggested – 1 mark per relevant point – Up to a maximum of 10 marks	
	Total for part (b) – Up to 14 marks	14
(b)	For calculating ROCE; revenue growth; average pay per employee, net profit margin; and two other appropriate measures – 1 mark each – up to 6 marks	
	For calculating economic value added – up to 3 marks	
	For justifying each of the two new indicators suggested – 1 mark per indicator	
	For evaluating the method of benchmarking – 1 mark per relevant point – up to 6 marks	
	For a reasonable conclusion on Boltzman's performance compared to General Machines – up to 3 marks	
	Total for part (c) – Up to 16 marks	16
(c)	For each relevant difficulty of implementing JIT – 1 mark	
	Additional marks awarded for relating the difficulty to Boltzman	
	Total for part (d) – Up to 7 marks	7
(d)	For each relevant point relating to the suitability of the balanced scorecard as a performance measurement system at Boltzman – 1 mark	
	(For answers structured around the four perspectives of the scorecard, no more than 2 marks are to be allocated to a single perspective.)	
	Total for part (d) – Up to 9 marks	9
	Professional marks – for style and structure of report – Up to 4 marks	4
		Total = 50

Report

To: Board of Boltzman

From: Consultant

Date: [today's date]

Subject: Performance management initiatives

Introduction

This report looks at a number of performance management issues at Boltzman, in particular the way Boltzman measures and manages its performance in relation to its key stakeholders, and whether the aspects of performance being measured are ones which are important to the stakeholders. We then also benchmark Boltzman's performance against General Motors, and look at the problems which Boltzman could face in its move towards just-in-time manufacturing. We finish by assessing the suitability of the balanced scorecard as a potential performance measurement system for the company.

(a)   **Stakeholder management**

The management approaches which are appropriate for different stakeholder groups depend on the **power** the groups have to influence strategic decisions at Boltzman and their **interest** in doing so.

Shareholders – Shareholders have high power but have little interest in the strategic decisions being taken by Boltzman – provided those decisions lead to satisfactory financial results. As such, they should be kept satisfied, and this can be done by ensuring that their financial targets are met.

Employees – Employees overall have little power, and only moderate interest; therefore the most appropriate way of managing them is to keep them informed of strategic decisions.

However, the sub-group of key employees who work in product development have high power because Boltzman cannot afford for them to leave. As such, these key employees need to be kept satisfied, for example by continuing to provide them with training and opportunities to develop their skills through working with new technologies.

Customers – Boltzman's customers appear to be its key stakeholder group, and they also appear to have a relatively high degree of bargaining power over it. The fact that Boltzman cannot afford to lose one of its major customers means that any strategic decisions needs to be acceptable to them.

Given that some of the parts are specifically designed for each customer, it would also seem appropriate to the key customers to be involved in product development, to ensure that the products meet their requirements. This level of cooperation should also help to strengthen the relationship between Boltzman and its customers.

Suppliers – Their low power and relatively low level of interest means that Boltzman's suppliers should require minimal effort.

The suppliers have low bargaining power in relation to Boltzman, which means that the company should be in a strong position to negotiate a favourable price for the goods it buys from them, and to ensure that the quality of them is maintained.

However, if Boltzman introduces JIT manufacturing it will need good relationships with its suppliers (as we will discuss in part (c) of this report), so this could increase the power of its suppliers.

Appropriateness of performance measures

Boltzman's performance measures should focus on the aspects of its performance which are important to its key stakeholders – which in this case, are its customers and its shareholders.

Customers – None of the suggested performance measures relate to the interests of Boltzman's customers, which is a major drawback. For example, it would be useful to have some measures looking at customer satisfaction, in terms of both quality and value for money.

Shareholders – The shareholders are interested in financial returns, and four out of the five suggested measures (return on capital employed, economic value added, revenue growth and net profit margin) relate to financial performance. This focus on financial performance is consistent with the shareholders' position as important stakeholders. Moreover, the use of economic value added suggests that Boltzman is specifically aware of the need to maximise shareholder wealth, rather than simply to generate short-term profits.

Employees – The suggested measure – Average pay per employee – makes no distinction between the key group of skilled employees and the other employees, which limits its usefulness. It would be more useful for Boltzman to compare the average of its product development staff (key staff) against a suitable industry benchmark, because retaining these staff is likely to be critical for the company's competitive success.

Suppliers – Given the relatively low power of Boltzman's suppliers, it is appropriate that none of the suggested measures relate to them. However, this will have to change if JIT is introduced – and, for example, the reliability of supplier deliveries becomes critical to Boltzman's internal processes.

(b) **Benchmarking**

Additional measures – The two additional indicators used in the benchmarking exercise have been chosen to provide some measures of Boltzman's performance in relation its customers. As we have previously identified, customers are key stakeholders, but none of the performance measures previously suggested are customer-focused. Therefore, including these additional indicators marks an improvement in the measures used.

Product development should help to maintain innovation in the business, which in turn should help to support on-going growth. The number of customers who recognise Boltzman as a top tier supplier provides some insight into its bargaining power with its customers, and it gives some indication of the customers' perception of the quality of Boltzman's products.

Benchmarking results

	Boltzman	General Machines
Return on capital employed (see Working)	15.5%	9.2%
Economic value added (see Working)	$97m	$(1,165)m
Revenue growth (20X3 – 20X4)	6.4%	1.0%
Average pay per employee	$54,618	$52,299
Net profit margin	8.2%	3.3%
Additional indicators:		
Product development cost (% of revenue)	11.2%	10.2%
Top tier supplier status (out of 20)	13	14

Performance analysis

Financial performance – Boltzman appears to be performing better than General Machines in relation to all the financial indicators (ROCE, EVA, and net profit margin).

Boltzman also appears to have better growth prospects than General Machines, and this may in part be a consequence of the greater attention it plays to product development.

Currently, General Machines is larger than Boltzman and has top tier status with marginally more large customers, but if Boltzman's growth rate (relative to General Machines) continues it may soon become larger than General Machines, and achieve top tier supplier status with more customers.

Benchmarking method

Competitive benchmarking – The benchmarking exercise is an example of competitive benchmarking, since Boltzman's performance has been compared against its main competitor, General Machines. This type of benchmarking can be useful for identifying areas where Boltzman needs to improve its performance to catch up with the General Machines. However, it will not identify how Boltzman can gain any competitive advantage from it.

Also, it is unlikely that a competitor will share any detailed performance information with Boltzman, so the only aspects of performance which can be benchmarked are high levels strategic ones, where the relative information is already publicly available (as is the case with the financial data currently being benchmarked).

As a result, however, this kind of benchmarking will not provide Boltzman with any insights into how to improve its processes.

Functional benchmarking – As well as comparing its performance against direct competitors, it may also be useful for Boltzman to monitor its performance against 'best in class' performers from other business sectors. Since Boltzman is not competing with these companies, they may be willing to share operational data with it in a way that General Machines would not be. As such, Boltzman could identify ways of improving its processes and capabilities which in turn should help to improve its overall financial performance.

Functional benchmarking could be particularly useful in relation to Boltzman's quality initiatives, since it could compare its performance with other companies which are recognised for the quality of their products, and then hopefully find ways to improve the quality of its products, and to support its aim of becoming the highest quality supplier in the market place.

(c) **JIT manufacturing**

As the head of aerospace has suggested in this email, the move to JIT manufacturing could have a significant impact on Boltzman's supply chain – both upstream (with suppliers), and downstream (with customers).

Forecasting demand – Under a JIT system, Boltzman will manufacture parts in response to customer demand, rather than holding any significant volumes of parts as inventory. However, to do this effectively, Boltzman will need to be able to forecast customer demand accurately and plan its manufacturing activities accordingly. This demand planning will require close links between Boltzman and its customers.

Suppliers – As well as not holdings stocks of finished parts, Boltzman will not hold any significant stocks of components under a JIT system. Therefore, Boltzman will be reliant on its suppliers to deliver orders on time, and without any defects, in order for the manufacturing process to run smoothly. Boltzman currently uses a large number of suppliers, and so it will need to review whether they are all sufficiently reliable to operate under a JIT system. Boltzman may find it more practical to reduce the number of suppliers it deals with, and to partner with a smaller number of suppliers whose reliability can be guaranteed (both in terms of the quality of the parts they supply, and in terms of delivering on time).

Disruption to the supply chain – However, reducing the number of suppliers it uses, and not holding any inventory makes Boltzman more vulnerable to any disruption in its upstream supply chain. One way of reducing the risk of disruption is to use local suppliers wherever possible. However, this would reduce the choice of suppliers available to Boltzman and also increases the suppliers' bargaining power over the company.

Factory design and factory processes – Introducing JIT will also have implications for the operational processes within Boltzman. For example, JIT organises production lines around the product or component being manufactured, rather than the type of work being done. Depending on how Boltzman's production lines are currently structured, they may need to be restructured to fit with the JIT approach.

Similarly, JIT requires staff to be multi-skilled and flexible. If Boltzman's operational staff currently have narrowly defined jobs, it is likely they will need to be retrained so that they have the variety of skills required to implement JIT successfully. However, this could cause problems in itself if the staff are resistant to changes in their working patterns.

(d) **Balanced Scorecard**

As we have identified in part (a) of this report, Boltzman's key stakeholders are its customers and its shareholders. However, none of the performance measures currently suggested relate to the interests of Boltzman's customers.

Customer perspective – The customer perspective of the balanced scorecard highlights the importance that successfully meeting customers' requirements will have on Boltzman's financial performance. Therefore, introducing the scorecard will reinforce the need for measures looking at customer satisfaction, which emerged from Initiative 1 (on stakeholder influence).

Financial perspective – The measures currently suggested concentrate mainly on financial aspects of performance. Again, as we noted in part (a), financial performance measures are important, especially given Boltzman's mission to maximise shareholder value.

The financial perspective of the balanced scorecard should ensure that financial indicators remain important performance measures at Boltzman.

However, the scorecard also highlights the importance that non-financial aspects of performance have in sustaining the company's financial performance. In particular, the scorecard suggests that a company's financial performance will be shaped how well it meets its customers' needs, the quality of its internal business processes, and the degree of innovation and learning within it.

Innovation and learning – The innovation and learning perspective of the scorecard is again important for Boltzman considering the company's reputation for innovation, and for the pursuit of engineering excellence identified in its mission. If Boltzman doesn't maintain its innovativeness this could affect its competitive position, which, in turn, could damage its performance in relation to the customer and financial perspectives of the scorecard.

Business processes – Boltzman's strategic aim to be the highest quality supplier in the market place suggests that it already needs efficient and effective business processes in order for it to achieve the levels of quality it wants to. However, the focus on business processes will become increasingly important as the company introduces lean production methods. As such, having some performance indicators focusing on process quality – as suggested by the business process perspective of the scorecard – would be suitable for Boltzman.

Shareholder concerns – Apart from their concerns about managerial autonomy, it is not clear what the shareholders' other concerns are, and therefore whether introducing the balanced scorecard will do anything to address them. Nonetheless, as the financial perspective of the scorecard addresses the question of how a company looks to its shareholders, by introducing the scorecard the board can demonstrate that they have recognised the importance of the shareholders and their concerns.

However, it is not clear how introducing the scorecard, by itself, will reduce the levels of autonomy managers will have. The shareholders' criticism in this respect appears to be about management styles and culture within Boltzman. Nonetheless, the 'balanced' nature of the scorecard means that managerial performance will be assessed under all four headings. Therefore, if the areas of performance against which manager's performance are measured are properly aligned to Boltzman's critical success factors (and, in turn, to its strategic aims and mission) this should reduce the scope for dysfunctional decision making, even if the managers still retain autonomy for their decisions.

Conclusion

Shareholders are a key stakeholder group, so the suggestion that Boltzman is not listening to shareholders' concerns needs to be addressed. The 'financial' perspective of the balanced scorecard reinforces the importance of measuring how well Boltzman is performing for its shareholders. However, the scorecard also highlights the importance of non-financial aspects of performance. Stakeholder analysis highlights that Boltzman's customers are a key stakeholder group, so the addition of customer-orientated indicators into the company's performance measures would be particularly beneficial.

The benchmarking exercise against General Machines indicates that Boltzman is currently performing well, relative to General Machines. However, it would also be useful to carry out a functional benchmarking exercise to compare some key operating processes against best-in-class performers.

> **Tutorial Note.** ROCE figures are based on year opening capital employed figures, because this is also the start point for working out capital employed in EVA. However, it would have been acceptable to use closing capital employed figures when calculating ROCE (although not EVA.)
>
> Treatment of Development costs – ACCA's suggested solution for this question assumed that the development costs had been capitalised, rather than charged to profit and loss. As such they have not been added back to profit when calculating EVA. Again, however, marks were given if an adjustment was made for product development costs.

	Boltzman $m	General Machines $m
Return on capital employed		
Profit before interest and tax	2,907	1,882
Capital employed:		
Equity	8,984	9,744
Non-current liabilities	9,801	10,629
	18,785	20,373
ROCE	15.5%	9.2%
EVA		
Profit before interest and tax	2,907	1,882
Less:		
Tax charge	(663)	(718)
Tax benefit of interest (28% of financing costs)	(81)	(88)
NOPAT	**2,163**	**1,076**
Capital employed	18,785	20,373
WACC: 11%		
EVA: NOPAT - (Capital employed × 11%)	**97**	**(1,165)**

77 Merkland Sportswear

> **Text references.** SWOT analysis is discussed in Chapter 1 of the BPP Study Text. The performance hierarchy linking strategic objectives and performance metrics is discussed in Chapter 2. Expected values are discussed in Chapter 6, and the value chain is covered in Chapter 4.
>
> **Top tips.**
>
> **Part (i).** There are two distinct parts to this requirement: assess the current metrics; and then make suggestions for improving them. As the marking guide illustrates, the marks available were distributed roughly equally between the two parts, so to score well you needed to give due weight to both parts of the requirement.
>
> The first part of the requirement asks you to 'assess' the existing metrics. A useful way to approach this requirement might be to ask yourself what the characteristics of effective performance metrics are, and then to consider how well MS's metrics demonstrate these characteristics. Importantly, performance metrics enable management to identify how well an organisation is performing against its critical success factors (CSFs), and how well it is achieving its strategy. In turn, this means that the aspects of performance which are being measured should be ones which are linked to key elements of an organisation's strategy.
>
> Therefore, before you can assess MS's performance metrics, you also need to identify its strategy. The third paragraph in the question scenario – which identifies MS's aims and then its broad strategy for achieving them – is crucial here. In effect, your assessment of the metrics should be an assessment of whether or not they will enable MS's management to determine if the company is achieving its aims and strategy.

Having assessed the current metrics, you are then asked to make suggestions for improvements. However, crucially, you must do so within the constraints outlined by the CEO – ie that the existing performance headings (financial, design and brand) are retained, and that there are no more than three financial metrics, and no more than two for each of 'design' and 'brand'. The post-exam review comments (see below) indicated many candidates in the real exam failed to adhere to these constraints.

Also, note that the requirement specifically asks you to use the SWOT analysis as the basis for your suggestions. Therefore a useful approach to this part of the requirement would be to ask if the current performance metrics will allow management to assess how the issues identified in the SWOT are affecting MS's performance. If factors in the SWOT are not being covered by the performance metrics, then these can provide the basis for your suggested improvements. However, remember, your suggestions must be within the constraints outlined by the CEO.

Examining team's comments for part (i): Although part (i) was often answered reasonably well, there were still a number of weaknesses in candidates' answers. A 'significant minority' of candidates chose to assess MS's performance, rather than the assessing the performance metrics.

Also, candidates need to remember that, when making suggestions, justifying the suggestion is crucial. Candidates will not score enough marks to pass the requirement by listing alternative performance metrics – to score the marks available candidates must explain why the metrics they are proposing would be beneficial to MS.

Most worryingly, however, the majority of candidates ignored the instructions from the CEO to limit the number of metrics suggested. Many answers contained long lists of new metrics, which was not what was asked for at all.

Part (ii). The requirement asks you to assess the qualitative and quantitative impact of a change of outsourcing partners for footwear manufacture. The qualitative issues (around the ethical implications of using child labour) should have been relatively easy to identify from the scenario.

The information needed to calculate the quantitative impact is provided in Appendix 3, and the comment 'It would be helpful to know how many units we would need to sell in order to cover these increased costs' should have been a clear instruction that a breakeven calculation was required here.

As the marking guide indicates, four out of the eight marks available for this requirement related to the breakeven calculation. However, when this question was examined, the post exam report suggested that a number of candidates appeared unable to perform the calculations, and the examining team reported that this was very worrying at P5 level.

Part (iii). You should have been able to score some relatively easy marks in the expected value calculation here – using the information you are given in Appendix 4 of the scenario. However, note that the requirement doesn't only ask you to calculate the operating profit, but you are also asked to evaluate expected value method as a method of decision-making under risk.

Part (iv). Here again there are two parts to the requirement: (i) evaluate the impact of the new factory on the figures in the dashboard (ie the results) and (ii) evaluate the impact of the new factory on the choice of metrics in the dashboard.

To identify the relevant issues here, it is crucial to think about the new factory in the context of MS's current business model. Currently, MS outsources all of its manufacturing. However, once the new factory is set up, MS will have its own manufacturing operation. This is particularly significant when thinking about the impact the factory will have on the metrics needed to assess performance.

The examining team's comments for this part of the question are also helpful here:

Examining team's comments: Many candidates attempted to recalculate the dashboard metrics but ignored the fact that the new factory was bringing in-house an existing process and so the change in operating profit was the different between the new factory's profit and that which was made from existing outsourced sales. However, even if no calculations were attempted a number of candidates earned enough marks to pass this requirement by simply going through the metrics and discussing how the new factory affected them and what changes should be made now that MS has a manufacturing operation – something which it did not have prior to this change.

Part (v). Note that the requirement here does not ask you to describe the value chain, or to explain the implications of the value chain for performance management in general term, but specifically to 'Explain the implications of using the value chain for performance management at MS'. Linking your answer to the scenario was important to score well here.

A useful way of approaching this requirement could be to think how MS generates value through the different activities in its value chain, and then to consider what implications this has for the choice of performance measures or the way performance is measured at MS.

Report format. Finally, note that you were asked to write a report, and remember that there are 4 'professional marks' available for the quality of your report. In this respect, markers are looking for suitable report headings, a brief introduction, and a logical structure to your report – signposted by the use of headings. They are also looking for your report to be written in a clear, concise style.

Marking scheme

Marks

(i)   For identifying MS's aims and broad strategies – up to 2 marks
For evaluating how well the metrics support each aim and strategy:
Growth – 1 mark
Shareholder wealth – up to 2 marks
Innovation – up to 3 marks
Marketing – up to 3 marks

For other comments / suggestions linked to SWOT analysis:
Comments about supply chain management – up to 2 marks
Comments about social media and IT expertise – up to 3 marks
Comments about brand ambassadors – up to 3 marks

For adhering to the constraint on the number of metrics on the dashboard – 1 mark

Total for part (i) – Up to 16 marks   16

(ii)   For calculations:
Increased Cost of sales – 1mark
Lost operating profit – 1 mark
New contribution per unit – 1 mark
Required sales 1 mark

Comments (on qualitative and quantitative issues) – up to 4 marks

Total for part (ii) – Up to 8 marks   8

(iii)   For calculations:
Variable costs – 1 mark
Revenue – 1 mark
Profit – 1 mark
Expected profit – 1 mark

For comments (on expected value method) – up to 2 marks

Total for part (iii) – Up to 6 marks   6

(iv)   For calculations:
Operating profit under 3rd part manufacturing – 1 mark
Loss of operating profit – 1 mark
New capital employed – 1 mark
New ROCE – 1 mark
No change to other metrics – 1 mark

For comments (about the impact of the new factory on the values in the dashboard, and/or on the choice of measures in the dashboard – up to 2 marks

Total for part (iv) – Up to 10 marks   10

(v) For relevant points about the implications of the value chain on performance management at MS – 1 mark per point

Total for part (v) – Up to 6 marks   6

Professional marks – for style and structure of report – Up to 4 marks   4

                                                                                    Total = 50

Report

To: Board of MS

From: Consultant

Date: [today's date]

Subject: Performance management at Merkland Sportswear (MS)

Introduction

This report looks at a number of performance management issues at MS, particularly in relation to the range of performance measures included in the dashboard. We begin by evaluating the existing measures used, before looking at the way the company's response to the child labour scandal in the sportswear manufacturing industry could affect its performance and its performance measurement system.

We finish by looking at how value chain analysis could influence performance management at MS.

(i) Evaluation of current metrics

MS's overall commercial aims are to grow as a business and to maximise shareholder wealth.

As these aims are essentially financial, it seems appropriate for the dashboard to include three financial measures, but only up to one each for 'design' and 'brand.'

Financial performance measures

Growth – Comparing the revenue figures to prior years can give an indication of the growth being achieved by the business. Including percentage change figure (for 20X5 compared to 20X4) on the dashboard also highlights the amount of growth achieved year on year. Similarly, the operating figures show whether this growth is profitable for MS.

However, because the dashboard doesn't give any revenue figures for the sportswear market as a whole, we cannot gauge how fast it is growing relative to its competitors, and whether its market share is growing or not.

Shareholder wealth – ROCE shows how profitably MS is using its assets, and, as such could provide some indication of how well MS is generating wealth for its shareholders. However, ROCE is ultimately not a good metric in this respect.

One of ROCE's weaknesses is that it could encourage strategic decisions designed to increase short-term profit, potentially at the expense of investment for the future. More fundamentally, though, ROCE is a profit-based measure, and shareholder wealth would be better assessed through a **value-based measure**, which provides some insight into MS's ability to generate future cash flows. In this respect, MS should consider using **economic value added** (EVA) as a metric instead of ROCE.

Non-financial performance

MS's broad strategy also identifies the need to create innovative products and to have an effective marketing operation – the best in Ceeland.

The current dashboard headings ('Design' and 'Brand') reflect the importance of these elements of performance. However, there are still some potential problems with the metrics used in each heading.

Design awards won – The design awards acknowledge the look and technology in a finished product, they do not directly measure the level of innovation in MS. (For example, the number of new features added to our products, or the number of new products developed would provide a more direct measure for innovation.)

MS's strategy also identifies that its products should help reduce the risk of injury and enhance sporting performance by their customers. The current dashboard does not measure how effectively the products are doing this. However, it could be difficult to provide metrics which cover all of these areas, given the constraints on the number of performance indicators to be included in the dashboard. As such, MS will have to decide whether reducing the risk of injury or enhancing sporting performance is likely to be the more critical success factor for its products.

Brand awareness – The level of brand awareness is likely to be influenced by the effectiveness of MS's marketing operations. The fact that brand awareness is increasing might suggest that MS's marketing operations have been effective. However, without any comparison showing brand awareness for rival brands it is difficult to tell how effective they are, and therefore whether MS has 'the best marketing operation in Ceeland'.

In this respect, market share might be a more appropriate measure – not least because it also links back to MS's aim to grow as a business.

Moreover, just because people can identify MS's logo or name one of its products does not mean they have a positive impression of the company or any desire to buy its products. By contrast, market share statistics can provide a measure of how well MS is identifying and satisfying customer requirements, and how effectively its marketing activities are influencing their purchasing decisions.

Potential improvements

Although the SWOT analysis suggests that supply chain management is a critical success factor for MS, the CEO's insistence that no new headings be added to the dashboard means that performance in this area cannot be reported directly.

However, MS's ability to manage its supply chain effectively will, indirectly, affect its revenue and operating profit margins. As such, it may be preferable to replace the absolute operating profit figures in the dashboard with percentage margin figures.

The following improvements could also be made to the non-financial performance metrics:

Design – We have already suggested that the number of new features added to our products might be a better performance measure than design awards won. The SWOT analysis suggests that, rather than just looking at new features, we could monitor innovation in relation to the number of new products introduced.

Brand – We have already suggested that market share would be a better metric than brand awareness.

However, the SWOT analysis also suggests that social media is going to become an increasingly important aspect of marketing activities – although MS's weak IT expertise may limit its ability to take advantage of this.

Linked to the overall performance metric of market share, MS could also monitor the number of followers it has on social media (eg on Twitter, or the number of 'likes' it has on Facebook) as an indicator of how effectively it is using these marketing channels.

Brand ambassadors – Despite the growth of social media, brand ambassadors still play an important role in promoting MS's brand, and the SWOT analysis highlights this by acknowledging the loss of a key brand ambassador as a strategic weakness. As such, it could be useful to include a metric for 'Number of ambassadors' under the 'brand' heading on the dashboard. However, as we have already suggested metrics for market share and social media followers – and can only have two in total for 'brand' – the board will have to decide whether including a metric for the number of ambassadors is more important than either of these.

(ii) **Impact of response 1**

Qualitative impact

Although there is not currently any evidence that MS's suppliers are using illegal labour, the fact that MS does not appear to have any assurance over the labour practices used by its suppliers (and is having to review them now) means there is a risk that this could be the case.

This means that the review proposed under Response 1 should be carried out as soon as possible. If MS does find that the appropriate employment terms and conditions have been breached (and, in turn, MS's own ethical code has been breached) it should be transparent and own up to these failings. However, at the same time, MS should also explain the actions it has taken (through either Response 1 or 2) to redress the problems and to prevent them from recurring. Taking action in this way should help to restrict the level of negative stakeholder reaction to any findings.

In particular, MS will have to manage the reactions of customers and the regulator if it finds evidence of any unethical practices in its supply chain.

Customers – Such findings will damage MS's reputation for ethical sourcing, and there is a danger that customers could boycott MS's products, threatening revenue and profit growth.

Regulator – The regulator will review MS's sourcing policies (as it did with Nush), and is likely to punish MS in some way for using suppliers who have acted illegally.

Employees – Any such breach would mean that MS has failed to follow the requirements of its own ethics code (to source goods responsibly) and this could damage employees' trust in the company as a responsible employer.

Assurance procedures – More generally, the review required by response 1 also suggests that MS could benefit from regular assurance processes over its supply chain – to ensure that its suppliers comply with relevant employment legislation on an on-going basis. Although the constraints on the performance headings in MS's existing performance dashboard mean there isn't scope to monitor performance there, it could perhaps be monitored at departmental level within the procurement department.

Quantitative impact

Impact on shareholders – The increased manufacturing costs, coupled with increased compliance and marketing costs, mean that MS's operating profit will fall by $5.5m if the number of shoes MS sells remains the same. MS will need to increase sales by 106,000 pairs of shoes to make good this shortfall.

However, since the problem of child labour appears to be a common problem among suppliers to sports footwear companies, if MS is able to demonstrate that it has responded rapidly and decisively to any potential problems in its supply chain, this action to help differentiate it from its competitors, and in doing so could help generate these extra sales.

Annual cost:

		$ m
Increase in cost of shoes purchased	$2.1 × 2 million pairs	4.2
Supplier audits		0.5
Marketing cost		0.8
Total (per year)		**5.5**

Contribution per unit	$
Price	75.0
Direct cost ($21 + $2.1)	(23.1)
	51.9

Number of units required to cover lost operating profit:	**105,973**

BPP
LEARNING MEDIA

(iii)   Expected operating profit of the new factory

	Bad	Medium	Good
Unit manufactured ('000s)	1,800	2,000	2,200
Revenue ($'000)	135,000	150,000	165,000
Variable costs ($'000)	37,800	44,000	50,600
Fixed costs	2,500	2,500	2,500
	94,700	103,500	111,900
Probability	0.3	0.6	0.1
Expected operating profit ($'000)	28,410	62,100	11,190	**101,700**

The expected operating profit from the new factory (before interest and tax) is $101.7 million.

In practice, however, this is not the level of operating profit which the factory will generate in any of the three economic scenarios. Instead, the actual profit (depending on which scenario applies) will be either: $94.7 million, $103.5 million or $111.9 million.

This highlights the underlying problem of expected value calculations: they only make sense if a scenario is played out a number of times, and therefore the expected value (as an average of the individual results achieved) is a meaningful figure. However, in this case, the decision to bring all of MS's footwear in-house is a one-off event, and therefore an average figure has little relevance in the decision-making.

Moreover, the expected value is also dependent on the probabilities assigned to each scenario. It is not clear how these have been determined, but it inevitably involves some degree of subjectivity.

(iv)   Impact of the new factory on the dashboard

Financial metrics (20X5)

	Existing factory	New factory	Change (%)
Revenue ($m)	273	273	-
Operating profit ($m) (see Working 1)	71	66	-7.0%
ROCE (Working 2)	41.7%	30.4%	-27.1%

The new factory will not affect the number of design awards won or brand awareness levels.

Impact on financial performance

Operating profit - The decline in operating profit indicates that manufacturing all of its footwear in-house will lead to an increase in MS's costs of approximately $5 million per year.

Although the variable cost of manufacturing footwear in-house ($21 - $23 per unit) is expected to be similar to that of buying footwear from an external supplier ($21 per unit), there will also be additional fixed costs associated with the new factory.

The increase in fixed costs will also lead to an increase in MS's **operational gearing**.

Non-current assets – As MS is primarily a product development and marketing operation – with no manufacturing operations of its own – it will have a relatively low level of fixed capital (buildings; equipment etc). As a result, it also has a relatively high ROCE.

However, establishing the factory will increase capital employed (as well as reducing operating profit), which explains the significant reduction in ROCE.

However, although establishing the factory (and taking full control of operations) may have a negative impact on ROCE in the short term, it could benefit MS in the longer term – for example, by helping it to avoid lost sales due to damaged reputation, or to avoid costs such as fines imposed by the regulator.

Impact on choice of metrics

Quality – If MS starts manufacturing footwear itself, then quality control will become an important aspect of performance management. Currently, product quality is not measured directly in the dashboard, but it would seem sensible to add an extra heading to reflect this new dimension – manufacturing – which has been added to MS's activities. (Alternatively, the 'design' heading could be expanded to allow additional metrics to be associated with it. But it would seem preferable to keep 'design' and 'manufacturing' as distinct activities.)

However, we must remember that MS has no experience of manufacturing. As such, it may be sensible to wait until the company has gained some operational knowledge of the factory operations before introducing a detailed metric for this area – for example, to avoid setting a performance targets which are not realistic.

Gearing – The factory will cost $36 million to build and equip, as well as increasing working capital by $11 million. It is not clear how this additional capital will be funded, but if it involves debt then this will increase the company's financial gearing, and therefore the level of financial risk. There is not currently any measure of such risk on the dashboard, but again it may be necessary to add one.

Workings

(1)

Average selling price ($)	$75
Cost of shoes ($)	$21
Operating profit per shoe	$54
Operating profit on 2m shoes bought/sold:	$108 million
Operating profit from the new factory (per Board's estimate given in the question scenario)	$103 million
Reduction in operating profit	$5 million

(2)

Current capital employed	
(where Operating profit (PBIT) is $71m and ROCE is 41.7%)	170.3
Additional capital employed: $36 m + $11m	47
New capital employed	217.3
Revised ROCE: ($66m / $217.3m)	30.4%

(v) **Value chain**

A value chain provides an overview of the different activities within an organisation which combine to create value for customers. By identifying the activities which create value, the organisation can then focus on improving its performance in those areas – with the result that it also improves its performance overall.

Equally however, the value chain can help an organisation to identify which aspects of performance are most important to measure – that is, those which relate to the key value-adding activities. In this respect, we might expect the metrics included in MS's dashboard to provide the board with information about how well the company is performing in these key activities. However, the current dashboard provides very little information about MS's performance in these activities.

Marketing and sales - To a degree, the dashboard heading for 'brand' could relate to the 'marketing and sales' activities in the value chain; but, as we have already suggested, simply monitoring brand awareness can only provide limited insight into the effectiveness of MS's marketing and sales activities.

Technology - In this respect, the linkage between technology (as a supporting activity) and marketing (as a primary activity) could also become increasingly important with the growth of social media as a marketing channel.

Logistics and operations - MS's current business model (with outsourced manufacturing and third-party retailers) means that a number of the primary activities (inbound/outbound logistics; operations; sales) are performed by third parties. Currently, MS does not appear to monitor the performance of its supply chain partners, but this is perhaps something it should consider doing, since these partners are responsible for generating a significant proportion of the value in MS's products.

Procurement – Although procurement is normally classified as a supporting activity on the value chain, MS's business model means that effective procurement (coupled with effective supply chain management, particularly with its upstream manufacturers) is likely to be crucial to the company's commercial success.

Moreover, the importance of outsourced manufacturers means that MS's performance management should not focus solely on its internal value chain, but also its value network (value system) more generally. (The Nush scandal provides an important reminder of this.)

Here again, the value chain also highlights the important supporting role that technology is likely to play – for example, in ensuring that the quantities of goods produced by different third party suppliers responds effectively to the requirements of MS's third-party retailers (for example, to avoid either over- or under-production of different product lines).

Product design – Technology could also be important at MS in relation to creating innovative products; either through the way technology is used in the design process, or the way that technological developments make new materials available for use in MS's products.

'Design' has already been identified as one of the three performance headings in the dashboard, but technology development is likely to be a key supporting activity in relation to product design.

Although we have already suggested this point (in part iv of this report) value chain analysis reiterates the idea that MS may need to include a wider range of metrics in its dashboard – to provide management with performance information about the range of activities which are critical in sustaining the company's commercial success.

BPP
LEARNING MEDIA

Mock exams

ACCA Professional Level

Paper P5

Advanced Performance Management

Mock Examination 1

Question Paper
Time allowed: 3 hours and 15 minutes
This paper is divided into two sections: Section A   ONE compulsory question to be attempted Section B   TWO out of THREE questions to be attempted

DO NOT OPEN THIS PAPER UNTIL YOU ARE READY TO START UNDER EXAMINATION CONDITIONS

SECTION A – This ONE question is compulsory and must be attempted

Question 1

JHK Coffee Machines Co (JHK) manufactures coffee makers for use in bars and cafes. It has been successful over the last five years and has built and maintained a loyal customer base by making a high quality machine backed by a three-year warranty. The warranty states that JHK will recover and repair any machine that breaks down in the warranty period at no cost. Additionally, JHK always maintains sufficient spare parts to be able to quote for a repair of any of its machines made within the previous 10 years.

JHK is structured into two divisions: manufacturing/sales (M/S) and service. The board are now considering ways to improve coordination of the activities of the divisions for the benefit of the company as a whole.

The company's mission is to maximise shareholder wealth. Currently, the board use total shareholder return (TSR) as an overall corporate measure of performance and return on investment (ROI) as their main relative measure of performance between the two divisions. The board's main concern is that the divisional managers' performance is not being properly assessed by the divisional performance measure used. They now want to consider other measures of divisional performance. Residual income (RI) and economic value added (EVA™) have been suggested.

A colleague has collected the following data which will allow calculation of ROI, RI and EVA™.

	Manufacturing/sales $m	Service $m
Revenue	880	17·0
Operating costs	494	11·0
Operating profit	386	6·0
Apportioned head office costs	85	1·0
Profit before tax	301	5·0
Capital employed	1,294	38·0
The notional cost of capital used is	9% pa	
The current cost of debt is	5·5%	
The tax rate is	30%	

Operating costs include:

	Manufacturing/sales $m	Service $m
Depreciation	88	2·7
Other non-cash expenses	4	0·3

All operating costs are tax deductible.

In addition to the divisional performance measures, the board want to consider the position of the service division.

The standard costs within the service division are as follows:

	$
Labour (per hour)	18
Variable divisional overhead (per hour)	12
Fixed divisional overhead (per hour)	25

Overheads are allocated by labour hours

Currently, the service division does two types of work. There are repairs that are covered by JHK's warranty and there are repairs done outside warranty at the customer's request. The service division is paid by the customer for the out-of-warranty repairs while the repairs under warranty generate an annual fee of $10m, which is a recharge from the M/S division. The company sells 440,000 units per year and in the past, 9% of these have needed a repair within the three-year warranty. Parts are charged by the M/S division to the service division at cost and average $75 per repair. A repair takes two hours, on average, to complete.

The board are considering amending this existing $10m internal recharge agreement between M/S and service. There has been some discussion of tailoring one of the two transfer-pricing approaches (market price or cost plus) to meet the company's objectives.

Although the service division has the capacity to cover all of the existing work available, it could outsource the warranty service work, as it is usually straightforward. It would retain the out-of-warranty service work as this is a higher margin business. It would then begin looking for other opportunities to earn revenue using its engineering experience. A local engineering firm has quoted a flat price of $200 per warranty service repair provided that they obtain a contract for all of the warranty repairs from JHK.

The board are also considering a change to the information systems at JHK. The existing systems are based in the individual functions (purchasing, production, sales, service, finance and human resources). The board are considering the implementation of a new system based on an integrated, single database that would be accessible at any of the company's five sites. The company network would be upgraded to allow real-time input and update of the database. The database would support a detailed management information system and a high-level executive information system.

Finally, at present, the management team at JHK are uncertain whether the purchasing function is maximising its potential in terms of purchasing efficiency and effectiveness.

The management team are currently considering the introduction of a system of benchmarking to measure the performance of the purchasing department.

Required

Write a report to the finance director to:

(a) Evaluate the divisional performance at JHK and critically discuss the proposed measures of divisional performance. **(12 marks)**

(b) Outline the criteria for designing a transfer pricing system and evaluate the two methods discussed of calculating the transfer price between the service and M/S divisions. (Perform appropriate calculations.) **(12 marks)**

(c) Evaluate the potential impact of the introduction of the new executive information system at JHK on performance management. **(6 marks)**

Professional marks will be awarded for the format, style and structure of the discussion of your report. **(4 marks)**

(d) Explain the concept of benchmarking, and briefly discuss the potential benefits that can be obtained as a result of undertaking a successful programme of benchmarking. **(5 marks)**

(e) Describe how a system of benchmarking could be introduced to measure the performance of the purchasing department at JHK. **(7 marks)**

(f) Discuss the problems that the management of JHK might encounter in implementing a system of benchmarking. **(4 marks)**

(Total = 50 marks)

SECTION B – Two questions only to be attempted

Question 2

The board of CMA Supermarkets is considering an upgrade of its company-wide IT system. The company has been opening new supermarket stores at a rapid rate in recent years, and has ambitions to rival the established supermarket chains in its country. The board believes that CMA could gain a significant competitive advantage from having a unified corporate database and from replacing its bar code technology with RFID, the radio frequency technology for labelling and identifying inventory.

The management accountant at CMA has been asked to explain to the board how a new network system and RFID technology may help to improve the management accounting system within the company, and also the company's performance.

At the moment, management accounts are prepared for each individual store, and monthly sales and profitability reports are presented to the store manager. Regional reports and a national report on company performance are also prepared each month, and presented to senior management and the board.

Because the company is trying to increase market share rapidly, it keeps its prices as low as possible, and whereas rival companies achieve a gross profit margin of about 55% on its sales, CMA's average gross margin is slightly below 50%.

In addition, a number of CMA's stores have reported an increase in out-of-stock products in recent weeks. The store managers are concerned that if customers keeping finding items out-of-stock they will stop shopping at CMA and will revert to one of the established supermarket chains.

The management accountant thinks that new technology will help to improve profitability and will influence the nature of performance reporting system. The benefits of improved IT will only be obtained however, if there is a radical re-thinking of how information is used within CMA.

Required

(a)   Explain how RFID technology for tracking inventory and inventory movements may help to improve the quality of management information in CMA Supermarkets, and may also help to improve CMA's operational performance. **(12 marks)**

(b)   Assess the changes which may be required to performance reporting in CMA Supermarkets in order to obtain the greatest value from a new IT system and RFID technology. **(8 marks)**

(c)   Suggest how the IT system for a supermarket might exploit information about individual customers to improve sales and profits. **(5 marks)**

(Total = 25 marks)

Question 3

XYZ is an expanding company. A year ago, its board of directors set a target of achieving above average growth in sales in its markets and increasing profit before tax by at least 5% each year for the next few years. In the year just ended, the markets grew by about 4%.

XYZ's current performance reporting system focuses on financial performance, and the following annual performance figures have been submitted to the Board of XYZ as a summary for the year just ended.

	This year		Last year
	Actual	Budget	Actual
	$m	$m	$m
Sales	61.5	64.0	60.2
Cost of sales	35.0	36.5	34.1
Gross profit	26.5	27.5	26.1
Other costs	17.3	18.0	17.0
Net profit before tax	9.2	9.5	9.1

In a report to the board, the operations manager stated that labour productivity had improved during the year, and although prices for raw materials and inputs had risen slightly more than expected, operational results appeared to be satisfactory.

In a separate report, the sales and marketing manager stated that sales had been disappointing, and XYZ's sales had grown more slowly than the market as a whole. However, the sales and marketing manager pointed out that some orders had been lost because the production department had been unable or unwilling to adapt product specifications to the requirements of the customer. Also, one of XYZ's larger customers had returned goods which it claimed did not meet its requirements, and the customer has subsequently not placed any further orders with XYZ. In addition, a delay in the completion of another large order meant that some revenue originally budgeted for this year would not now be earned until next year.

XYZ's sales department is organised on a regional basis, and sales targets had been set for each regional manager in the budget. The sales and marketing manager concluded his report with the opinion that the sales managers had done their best in the circumstances, and total sales revenue was higher than in the previous year.

The CEO expressed the view that the gross profit margin was satisfactory, and the increase in other costs had been kept below budget, so there were some reasons for satisfaction with performance for the year. On the other hand, there were also reasons for concern. The anticipated growth in sales had not been achieved, and the fact that XYZ's growth was below the market growth rate was particularly disappointing.

In the opinion of the CEO, the problem was a lack of co-ordination throughout the company in setting performance targets, and a structured approach to target-setting and performance measurement was required. In particular, the CEO believed that XYZ's performance measures needed to link operations to strategic goals more closely, and they needed to focus on non-financial as well as financial measures.

To this end, the CE has suggested that XYZ should use a structure for setting targets based on the concept of the performance pyramid.

Required

(a)   Briefly discuss the features of a performance pyramid (of Lynch and Cross).   **(6 marks)**

(b)   With reference to the performance pyramid, recommend how the system of performance measurement within XYZ could be improved.   **(6 marks)**

(c)   Assess how the introduction of a performance pyramid might help XYZ achieve its stated objectives for sales and profit growth.   **(8 marks)**

(d)   Assess the impact of introducing the performance pyramid on the information systems at XYZ.   **(5 marks)**

(Total = 25 marks)

Question 4

Action Buttons Co (AB Co) manufactures a range of electronic action toys for children. It was established eight years ago by two friends from university, Chris Booker and Sally Thomas, who still manage the company jointly. For the first five years, the company enjoyed rapid growth in sales and profits, which encouraged Chris and Sally to expand their product range. The growth was financed by a medium-term bank loan.

In the last two or three years, business has not been as good though. Sales have continued to rise in spite of competition from imported goods from China and, more recently, Eastern Europe. However, profits have fallen because the company has been unable to increase its selling prices despite operating costs rising. In addition, the company has incurred interest costs on its borrowings.

Chris and Sally recently received an offer from a venture capitalist firm that specialises in buying and turning round failing businesses, which wanted to buy AB Co. Chris and Sally were surprised to learn that AB Co was considered a failing business, but the venture capital representative informed them that AB Co had a mixed portfolio of products (some successful and others not), an excessive level of debt, and an apparent lack of strategic direction.

Chris and Sally recognise that they have only limited information about the profitability of each of their products. AB Co employs a head accountant who prepares an annual budget and monthly budgetary control reports comparing budget and actual revenue and expenditure, but they have little additional information about company or product performance. They do not employ a finance director because Sally manages the company's finances and relationship with the bank.

Chris and Sally agreed that they were fully in control of their business, but decided to call in a firm of consultants to give them advice about their business prospects. The consultants recommended a review of the company with a view to preparing a corporate failure prediction score, and the consultants suggested that this should be based on Argenti's 'A score' model, rather than a 'Z score' approach. This was agreed, although Chris and Sally did not know exactly what to expect from the review.

The consultants carried out the review and reported that the corporate failure prediction 'A score' for AB Co was 30, which put it in the category of companies that were at risk of corporate failure. Chris and Sally were shocked when they heard this. Chris asked how the consultants could be so confident when the scoring system seemed to be based on judgement and not on any hard evidence. Sally agreed, and commented that predictions and forecasts are often wrong. Even so, Chris and Sally were doubtful what they should do in view of the consultants' report.

Required

(a) Identify the different types of reason why business fail.   **(5 marks)**

(b) Explain the purpose and nature of Argenti's A score for corporate failure prediction and its advantages over a Z score approach.   **(6 marks)**

(c) Discuss Chris and Sally's criticisms that the A score is based on the judgement of the consultants, and that the corporate failure prediction could be wrong.   **(6 marks)**

(d) On the basis of the information available, advise Chris and Sally what measures they could take to deal with the possible problems revealed by AB Co's corporate failure prediction 'A score'.   **(8 marks)**

(Total = 25 marks)

Answers

DO NOT TURN THIS PAGE UNTIL YOU HAVE
COMPLETED THE MOCK EXAM

Plan of attack

What's the worst thing you could be doing right now if this were the actual exam paper? Panicking, and getting yourself in a right old state? Yawning, because you're exhausted from too much late night, last-minute revision? Wondering how to celebrate the end of the exam in 3 hours and 15 minutes time?

Well, they're all pretty bad. But what you should be doing is spending the first few minutes of the exam looking through the paper in detail, working out which questions to do, and the order in which to attempt them. So turn back to the paper and let's sort out a **plan of attack.**

First steps first

In our view, the compulsory Section A question is often the best place to start, since it is compulsory and accounts for 50% of the marks available in the paper. This means you cannot score enough marks to pass the paper without answering the Section A question.

However, make sure you look through the **whole** paper and carefully before starting in to answer any questions.

In the first five minutes of the exam, look through the case study scenarios and the question requirements and work out which questions you are going to attempt, and the order you are going to tackle them. We would then suggest you spend approximately the next five to ten minutes analysing the requirements of the Section A question and identifying the key issues in the scenario. Planning your answer is very important; don't just start writing your answer as soon as you open the exam paper.

If you are worried about the paper, it is likely that you believe the Section A question will be daunting. In this case you may prefer to do one, or both, of your optional (Section B) questions before tackling it. Don't however, fall into the trap of spending too long on the optional questions because they seem easier. Remember the Section A question accounts for 50% of the marks, so it is crucial to your chances of passing this exam.

It is dangerous to be over-confident, but if you're not too nervous about the exam, we suggest you should start with the compulsory Section A question. You know you've got to answer it, so you might as well get it over and done with straight away.

Make sure **you address every requirement and sub-requirement in the questions**, and also make sure you apply your answer directly to the scenario.

Remember that the basis of the P5 exam is **analysis and application, not simply performance measurement**. You are being tested on your ability to apply your knowledge to analyse and address the specific issues identified in a scenario.

The questions themselves

Question 1. The scenario introduces a company with two divisions, whose overall mission is to maximise shareholder wealth. However, the company currently uses ROI as its main measure of performance for the two divisions – but is ROI really the best measure to use in order to maximise shareholder value? This issue is one of the points which need to be evaluated in part (a), when you are asked to evaluate RI and EVA as alternative measures of divisional performance. However, note there are two distinct elements to part (a): evaluating the performance of the divisions; and discussing the measures which have been proposed for measuring that performance.

The second part of the question looks at issues to do with transfer pricing between the divisions. This part of the question involves a combination of calculation and discussion. You need to calculate the impact that the two different methods of transfer pricing will have on the division's profitability, but then evaluate the implications of this.

Information systems play an important role in performance management, because management are not able to get timely and relevant information about an organisation's performance it makes their job in controlling the organisation and making strategic decisions much harder. Part (c) picks up on this point, by introducing the idea that JHK is considering a change to its information systems.

Parts (d) – (f) look at different issues in relation to benchmarking: what are the potential benefits from it, how can it be implemented at the company, and what problems might the company encounter when implementing it?

Question 2. The context of question 2 is how IT developments (specifically RFID technology) can be beneficial to a supermarket. In part (a) you need to consider two aspects of how the technology could be used: to improve the quality of management information available to managers, but also how it can directly help operational performance; for example, by helping the supermarkets to manage their inventory more effectively. As such the focus of part (a) is how IT can help the supermarket improve its internal business processes, whereas part (c) of the question looks at how the supermarket can use IT to improve its relationship with customers.

Part (b) again picks up the idea that managers need information to make decisions, but in this case asks you to consider ways in which performance reports could be improved to provide managers with better information.

Question 3. One of the key features of modern performance measurement systems is that they are multi-dimensional - in other words, they look at non-financial aspects of performance as well as financial ones. Question 3 looks at one such multi-dimensional performance measurement system: the performance pyramid. Part (a) should be a source of some relatively easy marks, because it is a test of knowledge, rather than your ability to apply your knowledge to a question scenario. However, in parts (b) – (c) you do have to apply your knowledge in order to assess how introducing the pyramid could be beneficial to XYZ. The final part of question (part (d)) requires you to assess the changes which might be required to XYZ's information systems to enable it to report on non-financial aspects of performance as well as the financial aspects of performance it currently reports on.

Question 4 looks at issues relating to corporate failure. The first part of the question looks at the underlying reasons which could cause businesses to fail, and then the second part looks at one of the models (Argenti's A score) which can be used for predicting corporate failure.

The second part of part (b) of this question, in effect, is looking at the advantages of qualitative models for predicting corporate failure compared to quantitative ones. By contrast, part (c) of the question highlights some of the potential difficulties with qualitative models.

However, being aware that their business is at risk of failure will only be useful to managers if they then take action to deal with the problems which are causing it to fail. Part (d) picks up on this point, by asking what measures the owners of a company deemed to be at risk of failure should take to deal with the problems the company is facing.

No matter how many times we remind you...

Always, always **allocate your time** according to the marks for the question in total and for the individual parts.

And always, read the requirements carefully and **follow the requirements exactly.** Part (a) of question 1, for example, requires you not only to evaluate the divisions' performance at JHK but also to discuss the measures which are being used to assess the divisions' performance. To score well in a question like this, it is vital that you address both parts of the requirement.

If you ran short of time on this exam, or struggled to interpret the questions, have another look at the guidance on Passing P5 in the front pages of this kit.

You've got spare time at the end of the exam...

If you have allocated your time properly then you **shouldn't have time on your hands** at the end of the exam. If you find yourself with five or ten minutes to spare, however, go back to **any parts of questions that you didn't finish** because you ran out of time.

Question 1

Marking scheme

		Marks
(a)	Calculations:	
	3 marks for calculation of ROI and RI (1 for controllable ROI; 1 for divisional ROI; 1 for RI)	3
	3 marks for calculation of EVA (½ mark each for: adjusting for other non-cash expenses; tax; depreciation treatment; NOPAT; WACC used; EVA)	3
	For assessing performance from the calculated numbers – 1 mark per relevant point – up to 3	3
	For comments on the performance measures – 1 mark per relevant point – up to 3	
	Total for part (i)	3
		12
(b)	For outlining the criteria for designing a transfer pricing system – 1 mark per point	Up to 3
	Calculations:	
	Number of warranty repairs per year – 1 mark	
	Cost per repair – 2 marks	
	Contribution under current agreement – 1 mark	
	Contribution with market price – 1 mark	
	Prices for breakeven under cost plus – 3 marks	Up to 7

Commentary:
1 mark per relevant point evaluating the current transfer pricing system
at JHK – up to 4 marks   Up to 4

Total for part (ii)   12

(c)   1 mark per relevant benefit from introducing the new executive
        information system – up to 4 marks   Up to 4
        1 mark per relevant difficulty or problem associated with introducing the
        new executive information system – up to 3 marks   Up to 3
                                                                                                                                     6

Professional marks for presentation, style and structure of report   4

(d)   For explaining the concept of benchmarking – 1 mark   1
        For discussing potential the benchmarking which can be gained from
        benchmarking – 1 mark per relevant point   Up to 4   5

(e)   1 mark for each relevant step in the process of introducing
        benchmarking – up to 6   Up to 6
        1 mark for other relevant factors to consider when introducing a system
        of benchmarking – up to 2   Up to 2   7

(f)   For each relevant problem identified and discussed – 1 mark each   Up to 4   4

                                                                                                                          Total =   50

To: Finance Director

From: Ann Accountant

Date: [Today's date]

Subject: Divisional performance and information systems

This report will evaluate the performance of JHK's divisions and will then consider some of the issues raised by the transfer pricing between the service and M/S divisions. It will finish by looking at the potential impact the proposed new information system could have on performance management at JHK.

(a)   **Divisional performance**

        Profitability – The two divisions are very different in size, such that the M/S division generates over 98% of the company's total revenue and operating profits. However, both divisions are profitable and make positive returns on investment (as shown in the Workings at the end of the first section of this Report.)

        Return on Investment (ROI)

        The workings in the Appendix show an overall division ROI (based on profit before interest and tax divided by capital employed) and an ROI figure adjusted to exclude re-allocated head office costs.

        Controllable ROI – Apportioned costs account for approximately 10% of revenue in the M/S division, but only about 6% of revenue in the service division. The controllable ROI figure should exclude these apportioned head office costs, because they are not controllable at divisional level.

        Comparison between divisions – Both divisions are generating a positive return on investment, although it is noticeable that the return form the M/S division is significantly higher than that of the Service division. Nonetheless, the returns generated by both divisions are greater than the 9% which is JHK's current cost of capital.

        ROI as a performance measure – ROI is simple to calculate and therefore is often used as a measure of performance. However, one of the main criticisms of ROI is that it can lead to short-termism and a lack of goal congruence between divisions and their parent company as a whole. For example, ROI may discourage asset replacement in the divisions, which may ultimately not fit with JHK's aim to maximize shareholder wealth.

Residual income (RI)

Absolute figure – Unlike ROI which looks at a percentage return on assets, RI provides an **absolute** figure for the income generated by each department, based on the profit figure less an imputed interest charge based on the capital employed by the division.

As the figures in the Appendix again show, both divisions generate a positive residual income.

However, given the difference in size between the M/S and the Service it is **hard to use RI to compare the performance** of the two divisions.

Profit-based measures – Both ROI and RI are both derived from profit measures of performance, but it is unclear how closely they link with JHK's overall performance measure of total shareholder return. This depends on share price and dividends paid, rather than just profit. Although there is likely to be a degree of correlation between profit and share price performance, this is not necessarily the case.

Economic Value Added (EVA) – EVA, like RI, is calculated by deducting an imputed interest figure from a profit figure. However, unlike RI which uses conventional accounting profits, EVA involves a more complicated calculation to try to avoid the perceived distortion of results by accounting policies. For example, marketing costs which have been charged as expenses in determining the accounting profits, may be added back under EVA if, in effect, they are investments which will generate future value.

The adjustments made to accounting profit in EVA mean that EVA is more directly aligned to JHK's objective of increasing shareholder wealth than either ROI and RI. Therefore, if EVA is adopted as a measure of divisional performance, this should help improve goal congruence between the divisions and the company as a whole.

Historical data – However, EVA is still ultimately derived from historical data (adjusted profit figures) so its focus will be different to shareholders who are ultimately concerned with future performance. Nonetheless, the adjustments to profit made in EVA are designed to make it a better guide of future performance than traditional profit-based measures.

Comparison between divisions – However, the size difference between the M/S and Service divisions at JHK means that EVA will not be suitable as a measure for comparing performance between the divisions, because it looks at absolute values rather than percentage returns.

Appendix

Workings

	M/S division	Service
Controllable ROI (%)		
Operating profit / Capital employed	386 / 1,294	6 / 38
	29.8%	15.8%
Divisional ROI		
PBT / Capital employed	301 / 1,294	5 / 38
	23.3%	13.2%
RI ($m)		
Operating profit	386	6.0
Imputed interest charge (@ 9%)	(116)	(3.4)
	270	2.6
EVA ($m)		
Operating profit	386	6.0
Add: non-cash expenses	4	0.3
Less: Tax (@ 30% of operating profit)	(116)	(1.8)
NOPAT	274	4.5
Capital employed x WACC (@ 9%)	(116)	(3.4)
	158	1.1

Notes

1 Notional cost of capital used as best estimate for WACC

2 Economic depreciation assumed to be the same as accounting depreciation

(b) **Criteria for designing a transfer pricing system**

A transfer pricing system is a mechanism for charging for goods or services transferred between the divisions of a company, in this case for the warranty services provided to the M/S division by the Service division. If such a system were not in place, the Service division would not receive any income for the work it does for the M/S division. Equally, the M/S would not incur any costs for the warranty services carried out.

Performance evaluation – Transfer prices are necessary to prevent the warranty services having an unfair impact on the performance measures of either division, thereby meaning that divisional managers can still be assessed on the basis of divisional profit.

Divisional autonomy – By giving a price or a cost to the services transferred, transfer pricing allows the division managers to retain autonomy. For example, if the M/S division feels the proposed transfer price for warranty services from the Service division is more expensive than the price would be from an external service company, then the divisional managers can choose to buy the services externally.

Goal congruence – Transfer prices should be set so that divisional behavior is aligned to the best interests of the group as a whole. In this respect, the price should reflect the true cost (the opportunity cost) to the group of the transfer. For example, although the service division currently has capacity to cover all the existing work available, if the demand for out-of-service work increases and the service department needs to sacrifice revenue from this work in order to carry out the repairs under warranty guarantee, it is important that any such lost revenue is recognised in the cost of the internal work.

There are a number of possible ways of determining transfer prices, but here we are looking at market based pricing and cost based pricing as means of pricing the repair work the service division does for the M/S division under the warranties.

Market based pricing

Because there is already an external market price (of $200 per warranty service) has already been tendered, this can be used be used as the basis for a transfer price.

Divisional profits – If this were the case, the Service division's net profit from warranty repairs would fall from the current figure of $2.67m to $0.59m (see workings in Appendix). This suggests that, in terms of performance evaluation, the current $10m recharge seems to favour the Service division more than the M/S division, given the current levels of repairs.

Spare capacity – However, given that the Service division would left with spare capacity if it stopped carrying out the internal repair work, the fact that the market-based transfer price still generates it a profit (albeit a reduced one) should mean the division will continue to take on the work.

This position could change if the level of external work increases though. The out-of-warranty business generates higher margins, which would suggest the Service division should prioritise this work over the less profitable internal work. In which case, if the Service division may no longer have sufficient capacity to cover the internal work, and so would need to outsource it.

Outsourcing – The current proposal means that the Service cannot choose to outsource part of its warranty work: it either has to outsource all of it or none at all. Depending on the level of external demand, JHK may feel it necessary to adjust the market based transfer price in respect of this, to avoid a situation where the Service division outsources the warranty work but is then left with significant spare capacity because the increase in external demand is less than demand for warranty work foregone.

Moreover, JHK may also want to adjust the market based transfer price if it feels the warranty service is an important part of the company's overall offering to its customers. The warranty is currently an important selling point for JHK, but it may be unable to control the quality of the repair work if it is outsourced.

Cost based pricing

The warranties could also be charged in relation to the cost to the Service division of providing them, either at pure cost price, or with a degree of mark-up added to the cost.

An analysis of the Service division's costs per repair, (see workings in Appendix) shows that the current fixed price deal ($10m), with the current level of repairs, generates a significant profit for the division: $2.67m.

Divisional profits – If the level of repairs remains at its current level (39,600 per year) then the service department would need to charge $253 per repair in order to maintain its current level of divisional profit. However, it is unlikely that the managers in the M/S division would accept a cost above $200 given this is the cost they would have to pay if the work were outsourced.

Breakeven price – For the Service division to breakeven on the warranty work they do, a price of $185 should be charged. This would be acceptable to the M/S division because it means the cost of the work will be lower than if it were outsourced. This price may also be acceptable to the managers in the service division, because it covers their fixed overheads as well as their variable costs.

In this respect, the cost based pricing approach suggests that a price between $185 and $200 may be the best for JHK to choose.

Workings

Units sold per year			440,000
Number of these requiring warranty, per year		9% / 3	13,200
Number of warranty repairs per year (3 years warranty)			**39,600**

Cost per repair

	Rate	Quantity	Cost
Parts	$75 each	1	75
Labour	$18 per hr	2 hrs	36
Variable divisional overhead	$12 per hr	2 hrs	24
Variable cost			135
Fixed divisional overhead	$25 per hr	2 hrs	50
Total cost			185

Comparison of current agreement with market price approach

Based on 39,600 repairs per year:

	Current agreement ($'000)	Market pricing ($'000)
Revenue	10,000	7,920
Variable costs	5,346	5,346
Divisional contribution	4,654	2,574
Fixed costs	1,980	1,980
Divisional profit	2,674	594

Cost plus pricing

		$
To maintain current contribution levels	[$10m / 39,600]	252.53
To cover variable costs	[$5.346m / 39,600]	135
For division to breakeven	[(10 m - 2.674m)/39,600]	185

(c) Impact of new executive information system (EIS)

Benefits

Improved decision making – At the strategic level, management should be looking at how well JHK is performing in relation to its key performance indicators. However, the EIS should also allow management to drill-down to the more detailed operational records to help understand the reasons for any variances in performance, and to identify ways of improving performance.

Improved information – The new system will increase the amount of information that will be available to managers, and the analysis they can carry out on that information. In particular, the system will allow the managers to use more up-to-date information than they are currently able to use.

Data integrity – Having a single database should again improve the quality of data which is used in decision-making. For example, there is no longer the risk of inconsistency between data drawn from two different systems or sources.

Tactical information – The EIS will also give access to tactical information such as budgets, which will help the executives control the business; most obviously by comparing actual financial performance against budget.

Potential problems and issues

Information overload – Although allowing managers access to more information could be a benefit of the EIS, if the amount of information available is not controlled then information overload could become a problem. For example, managers could get obsessed with looking at detailed information rather than focusing on strategic issues and overall performance against key performance indicators.

Training – Because the EIS is a new system, in order to maximise the benefit which managers can get from using it, they will need to be trained in how to use it.

Conclusion

Divisional performance – Given the overall focus on maximising shareholder wealth, ROI and RI are unlikely to be the most appropriate measures of divisional performance to use. EVA is likely to be a more appropriate measure of performance.

Transfer pricing – The current fixed price recharge between the Service division and the M/S division allows the Service division to earn a significant profit from the internal repair work it carries out. However, it is possible that the current arrangement may not encourage both divisions to act in the best interests of JHK as a whole.

(d) Benchmarking and its benefits

Benchmarking is the establishment, through data gathering, of targets and comparators which allow relative levels of performance (and particularly underperformance) to be identified. The sources of data used in benchmarking can be internal (historical data; or data from other business units) or external (data from competitors; or best-in-class performers). By adopting identified best practices, it is hoped that performance will improve.

Potential benefits of benchmarking

(i)   Comparing an organisation's (or business unit's) performance with that of another highlights how much room there is for improvement.

(ii) Benchmarking focuses on key areas of performance and may be used to **set targets** which are challenging but evidently 'achievable' (because they have already been achieved by the comparator).

(iii) The sharing of information, comparing past failures and successes, can be a **spur to innovation**.

(iv) It should be possible to identify achievable **cost savings**, and realistic targets should help to improve **budgeting**.

(e) Introducing a system of benchmarking

The introduction of a system of benchmarking can be divided into stages. It needs to be carefully planned, and is likely to need significant resources in terms of management time.

Step 1   **Review and assess current practices**, and then **set objectives** for the benchmarking study.

Step 2   Establish **key performance indicators** and **targets** for the purchasing department. These may include a target level of negotiated discounts, cost of sales ratios, inventory levels, costs per order and overall costs of running the department.

Step 3   **Select external organisations** (or internal functions) which reflect 'best practice' to study. It is possible JHK may need to negotiate an agreement with an external organisation (not necessarily in the same industry) to obtain data from its purchasing department to use for benchmarking purposes.

Step 4   **Measure** the performance of JHK's purchasing division, and that of the division (or organisation) it is being benchmarked against.

Step 5   **Compare** performances so that management can focus on where improvements need to be made.

Step 6   Design and implement **improvement programmes** as necessary.

Step 7   **Monitor** improvements and refine programmes if necessary.

When selecting an appropriate benchmark basis, JHK should ask itself the following questions.

(i) Is it possible and easy to obtain **reliable** comparator information?

(ii) Is there any wide **discrepancy** between different **internal divisions** (if JHK is using internal benchmarking)?

(iii) Can **similar processes** be identified in **non-competing environments** and are these non-competing companies willing to co-operate?

(iv) Is there sufficient **time** to complete the study, or might management and/or staff time be more usefully spent on other things?

(f) **Problems when implementing benchmarking**

(i) It implies there is **one best way** of doing business – arguably this boils down to the difference between efficiency and effectiveness, which is what JHK is concerned with. A process can be efficient, in terms of man hours spent for example, but its output may not be useful (the suppliers may be too expensive, or the goods of poor quality).

(ii) There may be **behavioural issues** to consider, as the staff of the purchasing department may feel threatened by the study and resist any planned changes. Tactful management is essential, and the reasons for the study must be properly **communicated**.

(iii) It is often only a **catching-up exercise** rather than a means of developing anything distinctive. After the benchmarking exercise, a competitor might improve performance in a different way.

(iv) Benchmarking will only highlight differences in the relative performance of JHK's purchasing department and its comparator. Benchmarking will not necessarily illustrate the reasons for those differences. However, if there are underlying differences between the two departments, simply trying to replicate the processes and procedures from the comparator department in JHK's purchasing department may not lead to corresponding improvements in performance in the purchasing department.

Question 2

Marking scheme

			Marks
(a)	For explaining how RFID technology could help the quality of management information at CMA – 1 mark per relevant point	Up to 7	
	For explaining how RFID technology could help improve CMA's operational performance – 1 mark per relevant point	Up to 8	
			12
(b)	1 mark per relevant point about changes which could be made to CMA's performance reporting in the light of the new technology available	Up to 8	
			8
(c)	1 mark per relevant point about how the IT system could be used in relation to customer relationship management	Up to 5	
			5
		Total =	25

(a) IT technology in supermarkets commonly uses bar codes for identifying the products that are sold, and bar code readers enable a supermarket to monitor the quantities of items that it sells as well as to price them for customers. Bar code reader systems are therefore quite sophisticated.

Inventory tracking – Radio frequency ID systems replace bar codes with a chip, and the chip on each item of inventory can hold additional amounts of information, not just product identification data. This means that RFID readers are able to detect where an item of inventory is at any time and can track inventory movements.

In the case of a supermarket such as CMA, RFID readers could track the movement of inventory from a central stores depot to a supermarket store room, from the store room to the shelves in the supermarket and from the shelves to the customer checkout.

Inventory management – In an industry where fast throughput of items is a critical aspect of success, the ability to monitor the movement of items in such detail, and the time between receiving stores items and selling them, may be of operational value by helping management to adjust purchasing and deliveries in order to speed up sales.

From an accounting perspective, RFID may also be used for inventory counts. An RFID reader can gather information about all the product items held in store at any time, without the need for detailed manual counting.

The additional benefit of having up-to-date **'real time' data** about inventory will depend on the company's management information systems. In principle, a company-wide IT system should be capable of comparing throughput times for different types of product, and comparing the operational performance of different supermarket outlets. The ability to locate stores items may help management to transfer items from where they are turning over slowly to where customer demand is stronger.

Operational performance – CMA's store managers are rightly concerned that the number of out-of-stock products appears to be rising.

This is a problem for two reasons:

- If an items is out-of-stock, customers cannot buy it, and so this will reduce CMA's revenue (unless the customers find a direct replacement they are prepared to buy instead).

- If customers keep finding that the items they want to buy are out-of-stock they will stop shopping at CMA. This is potentially a bigger problem for CMA because, not only will its revenue and market share fall as a direct result of the lost customers, but it could find it harder to recruit new customers if it develops a reputation for not having items in stock.

Reducing out-of-stock products – RFID tags should lead to fewer out-of-stock products. In turn, keeping CMA's shelves fully stock should lead to increased sales and profits, and a more positive shopping experience for customers (leading to higher customer retention).

Inventory ordering – Because RFID technology provides real-time information it will enable CMA to manage its supply chain more efficiently, both between its stores and its warehouses, and from its stores back to suppliers.

Using RFID tagging, whenever a product is scanned through a till, stock levels for that product are updated. However, perhaps more importantly, CMA could also use RFID tagging to inform product suppliers of sales and inventory levels. For example, CMA's RFID system could send inventory messages to suppliers whenever their products are scanned through its tills. In this way, the suppliers are aware of the up-to-date inventories at the stores and can ship additional products as necessary. (If CMA pursued this approach, it might be able to switch to a vendor management inventory relationship with its suppliers, which could be used to help improve product availability.)

However, for CMA to maximise the benefit it can get from using RFID in the short term, it will need its supplier to implement RFID technology on all the products they supply to it. It is not how many of CMA's suppliers can currently do this, or even whether it will be possible to tag all the products CMA sells (for example, fresh fruit and vegetables).

(b) **Integrated system** – The greatest value may be obtained from a new IT system by integrating it across the company. The same system should record data for and report on the performance of central inventory and distribution depots as well as individual supermarket outlets. The system should also record information about costs (which could be held within the data on RFID chips) and selling prices, so that information can be reported about gross profits of stores and product groups within each store. Unexplained losses (due to theft by customers) could also be monitored as a cost item.

Real time information – The system should also operate in real time, so that users of the system are able to access information they want at any time. Stores managers, for example, should be able to obtain information about sales and gross profits for the store, and then if required drill down for further information about the profitability of product ranges, or manufacturers' brands or even individual product items.

Similarly, rather than having to wait until the end of the month for summary performance reports, senior management could receive summary trading updates at the end of each day or week.

Dashboards and drill downs – At the moment, individual store accounts are prepared for each store and then presented to the store manager, alongside summary reports for the senior management team. It would be more useful for CMA if this information was all available electronically, in a way that allowed managers to drill down from summary information to more detailed information for regions and then individual stores.

Having an integrated system in this way should help senior management make comparisons between different central inventory and distribution depots or between different supermarket outlets. Non-financial performance information (for example speed of product throughput) as well as financial information should be provided, all within the same system.

The system should also include external data, although much of this may have to be input by the company's own staff. For example, employees who visit rival supermarkets to check competitors' prices should be able to insert their current prices into the system, so that supermarket managers and senior management can monitor competitive pricing and respond to rivals' price changes.

Data mining – The information that is gathered about product sales should also be used to extract sales data and analyse it to produce information that might help the company to improve sales further – such as information about what products sell well in different areas and at different times of the day, week or year. Data analysis can also be used to 'mine' for data about individual customers.

(c) **Identify buying habits** – In order to exploit data about individual customers, CMA needs to obtain data about a customer's buying habits. For on-line sales (for home delivery), the system identifies individual customers, and it can prompt them to buy items (by presenting a list of the items they regularly buy as a pro-forma shopping list) or it can try to encourage them to buy more with discount vouchers.

Loyalty card schemes – For other customers, some supermarket groups use a loyalty card scheme. Customers who present their loyalty card at a store checkout may be awarded bonus points which eventually build up into money-off vouchers. The customer is identified through the loyalty card, and sales details are recorded by the check-out system. Through loyalty cards, supermarkets are able to gather data about what individual customers buy, how much they spend and when they do their buying. Offers to encourage customers to buy more can be related to the known buying preferences of the individual.

If required, a supermarket should be able to calculate the gross profit contributed each period by each 'loyal' customer. This may help the company to target particular types of customer who are more profitable than others.

Question 3

Marking scheme

		Marks
(a)	1 mark for each relevant point up to a maximum of 6 marks for features of the performance pyramid.	Up to 6
(b)	1 mark for each relevant point up to a maximum of 6 marks for recommendations linked specifically to performance measures at XYZ.	Up to 6
(c)	1 mark for each relevant point up to a maximum of 8 marks for assessing how the pyramid can help XYZ achieve its stated objectives.	Up to 8
(d)	Up to 2 marks on the need for additional (non-financial) information.	
	Up to 4 marks for comments on the issues around the collection of this information.	Up to 5
		Total = 25

(a) **Hierarchy and linkages**

A performance pyramid is a hierarchy of integrated performance targets and measurements, which highlights the linkages between operational performance in an organisation and the achievements of strategic goals. The pyramid identifies that it is vital that different departments in an organisation are aware of the extent to which they are contributing – both separately and collectively – to achieving strategic aims.

Non-financial performance measures

Unlike 'traditional' performance measurement systems, the pyramid does not have a narrow, financial focus.

The successful achievement of corporate objectives depends on meeting required performance standards with regard to **customer satisfaction**, **flexibility** and **productivity**. Although productivity can be monitored by financial targets and performance measures, customer satisfaction requires non-financial or 'market' measurements. Flexibility is achieved through a combination of internal and external factors, and should be monitored by both financial and market measurements.

Identify performance drivers

At an operational level, the key drivers of performance relate to quality and delivery (external effectiveness) and cycle time and waste (internal efficiency), and these should be monitored through suitable performance measures.

Measures of performance are inter-related both at the same level within the organisation (operational business operating system and business strategy level) and also vertically through these different hierarchical levels.

The performance pyramid therefore provides an integrated structure of performance targets and measurements, covering all key aspects of performance and at all levels in the organisation.

(b) **Non-financial performance measures**

The performance reporting system within XYZ appears to focus exclusively on financial performance, and does not provide information about effectiveness and efficiency issues which may be affecting the company's performance. For example, the improvements in labour productivity could be measured through the management accounting system, as well as increases in the cost of raw materials. Currently, the sales and marketing manager is only able to provide qualitative reasons for disappointing sales revenues – customer returns, and the loss of some orders – but the sales manager seemingly wasn't able to explain what XYZ *was* doing to meet customer expectations, for example, through measuring the quality of XYZ's products to ensure they were fit for purpose.

Link between corporate strategy and day-to-day operations

It would also appear that there is an absence of integrated performance measurements through the company, from corporate level down to operational level. The operations manager reported on labour productivity improvements (which affect cycle times) but not on waste. There was also no comment from the operations manager on the lack of flexibility in production (in adapting product specifications) that may have been the cause of lost orders.

The sales and marketing manager can report on sales performance at a market level – sales revenue and sales growth – but there is no obvious link between sales performance and the factors that contribute to that performance: customer satisfaction and flexibility and, at an operational level, quality and delivery.

XYZ should be able to improve its process for setting performance targets and monitoring performance by establishing a range of operational (non-financial) performance targets alongside its current financial performance measures, and by setting performance targets at **strategic business unit level** (for customer satisfaction, flexibility and productivity) and **operational level** (quality, delivery, process time and waste).

(c) **Establishing corporate level objectives** – Establishing a performance pyramid structure should begin with the overall corporate objective or corporate vision. In XYZ's case, this may be the objective of increasing profit by 5% each year, and increasing market share. The overall objective should then be used to establish targets at the next level down in the performance hierarchy.

Strategic business unit objectives – At the business strategy level, performance targets should then be established for both internal efficiency (financial targets) and external effectiveness (marketing and sales targets). The financial and marketing targets should be consistent with each other.

Operational objectives – At the next level down in the hierarchy, targets should be established for productivity, customer satisfaction and flexibility. XYZ has not recognised customer satisfaction or flexibility targets before, but these are key factors in achieving the targets for market growth and sales. Although productivity targets are fairly easy to establish, in financial terms, customer satisfaction and flexibility are not so easily measured. Targets for productivity, flexibility and customer satisfaction need to be integrated and consistent with each other.

Setting targets – Targets for flexibility may be qualitative in nature, relating to XYZ's ability to adapt product specifications to customer requirements. Targets for customer satisfaction may include targets for reducing the volume of customer returns. Achieving these targets will require collaboration between marketing and operations. Also when setting any 'flexibility' targets, XYZ needs to bear in mind the potential cost of customising potential orders. There may be occasions when it is simply not cost effective to make the adaptations a customer requests.

At an operational level, targets should be set for quality, delivery, cycle time and waste that are consistent with the targets for customer satisfaction, flexibility and productivity. For example, specific quality targets may help to reduce the volume of customer returns. Targets for cycle time and delivery may help the company to complete customer orders more quickly, thereby increasing the amount of orders it can complete in a year.

Achieving specific targets at operational level, if well selected, should enable XYZ to achieve its targets at the higher levels. In this respect, the pyramid can provide an integrated structure for performance management that should improve XYZ's ability to achieve its objectives.

Importantly, setting these targets highlights the importance of **understanding the processes** that drive XYZ's results, rather than simply looking at revenues, costs and profits as figures in the management accounts.

(d)   **Non-financial information** – In order to implement the performance pyramid, XYZ will need to monitor its performance in relation to a number of non-financial aspects, such as customer satisfaction, quality and productivity.

Therefore its information systems will need to include data for these non-financial aspects of performance, as well as financial data.

XYZ's current performance reporting system focuses on financial performance alone, and so XYZ's information systems may not currently record any non-financial data.

Availability of data – If XYZ introduces a range of new performance measures (based on both financial and non-financial information) it will also be important that the correct information is available as and when required to support control and decision-making at all levels across XYZ. For example, operational managers may need information about levels of waste (possibly even on a real time basis), while the directors will require more strategic information about XYZ's performance in relation to its market objectives. If XYZ's information systems are not able to provide the information required, then managers will not be able to measure and manage performance in the way envisaged by the pyramid.

Changes to database structure – XYZ may need to modify its existing database structure or add additional records in order to capture the non-financial data it needs to accompany the pyramid. These alterations could be costly, depending on how flexible or easily adaptable XYZ's existing systems are.

Implementing the pyramid may also prompt XYZ to look at systems which allow it monitor how efficiently it is making, accounting for, and delivering customer orders. In this context it might even consider implementing an enterprise resource planning system (ERPS), but again it would need to consider the cost of doing so.

Capturing data – XYZ will also have to introduce systems for capturing the non-financial data that it needs; for example, if it wants to record customer satisfaction scores, it may need to design a way that customers can complete a satisfaction survey online, with the results of that survey automatically feeding into XYZ's database.

Cultural shift – The focus of XYZ's current reporting system suggests that financial performance is currently seen as the most important aspect of performance. Therefore, the change to collecting and using data about non-financial performance could seem a significant change for XYZ's culture.

However, the pyramid suggests that there should ultimately be financial benefits from recording this non-financial information. For example, if the information which is collected helps to improve cycle time and reduce waste, in turn these could help improve XYZ's profits and cash flow.

Question 4

Marking scheme

		Marks
(a)	1 mark for each type of reason why businesses may fail – up to a maximum of 5	5
(b)	For explaining the purpose and nature of Argenti's A score model – 1 mark per relevant point – up to a maximum of 4	up to 4
	For explaining the advantages of the A score model over a Z score approach – 1 mark per relevant point – up to a maximum of 3	up to 3
		6
(c)	For discussing the degree of judgement involved in the A score (as a qualitiative model) – 1 mark per relevant point – up to 5	Up to 5
	For recognising the relative experience of the consultants in applying the model (compared to Chris and Sally – 1 mark per relevant point – up to 2	Up to 2
		6
(d)	1 mark for relevant measures and actions Chris and Sally could take to address the potential problems facing AB Co – up to 8	Up to 8
		8
		Total = 25

(a) **Human causes** – These causes include leadership and management failures. They include: self-deception (management believing things are going well when they aren't), an overly rigid organisation culture, and a tendency to conform and compromise. The symptoms of human causes may be seen in low morale and loss of leadership credibility. Competent staff leave while the remaining staff start scape-goating or blaming others for failure.

Internal and external causes
Firms often fail due to internal causes rather than external ones.

 Internal factors (like human causes) can include human resources issues such as a lack of appropriate management action and discipline, but internal factors may also include high operating expenses, a lack of cash control, a lack of capital, a lack of knowledge about the company's product or service, and an inappropriate marketing strategy.

External factors exist in the firm's operating environment and include recession and fiscal policy, the emergence of successful and aggressive competitors, or changes in technology which could affect demand for a firm's products or services.

Structural causes

These causes include a lack of long-term planning, a lack of innovation, and simply the stage of the **life cycle** the business is at.

However, it is not only older businesses that decline. In fact, younger firms are often more likely to suffer from resource and capability deficiencies than older firms, leading to the 'liability of newness' - for example, where a firm has **yet to establish credibility or legitimacy with suppliers**, clients, customers and other organisations in the industry. In this respect, the failure of older firms is more likely to be a function of internal market forces, with the failure of younger firms may well be a function of internal structural causes.

Tutorial note.

You may have suggested weak cash flow or falling profits as a cause of business failure. However, these are not actually the causes of failure; rather they result from business-related causes. For example, cash flow suffers if customers do not pay on time (through poor credit control) or if inventories cannot be sold.

(b)   Argenti's ' A score' model is a qualitative model for predicting corporate failure, which may provide useful information for investors and management about companies that may be in difficulty.

The 'A score' model assesses the risks of poor management causing corporate failure. The model identifies each weakness or deficiency in an organisation, and gives it a mark, or scores it as zero if the problem is not present.

A company's overall 'A score' is based on an assessment of three different elements: (i) **defects** in the company's management or its accounting systems; (ii) management **mistakes** made, and (iii) **symptoms of failure**.

The maximum acceptable score is 25, and companies which have an 'A' score of greater than 25 are likely to show many of the signs preceding corporate failure, and should therefore be seen as a cause for concern.

Within this overall score, Argenti also suggested that the maximum acceptable score for 'defects' should be 10 or less, while the score for management mistakes should be 15 or less. If a firm scores anything for 'symptoms of failure' this should automatically be seen as an indicator that the firm is at risk.

Overall, the 'A score' model is concerned primarily with the **quality of the management** and management information, and the past decisions or actions by management that may have led the company into difficulty.

In comparison, a **Z score** failure prediction model is based on **financial ratios**. The Z score is likely to be less subjective than A score, because it is quantitative, being based on calculations from published financial information.

However, the information required to compute a Z score may not be readily available (since financial information is not always up-to-date). Also, the Z score model is not appropriate for unquoted companies because one of the elements measured is the market value of equity. (Unquoted companies do not have a market value of equity).

Finally, experience seems to show that the Z score of failing companies deteriorates sharply in the period just before the company collapses. However, the accuracy of the Z-score model as a forecaster of corporate failure diminishes significantly if it is used more than two years before a ultimately company fails. Consequently, Z scores may be an unreliable longer-term predictor of corporate failure, so their value as a trigger for action to prevent collapse is reduced.

(c)   Chris is correct in stating that the A score is based on the judgement of the consultant and the 'A score' is a qualitative model. The score for **management defects** is based on factors such as whether the CEO is an autocrat, whether the finance director is weak, whether there are defects in the accounting system, (such as an absence of up-to-date cash flow forecasts and a poor costing system that fails to report the contribution earned by each of the company's products or services) and the ability of the company to respond to change.

The score for **management mistakes** is based on judgement about factors such as the extent to which the company is overtrading or whether the company has invested in a big project that has gone wrong.

However, although the 'A' score is based on the judgement of the consultants about these factors, the judgement is based on experience. Chris and Sally may not be able to produce a reliable 'A' score using their own judgement, but it should be expected that consultants claiming expertise in 'A' score failure predictions will have some professional competence in this area. Chris and Sally should respect this, rather than trying to dismiss it.

Sally is correct to state that the 'A' score may be misleading. Whenever predictions are based on statistical analysis (in this case, an 'A' score) there is the possibility of Type I and Type II errors.

A Type I error would be an A score indicating that the company is 'safe' when it subsequently fails. A Type II error would be an A score that predicts corporate failure when in fact the company is 'safe'. The consultancy firm should be able to provide some statistical evidence of its track record in successfully (or unsuccessfully) predicting failure, and if its past ability seems reasonably good, it would be advisable for Chris and Sally to accept the 'A' score for AB Co (of 30) is a matter of concern, because it is higher than the maximum acceptable score of 25.

(d)   Chris and Sally should make a decision about what to do in view of the A score for the company.

Potential sale of the company. One option would be to negotiate with the venture capital firm for the sale of the company, and leave it to the venture capitalists to tackle the problem of how to turn round the company's position and prospects.

On the other hand, if they decide to continue as owners and managers of AB Co, Chris and Sally should consider appropriate action to reduce the risk of failure. A possible approach would be to look at the component elements of the A score in turn. Each factor within management defects, management mistakes and symptoms of trouble will have an individual score in the consultants' analysis. The factors contributing to the high 'A' score should be reviewed and ways of reducing the score should be considered.

Current weaknesses - In the case of AB Co, probable weaknesses are the absence of a strong finance director (or head of accounting and finance) and weaknesses in the accounting system (the absence of up-to-date cash flow information and a poor costing system that fails to provide sufficient information about product profitability). The company may also have experienced problems in adapting to change, such as responding to the growth in competition. The leverage (gearing) of the company and overtrading may have contributed to a high score for management mistakes.

Improvements to make - Having identified the main problem areas, Chris and Sally should then take measures to deal with them. To reduce weaknesses in management, it would seem to be appropriate to appoint a finance director who should be required to improve the accounting information system, so that more information about the company's performance is available to be reviewed on a timely basis. If the company has been slow to respond to change and new competition, improvements in product innovation and in sales and marketing may be appropriate to help differentiate AB's toys from the cheaper imported goods. To reduce the threat from high gearing and overtrading, the company should perhaps consider a period of consolidation, when it does not chase sales growth but accumulates profits, and uses positive operational cash flow to pay down the bank loan.

Monitoring and control – Having initiated improvements, Chris and Sally – together with the finance director – should monitor the company's position and performance regularly. Unless improvements are made, the company may well remain exposed to a high risk of failure.

ACCA Professional Level

Paper P5

Advanced Performance Management

Mock Examination 2

Question Paper
Time allowed: 3 hours and 15 minutes
This paper is divided into two sections
Section A   ONE compulsory question to be attempted
Section B   TWO out of THREE questions to be attempted

DO NOT OPEN THIS PAPER UNTIL YOU ARE READY TO START UNDER EXAMINATION CONDITIONS

SECTION A – This question is compulsory and must be attempted

Question 1

Metis is a restaurant business in the city of Urbanton. Metis was started three years ago by three friends who met at university while doing courses in business and catering management. Initially, their aim was simply to 'make money' although they had talked about building a chain of restaurants if the first site was successful.

The three friends pooled their own capital and took out a loan from the Grand Bank in order to fit out a rented site in the city. They designed the restaurant to be light and open with a menu that reflected the most popular dishes in Urbanton regardless of any particular culinary style. The dishes were designed to be priced in the middle of the range that was common for restaurants in the city. The choice of food and drinks to offer to customers is still a group decision amongst the owners.

Other elements of the business were allocated according to each owner's qualifications and preferences. Bert Fish takes charge of all aspects of the kitchen operations while another, Sheila Plate, manages the activities in the public area such as taking reservations, serving tables and maintaining the appearance of the restaurant. The third founder, John Sum, deals with the overall business issues such as procurement, accounting and legal matters.

Competition in the restaurant business is fierce as it is easy to open a restaurant in Urbanton and there are many competitors in the city both small, single-site operations and large national chains. The current national economic environment is one of steady but unspectacular growth.

The restaurant has been running for three years and the founders have reached the point where the business seems to be profitable and self-sustaining. The restaurant is now in need of refurbishment in order to maintain its atmosphere and this has prompted the founders to consider the future of their business. John Sum has come to you as their accountant looking for advice on aspects of performance management in the business. He has supplied you with figures outlining the recent performance of the business and the forecasts for the next year (see the performance report below).

This table represents the quantitative data that is available to the founders when they meet each quarter to plan any short-term projects or initiatives and also, to consider the longer-term future. Bert and Sheila have often indicated to John that they find the information daunting and difficult to understand fully.

John Sum has come to you to advise him on the performance reporting at Metis and how it could be improved. He feels that the current report is, in some ways, too complex and, in other ways, too simple. He wants to look at different methods of measuring and presenting performance to the ownership group. As a starting point, he has suggested to you that you consider measures such as NPV, EVA™, MIRR as well as the more common profit measures.

John is naïve and wants the NPV and MIRR to be appraised as if the business was a three-year project up to 20X2 so he knows the performance of the business to date. He has requested that other calculations in your performance review should be annual based on the 20X2 figures although he is aware that this may be omitting in his words 'some important detail'.

At recent meetings, Sheila has been complaining that her waiters and waitresses are not responding well to her attempts to encourage them to smile at customers although her recent drive to save electricity by getting staff to turn off unnecessary lights seems to be working. Bert stated that he was not convinced by either of Sheila's initiatives and he wants her to make sure that food is collected from the kitchen swiftly and so delivered at the right temperature to the customer's table. Also, Bert has said that he feels that too much food is becoming rotten and having to be thrown out. However, he is not sure what to do about it except make the kitchen staff go through lengthy inventory checks where they review the food held in store. John is worried about these complaints as there is now an air of tension in the owners' meetings. He has been reading various books about performance management and has come across the quote, 'What gets measured, gets done.' He believes this is true but wants to know how it might apply in the case of his business.

John is also concerned at the potential impact the tension between his co-owners could have on strategic decisions at Metis.

At the last meeting, Bert expressed his concern at the impact the proposed building upgrade was forecast to have on the figures for 20X3, and he suggested that Metis should reconsider whether it needs to undertake the upgrade in the next year. However, Sheila retorted that this was a very short-term view, and if Metis didn't upgrade its restaurant, customers were likely to stop eating there. John explained that he could appreciate both Bert and Sheila's perspectives, because it was important that Metis considers its long-term future as well as its short-term position.

You should assume it is now June 20X2.

Metis Performance Report

Metis Restaurant		Year to 31 March			Latest quarter to 31 March 20X2	Previous quarter
	Actual 20X0 $	*Actual 20X1* $	*Actual 20X2* $	*Forecast 20X3* $	*(Q4 20X2)* $	*(Q3 20X2)* $
Revenue						
Food	617,198	878,220	974,610	1,062,180	185,176	321,621
Wine	127,358	181,220	201,110	219,180	38,211	66,366
Spirits	83,273	118,490	131,495	143,310	24,984	43,394
Beer	117,562	167,280	185,640	202,320	35,272	61,261
Other beverages	24,492	34,850	38,675	42,150	7,348	12,763
Outside catering	9,797	13,940	15,470	16,860	2,939	5,105
Total	979,680	1,394,000	1,547,000	1,686,000	293,930	510,510
Cost of sales						
Food	200,589	285,422	316,748	345,209	60,182	104,527
Wine	58,585	83,361	92,511	100,821	17,577	30,528
Spirits	21,651	30,807	34,189	37,261	6,496	11,283
Beer	44,673	63,566	70,543	76,882	13,403	23,279
Other beverages	3,674	5,228	5,801	6,323	1,102	1,914
Outside catering	3,135	4,461	4,950	5,395	941	1,634
Total	332,307	472,845	524,742	571,891	99,701	173,165
Gross profit	647,373	921,155	1,022,258	1,114,109	194,229	337,345
Staff costs	220,428	313,650	348,075	379,350	66,134	114,865
Other operating costs						
Marketing	25,000	10,000	12,000	20,000	3,000	3,000
Rent/mortgage	150,800	175,800	175,800	193,400	43,950	43,950
Local property tax	37,500	37,500	37,500	37,500	9,375	9,375
Insurance	5,345	5,585	5,837	6,100	1,459	1,459
Utilities	12,600	12,978	13,043	13,173	3,261	3,261
Waste removal	6,000	6,180	6,365	6,556	1,591	1,591
Equipment repairs	3,500	3,658	3,822	3,994	956	956
Depreciation	120,000	120,000	120,000	120,000	30,000	30,000
Building upgrades				150,000		
Total	360,745	371,701	374,367	550,723	93,592	93,592
Manager salary	35,000	36,225	37,494	38,806	9,373	9,373
Net profit/loss before interest and corporate taxes	31,200	199,579	262,322	145,230	25,130	119,515
Net margin	3.2%	14.3%	17.0%	8.6%	8.5%	23.4%

Additional notes:

1. The business was founded with $600,000 which comprised $250,000 of equity from the founders and the remainder in a loan from Grand Bank. Under the terms of the loan, all principal is repayable in 10 years' time and interest is charged at a fixed rate of 8·4% per year.

2. John has estimated the overall cost of capital to be 12·5%.

3. The company earns 4·5% on any returns in its deposit account.

4. John wishes you to use the $600,000 original investment as the capital employed figure for analysis purposes as no new capital has been input and the owners have taken out all residual earnings so far as dividends.

5. The corporation tax rate for Metis is 30%, paid in the same year as profits are generated. Accounting depreciation is a tax allowable cost.

6. Marketing spending is for the short-term promotion of offers only.

Required

Prepare a report to Mr John Sum addressing the following issues:

(a) Critically assess the existing performance report and suggest improvements to its content and presentation.

(12 marks)

(b) Calculate and briefly evaluate:

(i) The use of John's suggested performance measures, and

(ii) Other profit-based measures, using the most recent year's actual figures where appropriate as examples. **(14 marks)**

(c) Assess how the quote 'What gets measured, gets done' could apply to Metis. **(10 marks)**

Professional marks will be awarded for the format, style, structure and clarity of your report. **(4 marks)**

(d) With reference to the issues arising at the last owners' meeting, discuss the importance of managing both short-term and long-term performance at Metis. **(10 marks)**

(Total = 50 marks)

SECTION B – TWO questions ONLY to be attempted

Question 2

Tench Cars (Tench) is large national car manufacturing business. It is based in Essland, a country that has recently turned from state communism to democratic capitalism. The car industry had been heavily supported and controlled by the bureaucracy of the old regime. The government had stipulated production and employment targets for the business but had ignored profit as a performance measure. Tench is now run by a new generation of capitalist business people intent on rejuvenating the company's fortunes.

The company has a strong position within Essland, which has a population of 200 million and forms the majority of Tench's market. However, the company has also traditionally achieved a good market share in six neighbouring countries due to historic links and shared culture between them and Essland. All of these markets are experiencing growing car ownership as political and market reforms lead to greater wealth in a large proportion of the population. Additionally, the new government in Essland is deregulating markets and opening the country to imports of foreign vehicles.

Tench's management recognises that it needs to make fundamental changes to its production approach in order to combat increased competition from foreign manufacturers. Tench's cars are now being seen as ugly, pollutive and with poor safety features in comparison to the foreign competition. Management plans to address this by improving the quality of its cars through the use of quality management techniques. It plans to improve financial performance through the use of Kaizen costing and just-in-time purchasing and production. Tench's existing performance reporting system uses standard costing and budgetary variance analysis in order to monitor and control production activities.

The Chief Financial Officer (CFO) of Tench has commented that he is confused by the terminology associated with quality management and needs a clearer understanding of the different costs associated with quality management. The CFO also wants to know the impact of including quality costs and using the Kaizen costing approach on the traditional standard costing approach at Tench.

Required

In response to the CFO's comments:

(a)   Discuss the impact of the collection and use of quality costs on the current costing systems at Tench.

(6 marks)

(b)   Discuss and evaluate the impact of the Kaizen costing approach on the costing systems and employee management at Tench.
(8 marks)

(c)   Briefly evaluate the effect of moving to just-in-time purchasing and production, noting the impact on performance measures at Tench.
(6 marks)

(d)   Explain why the adoption of TQM is particularly important within a just-in-time (JIT) production environment.
(5 marks)

(Total = 25 marks)

Question 3

Two years ago, LC plc established a joint venture operation with HTB. LC is a large multinational gaming company, while HTB is a smaller electronics company, which is run and managed by its founder's family. However, HTB has recently developed a new virtual casino platform, and LC has been trying to expand its online casino side for several years now.

The two companies agreed to establish the joint venture to harness HTB's software and technological skills and LC's existing customer base and distribution network.

The initial equity investment in the joint venture was $10 million in cash, with 50% contributed by each of the joint venture partners. The partners agreed that any profits would also be split evenly between them. Since the initial investment, all additional long-term capital has been raised in the form of bank loans, secured against the assets of the joint venture operation.

The management accountant of LC has produced the following financial results for the joint venture in its first two years, together with forecasts for the next two years. These are shown below.

(Figures are in $millions.)

	Year 1 actual	Year 2 actual	Year 3 forecast	Year 4 Forecast
Revenue	14	19	25	31
Costs	13	17	21	26
Profit before tax	1	2	4	5
Tax	0	0	1	1
Profit after tax	1	2	3	4
Dividend	0	0	2	3
Net cash flow in year	(5)	0	(7)	(4)
Gearing	55%	45%	100%	123%

These figures have been shown to the management of HTB, who agree with most of the forecasts for the next two years, including the forecasts for sales and profits. They do not agree, however, with the dividend figures.

The management of LC have argued in favour of dividend payments out of profits, as an indication to their shareholders that the joint venture is successful. The management of HTB believe that in the early years of the venture, profits should either be reinvested for faster growth or should be used to pay back debt.

There have also been some disagreements between the joint venture partners about transfer prices. LC makes a fixed annual charge to the joint venture for marketing support and accounting services. HTB charges the joint venture for software support by its technicians, based on an hourly rate which includes a mark-up for profit.

In addition, there has been disagreement between senior management of the two joint venture partners about the measures being used to assess the venture's performance. The management of LC expressed the view that in the early years of the joint venture, the key performance statistics were profit, sales growth and profit growth. The management of HTB argued in response that, although growth and profitability were important, it was essential to recognise the liquidity and gearing risks facing the joint venture. They contended that cash flows and gearing levels should also be monitored.

Required

(a)   Evaluate the compatibility of the joint venture partners.   **(8 marks)**

(b)   Assess the difficulties that may arise in the joint venture in relation to identifying and agreeing key performance targets, and in monitoring performance.   **(9 marks)**

(c)   Evaluate the actual and expected performance of the joint venture, from the differing perspectives of the management of LC and HTB.   **(8 marks)**

(Total = 25 marks)

Question 4

Each year, the government of Erewhon publishes league tables ranking the performance of the schools in the country. All the schools in Erewhon are funded by the state, and are all ultimately accountable to the government's Education Department.

The Education Department argues that the league tables help identify those schools whose performance is appreciably greater or lower than expected, and to show the level of variation in performance between schools. However, the Education Department also argues it is important to identify why there are large and unexplained variations, and then work to bring about an early improvement in those schools which have performed worse than expected.

Critics have argued that the league tables only look at selected aspects of performance, and the indicators have been selected on the basis of what data is available rather than that which is valued by parents and pupils. Another criticism is that they have a negative impact on public confidence and professional morale.

An extract from the most recent schools league table (based on exam grades) showed the following:

Rank	School	% of pupils passing at least 5 final exams with Grade A - C	Value added score (Par = 100)
1	CAD School	85	103
52	HI School	62	94
103	SPO School	54	115

[The 'Value added' score indicates how well students performed in their final exams compared to their performance in intermediate exams.]

HI School and SPO School are neighbouring schools. In the last three years, SPO has been over-subscribed, while HI has a pupil roll that is below capacity.

The three schools (CAD, HI and SPO) have also recently had their routine inspections by the Education Inspector. CAD received a rating of 'Good'; HI received a rating of 'Satisfactory'; but SPO received a rating of 'Excellent.'

Here are some extracts from the Education Inspector's reports:

[CAD School]: 'Although the standard of teaching was very high, there seemed to be a concentration of resources on those students who were on the threshold of getting a Grade C in their exams.'

[SPO School]: 'There seemed to be a real sense of community and togetherness at this school. The number of after school clubs and study support clubs was particularly impressive, as was the pastoral care afforded to the pupils.'

Required

(a) (i)   Explain three possible problems accompanying the use of performance measures.   **(6 marks)**

     (ii) Evaluate the appropriateness of the league table for monitoring schools' performance in Erewhon.

                                                                                          (8 marks)

(b) Recommend, with reasons, two additional indicators (apart from those included in the league tables) which schools in Erewhon could use for evaluating their performance.   **(6 marks)**

Following the publication of the most recent Inspector's reports, the Governors of HI School have called for a review of the way performance is measured in the school.

Required

(c) Briefly discuss three factors which will influence the effectiveness of any performance standards selected for the school's new performance measurement system.   **(5 marks)**

                                                                                       (Total = 25 marks)

Answers

DO NOT TURN THIS PAGE UNTIL YOU HAVE
COMPLETED THE MOCK EXAM

Plan of attack

What's the worst thing you could be doing right now if this were the actual exam paper? Trying to find a pen which works? Panicking, and generally getting yourself flustered? Wondering how to celebrate the end of the exam in 3 hours and 15 minutes time?

Well, they're all pretty bad. But what you should be doing is spending the first few minutes of the exam looking through the paper in detail, working out which questions to do and the order in which to attempt them. So turn back to the paper and let's sort out a **plan of attack.**

First steps first

As we suggested with Mock Exam 1, in our view, the compulsory Section A question is usually the best place to start, but you may prefer to start by doing your best Section B question first. However, if you do decide to start with a 25 mark Section B question, make sure that you finish your answer in no more than 49 minutes (25 marks × 1.95 minutes per mark). Remember, the Section A question makes up 50% of the marks for the paper so you need to allow yourself enough time to answer these.

Make sure you look through the whole paper carefully before diving in to answer any questions.

In the first five minutes of the exam, look through the case study scenarios and the question requirements and work out which questions you are going to answer, and the order in which you are going to answer them. We suggest you then spend approximately the next five to ten minutes analysing the requirements of the Section A question and identifying the key issues in the scenario. Remember, planning your answer is very important; don't just start writing your answer as soon as you open the exam paper.

If you are worried about the paper, it is likely that you believe the Section A question will be daunting. In this case you may prefer to do one, or both, of the optional (Section B) questions before tackling it. Don't however, fall into the trap of spending too long on the optional questions because they seem easier. Remember the Section A question accounts for 50% of the marks, so it is vital to your chances of passing this exam.

It is dangerous to be over-confident, but if you're not too nervous about the exam, we suggest you should start with the compulsory Section A question. You've got to answer it, so you might as well get it over and done with straight away.

Make sure **you address every requirement and sub-requirement in the questions**, and also make sure you apply your answer directly to the scenarios. Remember that the basis of the P5 exam is **analysis and application**: you are being tested on your ability to apply your knowledge to analyse and address the specific issues identified in a scenario.

The questions themselves

Question 1 – The scenario identifies varies issues around the way performance is measured and reported in an organisation, and the first part of the requirement asks you to assess the performance report which is currently produced. Crucially, however, this is question is looking at the way the organisation's performance is reported, rather than how well the organisation itself is performing.

The second part of the question (part (b)) requires you to apply a number of different performance techniques – net profit, ROCE, Return on Equity, NPV, MIRR and EVA. Again, however, the primary focus of your answer should be the benefits (or limitations) of using the different techniques rather than the organisation's performance as such.

The quote at the heart of part (c) – What gets measured, gets done – is an important one in the context of performance management generally. If staff know they are being assessed on one aspect of performance they are likely to put more effort into performing well in that area compared to another area where they are not being assessed. However, it is important that you make sure you answer to part (c) remains applied to the scenario rather than becoming a generic discussion of the quote.

Part (d) looks at the importance of managing both short-term and long-term performance in organisations. The last paragraph of the scenario provides the context for this question, and you should make use of the issues raised in it in your answer. The quote from part (c) could also be relevant here – for example, if long-term performance is important as well as short-term performance, what implications will this have for the choice of performance measures in the business?

Question 2 looks at a number of issues surrounding quality and costs. However, at the heart of the question is the contrast between the traditional view of quality costs and the ideas of total quality management and continuous improvement .

The organisation described in the scenario currently follows the traditional approach to costing, but parts (b) and (c) ask you to consider the potential impact if the organisation replaces this with a system driven by kaizen costing and JIT purchasing and production. It is important to recognise that such a change won't simply affect individual aspects of performance, but it will also affect the whole culture within the organisation. Don't overlook this when evaluating the impact of the changes.

Question 3 – The main topic area in Question 3 is the performance management issues which can arise in relation to complex business structures – in this case, a joint venture.

The first part of the question looks at the two venture partners, but your findings in part (a) will have important implications for part (b) – assessing the difficulties in setting performance targets for the joint venture. If, for example, the venture partners have differing objectives for the joint venture, or have conflicting views about how it should be run, what implications is this likely to have for the partner's ability to agree performance targets for the joint venture?

The point about the differences between the venture partners is also relevant in part (c), where you have to evaluate the performance of the joint venture from the perspectives of both partners. Crucially, one partner is interested in the profitability of the venture, while the other partner is interested in its liquidity and gearing. **Question 4** looks at the use of performance league tables in public sector organisations –specifically, schools. Although league tables are becoming increasingly widely used, there are still a number of potential issues with using them – and this is the focus of part (a) of the question. Part (a) (i) looks at the possible problems in general terms, but then in (a) (ii) you have to evaluate the proposed league tables specifically in the context of the scenario.

Planning, and identifying the links between the parts of the question, is also important here. Your evaluation in part (a) (ii) should identify some of the limitations of the current league tables; but these, in turn, should help you identify additional factors – part (b) – which it would beneficial to add to the tables.

The question finishes with a requirement about performance standards, and the characteristics of effective performance standards.

Once, once more

You must **allocate your time** according to the marks for the question in total, and for the parts of the questions. And you must also **follow the requirements exactly**.

It's easy to waffle on this exam if you don't follow the requirements strictly. If you answer contains irrelevant material, you will not be scoring marks efficiently, and you will put yourself under increased **time pressure**.

All finished and quarter of an hour to go?

Your time allocation must have been faulty. However, make the most of any time you have left at the end of the exam. Go back to **any parts of questions that you didn't finish** because you ran out of time. Always write something rather than nothing if you possibly can, and try not to leave questions unanswered.

Question 1

Top tips.

Part (a). One of the key issues here is that the current report focuses solely on financial performance, (and within that, only really profit measures). Therefore, one significant improvement could be for the report to include a range of non-financial performance indicators alongside financial ones.

In this respect, you might have used one of the multi-dimensional frameworks such as the Balanced Scorecard or the 'Building Blocks' model to help you plan your answer (although these were not specifically required.) In particular the 'Results and Determinants' element of the 'Building Blocks' model could have been useful here - given that Metis is a service business.

However, if you do decide to use one of these frameworks as a guide you must still make sure your answer is tailored to the scenario. For example, although one of the dimension in the 'Results and Determinants' block is 'Innovation' the scenario does not provide you with any information about innovation at Metis. Therefore you should not have invented any, or included this dimension in your answer. To this end, the suggested solution below isn't structured around any given model.

However, remember that the question requirement is to critically assess the performance *report*, not Metis' performance itself.

Also, make sure you assess both the content and the presentation of the report. For example, how user-friendly is the layout and presentation of the report?

Part (b). The scenario identifies NPV, EVA and MIRR as three methods to use as performance measures, as well as the 'more common profit measures.' You should have identified that ROCE and Return on Equity were relevant here.

Although the requirement asks you to 'calculate' Metis performance using the different measures, it also asks you to 'briefly evaluate' the use of the different measures. In other words, once you have done the calculations you also need to consider how useful they are for assessing Metis' performance.

Part (c). The idea that 'What gets measured, gets done' is a key issue in performance management because people tend to focus on performing well in those areas which are being measured (possibly at the expense of other areas). The underlying suggestion is that the things which are measured are those that are important to an organisation, but what implications could this have for the way staff (or managers) treat those aspects of performance which are not measured? For example, is there too much emphasis on financial performance at Metis, rather than non-financial aspects such as customer service?

To score well here, though, it is important you don't just assess the quote in general terms, but apply it specifically to Metis. For example, how far does the choice of what is measured (or not measured) contribute to the performance issues identified in the scenario.

Part (d). In effect, this picks up on the ideas of the quote in part (c). If too much focus is given to short-term performance, will long-term performance suffer, or vice versa?

And again, as in part (c) make sure you don't just discuss the potential conflict between short-term and long-term performance in general terms, but link it specifically to the scenario; for example, in relation to the decision to upgrade the restaurant.

Examining team's comments. In part (a) any candidates used the report given in the scenario to make specific criticisms and suggestions for improvements in a practical way and scored well. However, a number of candidates chose to 'critically assess Metis' performance', rather than the report itself, and consequently these candidates only scored few marks for the question. It is vital you read the question requirement carefully and answer the question actually being asked.

Marks

(a) Strengths of current reporting (eg measures overall objective) – 1 mark per point, up to 2 marks

Weaknesses of current reporting – 1 mark per point, up to 12 marks
Possible weaknesses include:
Data overload; use of absolute numbers only; no breakdown into functional areas; timescales used; lack of non-financial performance indicators

Total for part (a) – up to 12 marks

12

(b) NPV calculation
Deriving free cashflows – up to 3 marks
Calculating NPV – up to 2 marks

EVA
Calculating NOPAT – 1 mark
Calculating EVA – 1 mark

MIRR
Present value of investment – ½ mark
Terminal value of returns – 1 ½ marks
Calculating MIRR – 1 mark

ROCE – 1 mark

Return on Equity – up to 2 marks

Evaluation of measures used – 1 mark per point; up to 4 marks

14

(c) General commentary on the quote – up to 2 marks

Specific examples appropriate to Metis – up to 3 marks per example; up to 10 marks.

10

Examples can include illustrations of how management responds to measures, or the problems which arise from the lack of certain measures in the performance report.

Professional marks for the format, style and structure of the discussion

(d) General commentary on the potential conflict between short-term and long-term performance measures – up to 2 marks

4

Specific examples appropriate to Metis – up to 2 marks per example; up to 10 marks.

10

Total = 50

REPORT

To: J. Sum

From: Accountant

Date: [Today's date]

Subject: Performance management at Metis

This report assesses the existing performance reporting pack and suggests improvements which could be made to it. It also evaluates different methods of measuring performance, and assesses the extent to which the choice of what gets measured could have an impact on the business' performance.

(a)

Current performance report

The existing report does provide some useful performance information; however, there are also a number of areas where it could be improved.

Profit information

Highlights profit – The existing report shows clearly how profitable the business is, both in terms of gross profit and net profit. Showing the net profit margin (%) is also useful, because, for example, it shows that not only has Metis been able to increase its revenue over the last three years, but also it has been able control its costs sufficiently well so that the **net margin** (%) has increased.

Absolute figures only – However, although the figures show that revenues and profits have increased over the three years under review, the figures would be more useful if they showed the percentage increases each year, rather than just showing each year's figures.

Product information

Revenue streams- It is also useful that the report shows revenues and costs for different product categories, because this could help identify if the revenues or costs for certain products are increasing more than for other products.

Again, however, this information could be more useful if it showed the percentage increases each year.

Margins by product – Equally, although the report shows revenues and cost of sales for different product category, it doesn't show the gross profit or gross profit percentage for each product category. However, such information would be useful for decision-making. For example, in 20X2, the gross margin Metis earned on food was 68% ($657k/$974k), the margin on beer was 62% ($115k/$186k) but on wine it was only 54% ($109k/$201k).

Performance comparison

Comparative figures – The report clearly shows how revenues and costs have changed over the last three years, and it also provides a **forecast** for the next year. This could be useful to assess how well Metis' actual performance compares to the forecast.

Budget controls – However, for any year of reported figures, the report only shows the actual results, it doesn't show any budget or forecast figures as a comparison. However, it would be useful if these were included, in order to gauge whether Metis is performing better or worse than had been anticipated, and therefore whether any corrective action is required to bring actual performance back in line with forecast.

Quantity of information – However, whilst it would be useful to have some additional information (% changes; performance against budget) it is important to avoid showing too much information in the report.

Given that the report is a quarterly summary, there is a danger that it already contains too much detailed information in the report; for example, instead of showing the detail of all the operating costs, this could be shown as a single line for 'Operating costs'. If this total line showed any unusual results, these could then be investigated separately by drilling down into the total.

Value of historical information – Equally, it is debatable how much value is added by showing three years of historical information. It could be useful to show the current year and the prior year, but any more than this seems to superfluous. As Metis was only started three years ago, there is likely to be little value in comparing performance in 20X2 with 20X0 as the business will have developed become much more established over the intervening period. Equally, market conditions could have changed over this period.

Seasonality – The comparison between the latest quarter and the previous quarter also appears to have little value. There is a fall in revenue of 42% between Q4 and Q3, which suggests Metis' business is seasonal. Therefore, it might be more useful to compare performance in the current quarter with the equivalent quarter in the previous year.

Presentation – The overall presentation of the report could also be improved. It might not be clear to a non-accountant what the most important figures, so the key figures (eg gross profit; net margin) could usefully be highlighted in bold. Similarly, the report might look less crowded if the figures were shown in thousands of dollars rather than to the last dollar.

Other areas for improvement

Cash flows – The focus of the current report appears to be exclusively on how much profit Metis is generating. Although the business' stated aim is to 'make money' this does not mean that profit is the only aspect of financial performance which should be monitored. For example, it would be useful for the report to include some measures relating to Metis' cash flow and liquidity.

Performance objectives – More generally, it might also be useful to define some more specific objectives of the business. These might then highlight which aspects of the business are most important to its success, and which should therefore be monitored in the performance report.

Functional areas – The report does not currently provide any information about how the different functional areas of the business are performing. For example, there are no measures which indicate how well the **service staff** are performing. Again, this issue could be addressed by identifying key objectives and establishing key performance indicators which will support those objectives. For example, Metis could use a customer survey to find out how satisfied its customers are with the service they have received, and average scores from these surveys could be used as an indicator of the quality of service being offered.

Similarly, there don't currently appear to be any indicators which relate to the performance of the **kitchen operations**. For example, it might be useful to monitor how long it takes for meals to be delivered from the kitchen, or how much food is wasted (for example, if the chef is not happy that a plate of food is up to standard and so it has to be thrown away).

Both of these points also highlight that the current report only looks at financial performance. However, the owners should also be monitoring how well Metis is performing in relation to its **non-financial performance indicators**. These are likely to be crucial in attracting and retaining customers, and hence to the longer term success of the business.

It is likely that **procurement** is another important functional area, because Metis will need sufficient food to satisfy customer demand, but it will need to avoid over-ordering perishable items. Equally, it will be important that Metis buys food and drink of high enough quality to satisfy its customers, yet secures it for the best price possible. The gross margins obtained for different product categories could be used as an indicator for this area, which again highlights the need for gross margin percentages to be provided rather than just an absolute figure.

External information – The existing report only looks at internal aspects of performance. For example, it does not give any indication of how Metis' margins or product mix compare against those of other similar restaurants. Such comparisons or benchmarking could be useful, although it may be difficult to obtain the necessary data. There may be a local restaurant association, or similar trade association, which Metis could join, which has a database of such information.

(b) **Summary of results for 20X2** (see Appendix for details)

Net profit after tax	$163,045
ROCE	43.7%
Return on Equity	65.2%
Net Present Value (20X0–20X2)	$(55,475)
MIRR (20X0-20X2)	6.75%
EVA (20X2)	$108,625

Profit and EVA – The results show that Metis is generating a healthy post-tax profit for the owners (equivalent to approximately $55k each), and it is generating a positive EVA which also suggests that the business is adding value for the owners (shareholders).

NPV – At first sight, the negative NPV figure does not look good, but it is important to remember the business has only been running for three years, and there was a significant initial investment to establish it ($600,000). Although it is not clear what period the owners wanted to appraise their initial investment, it is likely that it will longer than three years; for example, the bank loan was taken out for 10 years. Moreover, Metis' cash flows suggest that the NPV will be positive by the end of the next year, which presents the initial investment in a more favourable light.

MIRR – Similarly, although the fact that the MIRR is less than the overall cost of capital (12.5%) might normally be a concern this again is due to the timeframe under review. As with NPV, the MIRR figure should increase in subsequent years as the business generates additional cash inflows.

Longer term performance – In this respect, NPV and MIRR could both be useful in appraising the business' performance over the longer-term, but they are less useful in judging the current state of the business.

This issue of longer-term performance and short term results may also need to be highlighted next year. Profits for the year are forecast to decline as a result of the building upgrade, but the upgrade is necessary to maintain the business. In this context, EVA will be an important performance measure because it adds back 'value adding' expenditure, and so may help encourage a long term (rather than short term) focus. For example, the net profit margin for 20X3 is forecast to decline to 8.6%. However, the main reason for this is the $150,000 scheduled for building upgrades in 20X3. If this were excluded, the net margin for 20X3 would be 17.5%.

(c) **What gets measured, gets done**

Making money – The logic behind the quote is that staff and managers will pay more attention to those areas for which they know performance is being measured, compared to those areas which are not being measured. For example, Sheila's recent drive to save electricity seems to have been successful, utility costs only rose 0.5% between 20X1-X2, compared to 3% the previous year. Controlling costs in this way, will also help Metis 'make money' which is ultimately its aim.

Lack of non-financial measures – By implication, the quote also suggests that there is a danger that what doesn't get measured, might not get done. There appears to be a danger at Metis that non-financial aspects of performance are not receiving as much attention as they could.

While Sheila appears to have been successful in her electricity cost-saving campaign, she has not been successful in getting her waiting staff to smile at customers. Perhaps this is not surprising though. The staff are not currently assessed on how well they interact with customers, and there do not appear to be any customer-driven performance measures (such as customer satisfaction ratings). Therefore, the staff may feel there are no incentives for them to smile at customers.

Equally, it appears that Bert thinks that food could be collected from the kitchen more quickly, and also that the amount of food wasted could be reduced. Again, however, these aspects of performance do not currently appear to be measured, which may explain why performance in them is not as good as it could be.

Lack of management information – More generally, the quote also highlights that it could be difficult for the managers to improve Metis' performance if they do not have adequate information about its current performance. Although Bert 'feels' that too much food is becoming rotten and having to be thrown out, he does not seem to have any information about actual wastage levels to support his feeling. Consequently, he is making the kitchen staff go through lengthy inventory checks, when they could potentially be carrying out more value-adding activities.

Information for decision-making – Nonetheless, Bert's checks on inventory could be useful if they help highlight the reason for the wastage. There could be several different reasons why food is becoming rotten: the quantities ordered are too high creating surpluses of perishable products; Metis could be buying poorer quality goods to save costs; or the temperature and storage facilities in the kitchen, or the way produce is handled, may not be satisfactory.

However, it is important that Metis highlights the reason for the wastage, because the first two potential reasons are procurement issues, while the third falls under Bert's area of responsibility. Equally, this suggests that rather than simply looking at gross margin, the performance report needs to identify some separate critical success factors for both procurement and the kitchen operations.

Choice of measurements – However, the quote could also highlight that there is a danger that too much focus could be placed on the aspects of performance which are measured. For example, the current performance report seems to place too much emphasis on financial results, rather than encouraging analysis of the underlying operations and activities in the business. Moreover, because the report shows quarterly revenue figures, this might lead to a focus on quarterly growth. However, the seasonal nature of the business means there is little value in such a comparison. In fact it could be counter-productive; a decline in quarterly revenue may prompt managers to try to introduce new strategies to reverse the perceived decline, when such a change is not required. In this respect, a more useful measurement would be to compare revenue against the equivalent quarter in the previous year.

Conflicts between owners – John is rightly worried about the air of tension which now exists in the owners' meetings. Therefore, it is important that the owners choose carefully what aspects of performance to measure. If, for example, there is an increased focus on food wastage but not on customer service this could increase the tension between Bert and Sheila, because it could give the impression that kitchen operations are more important than the public areas. Consequently, the quote could serve as a reminder that Metis needs a balanced set of measures from across all three elements of the business, because ultimately they are all important to its continuing success.

Appendix:

Workings

	20X0 $	20X1 $	20X2 $	
Profit				
PBIT	31,200	199,579	262,322	
Interest ($350,000 @ 8.4%)	29,400	29,400	29,400	
PBT	1,800	170,179	232,922	
Tax (@ 30%)	540	51,054	69,877	
Profit after tax	**1,260**	**119,125**	**163,045**	
Cashflows & NPV				
PBIT	31,200	199,579	262,322	
Tax on operating cash flows (@ 30%)	9,360	59,874	78,697	
Depreciation (added back)	120,000	120,000	120,000	
Free cashflows	141,840	259,705	303,625	
NPV				
Initial investment	-600,000			-600,000
Present value of cashflows	126,080	205,199	213,246	544,525
(Discount factor 12.5%)				
Net Present Value				**-55,475**
MIRR				
Initial outlfow	-600,000			**-600,000**
Returns				
Cashflows	141,840	259,705	303,625	
Factor (Deposit account rate 4.5%)	$(1.045)^2$	1.045	1	
	154,893	271,392	303,625	**729,910**
MIRR =	$(-729,910/-600,000)^{1/(4-1)} - 1$			0.0675
MIRR				**6.75%**

		20X2 $
EVA		
NOPAT		
Operating Profit (PBIT)		262,322
Tax on operating profit		78,697
NOPAT		183,625
Capital employed	600,000	
WACC	12.5%	
		75,000
EVA		**108,625**
ROCE		
PBIT	262,333	
Capital employed	600,000	
		43.72%
Return on Equity		
PAT	163,045	
Equity invested	250,000	
		65.22%

Notes and assumptions re EVA and NOPAT:

Economic depreciation has been assumed to be the same as accounting depreciation so no adjustment required.

Since marketing spending is for short-term promotional offers only it has not been treated as capital and added back to profit in the EVA calculation. As it relates to short-term promotions only, it seems more prudent to retain marketing spending as a cost to the period.

(d)   **Strategic and operational issues**

The contrast between short-term and long-term performance could be seen as an illustration of the contrast between strategic and operational level performance in an organisation. For example, the focus for the kitchen staff or waiting staff is most likely to be on short-term operational issues which affect the number and quality of the meals they can prepare and serve to customers, and therefore their ability to meet short-term customer demands.

Strategic issues – However, alongside this, the owners should also be considering the more strategic issues which the business is facing. The owners have identified their aim as being to 'make money' but given that competition in the restaurant business in Urbanton is fierce, it would seem sensible for them to have an overall strategy for Metis; for example, to define how Metis might be able to distinguish itself from the competitors in the long term.

At the moment, Metis does not have any particularly culinary style (serving popular dishes regardless of style), and it prices its dishes in the middle of the range. So the owners might decide that the quality of service or the ambience within its restaurants is what will distinguish Metis from its competitors. However, this strategic decision will then have an impact on operational decisions, because, for example, if customer service becomes a key success factor for the business, it will be vital that the waiting staff provide Metis' customers with excellent service on a day-to-day basis.

Performance hierarchy – In this way, Metis could establish a performance hierarchy throughout the organisation. For example, if part of its overall mission is to provide excellent customer service, then the individual staff can also be set personal targets and goals which focus on the levels of customer service they provide, including – for example – smiling at customers.

Targets – One of the challenges which Metis will face is linking its strategy to its day-to-day operations. For example, if the owners decide to refine their aim to simply 'make money' into a more specific target to grow the business by a certain percentage each year, or to open a number of new restaurants over a given period of time, they will need to consider what practical steps need to be taken to generate this growth. Equally, setting targets in this way will provide the owners with a means of measuring how well the business is performing (for example, in relation to the level of profit it is generating, or in relation to the number of customers eating in the restaurant as a percentage of capacity.)

Trade-offs between long-term and short-term

Tension – The tension between Bert and Sheila also highlights the tension and conflict which businesses can face between long- and short-term priorities. Bert's opposition to the proposed building upgrade seems to be driven by a desire to reduce expenditure, or to maximise Metis' profits in the short term.

Short-term cost saving – Metis' net margin is forecast to fall to 8.6% in 20X3. However, if the $150,000 forecast for building upgrades was not spent, the forecast net margin for 20X3 would be 17.5%. This appears to be the logic of Bert's argument against doing the building upgrade work.

Longer term consequences – However, as Sheila has pointed out, this appears to only look at the short term rather than the potential longer term consequences of not doing the upgrade work. The restaurant needs to be refurbished in order maintain its atmosphere.

Consequently there is a risk that if Metis does not refurbish the restaurant customer may choose to eat at one of its competitors' instead, with a better atmosphere. This issue could be particularly important if the atmosphere and ambience of the restaurant is one of the key factors which Metis currently uses to differentiate itself from its competitors.

In this respect, the Bert's suggestion to try to reduce expenditure in the short term, could end up being counter-productive in the longer-term, as revenues and profits will fall if customers stop eating at Metis. In turn, this would also jeopardise the idea of expanding Metis into a restaurant chain, because this expansion is dependent on the first restaurant being successful.

Choice of performance measures

This relationship between short-term and longer-term objectives also has significant implications for the way Metis should **measure performance** and the performance measures it uses.

What gets measured, gets done – In this respect, the idea that 'What gets measured, gets done' is again important. For example, if ROCE is selected one of Metis' key financial performance measures, the owners are likely to want to maximise its ROCE.

However, one of the disadvantages of measures such as ROCE is that they can lead to too much focus on short-term performance. For example, ROCE can discourage capital investment – because it will increase capital employed and so potentially the ROCE figure generated in the following period, even if the operating profit figure remains unchanged.

Nonetheless, Metis must not overlook short-term aspects of performance. For example, it is important that it continues to have sufficient liquidity to meet its short term liabilities and obligations as they fall due. Nonetheless, its forecast performance suggests there shouldn't be any problem in this respect.

Question 2

Text reference. Quality issues and Japanese business practices and management accounting techniques such as kaizen costing and JIT are discussed in Chapter 13 of the BPP P5 Study Text.

Top tips.

Part (a). A common theme across a number of areas of performance management is: 'What gets measured, gets done.' And this theme is relevant here too. If Tench starts focusing on quality and quality costs, this should help it increase the quality of its cars.

However, before you start discussing the impact of quality costs in this way, it would be sensible to explain what quality costs are. The analysis of costs into 'prevention', 'appraisal', 'internal failure' and 'external failure' costs could be a useful way of thinking about the range of quality costs which could affect Tench.

Whereas part (a) asks you to discuss aspects of Tench's current costing system, parts (b) and (c) focus on its planned new systems. In effect, then this question as a whole is highlighting the contrast between traditional views of quality costs (part a) and the Japanese approaches based around the ideas of continuous improvement (kaizen) and just in time.

Part (b) picks up on this point specifically, and a key point to note here is the distinction between cost reduction (in kaizen costing) and cost control (in traditional approaches). However, note that there are two sub-requirements to this part of the question: the impact of Kaizen costing on: (i) Tench's costing systems, and (ii) employee management.

Part (c) then considers the related issue of moving to a JIT system. Note that you are asked to 'evaluate' the effect, so you need to consider the advantages and disadvantages of doing so. In this respect, it is important you appreciate the context in which Tench currently operates. It is based on a former communist state and still seems to have a very bureaucratic culture; how suitable is such a context for introducing JIT systems?

Part (d) then considers the related issue of TQM. This should have been a straightforward part of the question. However, time management is important here to make sure you get time to gain these easy marks.

Importantly, to score well in all four parts of this question, you need to answer the question set. Answers which simply **describe** quality costs, Kaizen costing, TQM and JIT systems in general terms will earn very few marks.

Marking scheme

		Marks
(a)	Impact of quality costs – 1 mark for each relevant point made, Up to 4 marks. Use of quality costs and explanation of traditional view of quality costs – 1 mark for each relevant point made, Up to 3 marks. Maximum of 6 marks	6
(b)	Description of Kaizen costing – Up to 4 marks Comparison of standard costing with Kaizen costing – 1 mark for each relevant point, Up to 3 marks Effect of Kaizen costing on employee management – 1 mark for each relevant point, Up to 3 marks Maximum of 8 marks	8

(c) Description of JIT purchasing and production – Up to 2 marks
Benefits of JIT for Tench – 1 mark for each relevant point, Up to 2 marks
Problems of introducing JIT at Tench – 1 mark for each relevant point, Up
to 3 marks.

Maximum of 6 marks   6

(d) Explanation of importance of TQM – up to 2 marks for each relevant and
fully explained point, up to 5 marks.   5

Total = 25

(a) **Quality costs hidden** – It is likely that Tench's quality costs are currently hidden within overheads and the standard costing system. Tench's quality costs are likely to relate to designing and developing quality control equipment; inspection and performance testing; and repairs and reworking. The current costing system will need to be modified to allow Tench to view its quality costs separately.

The quality costs can be categorised into two groups:

Costs of conformance – These are the costs of achieving the desired quality standards.

They will include **prevention costs** (such as staff training and building quality into the design of the cars and Tench's business processes) aimed at preventing cars being rejected on the grounds of poor quality.

They will also include **appraisal costs** such as the costs of inspecting components coming in from suppliers, and inspecting the cars while they are being built and once they are completed.

Costs of non-conformance – These are the costs which arise if Tench's cars do not meet the required quality standards. They will include internal failure costs and external failure costs.

Internal failure costs arise if a fault is identified before a car leaves the factory and has to be rectified. **External failure costs** arise if the fault is identified by the customer once they have bought the car. External failure costs could include both the cost of repairing cars returned from customers, and the administration costs of maintaining a customer complaints department.

Opportunity costs

There could also be opportunity costs related to quality which are not currently recognised by Tench. For example, the loss of possible future sales resulting from dissatisfied customers, or the impact on the manufacturing process of having to repair faults rather than working on new cars.

Impact of quality on Tench's costing systems

Tench's management appear to have already recognised the need to focus more on the quality of their cars in order to compete with the new (foreign) entrants into the market.

However, identifying and collecting quality costs will reinforce the importance of quality, and will sustain management's focus on quality. In addition, applying the logic that 'What gets measured, gets done' the focus on quality should allow Tench to make the quality improvements they need to compete more effectively with the new imports.

Traditional view of quality

The discussion of costs of conformance and non-conformance represents the traditional view of quality which suggests that there is any optimal effort that minimises quality faults, although it never entirely eliminates them. This approach recognises that there is a trade-off between the costs of conformance and non-conformance, up to a point where the cost of reducing the error rate any further is greater than the benefit from preventing that additional fault.

(b) **Kaizen costing** – In contrast to traditional costing systems which focus on **cost control**, Kaizen costing systems focus on **cost reduction**.

Kaizen costing involves a process of **continuous improvement** in which the costs of producing a product are constantly reduced over the product's life.

Functional analysis is applied at the design stage of a new product, and a **target cost for each function** is set. The functional target costs are added together and the total becomes the **product target cost**.

Once the product has been in production for a year, the actual cost of the first year becomes the starting point for further cost reduction in the second year, and so on into subsequent years.

Impact of Kaizen approach at Tench

Kaizen costing vs Standard costing – Tench currently applies standard costing system, where the focus is on **cost control** rather than **cost reduction**.

However, because Kaizen focuses on continuous improvement and cost reduction, standard costs have much less value for monitoring performance as they are fixed over the relevant period. However, the nature of kaizen costing means that the 'standard' costs themselves should be reduced over time.

Therefore, the impact of introducing Kaizen costing at Tench is likely to be significant. Whereas standard costing doesn't provide any motivation to improve performance levels, the whole focus of kaizen costing is on cost reduction and performance improvement.

Employee management

Attitude to employees – Kaizen costing will also have a significant impact on employee management at Tench, because the **management attitude to employees** will be different under Kaizen compared to a standard costing approach.

In standard costing systems, employees are often viewed as the **cause of problems** in an organisation. Under Kaizen, employees are viewed as the **source of solutions**, and they are **empowered** to find, and implement, these solutions.

Culture change – This idea of employee empowerment indicates the way that changing the costing system will also lead to a major **cultural change** at Tench. Tench appears to have a history of bureaucratic control, but now employee teams will be empowered to make changes themselves rather than having to have them approved by a management hierarchy first.

Implementing Kaizen – In time, the Kaizen system should increase staff motivation through empowerment. However, in the shorter term there could be difficulties in encouraging workers who are used to a command and control structure to change their behaviour and suggest possible improvements themselves.

(c) **Demand-pull system** – The essence of Just-in-time (JIT) systems is that they are demand-pull systems, rather than supply-push ones. Materials are only purchased (JIT purchasing), and finished products are only produced (JIT production) as needed to meet actual customer demand.

This is in contrast to traditional manufacturing systems in which manufacturers forecast demand for their products in the future and then try to smooth out production to meet that forecast demand.

Effect on Tench

Benefits of JIT systems – However, one of the main characteristics of traditional manufacturing systems is that they lead to high levels of inventory being held. By contrast, by only producing goods as they are needed, JIT systems significantly reduce **inventory levels, factory floor space required** and **reduce working capital requirements**, all of which could be beneficial to Tench.

Moving to a JIT system should also make Tench's **production processes more flexible** and should **reduce** throughput times, leading to faster response times to changes in product specification or customer demands.

Potential drawbacks of JIT systems

Supplier reliability – In order to implement JIT successfully, Tench will need to be able to rely on its supplier. With no inventories to fall back on, any disruption in supplies (in relation to either the quality or timeliness of deliveries) could force production to cease, which is likely to be costly for Tench.

If there is not already a **JIT culture** in Essland, it may be difficult for Tench to find **suppliers** who are capable of meeting the required **quality and delivery standards** needed to run a JIT system.

Performance measures

Quality measures/supplier performance – The increased importance of quality and reliability which are necessary in JIT systems, mean that Tench's performance measures will need to include quality measures, and will need to monitor supplier performance in delivering the quality required.

Multi-skilled teams – Another feature of JIT production is that teams are multi-skilled. Teams need to be formed to work by component or product rather than by the type of work performed. This means that **functional divisions of cost** become less appropriate. By contrast, performance measures focusing on **spare capacity** or **bottlenecks** in production are likely to become more important. Also, as staff will need training to work in the new teams, measures surrounding the **amount and effectiveness of training** will be required.

(d)　**Just-in-time (JIT) systems incorporate:**

(i)　**JIT production**, which is a system driven by demand for finished products so that work in progress is only processed through a stage of production when it is needed by the next stage. The result is **minimal** (or in some cases non-existent) **inventories of work in progress and finished goods.**

(ii)　**JIT purchasing**, which seeks to match the usage of materials with the delivery of materials from external suppliers. This means that **material inventories** can be kept at **near-zero levels.**

Production management within a JIT environment therefore needs to **eliminate scrap and defective units** during production and **avoid the need for reworking of units**. Defects stop the **production line**, creating **rework** and possibly resulting in a **failure to meet delivery dates** (as **buffer inventories** of work in progress and finished goods are **not held**). TQM should ensure that the **correct product** is made to the **appropriate level of quality** on the **first pass through production**.

For JIT purchasing to be successful, the organisation must have confidence that the **supplier** will **deliver on time** and will deliver **materials of 100% quality**, that there will be no rejects, returns and hence **no consequent production delays**. This confidence can be achieved by **adopting supplier quality assurance schemes** and stringent **procedures for acceptance and inspection of goods inwards**, which are integral parts of TQM.

Question 3

Text reference. Performance management issues in relation to joint ventures are discussed in Chapter 16 of the BPP P5 Study Text.

Top tips. A key issues in managing performance in joint ventures is establishing what the goals of the joint venture are – because the joint venture partners may have different goals for the venture. This idea of the differences between goals and objectives of venture partners is at the heart of this question.

In order to evaluate the compatibility of the venture partners [part (a)] you need to think about what each partners hopes to get out of the venture, but equally what each partner is bringing to it. For example, are their skills complementary?

The scenario has identified that there is disagreement among the venture partners about the most important aspects of its performance to measure. These disagreements will make it difficult to decide what performance targets to set for the venture (part (b)).

Similarly, the partners' different focus may mean that they have different opinions about how well the venture is performing (part (c)). Although the venture is profitable, there appear to be concerns about its liquidity and gearing. This suggests HTB are likely to be more concerned about its performance that LC (whose primary focus seems to be on profit).

Marking scheme

	Marks

(a) 1 mark per relevant point about the compatibility of the venture partners –
up to a maximum of 8

Relevant points could relate to:

Competences of the partners

Goals and cultures

Ownership and size (public vs private company)

Strategic interests in the venture

Total: up to 8

       8

(b) Assessment of the difficulties in identifying and agreeing key performance targets - 1 mark per point – up to a maximum of 5

Assessment of the difficulties in monitoring performance – 1 mark per relevant point – Up to a maximum of 6.

Total: up to 9

       9

(c) Evaluation of sales and profit growth – 1 mark per relevant point – up to 3 marks

Evaluation of liquidity and gearing – 1 mark per relevant point – up to 6 marks

Total: up to 8

       8

Total = 25

(a) **Fit between competences** – HTB appears to have the specialist technological skills which are required for the venture to be successful, while LC brings marketing skills and access to customers. In this respect, the partners' competences appear to complement each other well, although the scenario doesn't indicate how successful each company is in its own field.

Goals and cultures – Although the partners' competences appear to complement each other well, it is less clear how well the partners' goals and cultures are aligned. As a **publicly listed company**, LC is likely to be concerned about delivering value and growth to its shareholders. HTB as a smaller, **family-owned company** may have different expectations and pressures.

Equally, there may be differences in the cultures and attitudes among the staff and management from the venture partners which could diminish how well they work together, if they need to. (It is not clear from the scenario how far the staff will need to work together, given their differing areas of expertise. In practice, there may not be much overlap at an operational level.)

Size – The discrepancy in size between the venture partners may also be a cause for concern. Although the partners have equal shares in the venture (50% each) it is not clear whether they view each other as equal partners. Over time, LC may try to exert itself as the dominant partner, due to its larger size, and in time if the JV proves successful **LC make seek to buy out HTB's interest in it**.

Strategic interests – Although the scenario indicates that LC views the JV as an opportunity to bolster its presence in an area of online gaming where it currently seems to be weak, it is less clear what HTB's strategic interest is in the JV. For the JV to be a success, it will be important that the venture partners ensure that their strategic and financial interests are aligned.

(b) **Establishing financial objectives** – It appears that the partners have different financial objectives for the joint venture, which are, to some extent, incompatible with each other.

Establishing key performance metrics – This difference in objectives is also likely to mean that the partners will be looking at different key financial indicators; with LC focusing on aspects of profitability and growth, while HTB focuses more on liquidity and gearing. Establishing a dividend policy also seems to be an area of potential conflict; with LC wanting to make a dividend payment as a sign of the business' success, but HTB wanting to retain the JV's profits within the business.

Non-financial objectives – The principal objective of the JV is likely to be to achieve a financial return on investment, but there could also be subsidiary non-financial objectives and non-financial performance targets that the partners consider necessary. These may be expressed in the form of a **balanced scorecard** of targets. A problem with multiple targets and non-financial targets in a joint venture, however, is that the JV partners may have different ideas about what these targets should be. If the partners cannot agree on financial targets, they may have even more difficulty in agreeing on non-financial targets.

For example, it is likely that the quality and reliability of the software will be important factors in ensuring that it is accepted by customers and enabling LC to gain market share in the way it wants to. However, there is no indication in the scenario about how any quality or customer satisfaction scores will be agreed or monitored.

Inter-company charges and transfer pricing may also cause difficulties because of the profit margins for each JV partner within the prices that they charge to the JV. Each JV partner may be concerned with their combined profits from the joint venture's operations and the products or services that it provides to the JV. LC may therefore include fees for technical support and accountancy services within its targets, and HTB may include the profits from software support in its targets. If this is the case, the JV partners will have differing financial targets, and there may well be a lack of trust arising from these differences.

Management information systems – Problems for HTB with monitoring performance may also arise if the management information system is under the control of LC, and LC is not providing all the information that HTB would consider useful. (LC provides the accounting services for the JV and so presumably provides the financial information for management.)

This could be an issue for non-financial measures of performance (for example, monitoring the number or severity of software problems or quality issues) as well as obtaining financial performance information.

(c) **Sales and profit growth** – The joint venture has been profitable from Year 1, and it is forecast to show increases in revenue and profits until the end of Year 4. The net profit margin (profit before tax) is also expected to increase from 11% (Year 2) to 16% (in Years 3 and 4).

This growth in sales and profits will be seen as positive by LC. From HTB's perspective, this growth in sales and profits is also likely to be seen as positive. However, they will be concerned about the gearing and cash flow. In particular, gearing is forecast to increase significantly: from 45% at the end of Year 2, to 123% at the end of Year 4.

Concerns about gearing – This high level of gearing is a particular concern given the JV's intention to use bank loans to continue its expansion, because there is no guarantee a bank would be willing to lend it the amounts required or that the JV will have sufficient assets to offer as security.

Cash flow and liquidity – The JV's cash flow and liquidity may also be cause for concern. Although the business is profitable, it has a negative cash flow for three of its four years. It is possible that the business is generating cash from its operating activities, but this is then being reinvested in growth (through increases in working capital and new spending on non-current assets). This suggests that HTB's caution over the speed of growth is justified, because the business not be sustainable in the longer term if it is grown too quickly in the short term. This position also appears to justify HTB's concern about paying a dividend in Years 3 and 4.

Performance targets – The figures suggest that the JV could have problems in the future with its gearing and its cash flows and liquidity. It would therefore seem appropriate for the management of the JV to recognise these risks and to set performance targets for both gearing and operational cash flows. These should be combined with targets for profits and sales growth, but all the targets need to be consistent with each other. If the projected sales growth cannot be achieved without excessive gearing or liquidity risk, the JV partners should consider either reducing planned growth and investment, or injecting additional equity into the business.

Question 4

Top tips.

Part (a) (i). Berry, Broadbent & Otley provided a list of eight possible problems accompanying the use of performance measures (see Chapter 12 of the Study Text for the full list). You have only been asked to provide three here.

Although this part of the question doesn't specifically require you to link your answer to the scenario, thinking about these potential problems should help you identify some of the potential issues relating to the school league tables – which in turn should help you answer part (a) (ii) of the question. Note that you are asked to 'explain' the problems rather than simply to 'list' them, so you may find it helps to explain the problem by illustrating it with reference to the scenario – even though you do not have to.

In Part (a), you are asked to 'Evaluate the appropriateness...' In other words, how or why might it be beneficial to use league tables to measure school performance; and how / why might it be disadvantageous to do so?

Part (b). The logic behind this requirement is that instead of using a single measure (exam results) to monitor performance, schools should look at a 'balanced scorecard' of ratings. The idea of the balanced scorecard is a useful one here because it identifies the need to consider the customer perspective (students' views/student satisfaction) and the financial performance (financial health/financial management).

Part (c). Although there is no requirement to use any specific model here, the reference to 'standards' in the question, and the fact that a school is a service business, means that the 'standards' from the building block model (ownership, achievability, fairness) could be useful here. This is the framework we have used in our answer below.

Marking scheme

		Marks
(a)(i)	Up to 2 marks for each problem evaluated (for a maximum of three possible problems). Total: up to 6	6
(ii)	1 mark per relevant point explaining the benefits of using the league tables for monitoring the schools' performance – up to 2 marks 1 mark per relevant point explaining the limitations or disadvantages of using the league tables – up to 6 marks Total: up to 8	8
(b)	For identifying an appropriate indicator – 1 mark each – for a maximum of 2 indicators For reasons explaining why each indicator recommended would be appropriate or beneficial to use – up to 2 marks per indicator. Total: up to 6	6
(c)	Up to 3 marks per relevant factor; discussed in the context of the scenario; for a maximum of three factors. (Possible factors could include: ownership; achievability; and equity) approaches Total: up to 5	5
		Total = 25

(a) (i) **Tunnel vision** – Once staff or organisations know that performance in certain areas is being measured, there is a danger that there will be an undue focus on those performance measures to the detriment of other areas. This can be seen as illustrating the idea that 'what gets measured, gets done.' For example, if exam results in a school are seen as the only important measure and clubs or sports activities are not important, there is a danger that no resources will be given to the clubs or sports activities.

> **Sub-optimisation** – This problem is linked to the idea of tunnel vision. Sub-optimisation means focusing specifically on some objectives means that other objectives are not achieved. So, for example, if a school focuses solely on an objective to optimise exam results, this might mean it overlooks an objective to provide all of its pupils with a certain number of hours sporting activity each week.

Measure fixation – We have already identified that resources and effort are likely to be concentrated on those areas of performance which are being measured. However, this could be a problem for an organisation if the performance measures which have been selected are poorly designed. For example, if a school has an objective to reduce costs, this may lead to it employing fewer teachers, or less experienced teachers. However, whilst these actions may reduce costs, they could also reduce the quality of tuition pupils receive, which in turn could lead to a fall in the exam grades pupils achieve (which is clearly not a desirable outcome from the objective to reduce costs).

Gaming (or distortion of results) – This problem arises where a measure is deliberately distorted to secure some strategic advantage.

For example, we could suggest that by focusing disproportionately on pupils who were on the threshold of a Grade C, CAD School is trying to distort its results – favourably – by boosting the percentage of pupils who pass their exams with at least a Grade C. As a result, this may give the impression that CAD's pupils are higher achievers than they actually are, and equally could be misleading for parents and the Government education department alike.

(ii) **Measurable indicator** – Although there is some criticism about whether or not exam performance is the most appropriate metric, exam results do provide a quantifiable indicator which can be used to compare performance between schools. In this respect, it does enable the government to see the extent of the variation in performance, and to identify which schools are performing better than others.

Target selection – However, one of the criticisms of school league tables is that they encourage schools to focus on meeting certain targets at the expense of other important objectives, and this appears to be happening in the scenario.

Although CAD School has come top of the league table based on exam grades, the Inspector's report suggests that this is partly due to the focus on ensuring that marginal students achieve a Grade C in their exams. The implication here is that the desire to perform well in the league table has led to the school concentrating on meeting the target at the expense of other important objectives. This is likely to be an **unintended consequence** of having the league table, but as the Inspector's report identifies, it is also an undesirable consequence.

Value added – The ranking in the league tables is based solely on **academic results**. However, this doesn't reflect the value added by the teachers and support staff in the schools. If the pupils entering CAD school are academically more gifted, on average, than those entering SPO school, then (given the same standard of teaching in both schools) we would expect CAD's exam results to be better than SPO's.

In the scenario, it appears that SPO actually provides more value to its students (for example, through the study support clubs) even though its exam grades are lower than CAD and HI's.

Impact on client behaviour – Although SPO's exam grades are worse than HI's, SPO has been over-subscribed, while HI is operating below capacity. This suggests that parents are not basing their decisions about which school to select for their children on the exam results alone. In this respect,

SPO's grading as 'Excellent' in the Inspector's report could have a greater impact on parents' decisions about which school to select.

Impact on morale – Equally, it does not appear that SPO's relatively low position in the league table has had any detrimental impact on the morale or performance of the school staff. Therefore, even if the benefits of the league table are limited, it does not appear that the table is causing any harm.

(b) **Student satisfaction** – It is important that students have access to as high a quality of education as possible, and that they are satisfied with the education and other services they are receiving from the school. (Areas that could be covered by a student satisfaction survey include: teacher quality; the school environment and infrastructure; technology and learning resources; and personal development).

Students who have a positive view of their school and their tuition are more likely to be motivated to work hard than those who are not satisfied with their school. However, students' perceptions about their school are also valuable because they can give insights into ways that the education could be improved.

Measuring student satisfaction will be useful for the school management to identify its strengths and weaknesses, and to determine areas for improvement.

Financial operating position – Although it is important that the school provides it pupils with as good an education as possible it is also important that it manages its financial resources effectively.

It is likely that the majority of the funding the schools receive will come from the government, and this funding will need to cover the costs of teachers' salaries and the schools daily operations. In this respect, it will be important that the school keeps its expenditure under control, so that it does not exceed the funding it has received.

In this respect, it is important to recognise the extent to which the school's budget is a critical constraint on its other activities (for example, the number of teachers and support staff it can employ, or investments in new information technology.)

(c) The building block model highlights that there are three key elements of performance standards in service businesses: ownership, achievability, and equity.

(i) **Ownership**. One of the most important factors in setting up a system of performance measurement is that those who are being measured must feel that they 'own' the standards that have been established.

People who participate are more likely to feel comfortable with, and committed to, the targets that they have. This will make working relationships much more effective. It will be hard for people to be motivated to achieve targets set by someone else.

(ii) **Achievability**. Performance measures need to be realistic, and balance the need to perform to the best standards against the need to make sure that employees are not discouraged by impossible targets. They must accept their targets and consider them to be attainable. For example, if the school decides to set a target for the % of students who achieve Grades A – C in their final exams, this target must not be too taxing as to make it unattainable.

(iii) **Equity**. Measurement must be fair across all business units. For example, if the school decides to measure the exam performance of different departments, it will need to consider how far these can be fairly compared against each other if the national pass rates for certain subjects are lower than for others.

ACCA Professional Level

Paper P5

Advanced Performance Management

Mock Examination 3 (ACCA September/December 2015 exam)

Question Paper
Time allowed: 3 hours and 15 minutes
This paper is divided into two sections Section A   ONE compulsory questions to be attempted Section B   TWO out of THREE questions to be attempted

DO NOT OPEN THIS PAPER UNTIL YOU ARE READY TO START UNDER EXAMINATION CONDITIONS

SECTION A – This ONE question is compulsory and MUST be attempted

Question 1

Iron Chicken (IC) is a multinational business which manufactures commercial building control systems. Building control systems include heating and air-conditioning systems, lighting controls, power and water monitoring and security systems (eg keypad access, alarms and CCTV). IC's manufacturing takes place at a number of factory sites where some products have a long product life and are simple and mass-produced while other products are complex and have a short product life due to changing technologies. IC's mission statement is 'to create value for shareholders through control products which improve productivity, save energy and increase comfort and safety'.

A new chief executive officer (CEO) has been appointed to address a decline in IC's share price in the last three years. This CEO has identified that the business has grown through acquisition and as a result she stated, 'senior management have focused on making corporate deals and not making control systems.' The CEO has declared that the business must focus on optimising its value generation rather than just getting larger through acquisitions.

You are a performance management expert within IC. The CEO has tasked you with aiding her in aspects of her improvement programme. First, she wants your views on the use of EVA™ as the key performance metric at IC. You have been supplied with the current EVA™ calculation (Appendix 1) but there is some doubt about whether the junior management accountant who has done this work was sufficiently trained in the method. So, the CEO needs you to evaluate its accuracy and the assumptions which form part of the calculation.

Second, the CEO believes that the poor performance of the company can be addressed by ensuring that the mission statement flows down into the performance management of the business. To that end, the following critical success factors (CSFs) have been identified and the CEO wants you to suggest additional key performance indicators (KPIs) for these.

CSF	Associated current KPI
1. Greater staff productivity	Units produced per labour hour
2. Reduction of wastage in production	Power consumed per unit produced
3. Greater innovation of products	Number of new products launched

Your suggestions should be in addition to these current KPIs.

Third, in order to improve performance, the CEO plans to implement initiatives associated with 'lean' manufacturing.

Specifically, there are three projects which have been suggested and the CEO needs your advice on these:

1. Move to just-in-time manufacturing
2. Use kaizen costing
3. Examine the costs of quality in achieving a 'zero defects' approach to manufacturing

The CEO has stated, 'I need to know briefly how the improvement projects will meet the three CSFs and also how they will impact on the existing three KPIs.'

Finally, the CEO requested, 'You must tell me the implications of the improvement projects for our information systems as I feel that they are not currently suitable for the plan that I have.' The current information systems of the company are based around the functional departments of the business such as manufacturing, marketing, finance and logistics. Each department has developed its own system although all feed into the finance system which is the main one used for strategic decision-making. In order that the department systems can all feed through to the current finance system, these current systems only handle quantitative data. The company is considering the implementation of a new information system. This new system will introduce networking technology in order to bring together all of the departmental systems into a new, single, corporate database.

Required:

Write a report to the CEO of Iron Chicken to:

(i)   Evaluate the accuracy of the EVA™ calculation and the assumptions in Appendix 1. Advise the CEO on your results, providing calculations as needed.   **(15 marks)**

(ii)   For each of the three critical success factors at IC, briefly explain a weakness of the current KPI associated with that CSF and then provide a justified alternative KPI.   **(6 marks)**

(iii)   Explain what the three improvement projects are, how they will help to meet the CSFs at IC and comment on the impact of each project on the existing three KPIs.   **(15 marks)**

(iv)   Assess the impact of the proposed, new information system on the three improvement projects.

(10 marks)

Professional marks will be awarded for the format, style and structure of the discussion of your answer.

(4 marks)

(50 marks)

Appendix 1

Economic value added

	Year ended 30 June 2015	
	$m	Note
Operating profit	551.4	
Add back		
Non-cash expenses	15.1	
Marketing capitalised	23.1	5
Operating lease expenses	40.0	
Less		
Tax	134.8	6
Lost tax relief on interest	24.5	7
Net operating profit after tax (NOPAT)	470.3	
Capital employed		
From the statement of financial position	2,401.0	10
Marketing spend capitalised	23.1	5
Operating leases	115.0	8
Adjusted capital employed	2,539.1	

$WACC = (1/2 \times 16\%) + (1/2 \times 6.8\%) = 11.4\%$

$EVA™ = NOPAT - (WACC \times Capital\ employed) = 181$

Assumptions and notes:

1   Debt/Equity   100.0%

2   Cost of equity   16.0%

3   Tax rate   30.0%

4   Cost of debt (pre-tax)   6.8%

5   There has been $23.1m of marketing spent each year for the last two years in order to build the brand of IC long term.

6   Tax paid in the year was $130m while the tax charged per the accounts was $134.8m.

7   Interest charged in the period was $81.6m.
      Lost tax relief on this interest was 30% × $81.6m.

8   The operating leases have an average life of four years.

9   The only research and development spending identified in the last five years was $10m expensed during this year on a new product.

The product has not been launched yet.

10 Capital employed during the period (from the statement of financial position):

Opening	2,282.0
Change in period	119.0
Closing	2,401.0

Section B – TWO questions from the three given must be attempted

Question 2

Perkin manufactures electronic components for export worldwide, from factories in Ceeland, for use in smartphones and hand held gaming devices. These two markets are supplied with similar components by two divisions, Phones Division (P) and Gaming Division (G). Each division has its own selling, purchasing, IT and research and development functions, but separate IT systems. Some manufacturing facilities, however, are shared between the two divisions.

Perkin's corporate objective is to maximise shareholder wealth through innovation and continuous technological improvement in its products. The manufacturers of smartphones and gaming devices, who use Perkin's components, update their products frequently and constantly compete with each other to launch models which are technically superior.

Perkin has a well-established incremental budgeting process. Divisional managers forecast sales volumes and costs months in advance of the budget year. These divisional budgets are then scrutinised by the main board, and revised significantly by them in line with targets they have set for the business. The finalised budgets are often approved after the start of the accounting year. Under pressure to deliver consistent returns to institutional shareholders, the board does not tolerate failure by either division to achieve the planned net profit for the year once the budget is approved. Last year's results were poor compared to the annual budget. Divisional managers, who are appraised on the financial performance of their own division, have complained about the length of time that the budgeting process takes and that the performance of their divisions could have been better but was constrained by the budgets which were set for them.

In P Division, managers had failed to anticipate the high popularity of a new smartphone model incorporating a large screen designed for playing games, and had not made the necessary technical modifications to the division's own components. This was due to the high costs of doing so, which had not been budgeted for. Based on the original sales forecast, P Division had already committed to manufacturing large quantities of the existing version of the component and so had to heavily discount these in order to achieve the planned sales volumes.

A critical material in the manufacture of Perkin's products is silver, which is a commodity which changes materially in price according to worldwide supply and demand. During the year supplies of silver were reduced significantly for a short period of time and G Division paid high prices to ensure continued supply. Managers of G Division were unaware that P Division held large inventories of silver which they had purchased when the price was much lower.

Initially, G Division accurately forecasted demand for its components based on the previous years' sales volumes plus the historic annual growth rate of 5%. However, overall sales volumes were much lower than budgeted. This was due to a fire at the factory of their main customer, which was then closed for part of the year. Reacting to this news, managers at G Division took action to reduce costs, including closing one of the three R&D facilities in the division.

However, when the customer's factory reopened, G Division was unwilling to recruit extra staff to cope with increased demand; nor would P Division re-allocate shared manufacturing facilities to them, in case demand increased for its own products later in the year. As a result, Perkin lost the prestigious preferred supplier status from their main customer who was unhappy with G Division's failure to effectively respond to the additional demand. The customer had been forced to purchase a more expensive, though technically superior, component from an alternative manufacturer.

The institutional shareholders' representative, recently appointed to the board, has asked you as a performance management expert for your advice. 'We need to know whether Perkin's budgeting process is appropriate for the business, and how this contributed to last year's poor performance.'

However, the shareholder representative did also acknowledge that external factors had contributed to Perkin's poor performance in the last year, and suggested that it would be useful if Perkin's performance reports distinguished between variances which had resulted from its own operational performance as opposed to external circumstances which could not have been anticipated when the budgets were produced. You noted that many organisations address this issue by analysing variances into planning and operational elements.

Required:

(a) Evaluate the weaknesses in Perkin's current budgeting system and whether it is suitable for the environment in which Perkin operates.   **(14 marks)**

(b) Evaluate the extent to which Perkin's poor performance for the last year can be attributed to external factors.   **(6 marks)**

(c) Discuss the potential benefits to Perkin of analysing variances into planning and operational elements.   **(5 marks)**

(Total = 25 marks)

Question 3

Posie is a large business which manufactures furniture. It is made up of two autonomous divisions in Deeland.

The manufacturing division purchases raw materials from external suppliers, and performs all manufacturing and packaging operations. All sales are made through the retail division which has 95 retail stores in Deeland, as well as through Posie's own well-developed website. Posie has retail operations in eight other countries as well as in Deeland. These overseas businesses operate as independent subsidiaries within the Retail Division, each with their own IT and accounting functions.

The furniture is sold in boxes for customers to assemble themselves. About 10% of the products sold by Posie are purchased already packaged from other manufacturers. All deliveries are outsourced through a third party distribution company.

Posie's corporate objective is to maximise shareholder wealth by producing 'attractive, functional furniture at low prices'. This is how customers generally perceive the Posie brand. The CEO of Posie is concerned about increasing levels of returns made by customers and increasing numbers of consumers complaining on online forums about products purchased from Posie.

Concerned about the impact on the Posie brand and the cost-leadership strategy, the CEO has asked you, as a performance management expert, to help Posie implement the six sigma technique to reduce the number of products returned and in particular to define customers' requirements and measure Posie's existing performance. The production director has been appointed to sponsor the project and you will be supported by a small team of managers who have recently received training in six sigma. The board member responsible for manufacturing quality recently resigned because she thought it was unfair that the manufacturing division was being held responsible for the increased level of customer returns.

You have been given access to some information concerning the reasons why customers return goods to help you measure existing performance in this area (Appendix 1). This is an extract from the management reporting pack presented to the board at their monthly meetings. The returns data, however, are only compiled every six months due to the lengthy analysis required of data from Posie's overseas retail operations. It is included twice a year in the board report along with the KPIs for customer satisfaction. The last time this information was produced 93% of customers indicated they were satisfied with the quality of the manufacture of Posie's products.

The CEO has heard that six sigma requires 'large amounts of facts and data'. He suggested that the returns data contain insufficient detail and that as part of your project you may need to do more analysis, for example, on why customers are not satisfied with the manufacturing quality.

He also added, 'I'm not sure that our current IT systems are capable of generating the data we need to identify which responsibility centres within the manufacturing division are the root causes of the problem of customer returns. We are planning to change the designation of the overseas retail businesses from profit centres to revenue centres, but again we need to know first how this will affect the information requirements of the business and any potential problems with doing so.'

Appendix 1

Reasons given by customers for returning goods

Category	Reason for return of goods	% Responses
1	Difficult to assemble or pieces missing	48%
2	Goods arrived damaged	14%
3	Goods were not as described or were defective	25%
4	Goods were of poor quality or no longer wanted	11%
5	Arrived late	2%
Total		100%

Required:

(a) Advise the board how the six sigma project at Posie to reduce returns from customers could be implemented using DMAIC methodology. **(15 marks)**

(b) Evaluate the impact on Posie's information requirements arising from:

    (i)   The need to identify and improve on the level of customer returns. **(6 marks)**

    (ii)   The proposed re-designation of the overseas subsidiaries from profit centres to revenue centres.

(4 marks)

(25 marks)

Question 4

Soup operates passenger rail services in Deeland, a technologically advanced country, with high demand for fast, reliable rail travel from business and leisure passengers. Many passengers choose train travel because they see it as less harmful to the environment than other forms of transport.

Soup's main objective is to maximise shareholder wealth. Since becoming licensed to operate routes in Regions A and B by the Deeland government five years ago, Soup has consistently delivered increased dividends and share prices for investors. In its initial appraisal of the licensing opportunity, Soup expected to operate the routes for at least 15 years, however, their licence may not be renewed when it expires in three years' time. The government has warned Soup it 'is unhappy about high returns to shareholders while there are many reports of poor passenger service, overcrowded trains and unreliable services on certain routes and at busy times'.

Soup owns its fleet of diesel powered trains. Each train in Region A has seven coaches with 70 passenger seats available per coach. In the less busy Region B, each train has six coaches each with 70 seats. As a condition of the licence, Soup runs a set number of services at both busy and quieter times in both regions. Soup has two larger rivals, both operating electric trains, which cause less harm to the environment than diesel powered trains. They run on the same routes in both regions.

The government regulates fares charged to passengers, which are the same per distance travelled for every operator in that region. The railway track, stations and other infrastructure are managed by the government which charges the operators a fee. There are several stations along the route which are only used by Soup trains and others where Soup trains do not stop at all.

Soup's trains are 25 years old, originally purchased cheaply from an operator whose licence was withdrawn by the government. Soup believes the low price it paid is a key competitive advantage enabling them to steadily increase their return on capital employed, the company's main performance measure, to a level well in excess of their rivals. The shareholders are pleased with the growth in passenger numbers over the last five years, which is the other performance measure Soup uses.

Soup's ageing trains spend increasing time undergoing preventative maintenance, safety checks or repairs. A recent television documentary also showed apparently poor conditions on board, such as defective heating and washroom facilities and dirty, torn seating. Passengers complained in the programme of difficulties finding a seat, the unreliability of accessing wireless internet services and even that the menu in the on-board cafe had not changed for five years.

Soup's CEO responded that unreliable internet access arose from the rapid growth in passengers expecting to access the internet on trains. She said Soup had never received any formal complaints about the lack of choice in the on-board cafe, nor had she heard of a recent press report that Soup's trains were badly maintained, so causing harm to the environment.

The CEO has asked you, as chief management accountant, for your advice. 'In view of the government's warning, we must develop performance measures balancing the needs of passengers with the requirements of the shareholders', she has said. 'I don't want to know how to improve the actual performance of the business; that is the job of the operational managers, nor do I just want a list of suggested performance measures. Instead I need to know why these performance measures will help to improve the performance of Soup.'

The following data applies to Soup:

	Region A	Region B
Number of services per day		
Peak times	4	4
Other times	6	8
Number of passengers per day		
Peak times	2,500	1,400
Other times	2,450	1,850

Required:

(a) Advise the CEO on how the use of the balanced scorecard could improve the performance management system of Soup. **(10 marks)**

(b) Using the performance data given, evaluate the comments of the Deeland government that Soup's trains are overcrowded. **(7 marks)**

(c) Assess the problems Soup may encounter in selecting and interpreting performance measures when applying the balanced scorecard to its performance management system. **(8 marks)**

(25 marks)

Answers

DO NOT TURN THIS PAGE UNTIL YOU HAVE
COMPLETED THE MOCK EXAM

Plan of attack

What's the worst thing you could be doing when you enter the exam hall if this were the actual exam paper? Trying to find a pen which works? Wondering how to celebrate the end of the exam in about three and a quarter hours' time? Panicking, and worrying you haven't done enough preparation?

Well, they're all pretty bad. But what you should be doing is spending the first few minutes of the exam looking through the paper in detail, working out which questions to do and the order in which to attempt them. So turn back to the paper and let's sort out a **plan of attack.**

First steps first

As we have already suggested in Mock Exams 1 and 2, in our view, the compulsory Section A question is usually the best place to start, but you may prefer to start by doing your best Section B question first. However, if you do decide to start with a 25 mark Section B question, make sure that you do not spend too long on it, so that you don't subsequently have sufficient time to answer the Section A question properly. Remember, the Section A question accounts for 50% of the marks for the paper so you need to allow yourself enough time to answer it. You cannot pass without answering the Section A question!

Make sure you look through the whole paper and carefully before diving in to answer any questions.

To begin with, look through the paper and the question requirements and work out which questions you are going to do, and the order you are going to attempt them. If you are going to answer the Section A question first, you should then analyse the requirements in detail, before identifying the key issues in the scenario and how they relate to those requirements.

If you are **worried about the paper**, it is likely that you believe the Section A question will be daunting. In this case, you may prefer to do one, or both, of the optional (Section B) questions before tackling it. Don't however, fall into the trap of spending too long on the optional questions because they seem easier. Remember the Section A question accounts for 50% of the marks, so it is critical to your chances of passing this exam.

It is dangerous to be over-confident, but if you're **not too nervous about the exam**, we suggest you should start with the compulsory Section A question. You've got to answer it, so you might as well get it over and done with straight away.

Make sure **you address every requirement and sub-requirement in the question**, and also make sure you apply your answer directly to the scenario. Remember that the basis of the P5 exam is **analysis and application**: you are being tested on your ability to apply your knowledge to analyse and address the specific issues identified in a scenario, or to evaluate the methods being used to manage performance within an organisation.

The questions themselves

Question 1 – The narrative behind this question is that a new CEO has recently been appointed at an organisation with a view to improving its performance. The scenario then describes several aspects of the CEO's improvement programme.

The first part of the question focuses on Economic Value Added (EVA) and the adjustments which need to be made to accounting figures when calculating EVA. Although there are some marks for calculations, the key verbs here are 'evaluate' and 'advise' so it is important you get a balance between the numerical and narrative elements of this requirement.

Part (ii) focuses on the organisation's KPIs, and requires you to identify and explain the weaknesses of the current KPIs before recommending alternatives which overcome those weaknesses.

Part (iii) then looks at three specific initiatives the CEO wants to introduce as part of a move to 'lean' manufacturing at the organisation: JIT; kaizen costing; and zero defects (TQM). The requirement asks for an explanation of what the initiatives are, but then looks more specifically at how they will help the organisation achieve its CSFs, and what impact they could have on its KPIs.

Part (iv) then looks at the link between the 'lean' initiatives and the organisation's information systems. The scenario explains that the organisation is thinking about implementing a new information system, and, in effect, the requirement asks how the new information could help to support the three 'lean' initiatives.

Question 2 – The scenario focuses on a company which manufactures electronic components, but which has performed poorly in the last year. The scenario provides details of the company's budgeting process, and also identifies a number of factors which have contributed to its poor performance during the year. The closing paragraphs of the scenario raise the suggestion of whether the budgeting system has contributed to the poor performance. The final sentence also raises the idea of analysing variances into planning and operational elements.

Part (a) of the requirement focuses on the weaknesses in the company's budgeting system, and its suitability for the environment in which the company operates.

Part (b) then looks at the extent to which the company's poor performance can be attributed to external factors – as opposed to the company's own internal weaknesses.

Part (c) then looks at a possible suggestion to improve the company's budgeting and control system, by analysing variances into planning and operational elements.

Question 3 – The scenario focuses on a furniture manufacturing company, which is concerned by the number of products being returned by customers. The scenario highlights that the company is looking to implement a six sigma project in order to reduce the level of customer returns. However, the scenario also highlights that the data currently available is not sufficiently detailed to understand which divisions are responsible for the high level of returns.

Part (a) of the requirement focuses on the DMAIC methodology of six sigma, and how this methodology could be used to implement the project.

Part (b) (i) then looks at how the performance information the company produces will need to change in order to provide the information management needs to tackle the problem of customer returns.

Part (b) (ii) also focuses on performance requirements in the organisation, but looks at the impact that re-designating profit centres to revenue centres could have on the reports.

Question 4 considers the potential benefits and problems of introducing the balanced scorecard as a performance management system at a company which operates passenger rail services.

The scenario highlights that the primary focus of the company's current performance management system is on financial performance, and aspects of non-financial performance are suffering as a result of this. Part (a) of the requirement then asks how introducing the balanced scorecard could improve the company's performance management system.

By contrast, part (c) looks at the potential problems the company could face when selecting and interpreting the performance measures to be included in the scorecard.

In between those two parts, part (b) focuses on one particular aspect of the company's performance – occupancy rates, in order to evaluate a suggestion that the company's trains are overcrowded.

Once, once more

You must **allocate your time** according to the marks for the question in total, and for the parts of the questions. And you must also **follow the question requirements exactly**.

It's easy to waffle on this exam if you don't follow the requirements strictly. If you answer contains irrelevant material, you will not be scoring marks efficiently, and you will put yourself under increased **time pressure**.

All finished and quarter of an hour to go?

Your time allocation must have been faulty. However, make the most of any time you have left at the end of the exam. Go back to **any parts of questions that you didn't finish** because you ran out of time. Always write something rather than nothing if you possibly can, and try not to leave questions unanswered.

If you write nothing, then, by definition, you cannot score any marks. Even if you write a couple of points in answer to a requirement, you could earn some marks for these – which ultimately could be the difference between passing and failing the exam.

Forget about it!

Don't worry if you found the paper difficult. It is more than likely that other students did too. However, once you've finished the exam you cannot change your answers so don't spend time worrying about them. Instead, you should start thinking about your next exam and preparing for that. Or, if this is your last exam, forget about it for now.

Question 1

Text references. Economic Value Added – including the adjustments to accounting profit required to calculate it – are discussed in Chapter 9 of the BPP Study Text. CSFs and KPIs are discussed in Chapter 2. Lean systems and enterprise resource planning systems (ERPSs) are discussed in Chapter 7. Just-in-time, kaizen costing, and costs of quality are discussed in Chapter 13.

Top tips.

Part (i). The third paragraph of the scenario (which highlights the doubts over the junior management accountant's ability to calculate EVA™) should have alerted you to the likelihood that some of the figures in the calculation would be wrong. However, it doesn't mean that all of them as necessarily wrong.

As such, a sensible approach to this question would be to work through the calculation methodically (line by line) identifying whether each of the current figures is correct or not. Where a figure is incorrect, you then need to adjust the calculation accordingly. In addition – applying your knowledge of the adjustments to operating profit required when calculating NOPAT – you need to consider if there are any figures which have been (incorrectly) omitted completely.

However, note that the requirement asks you to 'evaluate the accuracy...' and to 'advise the CEO on your results...' as well as providing updated calculations. As the marking guide indicates, a maximum of 8 out of the 15 marks for this requirement are available for calculations, so the written element of this answer is equally important as the calculations.

And remember, that you are advising the CEO. So, as well as commenting on in individual items in the calculation, it would also be appropriate to consider the implications of the adjustments as a whole – for example, do they mean IC is performing better or worse than first suggested by the junior management accountant's figures?

Part (ii). The wording of the requirement – to explain 'a weakness' and to provide 'a justified alternative' – means that there are a number of possible answers to it. You may have recommended different alternatives to the ones suggested in the solution below, but provided they are relevant (ie they help to measure performance against the CSF) and you have justified your recommendation you would earn the mark available. Nonetheless, to score the mark it is important that you recommend a KPI (ie something that could be measured), not an alternative CSF.

Importantly, you should not spend too long on this part of the question though, as there are six marks available for it. Given that there are three CSFs, this means there are only two marks for each CSF: one for explaining a weakness of the current KPI associated with it, and one for providing a justified alternative KPI. The instruction in the question to 'briefly explain' is important – you shouldn't waste time giving a detailed explanation, particularly as there is only one mark available per weakness.

Part (iii). The short paragraph in the scenario above the three projects – with its reference to 'lean' manufacturing – provides some useful context for this requirement. In effect, the three projects are ways of (hopefully) making IC's manufacturing 'leaner'.

As the three projects are clearly identified separately, a useful way of tackling the requirement would be to address each project in turn. Then for each project you need to do three things:

– Explain what the project is (ie what are, respectively, just-in-time manufacturing, kaizen costing; and costs of quality/total quality manufacturing ('zero defects'))

– Explain how the project will help to achieve IC's CSFs. (Again the reference to 'lean' in the introductory paragraph here could provide a useful pointer here, since eliminating waste (CSF number 2) is one of the key aims of 'lean')

– Explain what impact the project will have on the KPIs. (**Note.** Your focus here should be on the levels of performance as measured by the indicators; not on the choice of indicators.)

Note, that for the second of the three parts you need to explain 'how' the project will help, whereas in the third you have to explain 'what' the impact will be. The distinction is important, because in some cases – eg in relation to the number of products launched – the projects may not affect the KPI. Make sure you state this though; saying that the project will not have an impact is a valid answer, and so would earn you a mark.

Part (iv). This final paragraph of the scenario describes the new information system. In essence, the new system is an enterprise resource planning system (ERPS), so, in effect the question is asking how an ERPS would help the three projects.

This requirement is quite challenging, but, of the three projects, the benefits can perhaps most easily be seen in relation to JIT. For example, in a demand-pull system, with no inventory, sharing information between different departments is likely to be crucial in avoiding stock-outs.

More generally, note that the scenario says that IC's current systems can only handle quantitative data. So, also think about the nature of the information required by the projects. For example, in order to reduce the level of defects, IC will presumably need to know what is causing those defects. But can a system which only handles quantitative data provide that information?

Overall. Remember that you have been asked to write a report, so make sure the style and structure of your answer, as well as its tone, is appropriate for a report.

Marking scheme

		Marks

(i) For calculation of corrected Economic Value Added:
1 mark for identifying correct treatment of each of the following and adjusting as necessary:

Non-cash expenses
Marketing expenses
Depreciation on leased assets
Research and development
Tax paid
Capital employed – opening figure
WACC
Economic value added
Maximum for calculation: 8 marks

1 mark per relevant point evaluating the assumptions and advising on the corrections
– up to 8 marks
Total for part (i) – up to 15 marks   **15**

(ii) KPIs for CSFs – up to 2 marks for each CSF
(1 mark for the weakness of the current KPI; 1 mark for the justified alternative)
Total for part (ii) – up to 6 marks   **6**

(iii) Quality improvement projects
Definitions and descriptions of the projects – up to 2 marks.
Analysis of the impact of the projects on IC's CSFs and KPIs – up to 6 marks per project
Maximum for part (iii) – up to 15 marks   **15**

(iv) New unified database
Definition and general points – up to 3 marks
Interaction with each project – up to 3 marks each
Other comments (eg quantitative vs qualitative information) – up to 3 marks
Maximum for part (iv) – up to 10 marks   **10**

Professional marks – up to 4 marks $\underline{4}$
                                                       Total = $\underline{50}$

Report

To: Board of Iron Chicken (IC)

From: Performance management expert

Date: [today's date]

Subject: Performance management issues at IC

Introduction

This report evaluates the accuracy and assumptions used in the calculation of EVA™. It then suggests new KPIs for the current CSFs at IC. Finally it considers the impact of three quality improvement projects on these CSFs and a proposed new information system.

(i)   **Economic value added (EVA™)**

Although some elements of it have been performed correctly, there are a number of errors in the existing calculation of (EVA™). The correct treatments are described below, and then the corrected EVA™ is calculated.

Non-cash expenses are correctly added back to profit as such costs are treated as unacceptable accounting adjustments on a cash-based view.

Marketing activities for long-term benefit are also correctly added back as they generate future value for the business. The prior year marketing expenditure is also added in to capital employed.

Operating leases should be added back to profit and to capital employed. However, a suitable additional depreciation should also be charged on the operating leases as these are now treated as assets of the business.

Research and development (R&D) expenditure should be added back to profit in the same way that the long-term marketing spending is. (**Note.** that there was no R&D expenditure in the prior year).

The **tax cost** in the calculation should be the amount paid, adjusted for lost tax on interest and not the adjusted amount of tax charged in the accounts.

The **WACC** is incorrectly calculated as it should be based on the post-tax cost of debt.

The **capital employed** figure should be based on the figure at the start of the year (opening capital employed) not the end of the year.

Economic value added	Year ended 30 June 2015
	$m
Operating profit	551.4
Add back	
Non-cash expenses	15.1
Marketing capitalised	23.1
Operating lease expenses	40.0
Research and development	10.0
Less	
Depreciation on leased assets (115/4)	28.8
Tax	130.0
Lost tax relief on interest	24.5
NOPAT	**456.3**
Capital employed	
At 2015 year start	2,282.0
Marketing spend capitalised from YE 30 June 2014	23.1
Operating leases	115.0
Adjusted capital employed at 2015 year start	**2,420.1**

$$\text{WACC} = (1/2 \times 16\%) + (1/2 \times 6.8\% \times (1 - 30\%)) = 10.38\%$$

$$\text{EVA™} = \text{NOPAT} - (\text{WACC} \times \text{Capital employed}) = \mathbf{\$205m}$$

The recalculated economic value added has increased from $181m to $205m which still indicates a positive position for the company as it adds to shareholder wealth.

In addition to the corrections above, the following assumptions in the calculation require comment:

1.   There is an implicit assumption that accounting depreciation (included in operating profit) is equivalent to economic depreciation (which should be used for EVA™ calculations). This is questionable generally, although there is no information to allow a more accurate calculation. Also, there is additional marketing spending which will probably have a limited economic life in building the brand. No estimation of this life and the resulting additional economic depreciation has been attempted in the above calculation.

2.   It has been assumed that no amortisation needs to be charged on the research and development costs since the product has not yet launched. This is in line with the accounting treatment of such items.

(ii) Key performance indicators for the critical success factors

Greater staff productivity

The current measure of units produced per labour hour does not reflect the skill and effort which goes into producing different units. The products of IC range from complex to simple and so revenue per employee would better reflect the different skill levels involved in production.

Reduction of wastage

The weakness of the existing measure is that it only looks at one cost area of production (power consumption). Inventory (stock) obsolescence will measure the wastage due to technological change which is present in the complex products produced by IC.

Greater innovation of products

Measuring the number of new products launched doesn't reflect the extent to which IC's innovations can become a sustainable source of value for its shareholders. The number of patents filed will reflect greater innovation at IC, but patents also legally protect groups of products. This will represent a stronger measure of innovation than new products launched, since the patent gives legal exclusivity.

Tutorial note.

There are many possible acceptable answers to this question. For example, alternatives you could have suggested are:

Greater staff productivity. Actual staff hours as a percentage of standard hours for actual production as this would measure staff efficiency in producing a wide range of products.

Reduction of wastage. Input/output analysis of material which looks at the percentage of material purchased which goes into the final product.

Greater innovation of products. Percentage of income earned from products which did not exist last year. This will measure the ability of IC to develop successful products. (The existing measure would record unsuccessful products as innovation.)

(iii) **Lean manufacturing projects**

The three projects link together as improvements to the quality of the manufacturing process at IC. There are common elements to these projects in the elimination of waste and empowerment of employees which will occur in the long term. In the short term, there may be increased costs due to these disruptive changes.

Just-in-time manufacturing (JIT)

JIT seeks to produce on a pull-basis to meet the customers' demands, rather than to produce products for inventory, which then acts as a buffer between production levels and demand. The main impact of JIT is the reduction of inventory which is held. The main enablers for such a system are a need for close links to customers and suppliers in order to predict demand and to quickly supply that demand.

In terms of IC's CSFs, this project will improve productivity as production lines must be made more flexible to meet changes in demand, although it should be noted that there could be a negative impact as constant changes in production lines will require more time to be spent setting up new production runs. It will also help to reduce wastage through losses in inventory as there will be less inventory. It also pushes some of the responsibility for improved quality of components (and reduced wastage) on to suppliers. However, it does not directly impact on product innovation.

The project will not necessarily immediately change any of the existing KPIs as it is about producing the right products at the right time not necessarily producing more products for any given input, and it does not impact directly on new product launches.

Use Kaizen costing

Kaizen costing aims to reduce current costs of production through continuous improvement. Each period, goals for lower costs are set and then performance monitored against these using variances. At the end of the period, a new lower cost goal is set for the next period. The process also often uses target costing to set the initial planned cost of a product thus incorporating the idea of only producing what the customer values. The purpose is to build into the control of the production process the idea of continuous improvement.

This project has the explicit aim of reducing waste and improving productivity and so is directly linked to the first two CSFs. As a result, it will have an impact on the KPIs which are related to productivity and resource consumption. The project will also require the empowerment of staff to make improvement decisions within their quality circles (teams) and so it may give scope for more innovative thinking. However, this thinking is not aimed at producing new products but at improving the production process, so new product innovation may only be affected indirectly.

Costs of quality and a 'zero defects' approach to manufacturing

Costs of quality can be broken down into four parts:

(1) Prevention costs which occur before or during production and aim to prevent the production of defective products;

(2) Appraisal costs which occur after production and aim to check that products meet quality standards;

(3) Internal failure costs which occur when products are identified as defective before delivery to the customer and so are scrapped or reworked; and

(4) External failure costs which occur when defective products are delivered to the customer.

The 'zero defects' approach is also known as 'total quality management' (TQM). The TQM philosophy is that it is better to spend money on prevention, which involves challenging all aspects of the production process in order to improve and so avoid failure costs.

This project will affect the CSFs relating to improved productivity and waste by reducing defective products, provided that staff time is not adversely affected by aiming for perfection in production. In terms of the KPIs, it may lead to increased time in production but reduced wastage. It will not have a direct impact on power consumption. Again, this project is unlikely to affect the number of new products launched as it focuses on the production process not product development.

(iv) **New information system**

The move to a single database for the organisation will integrate the subsystems from different functions (such as production and sales). It will require existing systems to be networked and compatible or else be replaced. It will affect overall decision-making by improving the visibility of each function's operations to the others and to the strategic decision-makers. This shift is often achieved by using an enterprise resource planning system and a strategic enterprise management system.

The unified database will be critical in achieving the goal of JIT manufacturing as close links between production scheduling and demand forecasts will be required in order to match production runs with demand forecasts/orders. Also, the production schedules will need links to inventory levels in warehousing so that inventory is run down before new production is initiated. As closer communication with suppliers and customers will also be required, some change to existing information systems will be necessary in any case. It may be worthwhile to consider including electronic data interchange (EDI) in the specifications of the new system.

In using kaizen costing, cross-functional communication will be important. The design team will need to communicate with the production team so that the design is more easily streamlined for production. The financial systems will need to be frequently updated for information from the quality circles as improvements are made. This will affect the kaizen cost targets which need to be continually monitored and new targets set regularly. Quality circles often involve groups from across the business and so a common information system will facilitate communications amongst them.

The introduction of TQM will require clearer reporting of quality costs to assist in the on-going motivation of staff, which is often a problem in TQM. Informing the quality teams of the impact that increased prevention costs are having on lowering failure costs will be important in maintaining the push to zero defects. The quality improvements and changes to production processes will need to be communicated across IC's different sites which the new database can facilitate.

The nature of the data used in the current system is quantitative but with the new projects, there will be a need to communicate qualitative information, for example, relating to the nature of defects or the new production processes put in place. This will require a fundamental change to existing systems which again motivates the change to a new database.

Question 2

Top tips. Although good exam technique is important in all P5 questions, it could be particularly useful in this one – especially reading all three requirements and identifying how the different parts of the question fit together. The issues being discussed in part (c) highlight one of the weaknesses in Perkin's current budgeting system (the lack of planning and operational variances). However, while it will be important to mention this weakness in part (a), you should not discuss it in detail there – in order to avoid duplicating your answer between parts (a) and (c). Similarly, although perhaps less immediately obviously, the extent to which internal factors have compounded external factors – part (b) – can also be seen as a result of the weaknesses in Perkin's current budgeting system.

Part (a). The scenario highlights a number of problems which Perkin has experienced, so one approach to this requirement could be just to work through the scenario and identify which of these are due to weaknesses in the current budgeting system, or its lack of suitability for the environment in which Perkin operates.

However, a more structure approach for trying to identify the weaknesses might be to use 'PRIME' as a framework for you answer.

Plan -– Does the budget process encourage budget holders to plan how to achieve targets which support the company's overall strategic objectives?

Responsibility – Do the budgets help to allocate responsibility, and specify which managers control which costs?

Integration – Does the budget structure help to ensure that the activities of one area support another?

Motivation – Do the budgets help to motivate managers?

Evaluation – Do the budgets allow trends in performance to be identified and investigated?

The scenario identifies a number of issues where Perkin's budgeting system does not help to achieve these 'PRIME' characteristics; and so you can then highlight these as weaknesses of the system.

However, note that you are asked to evaluate the system's suitability for Perkin's environment, as well as the weaknesses in the system. A key point to realise here is that Perkin is operating in a dynamic, fast-moving environment. Therefore, to what extent are incremental budgets, which are produced annually, and enforced rigidly likely to be suitable?

Although the requirement does not ask you to recommend an alternative budgeting system, it could be helpful to think whether the characteristics of alternative budgeting models (eg rolling budgets) would make them more appropriate than Perkin's current system. If another model seems more suitable, briefly mentioning this could help support your evaluation of the suitability (or unsuitability) of the current system.

Part (b). The scenario clearly identifies a number of external factors which have affected Perkin's performance during the year (eg rising silver prices; the fire at the customer), and these factors in themselves are outside Perkin's control.

In effect, however, this requirement is looking at the extent to which factors can fully be classified as controllable or uncontrollable. The key question in Perkin's case is: Although the initial factors was external (uncontrollable), has Perkin's internal response (controllable) also had an impact on its performance?

Part (c). As we noted at the start of these 'Top tips', the link between part (c) and part (a) in this question is important, because the change being suggested in part (c) addresses one of the weaknesses you could have identified in part (a) – the current lack of any analysis between planning and operational variances.

The third paragraph of the scenario is also important here. We are told that the main board significantly revises the budgets, but then divisional managers are appraised on the financial performance of their divisions. Does this seem a fair way of appraising the manager's performance?

Note, however, that the verb in part (c) is 'discuss' rather than evaluate. Therefore you need to focus specifically on the potential benefits of the change – not, for example, the extent to which those benefits could be limited by any difficulties associated with trying to analyse the variances.

Marks

(a) Evaluation of current budgeting system

Weaknesses in current system – 1 mark per relevant point – up to 12 marks
Suitability of the system for Perkin's environment – 1 mark per point – up to 5 marks
Conclusion – 1 mark

Total for part (a): up to 14

14

(b) Discussion of controllable and non-controllable aspects – up to 2 marks

Identifying external factors which contributed to Perkin's poor performance – 1 mark

Evaluating the extent to which the external factors as opposed to internal weaknesses were responsible for Perkin's poor performance – 1 mark per relevant point; up to a maximum of 4

Total for part (b): up to 6

6

(c) Definition of planning and operational variances – 1 mark

Discussing the benefits of distinguishing between planning and operational variances – 1 mark per relevant point; up to a maximum of 4

Total for part (c): up to 5

5

Total = 25

(a) Perkin uses a traditional approach to budgeting, which has a number of weaknesses.

First of all, the budgeting system does not seem aligned with Perkin's **corporate objective** which focuses on innovation and continuous product improvement. Innovation is a key competitive advantage to both component and device manufacturers in this industry and the products which incorporate Perkin's components are subject to rapid technological change as well as changes in consumer trends. The markets in which the two divisions operate appear to be evolving, as seen by the high popularity of the smartphone model which was designed for playing games. This may mean the distinction between smartphone and gaming devices could be becoming less clear cut. Management time would probably be better spent considering these rapid changes and currently the budgeting process does not facilitate that.

In reality, the budget process at Perkin is **time consuming** and probably therefore a costly exercise. Divisional budgets go through a lengthy process of drafting and then revision by the main board before they are approved. The approval often happens after the start of the period to which they relate, at which point the budgets are already **out of date**. This also means divisional managers are trying to plan activities for the next financial year without a set of finalised targets agreed, which could impact the effectiveness of decisions made.

Another weakness is that the budgets are **only prepared annually**, which is clearly too infrequent for a business such as Perkin. The process is also rigid and inflexible as deviations from the planned targets are not tolerated. Sticking to rigid, annual budgets can lead to problems such as P Division not being able to cope with increasing popularity of a particular product and even other short-term changes in demand like those driven by seasonal factors, or one-off events such as the factory fire. Linked to this problem of budgetary constraints is that to cut costs to achieve the budgeted net profit, managers closed one of the three research and development facilities in G Division. As identified at the outset, a successful research and development function is a key source of long-term competitive advantage to Perkin.

It also appears that Perkin **fails to flex the budgets** and consequently the fixed budgets had discouraged divisional managers from deviating from the original plan. P Division did not make technical modifications to its components due to the cost of doing so, which meant they were unable to supply components for use in the new model of smartphone and had to discount the inventories of the old version. It is unclear why G Division did not take on additional staff to cope with increased demand following reopening of their customer's factory, but it may be because managers felt constrained by the budget. This then caused long-term detriment to Perkin as they lost the preferred supplier status with their main customer.

Another problem created by annual budgeting is the **management of short-term changes in costs and prices**. A key component of Perkin's products is silver, which fluctuates in price, and though it is not clear how much effect this has on Perkin's costs, any problems in supply could disrupt production even if only a small amount of silver were required. Also Perkin exports goods worldwide and probably also purchases materials, including silver, from overseas. The business is therefore exposed to short-term movements in foreign currency exchange rates which may affect costs and selling prices.

Similarly, there also seems to be **considerable uncertainty** in sales volumes and prices which creates problems in the forecasting process for the two divisions. P Division did not anticipate the high demand for the new component which meant P Division had to discount products it had already manufactured in order to achieve its forecast sales volumes. G Division did correctly forecast the demand, but based on past growth in the market which may be too simplistic in a rapidly changing industry. Lack of up-to-date information will hinder decision-making and overall performance at Perkin. Perkin would perhaps be better adopting a rolling basis for forecasting.

The two divisions share manufacturing facilities and are likely to compete for other resources during the budgeting process. The current budgeting system does not encourage resource, information or knowledge sharing, for example, expertise in forecasting silver requirements. Divisional managers are **appraised on the financial performance of their own division** and hence are likely to prioritise the interests of their own division above those of Perkin as a whole. P Division would not re-allocate its manufacturing facilities to G Division, even though G Division needed this to cope with extra demand following reopening of the customer's factory. The current system is therefore not encouraging goal congruence between the divisions and Perkin as a whole and a budgeting system, if done effectively, should encourage co-ordination and co-operation.

Managers may find the budgeting process **demotivating** because it is **time-consuming** for them and then the directors override the forecast which they had made. It is also unfair and demotivating to staff to appraise them on factors which are outside their control. This also identifies another weakness in Perkin's budgeting system related to control, as there does not seem to be any planning and operating variance analysis performed to assess exactly where performance is lacking, and so no appropriate management information is provided. In fact it is not even clear just how often divisional managers receive reports on performance throughout the year. Any budgeting system without regular feedback would be ineffective. It should even be noted that for the industry in which Perkin operates the use of only budgetary targets as a measure of performance is narrow and internal. It should be utilising information from external sources as well to assess performance in a more relevant and contextual way.

Given the rapidly changing external environment and the emphasis on innovation and continuous product development, the current budgeting method does not seem appropriate for Perkin.

(b)   As the shareholder representative noted, external factors have adversely affected Perkin's performance over the last year. However, the way Perkin has responded to the external events has also contributed to the problems it has faced. As such, it is important that Perkin doesn't simply use the external factors as an excuse for its poor performance, thereby failing to acknowledge the internal factors and behaviours which have also contributed to it.

The current lack of any detailed analysis into the reasons why Perkins' actual performance varies from budget means it is difficult to hold managers to account for their performance. However, as the three examples we evaluate below demonstrate, the factors that affect performance cannot be categorised entirely as controllable (internal) or as uncontrollable (external). Instead, Perkin's performance reflects a combination of both types of factors.

The **unexpectedly high popularity of the new smartphone** with the large screen was an external factor. However, P Division's inability – or unwillingness – to make the necessary technical modifications to its own components to support the new screen was an internal factor, resulting – as we noted in part (a) – from the fact that Perkin does not flex its budgets.

Similarly, the **global shortage of silver** during the year (and the corresponding increase in silver prices) was an external factor. However, the lack of communication between G Division and P Division which led to G buying silver when P already held large inventories reflected an internal weakness. If the two divisions had liaised more effectively, the impact of the short-term increase in silver prices could have been reduced (or perhaps even avoided) if Perkin was able to wait until prices fell again to top-up its inventories.

Again, the **fire which affected G's main customer** was an external factor. However, G's refusal to recruit extra staff to fulfil increased demand when the customer's factory re-opened, and P's refusal to allow some of its manufacturing facilities to be used to meet this demand are both internal decisions. However, it was these responses – rather than the fire itself – which led to Perkin losing its preferred supplier status with the customer.

As we noted in part (a), the response to the silver price increase and the fire both reflect the lack of goal congruence between the divisions and Perkin as a whole. Again, though, this is an internal weakness, reflecting dysfunctional behaviour which has resulted from the way divisional performance is rigidly assessed against budget. Therefore, although external factors have contributed to G's poor performances, internal weaknesses have also played a significant part in G's poor performance.

(c) **Planning variances** result from actual events and circumstances differing from the assumptions used in the original budget. For example, the fire at its main customer meant that the annual growth of 5% anticipated in G's sales forecast was too high (because the budget had not anticipated the fire). The lost sales resulting from the fire should be treated as a planning variance.

In effect, a planning variance is the difference between the original budget and the budget as it would have been revised with the benefit of hindsight.

Operational variances then reflect the differences between this 'revised' budget, and actual performance. Operational variances result from the ongoing decisions of divisional managers, rather than issues with the original budget-setting process.

We have already noted – in part (a) – that the lack of planning and operating variance analysis is a weakness, because it means Perkin cannot accurately identify the reasons why actual performance is below budget. Given the dynamic nature of Perkin's markets (and the fact that budgets are only produced annually) it seems likely that there could be significant planning variances.

By isolating these planning variances, Perkin could then get a fairer reflection (through the operational variances) of how well the **divisional managers** are performing. This will also increase the effectiveness of the budgeting system as a **control mechanism** – comparing the manager's actual controllable performance against budgeted targets.

Currently, the divisional managers are appraised on the financial performance of their divisions, so they are being held responsible for planning variances as well as operational variances. However, as the budgets are determined by the main board, the managers should not be held responsible for planning variances over which they have little (or no) control.

Equally, however, by isolating the planning variances, Perkin can get a better insight into the degree to which the original budget was inaccurate. If it becomes clear that the majority of the variances result from changes in circumstance which couldn't have been known when the annual budget was originally set, this could reinforce the argument for moving away from the current budgeting system – for example, to rolling budgets.

Question 3

Top tips.

Part (a). Arguably the most important words in the requirement are 'could be implemented'. This is because they indicate that the advice you need to give the board is about how the project could be implemented; not how six sigma could help Posie to reduce the level of returns from customers.

The specific reference in the requirement to the 'DMAIC' methodology should help you structure your answer. If you use each of the five elements of 'DMAIC' as headings to provide a framework for your answer, you can then assess the activities which Posie need to undertake at each phase of the project.

Note, however, that the marking scheme indicates that there were more marks available for advice given in relation to the 'define' and 'measure' phases of DMAIC, than for the other three. The CEO's concerns about the quality of Posie's data should have alerted you to the fact that 'measurement' of performance is currently an issue at Posie. This, in turn, is reflected in the marking scheme – where up to 6 marks are available for advising about the 'measure' phase of DMAIC.

Part (b) (i). The last paragraph of the scenario sets up the context for this requirement – identifying that the data generated by Posie's current IT systems isn't sufficient to identify which responsibility centres are the root cause of the problem of customer returns. This reference should highlight the need to produce performance information at a responsibility centre level.

However, the requirement is not only about responsibility centres; you should also think more generally about the qualities of good performance reports (eg level of detailed provided, timeliness) and whether the current returns data enables Posie's management team to manage returns effectively.

Part (b) (ii). It should be obvious that re-designating the overseas subsidiaries as revenue centres means that their managers will only be held accountable for their revenue (rather than for revenues and costs, as they currently are). Hence, performance data will need to focus on revenues. However, simply stating this one point is only likely to earn you one mark (and there are up to 4 marks available here.) So, you also need to think more widely here: for example, even though the divisional managers' focus will be on revenue, there will still be costs associated with operating the subsidiaries. How will these be recorded and controlled?

Marking scheme

Marks

(a) Use of DMAIC

    Define – 1 mark per point – up to 4 marks
    Measure – 1 mark per point – up to 6 marks
    Analyse; Improve; Control – 1 mark per point – up to 3 marks for each heading

    Total for part (a): up to 15   15

(b)(i) Definition of responsibility centres – 1 mark

    Impact on information requirements of the need for greater detail about customer returns –
    1 mark per relevant point; up to a maximum of 6

    Total for part (b)(i): up to 6   6

(b)(ii) Impact on information requirements due to the re-designating overseas subsidiaries as revenue centres – 1 mark per relevant point; up to a maximum of 4

Total for part (b)(ii): up to 4

4

Total = 25

(a) The DMAIC process is a technique used to implement six sigma to improve existing processes. It is split into five phases as described below.

Define the process

The CEO is concerned that the increase in returns from customers is increasing costs and threatens to affect the Posie brand.

Six sigma focuses closely on the requirements of the customer, and it is important for Posie to be clear exactly what customers' requirements are, and specifically why products are returned.

The objective of the project needs to be clear – in this case to reduce the number of customer returns.

Customers will expect certain minimum requirements from the manufacturing and packaging process, for example, that they can assemble the furniture properly and all the necessary components for them to be able to do this are included in the box. Customers will also expect the goods to be delivered undamaged within a reasonable time, and at the time and date promised when the order was placed. Customers' perceptions of quality should correspond to the price paid, though different customers will have different expectations of this.

Beyond this basic requirement, there may be aspects of the manufacturing product which further enhance the customers' experience of the product, and presumably of the Posie brand. Customers may be particularly pleased with furniture which is delivered early or at a time especially convenient to them, or which is robust, durable and 'well-made'. These perceptions are subjective, and may equally relate to design or the quality of raw materials as to the manufacturing process. By identifying where the products exceed customers' expectations, it may be possible to focus more on these aspects in the future. While products which significantly exceed customers' expectations will enhance the Posie brand, it may also indicate a quality of manufacture which is too high and allow Posie to reduce manufacturing costs in accordance with its cost leadership strategy whilst still having mainly satisfied customers.

Measure the existing process

The current returns figures do give some data to as to why products are returned, but their usefulness is limited as it is unclear which of the categories relates to defective manufacture, and which relate to activities of other divisions. The ambiguity of the data and category definitions will need addressing to enable the process to be measured effectively.

Returns in Category 1 could be because the goods were not manufactured or packed properly in the manufacturing division, but could also be due to poor design, customers losing components or simply being unable to assemble furniture.

Damaged goods in Category 2 probably do not arise because of defective manufacturing either, though customers may wrongly categorise defective goods as damaged. For the other categories it is less clear. Though goods may become damaged by the distribution company, it seems that only a small number of returns relate directly to them.

Returns in Categories 3 and 4 could be due to defective manufacture or if the customer had simply changed their minds and no longer wanted the product. In Category 3, the identification of 'defective' items is too broad.

Returns in Category 5 which arrived late are clearly not due to manufacturing defects and as this causes only 2% of returns, is relatively insignificant.

Currently 10% of Posie's sales are of products from other manufacturers. There is no indication from the data given how many of the returns relate to these products, nor of the total number of returns relative to the number of items sold.

Therefore the existing data are insufficient to reliably measure existing performance and take no account of inputs such as raw materials. Only items which customers value should be measured. The CEO has suggested more detailed data are required, for example, on overall customer satisfaction with the manufacturing, but this is at 93% which already seems high and there is little point in incurring costs to measure what customers are already satisfied with. In the context of the six sigma project at Posie, there is little that can be done to improve this particular area and such items should not be measured.

Analyse the process

This stage is where the root causes of the problems are identified. Additional information may be needed, for example, to analyse customer returns by type of product, by country of sale or with a clearer definition of what is meant by 'defective'. By doing so, Posie may identify areas of the business where customer returns are particularly high and so be able to focus on these.

Improve the process

At this stage the proposals for improving the process are implemented and availability of resources and likely costs of making the improvements need to be carefully considered. Posie may need to consider which aspects of the production or packaging process could be improved, for example, by better maintenance or calibration of machinery. Additional training of staff may also be required.

Control

This is the on-going monitoring that the reduction in customer returns due to defective manufacturing is being maintained. Reporting on the number of returns may be done by exception if they reach a particular level. In Posie, it seems likely that the data on customer returns used to manage this process will need to be redesigned to make it clearer in which responsibility centre the problems arise. The ongoing monitoring may indicate that some of the earlier stages in the DMAIC process need to be revisited.

(b)   (i)   The CEO wants to identify which responsibility centres are the root causes of the problem of customer returns. A responsibility centre is a part of the business where a manager has specific authority and accountability for its performance and so Posie will need information relating to aspects of performance specific to the centre. For example, performance data relating to the reasons for customer returns need to be clearly segregated between responsibility centres. Currently, the information compiled on customer returns does not do this and some categories of return may result from manufacturing defects but some will be from problems outside the manufacturing division, or even outside Posie itself, for example, from poor quality raw materials purchased externally, or because of late deliveries or damaged goods caused by the distribution company.

Once information has been analysed and responsibility has been identified, then the managers of those areas will need the information drilled down into even further, as in order to improve they need to know which specific areas they can control. It would be unfair to make managers responsible for aspects of performance which they are unable to control, and the board member responsible for manufacturing quality has recently resigned because of this.

Posie needs to ensure it produces performance data to an appropriate level of detail so as not to overload the users with too much data. For board level reporting, the information in the current board reporting pack may be too detailed and it would be sufficient just to produce summary data on the overall level of returns relative to sales. Responsibility centres would need much more detailed information, perhaps even down to product or production line level.

However, Posie should also consider the costs and resources required to provide more detailed performance data. Given Posie's cost leadership strategy, the costs of data collection may outweigh the benefits of doing so.

Performance data should be provided at an appropriate frequency. For the Posie main board, monthly reporting may be sufficient to alert them to any problems. Responsibility centres will need much more frequent, even daily or weekly details of the levels of customer returns so that they can react quickly to any problems identified. At the moment, the returns data are compiled every six months, possibly due to the difficulties in obtaining data from the IT systems in the overseas businesses. Even for a board level report, this seems much too infrequent.

(b)   (ii)   At the moment, the overseas subsidiaries are being designated as profit centres and managers will be held accountable for both revenues and costs. As they do not manufacture, it seems reasonable to designate them as revenue centres. As such, managers would be held accountable for just revenues as they have little or no control over costs as most goods for resale are purchased from the manufacturing division.

The performance data produced by Posie's subsidiaries' IT systems will therefore switch to focus more on revenues rather than costs. As revenue centres they may well have some freedom to change selling prices. Posie will need to ensure the subsidiaries have information to monitor the impact of different pricing strategies and will need to provide the management of these subsidiaries with information gleaned from the external environment. It will be important to evaluate competitors' pricing strategies when making pricing decisions.

A potential problem with providing only performance data relating to revenue is that managers could focus too much on achieving revenue targets rather than maintaining or improving profitability. As they are autonomous subsidiaries, there will be aspects of their own costs, such as staffing costs and other overheads, which they will be able to have some control over. It is important that Posie ensures the management still has sight of this information to ensure that such costs are still controlled effectively.

Furthermore, if the overseas managers are only held responsible for sales, this may mean they do not focus sufficiently on addressing reasons why goods are returned, and so levels of returns may increase. This means that once Posie undertakes the exercise to identify the root causes of the returns from customers, this information is shared and monitored.

Posie needs to be aware of these issues when determining information requirements if the reclassification of the subsidiaries goes ahead. It will not be as simple as assuming that they will now only need information on revenues.

Question 4

Text reference. The balanced scorecard is discussed in Chapter 15 of the BPP Study Text.

Top tips.

Part (a). The number of times the word 'passenger' is mentioned in the scenario should have been an inherent clue that managing passenger (or 'customer' satisfaction) should be a key part of Soup's performance management process.

The last paragraph highlights this point even more clearly, with the reference to the need for performance measures which 'balance the need of passengers with the requirements of the shareholders'. The reason why the scorecard s called the 'balanced scorecard' is because it encourages organisations to develop performance measures which ensure a 'balance' between the four perspectives. As such, it is also important to try to think how performance information in each of the four areas could be useful for Soup – don't just focus, for example, on the benefits of having passenger-focused performance measures.

Also, make sure you take note of the instructions the CEO has given in the last paragraph. She has said, specifically, that she doesn't want a list of suggested performance measures; instead she wants to know **why** those performance measures will help to improve Soup's performance.

Similarly, note that the CEO has specifically said that she doesn't want to know about how to improve Soup's performance, but instead how to improve Soup's performance management systems. This distinction between 'performance' and 'performance reporting' is absolutely crucial in P5. In a question like this – where the focus is on Soup's performance management system – you will score no marks for suggestions about how to improve the company's underlying performance.

Part (b). Whereas your focus in part (a) should have been one Soup's performance management systems, the focus here is on the underlying performance – in particular, the occupancy rates on Soup's trains.

The third paragraph of the scenario provides details of the capacity of Soup's trains, so you need to use these details in conjunction with the data at the end of the scenario to work out how many seats are available per day compared to the number of passengers.

However, note that you aren't asked simply to calculate occupancy rates, but rather to evaluate the comment that Soup's trains are overcrowded. So, how far do the figures you have calculated support the comment?

Part (c). The focus in this third part of the question returns to the balance scorecard as a performance management system. However, whereas part (a) looked at the ways the scorecard could improve the performance management system at Soup, part (c) now looks at the problems which Soup could encounter when applying it.

There are two key points to note here though. First, the requirement is looking specifically at the problems which could be encountered in 'selecting and interpreting performance measures' – not, more generally, about the problems which could be encountered in introducing the balanced scorecard. Second, you are asked to assess the problems 'Soup may encounter...' rather than to discuss the problems in general terms. To score well in this part of the question, it is vital that you link your answer directly back to Soup.

Marking scheme

Marks

(a) For relevant points about how using the balance scorecard could improve Soup's performance management system – 1 mark per point, up to a maximum of 10 marks

No marks are to be awarded for a list of new measures without justifying why they would benefit Soup

A maximum of one mark is to be given for a generic description of the balanced scorecard without clear references to the scenario.

Total for part (a): up to 10 10

(b) For relevant calculations – 1 mark each, up to 4 marks
   – Seats available per train
   – Seats available per day by region/time
   – Seat occupancy by region/time
   – Total seat occupancy

Comment on whether the figures are consistent with government's claims about overcrowding – 1 mark

Other comments – up to 2 marks

Up to 2 additional marks for identifying journey time is an important factor and for attempting to quantify journey times from the data given

Total for part (b): up to 7   7

(c) For each problem Soup may encounter – 1 mark per relevant point, up to 2 marks per problem

Problems include:
   – Selection of appropriate measures
   – Prioritisation of measures
   – Difficulties of making measurements
   – Conflicting measures
   – Overload of measures

A maximum of 3 marks to be given, in total, for general problems of applying the balanced scorecard, but not applied to Soup

Total for part (c): up to 8   8

                                          Total = 25

(a) The balanced scorecard consists of four perspectives: customer, internal, innovation and learning and financial. It requires an organisation to have a number of goals supported by performance measures in each perspective. The customer perspective measures what it is that customers value from the business; internal looks at what processes does the organisation need to be successful; innovation and learning considers how future value can be created and financial measures whether performance is acceptable to investors.

It is useful because it uses both internal and external information to assess performance and measures **financial and non-financial aspects** of a business to ensure long-term future success, rather than just focusing on historic results. It can also be used as a mechanism to link KPIs into the CSFs which are vital to deliver strategy.

Financial perspective

Soup currently uses return on capital employed (ROCE) as its key financial performance measure, but this does not correlate directly with the **objective to maximise shareholder wealth** and could encourage short-term decisions to be taken at the expense of long-term success. This is the case at Soup which purchased old trains and subsequently failed to reinvest, meaning that Soup's ROCE is probably higher than its rivals. However, the trains are becoming unreliable and their condition is deteriorating. In the long term this will reduce customer satisfaction and financial performance.

Using the scorecard, Soup should have a **broader range of financial measures** which encourage managers to take decisions, such as investment decisions, consistent with the objective to maximise shareholder wealth in the long term. EVA would be a suitable measure to help achieve this, and would be preferable to the current focus on ROCE.

Customer perspective

Soup does measure growth in passenger numbers which could be a measure of customer satisfaction. However, it is a limited, quantitative measure. Though Soup does have rivals and is likely to be required to operate a specified level of service under the terms of the licence from the government, some passengers may be forced to travel on Soup trains, rather than those of another operator because of where they live or the times they need to travel. The number of operators (competitors) is limited by the capacity of the railway infrastructure as well as by passenger demand. This means that the level of repeat customers may not be appropriate for Soup.

Passenger numbers are also externally focused but again this fails to fully consider the environment in which Soup operates. Within the customer perspective Soup could use a range of performance measures. This will be beneficial as where passengers are able, they are likely to choose to use Soup if they provide a good service. This can be easily measured by surveying or asking passengers' opinions. This will give Soup more qualitative information about their customers and their expectations, which will vary, for example, passengers will have different perceptions of overcrowding, or what is an acceptable delay. Certain groups may be more affected by overcrowding like frequent travellers and the elderly. Passengers who are unable to find a seat will probably be the most dissatisfied, though this will depend on how long their journey is. Other aspects of Soup's service may be less valued than reliability and occupancy, like wireless access and the on-board cafe, but will be important to certain groups.

Another key element of customer satisfaction will relate to the amount of fare paid. Fares are regulated in Deeland so the interaction between fares and other aspects of the service is unknown. Many customers while valuing a particular aspect of the service may be unwilling to pay more for it; some may accept a reduction in the level of service if fares were reduced.

This detailed information about customers will allow Soup to focus performance improvements on key areas using more external data to make decisions.

Internal processes

Measures of the internal processes are likely to be closely linked to customer satisfaction. Soup apparently neglects this area in its performance management system. The scorecard could be used to help to address reliability, overcrowding and environmental factors.

Reliability will be highly valued by customers especially those who travel frequently and who rely on rail travel to get to work. The number of trains arriving late would be a suitable measure of reliability, as would the number of train services cancelled, though the length of the delay is also critical and should be carefully defined. The scorecard would allow more detailed measures as some of the factors affecting reliability will be within Soup's direct control but others such as failures in the railway infrastructure are controlled by the government. This is useful information for Soup to effectively assess their controllable performance and feedback as necessary to external parties.

Seat occupancy, the number of passengers on a train compared to the number of available seats on different routes and at different times, is a suitable measure of train overcrowding and is important for passenger safety. To fully utilise its trains and achieve its objective of maximising shareholder wealth, Soup must try and maximise both the seat occupancy and the amount of time its trains are actually running. These internal measures would then help to support financial targets.

Soup's licence to operate rail services in Regions A and B expires in three years' time, and as with the operator from whom Soup purchased the trains, it may not be renewed. Soup must balance the needs of shareholders for short-term increases in dividends and share price with the long-term need to renew to its operator's licence.

Innovation and learning perspective

The creation of long-term future value can be addressed by the innovation and learning perspective. The immediate scope to innovate the service experienced by the passenger is limited, but there are some quick wins available in the choice in the on-board cafe and improving the reliability of the internet access. Also time spent training staff may improve customer satisfaction and reduce maintenance time. Fundamental innovation like the use of faster or environmentally less harmful trains requires long-term planning and

large capital investment. The scorecard will encourage Soup to be forward looking, unlike the present system which is limited to historic performance.

(b) To measure the extent of overcrowding, some measure of occupancy is needed. The number of passengers per available seat can be used as a measure of occupancy.

		Region A		Region B	Total
Seats available					
Per service (70 per carriage)		490		420	
Seats available per day					
Peak times	4 services	1,960	4 services	1,680	
Other times	6 services	2,940	8 services	3,360	
Total		4,900		5,040	9,940
Passenger demand per day					
Peak times		2,500		1,400	
Other times		2,450		1,850	
Total		4,950		3,250	8,200
Occupancy (demand / availability)					
Peak times		127.6%		83.3%	
Other times		83.3%		55.1%	
Total		101.0%		64.5%	82.5%

Overall occupancy (82.5%) is significantly below 100%, which means on average there are more seats available than passengers. This not consistent with the government's claims that the trains are overcrowded. However, these averages may be misleading as trains running on certain days or at certain times may be relatively overcrowded. This may generate customer dissatisfaction even on services which are on average not fully occupied. The total number of passengers without seats would be a better measure.

There are **significant variations between regions and times travelled** with only the trains in Region A travelling at peak times being over occupied. This affects only 18% (4/22) of all services.

The people most affected by this will be the 28% of the passengers travelling at peak times in Region A who are unable to obtain a seat. This represents only 9% (28% × 2,500/8,200) of total passengers per day. There is some overcrowding, but the claim that Soup's trains are overcrowded seems exaggerated given the data provided. However, certain routes or specific times or sections of the trains may be more affected and more analysis is needed.

The impact of overcrowding on passengers also depends on the **length of journeys** passengers are making; with the lack of seating typically causing a greater inconvenience to passengers on long journeys compared to passengers only making a shorter journey. Equally, some passengers may board a service at intermediate stations, rather than travelling the full length of a route. These passengers are relatively more likely to have to stand, but will have to stand for a shorter length of time than passengers who are travelling the full length of the route.

(c) When applying the balanced scorecard in Soup, the measures need to be chosen carefully. A balance needs to be struck, and only measures which help Soup to **achieve its objectives** should be chosen. Currently Soup focuses on short-term financial measures such as return on capital employed, whereas the balanced scorecard considers more **long-term measures**.

Some measures are more important than others, so **prioritising measures** will be difficult. Customers may value some aspects of the service more than others, for example, the choice available in the on-board cafe is probably unimportant to most passengers provided they can obtain some food and drink. The punctuality of Soup's trains or whether they even run at all is fundamental to achieving customer satisfaction and needs careful measurement. Soup must have measures for regulatory or safety reasons too.

Some aspects of the business may be **harder to measure** than others. For example, it may be relatively easy to measure seat occupancy as a measure of overcrowding, but passengers' perceptions of overcrowding may differ. Non-financial aspects such as customer satisfaction may be subjective and any surveys done may not reflect the experience of the majority of passengers. Performing and analysing surveys would also be time consuming and resource intensive.

Measures chosen may conflict. Overcrowding may be unwelcome by passengers but making them less crowded conflicts with Soup's presumed objective of fully occupied trains. Time spent maintaining trains to reduce their impact on the environment or ensure reliability will mean they are not operational for periods of time, though safety will be a key factor here.

Care must be taken to **avoid overloading** with too many performance measures. The current objective to maximise shareholder wealth is very broad. Having a clearer strategy would enable Soup to determine suitable performance measures so it is not overloaded with KPIs which do not contribute towards achieving this strategy.

Review Form – Paper P5 Advanced Performance Management (02/16)

Name: _____   Address: _____

_____

_____

How have you used this Kit?
(Tick one box only)

☐ On its own (book only)

☐ On a BPP in-centre course_____

☐ On a BPP online course

☐ On a course with another college

☐ Other _____

Why did you decide to purchase this Kit?
(Tick one box only)

☐ Have used the complementary Study text

☐ Have used other BPP products in the past

☐ Recommendation by friend/colleague

☐ Recommendation by a lecturer at college

☐ Saw advertising

☐ Other _____

During the past six months do you recall seeing/receiving any of the following?
(Tick as many boxes as are relevant)

☐ Our advertisement in *Student Accountant*

☐ Our advertisement in *Pass*

☐ Our advertisement in *PQ*

☐ Our brochure with a letter through the post

☐ Our website www.bpp.com

Which (if any) aspects of our advertising do you find useful?
(Tick as many boxes as are relevant)

☐ Prices and publication dates of new editions

☐ Information on product content

☐ Facility to order books

☐ None of the above

Which BPP products have you used?

Text	☐	Passcards	☐	Other	☐
Kit	☑	i-Pass	☐		

Your ratings, comments and suggestions would be appreciated on the following areas.

	Very useful	Useful	Not useful
Passing P5			
Questions			
Top Tips etc in answers			
Content and structure of answers			
Mock exam answers			

Overall opinion of this Kit	Excellent	☐	Good	☐	Adequate	☐	Poor ☐

Do you intend to continue using BPP products?   Yes ☐   No ☐

The BPP author of this edition can be emailed at: accaqueries@bpp.com

Please return this form to: Head of ACCA & FIA Programmes, BPP Learning Media Ltd, FREEPOST, London, W12 8AA

Review Form (continued)

TELL US WHAT YOU THINK

Please note any further comments and suggestions/errors below.